Blessed Peacemakers

Blessed Peacemakers

365 Extraordinary People Who Changed the World

KERRY WALTERS
and
ROBIN JARRELL

CASCADE *Books* · Eugene, Oregon

BLESSED PEACEMAKERS
365 Extraordinary People Who Changed the World

Copyright © 2013 Kerry Walters and Robin Jarrell. All rights reserved. Except for brief quotations in critical publications or reviews, no part of this book may be reproduced in any manner without prior written permission from the publisher. Write: Permissions, Wipf and Stock Publishers, 199 W. 8th Ave., Suite 3, Eugene, OR 97401.

Cascade Books
An Imprint of Wipf and Stock Publishers
199 W. 8th Ave., Suite 3
Eugene, OR 97401

www.wipfandstock.com

ISBN 13: 978-1-60899-248-5

Cataloguing-in-Publication data:

Walters, Kerry S.

    Blessed peacemakers : 365 extraordinary people who changed the world / Kerry Walters and Robin Jarrell.

    xxii + 390 pp. ; 23 cm. Includes bibliographical references and index.

    ISBN 13: 978-1-60899-248-5

    1. Nonviolence. 2. Peace-building. 3. Peace—Religious aspects. I. Jarrell, Robin. II. Title.

BL629.5.C66 W30 2013

Manufactured in the U.S.A.

For Kim & Jonah. Always.
K. W.

For my mother, June, and my father, Bob.
R. J.

Contents

Introduction   xix

1 JANUARY Telemachus	1
2 JANUARY Willi Graf	2
3 JANUARY Takashi Nagai	3
4 JANUARY Albert Camus	4
5 JANUARY Lanza del Vasto	5
6 JANUARY Jacques Ellul	6
7 JANUARY Sadako Sasaki	7
8 JANUARY Emily Greene Balch	8
9 JANUARY Rigoberta Menchú Tum	9
10 JANUARY Henry Scott Holland	10
11 JANUARY Aldo Leopold	11
12 JANUARY Benny Giay	12
13 JANUARY Thomas Hurndall	13
14 JANUARY Martin Niemöller	14
15 JANUARY Nathan Söderblom	15
16 JANUARY Ormond Burton	16
17 JANUARY William Stafford	17
18 JANUARY Kenneth Boulding	18
19 JANUARY Helen Mack Chang	19
20 JANUARY Khan Abdul Ghaffar Khan	20
21 JANUARY Hildegard Goss-Mayr	21
22 JANUARY U Thant	22
23 JANUARY María Julia Hernández	23
24 JANUARY Absalom Jones	24
25 JANUARY Rufus Jones	25
26 JANUARY Thomas Gumbleton	26
27 JANUARY Roy Bourgeois	27
28 JANUARY Isaac of Nineveh	28

Contents

29 January
  Romain Rolland 29
30 January
  Vallalar 30
31 January
  Donald Soper 31
1 February
  Yevgeny Zamyatin 32
2 February
  Maximillian Vanka 33
3 February
  Carlos Filipe Ximenes Belo 34
4 February
  Rosa Parks 35
5 February
  John Nevin Sayre 36
6 February
  Asha Hagi Elmi 37
7 February
  Dom Hélder Câmara 38
8 February
  Martin Buber 39
9 February
  Alice Walker 40
10 February
  Frances Moore Lappé 41
11 February
  Muriel Lester 42
12 February
  Dorothy Stang 43
13 February
  Emil Fuchs 44

14 February
  Valentine 45
15 February
  Ben Salmon 46
16 February
  Simone Weil 47
17 February
  Jonah Jones 48
18 February
  Julia Butterfly Hill 49
19 February
  Krishnammal and Sankaralingam Jagannathan 50
20 February
  A. J. Muste 51
21 February
  John van Hengel 52
22 February
  Menachem Froman 53
23 February
  Wulfstan of Worchester 54
24 February
  Monika Hauser 55
25 February
  Jacob Hutter 56
26 February
  Naim Ateek 57
27 February
  Gautama Siddhartha 58
28 February
  Linus Pauling 59
1 March
  Loung Ung 60

Contents

2 MARCH
    Judi Bari   61

3 MARCH
    Miriam Makeba   62

4 MARCH
    Ludwig Quidde   63

5 MARCH
    Hussein Issa   64

6 MARCH
    Sulak Sivaraksa   65

7 MARCH
    Stanley Kubrick   66

8 MARCH
    Maria Skobtsova   67

9 MARCH
    Tom Fox   68

10 MARCH
    Asghar Ali Engineer   69

11 MARCH
    Rutilio Grande   70

12 MARCH
    Preah Maha Ghosananda   71

13 MARCH
    Ham Sok-Hon   72

14 MARCH
    Walter Brueggemann   73

15 MARCH
    SuAnne Big Crow   74

16 MARCH
    Rachel Corrie   75

17 MARCH
    Bayard Rustin   76

18 MARCH
    Fred Shuttlesworth   77

19 MARCH
    Vera Brittain   78

20 MARCH
    John Middleton Murry   79

21 MARCH
    Pocahontas   80

22 MARCH
    John McConnell   81

23 MARCH
    David Suzuki   82

24 MARCH
    Kalle Lasn   83

25 MARCH
    Norman Borlaug   84

26 MARCH
    Kate Richards O'Hare   85

27 MARCH
    Wally and Juanita Nelson   86

28 MARCH
    Pelagius   87

29 MARCH
    R. S. Thomas   88

30 MARCH
    Dith Pran   89

31 MARCH
    César Chávez   90

1 APRIL
    Wangari Maathai   91

2 APRIL
    John Paul II   92

3 APRIL
    Jane Goodall   93

4 APRIL
    Martin Luther King, Jr.   94

Contents

5 April	
Pythagoras	95
6 April	
Daniel Ellsberg	96
7 April	
André Trocmé	97
8 April	
Ivan Supek	98
9 April	
Dietrich Bonhoeffer	99
10 April	
Jessie Wallace Hughan	100
11 April	
Kurt Vonnegut	101
12 April	
Frederick Franck	102
13 April	
Amy Goodman	103
14 April	
Arun Gandhi	104
15 April	
Robert Purvis	105
16 April	
Iqbal Masih	106
17 April	
Albert Einstein	107
18 April	
Margaret Hassan	108
19 April	
Meng Tzu	109
20 April	
Lady Godiva	110
21 April	
Helen Prejean	111
22 April	
Käthe Kollwitz	112
23 April	
Adin Ballou	113
24 April	
Margaret Fell	114
25 April	
Ernesto Balducci	115
26 April	
Amy Biehl	116
27 April	
Dorothee Soelle	117
28 April	
Oscar Schindler	118
29 April	
Gordon Kiyoshi Hirabayashi	119
30 April	
Immanuel Kant	120
1 May	
Albert Bigelow	121
2 May	
Benjamin Spock	122
3 May	
Anthony Benezet	123
4 May	
Carl von Ossietzky	124
5 May	
Pete Seeger	125
6 May	
Ariel Dorfman	126
7 May	
Carl Upchurch	127

8 May		25 May	
Pat Barker	128	David Dellinger	145
9 May		26 May	
Sophia Scholl	129	Utah Phillips	146
10 May		27 May	
Beyers Naudé	130	Julia Ward Howe	147
11 May		28 May	
Mychal Judge	131	Rachel Carson	148
12 May		29 May	
Brother Roger	132	Leó Szilárd	149
13 May		30 May	
Fridtjof Nansen	133	Ruth Manorama	150
14 May		31 May	
Peter Maurin	134	Jean-Pierre Willem	151
15 May		1 June	
Frances Crowe	135	Mary Dyer	152
16 May		2 June	
Nhat Chi Mai	136	John XXIII	153
17 May		3 June	
Daniel Berrigan	137	Satish Kumar	154
18 May		4 June	
Bertrand Russell	138	Jim Wallis	155
19 May		5 June	
Laozi	139	Angie Zelter	156
20 May		6 June	
Wei Jingsheng	140	Marian Wright Edelman	157
21 May		7 June	
Elizabeth Fry	141	Seattle	158
22 May		8 June	
Betty Williams	142	John Perkins	159
23 May		9 June	
Max Walters	143	Bertha von Suttner	160
24 May		10 June	
Harry Emerson Fosdick	144	Sumaya Farhat-Naser	161

Contents

11 June
Jeanette Rankin — 162

12 June
Frédéric Passy — 163

13 June
Dante Alighieri — 164

14 June
David Low Dodge — 165

15 June
Paul Rusesabagina — 166

16 June
Charles Yale Harrison — 167

17 June
Viktor Popkov — 168

18 June
José Brocca — 169

19 June
Aung San Suu Kyi — 170

20 June
Jonathan Dymond — 171

21 June
Shirin Ebadi — 172

22 June
Paulinus of Nola — 173

23 June
William Sloane Coffin — 174

24 June
Raphael Lemkin — 175

25 June
Lois Marie Gibbs — 176

26 June
Justin Martyr — 177

27 June
Geoffrey "Woodbine Willie" Studdert Kennedy — 178

28 June
Danilo Dolci — 179

29 June
Samantha Smith — 180

30 June
Muhammad Yunus — 181

1 July
David Brower — 182

2 July
Birsel Lemke — 183

3 July
Kees Boeke — 184

4 July
Ron Kovic — 185

5 July
H.H. Dalai Lama — 186

6 July
Elise Boulding — 187

7 July
Ben Linder — 188

8 July
Peace Pilgrim — 189

9 July
Shane Claiborne — 190

10 July
Toyohiko Kagawa — 191

11 July
Abdulkadir Yahya Ali — 192

12 July
Mitch Snyder — 193

13 July
Toma Sik — 194

14 July
Woody Guthrie — 195

15 July
Barbara Lee — 196

16 July
Bartolomé de las Casas — 197

17 July
Ammon Hennacy — 198

18 July
Nelson Mandela — 199

19 July
Barbara Deming — 200

20 July
Mirabehn — 201

21 July
Albert Lutuli — 202

22 July
William Wilberforce — 203

23 July
Leopold Engleitner — 204

24 July
Stanley Hauerwas — 205

25 July
Walter Rauschenbusch — 206

26 July
Eberhard Arnold — 207

27 July
George Bernard Shaw — 208

28 July
Lupus of Troyes — 209

29 July
Dag Hammarskjöld — 210

30 July
Smedley Butler — 211

31 July
Ingrid Washinawatok el-Issa — 212

1 August
Conrad Grebel — 213

2 August
Niall O'Brien — 214

3 August
Martin Sheen — 215

4 August
Raoul Wallenberg — 216

5 August
Wendell Berry — 217

6 August
Hibakusha — 218

7 August
Helen Caldicott — 219

8 August
Gordon Zahn — 220

9 August
Franz Jägerstätter — 221

10 August
Peter Damian — 222

11 August
Clare of Assisi — 223

12 August
Benedict of Nursia — 224

13 August
John Dear — 225

14 August
Maximilian Kolbe — 226

Contents

15 August
Óscar Romero — 227

16 August
E. F. Schumacher — 228

17 August
Catherine Doherty — 229

18 August
Mozi — 230

19 August
Petr Chelčický — 231

20 August
Jonathan Daniels — 232

21 August
Raymond Hunthausen — 233

22 August
Ouray — 234

23 August
Iccho Itoh — 235

24 August
Howard Zinn — 236

25 August
Ginetta Sagan — 237

26 August
Jinzaburo Takagi — 238

27 August
Mother Teresa — 239

28 August
Smaragdus of St. Mihiel — 240

29 August
Arndt Pekurinen — 241

30 August
Gene Sharp — 242

31 August
Jaime Sin — 243

1 September
Siegfried Sassoon — 244

2 September
Dick Sheppard — 245

3 September
e. e. cummings — 246

4 September
Albert Schweitzer — 247

5 September
Jonathan Kozol — 248

6 September
Jane Addams — 249

7 September
Asoka — 250

8 September
Mother Ann Lee — 251

9 September
Ruth Fry — 252

10 September
Jean Vanier — 253

11 September
Vinoba Bhave — 254

12 September
Solange Fernex — 255

13 September
Aristophanes — 256

14 September
Cyprian of Carthage — 257

15 September
Jean Renoir — 258

16 September
Ursula Franklin — 259

17 September
Ron Sider — 260

18 September
Chris Hedges — 261

19 September
Paulo Freire — 262

20 September
Henry Salt — 263

21 September
Henri Nouwen — 264

22 September
James Lawson — 265

23 September
Eric Bogle — 266

24 September
Hildegard of Bingen — 267

25 September
Erich Maria Remarque — 268

26 September
Paul VI — 269

27 September
Nujood Ali — 270

28 September
Lillian Smith — 271

29 September
Lech Walesa — 272

30 September
Elie Wiesel — 273

1 October
Vida Scudder — 274

2 October
Mohandas Gandhi — 275

3 October
Robert Barclay — 276

4 October
Francis of Assisi — 277

5 October
Philip Berrigan — 278

6 October
Fannie Lou Hamer — 279

7 October
Desmond Tutu — 280

8 October
Penny Lernoux — 281

9 October
Jody Williams — 282

10 October
Ken Saro-Wiwa — 283

11 October
Thich Nhat Hanh — 284

12 October
Edith Stein — 285

13 October
Mordecai Vanunu — 286

14 October
William Penn — 287

15 October
Mahavira — 288

16 October
Günter Grass — 289

17 October
Richard McSorley — 290

18 October
René Ngongo — 291

19 October
John Woolman — 292

20 October
Wayne Morse — 293

21 October
Ernest Fremont Tittle — 294

Contents

22 October
  Eileen Egan — 295

23 October
  Anita Roddick — 296

24 October
  Denise Levertov — 297

25 October
  Micah — 298

26 October
  Paul Farmer — 299

27 October
  Klas Pontus Arnoldson — 300

28 October
  Desiderius Erasmus — 301

29 October
  Clarence Jordan — 302

30 October
  Marcellus the Centurion — 303

31 October
  Dick Gregory — 304

1 November
  Collateral Damage Victims — 305

2 November
  Samuel Ruiz Garcia — 306

3 November
  Martin de Porres — 307

4 November
  James Groppi — 308

5 November
  Vandana Shiva — 309

6 November
  Lucretia Mott — 310

7 November
  Eleanor Roosevelt — 311

8 November
  Dorothy Day — 312

9 November
  Thomas Berry — 313

10 November
  Seneca — 314

11 November
  Martin of Tours — 315

12 November
  Baha'u'llah — 316

13 November
  Karen Silkwood — 317

14 November
  Pedro Arrupe — 318

15 November
  Paul Moore — 319

16 November
  Adolfo Sansolini — 320

17 November
  Origen — 321

18 November
  Howard Thurman — 322

19 November
  Gillo Pontecorvo — 323

20 November
  Leo Tolstoy — 324

21 November
  Menno Simons — 325

22 November
  Aldous Huxley — 326

23 November
  Maude Royden — 327

Date	Name	Page
24 November	Arundhati Roy	328
25 November	Paul Jones	329
26 November	Adolfo Esquivel	330
27 November	Thich Quang Do	331
28 November	Arthur Carman	332
29 November	Elias Chacour	333
30 November	Etty Hillesum	334
1 December	Peter Rideman	335
2 December	Gamaliel	336
3 December	Aelred of Rievaulx	337
4 December	Benjamin Britten	338
5 December	Clement of Alexandria	339
6 December	Ryan White	340
7 December	Ivo Markovic	341
8 December	Elihu Burritt	342
9 December	Dalton Trumbo	343
10 December	Thomas Merton	344
11 December	Martyrs of El Mozote	345
12 December	Hafsat Abiola	346
13 December	Archibald Baxter	347
14 December	Andrei Sakharov	348
15 December	Ludovic Lazarus Zamenhof	349
16 December	Kabir	350
17 December	Craig Kielburger	351
18 December	Junsei Terasawa	352
19 December	James Peck	353
20 December	Sidney Lewis Gulick	354
21 December	Emma Tenayuca	355
22 December	Francis Sheehy-Skeffington	356
23 December	Abraham Joshua Heschel	357
24 December	Benjamin Rush	358
25 December	Jesus the Christ	359
26 December	Walter Wink	360

Contents

27 December
    Lactantius   361

28 December
    Child Soldiers   362

29 December
    John Howard Yoder   363

30 December
    Maurice McCrackin   364

31 December
    John Timothy Leary   365

For Further Reading   367
Alphabetical Index   387

Introduction

Becoming Instruments of Peace

PEACEMAKING IS HARD WORK because violence is the norm in our world. The going assumption in our schools, popular culture, governing bodies, and (sadly) religious institutions is that violence is inevitable and necessary: inevitable because evildoers will always try to harm good people, necessary because defensive or retaliatory violence is the only thing that will dissuade or stop them. The inconsistency of seeing violence as a tragic fact in some contexts but a virtue in others apparently doesn't trouble most of us. Violence remains our default assumption, peace but a fleeting interlude or interruption in the normal course of events. So peacemakers who deny that violence is either inevitable or necessary have their work cut out for them. Swimming against the current is a daunting and overwhelming task.

That's why we offer this book of peacemakers. In profiling the lives, thoughts, and deeds of people from all over the globe who offer alternatives to violence, we hope to inspire others who yearn and work for peace and justice. It helps to be reminded that one isn't alone in the task, and that people of good will from ancient times to the present have labored to become instruments of peace in a world that too often settles for violence. It helps to hear the stories of fellow peacemakers. We learn from them, we gain strength from them, and we pass their wisdom on to the next generation. A daily reading of how they swam against the tide and created new currents can be an uplifting tonic.

The lives of peacemakers are richly diverse. They share certain core convictions, but the various contexts in which they work make each of their stories unique. Profiled in these pages are men, women, and children from all points of the compass and whose lives span twenty-five hundred years of history. Many are persons of faith—Christian, Jewish, Muslim, Hindu, Buddhist, Bahai, Jain—but some are totally secular in their outlook. Some have familiar and even household names, while others are relatively unknown. They are human rights and anti-war activists, scientists and artists, educators and scholars, songwriters and poets, film directors and authors, diplomats and economists, environmentalists and mystics, prophets and policymakers. Some are unlettered, but all are wise. A few died in the service of nonviolence. All sacrificed for it.

What are some of the core convictions that peacemakers bring to the table?

First, peacemakers believe that peace and justice are so intimately linked that one is impossible in the other's absence. Justice is the establishment of right proportionality or fairness. When men, women, nonhuman animals, and the earth herself are treated fairly and with respect, justice reigns. Peace, as theologian Walter Brueggemann says, is characterized by a "persistent vision of joy, well-being, harmony, and prosperity." It is a healing of fragmentation and disunity which allows justice to flourish.

Second, peacemakers understand that violence is essentially a violation, transgression, or infringement that assaults and shatters well-being. When it comes to violence, there is a frighteningly wide spectrum that includes the global environmental devastation caused by unsustainable lifestyles and public policy, the large-scale destructiveness of warfare, unjust economic and political institutions, and the turmoil of self-hatred or neurotic guilt. Moreover, violence is indiscriminate, cutting a broad swath of destruction that engulfs everyone and everything in its path. It brutalizes those who wield it, even when they do so with good intentions.

Third, peacemakers agree that a genuinely fruitful response to violence must model the proportionality and resulting concord that are the ultimate goals. Peace sustains an organic relationship between means and ends, method and goal. Justice and peace can't be lastingly achieved through unjust policies or violent methods. To presume otherwise not only ignores lessons of history; it also violates right proportionality. As pacifist A. J. Muste famously put it, "There is no *way* to peace. Peace *is* the way." Responding violently to violence *could* lead to a temporary lessening of oppression or aggression. But it's bought at the terrible price of perpetuating the cycle of violence that breeds oppression and aggression in the first place. Genuine justice and enduring peace can't be imposed violently, because violence by its very nature fragments and destroys.

This doesn't mean that peacemakers turn a blind eye to injustices that rupture peace. The nonviolence most of them embrace is an active force rather than a passive acquiescence to injustice. Some peacemakers actually dislike the word *pacifism* because it sounds too much like "passivity." But nonviolence as both a lifestyle and a liberating strategy of resistance is powerful enough to convert cultures of oppression; witness the American civil rights movement and the "velvet revolutions" against Soviet domination that took place in Europe in 1989.

The fourth conviction shared by peacemakers is that conflicts between competing interests don't magically disappear. Pacifist author Aldous Huxley and civil rights giant Martin Luther King Jr. both pointed out that whitewashing inner turmoil and oppressive social structures for the sake of surface tranquility is a phony peace doomed to collapse. For genuine justice and peace to flourish, conflicts must be faced with honesty and courage whenever they arise. The key difference is that a solution will be sought through peaceful rather than violent means. Discussion, arbitration, and reconciliation are the tactics of nonviolent conflict resolution, and they're applicable to both international and interpersonal disputes.

Finally, most peacemakers, especially religious ones, believe that peace is both an external state of concord and an internal state of tranquility. Some twenty-five centuries ago, the philosopher Plato drew an analogy between political justice and individual virtue. Both, he argued, are defined by a right proportionality, or justice, that establishes harmony, or peace. His point was that the inner and the outer are mutually dependent. The lesson for the peacemaker is the importance of cultivating a harmony in her inner world similar to the one she hopes to nurture in the outer world. Without this integration

Becoming Instruments of Peace

of inner and outer, the strain of peace work becomes too burdensome. To paraphrase Gandhi, "You must be the [nonviolent] change you wish to see in the world."

Fortified by these five convictions, peacemakers from a mosaic of cultural perspectives continue to strive for a world in which, as pacifist Peter Maurin once said, it's a bit easier for men and women to be good. All peacemakers bring different talents and temperaments to the task, and each has something valuable to contribute. What links them—and us—together is the shared desire to be, as a prayer attributed to Francis of Assisi puts it, "instruments of peace." Our hope is that the entire year's worth of peacemaker stories offered in this book helps sustain and focus that desire.

❋ ❋ ❋

When we began thinking about this book, one of our worries was that we'd have trouble finding enough peacemakers to fill up an entire year's calendar. It was a silly concern. As we progressed, we realized that our real problem would be figuring out how to hone down the hundreds and hundreds of candidates to a mere 365. It was exhilarating to discover so many fascinating and worthy peacemakers who have made the world a better place, but it was challenging—not to mention humbling!—to decide which ones to include and which ones to leave out. So we want to acknowledge here what will be apparent to discerning readers anyway: there are hundreds of celebrated peacemakers not included in this volume and unsung thousands who labor every day to end violence and promote justice. We know that many of you who will read this book could easily have been profiled in it, or that you know someone who could have been included. Our apologies, and our gratitude, to you all.

The 365 profiles are snapshots rather than fully developed biographies. Sometimes we've offered a biographical summary, but more often we've focused on a particular event or theme in the individual peacemaker's life and work that especially reveals his or her character. In preparing the profiles, we combed through multiple resources: biographies and autobiographies, essays, letters, award citations, speeches, news articles, and obituaries. Readers wanting more information may consult the "For Further Reading" bibliography at the end of the book.

In organizing this book, we did our best to match up peacemakers and calendar days according to either their birth or death dates. We were usually successful. But because more than one peacemaker sometimes fit a single date, a few profiles had to be moved to nearby days of the calendar. Then, of course, there are a few other peacemakers, typically ancient but a few more recent, for whom we could find no definite birth or death days. We've scattered these throughout the book in a loving but calendrically arbitrary way.

We're grateful to many people for their advice and encouragement. First and foremost, we're glad to acknowledge that the initial inspiration for *Blessed Peacemakers* was Robert Ellsberg's wonderful book *All Saints: Daily Reflections on Saints, Prophets, and Witnesses for Our Time*. What he did for saints we hope, in a much more modest way, to do for peacemakers.

We are immensely grateful to our copy editor, Jacob Martin, for his expert and conscientious grooming of our text.

In addition, our families and friends have been enthusiastic and helpful supporters of the project from start to finish. It was a rare week when one or the other of them didn't suggest a new candidate for inclusion in the book or ask us who we happened "to be working on" at the moment. More specifically, Kerry thanks Karl Mattson and Sara Tower for their patience in listening to him think aloud about this project, and for their own inspiring peace work. But the bulk of his gratitude goes, as usual, to his wife, Kim, and his son, Jonah. Robin thanks the group PeaceWay for their continued inspiration and loving example in their daily working for justice and peace. Robin would especially like to thank Chris, Janine, and Sedona.

1 January
Telemachus

DIED 1 JANUARY 404

Opponent of Gladiatorial Games

THE CHURCH FATHER THEODORETUS reports that in the waning years of the Roman Empire, an ascetic monk "from the east" ventured into a gladiatorial stadium in Rome and tried to put a stop to the bloodthirsty contest that was a staple of Roman culture.

The gladiatorial game originated as a funeral gift for the dead. The first of these funeral rituals occurred in 264 BCE, when Decimus Junius Brutus ordered three pairs of slaves to fight in memory of his father. Over the next few centuries, gladiatorial combat became one of the symbols of Roman culture and authority easily recognized throughout the entire empire. It was also an integral part of the oddly named *Pax Romana*.

The *Pax Romana* kept the "peace" in three ways: the military, which used brutal and ruthless violence to keep the Roman "peace"; crucifixion, which served as a public method of execution to suppress any rebellion from conquered lands; and the stadium, the venue of violence for the common people that celebrated the military ideal of conquest through bloodshed.

In the latter part of the fourth century, Roman military might was fraying, stretched too thin by the hopeless task of policing the empire's borders. Crucifixion had been abolished in 337 by Constantine when he converted to Christianity. The stadium's gladiatorial combat, still as popular as ever, was the only aspect of the *Pax Romana* that remained relatively unscathed.

In Greek, Telemachus means "faraway fighter." It's an ironic name for a Christian who tried to put a stop to the gladiatorial games. He is said to have descended into the stadium "entreating the combatants" to cease fighting, but was beaten to the ground and killed.

The symbolism of Telemachus' name wasn't lost on the faithful in the fifth century. He "fights" (nonviolently) for Christ against the Roman Empire. From the "faraway" east, a place unsullied by the values of the violent Roman culture, he steps into a gladiatorial fight for the sake of the peace of Christ and is martyred.

The historical details about Telemachus' death are obscure. Some records claim he was killed by the gladiators he confronted, others that he was stoned to death by the spectators, who were furious that their sport had been interrupted. Regardless of how he met his end, Telemachus' fifth-century biographer Theodoretus clearly saw the death of the ascetic monk from the east as a symbol of Christianity's repudiation of violence. And whether killed by sword or stone, Telemachus' death was the catalyst that prompted the Emperor Honorius to end the practice of gladiatorial games in Rome. According to tradition, the final gladiator game in the empire took place on 1 January 404, which is also accepted as the day Telemachus met his end.

2 January

Willi Graf

1 January 1918—12 October 1943

Silence Is Complicity

BORN IN THE FINAL year of World War I to Anna and Gerhard Graf, Willi Graf was one of four children. His family was devoutly Roman Catholic. By the time he was fifteen, the same year that Hitler came to power in Germany, he was a leader in a Catholic youth organization with distinctly anti-Nazi sentiments. When the Nazis outlawed all young peoples' groups except the Hitler Youth, Graf distanced himself from friends who joined it, even refusing to associate with them. In 1934, disgusted with Nazi policies, he joined the illegal *Grauer Orden*, another Catholic youth group. His membership led to his arrest four years later. Luckily for him, authorities dismissed the charges as part of the national celebration of the German annexation of Austria.

Graf's first two years of medical studies in Munich were interrupted in 1940 by his conscription into the German army. His military service took him to the Polish ghettoes in Warsaw and Lodz, whose scenes of horror he never forgot, and finally to Russia. In 1942 he returned from the eastern front convinced that his Christian faith obliged him to resist the Nazis. To his dismay, he discovered that most of his Catholic friends were unwilling to join him. Although they were as opposed to Hitler as Graf himself was, they rejected any kind of action against the Nazis as hopeless. Graf found such inaction in the face of evil unconscionable. For him, silence was complicity.

Eventually Graf discovered and joined the White Rose, an underground organization dedicated to nonviolent resistance of the Nazi regime. Launched in the summer of 1942 with the publication of four anti-Nazi pamphlets distributed from Munich throughout Germany, the White Rose grew to a sizable student movement that outwitted the Gestapo for two years. During a time when buying paper or stamps in large quantities was a risky business, the White Rose printed and disseminated flyers that declared, "We will not be silent! We are your bad conscience. The White Rose will not leave you in peace." Night after night, Germans awoke to find subversive slogans like "Freedom!" and "Down with Hitler!" scrawled on walls.

Graf's main job in the White Rose was to recruit new members. But his work ended in February 1943 when the Gestapo arrested him and the organization's leaders. Two months later he was convicted of high treason and aiding the enemy, and sentenced to death. All appeals were denied, and Graf was beheaded on 12 October. Just before his execution, he wrote a final note to his family. "On this day I'm leaving this life and entering eternity. God's blessings on us. In Him we are and we live."

3 January
Takashi Nagai

3 January 1908—1 May 1951

The Saint of Urakami

WHEN THE ATOMIC BOMB exploded over Nagasaki, Takashi Nagai, a radiologist, was on duty at the city's medical college hospital. Although badly injured in the blast, he pitched in with the rest of the medical staff to treat the hundreds of wounded that began trickling into the hospital. It was only a day later that he was able to make his way to the suburb of Urakami where he lived with his wife, Midori, and their children.

The children had been sent to the mountains for safekeeping two days before the explosion. But Midori, and the house she and Nagai shared, were gone. He was able to recognize the carbonized remains of his wife only by the rosary clutched in the powdered bones of her right hand. Stricken with grief, Nagai prayed: "Jesus, you carried the heavy Cross until you were crucified upon it. Now You come to shed a light of peace on the mystery of suffering and death, Midori's and mine."

Nagai had come to Christianity as an adult. The son and grandson of physicians who practiced Shinto, Nagai went through a period of atheism during his medical training. He converted in his mid-twenties when his future wife, Midori, a devout Roman Catholic, slipped a catechism into a care package that she sent to him during his mandatory period of military service.

A month after the destruction of Nagasaki, Nagai was stricken by radiation sickness. Already diagnosed in the spring of that year with leukemia caused by his medical work with X-rays, Nagai remained near death for a month. But to the surprise of everyone he recovered. During his convalescence, he built a small hut from the rubble of his Urakami house where he lived for two years with his children, mother-in-law, and two other relatives. Eventually he built a smaller one for himself as a hermitage in which he spent hours in prayer and contemplation. He named the hut *Nyoko do*, "As Yourself House," from Jesus' command to "Love your neighbor as yourself."

It was in *Nyoko do* that Nagai began writing poems and books that commemorated the victims of Nagasaki, connected their suffering to the suffering of Christ, and praised the spirit of loving forgiveness. With chilling poetic finality he describes the incineration of young Christian schoolgirls "like lilies white" who died "burning red" chanting psalms. One of his poems, inspired by the death of Christian schoolgirls as they participated in morning prayer, is a stark reminder of the more than eight thousand Japanese Christians who perished in the blast. It was written as he lay dying of leukemia.

4 January
Albert Camus

7 November 1913—4 January 1960

Resisting Murder

PHILOSOPHER, NOVELIST, AND ACTIVIST Albert Camus was no stranger to violence. During the Nazi occupation of France, he was a member of the French Resistance and edited the illegal newspaper *Combat* under the *nom de guerre* "Beauchard." But by war's end, he was sick of the killing and destruction he'd witnessed. He knew there had to be a better way to resolve differences. He voiced his conviction in 1946 in a remarkable series of essays titled *Neither Victims nor Executioners.*

Camus argued that people today live in a constant state of fear and that this fear "implies and rejects the same fact: a world where murder is legitimate and where human life is considered trifling." The fear is often translated into patriotic zeal that encourages killing for one's country. But for his part, declared Camus, he can no longer "hold to any truth which might oblige me, directly or indirectly, to demand a man's life." He will not be a murderer, and will resist those who advocate murder. Camus admitted that he wasn't naïve enough to wish for a world in which violence is eliminated, "but rather one in which murder is not legitimated" by the state.

A first step toward resisting murder is defending the right of "universal intercommunication," or *"le dialogue,"* between humans. At the very least, this means refusing to see natives of other countries, cultures, beliefs, and tongues as strangers to be feared and resisted. It's difficult to wage war when the "enemy" wears a human face.

Camus lived by these principles for the rest of his life. He was an outspoken champion of pacifism and opponent of capital punishment. He became an advocate for human rights, working with UNESCO until resigning to protest the United Nations' recognition of Generalissimo Franco as Spain's ruler. He tried to arbitrate a peaceful settlement in the Algerian War, a conflict that especially disturbed him since he was born in Algeria to a *pied-noir* or French settler family. He spoke out against Soviet aggression at a time when it was unfashionable for intellectuals to do so. And in his writings—novels, plays, political essays, and philosophical monographs—he tirelessly urged his readers to join him in resisting murder. "All I ask," he wrote, "is that in the midst of a murderous world, we agree to reflect on murder and to make a choice. After that, we can distinguish those who accept the consequences of being murderers themselves or the accomplices of murderers, and those who refuse to do so with all their force and being."

Albert Camus died in a car accident three years after winning the Nobel Prize in Literature.

5 January
Lanza del Vasto

29 September 1901—5 January 1981

Servant of Peace

WHEN MANY PEOPLE HEAR the word *peace*, they automatically think of the absence of armed conflict or the intervals between wars. But this negative definition of peace only scratches the surface. Genuine peace—the kind that makes for an end to warfare—is a lifestyle that seeks to nurture just relations between people on a daily basis so that well-being may flourish. It involves an inner conversion as well as a certain kind of comportment in the world. It's not just an occasional cause. It's a way of life.

Few people have appreciated this more than the Italian nobleman Lanza del Vasto. He spent some months in India before the Second World War learning the principles of nonviolence from **Mohandas Gandhi**. After the war, he returned to India for a while to work with Gandhi's disciple **Vinoba Bhave**. Gandhi was so impressed by del Vasto's dedication to nonviolence that he gave him the name Shantidas, "Servant of Peace."

In 1948, del Vasto, his wife, and several friends began an experiment in communal nonviolent living, which they called the Community of the Ark. Located in France, Ark members embraced a simple lifestyle that aimed for self-sufficiency and incorporated nonviolence into every aspect of their life together. Believing that in order to help heal the world's violence they needed to distance themselves from its baleful influence, del Vasto and his fellow Ark members saw their community as a refuge in which to build their commitment to peace and rejuvenate their spirits. As he once said, "We are accused of going against the times. We are doing that deliberately and with all our strength." But the community was never intended to be a head-in-the-sand retreat. Del Vasto and his companions were frequently in the thick of public witnesses against war, torture, the nuclear arms race, and militarism, actions for which del Vasto was arrested many times.

Del Vasto's pivotal meeting with Gandhi convinced him that "the most efficient action and the most significant testimony in favor of nonviolence and truth is living a life in which there is no violence or unfairness, neither hidden violence nor brutal violence; neither legal and permitted unfairness, nor illegal unfairness." Trained by the Community of the Ark in this kind of life, he and his followers felt empowered to help others find "the nonviolent answer" to the world's economic and political problems. What matters, he said, is to discover whether there are such things as a nonviolent economy, nonviolent authority, nonviolent justice, nonviolent medicine, farming, and diet. And the necessary condition for all of these social forms of nonviolence "is to make sure that all violence, even of speech, even of thought, even hidden and disguised, has been weeded out of our religious"—that is, inner—"life." Only then could a world of "peace, strength, and joy"—the motto that the Community of the Ark adopted as its own—be born.

6 January

Jacques Ellul

January 6, 1912—May 19, 1994

Peaceful Anarchist

Born in Bordeaux, Ellul converted to Christianity at age twenty-two. He was a leader in the French Resistance in World War II, and, despite being greatly influenced by Marx's *Das Kapital* at age sixteen (and later by theologian Karl Barth, the "second great element" of his intellectual life), Ellul maintained that Christianity and anarchism are neither ideologically nor socially incompatible. "Biblical thinking," he argued, beginning with the Hebrew Scriptures, is intensely anarchist. Ellul believed that Jesus' teaching on the relationship between the Divine and the state has been skewed by the institutional church in order to wield power within the state, thereby stymieing real peace and true cooperation between people.

In 1937, Ellul married Yvette while serving as Director of Studies at the University of Strasbourg. In 1940, after his father was arrested and killed by the Nazis for being a "foreigner," Ellul fled with his Holland-born wife before she could suffer the same fate. For the next four years, the two lived a meager existence in the countryside while helping the French Resistance.

In 1944, Ellul became deputy mayor of Bordeaux and also served on the National Synod of the Reformed Church of France. Both these endeavors led him to become disillusioned and critical of both political and religious institutions.

Ellul was especially wary of technological advances, warning that technology in modern society is suspect if it becomes a vehicle for the mass media propaganda that serves to legitimate the sacrality of the state and thus acts as a means of manipulation and control. Ellul wrote, "When I say that I 'despise technology' . . . it is not technology *per se*, but the authoritarian power that the 'technocrats' seek to exercise, as well as the fact that technology determines our lives without our being able to intervene or, as yet, control it."

Ellul dedicated himself to writing philosophical and theological works on Christianity and anarchy. His anarchy, which he argued was modeled on Jesus' social teachings, specifically championed non-domination as opposed to disorder.

A sympathetic commentator once remarked that Ellul's sharp criticisms of the politics of modern society made him like the child who "blurted out that the emperor has no clothes." The "prophet of Bordeaux," as his admirers called him, died in Pessac, France. Thanks to his work, we're more attuned to invisibly oppressive structures that stifle freedom and foster violence.

7 JANUARY
Sadako Sasaki

JANUARY 7, 1943—OCTOBER 25, 1955

A Child's Hope for Peace

THE DEATH OF A single child due to the insanity of war may be the world's most heinous crime. In the city of Hiroshima, Japan, one monument dedicated in 1958 depicts a young victim of the atomic bomb. The plaque reads, "This is our cry. This is our prayer. Peace in the world."

Sadako Sasaki was only two years old and one mile away from ground zero when the atom bomb named "Little Boy" struck on 6 August 1945. Most of her family miraculously escaped destruction, but the radioactive black rain that subsequently fell upon the city stained Sadako's clothes. In 1954, at the opening of the Hiroshima peace park, Sadako told her best friend, Chizuko Hamamoto, "I can remember it. There was a flash, like a million suns, then a heat that felt like pricking needles."

Sadako was a strong, athletic eleven-year-old track runner when she was diagnosed with leukemia, which was most probably caused by her exposure to the bomb's radiation. Shortly after she was admitted to Hiroshima's Red Cross hospital, members of her track team visited her, bringing her gifts. One of them, Sadako's best friend Chizuko, told her the story of the "thousand cranes" after she noticed Sadako admiring the bright paper birds hanging over the hospital beds of other patients.

The tale Chizuko told was the legend of the crane, a creature sacred in Japan for its longevity; cranes were believed to live for one thousand years. Functioning like the prayer flags of India and Tibet, folded paper cranes in Japan connected the human and divine realms. It was believed that the sacred crane favored whoever made the effort to fold a thousand pieces of paper into its shape, and would grant the wish of the maker.

The story renewed Sadako's hope for recovery from her illness. She longed to rejoin her track team and run relay races once again. So she spent most of her time folding cranes, scrounging scraps of paper—sometimes using even the wrappers on medicine bottles—wherever she could find them. Inside each one, Sadako carefully wrote her wish: *Make me well.*

Sadako died at the age of twelve after folding thirteen hundred cranes. Her teammates began a campaign to raise funds for a memorial to her—a statue of Sadako holding a golden crane. It stands in her honor and to the memory of all the children who died as a result of the atomic bomb blast in Hiroshima. It is one of the world's most vivid monuments to peace.

8 January
Emily Greene Balch

8 January 1867—9 January 1961

Global Peace Is Ultimately Personal

THE SECOND WOMAN TO receive the Nobel Peace Prize (awarded to her in 1946), Emily Greene Balch was born in Boston, Massachusetts, the daughter of a prosperous and educated family dedicated to abolitionism in the years leading up to the Civil War. Taking advantage of the opportunities in higher education available to women of her generation, Balch was a member of Bryn Mawr's first graduating class in 1889.

Balch's commitment to social justice and peace began in her youth under the influence of the Reverend Charles Dole, whom she described as a preacher of "good will, not in the sense of mere kindliness, but of unceasing 'all out' willing the good." Along with **Vida Scudder** and Helena Dudley, Balch founded Denison House in Boston, named in honor of the British socialist theologian Frederick Denison Maurice and inspired by the burgeoning Christian Socialist movement in America.

Balch's religious views—founded on the liberal Unitarianism of her youth, which valued rational discourse over polemics—led her to view coercive force as "self-defeating" and to assert that "new methods, free from violence, must be worked out for ending abuses and for undoing wrongs, as well as for achieving positive ends." She became a Quaker in 1921.

After graduate studies in economics and social justice in Paris and Berlin, Balch joined the faculty of Wellesley College in 1896. When the United States entered World War I, she participated in anti-war movements because she believed that the violence of this and all other wars reflected "our whole economic and social system [and] our scale of value." Her socialist and pacifist views led to her termination from Wellesley after a twenty-two-year teaching career.

In 1919, Balch became the Secretary-Treasurer of the Women's International League for Peace and Freedom. In that position, she worked diligently for global peace, believing that nationalism was antithetical to real or enduring peace. Social change, Balch argued, came only through understanding that "the most precious thing we know of is personality." Personal relationships are the key to peace.

In 1939, Balch was again at the forefront of the anti-war movement. Soon, however, she reluctantly modified her pacifist stance toward Nazism, believing that military opposition to Hitler was a necessary although unspeakably tragic evil.

Balch's enduring work with the Women's International League for Peace and Justice helped shape policy decisions of the League of Nations and eventually influenced the principles promoted by the United Nations.

9 January
Rigoberta Menchú Tum

9 January 1959—

Respecting the Dignity of the Indigenous

Although her struggle for justice was famous throughout the rest of the world, Rigoberta Menchú Tum, the K'iche' Mayan peacemaker from Guatemala, was acknowledged by her own government as a force to be reckoned with only after she won the 1992 Nobel Peace Prize. The Nobel Committee honored Menchú for her advocacy for the rights of Guatemala's indigenous peoples.

Menchú inherited the struggle for economic equality from her Mayan ancestors. By 1679, the Spanish conquistadores had conquered all of the Mayan kingdoms and established colonial rule throughout Central America. For the next five hundred years, indigenous peoples were peasant slaves to wealthy European settlers, despite several violent attempts to throw off the yoke.

Menchú's father, Vicente, fell afoul of the law when he tried to cultivate land in the mountains of Guatemala that belonged to wealthy landowners. While he spent time in prison, his family was forced to work on the plantation or *finca* to earn enough money for his release. His later involvement in the Peasants' Unity Committee or *Comité de Unidad Campesina* (CUC), an organization that demanded the overthrow of the repressive Guatemalan government, eventually led to his murder by the Guatemalan army in January 1980. Two of Menchú's brothers died from malnutrition and the poisonous effects of pesticides used on the *fincas*, and a third was murdered. Their grieving mother was abducted by Guatemalan soldiers who raped, tortured, and killed her.

Inspired by her father's example, Menchú began working for the CUC. Her activism forced her into hiding soon after the deaths of her parents. Fleeing to Mexico, she returned to Guatemala in 1981 to continue the work her father started by joining with several groups (among them the Vicente Menchú Revolutionary Christians) as an educator. She traveled to Europe in 1982 as part of a coalition to raise awareness about the plight of indigenous Guatemalans. While there, she met the anthropologist Elisabeth Burgos. Burgos' interview with Menchú eventually became the book *I, Rigoberta*, which gained Rigoberta and the indigenous movement of Guatemala international attention when it was published in 1983.

Shortly after being awarded the Nobel Prize, Menchú founded the Rigoberta Menchú Tum Foundation, which continues to advocate tirelessly for the rights of the poor and indigenous Mayan people of Guatemala. Its "Code of Ethics for an Era of Peace" states: "There is no Peace without Justice; No Justice without Equality; No Equality without Development; No Development without Democracy; No Democracy without Respect to the Identity and Dignity of Cultures and Peoples."

10 January
Henry Scott Holland

27 January 1847—17 March 1918

Society's Christianization

If Henry Scott Holland's name is recognized today, it's most likely because of a one-liner of his, often repeated at funerals, that "death is nothing to us." The work that he considered his true calling—awakening his fellow Christians to the truth that "duty to God and duty to man are the same thing"—is nearly forgotten. And that's a shame.

Holland was an intellectual who enjoyed the scholarly life. But he was also an Anglican priest, and he believed it his duty to coax Christians out of their pews and into the unpleasant world of poverty, violence, and despair to which they often closed their eyes. Genuine Christianity, he believed, was much more than a set of creeds. It was the living experience of helping the poor, sick, homeless, imprisoned, and needy, just as Jesus did and just as he commanded his disciples to do. So in 1884, Holland left a comfortable lectureship at Oxford to become a member of the clerical staff at London's St. Paul's Cathedral. He wanted a better understanding of England's social problems.

His experiences in the streets of London, which he described as "reeking with human misery," led to the publication in 1889 of his most famous book, *Lux Mundi*. In it, he alarmed the ecclesiastical and political establishment of the day by calling for the "Christianization of the social structure whereby all men live in accordance with the principles of divine justice and human brotherhood." This was disturbing enough, but Holland's denunciation of capitalism as the primary obstacle to society's Christianization, and his recommendation that the state take over and supervise commercial transactions and industrial production in order to protect workers, absolutely scandalized the upper and middle classes.

On the heels of *Lux Mundi*'s appearance, Holland formed the Christian Social Union to "investigate areas in which moral truth and Christian principles could bring relief to the social and economic disorder of society." For years the Union published a magazine, *Commonwealth*, in which the plight of the poor—substandard housing, inadequate medical care, low wages, and so on—was regularly reported. *Commonwealth* also led the way on several campaigns for social and economic reform, especially in calling for a state-guaranteed minimum wage and unemployment benefits to workers who lose their jobs through no fault of their own.

Holland returned to Oxford in 1910 as the Regius Professor of Divinity to educate a rising generation of clergy in his vision of a Christian's social duty. The shock of World War I seriously undermined his already fragile health, and his final years were painful. But to the end, he cautioned his students against a smug or otherworldly churchiness by impressing upon them that duty to God and duty to one's fellow humans coincided.

11 January
Aldo Leopold

11 January 1887—21 April 1948

Making Peace with the Land

ALDO LEOPOLD EXPRESSED HIS passionate love for his wife, Estella, whom he married in 1912, in carefully copied lines of poetry in one of his many notebooks. He expressed his passion for a "land ethic" through a compilation of essays, *A Sand County Almanac,* published in 1949 and dedicated "to my Estella." It was a literary achievement that led future generations to view land not just as a commodity, but as a gift to be shared with and nurtured by all creation—a gift deserving the same tender affection we feel for a spouse or lover.

Leopold argued that "land" wasn't merely "soil." Land was the foundation and source of nutrition for the plants and animals that make up the biotic community. That community's natural integrity deserved careful guardianship because "man-made changes have effects more comprehensive than intended or foreseen." So far as Leopold was concerned, the pesticide DDT had as much potential destructive power as the atomic bomb.

"All history," wrote Leopold, "consists of successive excursions from a single starting point, to which man returns again and again to organize yet another search for a durable scale of values." He believed that the land was both the means and ultimate end in that scale, the lasting gold standard to which history, both human and animal, must always appeal.

Born in the relative wilds of Burlington, Iowa, Leopold spent his youth roaming his own backyard of prairies and woods and developing astute observational skills. An avid reader, he also began cultivating a vivid literary talent. He attended Yale and received a degree in forestry.

Upon graduation, Leopold was assigned to the Arizona territories by the U.S. Forest Service. In 1924, he was reassigned to the U.S. Forest Products Laboratory in Madison, Wisconsin, and he began teaching at the University of Wisconsin in 1928.

After the 1933 publication of his book *Game Management,* Leopold was appointed the first chair of the University of Wisconsin's new Department of Game Management. Two years later, he and his family bought and settled into a worn-out farm that became the laboratory for his "land ethic," whose main principle was "to stop thinking about decent land use as solely an economic problem. A thing is right when it tends to preserve the integrity, stability, and beauty of the biotic community. It is wrong when it tends otherwise."

Leopold died from a heart attack in 1948, two hours after trying to fight a brush fire on a neighbor's farm. His final moments were spent defending the earth he so loved.

12 January

Benny Giay

12 January 1955—

Creating a Zone of Peace

West Papua, the westernmost province of the large island of New Guinea, has its share of troubles. Part of the Dutch East Indies colony for over a century, it was claimed by Indonesia in 1949 after the Dutch gave up sovereign claims to the island. The Indonesian occupation that succeeded the Dutch one lasted some twenty years, finally ending when a UN-sponsored referendum allowed Papuans to decide whether to stick with Indonesia or to form a separate state. Although they chose to remain with Indonesia, a breakaway movement that favored independence rejected the decision. Since that time, West Papuans have endured years of civil warfare between the guerrilla separatists and the Indonesian armed forces.

To make matters worse, ethnic Indonesians, most of whom are brown-skinned and Muslim, tend to treat dark-skinned Papuans, who are predominantly Christian, as second-class citizens. This racial and economic discrimination continues to fuel the guerrillas' resistance to the government. It also prompts abuse of Papuans by the Indonesian military's anti-terrorist strike force, which arbitrarily targets churches, schools, and private Papuan homes. Displaced villagers whose homes and livelihoods have been destroyed are forced to flee into the jungles.

Rev. Benny Giay, an indigenous Papuan, has spent years trying to make West Papua a "zone of peace" by working for trust and reconciliation between his people and the native Indonesians. An evangelical minister who earned a doctorate in anthropology from a Dutch university, Giay rejects the violence practiced by the separatists while at the same time refusing to condone Indonesian persecution. But he believes that nonviolent resistance is a more effective response to the oppression than civil war, whose primary victims are innocent men, women, and children. So his efforts have been focused on educating West Papuans to take on leadership roles in their communities and writing and speaking about Muslim persecution of Papuan Christians to let the world know what's going on.

One of Giay's most successful campaigns at nonviolent empowerment was the founding of West Papua's first seminary in 1986. Prior to that time, Christian ministerial candidates were forced to travel far from West Papua to be educated at foreign institutions. Giay's seminary focuses on offering seminarians educational opportunities that emphasize the principles and methods of liberation theology. He believes that the homegrown training they receive best prepares them for future public leadership in a land that, for all practical purposes, is under military occupation, and whose best chance of liberation is through active nonviolence inspired by gospel principles.

Giay has suffered for his peace work. Many of his books have been banned by the Indonesian government, he has sometimes been arrested, and he regularly receives death threats. But he continues his labors for the "New Papua" he envisions: a land where light-skinned Muslims and dark-skinned Papuans live together without rancor or persecution.

13 January
Thomas Hurndall

27 November 1981—13 January 2004

Defying the Stars for Peace

Jocelyn Hurndall wrote about the death of her son Tom this way: "I am often asked, what is it like to lose a child? It's like this. Between the instant of receiving the news and the next instant in which you have to comprehend it, you somehow realize that every cell in your body is about to be shaken furiously, and you freeze to delay the moment of impact. Your entire existence becomes concertinaed into the space between the blow and the pain, and nothing will ever, or can ever be the same again."

Tom's is a tragically old story: a son who learns the value of the struggle for peace and justice from his mother and then loses his life in the effort; the mother who continues the tradition of peacemaking in memory of her son.

London-born Tom Hurndall was a twenty-one-year-old university student photographing activists acting as human shields to protect ordinary Iraqis in Baghdad when he heard about the death of **Rachel Corrie**. Rachel was a twenty-three-year-old peace activist crushed under an Israeli bulldozer as she tried to protect a Palestinian family's home.

In April 2003, Tom travelled to Gaza to investigate Corrie's story, joining the International Solidarity Movement (ISM) at a refugee camp in the Gaza strip. When shots began hitting the buildings, Tom left his safe position behind a roadblock to lift a small boy out of danger. He was returning for two small girls when an Israeli sniper in a tower shot him in the head. His transport to hospital, which should have taken seven minutes, took thirty minutes because of delays at Israeli checkpoints. Nine months later, never coming out of a coma, Tom was dead.

Jocelyn Hurndall began the frustrating task of making sense of her son's death within the conflicting context of the refusal of Israeli and British authorities to assume accountability (and their subsequent cover-up) and Yassar Arafat's praise of Tom as a martyr.

In the end, a Bedouin sergeant, Taysir Walid Heib, an Arab who couldn't read or write Hebrew, was convicted of Tom's murder and given an eight-year sentence—the longest for a Israeli soldier since the Second Intifada. Jocelyn wrote that "Tom was a victim of a victim." She believed the policymakers of the war deserved the heaviest recriminations.

Jocelyn wrote a book in memory of Tom, the title of which echoes the words he had tattooed on his wrist: *Defy the Stars*.

14 January
Martin Niemöller

14 January, 1892—6 March 1984

A Life Changed for Peace

MARTIN NIEMÖLLER'S EARLY CAREER was theologically distant from the Christian pacifism he later advocated. Born in Lippstadt, Germany, the second son of a Lutheran Pastor, Niemöller grew up in a traditional and perhaps anti-Semitic home. Devotion to his country led him to a career in the Kaiser's navy during World War I. He quickly rose through the ranks, becoming captain of a U-boat and receiving the Iron Cross for his success in sinking allied ships.

A religious turning point came in 1918 as he navigated through the Straits of Otranto. Niemöller wondered, "Will peace come to us—or shall we, like the Flying Dutchman, spend year after year without rest or respite?" He felt "instinctively conscious of a further mission of some kind awaiting me. Why, otherwise, should God Himself have directed our helm now?"

After the war, Niemöller resigned his commission and, as he later wrote in his memoir *From U-Boat to Pulpit*, began the transition from German nationalist to Lutheran pastor. Initially supportive of Hitler's ideals, Niemöller soon saw the dangerous way the Führer conflated German nationalism with "German" Christianity to further Nazi propaganda. In an attempt to stem the Nazi tyranny over the churches and to "obey God and not men," Niemöller and other dissenting theologians such as Karl Barth and **Dietrich Bonhoeffer** formed the Confessing Church.

For his activism, Niemöller spent eight years in Sachsenhausen and Dachau concentration camps as Hitler's "personal prisoner." His wife, Else, whom he married in 1919, was left to raise their children alone and was allowed only infrequent visits.

At the end of the war, critics called Niemöller to task for his early anti-Semitic stance, a charge that a repentant Niemöller did not deny. In 1959, he wrote that his years in prison were another religious turning point in his life. He initiated the Stuttgart Declaration of Guilt, which confessed that the German Protestant churches had not done enough to stem Nazi crimes.

Near the end of his life, Niemöller became a proponent of nuclear disarmament and an ardent pacifist. He visited communist leader Ho Chi Minh during the Vietnam War, remarking, "One thing is clear: the president of North Vietnam is not a fanatic. He is a very strong and determined man, but capable of listening, rare in a person of his position." Niemöller became president of the World Council of Churches in 1961 and earned the Lenin Peace Prize in 1966.

Looking back on his career on the occasion of his ninetieth birthday, Niemöller said he began as "an ultra-conservative who wanted the Kaiser to come back; and now I am a revolutionary. If I live to be one hundred, I shall maybe be an anarchist."

15 January
Nathan Söderblom

15 January 1866—12 July 1931

Ecumenical Pioneer

BORN IN THE COUNTRY parish of Trönö, Sweden, Soderblöm, the son of a Lutheran pastor, was destined for a life in Christian ministry. Possessing a keen intellect, he attended the University of Uppsala and graduated in 1883 with honors in Greek, Latin, Arabic, and Hebrew. At the time, the academic fields of the History of Religion and the Origins of Christianity were viewed by many clergy as threats to the Christian faith. But Soderblöm believed otherwise, and as a graduate student learned Old Persian to explore whether the Old and New Testaments had been influenced by the religion of Iran. He earned his BD degree in 1892 and was ordained in March 1893.

That same year, Soderblöm experienced "a direct perception of the holiness of God . . . , that God was far stricter than anyone could comprehend. God is a consuming fire. This apprehension was so powerful, so shattering, that [I] was unable to stay on [my] feet." For the rest of his life, Soderblöm's faith remained unshakable. He was "unable to doubt God in spite of everything."

Over the next seven years, he served the Swedish Church in Paris, among the members of which were the philanthropist Alfred Nobel and the playwright August Strindberg. Soderblöm returned to Sweden in 1901 to assume a professorship in the University of Uppsala's School of Theology. The author of several well-received books, Soderblöm was especially influential in making the field of comparative religion respectable in Christian circles. He remained at the university until his 1914 election as Primate and Archbishop of Sweden.

Soderblöm's work as an academic and pastor led him to the conclusion that Christians "find no difficulty in freely interpreting Jesus' words in the Sermon on the Mount" but were much less likely "to take the master's uncomfortable words completely seriously." He believed the Church must engage with the world in order to bring about the gospel vision of justice that leads to peace.

During the final seventeen years of his life, Soderblöm worked toward that vision through his efforts to found a worldwide ecumenical movement. He sought the intercommunion of all Christian denominations, and in 1925 he worked tirelessly to bring together leaders from Anglican, Reformed, Orthodox, and Lutheran traditions in what came to be known as the Stockholm Conference. The ecumenical conference, motivated in part by the impotence of the divided churches to prevent World War I, advocated "a Christian internationalism equally opposed to a national bigotry and a weak cosmopolitanism" and "affirmed the universal character of the Church and its duty to preach and practice the love of the brethren."

Soderblöm's ecumenism earned him election to the Swedish Academy in 1925 and the Nobel Peace Prize the year before his death.

16 January

Ormond Burton

16 January 1893—7 January 1974

Christian Peace without Compromise

In 1923, four years after the end of the "war to end all wars," Ormond Burton addressed a conference of the New Zealand Student Christian movement. He called his listeners to lives of radical discipleship. For Burton, such devotion required a commitment to the nonviolence preached and practiced by Christ, and he urged the students to put their faith into practice by refusing to join or serve in the military.

No stranger to combat, Burton served as a stretcher-bearer at Gallipoli, one of the bloodiest and most wasteful standoffs of World War I. When his best friend was killed in action, he volunteered to replace him. Commissioned a lieutenant in the infantry, Burton was decorated for gallantry several times. But the harsh Treaty of Versailles that the Allies forced upon a defeated Germany convinced him that genuine peace could never be won by military conflict. The victors, he concluded, would always demand concessions from the losers that inevitably stirred up resentments and kept old wounds fresh, thereby preparing the way for the next war. As he sadly noted at the end of World War I, "Victory had not brought a new world, and we saw in a flash of illumination that it never could. War is just waste and destruction, solving no problems and creating new and terrible ones." By the time he spoke to the New Zealand Student Christian organization in 1923, he was a committed pacifist.

After the war, Burton was barred for a time from teaching because he refused to sign an oath to the Crown that would have obliged him to fight if war broke out again. He finally secured a job in a remote district of New Zealand. In the 1930s, he began training for ordination in the Methodist Church. Upon completion, he took a run-down church in one of Wellington's worst slums and quickly revitalized it by dint of hard and dedicated work. He also cofounded the Christian Pacifist Society of New Zealand. When war erupted again in 1939, he spoke out against it and was promptly arrested, released, and arrested again. Sentenced to a year in prison, he spent his time behind bars writing an anti-war tract, *Testament of Peace,* for which the Methodist Church expelled him. He would not be reinstated or given another church until 1952.

Although Burton continued as a peace activist for the rest of his life, he steadfastly refused to cooperate with non-Christian peacemakers. When the Christian Pacifist Society he helped found voted to offer membership to non-Christians, he resigned in protest. He justified his position by arguing that without a strong commitment to the Prince of Peace, pacifism was merely an abstract philosophy. Of course he was mistaken. But he can be forgiven for the sake of his lifelong dedication to nonviolence.

17 January
William Stafford

17 January 1914—28 August 1993

Show Me a Good War

SOME TEN MILLION MEN were conscripted into the U.S. military during World War II. Fifty thousand of them requested and received conscientious objector status. Some served as noncombatant medics. Others chose to go to prison. Twelve thousand opted to serve in labor camps scattered across the nation. The poet William Stafford was one of the latter.

Born in Kansas shortly before World War I erupted, Stafford grew up hearing elders—teachers, relatives, neighbors—talk about how horrible the conflict had been. So he arrived at his pacifist convictions while still quite young. When drafted in 1942 during World War II, it was only natural that he petitioned for conscientious objector status. For the next four years he performed hard manual labor in the camps—first in Arkansas, then in Illinois, and finally in California—for $2.50 a month. In Arkansas he was nearly lynched by a mob infuriated by his pacifism. After his release from the camps and his return home, a childhood friend threated to kill him for his "treasonous" opposition to the war. His first book, *Down in My Heart*, was a semi-autobiographical novel about life in the camps.

Stafford didn't begin publishing poetry until nearly twenty years after the war ended. But his verse attests to his continuing opposition to it and to all wars. (Once asked whether he believed he could fight in a "good" war, he replied, "*Show* me a good war.") In "These Mornings," Stafford meditates on what happens when warplanes bomb cities. Both buildings and people are blown up into the sky or down into the earth, he writes, leaving nothing but hideous scars on the land. In "Ground Zero," he reflects on the uncanny sidewalk photographs of victims created by the flash of the atomic blast at Hiroshima. Their shadows, he muses, are now ours. Our condoning of such an unimaginable mass killing leaves us spiritually anemic, shadow-like. And in "For the Unknown Soldier," Stafford fleshes out the abstract word *enemy* by reminding readers that the "unknown enemy soldier" is a person who, just like us, marvels at a beautiful sky or carries a laughing baby to a park. He challenges the patriotic blindness that darkens our awareness of the "enemy's" humanness.

Stafford's lifelong opposition to war wasn't strident. Although he understood and sympathized with the motives behind loud anti-war demonstrations, he neither approved of them nor participated in them. His style was quiet conversation, poetic evocation, and "living a life of witness by seeing the good in the enemy." As he once said about his conscientious objection to World War II, "I can't stop war, Jesus couldn't stop war, Eisenhower couldn't stop it. [But] I could decide there would be one person not in it."

18 January
Kenneth Boulding

18 January 1910—18 March 1993

Economist of Peace

Born in England, the son of a Liverpool plumber, Kenneth Boulding was the first in his family to go beyond elementary school. In his early years, the memory of the horrors of World War I made him a pacifist and led him to reject his family's Methodism (British Methodists had endorsed the war) and to join the Society of Friends. Boulding's commitment to nonviolence exerted a profound influence on his life's work.

Boulding was a brilliant student, earning an Oxford scholarship and later a fellowship at the University of Chicago. After settling in the United States, he began his scholarly life as an economist. But his interests ranged far beyond the boundaries of his specific discipline to include philosophy, religion, poetry, and systems analysis. He was convinced that "in any applied field one had to use all the social sciences . . . as all the social sciences were essentially studying the same thing, which was the social system."

In 1937, Boulding joined the faculty of Colgate University where he stayed for thirty years before moving to the University of Colorado. Collaborating with his wife, **Elise Boulding**, whom he married in 1941 and with whom he raised five children, Boulding's theories on peace and conflict resolution, explored in over thirty books, mirrored his pacifism. His Quaker background especially drew him to explore self-interested modes of exchange, the relationship between warfare and fear, and the importance of social and cultural interdependence to individual flourishing. In his 1963 book *Conflict and Defense*, he argued that understanding the dynamics of conflict is essential in the struggle for peace. Contrary to the opinions of many of his fellow economists, Boulding denied that economic growth was effectively fueled by warfare. Instead, he argued, it rested on cooperation and collaboration.

Boulding was more than a scholar of peace; he was also a peace activist. In 1942 he authored a circular that denounced World War II. Twenty-three years later, he helped organize the first teach-in against the Vietnam War. Boulding was also one of the first economists to decry what he called the "cowboy" mentality of wasteful and nonsustainable consumption, and he coined the term "spaceship earth" (later made famous by Buckminster Fuller) to draw attention to the need for more ecologically minded lifestyles and public policies.

Boulding died in Colorado in his eighty-fourth year. In a tribute to him, futurist and economist Hazel Henderson called Boulding "a towering intellectual figure of the twentieth century who did more than most to open windows to the twenty-first century."

19 January
Helen Mack Chang

19 January 1952—

Rationality in Justice

BEFORE THE DEATH OF her sister, Helen Mack Chang described her life as conventional and comfortable. An ethnic Chinese whose family lived in Guatemala, Chang was in her late thirties when her younger sister Myrna was stabbed twenty-seven times by a young sergeant from the Estado Mayor Presidencial, the much-feared presidential guard.

Myrna's murder was an effort on the part of Guatemala's oppressive junta to stop her investigations into the deaths and displacements of thousands of indigenous Mayans. Killed or driven from their mountain homes over the course of Guatemala's thirty-five-year civil war, the Mayans were forced into squalid refugee camps. The Guatemalan government refused to acknowledge or take responsibility for their plight. Myrna, an anthropologist, traveled to a number of camps to document personal accounts of persecution and genocide. She had already published some of the material and planned to release more. That's why she was murdered.

Myrna's death, Chang said, changed her life forever. Correctly believing that the murder was politically motivated, she began a one-woman crusade to prove her suspicion and to break the culture of impunity for political crimes that Guatemala's various military regimes had fostered. After nearly a decade, hearings before no fewer than twelve different judges, and the assassination of the lead police investigator, the military commando who murdered Chang's sister was finally convicted. During that period, Chang's bulldog persistence in following the chain of evidence also led to the indictment of three high-ranking military officers who ordered the slaying.

During the course of her search for her sister's murderer, Chang received many death threats and was even occasionally accused by other anti-government activists of being motivated by a desire for revenge. But Chang insisted that she sought justice rather than reprisal. "This is a fight for rationality in justice and for the common happiness that is the fruit of justice," she said. Her sister's murder was the catalyst for calling into question the arbitrariness of a justice system that prosecuted some crimes but ignored those committed in the interests of the repressive government. In essence, she said, pursuit of the governmental forces that murdered her sister was "putting on trial the existing policy of terror in Guatemala during the last thirty years."

Chang's efforts were honored with the 1993 Right Livelihood Award, a recognition often referred to as the alternative Nobel Peace Prize. Shortly afterwards she founded the Myrna Mack Foundation, a human rights advocacy organization, to continue her struggle for "rational"—nonarbitrary—justice in Guatemala.

20 January
Khan Abdul Ghaffar Khan

1890—20 January 1988

Servant of God

In 1921, thirty-one-year-old Khan Abdul Ghaffar Khan was behind bars for defying British colonial law. His crime was working for educational reform in remote villages of present-day Pakistan. When the magistrate questioning him expressed doubt about Khan's professed loyalty to nonviolence, Khan replied that he was a follower of **Mohandas Gandhi**. "And what if you'd never heard of Gandhi?" he was asked. The tall, muscular Khan startled the magistrate by effortlessly pulling the iron bars apart. He was sentenced to three years.

Khan was born into a wealthy and devout Muslim family in the Pathan village of Utmanzai. Despite the Pathan tradition of blood feuds and honor killings, which made the tribe one of the most violent in British India's Northwest Frontier, Khan's father struggled to live peacefully and to instill an aversion to violence in his son. He raised Khan to see Islam as a religion that advocated harmony and reconciliation.

The roots of Khan's nonviolence thus lay explicitly in his religious faith. He was convinced not only that the basic message of Islam is peace, but that this message of peace was the key to reconciliation with all other faiths as well. As an adult, Khan's openness to other religious perspectives made him a close friend and collaborator of Gandhi. Together the two worked to reconcile Hindus and Muslims in their common quest for independence from the British Raj.

One of the most dramatic expressions of Khan's devotion to nonviolence was his 1924 founding of the Khudai Khidmatgars, or "Servants of God," a nonviolent army of Pathans whose members took an oath to serve "humanity in the name of God, to refrain from violence and revenge, and to forgive those who oppressed them or treated them with cruelty." The Servants of God, who eventually numbered approximately one hundred thousand, boasted all the trappings of a regular army. They wore uniforms, formed regiments, and trained and drilled. But their training was in nonviolent resistance and their weapons were patience and righteousness, which, according to Khan, "no power on earth can stand against." The Servants of God were at hundreds of strikes and public demonstrations against the British rulers of India to protect participants from British soldiers. British repression of them was particularly severe, in part because of the Pathans' legendary ferocity as warriors. In 1930, after one of Khan's periodic arrests by the authorities, the British killed three hundred of them as they conducted a nonviolent protest. Their resilient dedication to nonviolence and their courage amazed even Gandhi.

After India's independence in 1947 and subsequent separation from Pakistan, Khan worked with the new country to encourage the growth of democratic institutions. But he proved a thorn in the side of Pakistani leaders who wished to make the nation a military power. Repeatedly arrested and imprisoned—he once sadly noted that he had been treated more humanely in British prisons than in Pakistani ones—he became a worldwide symbol of the prisoner of conscience. Three years before his death, he was nominated for a Nobel Peace Prize.

21 January
Hildegard Goss-Mayr

22 January 1930—

Marked for Peace

In 1942, twelve-year-old Hildegard Mayr witnessed the growing terror in Vienna as communists, pacifists, and Jews were arrested and taken away by Nazi thugs. Even her own parents, both Catholic pacifists, were under surveillance. But despite the danger facing her whole family, she refused to go along with the "Heil Hitler!" waves of jubilation that swept over her fellow students every time another Wehrmacht victory was announced. As she recalled, "I felt a huge force pressing on me . . . and I said to myself, 'you have to resist . . . don't raise your hand even if they lynch you.'" This will to resist the evil of violence, developed at so young an age, marked her for life. She knew even then that she had to choose between "the forces of death and the spirit of revenge, or the forces of life that are able to overcome evil at its root." She chose life and nonviolence.

Hildegard and her family managed to survive the terrible Nazi years, and she went on to study philosophy in France and the United States, eventually earning a doctorate. She joined the International Fellowship of Reconciliation in 1953, a year before she married Jean Goss, a World War II combat veteran turned pacifist. The couple traveled around the world, teaching nonviolence and conflict resolution to laypeople, nuns, and priests in such countries as Brazil, Mexico, and the Philippines. Whether opposing the Cold War nuclear doctrine of mutually assured destruction (MAD) in the 1960s, working in Africa in the 1970s in the struggle against colonialism, or being arrested in Brazil in 1975 for teaching *firmeza permanente*, a tactic similar to Gandhi's practice of meeting violence with persistent firmness, Goss-Mayr and her husband were at the forefront of peace work in the second half of the twentieth century.

A regular feature of Goss-Mayr's approach to teaching peace was to remind her students that peace was as much an inner attitude as an external change in policy or economic and social structures. Without the cultivation of both, neither was possible in the long run. As she said in 1984 while helping Filipinos devise nonviolent strategies to end President Ferdinand Marcos's repressive regime, "The seed of violence is in the structure, of course, and in the dictator. But isn't it also in ourselves? It's very easy to say that Marcos is the evil. But unless we each tear the dictator out of our own heart, nothing will change."

Her husband and coworker, Jean, died in 1991. Goss-Mayr continues to train peaceworkers in nonviolence and to advocate for justice, proving herself, as fellow peace worker **John Dear** says, "the greatest living peacemaker."

22 January

U Thant

22 January 1909—25 November 1974

Searching for Peaceful Coexistence

On a September night in 1961, **Dag Hammarskjöld**, Secretary-General of the United Nations, died in a plane crash while on his way to negotiate a ceasefire between warring factions in what was then called Northern Rhodesia. Hammarskjöld had an international reputation. His successor, a soft-spoken Buddhist from Burma (now Myanmar) named U Thant, was unknown. But he would lead the United Nations with grace and skill during a decade of worldwide strife.

The son of a wealthy landowner and merchant, Thant was educated at the prestigious National High School in his native land and went on to study at University College in Rangoon. Upon graduation, he returned to teach at his alma mater and was appointed headmaster when he was only twenty-five. During his years as a school administrator, he became actively involved in Burma's struggle for independence from Great Britain. He struck up a working acquaintance and then friendship with U Nu, who became the first prime minister of independent Burma in 1947. Once in office, Nu assigned Thant to several government posts before appointing him Burma's permanent delegate to the United Nations in 1957.

Thant once said that as a Buddhist, he was "trained to be tolerant of everything except intolerance." His quiet manner and unassailable integrity gave him the authority to navigate tangled political crises during his tenure as UN Secretary-General. He was instrumental in defusing the 1962 Cuban Missile Crisis and in ending the first civil war in the Congo (1960–1966). He opposed the apartheid policy of South Africa and, frustrated by the hawkish posture of President Lyndon Johnson's administration toward Vietnam, unsuccessfully tried to engage Washington and Hanoi in peace talks. He was also a guiding force in helping establish UN environmental and development programs.

One of the convictions that guided U Thant's leadership of the UN was his belief that a different kind of war needed to be fought, one that was waged nonviolently for secure and peaceful coexistence rather than conquest. "Two world wars were fought to make the world safe for democracy," he told the General Assembly in 1964. "Today we have to wage a war on all fronts. This war has to be waged in peace time, but it has to be waged as energetically and with as much total national effort as in times of war. The war we have to wage today has only one goal, and that is to make the world safe for diversity. The concept of peaceful coexistence has been criticized by many who do not see the need to make the world safe for diversity. I wonder if they have ever paused to ask themselves the question: What is the alternative to coexistence?" In many ways, the search for peaceful coexistence was the ruling principle of U Thant's public life.

23 January
María Julia Hernández

30 January 1939—30 March 2007

Remembering the Slain

IN THE FEATURE FILM *Romero* about the life and martyrdom of El Salvadoran Archbishop **Óscar Romero**, there's a poignant scene in which the relatives of "disappeared" victims of death squads line up to look at hundreds of photographs of corpses to see if their missing loved ones are among them. They dread finding them—but they need to know what happened to them. And if they discover that their loved ones are among the slain, they want justice.

The scene isn't a cinematic invention. María Julia Hernández actually compiled a photographic encyclopedia of the victims of the civil war in El Salvador that claimed some seventy-five thousand lives between 1978 and 1992. Death squads and military units loyal to the ruling junta kidnapped, tortured, raped, and killed thousands of ordinary people whom they suspected of loyalty to the leftist guerrillas defying the government. For their part, the guerrillas also carried out kidnappings and killings of people whom they thought loyal to the government. Every morning maimed corpses could be found on the streets of San Salvador, dumped overnight by right-wing death squads or leftist guerrillas. Often their faces were burned with battery acid to delay identification of them.

After he became archbishop in 1977, Óscar Romero asked Hernández, then a law professor at the University of Central America, to help him document the atrocities. Romero was murdered three years later, and Hernández herself received regular death threats during the next decade; she began each day by praying, "Well, God, will I see you today, or will you leave me a bit longer, fighting?" But she persevered in her advocacy for the disappeared and the slain, eventually putting together a catalogue of the dead that contained several thousand photos. She was the first to break the news about the 1981 **El Mozote Massacre** in which nearly eight hundred peasant men, women, and children were abused and slaughtered by government forces. Eight years later, she was one of the lead investigators of the murder of six Jesuit priests at the university where she once taught. As the Human Rights Officer for the Roman Catholic Diocese of San Salvador, she pestered the government to investigate these and other murders and to prosecute those responsible. When the civil war ended in 1991, Hernández hoped that justice would finally be served. But the government issued a general amnesty for all participants in the long conflict. Hernández, undeterred, campaigned to overturn the amnesty.

Her dedication to chronicling human rights abuses in El Salvador and seeking justice for victims was unshakable. An intensely religious woman, Hernández never married, lived simply, and worked out of a sparse office decorated with a photograph of Romero, a man whom she loved and admired. She once described her vocation as a "mission to help the Salvadorian people, who live in a defenseless and precarious state. I know that, from a religious point of view, defending human rights is also a labor of evangelism because it is the defense of human dignity, of men and women in the image of God. It is a choice of love, a choice of faith. I shall never give up."

24 January
Absalom Jones

6 November 1746—13 February 1818

To Arise Out of the Dust

The vestry of Philadelphia's St. George's Methodist Episcopal Church decided that it was time to act. One of the few integrated churches in the United States at the end of the eighteenth century, St. George's black membership had increased many times over thanks to the active evangelization of two black parishioners, Absalom Jones and Richard Allen. So in November 1787, an alarmed vestry voted to require black members to sit in the church balcony during worship services. When Jones heard about the decision, he knew he had to defy it. On the following Sunday, he sat in the front pew of the church and was promptly thrown out. He and Allen left the church, taking most of the black parishioners with them, and founded the Free African Society (FAS).

The FAS was intended to be both an alternative nondenominational gathering of black worshippers and a relief society that offered aid financial assistance to freed slaves. Jones knew something about slavery. Born in bondage in Delaware, he was sold to a Philadelphia shopkeeper when he was sixteen. He learned to read and write by attending the night school for blacks run by Quaker **Anthony Benezet** and eventually managed to purchase his freedom as well as that of his wife.

In 1794, FAS members established themselves as the First African Church of Philadelphia and voted to affiliate with an official denomination. Jones and his followers decided to go with the Episcopal Church, while Allen and his followers opted for the Methodist one. Jones and his people were accepted by the Episcopal diocese—their congregation was renamed the African Episcopal Church of St. Thomas—and Jones was ordained a deacon in 1795. Nine years later, he became the first black Episcopal priest, and he ministered to St. Thomas until his death.

From the very beginning, the congregation of St. Thomas, under Jones's leadership, was defiant of slavery and racial discrimination. One of the church's founding documents records the determination of its members "to arise out of the dust and shake ourselves, and throw off that servile fear, that the habit of oppression and bondage trained us up in." Jones's sermons regularly denounced slavery as a sin, urged slave owners to free their human chattel, and tried to persuade lawmakers to offer protection for runaway slaves looking to find freedom north of the Mason-Dixon Line. But Jones carried on his crusade against slavery outside of the church as well. Working with his old friend Richard Allen, he lobbied against the Fugitive Slave Act of 1793, a law that stripped fleeing slaves of basic human rights; petitioned Congress in 1800 to abolish the slave trade; cofounded Philadelphia's Vigilance Committee twelve years later to aid runaways and protect them from slave catchers; and campaigned strenuously against plans to exile free slaves to Liberia. In everything he did to help his people, his guiding principle was that nonviolently speaking truth to power was the key to resisting oppression.

Jones was well named: Absalom means "Father of Peace."

25 January
Rufus Jones

25 January 1863 — 16 June 1948

Building the Beloved Community

The American Quaker Rufus Jones not only wrote important scholarly as well as popular books about mysticism. He was a mystic himself. His life was punctuated by three experiences that he believed were dramatically immediate contacts with the divine. But in addition to traditional mystical experiences, he was convinced that traces of God could be discerned in the everyday lived world and by looking within to discover the "inner light" so valued by the Friends. There was, he believed, only the thinnest of membranes between us and the Divine. "There is a Beyond, a More yet, within us, and it appears to be akin to us."

What this meant for Jones is that all of reality is a "spiritual Society—a blessed community—which includes God and the cooperative souls, who with Him form the growing Kingdom." Jones was especially attuned to seeing every human he encountered—including some particularly nasty ones he encountered in Nazi Germany when he went there on a mission, while in his seventies, to rescue Jews—as members of this blessed community, bound to them through the "More yet" within.

For the first half of his adult life, Jones was a prolific writer, journalist, editor, lecturer, and professor. He continued most of these activities in the second half of life—he was a man of unbounded energy—but in 1917, with the founding of the American Friends Service Committee (AFSC), a relief organization that embodied Quakerism's gospel-based advocacy of nonviolence, Jones the mystic became an activist as well. Between the wars he worked with the AFSC to bring economic and humanitarian relief to war-torn Europe. He traveled to Asia, met Gandhi during a visit to India—the two men were equally impressed with one another—and traveled the United States as head of the AFSC to drum up support for its mission. A year before his death, the AFSC was awarded the Nobel Peace Prize. Jones's wise steerage of the organization for thirty years was largely responsible for the honor.

Jones once wrote, "I assume that the major business we are here for in this world is to be a rightly fashioned person as an organ of the divine purpose." Being rightly fashioned for Jones meant cultivating the mystic's biblical faith, personal conversion, and inner yearning for God while at the same time working in the world for imaginative social transformation that lessens poverty, injustice, and warfare. Doing so honors the More yet within and our fellow humans without. It builds the beloved community.

26 January
Thomas Gumbleton

26 January 1930—

Peace Prelate

In late March 2003, a Roman Catholic prelate was led away in plastic handcuffs by Washington DC police. Along with other religious leaders and two Nobel Peace Prize recipients, he had been protesting the Iraq War in front of the White House. His arrest shocked many Americans, Catholic and non-Catholic, both those who opposed and those who supported the war. But for Thomas Gumbleton, Auxiliary Bishop of Michigan, it was nothing new. He'd been arrested once before, in 1999, also for peace witnessing at the White House.

The official Roman Catholic position on warfare—a position shared by all Christian denominations except a handful of historic peace churches—is that all wars are regrettable but some are morally justifiable if entered into for the right reasons and fought in the right way. But Gumbleton, a longtime pacifist who champions "peacemaking as a way of life," rejects this position despite being a member of the ecclesial hierarchy. He is one of the few prelates of the Church willing to take a public anti-war stance, much less to be arrested for his convictions.

Gumbleton was consecrated bishop in 1968 during the height of the Vietnam War, and he immediately took advantage of his new position to urge American withdrawal from a conflict that eventually killed fifty thousand Americans and hundreds of thousands of Vietnamese. At the time, he was the only Catholic bishop who publicly opposed the war.

Also while serving as bishop, Gumbleton became one of the founders of the American branch of Pax Christi, the international Catholic peace organization, as well as Bread for the World, an organization that addresses the problem of world hunger. As president of both organizations, he frequently traveled around the world to meet with victims of war and economic injustice. He has consistently spoken out for the protection of human rights and in support of international disarmament, particularly of nuclear weapons. One of his continuous messages is that Christians are confronted with a fundamental choice between what he calls "pax Americana" and pax Christi. The first entails "bombing, killing, wherever we decide." The second means heeding the life and message of Jesus as revealed in the gospels: "you listen to what Jesus says, you watch how He acts; you follow His life. If Jesus didn't reject violence . . . you may as well say you know nothing about Jesus of Nazareth. He rejected violence for any reason, any reason whatsoever."

Gumbleton's vocal defense of pacifism has made him a persistent thorn in the Vatican's side, as have his recent public declarations in defense of gay rights. But even in retirement, he continues to encourage people toward "the very profound conversion of mind and heart" to nonviolence.

27 January
Roy Bourgeois

27 January 1938—

Divine Obedience

LOUISIANA NATIVE ROY BOURGEOIS thought his education was over when he graduated from college. But the next four years as a naval officer, including ground combat in Vietnam that earned him a Purple Heart, taught him a new way of looking at the world. "I left Vietnam wanting to give peacemaking a chance," he recalls. So he joined the Roman Catholic Maryknoll order, was ordained in 1972, and was sent to Bolivia, where he lived for the next five years. It was in Latin America that he learned yet another lesson: the connection between militarism, violence, and the poor. He discovered that ministering to the oppressed was only half of his calling as a Christian. The other half was resisting the causes of oppression, which in Latin America's case too often were traceable to U.S.-backed military strongmen who ransacked economies and brutalized citizens.

Eventually Bolivian authorities, angered at Bourgeois' public calls for justice, sent him packing back to the United States. In 1980, shortly after his return, three nuns and a lay missionary were raped and murdered by El Salvadoran soldiers of the U.S.-supported military junta there. Two of the nuns were Bourgeois' friends. Their murders, as well as the slaying of Archbishop **Óscar Romero** and hundreds of others in El Salvador, prompted Bourgeois to take his activism against U.S. foreign policy in Latin America to the national level.

Bourgeois discovered that many members of the officers corps from repressive Latin American countries were trained at the School of the Americas (SOA), a U.S.-funded military training facility housed in Fort Benning, Georgia. Bourgeois also learned that SOA students were actually being trained in interrogation techniques and "counterterrorism" tactics. A frightening number of the school's graduates were implicated in the kidnapping, torture, murder, or disappearance of dissidents in their native countries. Although he didn't know it at the time, the El Salvadoran murderers of the four women were SOA alums.

Determined to do something to stop U.S. complicity in Latin American human rights violations, Bourgeois founded the School of the Americas Watch in 1990, an organization that seeks to close down SOA (now renamed the Western Hemisphere Institute for Security Cooperation). Every November, thousands of protesters gather at the gates of Fort Benning to remember all those slain by its graduates. They call out the names of victims, and the assembly shouts *"Presente!"* Hundreds of peace workers, including Bourgois and dozens of priests and nuns, have been arrested in these nonviolent demonstrations. When challenged on his activism, Bourgeois responds, "When a law of my country contradicts the law of God, then I have no choice but to disobey the law of my country. Some call it civil disobedience; I call it divine obedience."

In a further act of divine obedience, Bourgeois recently challenged the Roman Catholic Church's refusal to ordain women. In 2010, he was excommunicated for participating in a women's ordination ceremony.

28 January
Isaac of Nineveh

CA. 700

Radical Forgiveness

Recognized by the Orthodox Church as a saint whose feast day is 28 January, little is known about Isaac's life. His first biography, written in the eighteenth century by an anonymous Arab author, is more hagiography than history. But a few facts seem more or less trustworthy.

Isaac was probably born near present-day Qatar sometime in the eighth century. He appears to have entered a monastery at an early age, accompanied by a brother. His devotion to study and spiritual discipline quickly earned him a reputation as a holy man and teacher, and his brethren soon wanted to elect him abbot. But preferring a solitary life of prayer and meditation, Isaac fled the monastery despite the pleas of his brother and fellow monks and settled in a hermitage near Nineveh. Here too his reputation for sanctity brought him unwanted attention. Soon, against his will, the city elected him bishop.

He lasted five months, increasingly frustrated by his flock's worldly greediness. The final straw was a financial dispute he was called to resolve. When Isaac appealed to the gospel to suggest that the debtor be given more time to repay his loan, the indignant lender snapped, "Leave your Gospel out of this!" Astounded and saddened, Isaac replied, "If you will not submit to our Lord's commandments in the Gospel, what remains for me to do here?" Shortly afterwards, he retreated to a monastery in the mountains where he remained until his death.

The advice Isaac offered the intractable creditor is significant because it attests to his strong conviction that forgiveness is one of God's primary attributes as well as a fundamental human virtue. He was confident that divine love is too strong to allow anyone to be exiled from God forever. Even demons, he insisted, "will not remain in their demonic state." God will await their conversion and welcome it when it comes. This doctrine of universal salvation or reconciliation with God preached by Isaac was also seen by him as a model for proper human relationships. Radical forgiveness, which requires patience and courage, is the key not only to social harmony but also to individual happiness and rectitude.

For Isaac, the key to cultivating the virtue of forgiveness is simplicity, or what he called "voluntary poverty." His unhappy experience shepherding a city abuzz with greed and ambition could only have strengthened his Christian belief that lust for possessions encourages an adversarial spirit in which others are seen as threatening competitors or as apples ripe for the plucking. But the interior disquiet and external violence bred by this attitude can be avoided by the cultivation of simple desires. "Nothing gives peace to the mind as much as voluntary poverty," observed Isaac. "Fire does not blaze among fresh wood, and enthusiasm for God does not break forth into flames in a heart that loves comfort."

29 January
Romain Rolland

29 January 1866—30 December 1944

Betrayal, Imperialism, War

WHEN WAR ERUPTED IN Europe in 1914, it was greeted with jingoistic enthusiasm by the populaces of all the belligerent nations. Even more remarkable was the equally enthusiastic response of most of the Christian leaders in Germany, France, England, Russia, Austria-Hungary, and Italy. Each of them all but declared the conflict a holy war. Each of them piously assured their fellow countrymen that God was on their side and encouraged young men to enlist for God and country.

A few people refused to jump on the martial bandwagon, even though they were vilified—at least in the early years of the war, before its futility and waste of human life sunk in—by virtually everyone else. One of them was the French novelist Romain Rolland, Europe's leading man of letters. Rolland, an ardent pacifist for most of his life, had already condemned warfare in his epic novel *Jean-Christophe*. But after actual war broke out, Rolland's pacifism became unfashionable—and, according to many of his countrymen, even treasonous.

But Rolland was undeterred. In 1915 he published *Above the Battle*, a collection of essays in which he castigated the war as well as its supporters. The book infuriated nearly everyone who read it, not only because of its condemnation of the war but perhaps even more because it accused Christians of hypocrisy and governments of dissimulation.

To Christians who backed the war by saying that it "exalts the virtue of sacrifice," Rolland responded by saying that they "seek consolation for having betrayed their Master's orders." Is there no better way to encourage "the devotion of one people than the devastation of another?" he asked. To national leaders who insisted that the war was a necessary defense against external enemies, Rolland answered: "The worst enemy of each nation is not without, but within its frontiers, and none has the courage to fight against it. It is the monster of a hundred heads, the monster named Imperialism, the will to pride and domination, which seeks to absorb all, or subdue all, or break all, and will suffer no greatness except itself."

As Rolland saw it, religious hypocrisy and governmental dishonesty are each, separately, bad enough. But when they become allies they invent noble-sounding reasons for going to war that persuade a gullible public to take actions counter to its own good. The church and state alliance rarely suffers from its encouragement of warfare; the ordinary man who enlists to fight and the ordinary wife and children he leaves behind do.

In *Above the Battle*, Rolland called for the formation of an international tribunal that would hold the religious and secular authorities who pushed Europe into war responsible for their deed and would seek nonviolent resolutions of future international conflicts. Such a body was founded in 1919 as the League of Nations.

30 January

Vallalar

5 October 1823—30 January 1874

Breaking through Caste

For centuries, the caste system in India rigidly segregated unevenly privileged groups of people. Supposedly established by the god Krishna, the system imposed a kind of apartheid that divided people into various hereditary castes that defined their positions in society, whom they could marry, and what sorts of occupations they could pursue. The castes ranged from an elite aristocracy to a large group of "untouchables," members of the lowest caste considered so unworthy that mere physical contact with them required ritualistic cleansing.

The nineteenth-century Tamil saint who came to be known as Vallalar, or "Great Giver," waged a campaign against the caste system that earned him the love of generations of untouchables. Born Ramalinga Swamigal and orphaned while still a child, Vallalar was given into the care of his elder brother, a respected scholar. His learning soon surpassed his brother's.

In a series of mystical encounters with Lord Muruga, a popular native deity, Vallalar was inspired to become a solitary at the age of thirteen. Several years of meditation convinced him that compassion and mercy are the only genuine paths to God and that the cruelty of the caste system was an abomination in God's eyes. Dismissing formal religion because of its defense of caste—Vallalar disdainfully referred to temple worship as "a darkness"—he taught that feeding the poor was a more worthy form of homage than rituals. He opened a "feeding house" in 1865 in the city of Valadur and opened its doors to people of any and all castes. The institution still provides free food to the needy today. The feeding house was associated with the Society for Pure Truth in Universal Self-Hood, an organization established by Vallalar that advocated equal treatment of people across the castes. It exemplified his conviction that spiritual liberation or *moksha* is achieved through self-denying service to others.

One sort of food that Vallalar's feeding house *didn't* offer was animal flesh. He believed that the conventional moral divide between humans and animals was just another manifestation of the caste mentality, and he refused to go along with it. "When I see men feeding on the coarse and vicious food of meat," he wrote, "it is an ever recurring grief to me."

Vallalar denounced the caste system in thousands of poems, many of which later inspired Indian resistance to British colonial rule. British authorities encouraged traditional caste segregation, seeing it as a deterrent to social unrest, and repeatedly attempted to discredit the cult of Vallalar and its criticism of the caste system. But Indians venerated him as a saint and prophet of social justice both during and after his life.

31 January
Donald Soper

31 January 1903—22 December 1998

Tree of Justice, Fruit of Peace

Like so many British youth of his generation, Donald Soper grew up believing that he was a "member of the greatest empire the world had ever known." Still a boy when World War I erupted, the "possibility that the power conducting mass violence did not necessarily confer moral approval on the practice" never occurred to him. He was confident in a totally uncritical way that might makes right.

That all changed in 1921, when he matriculated at Cambridge to study history. An excellent athlete, Soper was devoted to the game of cricket. He had been relatively unmoved by the sight of older Cambridge students who had returned from the war maimed. But the horror and senselessness of violent death was brought home to him when a fast pitch of his accidentally killed a batman during a cricket match.

Soper never got over the spiritual and moral ramifications of this tragedy. Wrestling with bouts of depression and guilt, he reexamined his earlier patriotism and experienced a religious conversion. His study of the gospels led him to the conclusion that nonviolence was a requirement for a Christian. Pacifism and social reform, which improved the quality of life for those living in want, were, in his estimation, undeniably bonded with Christ's radical message.

Licensed as a Methodist minister in 1926, Soper soon became a respected preacher and debater. His fame spread nationally in 1942 when he began open-air preaching at Hyde Park's "soap-box parliament." He continued using his weekly open-air forums for the next sixty-five years to argue for peace, socialism, nuclear disarmament, and racial equality. Known affectionately as "Soapie" and "Dr. Soapbox," Soper was known for not sparing hecklers who interrupted his addresses. He was still climbing onto the soapbox at Hyde Park even in his ninetieth year.

Soper joined **Dick Sheppard**'s Peace Pledge Union in 1937. His public arguments for pacifism were so fervent and persuasive that the government banned him from speaking on the BBC during World War II. After the war, he remained one of England's most recognized spokespersons for peace with justice. "Peace is the fruit of justice," he insisted, "and can grow on no other tree. It is impossible to graft it on a society which is unjust. The rejection of war must go hand in hand with the rejection of the systems which have required war as a continuation of politics by other means."

Soper was a regular columnist for the socialist weekly *Tribune* for over twenty years. He also published numerous books on Christianity, social reform, and pacifism. Awarded a life peerage by the Labor Party in 1965, he wryly remarked that the honor was "proof of the reality of life after death." A controversialist until the end, he remarked shortly before his death that because capitalism is based on institutional theft, shoplifting at a supermarket by an impoverished and hungry person isn't necessarily a crime.

1 February

Yevgeny Zamyatin

20 February 1884—10 March 1937

Humanistic Heretic

IDEALS INSPIRE HUMANS TO transcend the here and now and struggle for a better future. Without them, we become frozen in the present, unable to envision alternatives to the here and now. But ideals can become deadly if they harden into dogma. Then, instead of liberating the spirit, they kill it. Instead of leading us to an open-ended future, they imprison us in the present.

The Russian novelist and essayist Yevgeny Zamyatin knew firsthand that dogmatized ideals can be made to justify violence and oppression. The son of a Russian Orthodox priest, he threw his lot in with the Bolsheviks while still in his teens. During his twenties, while studying naval engineering, he was arrested and exiled by the Tsarist government several times. When the 1917 revolution overthrew the Romanov dynasty, Zamyatin rejoiced that an era of oppression and violence had ended.

But he soon discovered that the old system of oppression was replaced by a new one. The very communitarian ideals that had led him to become a Bolshevik were soon exploited by Lenin and his lieutenants to suppress freedom of thought and action. In the name of Soviet solidarity, books were censured and authors silenced; life became increasingly regimented; private hopes and ambitions took backseats to collectivist goals; religion was persecuted and repressed; and surveillance became a way of life.

Zamyatin, who turned from engineering to writing, protested against what he called the "entropy of thought" cultivated by totalitarianism. In his essays he warned against embracing dead ideals that freeze the human spirit and transform people into facsimiles of "Lot's wife, already turned into a pillar of salt, already sunk into the earth." In his most famous novel, *We*, he describes a closed society encased within high and impenetrable walls in which personal names have given way to numbers, each moment of the day is strictly regimented and monitored, and creative thought is discouraged and severely punished whenever it crops up. Zamyatin's chilling portrait of what can happen when ideals go entropic inspired later novels such as Aldous Huxley's *Brave New World* and George Orwell's *1984*.

As an alternative to the dead ideals of totalitarianism, Zamyatin recommends what he calls "heresy." "The world is kept alive only by heretics: the heretic Christ, the heretic Copernicus, the heretic Tolstoy. Their symbol of faith is heresy." The heretic, the individual who insists on thinking for him or herself even to the point of risking persecution and death, is "the only remedy against the entropy of thought." In calling for heresy, Zamyatin, who eventually fled the Soviet Union to die in poverty in France, advocated a form of nonviolent resistance to oppressive structures that deny individuals their humanity.

2 February
Maximilian Vanka

11 October 1889—2 February 1963

Muralist for Peace

In 1937, Millvale, Pennsylvania, was a poor town on the north bank of the Allegheny River. A sizable percentage of the residents, many of them immigrants from eastern Europe, worked across the river in the Pittsburgh steel mills. They worshipped at St. Nicholas Croatian Catholic Church, a twin-towered Romanesque structure built on one of Millvale's hills and shepherded by Franciscan Father Albert Zagar.

Throughout eight weeks in the spring of 1937, worshippers at early morning mass observed a thin man with a goatee industriously working on a series of dry fresco murals on the interior walls of St. Nicholas. The artist, Maximilian Vanka, had been commissioned by Father Zagar to decorate the sanctuary with religiously themed paintings. Vanka worked from early morning to late night on the project, Father Zagar frequently praying at the altar while Zagar painted.

Vanka's eleven murals included stunning depictions of the four gospelists, St. Francis receiving the stigmata, the creation, and the crucifixion. Overall, the mood was celebratory. But when Vanka returned to St. Nicholas four years later to complete a second cycle of murals, the paintings took on a much more somber tone and message. War had been raging in Europe for months, and Vanka's anguish over the killing and destruction there was reflected in his work. The new murals included breathtaking images of a crucified Christ stabbed by a bayonet-wielding soldier, the Holy Mother throwing herself between opposing armies, and the burial of a lad killed in battle. The new murals also reflected Vanka's outraged realization that war was good business for unscrupulous profiteers. Two of his panels offer a grim contrast between an impoverished working family and a wealthy capitalist. Together, this second cycle of murals is one of the most haunting indictments of war-making ever created by an artist.

Maximilian Vanka had firsthand acquaintance with poverty and war. Born in Zagreb, he was a *fachook*, or noble bastard, sired by a member of the Habsburg nobility. Abandoned while still an infant, he was raised by peasants until he was eight, when his maternal grandfather learned of his existence and took him in. Vanka displayed a talent for drawing from an early age, and his grandfather encouraged him to study art in Zagreb and Brussels. When World War I erupted, Vanka, a firm pacifist, served with the Belgian Red Cross and witnessed horrors that later found expression in his St. Nicholas murals.

After the war he lived for a few years in Paris and exhibited throughout Europe. He married an American woman and in 1934 immigrated with her to the United States. They settled in Pennsylvania, where Vanka taught art at a number of colleges while continuing his work as a freelance artist. Today he's recognized as one of this nation's finest immigrant artists. But none of his work is more gripping than the St. Nicholas murals.

3 February
Carlos Filipe Ximenes Belo

3 February 1948—

Protector of East Timor

Until less than a decade ago, the Southeastern Asian state of East Timor was a troubled country. A Portuguese colony from the sixteenth century until 1974, the tiny island enjoyed its status as a free state for only two years before it was invaded and annexed by Indonesia. Over the next quarter-century, the East Timorese endured a foreign occupation marked by indiscriminate killings—well over one hundred thousand—and destruction. The ferocity of the Indonesian occupation was fueled by religious differences. East Timor's population is overwhelmingly Roman Catholic, while Indonesia is a Muslim nation.

The rest of the world knew little and cared less about the turmoil in East Timor until the Roman Catholic Apostolic Administrator and later Bishop of Dili, the nation's capital, demanded that it take notice. He was Carlos Filipe Ximenes Belo, a Salesian priest who had trained in Portugal and Rome before returning to his native land. Belo's appointment was approved by Indonesian governmental authorities because they thought he would be timid and pliable. They were mistaken.

In 1983, Belo's first year in office, Indonesian military forces on the lookout for Timorese resistance fighters swept over the village of Kraras. When they departed, they left behind three hundred dead villagers. The Sunday following the massacre, Belo delivered an impassioned sermon in Dili Cathedral denouncing the atrocities, appealing to the Indonesian occupiers to restrain themselves, and calling on the international community to intervene in the name of justice. Immediately after the sermon, he began initiating as much contact with the outside world as he could, reaching out to dozens of journalists, human rights activists, diplomats, and political and religious leaders, in the hope of bringing East Timor's plight to their attention.

Belo advocated nonviolent but firm resistance to the Indonesian occupiers and was tireless in his public denunciations of the torture, imprisonment, execution, and disappearance of East Timorese citizens. His work on behalf of his countrymen enraged the Indonesians, putting Belo himself at risk of assassination or disappearance. Conservative elements in the Roman Catholic Church also criticized him for using his position as the nation's religious leader to speak out against political injustice. But Belo saw no conflict of interest between his commitments to Christ and his advocacy for the East Timorese people, whom he described as "dying" under the Indonesian occupation.

Belo's commitment to nonviolent change, his persistence in denouncing atrocities, and his efforts to draw the world's attention to East Timor finally paid off. Bowing to international pressure, Indonesia surrendered its claims to Belo's country, and the newly independent East Timor elected its first president in 2002. Belo, who was awarded the Nobel Peace Prize in 1996, resigned his bishopric and traveled to Mozambique, where he remains today as a missionary.

4 FEBRUARY
Rosa Parks

4 FEBRUARY 1913—24 OCTOBER 2005

Tired of Giving In

On 28 August 1955, a black teenager named Emmett Till was brutally murdered in Mississippi because he flirted with a white woman. He was tortured, shot, and dumped in the Tallahatchie River. His mutilated body was recovered three days later.

Two months later, Rosa Parks, a black seamstress in Montgomery, Alabama, who had been a member of the National Association for the Advancement of Colored People (NAACP) since 1943, attended a meeting in which Till's murder was discussed. Three days later, anger at Till's murder and years of accumulated weariness at being mistreated because of the color of her skin prompted Parks to do something that would spark the first large-scale campaign of active nonviolence in the United States. As **Martin Luther King Jr.** later said, "no one can understand the action of Mrs. Parks unless he realizes that eventually the cup of endurance runs over, and the human personality cries out, 'I can take it no longer!'"

Coming home from work on 1 December, Parks refused to give up her bus seat for a white passenger, as local custom required. The enraged bus driver had her arrested. Within hours Montgomery's black population, which accounted for 75 percent of the regular riders on the city's buses, had heard about the incident. Two days later, Martin Luther King Jr., at the time an unknown young Baptist preacher, urged blacks to quit using public buses until the segregation policy was dropped. The boycott lasted for over a year, with forty thousand blacks getting to work—in some cases traveling as far as twenty miles from where they lived—any way they could without availing themselves of public transportation. City buses stood empty, the bus line lost thousands of dollars, and the eyes of the nation became focused on the problem of racism in the Deep South. In the end, the city agreed to the boycott organizers' demands. The boycotters had demonstrated to the nation that nonviolence works.

The general assumption after Parks' arrest was that she had refused to give up her seat because she was worn out from working all day. But she was quick to point out that she wasn't physically tired at all. Instead, she said, "the only tired I was, was tired of giving in. I did not want to be mistreated, I did not want to be deprived of a seat that I had paid for. It was just time. I had not planned to get arrested. I had plenty to do without having to end up in jail. But when I had to face that decision, I didn't hesitate to do so because I felt that we had endured that too long. The more we gave in, the more we complied with that kind of treatment, the more oppressive it became."

Parks' act of resistance cost her personally. She was fired from her job, and eventually she and her husband, now unemployable in Montgomery, had to leave the city in search of work. But her refusal to give up her bus seat had colossal consequences. Although she couldn't have known it at the time, it was the spark that ignited the civil rights movement.

5 February
John Nevin Sayre

4 February 1884—13 September 1977

Episcopal Peacemaker

WHEN THE UNITED STATES entered World War I in 1917, pacifists were generally loathed. They were ostracized socially, persecuted legally, and either forcibly inducted into the military or imprisoned. In both barracks and jail, they were frequently brutalized. As one Mennonite inductee recalled, "We were cursed, beaten, kicked, and compelled to go through exercises to the extent that a few were unconscious for some minutes."

It took a brave person to object publicly to the treatment of pacifists. John Nevin Sayre, Episcopal priest, pacifist, missionary, teacher, and author, was one such person. He protested directly to Woodrow Wilson, describing in chilling detail the abuse that was going on and challenging the president to do something about it. Thanks to his efforts, Wilson agreed to the recognition of conscientious objection as a legal alternative to military service.

A native of Pennsylvania, Sayre came from an economically privileged background, attending all the right schools and meeting all the right people, and after his ordination it was expected that he would rise to prominence in the church hierarchy. But after serving as a missionary teacher in China for a couple of years, he came to the conclusion that his true calling was preaching the message of Christ's peace. Following his defense of pacifists during World War I, he joined the Fellowship of Reconciliation (FOR), working as editor, administrator, and public lecturer. He also cofounded and taught at Brookwood Labor College, an institute aimed at educating blue collar workers in order to strengthen labor unions. So far as Sayre was concerned, a great deal of the world's violence was caused by economic injustice. He considered his work with Brookwood an extension of his pacifism.

In the years leading up to World War II, Sayre traveled around the world in the interests of peace. He toured Germany in 1921 as a FOR representative, speaking widely and collecting data on the destructiveness of war. In 1927 he traveled on horseback throughout Nicaragua, hoping to broker a peace agreement between Augusto Sandino, the guerilla leader resisting American military occupation of his country, and the United States government. Sayre never met Sandino, but his presence saved several Nicaraguan villages from bombardment at the hands of U.S. forces. During the 1930s he spoke widely on behalf of European Jews. In 1939 he helped found the Episcopal Peace Fellowship. Following the war, he traveled to a number of countries to urge the commutation of soldiers convicted of war crimes. Before ill health slowed him down, he was a frequent presence at rallies against the Vietnam War.

Two years after his death, Sayre's devotion to peace was honored by the Episcopal Peace Fellowship's establishment of the John Nevin Sayre Award, given every three years to a peacemaker who carries on his tradition of Christian pacifism.

6 February
Asha Hagi Elmi

6 February 1961—

The Sixth Clanswoman

In accepting the 2008 Right Livelihood Award, Asha Hagi Elmi reminded her audience that "it has always been the case in all armed conflicts that women and children are the first and last victims of war, though war is neither their desire nor their decision." She knows what she's talking about. As a Somali, she's endured a civil war that's lasted over twenty years. The long conflict has ravaged the nation's economy and infrastructure, killed nearly half a million people, and inflicted suffering on millions more.

The civil strife in Somalia is inseparably connected to the nation's traditional clan structure. There are five male-dominated clans or tribes within the nation, and the tensions between them are long-standing. Since these tensions erupted into outright civil war in the mid-1980s, women like Asha Hagi who married outside of their clan have been rejected by both their birth and their marriage clans. In describing her own situation, she speaks for thousands of Somali women. "My clan of marriage saw me as a stranger, an outsider and at times a traitor. They didn't want me to know or even listen to what was being said. In my clan of birth, they also saw me as an outsider. My relatives saw me as someone who did not belong to them because I had this 'other part' that was related to the enemy. They didn't want me to know their conversations and plans."

Realizing that the traditional clan system left no room for women's voices—voices that typically cry the loudest for peace—Asha Hagi organized the Sixth Clan, a unification of women from the five traditional clans. The Sixth Clan works to encourage women's political participation in Somalia, to advocate for the rights of women and children across all of Africa, and to ensure that women are a presence in the ongoing peace talks between the warring clans. In 1992, Asha Hagi cofounded the humanitarian organization Save Somali Women and Children in order to further the goals of the Sixth Clan.

Asha Hagi was elected to Somalia's transitional parliament in 2004 and served for five years. During that time she participated in UN-sponsored peace talks and traveled widely throughout Africa, advocating the rights of women and children and especially speaking out against female genital mutilation. Through her work with the Sixth Clan, women in Somalia have a louder voice in the political and peacemaking process. As she says, "Through the Sixth Clan, we have transformed the women's role from the traditional ululation to indispensable stakeholders for national peace and political process. We have also taken women from the periphery to the negotiating table as equal partners and decision-makers. Women are no longer passive observers, but instead active participants. We have challenged the social cultural paradigm and carved out women's political space in the national political dispensation."

7 February
Dom Hélder Câmara

7 February 1909—27 August 1999

Ending the Spiral of Violence

The "bishop of the slums," as Roman Catholic Archbishop Dom Hélder Câmara was called, was a tiny and stooped man, partly because of physical fragility but mainly because of his tireless advocacy, in the name of Christ, for the poor and oppressed of his native Brazil. But he never thought the work too much to bear. "If people are too heavy for you," he once said, "carry them in your heart, not on your shoulders!"

Câmara captured world attention in 1962 when, attending the Second Vatican Council in simple cassock and wooden cross, he urged his more resplendently dressed fellow bishops to give their gold and silver pectoral crosses to the poor. Conservative Catholic officials disapproved of his outspoken gospel-based concern for the poor and urged him to keep quiet. But Câmara defied them by issuing a statement at the end of the Council that made it clear to everyone where his ministry lay. "Almost 2,000 years after the death of Christ, at a time when the Declaration on Religious Liberty is to be promulgated, nearly two-thirds of humans live in a subhuman condition that makes it impossible for them to understand the true meaning of liberty."

For the next twenty-five years, until his retirement, Câmara agitated on behalf of Brazil's urban poor, chairing housing projects, encouraging the growth of labor unions, launching a national nonviolent movement called "Action, Justice, and Peace," and continually urging the U.S.-backed Brazilian junta to move closer to democracy. His voice was so troublesome that the government ultimately banned him from public speaking or publishing for nearly fifteen years.

One of Câmara's central convictions was that the violence that fragments the world is caused primarily by structural injustice that economically crushes the many for the benefit of the few. He called this the first and most basic level of violence. In desperate response to structural injustice, the oppressed rise up in violent rebellion—the second level of violence—which in turn is savagely repressed by the powers that be—the third level. Violence, Câmara saw, is a "spiral" that perpetuates itself ceaselessly as long as the first level endures. But violent revolution is no solution to oppression, he insisted. It will only bring more violence and not the longed-for justice. A much more effective tool for putting an end to the spiral of violence is stepping outside of it by engaging in nonviolent direct action against structural injustice—strikes, boycotts, appeals to public conscience. For Câmara, this strategy exemplified the spirit of Jesus.

Although detested and feared by governmental authorities, Câmara was beloved by the Brazilian people for his courage in living his faith. "Denunciation of injustice," he told them, "is an absolutely essential chapter in the proclamation of the Gospel." And, he added, it's "an absolute duty for shepherds."

8 February
Martin Buber

8 February 1878—13 June 1965

Inclusive Zionist

BY THE TIME HE immigrated to Jerusalem in 1938, Vienna native Martin Buber was already recognized as one of Europe's leading Jewish intellectuals. Raised in an Orthodox family, he spent most of his childhood studying Torah and Midrash. As a young man he studied philosophy before launching his career as a public intellectual. He became a professor at the University of Frankfurt in 1930 and helped cofound the Central Office for Jewish Education, an alternative institute of higher learning, when the Nazis forbade Jews from attending German universities.

Buber's writings, especially his books on Hasidism, earned him acclaim. But his best known book, *I and Thou*, became one of the twentieth century's most influential texts. In it, Buber argued that humans are relational, interdependent creatures rather than radically autonomous, self-sufficient ones. There are, he wrote, two modes of relating to other people: one in which we reduce them to the status of objects to be used, and one in which we recognize them as subjects valuable in their own right and essential to our own development as humans. When we relate in the first way, we transform people into "It"s and stunt their development. When we relate in the second way, we recognize them for the "Thou"s they are and allow them to flourish.

For Buber, the Thou-It distinction wasn't merely a philosophical abstraction. He saw it as the key to building community based on mutual respect and reciprocity rather than an often violent competition for control. "The most pernicious of all false teachings," he wrote, is the claim that "history is determined by power alone." Buber conceded that power is sometimes a necessary response to evil. The rise of European fascism and the horrors into which it led the world were stark reminders of that truth. But genuine community and individual flourishing are ultimately built on dialogue that aims at understanding and cooperation rather than manipulation and control.

Even before relocating to Palestine, Buber was a committed Zionist. But in keeping with his embrace of I-Thou rather than I-It relationships, he opposed all versions of Zionism that were nationalistically exclusivistic. Buber wanted a binational state in which Jews and Arabs recognized one another's humanity so that they could "develop the land together without one imposing his will on the other." Far from either group trying to exclude the other, each should see it as their "duty to understand and to honor the claim which is opposed to ours and to endeavor to reconcile both claims." The "disease of nationalism," Buber warned, would destroy any real prospect of a homeland for the Jews. Since Buber's death, the wisdom and humanitarianism of his call for a binational state of Israel has become increasingly apparent.

9 February

Alice Walker

9 February 1944—

Writing Down the Truth of Peace

In Alice Walker's 1983 novel *The Color Purple,* Celie pleads with her sister Nellie "to write." Nellie promises that "only death can keep me from it." Her response reflects Walker's own passion for writing.

When a freak childhood accident robbed her of vision in one eye, Walker longed for death. Once confident and self-assured, she became a shy, introspective child who battled bouts of depression. But the accident and its aftermath eventually turned her toward writing and what she described as "a need to tell the truth."

The eighth and last child of Georgia sharecroppers, Walker attended the only non-segregated high school in her county and graduated at the top of her class. In 1961 she enrolled in Spellman College and became immersed in the civil rights movement. Her mentor, conscientious objector and peace activist Staughton Lynd, urged her to transfer to Sarah Lawrence College to hone her already considerable writing talent.

In college, Walker combined activism with her passion for writing. She worked for the Legal Defense Fund of the National Association for the Advancement of Colored People, championing the rights of Southern blacks evicted from their homes because they registered to vote. It was during this period that she met and married Melvyn Leventhal, a Jewish civil rights lawyer. They divorced in 1976, five years after the birth of their only daughter.

Walker was instrumental in bringing the work of Zora Neale Hurston (*Their Eyes Were Watching God,* 1937) out of obscurity and into the literary mainstream. Her talent in multiple genres (fiction, nonfiction, and poetry) seamlessly weaves scholarly and imaginative focus onto the experience of oppression.

Her novel *The Color Purple* earned Walker the Pulitzer Prize; she was the first African American to receive it. The novel highlights the many variables, including the suppression of female spirituality, that inhibit a vision for peaceful human existence. More recently, Walker has been an outspoken critic of war in general and the Iraq War in particular, commenting before the war that "the women and children of Iraq are just as dear as the women and children in our families ... and so it would have felt to me that we were going over to actually bomb ourselves." She has also championed the cause of the Palestinians by visiting the people of Gaza in 2009 with the anti-war group Code Pink.

10 February
Frances Moore Lappé

10 February 1944—

Dietitian for a Small Planet

It's a truism to observe that the planet is shrinking. Cyber-technology, supersonic transport, and growing economic interdependence now bind together what to earlier generations seemed to be remote regions of the world. The communities in which we now live are as global as they are local, and this shift calls for a reconsideration of familiar ways of living in the world.

One of the things that needs to be reexamined is the standard American diet. Per capita, we Americans consume nearly three hundred pounds of meat per year. For several generations now, our national dietary assumption has been that meat should be the centerpiece of every meal; the well-fed American family is a meat-eating family. Moreover, meat—beef, poultry, and pork—is affordable to families in nearly all income brackets. A food that not so terribly long ago was considered the prerogative of the wealthy is now enjoyed by the majority of people in America. Meat is the great democratizer.

But our meat-centered dietary culture was called into question in 1971 with the publication of Frances Moore Lappé's *Diet for a Small Planet.* In her book, Lappé pointed out the enormous waste and extravagant cost of eating meat. Factory farming—the intensive cultivation of food-animals necessary to cater to the demand for meat—befouls land, water, and atmosphere. Farm land that otherwise could be used to grow food crops is instead used to cultivate the tens of thousands of tons of grain needed to feed factory-farmed livestock. Moreover, the return on the grain investment is poor: it takes up to sixteen pounds of grain to produce a single pound of meat.

There is, then, a huge but hidden domestic cost to America's love affair with meat. But because the planet is smaller, dietary habits in this country cost other countries as well. The grain that we use to feed the animals we eat is more than enough to feed the world's impoverished and hungry people. The problem of world hunger, argues Lappé, isn't caused by lack of food so much as by the maldistribution and ill-use of food resources. In many senses, as the old saying goes, I am what I eat. But as Lappé points out, *you* are also what I eat, because my dietary habits affect the worldwide distribution of food resources. Whenever I eat, my food choices impact the international community.

Through her many books and lectures as well as through the work of the Institute for Food and Development Policy, which she cofounded in 1975, Lappé has been a tireless advocate of nonviolent dietary reform. Her work continues to be inspired by the fundamental conviction that a smaller planet requires an American dietary lifestyle friendly to people, the environment, and animals across the world.

11 February

Muriel Lester

9 December 1885—11 February 1968

Ambassador of Peace

There was little in Muriel Lester's childhood that suggested what she would make her life's work. Born into a wealthy British shipbuilding family, she and her two siblings, Doris and Kingsley, were sheltered from the poverty endured by the lower classes in Victorian England. Once, when she was eight years old, Muriel passed through a London ghetto while riding on a train. Astounded at the "gardenless, sordid, unsavory dwelling houses," she incredulously asked the nanny accompanying her if people actually lived in them. "Oh yes," the nanny replied. "But they don't mind it. They're not like you. They enjoy it."

Lester never forgot this first experience of poverty, and while still in her teens she became a dedicated socialist. Deciding to forgo a university education in order to work for social justice, she and her sister used an inheritance from their brother, who died young, to open Kingsley Hall, a settlement house in East London. The house offered shelter and meals to the poor and served as a nondenominational chapel. Lester lived there for the next two decades, attending to the needs of London's least privileged.

Influenced by the pacifist writings of **Leo Tolstoy**, Lester opposed World War I and joined the newly formed Fellowship of Reconciliation (FOR) in 1914. During the years of the war, "God Save the King" wasn't sung in Kingsley Hall. She explained that the fourth line, "Send him victorious," could only mean "killing, wounding, gassing, starving, lying, spying, drinking, and venereal disease" in peacetime. The victory she wanted was "the conquest of slums, disease, ignorance."

Although a deeply religious woman who believed that warfare was antithetical to Christianity—it was, she said, a "daily crucifixion of Christ"—Lester grew dissatisfied with the failure of mainline churches to embrace pacifism or to condemn the capitalist system she believed encouraged warfare. "The doctrine of the Cross, self-giving, self-suffering, forgiveness, is the exact opposite of the doctrine of armies and navies," she wrote. "One must choose between the sword and the Cross." Institutional Christianity, she feared, had chosen the sword while paying lip service to the Cross.

In 1926 Lester traveled to India to meet **Mohandas Gandhi**, and the two established a close friendship that lasted until his assassination in 1948. In 1933 she became ambassador at large or "traveling secretary" for the FOR, a post she held for the next thirty years. She traveled around the globe nine times, speaking against war and in favor of nonviolent conflict resolution and reconciliation. By the time she retired in the late 1950s, she had been twice nominated for the Nobel Peace Prize and was internationally recognized as one of her generation's leading pacifists.

12 February
Dorothy Stang

7 July 1931—12 February 2005

A Sacrosanct Right

SHE TOLD FRIENDS THAT her age and status as a Roman Catholic nun would protect her, despite the many death threats she had received. But she was wrong. On her way to a community meeting in a town on the edge of the Brazilian rainforest, she was stopped by two men. They asked her if she was carrying weapons. She responded by opening up the Bible she always had with her and reading one of the Beatitudes: "Blessed are the poor in spirit." As she tried to walk past the men, they shot her and then pumped five more bullets into her as she lay face down in the dirt.

The murder of Sister Dorothy Stang shocked and saddened the thousands of Brazilian peasants whom she had represented for thirty years. Born into a large Catholic family in Dayton, Ohio, Stang joined the Sisters of Notre Dame de Namur, an order dedicated to aiding poor people, especially women and children, in the world's "most abandoned places." In 1966, ten years after taking her final vows, she was sent to Brazil as a missionary.

Stang fell in love with her new home. She became fluent in Portuguese and eventually acquired Brazilian citizenship. Early on she began championing the rural poor among whom she lived. Brazilian peasants, who scratched out a precarious existence on small farms in and around the rainforest, were being driven off their land by ranching and timber conglomerates that slashed and burned their way through the forest. The ranchers wanted cleared land either to graze beef cattle or to grow grain to feed cattle. Leaders in the timber industry wanted the millions of feet of straight and true lumber the rainforests supplied.

In standing against the ranchers and timbermen, Stang found herself defending both the poor who were being dispossessed and the rainforest that was being plundered. (To date, about 20 percent of its 1.6 million square miles has been destroyed.) The farmers, she insisted, "have the sacrosanct right to aspire to a better life on land where they can live and work with dignity while respecting the environment." And the "death of the forest," she believed, "is the end of our life," not just because its devastation means the displacement of farmers, but because the rainforest is one of the world's natural wonders. Its wanton destruction for commercial gain is an assault on God's earth and an impoverishment of the human spirit.

Stang's murder has galvanized resistance to the timber and ranching interests who wish to exploit the Brazilian rainforest. The apprehension and trial of her murderers, both of whom expressed regret at their crime, drew the world's attention to the plight of both the poor Brazilian farmers and the commercial destruction of the rainforest. In death as in life, Sister Dorothy's nonviolent campaign for economic and environmental justice continues.

13 February

Emil Fuchs

13 May 1874—13 February 1971

Accepting the Challenge of Peace

In June 1953, East Berlin exploded. A couple of months earlier, Communist Party leader Walter Ulbricht, under pressure from the Kremlin, had announced an acceleration of the "Sovietization" of the German Democratic Republic (GDR). Higher taxes would be levied, heavy industry would be promoted at the expense of food and consumer goods, and electricity would be rationed. East Berliners, already stretched to the breaking point by poverty, took to the streets in protest.

Ulbricht's response was to declare martial law and crack down on dissident groups already under suspicion. One of them was the Young Congregations, a Christian evangelical organization. Clergy members were arrested, churches associated with the group were closed down, and affiliated students were expelled from schools. It was obvious to everyone that Ulbricht, an outspoken atheist, was using the riots as an opportunity to attack religious faith.

One man publicly protested the persecution. Emil Fuchs, a Lutheran pastor turned Quaker, lifelong Christian socialist and pacifist, and loyal (even if sometimes reluctant) supporter of the GDR, bucked the government line by defending the Young Congregations. Even more, he pled—fruitlessly, as it turned out—for a reversal of Ulbricht's Sovietization agenda. A few years later, Fuchs, ever the gadfly, was more successful in his efforts to convince the GDR to allow young pacifists eligible for military conscription to perform alternative forms of nonviolent service.

Unusual for an East German socialist, Fuchs was convinced that the message of Jesus, if taken seriously, led to the establishment of an economically just social order and a world free of violence. He knew all too well the horror of warfare, having lived through both world wars as well as the crushing poverty that both caused and followed wars. He also knew about political persecution: he was imprisoned by the Nazis for helping refugees flee Germany, and he was always regarded with suspicion by the Stalinist leaders of the GDR. But through it all he never allowed his own misfortunes to blind him to the suffering of others. "Do not close your eyes before the sufferings of your neighbors," he wrote. "Do not fear that it will destroy your happiness if you live in sympathy with them. No. Hold it [sympathy] fast; take it into your life."

In fact, Fuchs believed that suffering for peace and justice is the challenge every Christian must face. Servility in the face of tyranny or oppression is never an option. "Let us hear the challenge of Christ. There may be hard disappointment and bitter suffering on the road he points to. He never promised quick or easy victory. Only by our suffering can we overcome prejudices bred in millions of people by the inability of Christians to speak to their times. Mahatma Gandhi led a great nation along his way of truth and came to a great creative success. When will the Christian conscience be strong enough to unite those who call themselves after Jesus in the building of a world of brotherhood? When will we be ashamed to call Christian those who trust in the sword?"

14 FEBRUARY
Valentine

DIED CA. 269

The Power of Love

ST. VALENTINE'S FEAST DAY has fallen on hard times. It's become an annual occasion marked by mawkish verse, images of fat cupids shooting arrows into hearts, and binge spending (in 2011, U.S. consumers blew nearly $16 billion on Valentine cards, candy, flowers, and jewels). Even the Roman Catholic Church contributed to the day's decline by taking if off the General Roman Calendar in 1969. But despite all the marketing hoopla that's almost swallowed up the day, peacemakers ought to remember it, because at its best it's a commemoration of the nonviolent power of love.

Not much is known about St. Valentine. He lived in the third century, was a priest in Rome, and was martyred in the final years of the Emperor Claudius II's reign. Stories about Valentine have him ministering in various ways to persecuted Christians. But the story that best expresses what the saint stands for has it that he secretly married dozens of young Christian couples during a time when Claudius had forbidden male youths from marrying because he wanted them as unencumbered soldiers for his legions. Valentine was discovered officiating at one such wedding and was hauled in chains before Claudius. Once there, he tried to convert the emperor. Enraged at the priest's presumption, Claudius had him beaten nearly to death and then beheaded.

At least two lessons may be taken from this story. The first is that Valentine is a figure who willingly risked his life for the sake of honoring love, concord, and union between couples. At a time when men of his class were concerned with fighting battles and defeating enemies, Valentine focused instead on blessing the love that binds people together. We still remember today, even if only vaguely and through consumerist lenses, Valentine's sacrifice and why he made it.

The other lesson is this: love always trumps power. Claudius wound up executing Valentine. But the empire that Claudius ruled has long since crumbled into dust, as must all empires. What endures is the creative, ever-renewing act of love between human beings, which, as history has shown, is powerful enough to resist any kind of illegitimate authority. Love is seditiously defiant of attempts to curtail it or stifle it; it will always find a way to express itself.

The subversive and expressive power of love has begun of late to take back Valentine's Day and reclaim it as the celebration of love it was intended to be. Environmental and human rights activists have used the holiday as an occasion to encourage lovers to forgo giving one another traditional gifts such as roses, chocolate, and diamonds because of the violence with which they're produced or acquired. Commercially grown roses pollute soils and waterways with chemical fertilizers and insecticides, chocolates are linked to rainforest despoliation, and diamonds are often mined by Third World workers who for all practical purposes are slaves. Weaning ourselves from the sentimental love of a consumerist holiday restores Valentine's Day as a celebration of the power of love.

15 February

Ben Salmon

1889—15 February 1932

In the Army of Peace

Coloradan Ben Salmon was a martyr for peace if ever there was one, persecuted by both state and religious powers for his refusal to serve in the military when the United States entered World War I. As he wrote his draft board, "Let those who believe in wholesale violation of the commandment 'Thou shalt not kill' make a profession of faith by joining the army of war. I am in the army of Peace, and in this army I intend to live and die."

Although Salmon was a deeply faithful Catholic, he rejected the just war doctrine endorsed by the Church since the fifth century. So when President Woodrow Wilson declared war against Germany in April 1917 and Cardinal James Gibbons of Baltimore shortly thereafter ordered American Catholics to support the war effort, Salmon knew he was in for trouble. He quickly wrote a letter to President Wilson explaining his religious opposition to participating in the war. "Regardless of nationality, all men are my brothers. God is 'our father who art in heaven.' The commandment 'Thou shalt not kill' is unconditional and inexcusable. By both precept and example, the lowly Nazarene taught us the doctrine of nonresistance."

If Wilson ever saw Salmon's letter, he was unimpressed, for no response was forthcoming. In the meantime, Salmon began giving anti-war speeches in Colorado that eventually brought him national attention as a "shirker" and "subversive." Secular as well as Catholic voices joined together in condemning his position. It was only a matter of time before authorities retaliated by drafting him. Salmon's induction papers arrived on Christmas Day 1917. He sent them back the next day along with a note saying that he already served in the army of Peace.

Two weeks later Salmon was arrested and charged with sedition and desertion, even though he had never been formally inducted into the army. Condemned to death, his sentence was "mercifully" reduced to twenty-five years of hard labor at Fort Leavenworth. Once behind bars, Salmon was regularly beaten by guards, thrown into isolation, and refused the sacraments by the prison priest. In protest, he went on a hunger strike and was forcibly fed for six months before officials declared him mentally unstable and shipped him off to a Washington, DC, hospital for the criminally insane.

Thankfully, the American Civil Liberties Union eventually took up Salmon's case. He was finally pardoned in 1920 and given a dishonorable discharge from the army—even though, once again, he had never been inducted. He returned to an unforgiving community in Colorado where he died twelve years later, his health prematurely broken by prison hardships and the poverty he endured after his release. But he went to his grave believing that "either Christ is a liar or war is never necessary"—and Christ is no liar.

16 February
Simone Weil

3 February 1909—24 August 1943

War Transforms Us into Things

PHILOSOPHER, POLITICAL RADICAL, CLASSICIST, factory worker, mystic, author: Simone Weil is hard, and perhaps impossible, to pin down. In her short lifetime, she journeyed from a youthful commitment to revolutionary Marxism to religious mysticism. But if there's a unifying theme that runs throughout her activities and her writings, it's her denunciation of the dehumanizing effects of violence.

Born into a solidly middle-class French family, Weil was a brilliant student who early on lived the double life of an intellectual and an activist. She taught school and wrote learned papers, but she also agitated for workers' rights and offered free classes to farm, railroad, and factory hands. She helped organize marches and demonstrations aimed at securing higher wages and better working conditions for manual laborers, and even left her teaching job to labor in a factory alongside the men and women whose courage and endurance she so admired. In 1937, she traveled to Spain to support the Republican cause in the Spanish Civil War. Although she tried hard to be a soldier, she was so inept that she put others at risk and was soon sent home. A Jew, she fled France in 1942, worked for the French Resistance from England, and died from a combination of tuberculosis and ascetic fasting.

Weil left behind dozens of published and unpublished essays. In one of them, "The *Iliad*, or the Poem of Force," she offers her most thorough defense of the claim that any form of violence, but especially the kind exemplified in war, dehumanizes. Her selection of the *Iliad* as the text around which her essay revolves intentionally challenges the widespread belief, exemplified in the ancient poem, that war is a glorious and heroic affair that brings out the best in combatants. On the contrary, Weil insists, glory and heroism are rendered irrelevant by war.

Violence, she argues, is a force "that turns anybody who is subjected to it into a thing. Exercised to the limit, it turns man into a thing in the most literal sense; it makes a corpse out of him." But even short of killing, martial violence saps humanity. It possesses "the ability to turn a human being into a thing while he is still alive." The person who is attacked becomes so focused on the dread of dying and the animal urge to remain alive that his soul disappears. He becomes an automaton. The aggressor is so focused on killing that his soul likewise disappears. He becomes an automaton as well. Like chess pieces, combatants forget their own and one another's humanity during the heat of battle. Minutes earlier, they were "thinking, acting, hoping." But in the clash of arms, they become "simply matter," stripped of autonomy and propelled hither and yon by the same laws of action/reaction that dictate the motion of any kind of matter.

For Weil, this robbery of humanity takes place wherever humans are forced into situations—the battlefield, the factory, the overly regimented schoolroom—that make them anonymous and dispensable. Before violence kills the body, it kills the soul.

17 February

Jonah Jones

17 February 1919—29 November 2004

Jonah Wrestles the Angel

The son of Welsh parents, Jonah Jones knew about the brutality of war from an early age. His father, a coalminer, was invalided in World War I, and Jones's earliest memories were of the suffering his father endured from his wounds. When the next world war erupted, Jones declared himself a conscientious objector. But even though he refused to kill in war, he volunteered for medical service with a parachute field ambulance. He was with the Allied troops who liberated Bergen-Belsen concentration camp in the spring of 1945. Although he never abandoned his personal commitment to pacifism, the horror of the camp persuaded him that some evils were so powerful that violence might be needed to defeat them. Jones was never comfortable with this possibility, especially after his conversion to Catholicism in 1955 following a near-fatal bout with tuberculosis. But he believed it couldn't be ignored.

As a youth, Jones had dropped out of school at the age of sixteen and attended night classes in the art of lettering. Later he studied sculpting and the art of staining glass. After the war he returned to his craft, specializing in church decorative art. His religiously themed carved stone and wooden statues and windows can be found throughout England and Wales, but he was especially known for his skill in lettering.

Jones often said that he was intrigued as both a man and an artist by "that great, flawed [biblical] character," Jacob. In Jacob, Jones sensed someone who shared his own ambivalences and struggles. Jones too had wrestled with an angel when it came to remaining loyal to pacifism in the face of the unmitigated evil he had encountered at Bergen-Belsen. Like Jacob, he came away wounded from the experience; nevertheless, he spent the rest of his artistically fruitful life trying to give expression to the peace and tranquility of God in wood, stone, and glass—and, toward the end of his life, in novels and memoirs as well.

One of Jones's loveliest pieces is a 1989 marble sculpture called *And David Danced before the Lord*. A young David, in the middle of a flowing pirouette, looks heavenward with an expression of longing expectancy, as if he waits for God to reveal a great secret to him. Perhaps in capturing David's deep need for a sign of assurance from God, Jones was also communicating his own tension between his dismay at the evil humans commit and his longing to stay the pacifist course. It is a tension that all peacemakers surely feel from time to time.

18 February
Julia Butterfly Hill

18 February 1974—

Friend of a Beautiful, Sacred Planet

A HORRIBLE CAR ACCIDENT changed Julia Butterfly Hill's life when she was twenty-two. Rear-ended by a drunk driver, she was thrown so violently against the steering wheel that its column penetrated her skull. It took a year of daily physical therapy before she could speak and walk properly again. But her convalescence gave her plenty of time to think about what she wanted to do with her life. "The steering wheel in my head, both figuratively and literally, steered me in a new direction."

Julia had always loved nature. (She gave herself the nickname "Butterfly" when she was six years old.) So when she recovered from her accident, she resolved to devote herself to protecting the environment. She headed to California and joined a group of environmental activists struggling to protect virgin redwood forests from clear-cutting by the Pacific Lumber Company. Petitions, litigation, and public demonstrations had been tried and had fallen short. The timber company was determined to cut. So Julia decided on a course of action that demanded a major lifestyle change on her part.

On the night of 10 December 1997, she climbed a 180-foot redwood that she named "Luna." Hoisting up a bag of food, a sleeping bag, and two six-by-six-foot wooden platforms that she secured in Luna's branches, Julia kept vigil in the redwood for the next 738 days and nights. Her presence in the tree not only prevented the Pacific Lumber Company from cutting it down; it drew national media attention and focused the public on the conflict between environmentalists, who sought to preserve the beauty of nature, and industrialists, who preferred to exploit nature for profit.

Julia's public witness, supported by a team of activists who regularly supplied her with food and water, paid off. In December 1999, an agreement was reached with the Pacific Lumber Company that spared Luna and surrounding redwoods. But Julia's yearlong nonviolent campaign had far-reaching effects. Besides saving Luna, it also drew attention to the possibility of a gentler relationship between humans and the environment, one in which nature is seen as a partner rather than merely a source of raw materials to be exploited. As Julia wrote, "Luna stands as a symbol. A symbol for all the old-growth forests that are smashing into the ground, into oblivion, every day. Luna stands for hope and the love that will always win over hate. She reminds us that there are no 'sides,' only 'us'; that love and hate are within us all. Luna reminds us that the hope for this beautiful, sacred planet that gives us life and thus hope for our humanity lies in our ability to transform the greatest obstacles and challenges into strength, endurance, commitment, and love. These are the essence of Luna."

19 February

Krishnammal and Sankaralingam Jagannathan

1926— AND 1912—

Land Reformers

JUDGED BY THE CASTE system, they were a mismatched pair. Krishnammal was from a poor Dalit or "untouchable" family, Sankaralingam from a wealthy and prestigious one. But in the years before World War II, when **Mohandas Gandhi** was inspiring millions of Indians to practice self-sufficiency and nonviolent resistance to the British Raj, they both became his disciples. They eventually married, but not until India had won her independence.

Krishnammal and Sankaralingam were impressed by Gandhi's insight that the future of India lay in the development of rural agriculture. But in the years following independence, most of the subcontinent's arable acreage was owned by powerful landowners and farmed by landless sharecroppers. The system was feudal, concentrating huge amounts of wealth in the hands of a few while keeping the peasantry in perpetual poverty. Throughout the 1950s and 1960s, initially with **Vinoba Bhave** and then on their own, the Jagannathans worked with the *Bhoodan* or land-gift program, a nationwide campaign to urge landowners to donate one-sixth of their acreage to landless peasants. The *Bhoodan* campaign was eventually able to redistribute some four million acres. Much of it, however, was so infertile that it required several seasons of careful tending before it was ready for planting.

Recognizing that the *Bhoodan* wasn't working as they had hoped, the Jagannathans created Land for the Tillers' Freedom (LAFTI) in 1981, an organization devoted to negotiating land sales to landless farmers, helping them learn better agronomical techniques, and making sure that they don't default on loans and lose their land. LAFTI also teaches such marketable skills as brickmaking and mat weaving to Dalit children in order to help them rise from their impoverished backgrounds. Finally, in a program similar to Habitat for Humanity, LAFTI helps poor farmers build affordable homes for themselves. The goal of all the organization's programs and campaigns is to find nonviolent solutions to the problems of rural poverty and landlessness.

In recent years, the Jagannathans have turned their attention to agricultural sustainability. Huge swaths of South India's coastlines have been transformed into aqua-industrial shrimp farms. These mega-operations salinate the soil and pollute groundwater, degrading the environment and forcing small farmers off their land and into already overcrowded and poverty-stricken cities. The Jagannathans have mobilized coastal peasants to fight the aquaculture conglomerate.

Krishnammal and Sankaralingam's labor on behalf of India's rural poor was recognized with a 2008 Right Livelihood Award, the alternative Nobel Prize. In accepting the award, Krishnammal spoke for herself and her husband by calling for a paradigm shift of the world's privileging those who already have more than they need at the expense of those who have too little.

20 February
A. J. Muste

8 January 1885—11 February 1967

Peace Is the Way

NIGHT AFTER NIGHT IN the mid-1960s, an elderly man in an oversized coat and hat stood in front of the White House with a lit candle in his hand. His vigil was both a protest against the Vietnam War then raging and a general witness for peace. His name was A. J. Muste, and he was once described by *Time* magazine as the "Number One U.S. pacifist."

Muste was born in the Netherlands but immigrated with his family to the United States when still a boy. Raised and eventually ordained in the Dutch Reformed Church, he left it in 1914 because he felt unable to endorse either its support of the war that erupted that year in Europe or its theological defense of apartheid in South Africa. He joined the more theologically liberal Congregationalists. But his relationship with that denomination came to an abrupt end as well. On Easter Sunday 1918, after preaching an anti-war sermon, Muste was immediately fired and ordered to vacate the parsonage that same day. He eventually joined the Society of Friends, but not before going through a period in the 1930s when he abandoned his Christian pacifism for Marxism-Leninism.

For Muste, it was Jesus rather than Marx or Lenin who was the real revolutionary. Muste saw the birth of Jesus as the harbinger of a new age in which human beings would build a new society based on peace with justice. The ideals taught by Jesus, Muste believed, radically challenged existing social, political, and economic institutions. They were revolutionary but nonviolent, because the kingdom of Heaven proclaimed by Jesus is nonviolent, and bad means simply can't lead to good ends. As Muste insisted, "There is an inextricable relationship between means and ends; the way one approaches one's goals determines the final shape which those goals take." That's why, Muste famously said, "There is no 'way' to peace. Peace *is* the way."

Muste was a longtime member of the Fellowship of Reconciliation, serving as its executive director for thirteen years, including during World War II. He was also a member of the War Resisters League's national committee. In the 1950s, he protested the proliferation of nuclear weapons by refusing to participate in civil defense drills and by joining fellow pacifists at various nuclear testing sites across the globe to witness for peace. When accused of laboring under a naïve idealism that failed to appreciate the dangers of the "real" world, he responded that in fact it's Christian pacifism that is realistic, because it renounces "obviously suicidal" war and war preparation and allows us instead to devote our funds and energies to "carrying a great 'offensive' of food, medicine, and clothing to the stricken peoples of the world."

In early 1967, Muste travelled to North Vietnam to meet with Ho Chi Minh to discuss ways of ending the war. He died two weeks later.

21 February
John van Hengel

21 February 1923—5 October 2005

A Crazy Little Thing Called Food Bank

Years after he invented the food bank, John van Hengel reflected with some amazement on what he and hundreds of volunteers had managed to do. "It's amazing how many people are being fed because of this crazy little thing we started," he said. "We're feeding millions and it's not costing anyone anything." Difficult as it is to imagine, given that food banks have become such familiar features of the cultural landscape—a fact that's cause for grief as well as gratitude—the first one appeared only in 1967. Van Hengel opened it in Phoenix, Arizona, on a shoestring budget.

Born in Wisconsin, van Hengel moved to southern California after graduating from Lawrence University. Calling himself a "first-rate beach bum," he held down an almost bewildering number of part-time or short-term jobs, working on different occasions as a publicist, ad man, waiter, truck driver, and salesman. He lived in California for nearly twenty years. But shortly after the breakup of his marriage, he moved back to his home state, where he continued to hold down a number of odd jobs until bad luck struck. Following a pretty brutal fistfight, van Hengel required spinal surgery that left him with a locked neck and palsy. After a lengthy recovery, he moved to Phoenix in the hopes that the warm climate there would improve his health. He volunteered at a local soup kitchen, where he also ate his meals, and lived modestly in a rented apartment over a garage.

Van Hengel got the idea for a food bank in 1967 after a homeless woman who regularly rummaged through trash cans told him how much perfectly good food was being thrown away by restaurants, bakeries, and supermarkets. She said that what the poor really needed was a place where food could be deposited and then drawn out—a food "bank." Inspired by her suggestion, van Hengel borrowed start-up money and the use of an empty building from his church, St. Mary's Basilica, scrounged food from local groceries, and gleaned vegetables and fruits from local farms.

In its first year, the food bank at St. Mary's, which is still up and running, distributed a quarter million pounds of food to the needy. Ten years later, van Hengel expanded the operation by founding America's Second Harvest, a national network of food banks that collects food from major corporations and then channels it to local charities. Second Harvest, now renamed Feeding America, routinely distributes about two billion pounds of food, feeding over twenty million Americans each year.

Van Hengel is estimated to have inspired or helped form at least one thousand food banks in the United States, Europe, Asia, and Latin America. Thanks to his vision and industry, the man who called himself a "first-rate beach bum" helped feed millions of hungry women, children, and men. His efforts were rewarded in 1992 when he was given an Americas Award, described as the "Nobel Prize for goodness," at a ceremony in Washington DC's Kennedy Center.

22 February
Menachem Froman

1945—

Meeting the Other Side

"The whole secret of religion," says Rabbi Menachem Froman, "is meeting the other side." When it comes to the Israeli-Palestinian conflict, that's exactly what he's been doing for over forty years: reaching out to Muslims in Israel and other countries—even to violent Muslim organizations such as Hamas—in the hope of building peace.

Froman is an unlikely candidate for this kind of reconciliation. In the wake of the 1967 Six-Day War, ex-paratrooper Froman and other Zionists founded Gush Enumin, a political group dedicated to populating the West Bank with Jews and edging out the Palestinian inhabitants. Froman still lives in the West Bank settlement of Tekoa—home of the ancient prophet Amos, another champion of social justice—and serves as its chief rabbi. But he long ago dropped his youthful insistence that Israel is only for Jews. Today, he is more than willing to live in a West Bank that's ruled by Palestinians. What's important is honoring the holiness of the land, not claiming ownership of it. So there's no reason, he believes, why the Holy Land can't be a peaceful home for all three Peoples of the Book. It's only proper, he says, that Israel be "the place where members of all faiths convene to renounce their breeding of prejudice, hostility, and war."

Although some Israelis consider him to be a traitor for it, Froman on various occasions met with both Yasar Arafat, the leader of the Palestinian Liberation Organization, and Ahmad Yassin, the leader of Hamas, to discuss the possibility of a peaceful accord between Arabs and Jews. In 2008, Froman teamed up with Khaled Amayreh, a Muslim journalist who has close ties with Hamas, to work out a ceasefire agreement between Israel and Hamas. The concord called for an immediate end to Palestinian attacks against Israelis in return for an Israeli withdrawal from the Gaza Strip. Hamas representatives endorsed the plan, but the Israeli government ignored it.

Rabbi Froman believes that Jewish and Palestinian populations are too mixed for a two-state solution to work if both sides insist on strictly demarcated borders. As an alternative, he advocates two countries without borders, Israelis and Palestinians being citizens of two sovereign nations who just happen to occupy the same land. Jerusalem, he argues, should be a free international city in which people of all faiths live in peace with one another. "The key to peace is peace in Jerusalem," he says, "to re-establish Jerusalem as the capital of peace in the world." But he's quite certain that the ultimate solution to the conflict must be religious rather than political. The externalities of the conflict obviously focus on geopolitical disputes over land. But the "core of the problem is religious," and only when all sides recognize that their worship of the same God binds them more than territorial spats divide them will the problem be solved.

23 February
Wulfstan of Worchester

CA. 1008—1095

A Medieval Abolitionist

ONE OF THE MANY changes wrought by William the Conqueror's 1066 invasion of England was the gradual replacement of all the island's native Anglo-Saxon bishops with Normans. Only one was left standing: Wulfstan of Worchester. That he survived spoke to his great reputation for holiness. He had been a confidant of King Harold, slain on the field at Hastings, and this alone would have made him persona non grata to the Normans.

From an early age, Wulfstan was renowned for his great dedication to prayer. One of the stories about his early life has it that he was once so distracted from prayer by the aroma of a roasting goose that he forswore meat for the rest of his life—the reason he's acknowledged as the patron saint of vegetarians. Although ordained a priest, Wulfstan left active parish ministry to live as a cloistered monk. But he was pulled back into the world in 1062 when he was consecrated bishop of a diocese whose seat was the town of Worchester.

During his episcopate, Wulfstan revealed himself as a social reformer who defended the poor and stood up to the Norman conquerors who oppressed them. Every day he washed the feet of twelve homeless men brought in from the street and distributed alms to them. He did this as both a reminder to himself of Christ's teaching and as an example of compassion to those around him. Concerned about the number of hungry people in Worchester, he once invited the town's wealthiest citizens to a banquet at the bishop's palace. As they arrived, they were told that the bishop was running late and would soon arrive. When he eventually showed up, he brought with him several hundred of the town's poor and quickly shamed the assembled dignitaries into serving them food and drink.

But Wulfstan's greatest nonviolent effort at restoring justice had to do with the slave trade carried out in Bristol, the busiest seaport in his diocese. The town was the center of a thriving slave industry. Anglo-Saxon peasants who fell into debt were sold as slaves there and shipped off to Ireland to spend the rest of their lives in miserable servitude. Apparently no one thought much one way or another about the practice until Wulfstan stepped up to condemn it. Perhaps living under the domination of the Normans sensitized him to the cruelty of slavery. Correctly viewing it as an evil inflicted on an already oppressed peasantry, the bishop was relentless in his denunciation of it, preaching sermon after sermon in Bristol exhorting slave traders to abandon their distasteful line of business. Whether because he touched the slavers' hearts or they wearied of listening to him, Wulfstan finally succeeded in stopping their traffic in human beings, making him one of the world's first abolitionists.

24 February
Monika Hauser

24 February 1959—

Helping Women Reclaim Their Lives

Too frequently, sexual violence against women in wartime is reported by the media as simple criminal assault. Monka Hauser, founder of Medica Mondiale, a women's advocacy organization, believes this is wrong-minded. Sexualized violence, says Hauser, is always a destructive "exertion of power over the immediate victim." But in wartime, sexual assaults take on an entirely new vehemence. "They always have strategic significance, regardless of whether they were explicitly planned, tacitly encouraged, or merely tolerated," because they "boost the morale of one's own fighters and terrorize the enemy." And it's for this reason that sexual violence in wartime should be considered a weapon of terrorism and users of that weapon indicted for war crimes.

Hauser, an Italian gynecologist who studied in Innsbruck and lives in Cologne, first became familiar with rape as a strategy of war when she traveled to Bosnia in 1993 to treat sexual assault victims of that region's conflict. Her experiences led her to found Medica Mondiale, which has worked with over one hundred thousand victimized women in such war-torn nations around the world as Afghanistan, the Congo, Israel, Liberia, Albania, and Bosnia-Herzegovina. Medica Mondiale's mission is to create local support structures and counseling centers for women who have been sexually violated in wartime, to advocate for women's rights, and to lobby for the official recognition of sexual violence in wartime as a war crime and not simply a civil one.

Hauser is especially concerned with eliminating the social stigma that wartime sexual assault victims often have to endure at the hands of their fellow countrymen. By ostracizing rape victims, notes Hauser, "society at home almost always continues the work of the rapists. Communities ostracize raped women and girls as blemishes on masculine/national honor or force them to remain silent if they want to survive socially." This "non-recognition of rape as a form of torture and grave human rights violation" constitutes an indifference to it that Hauser sees as nothing short of shameful.

Throughout the history of warfare, but especially in the conflicts of the last century, women and children have been the primary casualties of armed conflict. The poverty, famine, and diseases exacerbated by war are typically seen as the chief causes of their victimization. But Hauser and Medica Mondiale are helping the world to see that sexual assault is another powerful way in which women become wartime casualties who must live with the scars of their experiences for years afterwards. She has devoted her career to accompanying "tens of thousands of traumatized women on their path towards reclaiming their lives."

25 February

Jacob Hutter

CA. 1500—25 FEBRUARY 1536

Founder of the Hutterites

ON AN ICY WINTER day in 1536, Jacob Hutter was stripped of his clothing, whipped half to death, drenched in brandy to make him combustible, and then burnt alive before a mob of mostly jeering onlookers. According to one of the few sympathetic witnesses to his execution, Hutter "gave a great sermon through his death, for God was with him." Hutter's crime was subversion of both political and religious authorities. A member of the Radical Reformation group that came to be called "Anabaptists," Hutter preached a Christianity closely modeled on the Acts of the Apostles' description of the communal life of the early church and Paul's second letter to the Corinthians extolling the primacy of love in the Christian life. Christians, he told his congregations, should hold property in common and distribute a sizable chunk of it to the needy; practice absolute pacifism, which included a refusal to pay war taxes; and practice as best they could the lifestyle taught and modeled by Jesus.

Hutter was born in the Tyrol region of modern-day northern Italy. A hatmaker by trade, he was exposed as a young man to the teachings of wandering Anabaptists, converted, and soon began preaching himself. Leaving his homeland in 1533 to escape persecution, Hutter traveled to Moravia, a region in what is now the Czech Republic, and lived there for two years, building and shepherding a number of congregations. When largely Catholic Moravia expelled the Anabaptists two years later, Hutter was arrested and transported to prison in Innsbruck. He was held there for several months and regularly tortured to force him to recant his religious views and to divulge the whereabouts of other Anabaptist leaders. Hutter refused to be broken, however, and the authorities, enraged by his stubbornness, sentenced him to his horrible death. Had Hutter cooperated, they would have settled for "mercifully" beheading him.

The followers of Hutter, who call themselves Hutterites, continue to practice the communal ownership and absolute pacifism he defended and died for. Persecuted numerous times by both church and state over the past four hundred years, the Hutterite community nearly died out in the nineteenth century. But several rural settlements in North America are now flourishing, keeping Jacob Hutter's ideal of Christian nonviolence alive.

26 February
Naim Ateek

2 February 1937—

Following the Way

ONLY TWO PERCENT OF the people in Israel and the Occupied Territories identify themselves as Christian. The overwhelming majority of their neighbors are Jewish and Muslim. So a Christian Palestinian is apt to feel doubly vulnerable: first as a second-class citizen because of Jewish domination, second as an outsider among his own mainly Muslim people.

The Reverend Naim Ateek knows this vulnerability firsthand and has turned it into a tool with which to promote justice and reconciliation. Born in the Galilee region, he and his family were forcibly relocated by Israeli soldiers to Nazareth in 1948 when their family home was taken over by Jewish settlers. He studied in the United States, was ordained an Episcopal priest, and returned to Nazareth to practice his ministry.

During his many years of parish work, he had ample opportunity to reflect on the parallel between the story of Jesus' persecution and crucifixion and the ongoing plight of the Palestinian people. Ateek came to see the subordination of Palestinians, especially Christian ones, as a replay of Christ's passion. Influenced by the liberation theology then being developed by Latin American thinkers, he came to the conclusion that the very vulnerability of Christian Palestinians gave them a vantage point from which to preach Christ's message of peace, nonviolence, and reconciliation. "We are Palestinian Christians," he writes. "This is certainly not our only agenda, but if we are not concerned with justice and peace and reconciliation, what is our faith really about? It's part of our responsibility as Christians—part of being faithful to the truth and to our baptismal covenant—to respect the dignity of every human being and speak out about injustice."

To help his fellow Palestinian Christians grow into the ministry of justice and peace, Ateek founded the Sabeel Ecumenical Liberation Theology Center in 1989. Based in Jerusalem, Sabeel strives to "make the gospel relevant ecumenically and spiritually" by defending the Christ-centered "sanctity of life, justice, and peace." Through education, advocacy, and public witness, the Sabeel Center's intent is always to preach a "spirituality based on love, justice, peace, nonviolence, liberation and reconciliation for the different national and faith communities," and thereby break the cycle of violence between Israelis and Palestinians on the one hand and Christians, Jews, and Muslims on the other.

Ateek chose the name "Sabeel" carefully. It's the Arabic word for "the Way," a reference to what the earliest Christians called the nonviolent teachings of Christ. But it also means "a spring of water," testifying to Ateek's deep conviction that nonviolence offers living and revivifying water to a land long parched by conflict.

27 February
Gautama Siddhartha

CA. 563 BCE—CA. 483 BCE

Nonviolence and Enlightenment

PRINCE SIDDHARTHA, BORN INTO the powerful warrior caste in what is now Nepal, had a protected and pleasure-filled childhood. His father, hoping to insulate the boy from life's miseries, kept him a virtual prisoner inside the extensive palace grounds. But young Siddhartha, increasingly curious about the outside world, finally persuaded a servant to take him beyond the palace gate. Once outside, he encountered scenes that shocked him to his depths: hungry and emaciated children, ill, lame, and aged people, and corpses being prepared for cremation. In one fell swoop he realized that life is full of suffering. Shaken to his roots, he fled the palace in the dead of night and retreated into the forests to search for meaning. He finally discovered it—his title, the Buddha, means "the enlightened or awakened one"—and shared his insights with the world.

The Buddha taught that the world's suffering is the result of unfulfilled craving. Our desires upset the equilibrium of our minds, giving rise to thought patterns that create artificial polarities such as mine/yours, desirable/undesirable, and love/hate. This fragmentation of our awareness of the world encourages a fixation on self, which the Buddha argued is itself an illusory construct created by craving, and this in turn breeds animosity toward those whom we fear pose a threat to the self's satisfaction. Violence, then, springs from self-deception spawned by the failure to control craving. It's a habit of thought that risks becoming so engrained as to seem natural.

To shed the delusional tendency to violence, the Buddha recommended a regimen of behavioral therapy: gradually rid oneself of craving by recognizing that desires only enslave and that it's better to be free, and practice behavior that encourages the letting go of craving. The Buddha summarized this teaching in the Four Noble Truths, recommendations for cultivating inner equilibrium and a right relationship with the world.

One of the central principles in the Buddha's teaching is the importance of nonviolence, or *ahimsa*. If we control our cravings, we control the fear, ignorance, egoism, and self-deception that create violence. Not wishing to suffer ourselves, we recognize that it's wrong to inflict suffering upon any living thing. One of the most eloquent expressions of this commitment to nonviolence is in the *Brahmajala Sutta*, a summary of Buddhist ethics from the Theravada tradition. In it, the Buddha instructs his *bhikkhus* or monks by using himself as an exemplar. He tells them that he "abstains from the destruction of life. He has laid aside the rod and the sword, and dwells conscientious, full of kindness, compassionate for the welfare of all living beings." He has laid aside all weapons, mental as well as physical, doesn't take what isn't given, blocks his ears to idle chatter or hurtful words, doesn't start or end quarrels, and strives to be trustworthy by refusing to utter falsehoods. The Buddha's point is that nonviolence, the mastery of craving which too often leads to rancor and strife, is both the path to and the fruit of enlightenment.

28 FEBRUARY
Linus Pauling

28 FEBRUARY 1901—19 AUGUST 1994

Prophet of Sanity

AFTER HIS DEATH, THE magazine *New Scientist* named Linus Pauling one of the greatest scientists of all time. But during his lifetime, particularly in 1962, when he was awarded the Nobel Peace Prize for his anti-nuclear weapons work, many people in the United States saw him as at best a Soviet stooge. A decade earlier, the State Department had refused him a passport because of his activism. *Life* magazine called the conferring of the Nobel Peace Prize a "weird insult [to the people of America] from Norway." The Senate Internal Security Committee, the Senate equivalent of the House Un-American Activities Committee, blasted him as a mouthpiece for the "Communist peace offensive" against American military preparedness. And his own colleagues in the chemistry department at Caltech studiously avoided congratulating him.

But Pauling, who'd already won the 1954 Nobel Prize in Chemistry for his research into chemical bonding, was immune to Cold War–era paranoia. As he said in his 1962 Nobel lecture, he was convinced of two things: "The only sane policy for the world is that of abolishing war," and it was the responsibility of the very scientific community that helped develop "terrible weapons" like those that destroyed Nagasaki and Hiroshima to take a lead in eliminating them. Pauling spoke from conviction but also from an uneasy conscience. Although he had declined to participate in the Manhattan Project during World War II, he did work on projects that had direct military application.

Due partly to the horrors of the world war and partly to the influence of his pacifist wife, Pauling became an outspoken advocate of nonviolence immediately after Germany and Japan surrendered. In 1946 he joined the Emergency Committee of Atomic Scientists, an organization chaired by **Albert Einstein** devoted to the elimination of nuclear weapons. He was one of the distinguished signatories of the 1955 Russell-Einstein Manifesto, a declaration cowritten by Einstein and British philosopher **Bertrand Russell** calling on the leaders of the world to seek nonviolent alternatives to international conflicts. In the late fifties he began agitating for a ban on above-ground nuclear testing, arguing that the radiation fallout was much more damaging to public health than government experts admitted.

The culmination of Pauling's anti-nuclear work was his cooperation with a Missouri-based organization called Committee for Nuclear Information. Pauling collaborated with other scientists in what has come to be called the "Baby Tooth Study," a long-term project that established indisputable links between nuclear testing and radiation poisoning by measuring levels of strontium-90, an element dispersed in above-ground testing, in the baby teeth of American children. The study frighteningly demonstrated that above-ground testing contaminated grasslands with strontium-90, which was then passed on to children through cow milk. It was a chilling conclusion and quickly led to a moratorium on open-atmosphere nuclear testing.

1 March
Loung Ung

1970—

Worth My Being Alive

By the time she was eight years old, Loung Ung's parents and two of her siblings were among the two million Cambodians killed by Pol Pot's brutal Khmer Rouge regime. Prior to the Khmer takeover in 1975, Ung and her family lived a comfortable life in the capital city of Phnom Penh, where her father was a senior police officer. Because of their wealth and her father's rank, Ung's family was targeted by Pol Pot's thugs. They were forced to evacuate Phnom Penh, her father was taken away by soldiers and never seen again, and Ung was put in a training camp for child soldiers. She finally escaped to a refugee camp in Thailand with the aid of her older brother Meng.

Ung was one of the lucky refugees who managed to get out of war-torn Southeast Asia. Through the auspices of the U.S. Catholic Conference of Bishops, she eventually wound up with a foster family in Vermont when she was ten years old. During the next few years she attended high school, living more or less like a typical American teen except for recurring nightmares about her ordeal in Cambodia.

After graduating from college, Ung returned to Cambodia to be reunited with the members of her family who survived the Pol Pot years. The devastation she encountered there, even fifteen years after the Khmer Rouge had been defeated, horrified her. She was especially struck by the number of adults and children she met who were maimed from stepping on undetonated landmines left over from the war years. An estimated four to six million of them are still scattered just beneath the ground throughout Cambodia.

Shortly after her visit to her homeland, Ung, determined to do something about what she witnessed there, got involved with the Campaign for a Landmine-Free World. For several years she toured the United States, speaking at colleges and universities, churches, and other venues to tell her own story and to raise support for a multilateral agreement to impose a ban on the use of landmines. (Several nations throughout the world have since signed onto an anti-landmine pledge. The United States isn't one of them.) In 2000, she published a best-selling memoir, *First They Killed My Father*, which described the Pol Pot years; raised awareness about Cambodian genocide, child soldiers, poverty, AIDS, and child prostitution; and served as a vehicle for her anti-landmine activism.

For Ung, her participation in the campaign to ban landmines is "the chance to do something that's worth my being alive": helping to heal Cambodia's wounds and to rid other countries of explosive remnants from past war that continue to maim innocent men, women, and children. But her activism does something else as well. "The more I tell people," she says, "the less the nightmares haunt me. The more people listen to me, the less I hate."

2 March
Judi Bari

7 November 1949—2 March 1997

Redwood Friend

They called it Redwood Summer. Sponsored by the radical environmentalist group Earth First!, the plan was to launch an entire summer's campaign against northern California timber companies seeking to log the state's old-growth redwood forests. Hundreds of environmental activists, veterans as well as newcomers, were expected to participate in the protests.

One of the leaders was Judi Bari, longtime environmental activist and Earth First! organizer and spokesperson. She had become an environmentalist a few years earlier when, working as a carpenter, her boss indifferently informed her that some siding she was nailing on a house came from a 1,000-year-old redwood. "A light bulb went on," she later remembered. "We are cutting down old-growth forests to make yuppie houses."

Like the other activists who participated in Redwood Summer, Bari frequently chained herself to at-risk trees to prevent their cutting and blocked the paths of bulldozers with her own body. But unlike other Earth First! members, many of whom were ready to use violence against the loggers, Bari insisted on a nonviolent approach. She condemned some environmentalists' practice of tree-spiking, in which metal nails are driven into tree trunks in order to ruin chainsaws and potentially injure loggers. Her inspiration was the nonviolent approach adopted by **Martin Luther King Jr.** during the struggle for civil rights. Because she was one of the most visible organizers of Redwood Summer, she became the target of an avalanche of hate mail and death threats. Although she reported the threats to local police, she couldn't persuade authorities to take her seriously.

In May 1990, an explosion ripped through Bari's car as she drove through Oakland, California. Caused by a nail-stuffed pipe bomb with a motion-sensitive trigger, the explosion nearly killed Bari, leaving her permanently disabled. She and the companion riding with her (his injuries were minor) gave police at the scene the names of several individuals and organizations who might have been responsible, but Oakland officials and the FBI instead chose to arrest Bari, claiming that she had made the bomb for the purposes of harming loggers but had accidentally set it off in her car. Given Bari's reputation as an advocate of nonviolence, it was an outrageous indictment. The charge was dropped for lack of evidence a couple of months later. But Bari and her companion sued the FBI and Oakland Police for false arrest and violation of their civil liberties. The courts eventually decided in their favor and awarded them over $4 million in damages. By that time, however, Bari had died of breast cancer.

The tragedy of Bari's attempted murder, although it brought immense personal suffering to her, led to something that the bomber, whose identity is still unknown, neither anticipated nor intended. The publicity surrounding the attempt on her life drew national attention to the destruction of old-growth redwoods, leading to the creation of Headwaters Forest Reserve in northern California, the nation's largest area of protected redwoods.

3 March
Miriam Makeba

4 MARCH 1932—10 NOVEMBER 2008

Mama Africa, Singer of Truth

So long as she stuck to singing African standards like "Pata Pata" and the "Click Song," Miriam Makeba was a hit in America. Born into poverty in Johannesburg, South Africa, but eventually, despite the restrictions of apartheid, making an international name for herself as a singer, Makeba delighted audiences with the richness of her voice and her exotic African songs. Harry Belafonte took her under his wing (together they recorded a Grammy-winning album), President John Kennedy insisted on meeting her, and Marlon Brando was one of her admirers. Her only regret was that South Africa revoked her passport in 1959 in retaliation for her public criticism of her home country, her performances at Martin Luther King-led civil rights demonstrations, and especially her appearance in the anti-apartheid film *Come Back, Africa*.

Things changed for the worse almost overnight when Makeba married Black Panther Stokely Carmichael in 1968. Scheduled concerts were cancelled, radio stations refused to play her music, and recording studios refused to work with her because of her association with Carmichael. Dismayed and angry at the racism she encountered in the United States, Makeba soon moved with Carmichael to Guinea, where she lived for the next fifteen years (she and Carmichael divorced in 1973). She continued to sing around the world, but refused for years to perform in the United States even after public outrage over her marriage had died down. In addition to opposing South African apartheid, she became a vocal critic of racism around the world. Her enemies tried to play down her outspoken anti-racism by claiming that she was a disgruntled hater of whites or a political opportunist. But Makeba vigorously rejected the accusations. "People have accused me of being a racist," she said, "but I am just a person for justice and humanity. People say I sing politics, but what I sing is not politics, it is the truth. I'm going to go on singing, telling the truth."

During the final years of apartheid, Makeba kept up the pressure by publicly urging an economic boycott of South Africa. She was awarded the United Nation's Dag Hammarskjöld Peace Prize for her energetic opposition to racism, and admirers of both her social activism and her music began calling her "Mama Africa." When apartheid officially ended in 1990, she returned to the land of her birth after a thirty-year exile. Although popular in Europe and North America, especially after her musical collaboration in the 1980s with Paul Simon that resulted in the album *Graceland*, she was largely unknown by young South Africans. That the younger generation who benefited from her years of opposition to apartheid neither knew nor cared much about her music was an irony that she took in stride. To the end of her life, Mama Africa continued performing internationally, and actually died while giving a benefit concert in Italy.

4 March
Ludwig Quidde

23 March 1858—4 March 1941

The Foolishness of Vengeance

KAISER WILHELM II, THE vainglorious and mustachioed German emperor who led his nation into the disastrous First World War, loved all things military. Diverting a goodly portion of the national economy to building up his army and navy and surrounding himself with generals and field marshals, he seemed out of touch with the real world in which ordinary people lived. So in 1894, a mild-mannered stutterer named Ludwig Quidde wrote a short pamphlet he hoped might serve as a reality check for the emperor. Titled *Caligula: A Study of Imperial Insanity*, Quidde's essay was ostensibly a study of ancient Rome. But anyone with a discerning eye quickly saw that in fact it was an implicit criticism of the Kaiser's infatuation with the military.

Caligula didn't land its author in jail, although Quidde was imprisoned on several other occasions for his outspoken pacifism. A member of the German Peace Society, an organization that still exists despite being suppressed under Hitler, Quidde advocated disarmament and international law under three German regimes: the Wilhelmine reign, the Weimar Republic that replaced it, and the Nazi stranglehold that destroyed the Republic. He suffered for his convictions under all three. The Kaiser charged him with *lèse-majesté* several times and had him thrown into jail. When World War I erupted, Quidde was accused of treason after he traveled to The Hague to dialogue with French and British pacifists. The charge was dropped, but he was hounded by German authorities for the war's duration. In 1924 the Republic imprisoned him for blowing the whistle on its secret buildup of the German Army. And when the Nazis came to power in 1933, Quidde was forced to flee the country. He settled in Switzerland, where he lived for the remainder of his days.

At the end of World War I, Quidde was one of the most vocal opponents of the harsh reparations levied against Germany by the Treaty of Versailles. Many of the treaty's critics disliked it because they believed it besmirched the honor and autonomy of the German state. Quidde's opposition was based on something else entirely: he feared that the economic penury into which the reparations would throw Germany would create a climate of anger that would inevitably spawn another war. "A humiliated and torn German nation condemned to economic misery," he warned, "would be a constant danger to world peace, just as a protected German nation whose inalienable rights and subsistence are safeguarded would be a strong pillar of such world peace." War is a bad enough destroyer of peace. But post-war acts of vengeance by the victors upon the losers only perpetuate the cycle of violence.

Awarded the Nobel Peace Prize in 1927, Quidde argued in his acceptance speech that world peace could only be based on the security provided by international law and order, not by military might. His hope was that new technology would make the killing power of weapons so terrible that nations would recoil in horror from their use. That hope has yet to be realized.

5 March
Hussein Issa

September 1947—5 March 2000

Peace as Mother's Milk

PALESTINIAN PEACEMAKER HUSSEIN ISSA once said that "peace and democracy education should be given to infants with their mother's milk." In light of the events that overtook him and his family when he was still an infant, it was a remarkable observation.

Issa was born just two months before the UN voted to partition British Mandate territory into two states, one Jewish and the other Arabic. The following year, when Israel declared itself sovereign, Issa's family was relocated from their ancestral farm in Ramle to a refugee settlement just outside of Bethlehem. His father died soon afterwards—of a "broken heart," according to Issa's son Ibrahaim—and Issa grew up in abject poverty. His harsh childhood and youth inspired him to find ways to rescue future Palestinian children from the same fate. Graduating from Bethlehem University in 1980 with a degree in education, Issa shortly afterwards opened a day care center that blossomed in a few years into a primary and secondary school. It was called "Hope Flowers."

From the very beginning, Issa's vision for Hope Flowers was to educate children in conflict resolution and reconciliation. Recognizing that enmity between Israeli and Palestinian adults in most cases was too entrenched to allow for fruitful dialogue, he pinned his hope on their children. Separatists on either side, he believed, were misguided. Because "Israeli and Palestinian destinies are inevitably tied," he was convinced that there was "no choice but to work together to try and forge a culture of peace." To that end, Issa regularly brought Israeli and Palestinian kindergarten children together so that they could see beyond the stereotypes and begin to build relationships.

After coming of age in a cramped and noisy refugee camp, Issa knew how starved Palestinian settlement kids can be for glimpses of nature. So he purchased land for a communal farm where Hope Flowers students could work, making contact with the soil as well as producing fruits and vegetables to eat and sell. He also arranged regular day trips out of the refugee camp that took students into the countryside. He believed that the excursions were essential for the development of inner tranquility, which in turn was the foundation for nonviolent conflict resolution.

Issa died of a heart attack when he was only fifty-two. But Hope Flowers, now supervised by his son, continues its work of teaching rising generations of Israeli and Palestinian children the way of peace. It is the mother's milk that will nourish them throughout their lives, and hopefully help build a less troubled relationship between Israelis and Palestinians.

6 March
Sulak Sivaraksa

27 March 1933—

Sowing Peace

"At the deepest level," says Buddhist peacemaker Sulak Sivaraksa, "the causes of suffering are always greed, hatred and delusion. At the more immediate level these causes have become embodied in consumerism, militarism, compartmentalization of thought and practice, and the separation of efforts to resolve social problems from the process of personal transformation." His life's work, both in his native Thailand and in the world at large, is to "sow seeds of peace" in place of the weeds of violence.

Long a voice of democratic reform in Thailand—an enterprise that has earned him death threats, arrest, and exile—Sivaraksa advocates a Buddhism engaged with the social, economic, and environmental problems of the day. He argues that the Buddhist notion of mindfulness is the key to overcoming the consumerism, militarism, and compartmentalization he believes characterizes the West and is beginning to encroach upon the East.

Aware that explicitly religious language is regarded with suspicion by many social reformers, Sivaraksa defends what he calls "Buddhism with a small *b*." Stripped of "ritual, myth, and culture," small-*b* Buddhism seeks to show that traditional Buddhist ideals such as mindfulness—"especially the breathing which brings us back to what is happening in the present moment. With what is wondrous, refreshing and healing both within and around us"—compassion, and a sense of the deep interconnectedness of all creation are also invaluable when invoked in political and economic contexts. They encourage a nonviolent approach to problem solving that's quite contrary to the usual adversarial way in which governments tackle issues.

For Sivaraksa, nonviolence is an active rather than passive way of life. The key is compassion. To see and empathize with the suffering of any sentient being is to be moved to do something to help alleviate its pain. Sometimes relief isn't possible. But frequently it is, and in those cases, to do nothing is to silently acquiesce to and collaborate in the damage that's inflicted on the victim. Passivity in the face of suffering, in other words, can be an often overlooked form of violence. Similarly, a consumer-driven indifference to wasteful modes of production, exploitative uses of human labor, and unsustainable wreckage of the environment, is a type of passivity that in fact is violent. Buddhism with a small *b* seeks to awaken people to this fact.

Sivaraksa has received international recognition for his efforts, as he says, "to continually plant seeds of joy, peace and understanding in order to facilitate the ongoing work of transformation in the depths of our consciousness." One of his many honors was a 1995 Right Livelihood Award, the alternative Nobel Peace Prize.

7 March
Stanley Kubrick

26 July 1928—7 March 1999

Satirizing Nuclear Madness

Herman Kahn's 1960 *On Thermonuclear War* wasn't exactly a best seller, but it *did* ratchet up the Cold War a degree or two. Kahn, a RAND military strategist, argued that a thermonuclear war was winnable. True, the killing power of such a conflict would be so great that its destructiveness, Kahn argued, would have to be measured in terms of "megadeath." But eventually one side would emerge victorious from the rubble.

Four years after Kahn's book, and two years after the world nearly tested Kahn's theory in the Cuban Missile Crisis, reclusive film director Stanley Kubrick made a movie that showed just how dangerous and ridiculous the idea of a winnable nuclear war was. The film carried the bizarre title of *Dr. Strangelove or: How I Learned to Stop Worrying and Love the Bomb*. Of Kubrick's thirteen films, three (counting *Strangelove*) were stridently anti-war—the other two were *Paths of Glory* in 1957 and *Full Metal Jacket* in 1987—but *Strangelove* was the best. Although the Cold War gave rise to an entire genre of apocalyptic films about nuclear war, Kubrick's stands out as the only one that uses satire and dark humor to protest nuclear proliferation. Kubrick himself described it as a "nightmare comedy." In terms of writing, directing, cinematography, and acting, it's a genuine tour de force.

The plot turns on a preemptive nuclear strike against the Soviet Union engineered by General Jack D. Ripper, an insane Cold Warrior. (Kubrick's insinuation is that *all* Cold Warriors are insane.) He sends nuclear bomb–laden B52s to Russia, deceptively telling the pilots that the Soviet Union and the United States are at war, and refuses to surrender the radio codes needed to order the pilots to abort the mission. His justification for launching the strike comes straight from Kahn: although the nuclear war that's bound to ensue will kill thousands of millions of Russians and Americans, it's winnable if the U.S. hits first.

The film shifts back and forth between Ripper's headquarters at the fictional Burpelson Air Base and an operations room, presumably at the Pentagon, where the U.S. president, an ex-Nazi named Dr. Strangelove (both played by Peter Sellers), and a cabal of generals and advisors gather to figure out how to deal with the rogue General Ripper's nuclear launch. Along the way, the Soviet ambassador to the United States reveals that his country's scientists have invented a Doomsday machine, fifty fail-safe nuclear bombs buried around the world that will automatically detonate if the Soviet Union is attacked. But there's no calling the American pilots back. They drop their payloads on Russia, and the film ends with nuclear mushrooms from the Doomsday machine blossoming all over the world. Kubrick's message was clear: there may be survivors in a nuclear standoff, but they won't be human. The idea of a winnable nuclear war is as absurd as it is terrifying.

8 March
Maria Skobtsova

8 December 1891—31 March 1945

The Giving of One's Soul

LIKE SO MANY OTHER Russian refugees fleeing from the Bolshevik Revolution, Maria Skobtsova made her way to Paris. The disruption of her old life and the additional blow of the death of one of her three children provoked a profound spiritual crisis in the woman known in Russia as a poet and political activist. She began a search for a more "purified" way of life that eventually led her, in 1932, to monastic vows in the Orthodox Church.

But as a nun, she refused to live a cloistered life. Instead, she ministered to the poverty-stricken and spiritually despairing refugees in Paris. She rented a large house and opened it up to the hungry and the homeless, reserving for herself only a cot in the basement. Her goal, she said, was to discern and revere the living God in every person she encountered, no matter how broken they were or how great the cost of serving them was. "I think service to the world is simply the giving of one's own soul in order to save others."

Hitler launched his signature blitzkrieg attack against France in May 1940. Five weeks later, the Nazis were in Paris and the persecution of Jews began. With no hesitation, Skobtsova began defying the Nazis by offering shelter and assistance to Jews on the run. She worked closely with an Orthodox priest, Father Dimitri Klepinin, who gladly issued baptismal papers to Jews who requested them. Together, the two of them moved fleeing Jews along escape routes to Switzerland. On more than one occasion, they smuggled Jewish children to safety by hiding them in trash bins and bribing garbage collectors to take them out of the city.

In 1942, French Jews were ordered to wear the infamous yellow star. Skobtsova immediately protested and called Christians to display solidarity with their Jewish brothers and sisters. "If we were true Christians," she said, "we would all wear the Star." Although she hated war, seeing it as "the brutalization of nations, the lowering of the cultural level, the loss of creative ability, the decadence of souls" that "throws the whole of mankind back," she also believed that it offered a profound opportunity to serve and sacrifice for war's victims.

For Skobtsova, the sacrifice came in February 1943 when she, Father Dimitri, and her son Yura, a collaborator in their aid to the Jews, were arrested by the Gestapo. They were interrogated and tortured. Skobtsova was eventually sent to Ravensbrück and Dimitri and Yura to Buchenwald. All three of them perished in the camps, Skobtsova surviving until 31 March 1945. She was sent to the gas chamber just days before the camp was liberated. During her two years at Ravensbrück, she ministered to her fellow prisoners, and there is testimony that she died taking the place of another prisoner who had been "selected" for the gas chamber. If so, Skobtsova's manner of dying, like her manner of living, exemplified her dedication to serving others.

9 March

Tom Fox

7 July 1951—9 March 2006

Standing with the Dehumanized

Christian Peacemaker Teams (CPT) is an organization founded by members of historic peace churches that sends volunteers to hot spots across the globe where the well-being of local people is threatened by violence. The hope is that the presence of nonviolent witnesses with ties to international media will tamp down the level of violence. As Peacemakers says, its goal is "to get in the way."

Tom Fox joined the CPT following a twenty-year career as a musician in the Marine Corps Band and after becoming a Quaker. In 2004 he joined three other CPT members on a mission to Iraq. Their work in Baghdad consisted of helping the families of imprisoned Iraqis secure financial assistance, making sure that medical supplies wound up in hospitals and clinics instead of on the black market, and working to build a strong CPT presence in Iraq.

In late November 2005, Fox and his fellow CPT volunteers were kidnapped by Al-Qaeda guerrillas who threatened to execute the four men unless the United States released all Iraqi prisoners. Three of the hostages were eventually rescued after being held for five months. Fox wasn't one of them. His body was found on 9 March 2006. He had been shot several times and dumped on a garbage heap in Baghdad. Cuts and bruises on his body suggested that he might have been tortured.

It's still unclear why Fox was singled out for execution. Perhaps it was because of his service in the Marine Corps. Before his abduction, knowing the danger he and his fellow CPT volunteers faced, Fox made his friends promise that they wouldn't seek vengeance if he was abducted.

During his time in Iraq, Fox wrote a blog recording his activities and impressions. In an entry titled "Why are we here?"—posted the day before he was snatched by Al-Qaeda—Fox wrote this: "If I understand the message of God, his response to that question is that we are to take part in the creation of the Peaceable Realm of God. As I survey the landscape here in Iraq, dehumanization seems to be the operative means of relating to each other. We are here to root out all aspects of dehumanization that exists within us. We are here to stand with those being dehumanized by oppressors and stand firm against that dehumanization. We are here to stop people, including ourselves, from dehumanizing any of God's children, no matter how much they dehumanize their own souls."

In the way he conducted himself during the last few years of his life, as well as in the way he died, Fox truly did stand with the victims of dehumanization.

10 March
Asghar Ali Engineer

10 March 1940—

De-politicizing Religion

When he was a boy, Asghar Ali Engineer's father, a Muslim Bohra priest (Bohra is an India-based Shi'a sect), told him two things. The first was that violence is never justifiable. "He often drew my attention," recalls Engineer, "to the verse of the Qur'an that to kill a person without justification amounts to killing whole humanity and to save a human life amounts to saving whole humanity." The second bit of advice from his father was "to do what my conscience dictated and not to care for the consequences." Engineer took both to heart.

After working as a municipal engineer in Bombay for twenty years, Engineer retired to serve as a leader in the Bohra community. But over the years his progressive interpretations of Islam proved too controversial for his fellow religionists, and he was formally expelled from the community in 2004. Views that got him into trouble included his conviction that women deserve the same legal and civil rights as men; that violence, especially when perpetrated in the name of religion, is an affront to all genuine religious sensibilities; and that sectarianism—or what he calls "communalism"—is a disrupter of domestic and international peace.

Engineer first became worried about sectarian violence as a youth, when murderous confrontations between Muslims and Hindus raged across India. Such cruelty perpetrated in the name of religion, he concluded, was a corruption. "Religion to me never could be a source of hatred. It always was a source of compassion and love."

Problems arise, Engineer believes, when religion becomes politicized as a weapon wielded by special interest groups. "It is not religion but misuse of religion and politicizing of religion, which is the main culprit." The collapse of religion into sectarianism or communalism too easily encourages adherents to see nonbelievers as less-than-human outsiders, and this in turn induces a forgetfulness of the core religious insight that each person represents the whole of humanity. When that happens, sectarian violence is just around the corner. It follows, argues Engineer, that the key to avoiding it is to keep politics and religion distinct from one another. When it comes to criminal law, human rights, civil liberties, and social entitlements, the best framework is a secular one. Religion as "a source of moral and spiritual richness" remains independent and consequently is able to serve as society's moral and spiritual barometer. Moreover, because it's not dragooned as an ideological weapon by any one sect, it "does not pose any challenge for a secular political set up." Used as an "instrument of power" by sectarians, religion becomes dangerous. Embraced as a foundation for compassion and virtue, it enriches individual lives and the moral fabric of society. It honors the insight that each human contains all of humanity.

11 March

Rutilio Grande

5 July 1928—12 March 1977

Proclaiming Subversion

It didn't take long at all. Just a few bursts from a couple of machine guns, and Jesuit father Rutilio Grande was silenced. The spray of bullets that took his life also killed an old man and a teenage boy who just happened to be passengers in the car Grande was driving when the murderers caught up with him. But in every war, there's so-called collateral damage.

Grande was murdered because the El Salvadoran military thought him a threat to the small country's elite class who controlled the government and most of the national wealth. Grande, a native El Salvadoran who studied in Rome, taught at the Catholic seminary in San Salvador, and served the parish of Aguilares, sought to empower hitherto voiceless peasants by giving them some control over their spiritual and material destinies. For generations, they had been stifled by a hierarchical Church on the one hand and an oppressive economic and political system on the other. Grande encouraged their liberation through the establishment of Christian base communities, self-reliant groups of peasants who regularly met to discuss the gospels and the ways in which Jesus' message shed light upon their situation. The base communities, serving as they did to raise consciousness among the peasantry, were condemned by the authorities as dangerously seditious, and it became increasingly risky for priests like Grande to remain in El Salvador.

The beginning of the end for Grande came in early 1977. In January a meddlesomely "subversive" priest had been snatched by government authorities and thrown out of the country. Two weeks later, Grande delivered a sermon at his Aguilares church that blasted the climate of fear and oppression created by the ruling junta. "I am fully aware," he said, "that very soon the Bible and the Gospels will not be allowed to cross the border. All that will reach us will be the covers, since all the pages are subversive—against sin, it is said. So that if Jesus crosses the border, they will not allow him to enter. They would accuse him, the man-God . . . of being an agitator. . . . Brothers, they would undoubtedly crucify him again." This sermon was Grande's death warrant, as he must have known it would be. A month later he was dead.

But Grande's murder bore fruit. It energized his friend **Óscar Romero**, who had just been appointed archbishop of San Salvador, into active opposition to the government and solidarity with the peasantry. Romero himself would be murdered three years later. In all, seventeen priests would die at the hands of the El Salvadoran junta. But their efforts to preach the subversive good news of spiritual and material liberation helped build a society in which wealth was a little more evenly distributed and a Church better able to see Christ in the faces of the people. So the bullets that cut him down didn't silence Grande after all.

12 March
Preah Maha Ghosananda

23 May 1929—12 March 2007

Joyful Proclaimer of Peace

In Cambodia, the new Khmer Rouge regime declared 1975, the year of its takeover, "Year Zero." Everything was to be started over. The old would be torn down and the new would be built.

By the time the regime hit Year Four, its final one in power, it had slaughtered or starved to death an estimated one-fifth of the nation's population, upwards of two million people. Buddhist monks and nuns—"social parasites" whom Khmer Rouge fanatics especially loathed—were driven into exile, forced at gunpoint to recant their vows, or murdered. Before the Khmer Rouge there were around sixty thousand of them in Cambodia. Afterwards, there were scarcely three thousand.

Preah Maha Ghosananda, whose name in Pali means "Joyful Proclaimer," had missed the killing years in his native Cambodia. For over a decade, from 1965 to 1978, he lived in deep seclusion in a Buddhist monastery deep in the forests of Thailand. After earning a doctorate from an Indian university, he had gone there to practice meditation. By the time he emerged from his hermitage, the Khmer Rouge had all but eradicated the Buddhist presence in Cambodia. It had also massacred all of Ghosananda's family.

Thousands of Cambodians had fled to refugee camps just across the Thai border. Ghosananda began visiting them, building temporary hut-temples wherever he went, blessing the people, and offering them consolation. Although a man temperamentally inclined to solitude, study, and meditation, Ghosananda threw himself into alleviating suffering in the world around him and never looked back. "We must find the courage to leave our temples," he said, "and enter the suffering-filled temples of human experience."

By the time the Khmer Rouge thugs were overthrown in 1979, Cambodia was in ruins, its economy and infrastructure shattered and its people demoralized. Moreover, guerrilla fighting in the Cambodian jungles between feuding factions continued, and hundreds of thousands of hidden landmines, a legacy from the years of violence, dotted the landscape. In order to inaugurate the spiritual rejuvenation of his homeland, Ghosananda undertook annual *Dhammayietra*, or "Pilgrimages of Truth" from one end of Cambodia to the other. Dressed in the saffron robes of a monk, he led groups of fellow Buddhists, laypersons as well as monks and nuns, on a "step-by-step" proclamation of peace and healing to some of Cambodia's most war-torn and damaged areas. Year after year he and his companions risked landmines, guerrilla hostility, weariness, and illness to walk across the land and bring hope and reconciliation to the people they met. At the start of each pilgrimage, Ghosananda announced: "Our journey for peace begins today and every day. Each step is a prayer, each step is a meditation, each step will build a bridge." Everywhere they went, the Pilgrims of Truth chanted: "Hate can never be appeased by hate; hate can only be appeased by love."

13 March

Ham Sok-Hon

13 March 1901—4 February 1989

Two Roads

IF THE EFFECTIVENESS OF a peacemaker is determined by how many repressive regimes he angers, Ham Sok-Hon has excellent credentials. Over his long career as an advocate of nonviolence, he was persecuted by the Japanese, the Soviet Russians, and finally by his fellow Koreans.

Born the son of a well-off physician in North Korea, Ham was expelled from one of the country's best schools in 1916 for protesting Japan's colonial rule of his homeland. Although a public apology could have gotten him reinstated, Ham refused. He eventually earned a degree in history, however, and taught for a number of years. But his nonviolent resistance to Japanese imperialism never wavered, earning him imprisonment four times in the years leading up to World War II. When the Soviets occupied Korea after the war, Ham also refused to cooperate with them. After he rejected the offer of a professorship at Kim Il-sung University because he realized it was simply a bid for his cooperation, he was arrested, beaten, and nearly executed before managing to escape to South Korea. During the Korean War three years later, he met members of the American Friends Service Committee and became a Quaker. Ham was attracted to the religion because of its pacifism and its lack of exclusionary doctrines. For Ham, there were many different paths to God, and he saw Quakerism, which he thought especially compatible with Buddhism and Taoism, as sharing that conviction.

In South Korea, Ham continued his public witness for peace and democracy, frequently opposing the repressive regimes of South Korean presidents Syngman Rhee, Park Chung-hee, and Chun Doo-hwan. He was jailed or placed under house arrest many times in retaliation for his criticisms of them.

Ham's social activism was based on fidelity to what he called the two "roads": the road to freedom and the road to love. By the first, he meant a political and economic democracy that protects human rights and allows individuals to flourish. By the second, he meant a religious perspective that embraces human suffering and seeks to ameliorate it.

Like **Mohandas Gandhi**, to whom he was often compared, Ham believed that sometimes the roads to freedom and love are so blocked by evil that force may ultimately be necessary to clear them. But he always considered it a last rather than a first resort. "We should keep to the principle of nonviolence," he said, "but not leave the people who are struggling. We should try to keep with them and to educate them. In the struggle there are several degrees or states—the best one, the second best one, the third best one. If you feel that it is impossible to follow the best one you should choose the second best or the third one. Just to keep silent and remain unmoved is much worse than to choose the second or even third state. Still, we must always urge the people to use the best method."

14 March
Walter Brueggemann

1933—

Shalom

WALTER BRUEGGEMANN IS THE most insightful Old Testament scholar the United States has produced. Many of his sixty-odd books are required reading in seminaries and religious studies programs across the nation. One of them, *The Prophetic Imagination* (1978), has become a classic.

But Brueggemann isn't only a scholar. Ordained in the United Church of Christ, he's also an astute Christian commentator on current social and political issues who frequently draws parallels between them and lessons from the Old Testament prophets. One of his most valuable contributions has been to remind Christians and others of the deep meaning of the ancient Hebrew word *shalom,* or "peace."

In the minds of many today, peace is just an interval between war. But Brueggemann points out that the Old Testament notion of *shalom* is much richer. It is the "persistent vision of joy, well-being, harmony, and prosperity" often expressed in words such as "love, loyalty, truth, grace, salvation, justice, blessing, and righteousness." *Shalom* is a recovery of creation's wholeness fragmented by violence and cruelty between humans. It is, says Brueggemann, "a dream of God that resists all our tendencies to division, hostility, fear, drivenness, and misery."

What Brueggemann's analysis suggests is that even though *shalom* is the natural order of things, its recovery depends in part upon the willingness of humans to practice lifestyles that express it in concrete terms. *Shalom,* he says, is an "incarnational" word. The only *shalom* we can imagine is one that responds to specific historical realities. To think of it in abstract terms is to fail to take it as a real possibility. But this doesn't mean that *shalom* is exclusively situational, much less relative.

Consider the Babylonian captivity, for example, that historical period when, after Babylon conquered the Kingdom of Judah, two generations of Jews endured bitter exile "by the waters of Babylon." During this period, the prophet Jeremiah recommended a *shalom* to the captives that spoke specifically to their predicament but that also pointed beyond it to a more general understanding of peace. He advised them to seek the *shalom* of the city—Babylon—in which they dwelt, for in its *shalom* they would find their own (Jer 29:7). When it came to the particular historical period in question, Jeremiah's point was that the Jews could create peace by forgiving and reconciling themselves to their captors. The broader lesson we can take from Jeremiah's advice is that the willingness to seek reconciliation whenever one has been violated is a necessary condition for *shalom.* But the specific contours of the reconciliation are fashioned case by case.

In Brueggemann's hands, the Old Testament notion of *shalom* becomes an active striving towards community and well-being, which in turn sets the stage for the later Christian understanding of the kingdom of God. In either case, peace, the "dream of God," is the fulfillment for which all creation yearns. It is our ultimate hope.

15 March

SuAnne Big Crow

15 March 1975—9 February 1992

Happytown

The 3,500-square-mile Pine Ridge Oglala Sioux Reservation in South Dakota is the largest and poorest Indian reservation in the United States. Half of its nearly thirty thousand residents live below the national poverty level, with unemployment at around 85 percent. Scores of homes are without electricity and plumbing. The life expectancy, forty-seven years for men and fifty-two for women, is the shortest in the entire Western Hemisphere. As if the living conditions aren't bad enough, the Sioux who live at Pine Ridge regularly endure local racism and federal indifference. Tussles between whites and Indians aren't uncommon.

But in 1987, a thirteen-year-old girl named SuAnne Big Crow demonstrated another way of dealing with the hostility directed at her and her people. She did it at a high school basketball game between the girls of Pine Ridge and Leads, a mostly white town about one hundred miles north of the reservation.

The Pine Ridge team traveled to Leads for the game. Although memories of what happened are mixed, the standard version is that fans on the Leads side of the gym began hurling racial epithets the moment the Pine Ridge team walked onto the court. Some hollered "Squaw!" and "Gut-eater!" and the Leads school band started thumping out a fake Indian drumbeat.

Then the unexpected happened, one of those breaks with convention that can defuse violent situations. SuAnne, a member of the Pine Ridge team, took off her warm-up jacket, draped it over her shoulders, and began a Sioux shawl dance while chanting a traditional song. The gym went silent. When she finished the dance, SuAnne grabbed a ball, dribbled to a hoop, and shot a basket. The gym roared with approval.

Even though parts of the story may be mythic, the whole perfectly fits SuAnne Big Crow's character. As a teenager, she toured the reservation and then the country encouraging Native Americans to avoid the use of drugs and alcohol. She was an outspoken critic of bigotry but always sought to reconcile with racists rather than condemn them. She dreamt of a youth center at Pine Ridge, a place she called "Happytown," where Sioux kids could gather for recreation and self-improvement. And along the way, she became a basketball star who set several athletic records while graduating at the top of her class. She was the pride of her community, and her people were crushed when she was killed in a car accident at the age of seventeen. Her funeral procession was six miles long.

But SuAnne's spirit of creative reconciliation remains a living memory at Pine Ridge. Admirers collected funds after her death to build what's now called the SuAnne Big Crow Boys and Girls Club. The Club serves twenty-six hundred reservation youngsters. Its facilities include a restaurant named "Happytown."

16 March
Rachel Corrie

10 April 1979—16 March 2003

Shielding Dignity

In the Israeli-Palestinian conflict, one common tactic of the Israeli army, whose official name is Israel Defense Forces or IDF, is house demolition. Called a counterinsurgency security measure by its defenders, critics argue that it's often an excuse to seize territory for Israeli settlers. The demolitions are carried out by armor-plated bulldozers that the military for some reason calls *doobis,* or "teddy bears." The heavily screened windows of these huge vehicles protect their drivers from sniper bullets and shrapnel, but also limit their range of vision.

On 16 March 2003, one of these bulldozers ran over and crushed Rachel Corrie, a young American member of the International Solidarity Movement (ISM), an organization dedicated to nonviolent direct action in defense of West Bank and Gaza Strip Palestinians. In a typical ISM action, volunteers stand as human shields between IDF *doobis* and Palestinian buildings earmarked for demolition. The hope is that their presence will inhibit the destruction of homes and the displacement of families, or at least draw international media attention to it. People from around the world travel to Israel to participate in ISM actions.

Rachel Corrie was one of them. A native of Washington State, she decided to delay her graduation from Evergreen State College to volunteer for a while with ISM. After arriving in Israel in early 2003, in the third and especially violent year of the Second Intifada, she was sent to the Gaza Strip city of Rafah, home to seventy thousand Palestinians. Corrie's initial assignment was guarding the Canada Well (so-called because of its funding source), which had been heavily damaged by IDF bulldozers. Rafah municipal workers trying to repair the well, which supplied upwards of 50 percent of the city's water, were regularly fired on by Israeli troops. While protecting it, Corrie reported that bullets hit the ground so close to workers and volunteers that bits of debris hit their faces.

On the day of her death, Corrie and six other ISM volunteers where shielding a number of Palestinian homes in Rafah that the Israeli military claimed were guerrilla hideouts. Reports differ about exactly what happened. Some say that the bulldozer operator, angered at an insurgent grenade that had exploded nearby, deliberately ran over her. Others say that she was in his blind spot. What's certain is that Corrie was hit by the vehicle and crushed to death as she stood or knelt as a human shield.

In an e-mail message to her mother written two weeks before her death, Corrie confessed to occasional moments of fear and despair at the violence surrounding her. But she also spoke of finding inspiration from the Palestinians. Through them, she said, "I am discovering a degree of strength and the basic ability for humans to remain human in the direst of circumstances—which I also haven't seen before. I think the word is dignity."

17 March

Bayard Rustin

17 March 1912—24 August 1987

Marching for Freedom

On 28 August 1963, **Martin Luther King Jr.** stood on the steps of the Lincoln Memorial. Looking toward the Washington Monument in the distance, he took a deep breath and launched into one of the most famous speeches ever given in American history. Addressing the estimated quarter of a million people gathered to hear him, he memorably told them that he had a dream that one day segregation would be a thing of the past in the United States.

The man who was responsible for putting together the March on Washington for Jobs and Freedom was Bayard Rustin, a longtime pacifist and civil rights advocate. Because he had ties with the Communist Party and was gay, several of King's closest advisors warned him against associating too closely with Rustin. They were afraid that the authorities, particularly FBI head J. Edgar Hoover, would use Rustin's past to smear the movement. But King stood by Rustin, recognizing that he was one of the most skilled members of his team. The success with which Rustin coordinated the march proved King right.

Rustin was born in West Chester, Pennsylvania. Moving to Harlem in the 1930s, he joined the American Communist Party, later saying that it was the only organization in the United States at the time that opposed segregation. He soon broke with the party, however, because of its endorsement of violence as a political weapon. His reading of Henry David Thoreau and **Mohandas Gandhi** had converted him to nonviolence.

When the United States entered World War II, Rustin refused induction and was sentenced to three years imprisonment. Upon his release, he began working with the Congress on Racial Equality (CORE) and became an advocate of nonviolent direct action in the struggle against segregation. He joined a team of sixteen men—eight blacks and eight whites—who intended to travel throughout the South on a "Journey of Reconciliation." Their action was a protest against the interstate law that forbade blacks and whites from riding on the same bus. The journey was launched on 9 April 1947. In North Carolina, the bus was stopped and several members, including Rustin, were beaten by local cops and then given hard labor jail sentences. But their treatment helped direct the nation's attention to the evils of segregation.

His participation in the Journey of Reconciliation earned Rustin the reputation of being someone skilled in the art of nonviolent resistance. When Martin Luther King Jr. organized the Montgomery bus boycott in 1955, it was only natural that he would turn to Rustin for advice. Their collaboration led two years later to the formation of the Southern Christian Leadership Conference (SCLC), an organization committed to using nonviolence in the struggle for civil rights. Its motto, inspired by Rustin, was "Not one hair of one head of one person should be harmed." Rustin's and King's efforts finally paid off with the passage of the Civil Rights Act of 1964 that ended racial segregation.

18 March
Fred Shuttlesworth

18 March 1922—5 October 2011

Architect of Project C

Reverend Fred Shuttlesworth, born and raised in Birmingham, Alabama, was one of the founders of the Southern Christian Leadership Conference, the civil rights organization dedicated to nonviolent opposition to segregation. As such, he was both a practitioner and defender of nonviolence. But as a native of a city that had a well-deserved reputation of being one of the most racist in the United States, Shuttlesworth was well aware of just how entrenched was the hatred of blacks by whites. Eugene "Bull" Connor, the city's longtime police chief, enforced Jim Crow with an iron fist, and Klan intimidation, both overt and thinly disguised, was common. Shuttlesworth's own home had been destroyed by a bomb in 1956 in retaliation for his involvement with the National Association for the Advancement of Colored People (NAACP). One of the investigating officers, himself a Klansman, ominously advised Shuttlesworth to get out of town.

So Shuttlesworth had a pretty good idea of what he was up against when he spearheaded an anti-segregation campaign in the spring of 1963 that he called "Project C." The "C" stood for "confrontation." Recognizing that appeals to conscience alone wouldn't budge the city's diehard segregationists, Shuttlesworth determined that nonviolent direct action was necessary. His goal was to provoke a situation so fraught with crisis that Birmingham authorities would be driven to the negotiation table.

The primary kinds of direct action launched by Shuttlesworth were protest marches and sit-ins in restaurants, stores, and such public facilities as libraries. Some blacks also volunteered to conduct "kneel-ins" at all-white churches. Bull Connor and his deputies moved in quickly, swinging their clubs. Connor requested and easily received a city injunction against all protests (a move that was later declared illegal by an appeals court), made dozens of arrests, and increased bail for jailed demonstrators, thereby keeping many of them from posting it. Eventually even **Martin Luther King Jr.** was arrested

Connor's aim was to quash the demonstrations by eventually throwing all of Shuttlesworth's followers behind bars. But the strategy backfired, because black high school students began taking their place in the streets and at the lunch counters. Connor, enraged at the youngsters' participation, turned attack dogs and fire hoses against them and arrested so many that the city jails were filled to overflowing. Film crews from television networks recorded the brutal confrontations. When the scenes were aired, the nation was horrified, costing Birmingham's segregationists sympathy and support. Finally some of the city's leading businessmen, worried that the bad press was damaging Birmingham's reputation, insisted on negotiating with the protesters. By July 1963, most of Birmingham's segregation ordinances were gone. So was Bull Connor. Shuttlesworth's Project C had succeeded, showing that nonviolent direct action worked if enough people were willing to take risks in opposing injustice.

19 March

Vera Brittain

29 December 1893—29 March 1970

Never the Same Person Again

Youth should be a time of exuberance, love, and anticipation. But for those generations whose youth is blighted by war—for the god of war especially devours the young—it becomes a time of despair. Killed on the battlefield or spiritually wounded back home, the youths who endure war are all victims of it.

One of the most gripping accounts of how war especially ruins the young is Vera Brittain's 1933 *Testament of Youth,* a memoir of World War I. Vera and her only brother, Edward, grew up in a comfortable middle-class household. Like so many other members of their generation, they were patriotically enthusiastic when war erupted between the European powers in 1914. Edward and all his chums immediately enlisted in the army. Vera, regretting that she couldn't follow them as a soldier, soon dropped out of university to train as a nurse. During the war years she served at military hospitals in London, Malta, and France.

It didn't take long for Vera's initial support for the war to sour. As she treated soldiers maimed by bullet and shell or burned by poison gas—her descriptions of their wounds are both ghastly and heartbreaking—she came to realize that her earlier notions of war had been romantic nonsense. After a particularly grueling night nursing gas-poisoned soldiers, she wrote, "I wish those people who write so glibly about this being a holy war, and the orators who talk so much about going on no matter how long the war lasts and what it may mean, could see a case." She sensed that the harsh reality of war was changing her. "I feel I shall never be the same person again," she confessed, "and wonder if, when the war does end, I shall have forgotten how to laugh. One day last week I came away from a really terrible amputation dressing I had been assisting at—it was the first after the operation—with my hands covered with blood and my mind full of a passionate fury at the wickedness of war, and I wished I had never been born."

This was written in 1915, scarcely a year into the war. By the time the fighting finally ceased three years later, Vera had lost, one by one, her fiancé, her beloved brother, and three of her childhood friends. Her *Testament of Youth* was an effort to come to terms with the disaster that had befallen her and her generation, and that had robbed them of their youth.

After the war, Vera returned to university. She studied history in the hopes of understanding "how the whole calamity of the war had happened, to know why it had been possible for me and my contemporaries, through our own ignorance and others' ingenuity, to be used, hypnotized and slaughtered." She became a leading figure in the pacifist and feminist movements in England, wrote books, and acquired fame. But she never ceased mourning the lives—her own included, perhaps—that the war had consumed.

20 March
John Middleton Murry

6 August 1889—12 March 1957

Adelphi Center Founder

Not all advocates of peace lead peaceful personal lives. Despite their admirable public work for nonviolence, they never quite seem to achieve a harmony or equilibrium in their private affairs. Such a one was the author John Middleton Murry.

Although largely forgotten today, Murry was one of the most prolific British authors of his generation, writing nearly sixty well-received books and hundreds of essays. He was married four times—one of his wives was the writer Katherine Mansfield; had numerous love affairs (the primary reason his marriages didn't last); and went through any number of ideological phases. At one time or another, he embraced Christianity (he even thought for a while of becoming an Anglican priest), Marxism, pacifism, and anti-Soviet militarism. But despite his unsettled private life and his leapfrogging from one cause to the next, he was a leading British pacifist in the 1930s. His most significant achievement was the founding of the Adelphi Center, intended, as he wrote, to be "a meeting place for pacifists of all ages who believe there is a need for co-ordinated effort to realize pacifism as a way of life."

Founded in 1934, Adelphi was envisioned as a nonsectarian experiment in communal living in which participants would practice nonviolence, pool resources, and together create an alternative to the going capitalism model. In his 1937 *The Necessity of Pacifism,* Murry argued that capitalism is "a social morality, an all-pervading spiritual atmosphere—nothing less, indeed, than a total life-mode," and that therefore reformist tinkering with it would do little to bring about fundamental change. What was needed, he believed, was the living example of a distinctly different "life-mode," and his hope was that the Adelphi Center would be just that.

The Center consisted of a large house situated on seventy acres of farmland. Murry's intention was that the community would become self-sufficient, growing most of its own food and selling or bartering the rest. He hoped for a core membership of twelve pacifists—despite his claim of nonsectarianism, Murry's Christianity was apparent in his plans for Adelphi—composed of both middle class and blue-collar workers. The commune hosted a summer school in which some of the day's leading thinkers lectured. They included George Orwell, Reinhold Niebuhr, and Herbert Read. In addition, it served as a haven for conscientious objectors to military service.

Despite Murry's communitarian vision, the core members of Adelphi were rugged individualists who found it difficult to cooperate with one another. The experiment collapsed in 1937, and the house was used shortly afterwards to shelter fifty refugee Basque children whom the Spanish Civil War had displaced. As sometimes happens, the reality fell short of the ideal when it came to Adelphi. But Murry's dream of a community in which practitioners of nonviolence could serve as examples to the rest of the world was and remains noble, despite its failure and Murry's own personal shortcomings.

21 March

Pocahontas

CA. 1595—MARCH 1617

New World Peacemaker

Every kid in America knows the story of Pocahontas, the Indian princess who saved Captain John Smith's life. Scholars have squabbled over whether Smith's rescue actually happened or, if it did, what it signified. But there's little doubt that Pocahontas played an important role in the establishment and preservation of peace between Jamestown settlers and the Native American inhabitants of the New World.

Pocahontas was the daughter of Powhatan, chief of a union of Algonquin-speaking tribes in present-day tidewater Virginia. She was probably in her early teens when the English founders of Jamestown arrived in 1607. One of their leaders, Captain John Smith, was captured by Powhatan's hunters a year later. As Smith related the story to Britain's Queen Anne, he was forced down on two flat stones and ringed by warriors prepared to beat him to death with clubs when Pocohantas broke through them and threw herself on Smith. She "hazarded the beating out of her own brains to save mine; and not only that, but so prevailed with her father, that I was safely conducted to Jamestown."

Whether or not the story is true, it's clear that Pocahontas was an important pacifying link between Jamestown settlers and Powhatan's people. She grew quite close to Smith, calling him her "father," played with settler children, and prevailed on her father and his hunters to supply the starving colony with stored grain and meat. As Smith put it, "once in every four or five days, Pocahontas with her attendants brought so much provision that saved many of their lives that else for all this had starved with hunger."

There was a third way in which Pocahontas ensured some degree of peace between settlers and Indians, but the telling of it speaks ill of the settlers. Despite Pocahontas's efforts, hostilities erupted in 1609, and at one point in the conflict she was taken hostage by the settlers. Held a prisoner for the next five years, she learned English, converted to Christianity, and married an Englishman named John Rolfe. At least on Rolfe's side, the marriage seems to have been motivated more by a desire to forge a peaceful alliance between the settlers and Powhatan than anything else. He was, he wrote, "motivated not by the unbridled desire of carnal affection, but for the good of this plantation, for the honor of our country, for the Glory of God, for my own salvation."

We don't know what Pocahontas felt about the marriage. All we do know is that she and Rolfe had a son, and that she died shortly after the child's birth of an unspecified illness. But the marriage with Rolfe did in fact ease the tension between the English and the Indians. It's sobering to think that Pocahontas, who did so much on her own to make peace between the two peoples, continued her peace-building even after she was kidnapped and held captive by the men who sailed to her shores on strange boats. In one manner of speaking, Pocahontas may be the New World's first peace martyr.

22 MARCH
John McConnell

22 March 1915—

Father of Earth Day

WHEN JOHN MCCONNELL SAW the first color photos of planet earth taken from outer space on the cover of *Life* magazine, he was speechless. The beauty of the planet's blues and greens swathed in white clouds convinced him that the same concern for peace among people that he'd championed his entire adult life needed to be extended to the planet itself. So he pitched an idea to the 1969 National UNESCO Conference: that the United Nations proclaim that a day be set aside each year to celebrate the earth and encourage responsible stewardship of it. He proposed the vernal equinox, the twenty-four-hour period in the spring evenly divided between night and day, as an appropriate date for the celebration. The vernal equinox is a period of equilibrium that McConnell hoped would serve as a symbolic reminder of the importance of harmony between humans and the environment.

The city of San Francisco, host to the UNESCO conference, enthusiastically endorsed the idea, as did **U Thant**, Secretary-General of the UN, and the first Earth Day was observed in 1970. In the United States, it's now generally celebrated on 22 April rather than the vernal equinox. But the spirit of harmony with the earth remains the same.

McConnell's concern for the environment was sparked in 1939, long before ecological sensibilities were on the map. While working in a plastics factory, he grew worried about the threat of pollution posed by nonbiodegradable plastics. World War II and the Cold War that followed it pushed McConnell's environmentalism to the background. During those years, his primary focus was on doing something to ameliorate world hunger and militaristic buildup. But the 1969 *Life* cover reawakened his awe for the planet and reminded him that the welfare of "earthlings" was necessarily bound up with the health of the planet itself.

In June 1970, McConnell wrote and published the "Earth Day Proclamation," a document that outlined the importance and purpose of the annual observation. In it, true to his conviction that human welfare is bound up with planetary welfare, he argued that the same economic and political institutions that create poverty and oppression also harm the environment. He laid out three goals, which he intended Earth Day celebrations to remind people of each year: to "peacefully end the scourge of war"; to "provide an opportunity for the children of the disinherited poor to obtain their rightful inheritance in the Earth"; and to "redirect the energies of industry and society from progress through products to progress through harmony with Earth's natural systems for improving the quality of life." McConnell's inspiration for Earth Day, celebrated internationally each year, has awakened millions of people to the need to cherish and protect both earthlings and the "beautiful Spaceship Earth," as U Thant put it when the United Nations endorsed Earth Day, that we earthlings call home.

23 March

David Suzuki

24 March 1936—

Maintaining the Sacred Balance

The Canadian-born geneticist David Suzuki knows something about disruption. During World War II, he and his family, despite having lived in British Columbia for three generations, were interned and then forcibly relocated east of the Rockies. The memory of this break in equilibrium, as well as the beauty of the Canadian Rockies through which he and his family were transported, inspired Suzuki's later dedication to preserving environmental stability.

Although he spent close to forty years as a university professor, Suzuki is at heart a public intellectual. He's a pioneer in popularizing science who began hosting a string of television shows as early as 1970. Since then he has written and hosted several immensely popular series that focus on issues of environmental sustainability and climate change. In recent years, he has become one of the world's most eloquent and informed defenders of the claim that human activity is dangerously accelerating the temperature of the planet. In lectures, books, and articles—and through the work of the David Suzuki Foundation, whose mission is to "protect the diversity of nature and our quality of life, now and for the future"—he advocates for an interdependent perspective on the planet and encourages humans to reduce their carbon footprints. The recipient of dozens of honorary degrees honoring his environmentalism, Suzuki was presented with a Right Livelihood Award in 2009 for his "advocacy of the socially responsible use of science, and for his massive contribution to raising awareness about the perils of climate change and building public support for policies to address it."

Perhaps Suzuki's trademark claim is that the earth's ecosystem is a "sacred balance" that humans are both morally and prudentially obliged to honor. The "sacredness" of nature is revealed whenever we're "spiritually uplifted by the beauty of a forested valley or an ice-coated Arctic mountain, overwhelmed with awe at the sight of the star-filled heavens, and filled with reverence when we enter a sacred place. In the beauty, mystery and wonder that our brain perceives and expresses, we add a special gift to the planet." But our flexing of "technological muscle power" has seriously jeopardized the balance that creates such beauty. It is no mark of shame, says Suzuki, to "acknowledge our dependence on the same biophysical factors that support all other life-forms" and resolve to change our individual and social behaviors in order to live in harmony with those factors. But in our drive to control the environment, we "seem to have forgotten the real things that matter"—the majestic beauty of the natural order that awakens awe in us—for the sake of a merely utilitarian relationship with nature. Suzuki's hope is to recall us to our proper relationship with the ecosphere so that the "sacred balance" can be restored.

24 March

Kalle Lasn

24 March 1942—

Culture Jammer

THERE ARE MANY FORMS of violence, but one of the most recent—and most insidious—is the phenomenon known as consumerism, the mania to buy and consume more and more and more. Americans are particularly prone to consumerism, a malady sometimes referred to as "affluenza," but most other so-called developed nations suffer from it too. Alarmingly, less developed regions around the world also feel its allure. Many of them suffer from what might be called consumer envy.

But why is consumerism a form of violence? It harms the environment because the frenetic production of goods to meet demand is unsustainable, and so exploits and pollutes earth and atmosphere. It harms people because it siphons off goods and natural resources from poor regions of the world to fuel the feeding frenzy of the richer ones. And it harms consumers themselves because, like all addictions, it increases craving without offering anything that ultimately satisfies it.

The Estonian-born Canadian social critic Kalle Lasn has declared war on consumerism, but it's a war fought with "memes," or units of meaning, rather than physical weapons. According to Lasn, "America is no longer a country. It's a multitrillion-dollar brand." What he means is that the average citizen is so surrounded by marketing memes—print and electronic ads, jingles, slogans, images, and sounds, all aimed solely at pushing products—that the default position for most of us from infancy to old age is *buy*. We're so drugged by the market-memed culture in which we live that we rarely come out of our daze long enough to get a bit of perspective.

What Lasn suggests as a form of resistance to the culture of consumerism is clogging up its works—"culture jamming"—by manipulating marketing memes in ways that make them convey messages contrary to their original intent. Lasn and his fellow culture jammers tweak ads for high-end jeans featuring body-perfect models by insinuating that our cultural fixation with slimness encourages eating disorders. Similarly, they jam full-page glossy ads for hard liquor by juxtaposing photos of drunks bent double spewing in alleyways. The purpose in their ad "rewriting" is to counteract the marketing memes that are such integral parts of our cultural scene that they just seem natural. Culture jamming uses the "element of surprise" to "stop the flow" of conventional memes. It shocks us in the hope that the ensuing moment of clarity will break us free from our addiction to the "consumerist script."

The point, says Lasn, is to practice an "ecology of the mind." We're pretty aware of the importance of cleaning up the environment or city hall, but much less conscious of the "infotoxins" that pollute our inner landscape. But just as physical and moral contamination violates the earth and politics, meme contamination commits violence against clear thinking and wise decisions. Lasn wants to do something about that.

25 March

Norman Borlaug

25 March 1914—21 September 2009

Feeding the World

MOST OF US WILL never save the life of a single person. Norman Borlaug, the "Father of the Green Revolution," is credited with saving one billion lives by introducing agricultural methods which immensely increased the world's food supply.

Borlaug, an agronomist who grew up on a family farm in Minnesota, tackled the problem of world hunger in the 1960s. At the time, impoverished nations like India, the Philippines, and Mexico were in danger of widespread famine because of soil depletion, low-yielding crops, and arid conditions. Borlaug brought modern science to the table in order to do something about the problem. He focused on the hybridization of food crops, especially wheat and rice, to enhance their yield; encouraged the use of chemical fertilizers, pesticides, and insecticides to stimulate growth and minimize disease and infestation; and stressed the vital importance of adequate irrigation.

One of Borlaug's greatest successes was coming up with a variety of high-yielding short-stalked wheat. Wheat is one of the world's most widely used grains. But older strains of it tended to produce relatively low yields and were easily damaged by bad weather or blight. Borlaug created new varieties that produced more abundant heads of grain on shorter stalks, which meant that the top-heavy wheat was less likely to collapse before harvest from its own weight or from high winds and heavy rains. The new strain also was more disease resistant than earlier ones. In just a few years, Borlaug's wheat, coupled with increased uses of chemical fertilizers and irrigation, rescued famine-endangered nations. Yields doubled in India, which was the most at-risk country, and by the mid-1960s Mexico was actually exporting grain. Borlaug was awarded the Nobel Peace Prize in 1970, the Nobel Committee wisely recognizing that making sure people around the world have enough to eat goes a long way towards reducing violence.

Since the heyday of the explosion in food production, quickly dubbed the "Green Revolution," Borlaug's farming methods have come under critical scrutiny. Environmentalists worry that the sustained use of chemical fertilizers, pesticides, and insecticides is slowly poisoning the earth, and that increased irrigation is both depleting aquifers and salinating the soil. Public policy makers and human rights activists are concerned that the intensive farming promoted by the Green Revolution tends to focus on exportable cash crops rather than locally consumed food crops, and that this too often encourages already poor countries to neglect feeding their own hungry. Finally, biologists and food activists warn against the trend towards genetically modified food crops that Borlaug especially championed during the last two decades of his life.

These reservations about the Green Revolution deserve to be taken seriously. But the fact remains that the extent of world hunger was so calamitous in the 1960s that something had to be done, and done quickly, to save millions of people from starvation. Borlaug fed them.

26 March
Kate Richards O'Hare

26 March 1877—10 January 1948

Women Pay the Price of War

THE PASSAGE OF THE 1917 Espionage Act is one of the lowest points in U.S. history. Enacted after the country entered World War I, the law prescribed a $10,000 fine and up to twenty years imprisonment for anyone who interfered with the recruiting of soldiers. The act was deliberately written in such general terms that merely speaking out against the war could be interpreted as a violation of the law. So it quickly became a legal opportunity for rounding up people whom the authorities considered to be troublemakers. Before the war was over, nearly one thousand U.S. residents were convicted of breaking the Espionage Act. They included well-known left-leaning war resisters such as perennial presidential candidate Eugene Debs, anarchist Emma Goldman, and union organizer "Big" Bill Haywood.

Among those arrested and imprisoned was the socialist activist and author Kate Richards O'Hare. As early as 1914, three years before the United States went to war, she passionately condemned militaristic adventurism and pointed out that the victims of war include the mothers whose sons are devoured by it. "It is the women of Europe who pay the price while war rages," she wrote, "and it will be the women who will pay again when war has run its bloody course and Europe sinks down into the slough of poverty like a harried beast too spent to wage the fight. It will be the sonless mothers who will bend their shoulders to the plough and wield in age-palsied hands the reaphook."

Such declarations, not to mention her 1904 socialist novel *What Happened to Dan?* and the radical journal *Rip-Saw* which she edited with her husband, brought O'Hare to the attention of the authorities. Ready to arrest her at the slightest provocation, they took action against her in 1917 when she blasted the war in a speech delivered in Bowman, North Dakota. She was quickly convicted of violating the Espionage Act and sentenced to five years in prison, despite the fact that she was a mother of four. While serving her time in Missouri State Penitentiary, she wrote two books. One of them, *In Prison*, was a stark exposé of the conditions women prisoners endured behind bars. O'Hare's graphic descriptions of guard brutality and lesbian sex between prisoners shocked the nation.

Although she didn't lose a son in battle, O'Hare's incarceration made her one of the women who pay the price for war. By the time her sentence was commuted by President Warren Harding in 1920, she had served close to four years. Upon her release, she worked hard for prison reform, especially for women inmates.

27 March
Wally and Juanita Nelson

27 March 1909—23 May 2002
1923—

War Tax Resisters

A CHANCE MEETING, WHEN she was a journalist and he was serving a jail term for participating in the Journey of Reconciliation, an effort to end segregation in the South, brought Wally Nelson and Juanita Morrow together. That was in 1948. For the next half-century, the two were life partners and collaborators in active nonviolence.

Both had been involved in civil rights actions before they met; both were members of the Congress of Racial Equality (CORE). In addition, Wally had spent nearly four years in a federal penitentiary for refusing to serve in World War II. As African-Americans, they were dedicated to securing civil rights for blacks. As advocates of nonviolence, they were equally devoted to resisting what they saw as the American war machine.

In the same year they met, the couple collaborated in the founding of Peacemakers, a national organization dedicated to "revolutionary pacifist activity." Members of Peacemakers pledged to live radically countercultural lives by refusing to serve in wartime, participate in the production or transportation of weapons, or pay war taxes. They also promised to spread the good news of pacifism in word and deed. The Nelsons were two of the first members to take the plunge into war tax resistance. It's a form of protest that, then and now, can have severe consequences, including seizure of property by the government and even imprisonment.

The basic purpose of war tax resistance is a refusal to fund military spending through tax dollars. There are several strategies that resisters have adopted over the years. Some refuse to pay any taxes, whereas others deduct the percentage of their tax that goes to the Pentagon but pay the rest. Some donate to charities the amount of money they would otherwise pay in taxes, and others don't. And some avoid the whole problem of paying taxes by adopting a lifestyle of voluntary simplicity in order to keep their income below taxable levels.

This last option was the one chosen by the Nelsons. They built their own home out of salvaged supplies and grew most of their food in a half-acre organic garden. They refused to buy insurance or automobiles, and earned what little cash they needed through odd jobs that deducted no social security tax from their wages. Their decision to live on a drastically reduced income and to forgo conventional insurance or governmental benefits, difficult as it was at times, was sustained by their conviction, as Wally put it, that "our entire economic life is tied into violence. It seemed logical that the less we participated, the less we'd be giving to that system."

But the Nelsons weren't just refuseniks. They continued their work with CORE through the 1950s, actively supported César Chávez's United Farm Workers campaign, and helped build tax resistance as a national movement. Wally died in 2002, advocating active nonviolence to the end. Juanita continues to live in their hand-built Massachusetts home, still refusing to pay taxes.

28 March
Pelagius

CA. 354—CA. 430

Wealth and Violence

PELAGIUS, WHO MAY HAVE been born somewhere in the British Isles, is quite possibly the earliest Christian humanist. A monk and theologian of the Celtic Johannine Christian Order, he argued against the doctrine of original sin and defended the position that humans, made in the likeness of a good God, are capable of willing and performing good works on their own. In saying this, he placed himself squarely on the side of those who taught that humans possess inherent dignity and a native attunement to virtue. This humanistic and hopeful position was blasted by Augustine, Pelagius was excommunicated in 417, and his writings were condemned as heretical by the Council of Carthage a year later.

Because of the Church's suppression of his works, not many of Pelagius's writings survive. But one of them, *On Riches*, is a thoughtful analysis of why, in his estimation, the acquisition of wealth is incompatible with a commitment to Christ. The heart of his argument is that there is an inseparable connection between wealth and violence, and violence is antithetical to Christian discipleship.

Pelagius argues for the connection between wealth and violence in three ways. First, he says, the temperament of a person who possesses wealth is prone to moods and responses that corrode his character, potentially harm others, and certainly fail to reflect Christ's example. The rich man is haughty, proud, full of fury and anger, boastful, and disdainful of the poor. Christ and his disciples, on the other hand, are downcast, humble, gentle, long-suffering, self-effacing, and compassionate of the poor. In the second place, wealth breeds violence because of the lengths the rich will go to in order to protect what they own. They will "oppress, rob, torture, and finally kill" to make sure that no one threatens their possessions. Finally, given the way the world is, it's entirely likely that the wealthy acquired their riches in the first place by force of arms or some kind of skulduggery. "It is difficult," writes Pelagius, "to acquire riches without committing every kind of evil. They are procured by calculated lies or clever theft or fraudulent deceit or robbery with violence or barefaced falsification. They are frequently accumulated by plunder of widows or oppression of orphans or bribery or, much crueler still, by the shedding of innocent blood."

It's clear from what Pelagius says that he doesn't think material possessions are wicked in themselves, but rather that their owners are tempted by violence in their pursuit or their protection and eventually succumb to greed, the foundation of all human sin. It's not accidental, he says, that Jesus embraced poverty, knowing as he did that ownership leads to greed and greed leads to violence. People who "profess themselves as Christ's disciples," concludes Pelagius, "should follow their teacher's example" and avoid falling into the spiral of wealth and violence.

29 March

R. S. Thomas

29 March 1913—25 September 2000

Troubler of the Welsh Conscience

Most people have heard of the Welsh poet Dylan Thomas, but fewer are familiar with the poetry of his fellow countryman R. S. Thomas. This is a pity, because the "other" Thomas is reckoned by many critics to be one of the finest poets of the twentieth century. He narrowly lost the 1996 Nobel Prize in literature to the Irish poet Seamus Heaney.

One of the reasons R. S. Thomas is relatively unknown is that he chose to live remotely and obscurely. An Anglican priest, he intentionally served rural parishes in western Wales far away from bustling town and city centers. He disliked giving interviews and discouraged visitors. He also had a somewhat curmudgeonly reputation for his distrust of modern technology, living for most of his life without central heating, refrigerators, or television. He rarely read newspapers.

Thomas may have been a recluse and an occasional curmudgeon, but he was hardly a misanthrope. His poetry, although always lean and unsentimental, sympathetically chronicled the harsh lives of Welsh famers and laborers. Thomas was generally unexpressive in his personal relationships, but he felt the impoverishment of his fellow Welshmen keenly and was a long-standing critic of what he saw as their oppression by the forces of capitalism.

Another continuous theme in Thomas's poetry was his love of the fierce Welsh landscape, especially the western seacoast. He was an ardent conservationist and wildlife preservationist his entire adult life, resisting mightily development of the countryside by both British and Welsh entrepreneurs. To the end of his life, he spoke out against the urbanization of rural Wales as well as the miserable living conditions of many of his fellow countrymen. As one commentator noted, he became the "troubler of the Welsh conscience."

Thomas's sympathy for the poor as well as his deep love of the Welsh countryside were fueled by a Christian-inspired dislike of violence. He became a pacifist shortly after his ordination in 1937, despite his awareness that "the general attitude of the Church to war between states" was "completely contrary to the teaching of Christ, who was that most unpopular creature in most circles, a pacifist." But even though he criticized the Church of England for its refusal to condemn warfare, he also expressed gratitude that his ordination gave him immunity from the draft during World War II. Looking back, he suspected that had he been a layperson in 1939, his "pacifist and conscientious objections" might not have been enough to motivate a resistance on his part to conscription.

In his later years, Thomas became an active member of the British-based Campaign for Nuclear Disarmament, the pacifist organization cofounded by **Bertrand Russell**.

30 March
Dith Pran

27 September 1942—30 March 2008

Messenger from the Killing Fields

APRIL, 1975: THE CAMBODIAN capital of Phnom Penh was in chaos as thousands of residents fled from approaching Khmer Rouge soldiers. American diplomatic and military personnel left quickly too. Just about the only foreigners remaining in the city were journalists. One of them was *New York Times* war correspondent Sydney Schanberg. Accompanying him was Dith Pran, a Cambodian photographer and general troubleshooter, one of those people an editor of the *Times* once described as "the local partner, the stringer, the interpreter, the driver, the fixer, who knows the ropes, who makes your work possible, who often becomes your friend, who may save your life, who shares little of the glory, and who risks so much more than you do."

Dith Pran lived up to the job description of "the fixer who may save your life" on that April day. He accompanied Schanberg and a few other reporters to a Phnom Penh hospital to check out rumors that the Khmer Rouge was shooting people left and right. Once there, they were confronted by a group of Khmer soldiers who, but for the fast talking of Dith, would have killed them all on the spot. Schanberg, who had been friends with Dith for two years, managed to get out of Cambodia shortly afterwards. Dith wasn't as lucky. He was stuck in Kampuchea, as the Khmer Rouge renamed Cambodia.

Dith later said that "you had to pretend to be stupid" if you wanted to remain alive under the new regime. Intellectuals and artists were ruthlessly exterminated, as was anyone who displayed such evidence of "Western corruption" as eyeglasses, perfume, or watches. Pretending to be a peasant, Dith fled Phnom Penh and landed up in a village twenty miles away, where he was put to work planting and harvesting rice. Along with millions of other Cambodians, he became a virtual slave of the Khmer Rouge, forced to labor in the daytime and attend indoctrination classes at night. Rations were miniscule; for months, Dith was allowed only a single spoonful of rice per day. He and his fellow workers supplemented their diets by surreptitiously eating bark, snails, and even the flesh from exhumed corpses. He endured this misery for nearly five years until the Khmer Rouge was finally overthrown. His friend Schanberg had given him up for dead. Their joyful reunion was dramatically captured in the feature film *The Killing Fields,* an allusion to the green fields fertilized by the bones of victims that dotted the Cambodian landscape during the Khmer regime.

Dith moved to the United States in 1980, where he became a tireless advocate for the Cambodian people and especially Cambodian refugees. Describing himself sometimes simply as a "messenger" and other times as a "one-person crusade," Dith believed it was his duty as a survivor of the killing fields to make sure that the world knew what had happened, lest the violence that killed most of his relatives and millions of Cambodians explode elsewhere. He served peace by warning of the horrors its collapse brings.

31 March

César Chávez

31 March 1927—23 April 1993

Not Beasts of Burden

THE HISTORY OF THE struggle for workers' rights is heavy with labor leaders who, either out of commitment or desperation, were ready to resort to violence. The Mexican-American cofounder of the United Farm Workers (UFW), César Chávez, wasn't one of them. His campaign for the rights of agricultural workers was openly and unapologetically based on nonviolent principles and tactics—and it worked. What **Martin Luther King Jr.**'s nonviolence did for civil rights, Chávez's did for labor rights.

Raised in a migrant farmworker family—his father lost his ranch after falling behind in the mortgage payments—Chávez had firsthand acquaintance with the miserable wages, brutal treatment, and unsafe conditions endured by western migrant farmworkers, most of whom were Mexican, Filipino, or Asian. He worked in the fields, with the exception of a "miserable" two-year stint in the Navy, until 1952, when he became an organizer for a Latino civil rights group. Ten years later, he cofounded the UFW.

In 1965, the UFW participated in its first major struggle, a strike against California grape growers. It was during this action that Chávez wrote his famous "Letter from Delano" to California's vineyard owners, a document that eloquently defends the humanity of workers too often looked down upon because of their color and their poverty. "We are not saints because we are poor," he wrote, "but by the same measure neither are we immoral. We are men and women who have suffered and endured much, and not only because of our abject poverty but because we have been kept poor. The colors of our skins, the languages of our cultural and native origins, the lack of formal education, the exclusion from the democratic process, the numbers of our slain in recent wars—all these burdens generation after generation have sought to demoralize us, to break our human spirit. But God knows that we are not beasts of burden, agricultural implements or rented slaves; we are men."

Chávez's letter testifies to his conviction, born of his commitment to nonviolence, that an appeal to conscience was more effective in the long run than physical coercion. And so it proved in the grape strike. The courage and patience of the thousands of strikers—Chávez once said that "the rich may have money, but the poor have time"—moved the entire nation, launched a widespread consumer boycott of grapes, and eventually led to concessions from the grape growers. Future strikes and boycotts, including the 1970 "Salad Bowl" action, the largest farm worker strike in U.S. history, were likewise successful, resulting in better working conditions for field laborers as well as state and federal regulations protecting their rights.

Chávez often said that his two greatest influences were **Jesus** and **Mohandas Gandhi**. Jesus' teachings and life assured Chávez of the virtue of nonviolence, and he frequently employed Gandhi's nonviolent tactics of boycott, strike, and hunger fast protests. From first to last, he remained loyal to what he often called "militant nonviolence" as both a way of life and as a means of addressing injustices.

1 April
Wangari Maathai

1 April 1940—25 September 2011

Green Belt Pioneer

HER HUSBAND DIVORCED HER, claiming that she was too headstrong to be a good wife. She was labeled a dangerous subversive by her own government. During one public demonstration, she was beaten into unconsciousness by police. In another, she was struck by a thrown tear gas canister. She was also jailed several times. And all because Wangari Maathai devoted herself to environmental and democratic reform in her native Kenya.

As a young academic biologist at the University of Nairobi in the 1970s—she was the first woman in Central Africa to obtain a doctorate in veterinary anatomy—Maathai grew concerned about the environmental devastation created in Nairobi by widespread deforestation. She recognized that a massive replanting program could both save the land and provide a source of income for Nairobi's poor. So in 1977 she founded a small local organization that paid Nairobi women to plant trees. The organization soon grew into a nationwide and then pan-African one known as the Greenbelt Movement. Since its inception, the movement has planted upwards of forty million trees in Africa and provided sources of income for nearly one million women.

The genius of Maathai's vision was its holistic awareness of the linkage between environmental sustainability and economic opportunity. Replanting Nairobi's forests with indigenous species was good for the environment because it improved soil health, cut down on erosion, created shade and windbreaks, and served as habitats for birds and small animals. But it was also good for economically distressed people because the reforestation provided them with a steady source of income, richer farmland, and firewood for personal use and for selling. It was a win-win situation.

Maathai's efforts on behalf of the land and its people earned her powerful enemies, especially longtime Kenyan president Daniel arap Moi. The clash between them came to a head in 1989 when Maathai rallied opposition to a plan, endorsed by Moi, to build a large business and residential complex in Nairobi's main park and wildlife refuge. Moi's government fought her every step of the way, and eventually the Kenyan courts ruled against her. But she brought so much negative publicity to the project that the foreign backers of the complex pulled out of the deal, and the Nairobi park was left undamaged.

Maathai was awarded the Nobel Peace Prize in 2004 for her "holistic approach to sustainable development that embraces democracy, human rights, and women's rights in particular." In her acceptance speech, she said that sometimes in history, moments arise that call for a "shift to a new level of consciousness to reach a higher moral ground," shedding fear and offering hope to one another. "That time," she concluded, "is now."

2 April

John Paul II

18 May 1920—2 April 2005

Justice and Forgiveness

Perhaps because he suffered as a youth under the brutal Nazi occupation of Poland and later, as a priest, under the repressive heel of Soviet-style communism, Pope John Paul II was especially concerned with ending violence and human rights abuse. His long papacy was marked by humanitarian criticisms of both communist and capitalist oppression; periodic calls for international arbitration of disputes, the abolition of capital punishment, and disarmament; and ecumenical and interfaith dialogue. He asked forgiveness and did public penance for the Church's long history of persecuting Jews. His support of the Solidarity movement in Poland heartened resistance to Soviet domination and contributed to the downfall of the Soviet empire. When it came to such matters as birth control, the ordination of women, papal authority, and liberation theology, John Paul was conservative and, according to his critics, even reactionary. But no one can fault him on his gospel-based advocacy of nonviolence and humanitarianism.

Actually, John Paul's perspective on peace and justice was traditional, following as it did Jesus' teachings and example as well as the social encyclicals of earlier popes. The twin pillars of peace, the Pope argued, are justice and forgiveness. Peace without justice is a false calm that may smooth over the surface of social discontent but does nothing to ameliorate its underlying causes. Peace without forgiveness carries within it potentially explosive resentment of past real or imagined transgressions.

Working for justice, on the other hand, necessarily involves the often unpleasant chore of getting so close to the victims of economic and political oppression that their suffering becomes our suffering. Only through the creation of this sort of empathic bond—a sensing of the suffering Christ in the other—are we truly motivated to seek fundamental legal and public policy changes. Similarly, unless victims can bring themselves to forgive their oppressors, genuine reconciliation is impossible. Reprisal may be psychologically satisfying in the short run, but it ultimately brings about "a real and permanent loss" because "violence kills what it intends to create." Forgiving is a lengthier and more painful process that "demands great spiritual strength and moral courage" on the part of forgivers. But it creates instead of destroys the possibility of real dialogue and community.

In his final annual World Day of Peace message, released only four months before his death, John Paul reminded the world that peace built on the twin pillars of justice and forgiveness is the responsibility of all people of good will, not just heads of state. Because the world in which we now live is so interconnected, the "common good," which "concerns every expression of [an individual's] social nature: family, groups, associations, cities, regions, states, the community of peoples and nations," must be everyone's responsibility.

3 April

Jane Goodall

3 April 1934—

Roots and Shoots of Hope

MOST BABY BOOMERS REMEMBER devouring each and every 1960s *National Geographic* magazine article about Jane Goodall and her work with the Gombe Basin chimpanzees. The young woman's ability not only to observe chimps in the wild but actually to live with them, not to mention the fascinating discoveries she made about their behavior, mesmerized tens of thousands of readers. It's not too much to say that her work helped lay the foundations of environmental awareness.

Since her early fieldwork, Goodall has been a tireless celebrator and protector of the planet. In 1977 she founded the Jane Goodall Institute, an organization that both supports ongoing primate research in the Gombe Basin and strives to encourage sustainable lifestyles and public policies. Always an ecologically minded thinker, Goodall sees the health of the natural world and its nonhuman inhabitants as necessarily connected with the well-being of humans. To advocate for the environment is also to champion social, political, and economic reforms that improve the lives of humans.

In 1991, after meeting with a group of teenagers who wanted to know how they could do something for the environment, Goodall created a youth branch of the Institute called Roots & Shoots. Goodall explains the name by pointing out that "roots creep underground everywhere and make a firm foundation. Shoots seem very weak, but to reach the light, they can break open brick walls. Imagine that the brick walls are all the problems we have inflicted on our planet. Hundreds of thousands of roots and shoots, hundreds of thousands of young people around the world, can break through these walls. We CAN change the world." The organization's mission is to help kids create projects that improve the environment and the quality of life for both animals and humans. Roots & Shoots groups, whose members range in age from kindergarteners to college students, have been established in over one hundred countries. They have participated in such projects as fundraising for animals orphaned by poachers, launching recycling programs, and organizing peace celebrations.

The founding of Roots & Shoots speaks to Goodall's hope for the future, despite the grim realities of environmental degradation, overpopulation, and human cruelty. She senses a "tremendous energy, enthusiasm, and commitment" on the part of young people to "fight to right the wrongs" that currently exist. It's they, she believes, who will adopt lifestyles less harmful to the environment, find more equitable ways to distribute the world's wealth, and "replace violence and intolerance with understanding and compassion. And love."

4 April
Martin Luther King Jr.

15 January 1929—4 April 1968

Righteous Extremism

In only thirteen years, Martin Luther King Jr.'s leadership of a peaceful revolution changed the face of the United States. Beginning with the 1955 Montgomery bus boycott and ending in 1968 with a campaign against the Vietnam War, King became the best-known practitioner of active nonviolence in the United States and acquired an international reputation second only to **Mohandas Gandhi**'s. He broke the back of Jim Crow in the South through the disciplined use of boycotts, sit-ins, and public demonstrations that both appealed to the nation's conscience and pinched the pocketbooks of white powerbrokers. He was imprisoned many times for his witness, endured countless death threats, and survived the bombing of his home. Eventually, his dedication to nonviolent revolution led to his murder. But his legacy is immeasurable.

In one of his most important essays, the 1963 "Letter from Birmingham Jail," King explained his nonviolent tactics and defended using them to bring about social and economic change. Most immediately, the letter is a reply to eight Alabama clergymen who accused King of extremism. But it's also as fine a statement of active nonviolence as he ever wrote.

King argued that there are four steps in any nonviolent campaign: an honest appraisal of the facts of oppression, an earnest effort to negotiate with oppressors, a self-disciplined purification of motives and control of behavior, and finally direct action in the form of nonviolent resistance to oppressors who refuse to negotiate. In each of his campaigns against racism, economic injustice, and warfare, King preached and practiced this basic approach.

But nonviolent resistance, because it may well involve a breaking of law, was looked upon by many of King's contemporaries as an "extreme" measure. Far better, they argued, to wait patiently for gradual change instead of "forcing" the issue with illegal boycotts and public marches. King responded by arguing that honest and loving acts of civil disobedience to unjust laws "arouse the conscience of the community over its injustice," and so actually express "the highest respect for law." Moreover, he said, some situations not only allow for but require extremism. Jesus, for example, was an extremist for love, and the prophet Amos an extremist for justice. It's not extremism in itself that is good or bad, but the cause that it serves. "Will we be extremists for hate or for love? Will we be extremists for the preservation of injustice or for the extension of justice?" Moderation in some situations is a betrayal. To stand by doing nothing in the face of evil for fear of extremism is worse than cowardice. It's collaboration with evil, for it "prefers a negative peace which is the absence of tension to a positive peace which is the presence of justice."

5 April

Pythagoras

CA. 570—CA. 490 BCE

How Not to Stir the Flame

It's remarkable that we know so little about the life of a philosopher who exerted as much influence on the ancient world as Pythagoras did, but so it is. All of his biography that we can be moderately sure of is that he was born on the Greek isle of Samos, perhaps traveled as far as Egypt in search of learning, and starved himself to death following the persecution of his followers in the Italian colony of Croton.

Fortunately, we know a bit more about his teachings, despite the fact that his followers were sworn to secrecy. In addition to his mathematical genius—he was the discoverer, as every schoolchild knows, of the theorem named in his honor—Pythagoras founded a wisdom school that taught, among other things, nonviolence. There seem to have been at least three principles on which he based this teaching.

To begin with, Pythagoras believed in the essential kinship of all living things, based primarily on his conviction that souls reincarnate after bodily death. No animal is dumb or soulless, and so he forbade his followers to kill them or to profit from their killing. Instead, he urged his students to follow a vegetarian diet. Second, Pythagorean nonviolence was also based on the conviction that coercion and force of arms are impractical ways of resolving conflict. Although they might appear to work in the short run, they inevitably fuel resentment that bursts into flame later. One of the sayings attributed to Pythagoras actually uses the metaphor of flame to make the point. "Don't stir the fire with a knife," he told his students. Doing so only causes the flame to burn even fiercer, and it also makes the knife too hot to handle.

The third principle that grounded Pythagoras's espousal of nonviolence was his conviction that a life of virtue was the end toward which humans properly strive, and that virtue in turn is cultivated by a lifestyle of simplicity, inner harmony, and just treatment of others. In the school he established, all possessions were held in common to guard against greed and envy, and students were trained to cultivate inner tranquility so as not to "waste their life in troubles and pains" by being "too much attracted by the pleasures of this life." They were also encouraged not to "step over the beam of a balance" and not to "overstep the bounds of equity and justice." This wasn't an unimaginative recommendation for them to slavishly follow the laws of the land, which after all might be unjust or tyrannical. Instead, Pythagoras seems to have had two other things in mind: first, to strive for a balance between inner tranquility and outward behavior, a right ordering of intent and deed that many ancient philosophers saw as a form of justice; second, to respect the dignity, well-being, and fair treatment of others.

At the end of the day, Pythagoras's advice to his students was summed up by this: "Let no man by word or deed persuade you to do or to say that which is not best for you." And what's best is a life of nonviolence.

6 April
Daniel Ellsberg

7 April 1931—

The Man Who Ended a War

THE *NEW YORK TIMES* headline for 13 June 1971, "Vietnam Archive: Pentagon Study Traces 3 Decades of Growing U.S. Involvement," was surprisingly tame for the story attached to it. It should have read: "The Beginning of the End of the Vietnam War." And the man responsible for the story was Daniel Ellsberg.

The "Pentagon study" to which the *New York Times* referred was a four-thousand-word history of U.S. involvement in Vietnam dating all the way back to the mid-1940s when most of Indochina was still a French colony. The study was commissioned by Secretary of Defense Robert McNamara, who left office before its completion in 1969.

The Pentagon Papers, as the study was called after it was made public, revealed that the U.S. government and military had consistently lied to the American people about the reasons for the war and the extent of U.S. involvement in Vietnam. Although the war was billed as a humanitarian struggle to protect the Vietnamese people from communist aggression, the Pentagon Papers offered evidence that American involvement was almost exclusively self-serving and that covert military action, including raids into Laos and Cambodia, was the order of the day. The study also opined, contrary to official White House and Pentagon statements, that the war was unwinnable.

Daniel Ellsberg, the man who leaked the Pentagon Papers to the *New York Times*, had been an ardent Cold Warrior for most of his adult life. Harvard educated (he earned a PhD in economics in 1962), ex-Marine officer, analyst for the RAND think tank, and advisor to the Defense and State Departments, Ellsberg also spent two years in Vietnam as part of a "pacification" effort to "win the hearts and minds" of Vietnamese peasants.

When the Pentagon study was completed, a copy of it was sent to the RAND Corporation. Ellsberg, already disillusioned with the war, read it, realized that the government was systematically deceiving the American public, and began secretly photocopying the report. As he later said, "I was part, on a middle level, of what is best described as a conspiracy by the government to get us *into* war." He decided that it was his moral duty to help get us *out*.

Ellsberg initially tried to convince U.S. congressmen to enter the Pentagon Papers into the congressional record, thus making them publicly accessible, but he got no takers. So he began leaking them to the *New York Times*, fully aware that doing so could put him in jail for the rest of his life. The Nixon Administration unsuccessfully tried to block their publication. The legal case against Ellsberg, an indictment on twelve separate felony counts for a total of 115 years behind bars, was dismissed because of misconduct on the government's part. And public outrage at the revelations of the Pentagon Papers guaranteed that the war would soon be over.

No small achievement for an ex-Cold Warrior.

7 April
André Trocmé

7 April 1901—5 June 1971

Knowing Only Human Beings

SEEMINGLY UNSTOPPABLE IN 1940, Hitler's armies rolled over France, conquering the nation and installing a puppet regime, the Vichy government, in just five short weeks. French Jews, as well as Jewish refugees who earlier had fled from Germany to France, were now at great risk, as were any Gentiles who sheltered them.

André Trocmé, Protestant pastor of Le Chambon-sur-Lignon in the mountainous country of south central France, urged his flock—which was nearly everyone in the village—to refuse to "give up their consciences" by participating in "hatred, betrayal, and murder." Instead, he encouraged them to offer shelter to fleeing Jews. Beginning in 1942, Le Chambon-sur-Lignon began doing just that. Between then and the end of the war, upwards of five thousand Jews were offered sanctuary in the village and surrounding forests. Villagers under Trocmé's leadership fed, housed, and sometimes nursed refugees, supplied them with fake papers, and smuggled them across the border into nearby Switzerland. The rescue operation was assisted by funds from American Quakers and the International Fellowship of Reconciliation.

The villagers' nonviolent resistance to Nazi oppression and Vichy collaboration was grounded on two abiding principles stressed by Trocmé in sermon after sermon. The first was that the first loyalty of Christians should be to God and the good news preached by Jesus Christ, even if it meant disobeying the laws of the land. Their duty, Trocmé told the villagers, was to "obey God rather than man when there is a conflict between the commandments of the government and the commandments of the bible." The second principle was that resisting evil by responding in kind is in effect collaboration with the enemy, because it contributes to the hatred and will-to-destroy that animates the enemy. But resisting violence with nonviolence breaks the cycle, thereby refusing the enemy the parasitic nourishment gleaned from the cycle's perpetuation.

Vichy officials were perfectly aware of what was going on in Le Chambon-sur-Lignon, but the villagers were so ingenious at eluding authorities that there was only one successful raid during the three years in which Jews were given sanctuary. Tragically, however, this raid captured mostly children whose parents had sent them to the village in the hope of eventually getting them to Switzerland. Trocmé himself was arrested in 1943. He refused to deny that he was sheltering Jews, but also refused to quit doing so. "These people came here for help and for shelter," he told the Vichy authorities. "I am their shepherd. A shepherd does not forsake his flock. I do not know what a Jew is. I know only human beings." He was released after only four weeks. Apparently, his captors didn't quite know what to do with him—a not unusual response to wielders of the unconventional "weapon" of nonviolent resistance.

8 April
Ivan Supek

8 April 1915—5 March 2007

Anti-Nuclear Humanist

THE IDEAL OF A world unified by humanistic values was bread and butter to the Croatian-born physicist-turned-philosopher Ivan Supek. In dozens of books on physics and philosophy as well as novels, plays, and memoirs, Supek urged readers to look beyond their differences to honor a common core of values centered on the mandate to preserve life and celebrate truth.

A major part of Supek's message was his call for total nuclear disarmament. As early as the summer of 1944, in the midst of World War II, he issued a warning about the misuse of atomic energy and called for moral responsibility on the part of the scientific community. His was probably the first public expression of concern about what at the time was still only a theoretical possibility of converting nuclear energy into weaponry. After the atomic blasts over Hiroshima and Nagasaki, Supek became even more convinced of the immorality of nuclear bombs. In 1960 he founded the Institute for the Philosophy of Science and Peace, an international center for the advocacy of nuclear disarmament. Fifteen years later, in collaboration with noted peacemakers such as **Linus Pauling**, Supek founded the International League of Humanists for Peace and Tolerance. He served as its president until his death.

The International League adopted as its own Supek's humanistic worldview. After leaving physics in the 1950s for philosophy and literature, Supek devoted himself to the advocacy of a humanism that called for an end to nationalism, a global sharing of scientific knowledge and technology, and an unqualified respect for human rights and freedoms. Political tyranny's drive toward ideological and cultural homogeneity, he believed, was ill-equipped to handle the world's diversity. Transnationalistic humanism was a better alternative, and in recommending it Supek defended a set of ten principles of global unity: (1) the preservation of life; (2) the affirmation of human equality; (3) the affirmation of human freedom; (4) transnational solidarity; (5) an ardent search for truth; (6) welfare for the disadvantaged; (7) the celebration of artistic beauty; (8) the humanization of law; (9) the practice of global nonviolence, including the elimination of weapons of mass destruction; and (10) good behavior on the part of individuals.

Supek's passionate defense of humanism as the key to a nonviolent world was founded on his conviction that people by and large are products of their environments. He believed that social conditions can turn citizens into either jingoistic brutes intolerant of others or civilized citizens of the world who celebrate their own cultures without condemning others. His ten humanistic principles are aimed at creating social environments that encourage the emergence of the latter while minimizing the possibility of the former.

9 April
Dietrich Bonhoeffer

4 February 1906—9 April 1945

A Spoke in the Wheel

Are there limits to pacifism? Are there situations in which the morally right thing to do is to embrace, howsoever reluctantly, violence? These are questions that keep peacemakers awake at night, especially ones whose pacifism is faith-centered. It is a perpetual worry.

The German theologian and pastor Dietrich Bonhoeffer knew this. In his mid-twenties, as he witnessed the rise of the Nazis, he grew convinced that a Christian's duty was to resist their hateful worldview by living as an ambassador of Christ. This not only meant serving the poor, the lonely, the oppressed, and the forgotten, but also required a courageous commitment to nonviolence. As Bonhoeffer said shortly before the Nazis came to power in 1933, "Every form of war service, unless it be Good Samaritan service, and every preparation for war, is forbidden to the Christian."

After Hitler became chancellor, most German Protestant clergy lined up to offer him their allegiance. Bonhoeffer was dismayed and angered by what he saw as their betrayal of Christ, and he rebuked them by pointing out that, at the least, the Church has a responsibility to challenge an unjust state's illegitimacy and to offer its victims aid. And even that wasn't enough. The core of the Church's duty, he said, was "not just to bandage the victims under the wheel, but to put a spoke in the wheel itself."

But as Hitler's killing machine continued to consume victims, Bonhoeffer began to suspect that the only effective spoke in the Nazi wheel would be the assassination of Hitler, and that a Christian's refusal to consider removing Hitler by force might be a grave injustice to those suffering from his bloodthirsty madness. Backing away from such a possibility, Bonhoeffer wrote, would be for a person to set "his own personal innocence above his responsibility for men . . . blind to the more irredeemable guilt which he incurs precisely in this." Sometimes, in situations where the beast is unleashed upon a helpless and tortured world, a "deed of free responsibility" that "leaves behind it the domain of principle and convention" might be called for.

Bonhoeffer agonized over his dilemma, and ultimately he decided that he had no choice but to participate, however marginally, in what he believed to be a sin: the plot to assassinate Hitler. He decided that the right thing would be to do the wrong thing. He made no excuses, either to himself or others. He recognized that in acquiescing to violence he was betraying the Prince of Peace, and he accepted the spiritual possibility of eternal damnation. He also accepted the temporal one of discovery and execution by the Nazis, which in fact happened.

Some see Bonhoeffer's decision as an irresponsible betrayal of the principle of nonviolence, and others as a tortured attempt to do the right thing. Regardless of which interpretation is correct, the example of Bonhoeffer's personal wrestling with the question of how best to be a spoke in the wheel is well worth keeping in mind. It's one that ought to haunt peacemakers.

10 April
Jessie Wallace Hughan

25 December 1875—10 April 1955

Coveting Peace

Brooklyn-born Jessie Wallace Hughan was considered an oddball by most of her fellow citizens. On the one hand, she was a committed socialist in a day and age when mainstream America feared and deplored anything associated with bolshevism. On the other hand, she was a deeply religious woman whose faith was distrusted and disliked by the secular-leaning majority of the country's socialists. But her courageous advocacy of nonviolent resistance to war and economic injustice earned her the respect, even if it was sometimes grudgingly given, of most of her fellow socialists—enough so, in fact, that they nominated her for political office in New York numerous times, including a 1920 run for the U.S. Senate.

Hughan's socialism was based on a solid understanding of economics. She earned a doctorate in the discipline from Columbia University in 1910. But it was difficult at the time for a woman to land a position at a college or university, and Hughan wound up teaching at a number of public high schools in New York and Connecticut throughout her entire career. Always under suspicion because of her socialism, she came dangerously close to dismissal on more than one occasion.

Like many of her fellow socialists, Hughan condemned World War I as a conflict fueled by capitalist-driven nationalism. Fearing that the United States would eventually get involved, she cofounded the Anti-Enlistment League, which encouraged young men to refrain from joining the military as a matter of conscience. By the time the United States entered the war in 1917, more than thirty-five hundred men had signed the League's pledge. In that same year, government agents seized the League's files and considered prosecuting Hughan for sedition.

In 1915, Hughan became a charter member of the Fellowship of Reconciliation, the faith-based international pacifist association. In 1922 she was a member of the Committee for Enrollment Against War, a revitalized version of the 1915 League, and the next year she cofounded the War Resisters League, remaining its secretary until ten years before her death. When a new war erupted in Europe, she cofounded the Pacifist Teachers League. On the United States' entry into the conflict following the attack on Pearl Harbor, Hughan became a tireless advocate for conscientious objectors.

Her experience of both world wars convinced her that nations perversely prided themselves on their capacity for war-making and that governments believed it their moral responsibility to go to war to protect their citizens. But Hughan saw the waging of war as an occasion for shame and an obstacle to prosperity. "War," she wrote, "rather than any foreign state, is the supreme enemy of country and mankind. One day citizens will covet for this nation the prestige of being the first to escape the shackles of war."

11 April
Kurt Vonnegut

11 November 1922—11 April 2007

War as Blasphemy

It seems strange that a convinced secularist like author Kurt Vonnegut would seriously invoke religious language. Yet he willingly called war a blasphemy, not in the sense that it was an affront to God's name but in that it offended against the name of everything decent and worthwhile in life. Vonnegut's aversion to warfare appeared again and again in his novels, short stories, and essays. It was one of the most recurrent themes throughout his writings.

Vonnegut came by his aversion the hard way, while serving as a soldier in World War II. In the closing months of the war he was captured by the Germans, packed into a boxcar with other POWs, and shipped off to a detention camp in Dresden. The city was bombed by the Allies in mid-February 1945, using a potent new kind of incendiary bomb that whipped up a firestorm so fierce that the city was destroyed in a single day. More people perished in the inferno than would die in Hiroshima later that year. Vonnegut and other prisoners who somehow managed to survive were ordered to drag burnt bodies out of the rubble. Given the doom that had fallen on Dresden, they were lucky that the surviving Germans didn't kill them on the spot out of sheer fury.

The utter horror that befell Dresden haunted Vonnegut for the rest of his life. He could never quite exorcise its memory. His most obvious attempt to do so was the novel *Slaughterhouse-Five*, but traces of the Dresden nightmare also appear in *Mother Night*, *God Bless You, Mr. Rosewater*, and even *Cat's Cradle*. It was toward the end of his life, still struggling with the memory, that Vonnegut declared the burning of Dresden and war in general a blasphemy. "There can be no doubt that the Allies fought on the side of right and the Germans and Japanese on the side of wrong," he wrote. "World War II was fought for near-Holy motives. But I stand convinced that the brand of justice in which we dealt, wholesale bombing of civilian populations, was blasphemous. That the enemy did it first has nothing to do with the moral problem. What I saw of our air war, as the European conflict neared an end, had the earmarks of being an irrational war for war's sake."

As a satirist, Vonnegut excelled in revealing the absurdity and sometimes harmfulness of sacred cows. The one he most delighted in deflating was the myth that war encouraged heroism and nobility. Wars, he countered, are "children's crusades" for the most part, fought by terrified young men who aren't trying to be heroic but only want desperately to stay alive and will do almost anything to make sure they do. And as for the nobility of war, Vonnegut had this to say: "Perhaps, when we remember wars, we should take off our clothes and paint ourselves blue and go on all fours all day long and grunt like pigs. That would surely be more appropriate than noble oratory and shows of flags and well-oiled guns."

12 April

Frederick Franck

12 April 1909—5 June 2006

Seeing the Original Face

FIVE YEARS BEFORE HIS death, Franck noted that he early on developed "a severe allergy against all physical violence." Born and raised in a Dutch town just a few miles from the Belgium border, he remembered how his house was regularly shaken "by the booming of the German field guns" during World War I. In the years after the war, he endured the economic and political crises that devastated Europe after the armistice and paved the way for Hitler and Mussolini. By the time he fled the Old World for America in 1940, he'd had enough violence to last a lifetime.

Franck was trained as a dental surgeon in Belgium, Scotland, and the United States. But his real love was art. Settling in New York City, he practiced dentistry two days a week and spent the rest of his time in a studio he rented on Bleecker Street. In a short while, exhibitions of his paintings, drawings, and sculptures earned him critical praise. He also began writing; he authored more than thirty books throughout his life. His creativity remained undiminished for the rest of his life, with the exception of a two-year hiatus in the late 1950s when he worked at **Albert Schweitzer**'s hospital in Lambarene, Gabon.

The abiding theme in both his art and books was Franck's conviction that personal dissatisfaction and interpersonal violence were the results of spiritual blindness. The busyness of everyday life and the clamor of our desires distract us from exploring the quiet, still place within ourselves where peace is to be found and from which a nonviolent attitude toward others originates. Using a phrase from Zen Buddhism, Franck referred to that place as the Original Face and insisted that it's the "specifically human core that differentiates us from the Naked Ape." In 1973 he published his best-known book, *The Zen of Seeing*, a guide on how to become more alert to the external world as well as the Original Face. "The meaning of life," he wrote, "is to see."

In the late 1960s, Franck and his wife moved to Warwick, New York, where they created a transreligious garden sanctuary called Pacem in Terris (Peace on Earth). Filled with Franck's paintings and drawings, Pacem in Terris was intended as an embodiment of the tranquility that comes when we learn to see our Original Face. Franck described the place as "one man's work of art that aspires to be an oasis of quiet, of sanity, where spirit and nature may reconnect." At the entrance to Pacem in Terris is the sculpture of a human figure waving an olive branch, the symbol of peace.

13 April
Amy Goodman

13 April 1957—

Trickle-Up Journalist

IT WAS A HORRIBLE day. Independence advocates, most of them students, marched in the East Timorese capital of Dili to protest against Indonesian rule of their country. They eventually gathered in a cemetery where one of their leaders, murdered by Indonesian troops a week earlier, had just been buried. Without warning, onlooking soldiers suddenly began firing into the crowd. Before it was all over, some four hundred people were slaughtered.

We know as much as we do about the Dili Massacre of November 1991 because Amy Goodman, an American journalist, was there. She not only witnessed the brutality. She was also a victim of it, beaten in the heat of the moment by the rampaging troops; she was lucky to escape with her life. But as an investigative reporter who believes it her duty to report world events typically ignored by mainstream media, Goodman is used to being in hot spots. In 1998, for example, she covered the standoff between Nigerian Army troops and civilian protesters of Chevron's exploitation of African oil fields. Closer to home, she was arrested and manhandled at the 2008 Republican National Convention while reporting on an anti-war protest taking place outside the convention center.

Goodman, who since 1996 has hosted the alternative media news program *Democracy Now!* for Pacifica Radio, believes that journalism in the United States and abroad is too often straightjacketed by governmental pressure and corporate special interests. She's dedicated to a model of independent political journalism that, although committed to social justice, is scrupulously factual and carefully documented. Her approach focuses on reporting events and people typically ignored by the mainstream media. She's known as a "trickle-up journalist" because she reports at the grassroots level—"it's our responsibility to go to where the silence is"—and because many of the stories she breaks work themselves "up" to the level of the major network news programs.

Goodman's abiding conviction is that democracy works only if citizens are fully informed about events, and that public policy decisions that affect everyone ought to be made by everyone, not merely a handful of leaders in Washington. When it comes to war, for example, she insists that "everyone must participate in that decision! Everyone should be heard!" But effective participation presupposes access to pertinent information, and that's where Goodman's style of journalism comes into play. "I see the media as a huge kitchen table that stretches across the globe that we all sit around and debate and discuss these critical issues."

Goodman received a Right Livelihood Award in 2008 for "developing an innovative model of truly independent grassroots political journalism."

14 April
Arun Gandhi

14 April 1934—

Violence Has Two Children

When Arun Gandhi was twelve years old, he was sent from his native land of South Africa to live in India with his grandfather, **Mohandas Gandhi**. His grandfather was murdered two years later. But during their time together, the old man taught the young boy the principles of *satyagraha,* or the pursuit of truth, and *ahimsa,* or nonviolence. Arun would grow up to be a practitioner and advocate of both, eventually founding the M. K. Gandhi Institute for Nonviolence, now located in Rochester, New York.

One of the centerpieces of Arun Gandhi's analysis of nonviolence originated in something his grandfather told him: "Violence has two children, the physical and passive forms." Most of us readily recognize physical violence—fistfights, wars, torture, rape—but we tend to overlook passive violence. Part of the reason is that physical violence is often dramatically headline-capturing, but passive violence, as its very name suggests, is less obvious. But, more significantly, focusing on physical violence allows us to point the finger at others, whereas recognizing and naming passive violence implicates us as well.

Passive violence, as Arun Gandhi understands it, can range from a sullen passive-aggression intended to manipulate others to more direct "name-calling, teasing, insulting, and disrespectful behavior." It never rises to the level of physical abuse and thereby allows its perpetrators to deceive themselves into thinking that they have done nothing to harm the target of their passive violence: "What's the big deal? It was just a little teasing. I didn't hit anybody!" But what this "sticks and stones can break my bones but words will never hurt me" excuse ignores is the fact that passive violence often ignites physical violence. The relationship between the two, says Arun Gandhi, "is the same as the relationship between gasoline and fire. Acts of passive violence generate anger in the victim, and since the victim has not learned how to use anger positively, the victim abuses anger and generates physical violence. If we wish to put out the fire of physical violence we have to cut off the fuel supply."

This is where the importance of *satyagraha* emerges for anyone who wishes to be a peacemaker. In the pursuit of truth—the truth that sets us free, so to speak—we must be able to scrutinize our own motives and actions in addition to the behavior of others. How much violence do we carry within our own thought patterns and scripted ways of responding to others? Is the physical violence that we condemn in others actually a by-product of our own passive-aggression? Are we fueling conflicts with thoughtless teasing or disrespectful behavior—doing so, perhaps, even as we believe we're working to resolve conflicts? These are questions that must be perennially asked because, as Arun Gandhi reminds us, physical aggression, the younger child of violence, is always accompanied by her insidious elder sister.

15 April
Robert Purvis

4 August 1810—15 April 1898

President of the Underground Railroad

"In the matter of rights," Robert Purvis always insisted, "there is just one race, and that is the human race." He pushed this point home in hundreds of speeches, beginning in the early 1830s and continuing until his death. It was the central conviction of his long life.

Purvis was born in South Carolina to a British father who was a successful cotton broker and a mother who was a free woman of color. Searching for a social environment friendlier to mixed marriages than the South, the family relocated to Philadelphia when Purvis was still a child. He spent the rest of his life there.

After attending Amherst College, which expelled him for an unspecified prank, Purvis threw himself into the abolitionist movement. In 1833 he partnered with William Lloyd Garrison to form the American Anti-Slavery Society. The Society advocated pacifism, denounced slavery, condemned slave owners as "man stealers," and called for an immediate and uncompensated end to the practice.

Between 1845 and 1850, Purvis was president of the Pennsylvania Anti-Slavery Society. Shortly before the Civil War, he famously denounced the Supreme Court's Dred Scott decision, which ruled that African Americans, free or enslaved, had no constitutional rights. "It is a fair example of the cowardly and malignant spirit that pervades the entire policy of the country," thundered Purvis. "The end of the policy is, undoubtedly, to destroy the colored man, as a man." As a man of color himself, he declared, he owed no allegiance to a nation that embraced the belief that a black man had "no rights a white man was bound to respect."

But it is Purvis's involvement with the Underground Railroad, the surreptitious network of south-to-north escape routes used by thousands of slaves, which was his noblest achievement. Unlike many supporters of the railroad, Purvis made his own home a way station for African Americans fleeing slavery. He estimated that for thirty years, an average of one escaped slave daily ate or rested in his house. The Purvis home became so famous as a haven for runaway slaves that it was known as "Saints' Rest" where, as one observer noted, "the wicked ceased from troubling and the weary are at rest." Purvis himself was hailed as the "President of the Underground Railroad."

After the Civil War and the end of slavery, Purvis continued his struggle for human rights, speaking out on behalf of women's suffrage, prison reform, justice for Native Americans, and—doubtlessly with his British roots in mind—Irish home rule. At the time of his death, he was the last surviving member of the American Anti-Slavery Society.

16 April

Iqbal Masih

1982—16 April 1995

Child Labor Activist

IT WAS A MOMENT that stunned viewers. In late 1994, a twelve-year-old-boy whose stunted body size and weight made him look half his age appeared on *ABC World News* to describe his years as a virtual slave in Pakistan. At the age of four, Iqbal Masih had been offered to a carpet manufacturer as collateral for a loan of about $16. For the next six years, twelve to fourteen hours a day, six days a week, the boy worked at a loom in a carpet factory. As "bonded laborers" working to pay off family debts, Iqbal and the other children in the factory were forbidden to leave and punished severely if they tried. "They threaten us not to even think of leaving," he said in the ABC interview. "They tell us, 'We'll burn your fingers in oil if you even try to leave. We'll put you in oil.'"

Iqbal ran away from the factory twice. The first time he headed straight for a police station, thinking he would be offered protection, and was promptly returned to his owner. As punishment, he was hung upside down by his heels and then chained for a time to his loom. He was luckier on his second try. After wandering the countryside for a few days, Iqbal eventually met a representative of the Bonded Labor Liberation Front (BLLF), an activist organization seeking to end the enslavement endured by over twenty million adults and nearly eight million children in Pakistan. Risking life and limb, Iqbal led the BLLF to the factory where he'd worked. When photos of malnourished children chained to looms were released, public outcry forced the police to close the place down.

Iqbal became an internationally known spokesperson for the BLLF, participating in dozens of raids on sweatshops and liberating over three thousand Pakistani child laborers. In the last year of his life, he toured Europe and the United States, drawing world attention to forced child labor and urging an international boycott on Pakistani carpets.

Although illiterate when he escaped from the factory, Iqbal was a bright child, mastering five years of schooling in less than three. His dream was to become a lawyer to continue his struggle against bonded labor. But Iqbal's courageous opposition to what has been called Pakistan's "carpet mafia" made him a target. On Easter Sunday, 16 April 1995, Iqbal was killed by a shotgun blast while riding a bicycle.

Iqbal Masih's life was short but powerful. His work inspired the creation of the international organization Free the Children, the goals of which are to "free children from poverty and exploitation and free young people from the notion that they are powerless to affect positive change in the world."

17 April
Albert Einstein

14 March 1879—18 April 1955

The Only Sensible Goal

ONE OF THE ICONIC images of our age is the bushy white mane, wrinkled face, and tired smile of Albert Einstein. He's one of the best known but least understood of all humans. Although "it's relative" has become a catchphrase in our everyday language, and although everyone knows that Einstein came up with something called the special theory of relativity, very few know much more about it than that it has something to do with the famous (and mysterious) formula $E = mc^2$.

What's not as well known, but much more comprehendible, is Einstein's lifelong aversion to the violence of war. In his thirties he witnessed the destructiveness of World War I and the ensuing collapse of Europe. When the Nazis came to power, he was condemned as a "Jewish intellectual," his books were publicly burned, and a bounty of $5000 was put on his head. Although he urged President Roosevelt to authorize nuclear research out of fear that Hitler's scientists would win the race to develop an atomic bomb, he joined other scientists after the war in arguing for disarmament. Toward the end of his life, he said that advocating for the development of the atom bomb was the "great mistake" of his life, but that circumstances had given him no choice.

To Einstein's way of thinking, any war—even one to stop Hitler—was a "disease" in two senses: it represented a weakening of the social immune system's ability to resolve conflict nonviolently, and it damaged and destroyed life. Nation-states pile up weapons in the false hope that they will serve as inoculations against the disease of war. But the sense of security they offer is "imaginary," especially in an age when nuclear as well as conventional weapons possess incredible killing power.

A surer protection against war than the stockpiling of weapons by each nation was, in Einstein's judgment, the establishment of an international governing body. "A nation can be considered peace loving only if it is ready to cede its military force to the international authorities and to renounce every attempt to achieve its interests abroad by the use of force. Peace can never be secured by threats, but only by an honest attempt to create mutual trust. One sided armament on a national basis only heightens the general uncertainty and confusion without being an effective protection." Although he wrote these words in 1948, he had endorsed the notion of a world government for at least two decades. After its formation in 1945, Einstein was a public and frequent champion of the United Nations.

Einstein recognized that a peace-keeping world government could come about in more than one way. One dark possibility was the enforcement of a false peace among subjugated nations by a militarized superpower. Einstein hoped that human reason would create the alternative possibility of a voluntary compact between the nations of the world to abide by international "law and order." It was, he said, the "only sensible goal."

18 April
Margaret Hassan

18 April 1945 — 8 November 2004

A Slender Woman with a Spine of Steel

THE VIDEO DELIVERED TO the Al-Jazeera television network was chilling and heartbreaking. Irish-born Margaret Hassan, kidnapped in Baghdad by Islamic terrorists, pled before the camera for the withdrawal of British military forces from Iraq. Towards the end of the recording she broke down in sobs. If the demands of her kidnappers weren't met, she said, she would be killed.

The British authorities refused to negotiate with the kidnappers. Several days later another videotape was delivered to Al-Jazeera, this one showing the cold-blooded murder of Hassan.

That someone like Margaret Hassan should be abducted, mistreated, and finally killed by Iraqis was a tragic irony. Although not a native of the country, she had lived in Iraq for most of her adult life. At twenty-seven she married an Iraqi engineering student studying in England and moved with him to Iraq. She learned Arabic, became an Iraqi citizen, and, like most other citizens of her adopted country, endured the brutal regime of Saddam Hussein.

Following the 1991 defeat of Hussein's army in the Persian Gulf War, Hassan joined the Baghdad branch of CARE, an international relief organization. The effects of the economic embargo imposed against Iraq by the United Nations, while doing little to damage Saddam's hold on power, were depriving citizens of basic foodstuffs and medicines. Moreover, depleted uranium weapons used by the U.S. military during the war had resulted in a high percentage of leukemia in children who lived in the affected zones. Hassan threw herself into the task of finding ways to get food and medical aid to those Iraqis most in need of them. She also became one of the most outspoken critics of the economic sanctions. Regardless of what she may have thought of Saddam and his thugs, she saw no reason why innocent Iraqis should suffer. Sanctions, she said, "are inhuman."

Hassan publicly condemned the 2003 U.S. invasion of Iraq, foreseeing that it would impose additional suffering on the Iraqi people. One year later, CARE appointed her head of its operations in Iraq. Most likely, this high-profile appointment is what brought her to the attention of her kidnappers. Instead of seeing a woman who had worked for the well-being of the Iraqi people for nearly fifteen years, they viewed her as a white European Christian who was both outsider and infidel.

When she was appointed head of Iraqi CARE, an acquaintance described the physically diminutive Hassan as "one of those slender people with a spine of steel." Her resolve, courage, and love of the Iraqi people were ill-rewarded by her abductors. But she went to her death knowing that she had made life better for thousands of Iraqis.

19 April

Meng Tzu

CA. 372—CA. 289 BCE

How to Rule Benevolently

The Confucian philosopher Meng Tzu, or Mencius, as he's better known in the West, was an itinerant political advisor who traveled from king to king in ancient China offering counsel. It was dangerous but badly needed work, because Meng lived during the two-hundred-year Warring States Period, a turbulent time when warlords fought almost constantly among themselves. Meng's advice to them wasn't what they wanted or expected to hear. Instead of praising them for their martial strength or tipping them off to innovative battle tactics or new war machines, he consistently admonished them to rule with benevolence and to cease their warfare.

Meng was raised by his widowed mother, who encouraged his scholarly bent. According to legend, she relocated to three separate dwellings during his childhood until she found just the right environment for her son. Their first house was next to a cemetery, and the second next to the town's marketplace. She feared that if they stayed in the first house, her son would want to become a professional mourner; if in the second, a merchant. So she located their third and final home next to a school so that her son would want to become a scholar.

The advice offered by Meng to King Hui of Liang was typical of his approach. The king, a powerful warlord, assumed that Meng had come to his court to tell him how to strengthen and enrich his kingdom. Meng astounded Hui by instead warning him that kings obsessed with power and riches made bad rulers because their ambitions always harmed their people. They force healthy and hardworking peasants into the army and off the land, delaying the ploughing and ruining the harvest. If that's not bad enough, the constant warring of bad rulers cripples their kingdoms. It indiscriminately kills without even trying to look ahead and prepare for the future. It's as if, Meng said, a fisherman used such a finely woven net that he trapped both large fish and tiny young ones, thus nipping future generations in the bud. Or it's as if a woodsman randomly and thoughtlessly cut down saplings along with dead underbrush.

Moreover, Meng told Hui, it's no good blaming hunger and unrest in the land on drought or bad growing seasons or peasant stupidity. The buck stops with the ruler, especially one who squanders resources and people to make war. "To argue that people died not because of mismanagement but because of natural disaster and bad weather conditions," said Meng, "is like distorting the fact that it is not the person who did the killing but the dagger in his hand."

Meng Tzu's counsel to the warlords may seem naïve and foolishly risky. After all, why would men accustomed to strong-arming their way through life embrace benevolence? But Meng believed that all humans are innately good and that a good word at the right time has the power to reawaken those who have lost their way. Even bad rulers can be reformed.

20 April

Lady Godiva

11TH CENTURY

Becoming Vulnerable for the Sake of the Poor

MOST EVERYBODY HAS HEARD of Lady Godiva. She shows up as a brand name, as a character in comedy sketches, and as a figure in paintings, sculptures, and novels. Occasionally, salacious versions of her even find their way into the porn industry. This last venue points to something else everybody knows about Godiva: she rode publicly, nude as the day she was born, on the back of a horse.

What often gets forgotten, however, is *why* Godiva made her famous horseback ride. According to the story, her husband Leofric had saddled the people of Coventry, a town in his domains, with a crushing burden of taxes. The townspeople, already poor, implored him to reconsider, but Leofric heartlessly refused. Godiva was touched by their misery and soon joined her voice to theirs. Finally, worn down by his wife's unending pleas—Leofric, after all, couldn't dismiss Godiva as easily as he could the townspeople—he promised to lift the taxes if she would ride up and down Coventry streets at high noon in the nude. It's clear that Leofric hoped this would put an end to the nagging, because it was unimaginable that a nobly born woman would humiliate herself in this way. But Godiva called his bluff. Clad in only her long tresses, she did exactly what her husband demanded. A chastened Leofric lifted the taxes, and Godiva's ride entered into legend.

Sticklers today might claim that there's no evidence to suggest that the Lady Godiva story is based on historical fact. We know that Godiva, or Godfigu ("God gift"), was an actual Anglo-Saxon noblewoman, that she was married to Leofric, Earl of Mercer, and that she died sometime in the two decades following the 1066 Norman invasion. The story of her famous ride wasn't written until a century after her death, however, thereby casting doubt upon its historical reliability.

But who cares? The truth of the story doesn't rely on its facticity but rather on its message. Godiva is a person of means willing to dispossess herself of everything for the sake of those who have little or nothing. To strip naked in public betokens a willingness to make oneself utterly vulnerable, totally without protection. In Godiva's case, this radical renunciation was done for the sake of lifting an unjust burden from people who were already barely scraping by. It was an act of voluntary humiliation undertaken out of a sense of justice, and is a perfect example of nonviolent conflict resolution. In making her ride, Godiva not only won the hearts of the people but also touched the conscience of her husband.

The details of her ride may be but dimly remembered today. But the very fact that the Lady Godiva legend has endured for so long suggests that the core truth embedded in it appeals to something in the human breast. All of us sense the virtue—the moral beauty—of sacrificing for the sake of others, as Godiva did for her people. At the deepest level, that's why we remember her.

21 April
Helen Prejean

21 April 1939—

Death Penalty Opponent

In the United States, more than three thousand prisoners, pretty evenly divided between whites and blacks, languish on death row. Locked in single cells for twenty-three out of twenty-four hours, utterly removed from the world, death row inmates are more marginalized than any other group of people in the country. And for most of the population on the other side of the prison walls, that's just fine. Nearly three-fourths of Americans believe that some crimes deserve death.

Sister Helen Prejean, a St. Josephite nun, isn't one of them. For three decades she's advocated for death row inmates. She doesn't for a moment whitewash their crimes if she believes they're guilty. Nor does she neglect the families of their victims. But she insists that capital punishment, even for heinous crimes, is wrong; violence doesn't wash away violence.

The moment of truth came for Prejean when she was forty years old. In 1981 she began a correspondence with a death row inmate at Angola, Louisiana's state prison, named Elmo Patrick Sonnier. Convicted of rape and murder, Sonnier was a hard case who came from a troubled family background. Soon Prejean was visiting him on a regular basis, and during the next three years, before he was executed by electrocution, she served as his spiritual director. Sonnier, in turn, helped Prejean realize that each death row prisoner is a unique person with a story worth hearing.

Sonnier was the first of many death row inmates Prejean has since ministered to and advised. In 1993, she published a memoir of her experiences on death row titled *Dead Man Walking*. Three years later the book was made into a feature film. Since then, Prejean has spoken around the world about capital punishment and led several campaigns for its abolition in the United States.

Prejean opposes the death penalty for two reasons. The first is that she sees it as a violation of basic human rights. "There are some human rights that are so deep that we can't negotiate them away. I mean people do heinous, terrible things. But there are basic human rights I believe that every human being has. The Universal Declaration of Human Rights in the United Nations says it for me. And it says there are two basic rights that can't be negotiated, that government doesn't give for good behavior and doesn't take away for bad behavior. And it's the right not to be tortured and not to be killed."

The second reason is her deep commitment to her Christian faith. She believes that no one, regardless of how socially marginalized or guilty of wickedness he or she may be, deserves to be separated from the People of God. "To me," she says, "to find God is to find the whole human family. No one can be disconnected from us. Which is another way of talking about the Body of Christ, that we are all part of this together." Sister Helen's calling is to remind death row prisoners, the families of victims, and the rest of us of this truth.

22 April
Käthe Kollwitz

8 July 1867—22 April 1945

Portrait of the Artist as Grieving Mother

ONE OF THE MOST powerful pieces of anti-war art to come out of World War I is Käthe Kollwitz's sculpture *The Grieving Parents*. Kollwitz's youngest son, Peter, was killed in the opening months of the war, sending Kollwitz into a spiral of grief from which she never completely recovered. For years her loss inspired dozens of drawings depicting mothers, maddened with sorrow, clutching their dead children. Her own mourning culminated in 1932 with the creation of *The Grieving Parents*, which portrays her husband and her hunched over in despair at the loss of their son.

Born in Königsberg, East Prussia, Kollwitz was raised in a religiously strict household—"A loving God," she later wrote, "was never brought home to us"—and studied art in Berlin and Munich. At twenty-four, she married Dr. Karl Kollwitz, a physician who treated the poor of Berlin, and she lived with him in one of the city's most impoverished areas. Her daily exposure to poverty, hunger, misery, and death provided some of the most common themes in her art. Her experiences with the city's down-and-out convinced her that the violence of social injustice was akin to the violence of warfare, and she became an outspoken socialist and pacifist.

When the Nazis took over in 1933, Kollwitz's political beliefs immediately targeted her as an artist whose work was unfriendly to the regime. She was forced to resign from the Prussian Academy of Arts, her paintings and sculptures were removed from exhibits and museums, and she and her husband were threatened by the Gestapo with the possibility of imprisonment in a concentration camp. Karl died in 1940, and one of Käthe's grandsons, also named Peter, perished in battle in 1942. A year later, her Berlin home fell victim to Allied bombs, and Kollwitz—alone, depressed, and in poor health—was evacuated to Dresden. "War follows me to the end," she wrote shortly before her death.

Kollwitz's last thirty years were lived during a period of turmoil and destruction: the two world wars, separated by a devastating economic depression and a horrifying escalation of political violence. Through it all, she pled for an end to the fighting that robbed her and tens of thousands of other mothers of their sons and their hope. "Every war already carries within it the war which will answer it," she warned. "Every war is answered by a new war, until everything, everything, is smashed. There has been enough of dying! Let not another man fall!" But her art was more powerful than her words in denouncing warfare. As one critic put it, "Her silent lines penetrate the marrow like a cry of pain."

23 April
Adin Ballou

23 April 1803—5 August 1890

Rejecting Carnal Weapons

AN EXTRAORDINARY GATHERING OF clergy and laypeople took place in 1839 in Massachusetts. The purpose of the meeting was to craft a statement that proclaimed the signatories' fidelity to what one of them, Adin Ballou, called "that original peculiar kind of non-resistance which was enjoined and exemplified by Jesus Christ." The document that was crafted, titled "Standard of Practical Christianity," urged Christians to withdraw their support from any of the "governments of the world" that dishonored Christ by using force to maintain order. As for themselves, they said, "we cannot employ carnal weapons nor any physical force whatsoever, not even for the preservation of our lives. We cannot do otherwise than love our enemies."

The driving force behind this bold proclamation of fidelity to nonviolence was the same Adin Ballou who advocated Jesus' peculiar kind of nonresistance. Ballou was a New England Baptist preacher who converted to Universalism, the belief in universal salvation, and was promptly disinherited by his father and excommunicated by the Baptist community. One of the reasons for Ballou's conversion was his refusal to believe that a loving God would commit the violence of damning souls to an eternity of pain for finite sinful acts. God is love, Ballou believed, and love is compassionate and forgiving.

Ballou also believed that Christians should imitate God's indiscriminate love by adopting a lifestyle of nonresistance modeled on the life and teachings of Jesus Christ. To his mind, nonresistance was anything but passive acquiescence to evil. It renounced physical force but embraced moral resistance and, if the occasion called for it, "non-injurious, benevolent physical resistance"—for example, restraining a violent madman bent on hurting a third party. Ballou summarized his reasons for rejecting "carnal weapons" in his 1846 book *Christian Non-Resistance,* one of the classics of American religious pacifism.

In 1842, Ballou and a few like-minded individuals decided to put the withdrawal advocated by the "Standard of Practical Christianity" into practice. They purchased some land in central Massachusetts and founded the Hopedale community, a utopian experiment in collective living inspired by the early Christian communities described in the Acts of the Apostles. Hopedale, whose principles Ballou explored in his book *Practical Christian Socialism,* continued until 1856.

Long an opponent of slavery, Ballou became a public advocate of abolitionism in the 1840s. Unlike many abolitionists who supported the Civil War, including even the onetime pacifist William Lloyd Garrison, Ballou remained an advocate of nonresistance, arguing that moral suasion and economic compensation to slave owners were viable alternatives to armed conflict. His loyalty to Christian nonresistance was admired by **Leo Tolstoy** and inspired such twentieth-century pacifists as **Martin Luther King Jr**.

24 April

Margaret Fell

1614—23 April 1702

Mother of Quakerism

Until she reached her late thirties, Margaret Fell's life was as conventionally respectable as anyone could wish. She was married to a well-born and well-bred member of the Lancashire gentry, Thomas Fell, a barrister who served as Justice of the Peace and a member of Parliament. Their home, Swarthmore Hall, was a place of beauty and refinement.

Then, in the summer of 1652, George Fox, founder of the Religious Society of Friends, visited the home of Thomas and Margaret, and nothing would ever be the same. Fox's preaching, Margaret later said, "opened us a book that we had never read in, nor indeed had never heard that it was our duty to read in it, (to wit) the Light of Christ in our consciences, our minds never being turned towards it before." Almost overnight, Margaret embraced the Quaker principles of silent worship, the Inward Light, and radical nonviolence. It wasn't long before Swarthmore Hall became a hub of Quaker activity, with Margaret at its center.

In its early years, the Society of Friends was feared and distrusted by the Church of England, and its members were regularly persecuted, fined, and imprisoned. In 1660, Margaret took advantage of her position as a member of the gentry to petition King Charles II on behalf of the Friends for the right of freedom of conscience. "We do not desire any liberty that may justly offend anyone's conscience," she insisted, "but the liberty we do desire is that we may keep our consciences clear and void of offense towards God and towards men, and that we may enjoy our civil rights and liberties." Two years later, Margaret submitted a similar petition, assuring the king that he had nothing to fear from the Quakers. "We are a people that follow after those things that make for peace, love, and unity."

Be that as it may, the civil authorities arrested Margaret in 1664. Charging her with sedition, they held her in jail for six months before sentencing her to life imprisonment and a forfeiture of her property. While behind bars she wrote numerous pamphlets, including a defense of women preachers titled "Women's Speaking Justified." She was pardoned in 1668 by the king, and a year later, now widowed, she married George Fox. But she also resumed her preaching, which eventually landed her in prison for another full year.

Thanks in part to Margaret's courageous defense of religious freedom, most of the legal strictures against Quakerism were lifted in the final decade of her life. By the time she died, she was known in the Society of Friends as the Mother of Quakerism.

25 April
Ernesto Balducci

6 August 1922—25 April 1992

Unearthing the Hidden Man

It was a legal case that riveted everyone in Italy. The defendant was a young man named Giuseppe Gozzini, charged with treason for declaring himself a conscientious objector and refusing to serve in the armed forces. Although the right to conscientious objection wouldn't be recognized by the Italian courts for another nine years, the public debate generated by Gozzini's 1963 trial prepared the way.

One of the primary voices in the national debate belonged to Ernesto Balducci, a Florentine priest long active in peacemaking. His eloquent and tireless defense of Gozzini inspired many but earned him the enmity of his conservative bishop, who banished Balducci from his diocese. For the next two years, Balducci lived in Rome, finally returning home only by the intervention of the pope. Even then, Balducci thought it prudent to remain out of the reach of Florence's bishop: he settled in a monastery two hundred yards beyond the diocese's border.

Born in a Tuscany mining town, Balducci was raised in poverty. Awarded scholarships by the Church, he studied theology in Rome and Florence before taking Holy Orders. His early years sensitized him to both the economic misery of the underclass and the indifference of the wealthy, and his ministry quickly took a social turn. In 1958 he founded *Testimonianze,* a monthly review of social and theological commentary that he edited until his death. Later, as a staunch anti-war advocate, he served as head of the publishing house *Cultural della pace,* "Peace Culture." His abiding concern in his editorial work as well as his public advocacy was the task of eroding the ideological barriers between people that encourage misunderstanding and conflict. "Act only according to that maxim," he wrote, "by which you can at the same time will that the human species would find the reasons and the guarantees of its survival."

Balducci believed that the key to creating a culture of peace was nurturing what he called the "hidden" as opposed to the "cultural" man. The latter is that generally unreflective part of us molded by our culture. It conforms easily to social conventions and attitudes. But underneath this artificial veneer lurks the "hidden man," the child of God who responds to prophetic calls to biblical values such as justice, nonviolence, compassion, and love. When the cultural man hears countercultural pronouncements such as those proclaimed in the Sermon on the Mount—blessed are the peacemakers, the merciful, the meek—he either mocks them or cynically dismisses them as impossibly utopian. But when the hidden man hears them, he "rises to his feet" in thrilled recognition of their truth. It's to the task of unearthing and awakening the hidden man in everyone that Balducci dedicated his life.

26 April

Amy Biehl

26 April 1967—25 August 1993

Weaving a Barrier against Violence

AMY BIEHL STOOD OUT in South Africa's black townships. A tall woman with long blonde hair and strikingly blue eyes, she was born into a Roman Catholic family in California, graduated with honors from Stanford University, and was a PhD student when she won a Fulbright Scholarship in 1992 to study at Cape Town's University of the Western Cape. She went there to research women under oppression. But once in South Africa, she threw herself into work in the impoverished townships that surrounded white and affluent Cape Town.

South Africa's first all-race national election had been called for April 1993, and one of Amy's principal tasks was to visit the townships to register voters. Biehl had been an opponent of apartheid for as long as she could remember and was excited to be a part of its dismantlement. It was fulfilling work. She came to love the South Africans she met during the registration drive, and she looked forward to the upcoming "Freedom Day" elections.

On Wednesday, 25 August 1993, after nearly a year in South Africa and less than a week before she was to return home to visit her family and fiancé, Biehl gave some black student friends a lift in her car to Gugulethu Township. As she drove through the township, a gang of angry young men, seeing a white woman behind the wheel, began pelting her car with stones and shouting "Kill the settler!" and "One settler, one bullet!" Finally forced to stop, Amy and her companions tried to flee. But a brick knocked her to the ground, and the mob beat and stabbed her to death.

Amy's murder shocked South Africa. Four of her assailants were quickly captured, tried, and convicted. Five years later, with the approval of Amy's parents, the four were granted amnesty by the Truth and Reconciliation Commission headed by Anglican Archbishop **Desmond Tutu** and released from prison. Amy's parents, Linda and Peter, established the nonprofit Amy Biehl Foundation, the motto of which is "weaving a barrier against violence," to celebrate their daughter's life and passion for social justice. Among its many projects, the foundation sponsors fifteen educational programs ranging from technical training to college preparation in Gugulethu Township, the community where Amy died.

Archbishop Tutu was just one of thousands touched by both Amy's devotion to ending apartheid and her parents' willingness to forgive and reconcile with their daughter's murderers. "The logic would be that the South Africans should be giving some kind of reparation to the Biehls," he said. "They've turned it upside down. It is the victims, in the depth of their own agony and pain, who say, 'The community—which produced these murderers—we want to help that community be transfigured.'"

27 April
Dorothee Soelle

30 September 1929—27 April 2003

Mysticism and Nonviolence

SOCIETY'S CONVENTIONAL IMAGE OF a mystic is that of a person who withdraws from the world in order to journey inward—"navel-gazing," as it's often disdainfully called—and discover some kind of spiritual enlightenment. The mystic is stereotyped as a guru sitting in splendid isolation on a mountaintop, utterly unconcerned with the world's affairs.

But theologian Dorothee Soelle, herself something of a mystic, argued that there's actually little accuracy in this portrayal. Far from being withdrawn from the world or indifferent to the suffering that goes on in it, the mystic is uniquely motivated and qualified to respond to social and economic injustices. Genuine mystics, like Buddhist bodhisattvas, don't renounce the world for the sake of a private spiritual illumination. Rather, they use the enlightenment they've achieved to do something about the world's ills.

The reason for this, says Soelle, is that mystics have been liberated from the three powers that typically hold humans in bondage: ego, possession, and violence. They recognize that the standardly accepted division between I and not-I is an artificial one born from overvaluing oneself and competing with others for possessions. This "delimitation of the self from others" in turn sets the stage for the "onset of violence." But the genuine mystic understands that his or her connection with the divine is likewise a connection to all other humans and, indeed, to all of creation—a relationship, as Soelle said, that "borrows the eyes of God." Patterns of opposition and resistance bred by the division of I and not-I collapse to be replaced by ones of mutuality and community. Violence becomes obsolete, because the conditions necessary for its eruption disappear.

Soelle became interested in questions of religion and politics at an early age. She grew up under the Nazi regime and, like many Germans of her generation, never got over the shame of belonging to a nation that willingly collaborated with mass murderers. She was especially worried by the acquiescence of so many people who claimed to be Christian, and eventually concluded that part of the explanation was that they had compartmentalized their faith, transforming it into a private and "otherworldly" thing. Convinced that such privatization is a perversion of faith, Soelle worked as a theologian to demonstrate the social responsibility of religion and as an activist to put her theology into practice. She became one of the Cold War's leading anti-nuclear voices, a dedicated opponent of both American involvement in Vietnam War and Soviet-style communism, and a proponent of liberation theology. The spiritual fuel of these activities was her conviction that the mystical worldview is revolutionary enough to resist "powerful but petrified institutions" that trade in oppression and violence. Consequently, her "most important concern" was to "democratize mysticism" so that society might be truly democratized as well.

28 April

Oskar Schindler

28 April 1908—9 October 1974

Behaving Like a Human Being

Some people who knew him called him an opportunist, a smooth-talking entrepreneur who knew all the angles. They weren't mistaken. Oskar Schindler *was* a slick operator. But during the course of World War II, he showed himself to be a humanitarian as well.

Born of German parents in what is now the Czech Republic, Schindler was a small-time and generally unsuccessful businessman throughout the 1930s. His luck changed when he joined the Nazi party in 1939 and followed the German army into conquered Poland. In hindsight, it was clear that he had no real sympathy with Nazi doctrine. He joined the party because he sensed golden opportunities in the German-occupied territories for an enterprising businessman. But to take advantage of them, he needed party credentials.

Schmoozing with high-ranking Nazis paid off immediately. Schindler was able to buy a formerly Jewish-owned enamelware factory in Krakow for a song, and he hired, at rock-bottom wages, about twelve hundred Jewish laborers to work in it. After he secured lucrative contracts from the military, the money began rolling in.

At first Schindler tried to turn a blind eye to Nazi persecution of Polish Jews. But even he had to take notice when the Krakow ghetto, a section of town into which German authorities crammed fifteen thousand Jews, was emptied in March 1943. Ghetto residents were either shot in the streets or rounded up for transport to the death camps. Horrified by what was happening, Schindler bribed Nazi officials with huge amounts of money to spare his factory workers.

Toward the end of the war, when Krakow had to be abandoned to the advancing Soviet army, Schindler saved his workers from certain death at the hands of the retreating Nazis by transporting all of them to a factory in the Sudetenland. There they were put to work making munitions for the German army. But by then Schindler, disgusted with the atrocities committed by Hitler and his thugs, was determined to undermine the German war effort. So he made sure that all the munitions produced in his factory were defective. With no money coming in and thousands of marks going out to protect his factory workers—who by now were known as "*Schindlerjuden*"—Schindler soon ran through his fortune. By the war's end, he was utterly broke.

Schindler was as unsuccessful a businessman after the war as he'd been before it. But his willingness to bankrupt himself in order to save human lives won him recognition by the State of Israel as one of those Gentiles who are "Righteous among the Nations." Today, there are more than seven thousand descendants of the Jews he saved. When asked why he risked everything to protect Jews during the war, Schindler's response was simple. "When you know people," he said, "you have to behave towards them like human beings."

29 April
Gordon Kiyoshi Hirabayashi

23 April 1918—2 January 2012

Internment Resister

In February 1942, just weeks after the Japanese attack on Pearl Harbor, President Franklin Roosevelt authorized the expulsion of Japanese-Americans from all zones in the United States considered to have military significance. This included the entire Pacific Coast. The 110,000 people of Japanese descent who lived there were moved to "War Relocation Camps" further east. It made no difference whether or not they were American citizens.

Gordon Kiyoshi Hirabayashi, one of those Japanese-American citizens, was a student at the University of Washington when the internment order was issued. A Christian pacifist who also belonged to the American Friends Service Committee, Hirabayashi originally intended to obey the order. But at the last moment, right before he was to step onto a bus waiting to take him and others to a camp, he realized that he couldn't go. As he later recalled, he suddenly understood that he had no right to "allow my citizenship to be warped without my protest." So he stepped away from the bus and decided instead to challenge the constitutionality of the War Relocation Camps.

When Hirabayashi was arrested and sentenced to ninety days hard labor for resisting relocation, as he knew he would be, he appealed his conviction all the way up to the Supreme Court. The judges unanimously ruled against him in 1943, arguing that the United States was justified in enacting restrictions against aliens during wartime if those aliens originated from the country against which the United States was fighting. Curiously, however, the government refused to pay for Hirabayashi's transportation to the Arizona federal prison where he was to serve his sentence. So the young man hitchhiked to Arizona and turned himself in to authorities there. It was a surreal situation.

After the war, Hirabayashi became a professor of sociology at the University of Alberta in British Columbia. His conviction was overturned in 1987 after the discovery that the U.S. federal government had exaggerated the threat to military security posed by Japanese residents of California. Hirabayashi, a mild man who always denied that he was "a rebel looking for a cause" when he violated the internment orders, says that the primary lesson he took away from the experience was the need for "constant vigilance" when it comes to civil liberties.

In 2007, a Los Angeles theatre premiered a play, *Dawn's Light*, based on Hirabayashi's nonviolent resistance to forced internment.

30 April

Immanuel Kant

22 April 1724—12 February 1804

Perpetual Peace

IMMANUEL KANT, WHO LIVED his entire adult life in the Prussian town of Königsberg, is unquestionably one of the most important figures in the history of Western philosophy. But his writing is generally so obscure as to be beyond the reach of nonprofessional (and some professional!) philosophers. One of his works, however, is perfectly accessible: a 1795 pamphlet titled *Perpetual Peace: A Philosophical Sketch*. When he sat down to compose it, Kant appreciated the importance of writing in a clear and understandable style. His hope was that the pamphlet would change the world.

Kant's little book proposed a program for peace within and between nations. He and the rest of Europe had witnessed the brutal wars of the eighteenth century, capped off by the savagery of the French Revolution, and Kant wanted to find a way to avoid them in the future.

In order to secure world peace, Kant argued that certain "preliminary articles" had to regulate the behavior of nation-states. There needed to be an end to secret treaties that bound nations to come to one another's defense in the outbreak of war; states needed to be economically and politically autonomous; there needed to be a total abolition over time of standing armies; and if war did erupt, nations needed to refrain from actions such as assassinations and terrorism, which would breed deep-seated resentment and make genuine peace unlikely.

But Kant recognized that these preliminary conditions for perpetual peace, while necessary, weren't enough to keep nations from warring with one another. So he recommended the establishment of an international governing body—a sort of league of nations—to safeguard the peace. This governing body rested on three "definitive" principles: all states should be republican rather than despotic in government; the relationships between nation-states should be regulated by international law; and each state should bind itself to the practice of "universal hospitality," which Kant defined as "the right of the stranger not to be treated as an enemy when he arrives in the land of another."

It took another century and a half of war before the league of nations Kant envisioned finally came to fruition with the emergence in 1945 of the United Nations. His articles and principles that serve as necessary conditions for perpetual peace have still to be fully realized. But they continue to serve as an inspiring model for the U.N.'s mission to bring perpetual peace to the world.

1 May
Albert Bigelow

1 May 1906—6 October 1993

The Voyage of the Golden Rule

As a lieutenant commander in the U.S. Navy during World War II, Albert Bigelow had captained submarine chasers and destroyer escorts. But when he heard about the atomic blast over Hiroshima, something inside him broke. At that moment, he realized that "morally war is impossible" in a nuclear age. He remained in the Naval Reserves for a few more years, but his conscience finally led him to resign in 1952, just one month before he would have been eligible for a military pension.

In 1955, as the United States was ramping up its nuclear arsenal and regularly testing atomic weapons in Nevada and the Pacific Ocean, Bigelow and his wife, now Quakers, hosted two of the so-called Hiroshima Maidens—women horribly burned in Hiroshima who had come to the United States for reconstructive surgery. Seeing their scars and listening to their stories convinced Bigelow that he had to do something to stop the madness of nuclear proliferation. He soon joined the Non-Violent Action Against Nuclear Weapons (NVAANW), a grassroots organization dedicated to protesting the manufacturing and testing of atomic bombs.

In January 1958, Bigelow and three other members of NVAANW sent a letter to President Eisenhower to tell him that they planned to sail a thirty-foot ketch, the *Golden Rule*, into a nuclear test zone in the Pacific Ocean. "For years we have spoken and written of the suicidal military preparations of the Great Powers," they wrote, "but our voices have been lost in the massive effort of those responsible for preparing this country for war. We mean to speak now with the weight of our whole lives." In a press conference shortly before they sailed, the crew of the *Golden Rule* said that they wanted their action to awaken a public that had been "benumbed [and] morally desensitized by ten years of propaganda and fear."

By the time the *Golden Rule* reached Hawaii, an alarmed Atomic Energy Commission had secured an injunction against its proceeding to the test zone. Bigelow and his crew ignored it, sailed on, and were arrested. Placed on probation, they sailed again. This time they were jailed. Their voyage for peace had apparently failed. But Earle Reynolds, a Quaker and peace activist, stepped up. He and his wife sailed their yacht, which they renamed the *Phoenix of Hiroshima*, into the Pacific Island test zone that Bigelow and his crew had tried to reach. When they arrived, they radioed that they were "in the U.S. nuclear test zone as a protest against nuclear testing." Arrested by the Coast Guard, Reynolds would serve six months for his "crime."

The voyages of the *Golden Rule* and the *Phoenix of Hiroshima* didn't end nuclear testing, but they did break through the "moral desensitization" that Bigelow feared had "benumbed" the American public. Citizens across the country protested the government's prosecution of Bigelow's and Reynolds' nonviolent resistance, and organizations sprang up from coast to coast to protest nuclear proliferation. Opposition to atomic weaponry was now part of the cultural landscape.

2 May
Benjamin Spock

2 May 1903—15 March 1998

The Point of Raising Kids

At the height of the Vietnam War, Vice President Spiro Agnew publicly blamed pediatrician and anti-war activist Benjamin Spock for the public protests rocking the nation. The alleged culprit was Spock's book *Baby and Child Care*, the best-selling guide to raising children first published in 1945. The "permissiveness" advocated in it, charged Agnew, had created an entire generation of spoiled brats who preferred marching in the streets to settling down as productive citizens.

Dr. Spock's child-rearing advice was never as permissive as Agnew (and others such as clergyman Norman Vincent Peale) claimed, but the vice president was right to see a connection between Spock's views about children and public demonstrations against the Vietnam War in the late 1960s and 1970s. The war was consuming the youth of America—not to mention Vietnam's—both physically and spiritually. Spock saw this for the tragic waste it was. "There's no point in raising children," he pointed out "if they're going to be burned alive," especially in a war that can't be won. The only way for the United States to emerge victorious, Spock said, would be to "exterminate an entire country." And that was unacceptable.

So as someone passionate about the well-being of children everywhere, Spock believed he couldn't stand on the sidelines. Following his own oft-quoted advice to parents to "follow your own common sense," he became an advocate of nuclear disarmament and an end to what he saw as American military adventurism. For five years in the 1960s he was co-chair of the National Committee for a Sane Nuclear Policy (SANE), a grassroots organization dedicated to disarmament. Arrested at a number of peace demonstrations, he was indicted in 1968 on federal charges that he conspired with others, including **William Sloane Coffin**, to counsel draft evasion. He was convicted and sentenced to two years in prison, but the verdict was overturned on appeal the following year.

It was during the Vietnam War that Spock became a national icon of resistance to governmental authority. He publicly announced his intention to become a war tax resister, and in 1972 he was the presidential candidate of the newly formed People's Party, running on a platform that advocated free medical care, a guaranteed minimum income for American families, dismantlement of the military, and the legalization of homosexuality, abortion, and marijuana. Spock was also the party's nomination for vice president four years later. Throughout the 1980s he remained a visible opponent of the nuclear arms race between the world's superpowers.

Spock never claimed to be an absolute pacifist. He willingly served as a medical officer during World War II, and never regretted his time in uniform. But he believed that the invention of atomic weapons in 1945 was a game changer, transforming warfare overnight into a dangerously outdated way of resolving conflict. This conclusion, he said, was just common sense.

Anthony Benezet

3 MAY

31 JANUARY 1713—3 MAY 1784

Defender of the African Genius

SOMETIMES A RUN OF bad luck is providential. By the time he was in his mid-twenties, French-born Anthony Benezet, who later become known as the father of the anti-slavery movement in America, had failed as a Philadelphia merchant. So he took up schoolteaching, a career that had little social prestige in eighteenth-century America. Since he was a Quaker, he soon landed a position in the city's Friends' English School, where he proved himself a superb teacher, although a lax disciplinarian by the day's standards.

Had Benezet been a more successful merchant, he would never have become a teacher. And had he not become a teacher, he wouldn't have started tutoring slave children in the evenings at his home. Benezet began offering the private instruction in 1750 as an act of charity. But in teaching the slave children, as he wrote years afterwards, he "had opportunity of knowing the temper and genius of the Africans." Benezet discerned in them "as great a variety of talents as amongst a like number of whites, and I am bold to assert, that the notion entertained by some, that the blacks are inferior in their capacities, is a vulgar prejudice, founded on the pride or ignorance of their lordly masters, who have kept their slaves at such a distance, as to be unable to form a right judgment of them." If African slaves appear abject and ignorant, he insisted, it's not because they are so by nature, but rather because of the dispiriting bondage in which they are held.

Benezet's interaction with black children made final his opposition to slavery, and for the rest of his life he waged a campaign against both the "peculiar institution" and the racism that usually accompanied it. He wrote pamphlets, spoke publicly, and began a widespread correspondence with influential men on either side of the Atlantic to persuade them of the wickedness of slavery. He worked on two fronts. First, he encouraged his fellow Quakers to liberate the slaves they owned and to join him in public denunciations of slavery because, he argued, slavery was inconsistent with Jesus' message. Second, he labored to turn public opinion against slavery by providing graphic examples of its cruelty on the one hand and inspiring accounts of the "African genius" on the other. In 1775 he organized the Society for the Relief of Free Negroes Unlawfully Held in Bondage, the first abolitionist society in America. Among its charter members was Thomas Paine.

In 1770, Benezet opened the first school for black children in Philadelphia, where he taught until his death. Although he didn't live to see the end of slavery in the United States, his influence was far-reaching in both the Quaker and non-Quaker communities.

4 May
Carl von Ossietzky

3 October 1889—4 May 1938

Exposer of Abteilung M

THE 1919 VERSAILLES TREATY that followed World War I imposed draconian penalties on a defeated Germany. It saddled the war-torn nation with financial reparations of close to $400 million (finally paid off only in 2010), stripped it of some of its territory, and severely limited the size of the German army.

Diehard German nationalists and the Prussian military caste found the treaty intolerable. But so did many supporters of the post-war democratic Weimar Republic that replaced the German monarchy. And they resolved to do something about it. So in the late 1920s, the German government began secretly building an air force and sending fighter pilots to the Soviet Union for training. It was a deliberate defiance of the Versailles Treaty and an arrogant affirmation of the German glorification of all things military.

Carl von Ossietzky, a journalist who had opposed German militarism since 1913 and whose anti-war attitude was confirmed by his frontline experience after he was drafted in 1916, broke the story of *Abteiling M* (Battalion M), as government memoranda called the secret air unit. His exposé appeared in 1929 in *Die Weltbuhne*, a Berlin-based leftist periodical already under surveillance. Von Ossietzky, whose long history of peace activism marked him as a subversive, was charged with stealing state secrets, convicted in a quick trial, and sentenced to nearly two years in prison. He was released in late 1932.

His freedom didn't last long. In January 1933, Hitler became the chancellor of Germany, ushering in the "Thousand Year Reich." One month later, von Ossietzky was seized at his home by Nazi thugs and taken into "protective custody." From then until his death, he was imprisoned in a number of concentration camps across the country. Regularly beaten, starved, and forced to perform backbreaking labor, even though he had a bad heart and suffered from tuberculosis, von Ossietzky suffered horribly for his pacifist whistle-blowing.

But the world hadn't forgotten him. In one of the most hotly criticized decisions the Nobel Prize Committee ever made, von Ossietzky was awarded the 1935 Peace Prize. Conservatives throughout Europe and the United States expressed outrage that a "criminal" convicted of leaking state secrets would be so rewarded. Two members of the Nobel Committee resigned in protest, and Norway's King Haakon refused to attend the award ceremony. Needless to say, the Nazis were outraged and insisted that von Ossietzky repudiate the award. He refused, saying that "the Nobel Peace Prize is not a sign of an internal political struggle, but of understanding between peoples." In retaliation, the Nazis decreed that German citizens would no longer be allowed to accept Nobel Prizes.

In 1992, over half a century after his death, German courts shamefully upheld von Ossietzky's 1931 conviction.

5 May
Pete Seeger

3 May 1919—

A Hate-Surrounding Machine

They say that music tames the savage beast. If the long career of Pete Seeger is any evidence, music is also a powerful force for peace and justice. For over seventy years, Seeger has used song, banjo, guitar, and ukulele in an ongoing campaign for human rights, environmental protection, and an end to war. Folksinger **Woody Guthrie** famously wrote on his guitar, "This machine kills fascists." Seeger's long-neck banjo carries a less violent but equally resolute slogan: "This machine surrounds hate and forces it to surrender."

Born into a prosperous, musical, and left-leaning Manhattan family, Seeger dropped out of Harvard in 1938 to begin his musical career. In 1941 he cofounded The Almanac Singers, a folksong group that specialized in tunes supporting such progressive causes as unionization and racial desegregation. Nine years later the group renamed itself The Weavers. Despite their reputation for radicalism, The Weavers had several hits in the early years of the 1950s: "Goodnight Irene," "Kisses Sweeter than Wine," and "Wimoweh." Although criticized by other progressive musicians at the time for selling out, Seeger insists that the popular music performed by The Weavers helped make their political and economic agenda more palatable to the general public. Be that as it may, Senator Joe McCarthy's House Un-American Activities Committee was not impressed, and The Weavers found themselves blacklisted as communists in 1953. Seeger, who joined the Young Communist League when he was seventeen, drifted away from the party during the Stalinist years. (Despite his anti-Sovietism, he still considers himself a communist because, as he says, "communism is no more what Russia made of it than Christianity is what the churches make of it.") But aside from a couple of reunion concerts, the McCarthy blacklisting put an end to The Weavers.

Since the 1950s, Seeger's musical talents have consistently been in the service of progressive social issues. Although he served in the military during World War II and supported the Republican cause during the Spanish Civil War, he has since been a consistent critic of militarism and the arms race. He was an especially vocal opponent of the Vietnam War. True to his early support of unions while with The Almanacs, Seeger remains an advocate of labor rights, and in the last three decades has also become an outspoken champion of the environment.

Seeger is fond of saying that the "wrong kind of music"—the kind he makes—is "dangerous" to wealth, power, and privilege. His own career attests to the truth of that statement. "Where Have All the Flowers Gone?," "Turn, Turn, Turn," "Talking Union," "Little Boxes," "Which Side Are You On?," "We Shall Overcome," and "Guantanamera," all songs recorded or written by Seeger, have become fixtures in the American cultural landscape. It's not too much to claim that their progressive message influenced the political thinking of an entire generation.

6 May

Ariel Dorfman

6 May 1942—

The Danger of Losing It All

Torture is a tragic fact of life in today's world. It's wielded as a military and political weapon by too many nations, including the United States (where it's euphemistically referred to as "enhanced interrogation"), despite the fact that it's universally condemned by human rights advocates. But very few of us, whether we despise it or sanction it, fully appreciate its full impact.

Ariel Dorfman does. The playwright, who fled Chile after the 1973 murder of Salvadore Allende and the ascendency of military strongman Augusto Pinochet, recognizes that torture is more than a crime committed against a particular body. It's also a deadening of the human ability to empathize with the suffering of others. Torture requires "the abrogation of our capacity to imagine others' suffering, dehumanizing them so much that their pain is not our pain. It demands this of the torturer, placing the victim outside and beyond any form of compassion or empathy." Even worse, it also "demands of everyone else the same distancing, the same numbness, on the part of those who know and close their eyes." Torture, therefore, "corrupts the whole social fabric because it prescribes a silencing. Torture obliges us to be deaf and blind and mute."

Dorfman's most gripping play is *Death and the Maiden*, the story of Pauline Salas, a woman tortured and repeatedly raped while held captive by a totalitarian government modeled on Pinochet's Chile. One of the rapists, a prison doctor named Roberto Miranda, was a fan of classical music and regularly played a recording of Schubert's "Death and the Maiden" during his assaults. Pauline never saw him—she was blindfolded during the rapes—but she's haunted by the memory of his voice. Years after her release, through a series of unexpected events, a man she believes to be Miranda arrives on her doorstep. She takes him captive and physically abuses him in order to solicit a confession. Miranda finally does confess out of fear for his life, but the audience is never quite sure if he's the torturer/rapist Pauline thinks he is or an innocent victim.

Death and the Maiden chillingly illustrates Dorfman's fear that the culture which permits torture becomes a victim of the torture. Pauline has most obviously been brutalized by the atrocities she experienced at the hands of her captors. But she's been brutalized spiritually as well, evidenced by her willingness—her eagerness—to inflict the same kind of pain and humiliation on Miranda. This willingness symbolizes the broader point that a society that tortures risks accepting it as nothing more than a conventional interrogatory technique. Moral inhibitions become increasingly elastic, even stretching to the point where the tortured who condemn their own abuse practice torture in the name of justice. From their wounded perspective, torture becomes the right thing to do. As Pauline cries out toward the play's end, "This time I am going to think about myself, about what I need. If only to do justice in one case, just one. What do we lose? What do we lose by killing one of them?"

Dorfman's implied answer is that, becoming morally blind and deaf and mute, we lose everything.

7 May
Carl Upchurch

26 January 1950—2 May 2003

"Deniggerization"

THE CARDS WERE STACKED against him from the moment of his birth—or maybe, as he said in his autobiography, from the very moment of his conception. Born and raised in a Philadelphia ghetto, Carl Upchurch quit school when he was nine years old and started running with a street gang. A series of petty crimes eventually culminated in an unsuccessful armed robbery for which Upchurch was convicted and sentenced to prison. He served more than ten years at Pittsburgh's Western Penitentiary. Released in 1981, he earned a college degree and founded the Progressive Prisoners' Movement, an organization that offered emotional and material support to prisoners. In 1992, he put together the Council for Urban Peace and Justice to offer counseling to gang members. The hope was to turn youths away from lives of crime before they wound up in prison. A year after its inception, the council sponsored a national summit on gang violence that brought together 150 gang leaders from 26 cities.

Upchurch's efforts on behalf of prisoners and gang members—potential prisoners—was fueled by his conviction that many of them, like he, were marked from birth for failure. In describing his own childhood, he coined an ugly word—"niggerization"—for an ugly process. Niggerization is the insidious mutation of a black child into a self-loathing, self-destructive, and violent youth who has internalized the white world's contempt. The devolution is fueled by legal and social discrimination, poverty, broken family life, lack of educational opportunity, and an environment of violence in which the likelihood for black youth of keeping out of jail or even surviving into adulthood is dismally low. It was no surprise to Upchurch that "niggerized" young men often wound up in street gangs and on the wrong side of the law.

But Upchurch's hope was that the cycle could be broken and reversed. He called the process "deniggerization." In his own case, deniggerization began while he was serving time in Western Penitentiary. He read deeply in such writers as Shakespeare, James Baldwin, Mark Twain, and Dostoevsky, and they awakened in him a new sense of identity and the conviction that humans were made for greater things than he had known on the streets of Philadelphia. He began to realize that he was a human being rather than a "nigger," inherently capable of greatness and worthy of respect, and this in turn began to erode the self-hatred and despair that had poisoned his life. It also gave him the strength and hope to do something about a social system that allowed kids like he had been to fall through the cracks. For Upchurch, the way to individual and social nonviolence was facilitating on a large scale the process of deniggerization that had personally liberated him. He always thought of his advocacy for prisoners and gang members as peacework.

Before his too early death, Upchurch's dedication to changing the lives of prisoners and young people was recognized by the Southern Christian Leadership Conference, the Rainbow Coalition, and the Fellowship of Reconciliation.

8 May
Pat Barker

8 May 1943—

Hidden Victims of War

DIFFERENT WARS HAVE GIVEN it different names. In World War I, it was called "shell shock." In World War II and Korea, "combat fatigue." Most recently, it's designated "post-traumatic stress disorder." But all the labels refer to the same thing: the psychological fragmentation inflicted by the horrors of battle. Sometimes the symptoms reveal themselves during combat, sometimes only afterwards. The worst cases—veterans who suffer from addiction, suicidal depression, rage, and even psychosis—are the ones that get the most press. But recent studies suggest that all combat soldiers suffer from psychological trauma to one degree or another. How could they not?

The actual trauma is tragic enough. But the social onus attached to it makes a bad situation worse. Historically, veterans suffering from battlefield trauma have been disdainfully dismissed as cowards, weaklings, or shirkers who let down their country and betray their comrades-in-arms.

The British author Pat Barker, in a gripping trio of novels collectively called the *Regeneration Trilogy*, explores the tragedy of battlefield trauma. Her novels are set during World War I, and some of the characters—the poets **Siegfried Sassoon** and Wilfred Owen, or psychiatrists W. H. R. Rivers and Lewis Yealand—are actual historical figures. The novels focus on the relationship between combat veterans who have cracked under the stress of war and the physicians who treat them. Barker's portrayal of the intense mental anguish experienced by veterans is painful to read, but it's not contrived. A trained historian, Barker researched hundreds of case histories of World War I–vintage shell shock before writing her novels.

One of the most gripping scenes in her trilogy appears in the first volume, *Regeneration*. It juxtaposes the therapeutic approach of Rivers, who feels great compassion for the broken men he treats, and Yealand, who regards them as cowards who simply need some bracing up. Rivers invites his patients to speak about their experiences at their own pace. Yealand subjects them to electric shock treatment that is nothing short of torture. His working assumption is that even shirkers would prefer to return to the battlefield than endure long bouts of his sort of "therapy." Barker describes Yealand's way of handling a veteran whose battlefield trauma has made him mute; Yealand ominously promises the soldier that he will be electrically convulsed until he agrees to speak, and then proceeds to follow through with his threat. By the end of the scene, the man has gasped a few broken words, and Yealand triumphantly pronounces him cured and ready to be sent back to the front line.

This scene alone is one of the most damning indictments of warfare ever penned. In writing it, Barker speaks for all veterans whose lives have been muted by war.

9 MAY
Sophia Scholl

9 MAY 1921—22 FEBRUARY 1943

Death on a Sunny Day

IN A PHOTOGRAPH TAKEN of her when she was twenty-one, "Sophie" Scholl stares at the camera with unusual intensity. There was good reason for her seriousness. Along with her brother Hans and a few close friends, she was a member of the White Rose, a small group devoted to nonviolent resistance to the Nazi regime. Sophie would have liked nothing better than to live like an ordinary university student. But her conscience wouldn't allow that.

Born in Forchtenberg am Kocher, where her father was once mayor, Sophie joined a Nazi youth organization when she was twelve. Although membership was mandatory, she was initially enthusiastic about her involvement. But she quickly became disenchanted, partly because of her father's opposition to the Nazi government.

Early on, Sophie displayed a talent for drawing and painting as well as a passion for theology and philosophy. After graduating from secondary school, she hoped to substitute kindergarten work for the mandatory *Reichsarbeitdienst,* or National Labor Service. But Germany was at war, and she was still required to serve in the quasi-military auxiliary, which she loathed and which ultimately inspired her to practice nonviolent resistance.

In May 1942 she enrolled at the University of Munich, where her brother was already a medical student, to study biology and philosophy. Hans introduced Sophie to a cadre of friends who would later form the core of the White Rose resistance movement. In long, late-night sessions, Sophie, Hans, and their friends debated the responsibility of the individual citizen in a society gripped by dictatorship.

Although raised a Lutheran, Sophie was greatly influenced by her reading of Cardinal John Henry Newman's "theology of conscience." The conscience, Newman argued, was an echo of the voice of God and took precedence over all other considerations. Eventually she and her friends resolved to act on their own consciences, and the White Rose was the result. From the early summer of 1942 until mid-February 1943, White Rose members wrote and distributed in Munich six leaflets urging Germans to resist the Nazis nonviolently. Hans initially discouraged his sister from participating in the group's activities. But he soon realized that as a woman she was much less likely to be stopped and questioned by the Gestapo, and before long Sophie was distributing White Rose leaflets.

Sophie and the other White Rose members were arrested on 18 February 1943 and charged with treason. Her courage and determination under interrogation were heroic. When she appeared before the People's Court for trial, it was apparent that her captors had broken one of her legs.

Sophie was condemned to death four days after her arrest, and beheaded shortly afterwards. As she walked to the guillotine, she is reported to have said: "Such a splendid sunny day, and I have to go. But what does my death matter, if through us thousands of people are awakened and stirred to action?"

10 May

Beyers Naudé

10 May 1915—7 September 2004

Anti-Apartheid Leper

DURING THE APARTHEID YEARS in South Africa, blacks were required to carry "passbooks" when traveling in white communities. The regulation was essentially a legal stratagem to restrict the movement and assembly of blacks. Pass holders who lacked the appropriate stamps of permission could be turned back from entering certain areas or even arrested. The passbooks came to be seen by black South Africans as one of the most potent symbols of apartheid oppression, and demonstrations against them regularly erupted. One of these public protests, held on 21 March 1960 in the town of Sharpeville, resulted in tragedy. Afrikaan policemen fired on the crowd, killing sixty-nine men, women, and children and wounding nearly two hundred others. Many were shot in the back as they fled.

The Sharpeville Massacre was a turning point for the Reverend Beyers Naudé, son of a Boer general, active member of the pro-apartheid organization the *Broederbond*, and Dutch Reformed Church (DRC) pastor who regularly delivered apartheid-justifying sermons to his all white Afrikaner congregation. News of the slaughter shocked him to his core and forced him to acknowledge the evil of apartheid. Naudé made a resolution. He had spent the first half of his life defending the inherent racial superiority of whites over blacks. He would spend the second half laboring to undo the damage he and his fellow Afrikaners had done. One of his first steps was to publicly agree with the World Council of Churches' condemnation of South African apartheid. In doing so, he publicly broke with the DRC, which quickly stripped him of his pulpit.

Over the next fifteen years, Naudé continued protesting apartheid. He cooperated with others in leaking internal *Broederbond* papers that documented the organization's rabid racism and willingness to use violence against outspoken blacks. He spoke publicly against apartheid and in favor of a nonviolent end to it whenever he had the chance, both in South Africa and abroad. International coverage of his opposition to apartheid became so embarrassing to the South African government that it temporarily suspended his passport in 1972. Five years later, authorities sought to silence Naudé further by placing him under the "ban," a form of house arrest that reduced his rights to travel or assemble with other people to much the same degree that passbooks restricted black South Africans. Archbishop **Desmond Tutu**, a friend and collaborator of Naudé's, said that his anti-apartheid stance had made him a leper in the eyes of Afrikaners.

After the ban on Naudé's activities was lifted in 1984, he worked with African National Congress leaders to bring about the official dismantling of apartheid that began in 1990. Towards the end of his life, Naudé returned to the same congregation that had ousted him forty years earlier. He must have been gratified to see how things had changed during that time both in the Dutch Reformed Church and in South Africa as a whole.

11 May
Mychal Judge

11 May 1933—11 September 2001

Overcoming Hell

THE PHOTOGRAPHIC IMAGE WENT viral: five men—cops and firefighters grimed with dust, soot, and grief—carrying an obviously dead man away from the falling tower on a jerry-rigged stretcher. The date was 9/11, and the man was Franciscan priest Mychal Judge. He would be counted as the first recorded fatality of the terrorist attacks on the Twin Towers in Manhattan.

Many people have heard of Judge's rush to the World Trade Center shortly after the attack. He was chaplain to the New York City Fire Department, and since firemen were in the thick of things on that September morning, it was only appropriate that he be there too. He was in the lobby of the North Tower, ministering to the dead and dying, when the South Tower collapsed, shooting murderous debris through North's windows. Judge was hit and died instantly.

What is less well known than his manner of dying is Judge's manner of living. He was a man who devoted himself, like his spiritual master St. Francis, to serving the down-and-outs in society, those people who are marginalized because of who or what they happen to be—or, more likely, because of who or what they're *not*.

Everyone who knew him remembered how uninhibited and nonjudgmental he was when it came to helping the vulnerable. He rarely left his apartment without a wad of $1 bills to hand out to the homeless people he knew he would meet that day. He ministered joyfully to alcoholics and drug addicts, to gays and lesbians who felt rejected by the Church, and to street people who suffered from mental illness. In the dead of winter, he once gave his coat to a homeless woman. When mildly rebuked about the deed, he simply responded that she needed the coat more than he did. Another time, while he ministered to a dying AIDS patient, he responded to the man's despairing fear that God hated him by holding him until he died.

Judge's endless service to broken people stemmed in part from his humble acknowledgment of his own vulnerability. A recovering alcoholic, he struggled each day to stay dry. As a celibate homosexual, he was all too aware of the feeling of abandonment, like that expressed by the dying AIDS patient, that many gay and lesbian Christians feel. His own wounds helped him to be more sensitive to and compassionate of the wounds of others. He was willing to enter into their suffering, sharing their burdens in the hope that he could bring them some relief. As he once said, "If you descend into somebody else's private hell and stand there with them, it ceases to be hell."

Judge's final entry into hell was that morning on 9/11 when he rushed to the Twin Towers. Cops and firemen who saw him in the final moments of his life recall that he was beseeching God to stop the destruction even as he ministered to those who were dying. Nine years before that day, Judge wondered during an interview: "I wonder what my last hour will be. Will it be trying to help someone, trying to save a life?" It was.

12 May

Brother Roger

12 May 1915—16 August 2005

A Little Parable of Communion

WHEN HE FIRST CAME to the French village of Taizé, arriving after a seventy-mile bicycle ride from his native Switzerland, Roger Schutz was struck by both its silent remoteness and its proximity to the ruins of the great medieval monastery of Cluny. He had been searching for a location to begin an experiment in monastic living. He decided to stay, and invited a few friends to join him.

Roger used the two houses he bought in Taizé as a refuge for Jews fleeing occupied France until he and his companions were forced to retreat to Switzerland with the Gestapo at their heels. But they returned when the Nazis were pushed out of France, took monastic vows that they wrote themselves, and in 1944 officially created the religious community of Taizé. Roger Schutz became Brother Roger and served as the community's prior.

From the very beginning, the special charism of the Taizé community was reconciliation of the differences between the various Christian traditions. Roger came from a Protestant background but was deeply sympathetic with Catholic liturgy, theology, and spirituality. Taizé was consciously nondenominational in order to attract clergy and visitors from Protestant, Catholic, and Orthodox traditions, and incorporated elements from all three in its simple liturgies. Denominational doctrines and demarcations took a back seat to Taizé's three guiding principles of "joy, simplicity, and compassion." During worship, the Taizé community stressed silent prayer—where, as Roger said, "with a childlike trust, we let Christ pray silently within us"—simple chant, and listening rather than preaching or credal affirmations. The point was to create a place for ecumenical fellowship and reconciliation.

Brother Roger was the inspiration and spiritual center of gravity for this ministry of reconciliation. It had always been his vision for Taizé. "In my youth," he wrote, "I was astonished to see how Christians—who nevertheless live from a God of love—use so much energy to justify their separations. So I said to myself that it was essential to create a community where people search to understand one another and to be reconciled with one another always, and through this, to render visible a little parable of communion."

The "little parable of communion" made visible by Brother Roger grew from its original 15 monks to 120. Each year over one hundred thousand visitors, many of them young people, come to Taizé on retreats and pilgrimages. All of them are drawn there by Brother Roger's message of spiritual reconciliation.

Roger was killed by a deranged woman at a Taizé prayer service. It was a startlingly violent end for a man who had spent most of his life cultivating the spirit of peace between Christians. Afterwards, the new prior of Taizé called upon the world to forgive Roger's murderer. The request honored Roger's legacy.

13 May
Fridtjof Nansen

10 October 1861—13 May 1930

Helping People Go Home

FRIDTJOF NANSEN SEEMED LARGER than life. A zoologist who conducted groundbreaking work in the study of nervous systems, a pioneer in the science of oceanography, an explorer who traversed the unpopulated interior of Greenland in one expedition and nearly made it to the North Pole in another, an author, inventor, and favorite son of Norway: he had it all. But nothing he did during the first fifty years of his life compared with his humanitarian work in his final decade.

In addition to slaughtering thirty-five million people, inflicting billions of dollars of damage on property, and changing the European map, World War I also produced half a million prisoners of war and millions of civilian refugees who had fled before advancing armies. In 1920 Nansen, who was already one of Norway's delegates to the new League of Nations, was asked to take on the repatriation of these homeless victims of war. In touring the settlement camps where they were kept, he was stunned by what he saw. "Never in my life," he said, "have I been brought into touch with so formidable an amount of suffering." Even the suffering he witnessed and personally endured in his Arctic explorations paled in comparison.

Nansen threw himself into his work, and was so efficient that within three years nearly all of the prisoners of war had been returned to more than thirty different countries. Having been named the League of Nation's High Commissioner for Refugees in the meantime, he worked with the International Red Cross not only to repatriate two million displaced Russian civilians, but also to get supplies into a famine-stricken Soviet Union. But governments unfriendly to the Bolshevik regime donated only reluctantly and stingily, and Nansen was forced to appeal to private foundations. At one point, in order to raise funds, he had photographs of starving Russian children made into postcards and sold. When he won the 1922 Nobel Peace Prize for his efforts to help displaced persons, he plowed the entire purse into refugee relief. But Nansen's efforts were stymied by uncooperative governments. Millions of Russians starved to death in the 1920s despite, as Nansen bitterly pointed out, such "an abundance of maize that the farmers had to burn it as fuel in their railway engines. All this, while thirty million people in the Volga region were allowed to starve and die."

Nansen also coordinated two other relief programs as High Commissioner for Refugees, one on behalf of Greeks returning to their home and the other on behalf of Armenians, both of whom had suffered at the hands of the Ottoman Empire. He also convinced over fifty governments to recognize what came to be known as the "Nansen Passport," an identification card for stateless persons that allowed them to cross borders. Taken together, millions of disrupted lives were influenced for the better by his dedication to returning people to their homes.

14 May

Peter Maurin

9 May 1877—15 May 1949

Making It Easier for Us to Be Better

THE CATHOLIC WORKER MOVEMENT was founded in 1933 by **Dorothy Day** and the vagabond Catholic philosopher and theologian Peter Maurin. Day is the person most closely associated in the public mind with the movement. But as she said many times, it all started with Maurin. He was, she remarked, "a revelation to me."

Born to a French peasant family, Maurin worked for a few years with the Christian Brothers before immigrating to western Canada to try his hand at homesteading. Following that, he traveled southward to the United States, working odd jobs, teaching French, reading voluminously in public libraries, and voluntarily living a hand-to-mouth existence. He slept in flophouses or barns, wore secondhand clothes, and ate inexpensively. Maurin, like St. **Francis of Assisi** before him, seemed to have absolutely no interest in possessions or money.

What he *was* intensely interested in was applying the social teachings of the Catholic Church to society at large. Maurin was convinced that Catholic principles of social and economic justice, based on the gospels as well as Church documents such as Pope Leo XIII's 1891 *Rerum Novarum,* were powerful blueprints for so transforming the world that, as Maurin liked to say, it became a bit easier for men and women to be better humans. An economy based on agrarianism, local craft, and an equal distribution of wealth, a nation based on nonviolent domestic and foreign policies, and a citizenry that prays, thinks, and practices radical hospitality: these were Maurin's ideals.

But he was sadly aware that this message was unwelcome to Church authorities who defended the social as well as ecclesial status quo. In one of his "easy essays," rhythmic pieces in which he presented his ideas in short repetitive sentences that made it easier to remember his points, Maurin criticized the Church for failing to detonate the power—the "dynamite," as he says—of its message. Instead, Church leaders and theologians have decided to "play a waiting game." They

> have taken the dynamite
> of the Church,
> have wrapped it up
> in nice phraseology,
> placed it in an hermetic container
> and sat on the lid.
> It is about time
> to blow the lid off.

In founding the Catholic Worker Movement with Dorothy Day, Maurin intended to light the fuse that would blow off the lid.

15 May
Frances Crowe

15 March 1919—

An Open Life of Peace

SHE IS A GENTLE force of nature. For over sixty years, Massachusetts resident Frances Crowe has been advocating for peace in a variety of ways. She became a convert to pacifism during World War II while working in a factory. Shocked by the firebombing of Dresden and Tokyo and the atomic attacks on Hiroshima and Nagasaki—they were, she says, "her epiphany"—she has since worked unstintingly to end war and the preparations for war.

A Quaker, Crowe sees armed combat as just one form of violence among many. So although a large part of her activism has been against war, she has also dedicated long hours in public witnesses against apartheid in South Africa, nuclear power plants in Vermont (for which she has been arrested seven times, the latest when she was ninety-one), and environmental degradation. Crowe's especially passionate about saving the planet. She tries to walk to as many places as she can so as not to use fossil fuels, lives simply, and eats locally and vegetarian. On her ninetieth birthday she urged friends and admirers who wished to observe the anniversary to do so by boycotting their cars for the day.

Crowe has been associated with just about every anti-war organization in the United States, including the War Resisters League, the Women's International League for Peace and Freedom, the American Friends Service Committee, and the Sane Nuclear Policy Committee. She was also a cofounder of the Taprock Peace Center in Deerfield, Massachusetts, one of the nation's best-known resources for peace and justice information and advocacy, and has been a war tax resister since the first Iraq War. "Unable to move congress to stop the war in Iraq," she says, "I stopped paying for war. I file my tax return, send a letter explaining that my conscience will not permit me to pay, and I send the taxes due to groups working to stop war and to public education."

Crowe's signature contribution to the peace movement has been her dedicated counseling of thousands of young men and women seeking conscientious objector status. She began the work during the Vietnam War and estimates that she advised two thousand men before the conflict finally ended. She continues draft counseling to the present day, offering advice to young men who are obliged by law to register for any possible future draft as well as to service men and women who wish to be discharged from the armed forces as conscientious objectors. She hopes that her counseling does something to help the nation get out of the cultural habit of solving conflict through warfare, and she dreams of the day when future generations will say, "Once people believed in war as the answer—not any more."

Crowe has, she says, "lived an open life" when it comes to her principles. She doesn't worry about legal prosecution or public condemnation. Instead, her "only fear is being indifferent to the suffering of others." That's not likely to happen.

16 May

Nhat Chi Mai

20 February 1934—16 May 1967

My Body a Torch

In the spring of 1967, a young Vietnamese Buddhist woman sat down in the courtyard of Saigon's Tu Ngheim Pagoda nunnery. She placed two statues next to her, one of the Virgin Mary and one of Avalokitesvara, the bodhisattva who embodies compassion. Calmly reciting a poem about the renunciation of hatred written by her friend and teacher **Thich Nhat Hanh**, she poured gasoline over her head and body and struck a match. In seconds, Nhat Chi Mai was a ghastly bonfire. A few minutes later, she was dead.

Self-immolation strikes many of us as the act of a crazed person, and doubtlessly it sometimes is. But in Nhat Chi Mai's case, it wasn't. She burned herself as an act of sacrifice in protest of the war that was ravaging her country and killing tens of thousands of her countrymen. She had already expressed her dismay at what she saw as the empty rhetoric of statesmen who preached peace while making war. "I am only an ordinary Vietnamese woman, without talent or ability," she wrote. "But I feel pain every time I look at the situation of my country. I want to say that the empty words you have been using, 'to defend freedom and happiness for Vietnam,' have lost all their meaning." So in a final effort to shock people of good will into action, and especially to unite Vietnamese Catholics and Vietnamese Buddhists in opposition to the war, Nhat Chi Mai offered herself as a sacrifice. She left behind a letter to the American government that expressed her hope for peace: "I offer my body as a torch to dissipate the dark, to waken love among men, to give peace to Vietnam, the one who burns herself for peace."

Nhat Chi Mai was a member of Nhat Hanh's Order of Interbeing, a Buddhist religious order dedicated to working for peace and unity among people. She was a talented young woman who wrote poetry and loved life. She spent the month leading up to her self-immolation with her parents and family, apparently wanting to gift them with happy memories of their final time spent together. She seemed so happy toward the end that her friends all thought she had fallen in love and was engaged to be married. In those final days, her mood, as Thich Nhat Hanh described it, was "honey and sweet rice." There was nothing neurotic or self-hating about her death, nor is it appropriate to consider it a suicide. It was an act of ultimate sacrifice made out of love and the desire for peace.

The South Vietnamese government tried to black out news of what had taken place in the nunnery courtyard, fearing that it would ignite anti-war sentiment. But word traveled fast. An estimated fifty thousand people marched in Nhat Chi Mai's funeral procession, and the Catholic and Buddhist communities in and around Saigon, inspired by her sacrifice, began collaborating with one another in opposing the war. Today, an urn marks the spot where she died.

17 May
Daniel Berrigan

9 May 1921—

Apologies, Good Friends

ONE OF THE VILEST "low-tech" weapons in the modern army's arsenal is napalm, a mixture of gas or petroleum, white phosphorus, and a thickening agent. Whether dropped as incendiary bombs or jetted in flamethrowers, napalm kills by burning its victims alive. Because of the phosphorus in it, it's difficult to wipe from skin and clothes. Once it makes contact, napalm will burn to the bone.

Napalm became a favorite weapon in the Vietnam War, dropped by the ton from American airplanes on jungle trails and camps as well as villages suspected of harboring the enemy. It killed indiscriminately, claiming women and children as well as Viet Cong; burnt forests, crops, and farm animals; and destroyed property.

On 17 May 1968, Jesuit priest Daniel Berrigan, his brother **Philip**, and seven other Catholic pacifists entered a municipal building in Catonsville, Maryland. They scooped nearly four hundred draft files into wicker baskets, took them outside, poured homemade napalm over them, and set them on fire. Then they prayed until the police arrived to arrest them on federal charges of violating the 1967 Selective Service Act. Dan Berrigan, who was sentenced to two years in prison for his "crime," later explained in free verse why he and his companions, who became known as the Catonsville 9, deliberately broke the law:

> Our apologies good friends
> for the fracture of good order the burning of paper
> instead of children the angering of the orderlies
> in the front parlor of the charnel house
> We could not so help us God do otherwise
> For we are sick at heart our hearts
> give us no rest for thinking of the Land of Burning Children

Berrigan, along with his brother Philip, has been fracturing good order for the sake of peace and justice ever since the Catonsville action. He has consistently witnessed against war, economic inequality, and political oppression, and he embraces a consistent ethic of life by also taking stands against capital punishment and abortion. In the heyday of the Cold War, he participated in anti-nuclear actions sponsored by the Plowshares Movement, cofounded by him and his brother. Taking the biblical injunction to hammer swords into plowshares seriously, people associated with the movement risked stiff prison sentences to symbolically hammer on nuclear warheads at military installations. As a Christian and person of conscience, Berrigan has never believed he had any other option than to be a peacemaker. As he says,

> Killing is disorder
> life and gentleness and community and unselfishness
> is the only order we recognize

18 May
Bertrand Russell

18 May 1872—2 February 1970

One or the Other

In 1966, an International War Crimes Tribunal convened to investigate charges that one of the world's nations was engaging in war-related crimes against humanity. The offenses included treaty violations, the use of chemical weapons, the torture of prisoners, the bombing of such civilian targets as hospitals, and the pursuit of genocidal policies. The tribunal was organized and headed by the British philosopher Bertrand Russell. The nation in the dock was the United States. The war in question was with Vietnam.

Americans were stunned. The International War Crimes Tribunal obviously evoked the Nuremberg Trials at the end of World War II, and the implied similarity between the United States and Nazi Germany, not to mention the guilty verdict rendered by the tribunal judges, were both infuriating and humiliating. Russell, however, made no apologies. The "arrogance" of U.S. leaders, he argued, had led them "to believe that they are above the law." But might didn't make right.

Russell's anti-war sentiments stretched as far back as the turn of the twentieth century, when he came to believe that "war is wrong and the use of force is to be deprecated." He resisted Britain's entry into World War I and agitated against the conflict throughout its duration, finally provoking a six-month jail sentence from the authorities. Seeing war clouds looming again in the 1920s and 1930s, Russell publicly criticized isolationism, arguing that it was built on the fear, pride, and greed that necessarily bred wars, and instead advocated the formation of an international peacekeeping force and a pledge for multilateral disarmament. When war broke out between Nazi Germany and the rest of the world, Russell reluctantly supported it, believing that Hitler had to be stopped. But he was convinced that Hitler's rise to power in the first place was facilitated by the refusal of the international community to come to Germany's economic aid. Had living conditions been less chaotic there between the wars, there would have been no vacuum in leadership and morale for a thug like Hitler to fill.

After the war ended, Russell turned his attention, especially during his final two decades, to anti-nuclear activism. The new weapons introduced at Hiroshima were, Russell correctly feared, capable of destroying humanity. "Either man will abolish war," he warned, "or war will abolish man." He recruited the world's top scientists to sign onto a public denunciation of nuclear weapons, and organized the Pugwash Conferences on Science and World Affairs, a Nobel Peace Prize–winning organization dedicated to eliminating nuclear arsenals. At the height of the Cold War, concluding that the growing nuclear threat called for direct action, he began calling for and practicing civil disobedience as a form of anti-nuclear witness. In 1963, he created the Bertrand Russell Peace Foundation, which worked both to draw attention to the threat of nuclear holocaust and to free political prisoners around the world. To the end of his long life, Russell continued speaking and acting for peace, convinced that the world had to choose either peace or destruction. It was one or the other.

19 May

Laozi

6TH CENTURY BCE

Wei Wu Wei

WE HUMANS ARE IMPATIENT creatures with a mania for control. We want things to get done quickly, and we want to be the persons who get them done. This go-get-'em attitude is especially characteristic of the American temperament, but it can be seen in all ages and all cultures of the world. We force things too quickly, not waiting for a natural unfolding to take place. We seem to have an aversion to simply letting things be.

Our impatient need to control things can create technologies that improve our lives. But it's also inflicted a lot of damage. Impatience and the will to control frequently lead to aggression against other people, animals, ideas, and the very planet itself. Our intentions may be noble and altruistic. But in our rush to dominate, we oppress people, inflict untold suffering and death on animals, condemn ideas with which we disagree, and pollute the earth.

The ancient Chinese sage Laozi, author of the Taoist text *Tao Te Ching*, advised us to calm down. According to him, the universe pulsates to the rhythm of the Tao, or the "Way." The Tao can't be seen, felt, described, or even thought. But it's the natural underlying order to which all things, when they're existing properly, conform. The Tao is the cosmic harmony that runs through all of creation and keeps everything in balance.

Our rush to "fix" things frequently upsets the Tao, throwing us off balance and creating destructive fragmentation in the world. Wars, famine, oppression, confusion, lusts, and negative emotions such as fear and hatred are the products of human impetuosity that disturb the natural rhythm. The wise person knows that it is in his or her best interests, not to mention the interests of everything else, to cooperate with the Tao rather than run against it. Harmony with the Tao, or what Laozi called *ziran*, means living in such a way as to relinquish aggressive drives, impatience, and the urge to run ahead of the game. Instead, steadiness and calmness are cultivated.

The goal, ultimately, is to achieve a state of equilibrium in which *wei wu wei*, or "action without action," becomes habitual. The practitioner of this kind of action lives simply in order to be receptive to the Tao; practices nonviolence in order to harmonize with the currents of the Tao; and flows with the moment rather than trying to freeze-frame and control it. The point is to let the Tao be, and in so doing to eliminate the destructiveness that erupts from either ignoring it or trying to force it. Laozi doesn't advocate passivity or indifference to the world. On the contrary, his hope is to awaken a sharper awareness of the beauty of creation and the joys of a simple, nonaggressive life, while at the same time nurturing a greater sensitivity to the suffering of others. As he wrote, "Simplicity, patience, compassion. These three are your greatest treasures. Simple in actions and thoughts, you return to the source of being. Patient with both friends and enemies, you accord with the way things are. Compassionate toward yourself, you reconcile all beings in the world."

20 May
Wei Jingsheng

20 May 1950—

The Fifth Modernization

In 1963 Zhou Enlai, Premier of the People's Republic of China and Mao Zedong's right-hand man, introduced a program intended to make China an economic world power. The program came to be known as the Four Modernizations, named after the four areas of commerce stressed by Zhou: agriculture, industry, science and technology, and national defense. It was left to Deng Xiaoping, who succeeded Zhou, to ramp up the campaign by accelerating China's volume of foreign trade.

In 1978, in the midst of the short-lived "Beijing Spring" period in which Chinese dissenters were allowed some degree of freedom to criticize their government, a young electrician who worked at the Beijing Zoo named Wei Jingsheng galvanized the nation by publicly posting a document titled "The Fifth Modernization." It was an eloquent plea for the addition of one more national goal: democracy. The document also blasted Deng with sarcastic innuendoes, basically calling him a dictator and implying that he was a "political swindler."

In "The Fifth Modernization," Wei declared that the Chinese government was an "autocracy" that denied people the right to be "masters of their own destiny." What's the point of economic wealth—the focus of the first four modernizations—without "true democracy"? "We want a modern lifestyle and democracy for the people. Freedom and happiness are our sole objectives in accomplishing modernization. Without this fifth modernization all others are merely another promise." As Wei saw it, true democracy "means the right of the people to choose their own representatives to work according to their will and in their interests. Only this can be called democracy. Furthermore, the people must also have the power to replace their representatives anytime so that these representatives cannot go on deceiving them in the name of the people." In true democracies, Wei observed, citizens have the right to openly criticize their leaders. But in China, a dissenter risks legal retribution. "Jail will be ready for him with open door and various unpredictable calamities may befall him."

Wei knew that in publishing his appeal for democracy, the very legal retribution he wrote about would likely befall him. He wasn't mistaken. Arrested shortly after "The Fifth Modernization" appeared, Wei was convicted on the trumped-up charge of selling military secrets to Britain and sentenced to fifteen years in prison. His arrest also spelled the end of the Beijing Spring. Wei was released one year short of his full term, largely through U.S. President Bill Clinton's intercession. But less than a year later he was back in prison for speaking out about human rights abuses in China. This time he served three years before he was suddenly deported to the United States, again through Clinton's intercession, where he's lived ever since and continues advocating for human rights.

21 May
Elizabeth Fry

21 May 1780—12 October 1845

The Angel of Prisons

London's Newgate prison in the eighteenth and nineteenth centuries was an abysmal place. Housing both felons and debtors, with a gallows on the grounds from which condemned men and women were frequently hanged before enthusiastic crowds, the place was deliberately kept filthy and cramped as a deterrent to crime. Unless prisoners were able to pay for better accommodations, they slept on filthy straw in damp, packed cells and were given just enough to eat to keep them alive. Debtors frequently brought their entire families with them to Newgate because there was nowhere else for their children to go. A large women's section held up to three hundred inmates.

In 1813, Quaker Elizabeth Fry was feeling at loose ends. She had birthed her eighth and final child the year before. She was financially comfortable, the daughter of one banker and the wife of another. Looking around for opportunities for charity work, she decided, on the urging of an acquaintance, to visit the women's cells at Newgate. What she saw shocked her and changed her life. Women walked around in filthy clothes, shrieking or cursing and neglecting their children. Some of the inmates were obviously insane. And everywhere there was "swearing, gaming, and fighting." There was also a lot of singing and dancing, which offended Fry's somewhat prudish Quaker sensibilities.

Still, she had found something she could devote herself to: prison reform. During the next few years, the trajectory of her prison work moved from delivering clothes and food to individual prisoners to lobbying Parliament to rethink the way England treated its prisoners. Her cries for prison reform made her so well known that she was actually invited to testify before Parliament in 1818, the first time a woman had ever done so. While there, she took the opportunity to blast capital punishment, an offense that at the time could be handed down by an English court for any one of over two hundred offenses. She continued her criticism of the death penalty in a 1827 book that recorded her observations of various prisons around England. In it she also noted that women and the poor, having little in the way of legal rights, were especially persecuted under the nation's penal code.

Fry's agitation for prison reform was well received by many in England, including no less a person than Queen Victoria herself, and it wasn't long before the press was calling her the "Angel of Prisons." But in 1828, Fry's campaign was almost derailed by her husband's abrupt bankruptcy. Her family was thrown into penury and debt—one of the crimes that could earn someone a sentence in Newgate—and her husband was disowned by London's Quakers for financial malfeasance. Were it not for her brother, she and her children would have been left in deep want. One can only imagine that Fry's own experience of unexpected poverty and social disgrace deepened her compassion for the prisoners for whom she continued to advocate once her own crisis had been resolved.

22 May

Betty Williams

22 May 1943—

Peace People

Rarely a day went by during the Troubles, that period of violence and turmoil in Northern Ireland that spanned the last three decades of the twentieth century, when tragedy didn't hit at least one family. Irish Republican Army soldiers and Protestant paramilitary ones kidnapped or killed one another as British soldiers unsuccessfully tried to keep peace. Women, children, and noncombatant men too frequently got caught in the crossfire. Surprise bombings of public houses and vehicles terrorized everyone.

But in 1976, the people of Belfast, mobilized by Betty Williams, publicly declared that they'd had enough of the killing. In August of that year, a young IRA man by the name of Danny Lennon was shot and killed by British troops as he tried to speed away from them in his car. His runaway vehicle careened onto the sidewalk and into a family of four, killing all three children and severely injuring their mother. Betty Williams heard the crash and rushed to the scene. She was sickened by what she saw.

The carnage of that August day was the tipping point for Williams. Like many other natives of Belfast, she had been personally affected by the Troubles. Coming from an extended family of Catholics as well as Protestants, she had lost two cousins, one from each religion, in the civil war. Other relatives of hers, including a grandfather, had been intimidated or beaten at various times. Each time she'd kept her head down. This time she didn't.

Williams immediately began to circulate a petition that called for an end to the violence ripping Belfast apart. In just a few hours after the horrible accident over six thousand people had signed it. One of the children's aunts, Mairead Corrigan, and a reporter, Ciaran McKeown, joined with Williams, and together they founded Peace People, a grassroots organization dedicated to bringing peace to Northern Ireland. Their call for peace rallied over ten thousand people to the children's funeral the following week. A few days later, nearly forty thousand more joined them in a peace march through the streets of Belfast. They were all Peace People. Like Betty Williams, they had long craved an end to the sectarian violence but had been afraid to speak out against it. Now, they mobilized.

Participants at that peace march signed onto a declaration that affirmed that they wanted "to live and love and build a just and peaceful society" for themselves and their children. They also affirmed their dedication to building peace by pledging to "work with their neighbors, near and far."

Williams and Corrigan were awarded the 1976 Nobel Peace Prize for their efforts to rally Peace People against violence. In her acceptance speech, Williams noted that the kind of nonviolent resistance practiced by Peace People demands that "we believe in the most energetic reconciliation among peoples by getting them to know each other, talk each other's languages, understand each other's fears and beliefs, getting to know each other physically, philosophically and spiritually."

23 May
Max Walters

23 May 1920—11 December 2005

Growing Peace

As a boy in Yorkshire, Max Walters grew to love the beauty of the moors and the growing things that made their home there. He acquired a green thumb at an early age, delighting in the quiet and simple tasks of nurturing life in the family garden. When World War II erupted, Walters found himself unable to endorse its wholesale destruction. His Christian faith, he believed, precluded him from participating in violence. Declaring himself a conscientious objector, he spent the war years as a hospital orderly. He later said that he derived great spiritual comfort during that dark time from T. S. Eliot's *Four Quartets*.

When peace returned, Walters studied botany at Cambridge University. As a student, he joined the Fellowship of Reconciliation and the Campaign for Nuclear Disarmament, and remained active in them his entire adult life. After taking his degree, he lectured at Cambridge and eventually became director of the University Botanic Garden. The high-water mark of his academic career was supervising a research team that compiled a taxonomic record of all European plant species.

Walters' dedication to peacemaking remained strong throughout his long life and led to his involvement, when he was in his seventies, in a humanitarian project. The Bosnian War that raged between 1992 and 1995 destroyed the botanical gardens in Sarajevo. Laid out in 1913, the pre-war gardens boasted three thousand species of plants and eight hundred species of trees and bushes. They had an arboretum and numerous greenhouses, and offered dozens of educational opportunities for students and visitors. But the fighting during the siege of Sarajevo nearly destroyed the gardens. Over four hundred shells exploded in them, damaging or killing every tree or bush. Volunteers tried desperately to save what seeds and plantings they could. But when the hostilities finally ended, the gardens were a wreck.

For Walters, the tranquility experienced in a well-cultivated garden was a symbol of the nonviolence he'd practiced and quietly proclaimed his entire life. So he put together another team, the members of which included his son, Martin, to collect cash, books, plants, and seeds to restore the Sarajevo botanical gardens. His efforts paid off. The gardens reopened in 2002, and the grateful people of the city erected a fountain in honor of Walters. But the real monument to this grower of peace was the restored botanical gardens themselves.

24 May
Harry Emerson Fosdick

24 May 1878—5 October 1969

War Prostitutes the Noblest Ideals

During his long career in ministry, Harry Emerson Fosdick's nationally broadcast radio addresses and fifty-plus books make him one of the best known preachers in America. Longtime pastor of New York's Riverside Church, he was a champion of progressive Christianity, doing battle with biblical fundamentalism as well as racism and injustice.

But a sermon that he delivered in November 1921 when he was pastor of a Presbyterian church so shocked his congregation that they soon ousted him from the pulpit. The immediate occasion for the sermon was the national dedication of the Tomb of the Unknown Soldier, the ceremonial burial of an unidentified victim of World War I.

Fosdick, who had served as an army chaplain in that war and regularly had given morale-boosting talks to troops about to go over the top, told his congregation a horrifying tale he had heard from a veteran. At an officer's mess one night during the war, the veteran recalled, "there was great laughter at the story of one of our men who had spent his last cartridge in defending an attack. 'Hand me down your spade, Mike,' he said; and as six Germans came one by one round the end of a traverse, he split each man's skull open with a deadly blow."

Fosdick, whose war experiences converted him to pacifism—previously, he told his congregation, he had been "a gullible fool" who actually believed that "modern war could somehow make the world safe for democracy"—told the story to illustrate one of his fundamental objections to war. Like the ancient Hebrew sacrifice of unblemished animals at the temple altar, young and healthy men were offered up at the altar of modern war. These youths generally brought high ideals to the battlefield. Like the young Fosdick, they believed that war, horrible as it is, could serve good ends, and they were eager to offer their bit. But the inescapable brutality of battle so corrupts even the highest ideals that soldiers reach the point where they cynically laugh at tales of bloody-handed slaughter, and civilians back home repeat the same tales as examples of battlefield valor. "I watched," Fosdick told his congregation, "as war lay its hands on these strongest, loveliest things in men and used the noblest attributes of the human spirit for what ungodly deeds! Is there anything more infernal than this, to take the best that is in man and use it to do what war does? This is the ultimate description of war—it is the prostitution of the noblest powers of the human soul to the most dastardly deeds, the most abysmal cruelties of which our human nature is capable. That *is* war."

If war were "fought simply with evil things like hate," said Fosdick, it would be bad enough. "But when one sees the deeds of war done with the loveliest faculties of the human spirit, he looks into the very pit of hell." The conclusion, for the Reverend Fosdick, was clear. We can have the "monstrous thing" of war, or we can have Christ. "But we cannot have both."

25 MAY
David Dellinger

22 AUGUST 1915—25 MAY 2004

Fraternity and Resistance

HE DESCRIBED HIS ROLE as "the older brother siding with the rebellious younger child against his parents." David Dellinger, one of the most committed and active pacifists the United States has ever produced, was referring to the part he played as a member of the Chicago Eight, the group of war protesters that disrupted the 1968 Democrat Convention in Chicago and whose conviction on conspiracy charges was eventually overthrown. Dellinger was considerably older than the other members of the Chicago Eight; his pacifist commitment stretched back to before most of them were born.

The son of a wealthy and conservative Massachusetts attorney, Dellinger became an advocate of what he usually called "radical" or "revolutionary" pacifism while a student at Yale. His revolutionary zeal for social change was fueled by his participation in unionization demonstrations, summer work in factories, and time spent riding the rails with hoboes. But he became a pacifist after punching someone during a brawl at a football game and feeling overwhelmed with remorse and shame. "The lesson I learned was as simple, direct and unarguable as the lesson a child learns the first time it puts its hand on a red-hot stove. Don't ever do it again!"

When World War II erupted, Dellinger refused to register for the draft and wound up serving three years in prison as a conscientious objector. After his release, he joined with **A. J. Muste** and **Dorothy Day** to launch the magazine *Direct Action*. Over the next three decades, he combined activism with progressive journalism, editing several other journals, most notably *Liberation*. In the years leading up to the Vietnam War, Dellinger was especially involved in the anti-nuclear movement. After the war started, in addition to his participation in the Chicago Eight demonstrations, he visited North Vietnam to negotiate for the release of captured American GIs. During the final two decades of his life, his focus was on Native American rights and the dangers of corporate globalization.

Throughout his long career as an activist, Dellinger remained faithful to the pacifism he had embraced as a Yale student. He believed that there were two "weapons of the spirit" in the pacifist arsenal: fraternity and resistance. The first involved an embrace of all peoples as brothers and sisters equally deserving of justice. The second involved methods of nonviolently opposing and counteracting. Pacifism isn't a passive kind of feel-goodism. "Commitment to nonviolence must not be based on patient acquiescence in intolerable conditions." Instead, "true pacifists are uncompromising fighters against fascism, totalitarianism, and every form of injustice and oppression." When the injustices are especially egregious, the temptation to resort to the "quick fix" of violent retaliation can be nearly overwhelming. But the true pacifist realizes "the self-defeating, self-corrupting effect of lapses into violence." Nonviolent action aims not to bring about a situation in which there are clear-cut losers and winners, but rather to liberate both victims and aggressors. It seeks to disarm all parties in order to build fraternity—a goal that Dellinger saw as genuinely revolutionary.

26 May

Utah Phillips

15 May 1935—23 May 2008

Pacifist Hobo

THE MOMENT OF TRUTH for Utah Phillips—born Bruce Duncan Phillips in Cleveland, Ohio, but later changing his name to reflect his adopted state—came during an army tour of duty in Korea. Sent there just after the war ended, he was shocked by the destruction and poverty he encountered. "It was absolutely life amid the ruins," he recalled in an interview shortly before his death. "Children crying—that's [my] memory of Korea. Devastation. I saw an elegant and ancient culture in a small Asian country devastated by the impact of cultural and economic imperialism. And the impact of an army of young men given unlimited license for excess of every kind, of violence, sex, booze, what have you, drugs—a blueprint for self-destruction. And I knew that if I endured that, I would perish, I would simply perish."

After his discharge from the army, Phillips made his way to Salt Lake City, where he worked with pacifist **Ammon Hennacy** at the Joe Hill Catholic Worker House for the next eight years. Even though he considered himself an anarchist, he ran for public office as a protest candidate in 1968 and 1976 in order to secure a platform for his anti-militarist and pro-union convictions. However, he always advised people to vote with their bodies and not just their ballots, to accept personal responsibility for ending injustice rather than handing it off to elected officials.

But Phillips' primary way of advocating pacifism and workers' rights was through song. Raised in a leftist family, he early on joined the Industrial Workers of the World (IWW), the anarchist labor union, and remained a card-carrying Wobbly for over half a century. Leaving home at an early age, he rode the rails across the country, working odd jobs along the way and sleeping rough in the countryside. He met hundreds of fellow hobos and picked up scores of working men's and folk songs from them. A skilled ukulele player from childhood, Phillips began performing the old songs he'd learned, as well as ones he'd written himself, in Salt Lake City coffeehouses. It wasn't long before he was touring the country doing benefit concerts for labor unions and progressive groups. His repertoire included such Wobbly favorites as "Hallelujah, I'm a Bum!" and "Joe Hill," ballads he'd learned while hoboing around the country.

One of Phillips' best-known compositions is "Enola Gay," a commemoration of the atomic bombing of Hiroshima and Nagasaki in which Japanese schoolchildren are hauntingly invited to look up "from their play" as the Enola Gay, the airplane that dropped the bomb, rains fire and destruction upon them. "Your bright young eyes will turn to ashes in the blinding light of Enola Gay," sang Phillips. His life's ambition was to try to ensure through song and story that no future Enola Gays would drop death on other children.

27 MAY
Julia Ward Howe

27 May 1819—17 October 1910

What Mother's Day Was Meant to Be

MOTHER'S DAY HAS BECOME one of the most commercialized holidays in the United States, a country that commercializes *all* its holidays. Americans spend over $4 billion each Mother's Day on flowers, gifts, and syrupy cards. The advertising blitzkrieg leading up to Mother's Day, and the colossal volume of sales it generates, lead many people to suspect that the holiday is nothing but a marketing gimmick invented by the retail industry.

But not so. The holiday is real—it was signed into law by President Woodrow Wilson in 1914—and its original intent was quite different from the saccharine shopfest it's become. Far from being a gimmick, Mother's Day was supposed to be a cry on the part of mothers across the world for an end to war.

Ironically, it was the author of "The Battle Hymn of the Republic," one of the most popular and bellicose songs of the Civil War, who first championed the idea of a day on which mothers called for peace. Julia Ward Howe, a Bostonian poet, author, abolitionist, and society wife, published the patriotic song in 1862 as a rallying cry for the North at a low point in the war.

But after the war, sickened by its carnage, Howe became an ardent pacifist. In 1870, she wrote the "Mother's Day Proclamation," which opened with "Arise, then, women of this day!" The proclamation encouraged all women to refuse their husbands caresses and approval when they come "reeking with carnage" and to refuse to give up their sons to the military, in which they will "unlearn all that we have been able to teach them of charity, mercy, and patience." Men believe that honor must be defended with sword and gun. But "blood does not wipe out dishonor, nor violence indicate possession." So it's up to women everywhere to cry, "Disarm! Disarm! The sword of murder is not the balance of justice!" Howe goes on to call for a "general congress of women without nationality" to promote peace and nonviolent resolution of international conflict. Given her faith in the ability of mothers to counterbalance the warlike tendencies of men, it's not surprising that Howe also became an outspoken champion of women's suffrage.

After writing the "Mother's Day Proclamation," Howe went on speaking tours across the United States and Britain to promote the idea. By 1873, nearly twenty cities in the United States, as well as Rome and Constantinople, celebrated Mother's Day. But Howe wasn't successful in getting national recognition for the holiday, which didn't come until four years after her death. Even though the modern holiday isn't at all what she envisioned, the concluding hope of her proclamation still inspires. "Let [mothers] solemnly take counsel with each other, as the means whereby the great human family can live in peace, and each bearing after her own time the sacred impress, not of Caesar, but of God."

28 May

Rachel Carson

27 May 1907—14 April 1964

Choosing the Right Road

SHORTLY AFTER WORLD WAR II, the U.S. chemical industry introduced a slogan it hoped would become a post-war mantra: "Better living through chemicals." For an entire generation, chemical pesticides, herbicides, and fertilizers became the order of the day. One of the favorite pesticides was DDT, a compound that had been used with great success during the war to keep down mosquito-borne malaria and lice-borne typhus among troops. After the war, DDT was used commercially to control insects, especially fire ants, on American farms. It was typically sprayed over fields by crop dusters.

But there were warning signs for those who chose to see them. The widespread use of DDT was beginning to damage biological populations for which it wasn't intended. Birds in particular were affected; toxic levels of DDT killed chicks in their shells before they could hatch.

Although a few biologists tried to draw attention to the hazards involved in DDT spraying, it wasn't until the 1962 appearance of Rachel Carson's *Silent Spring* that the possibility of widespread chemical poisoning was taken seriously. In the book, Carson carefully exposed the effects of DDT and other pesticides on insects, mammals, amphibians, birds, mammals, and humans. Because of their indiscriminate killing range, she preferred to call chemical pesticides "biocides." The title of her book gestured at more than the horrible possibility of a spring without birdsong. It was also a chilling way of warning about a disastrous breakdown of ecosystems if chemical pesticides continued to be used indiscriminately as "weapons" against nature.

Part of the reason *Silent Spring* finally drew public attention to the dangers of artificial pesticides was Carson's talent as a writer of popular science. She was already famous because of an enthusiastically received trilogy on marine biology she had published between 1941 and 1955. The beauty of her prose in *Silent Spring*, even as she warned of looming environmental disaster, captivated her readers.

Although Carson was immediately concerned with pesticides in *Silent Spring*, she prepared the way for a total rethinking of our responsibilities to nature. Since the industrial revolution, she argued, when humankind's "announced goal" became the "conquest of nature," a "depressing record of destruction" has been set. The thoughtlessly exuberant use of chemical pesticides—"nothing must get in the way of the man with the spray gun"—was just the latest chapter of that conquest. But, Carson assured her readers, the assault against nature could be halted and reversed. "We stand now," she wrote, "where two roads diverge. The road we have long been traveling is deceptively easy, a smooth superhighway on which we progress with great speed, but at its end lies disaster. The other fork of the road—the one 'less traveled by'—offers our last, our only chance to reach a destination that assures the preservation of our earth."

In writing these words, Rachel Carson launched the environmental movement.

29 May
Leó Szilárd

11 February 1898—30 May 1964

Principle, Not Expediency

As he tells it, the Hungarian physicist Leó Szilárd first conceived of the possibility of a nuclear chain reaction while standing on a London street corner. That was in 1933, shortly after he fled from Nazi Germany. Six years later, with Europe in the midst of World War II and Szilárd anxiously aware that German scientists were trying to make nuclear weapons, he urged **Albert Einstein** to warn President Franklin Roosevelt. Roosevelt agreed to fund nuclear research, and within two years Szilárd and his colleagues successfully created a chain reaction at the University of Chicago, a necessary condition for weaponizing the atom.

Szilárd reluctantly collaborated with the Manhattan Project, the U.S.-sponsored effort to build an atomic bomb, because he worried about Nazis winning the nuclear race. But as soon as Germany surrendered, he began urging restraint. He coauthored the Franck Report, a letter signed by several nuclear physicists in June 1945 recommending that the newly developed atomic bomb not be used as a weapon against Japan. Truman, of course, ignored the plea. Szilárd was so disgusted by the devastation caused by the nuclear strikes on Hiroshima and Nagasaki that he left physics and devoted the rest of his scientific career to biology. During the Cold War, he was the subject of continuous FBI surveillance.

The main reason for the FBI interest in Szilárd is that he became a social activist who spoke across the country advocating nuclear arms control. As early as 1947 he called upon world leaders to dismantle nuclear weapons, and he was instrumental in the formation of the Pugwash Conference, a gathering in which scientists from around the world regularly meet and exchange ideas about how to harness science in the service of peace.

Szilárd also became a vocal advocate of a unified world government because he was convinced that global cooperation was the only safeguard against potentially nuclear clashes between different countries. Truman's decision to drop atom bombs on Japan as well as the subsequent nuclear race between the superpowers made Szilárd distrustful of patriotism. In an interview given four years before his death, he noted, "By and large, governments are guided by considerations of expediency rather than by moral considerations. And this, I think, is a universal law of how governments act. Prior to the war I had the illusion that up to a point the American Government was different. This illusion was gone after Hiroshima." A single world government, he hoped, would be better able to base decisions on moral principle rather than expediency.

To the end of his days, Szilárd never underestimated the horrific killing power of so-called conventional weapons, and often cited the loss of life in Dresden and Tokyo caused by incendiary bombs. But atomic weapons, he believed, were something else entirely—a "new force of nature for the purpose of destruction," as he said. He had helped uncap that force in the 1930s and early 1940s, and he devoted the final twenty years of his life to trying to put it back in the bottle.

30 May

Ruth Manorama

30 May 1952—

Defender of the Dalits among the Dalits

Today in the Indian subcontinent, there are over two hundred million Dalits, or people who belong to the caste commonly called "untouchable." The Sanskrit word *Dalit* means "ground up," "suppressed," or "broken to pieces," suggesting the contempt with which members of the caste have been regarded. Traditionally performers of "impure" labor such as butchering and latrine cleaning, Dalits are now legally protected from discrimination by India's constitution. But prejudice against them remains strong, especially in rural India.

Ruth Manorama, herself born into the Dalit caste, has spent her adulthood trying to improve the living conditions of one group of Dalit people in particular: the eighty million untouchable women. She calls them the Dalits among the Dalits because they suffer discrimination three times over: first because of their caste, second because of their gender, and third because of the grinding poverty they typically endure as a result of their caste and gender. As Manorama points out, these women "are denied their dignity, livelihood and social security and everything that is humane and just." Sexual violence against them is especially common.

Born in southern India, Manorama, who converted to Christianity while a teenager, earned a graduate degree in social work before embarking on her advocacy for Dalit women. In the mid-1980s she collaborated in a research project that compared the living conditions of Indian Dalit women and African American women, and she was struck by the similarity of discrimination endured by both groups. A couple of years later she began mobilizing slum-dwelling Dalit women into massive demonstrations aimed at drawing public attention to their economic and social plight. She helped organize the National Federation of Dalit Women in 1995 and raised international awareness of the discrimination against Dalit women by making sure that the issue became a centerpiece of the UNESCO-sponsored World Conference Against Racism held in 2001 in Durban, South Africa. In recognition of her work, Manorama was given the 2006 Right Livelihood Award, known as the alternative Nobel Peace Prize.

Manorama believes that her advocacy for Dalit women has global implications. Because they have suffered so much from discrimination, poverty, and violence, the female untouchables of India are in a privileged position to empathize with other victims throughout the world. As Manorama says, "Dalit women's rights are a global responsibility. Our sufferings encourage us to have a common cause with other oppressed and struggling people of the world. We as Dalit women pledge ourselves to liberate all our people from continuing bondage of poverty, deprivation, suffering, gender and other discrimination."

31 May
Jean-Pierre Willem

24 May 1938—

Founder of Barefoot Doctors

IN THE EARLY 1960s, the People's Republic of China had a big problem: too few doctors (around forty thousand) and too many patients (over five hundred million). Moreover, most of the nation's doctors were centered in urban areas, whereas most of China's inhabitants lived in the country. So in 1965, Mao had a great idea: give rural healers a three- or four-month crash course in basic medicine, let them combine their new skills with tried and tested local folk remedies and herbal medicines, and set them loose. These "barefoot doctors," as they came to be called, were a huge success—so much so that five years later the United Nations' World Health Organization recommended barefoot doctors for all developing nations.

Dr. Jean-Pierre Willem, a French-born and trained physician, had firsthand acquaintance with the need for local healers to make up for the lack of university-trained physicians. In 1959, while still in medical school, he traveled with other French students to Algeria to provide medical care for locals caught in the middle of that nation's civil war. Five years later he worked a few months at Albert Schweitzer's clinic in Gabon, Africa, before moving on to another clinic in Rwanda. In the 1970s he spent nearly a year in Laos.

Willem's experiences in these countries confirmed his sense that developing nations were woefully short of trained physicians. As a result, thousands of people, especially children, died each day of easily treatable illnesses. His time abroad also convinced him that there was a wealth of medical knowledge that the West could learn from local healers. They were familiar with plants and insects in their areas that had medicinal value that conventional medicine knew nothing about, and they were experts about the diseases and illnesses to which their own people were especially susceptible. Additionally, Willem recognized that local medicine practiced in Asia and Africa tended to take a comprehensively different view of human health. Unlike Western medicine's focus on specialization, traditional medicine tends to adopt a broader perspective. Willem was convinced that organizing local healers, supplementing their skills with supplies and a bit of training, and encouraging them to circuit ride throughout their regions, offering medical assistance, would benefit local peoples, just as Mao's barefoot doctors program had. He was also confident that Western physicians could learn much from working with traditional practitioners.

So in 1987, Willem founded the international NGO *Medecins aux Pieds Nur* (MAPN), or "Barefoot Doctors," to offer medical assistance to the developing world. MAPN advocates the basic right to health care of all people by encouraging local practitioners in regions without physicians. With programs in Burundi, Guatemala, Vietnam, Colombia, Brazil, Togo, Niger, and Peru, Barefoot Doctors offers healing and hope to the developing world.

1 June

Mary Dyer

CA. 1611—1 JUNE 1660

Quaker Martyr

A QUICK PERUSAL OF human history reveals how much violence religious intolerance has spawned. Nearly all faith traditions have been guilty at one time or another of breaking God's peace by persecuting dissenters within their own ranks or declaring war against outside "infidels." Happily, every age also produces courageous persons of faith who counterbalance these misguided crusades by championing freedom of conscience through their actions and their words. The Quaker Mary Dyer, who was hanged by authorities in the Massachusetts Bay Colony for her defense of religious liberty, is one of them.

We don't know much about Mary's early and middle years. Married in London in 1633 to William Dyer, the couple migrated soon afterwards to Boston to join the Puritan community established there a generation earlier. In 1637, Mary became involved in the Anne Hutchinson controversy. Hutchinson riled Puritan officials by teaching the primacy of individual conscience over clerical authority and was eventually banished from the Massachusetts Bay Colony. When she resettled in Rhode Island, Mary apparently followed her, at least for a while.

Seventeen years later, on a trip back to England with her husband, Mary was converted to Quakerism by **George Fox**. William, who remained a Puritan and almost certainly condemned Mary's decision, went back to Boston without her. After a few years of preaching in England, Mary returned to Boston in 1658 and publicly protested a recent law banning Quakers—whose beliefs uncomfortably reminded Puritan officials of Anne Hutchinson's teachings—from the Massachusetts Bay Colony. Mary was arrested, banished from the colony, and warned not to return. But return she did, and the second time she was arrested she was condemned to death. Only the intervention of her son saved her. Banished again, she eventually returned to Boston, saying that she was duty-bound to protest any law that forbade freedom of conscience. Arrested once more, she was charged with "rebellion, sedition, and presumptuous intruding upon us," and sentenced to death. This time the sentence was carried out. As she was led to the scaffold erected on Boston Common, drums were beaten by militia to drown out any words she might say to the onlookers. But one of her guards, who begged her to repent and save her life as he led her to the scaffold, reported her final words. "I came to keep bloodguiltiness from you," Mary told him, "desiring you to repeal the unrighteous and unjust law made against the innocent servants of the Lord. Nay, man, I am not now to repent."

King Charles II was horrified when he learned of Mary's execution, and soon issued a decree forbidding the execution of Quakers and other dissenters. Thirty years after her death, Parliament passed the Toleration Act, which guaranteed freedom of worship and conscience to all "nonconformist" Protestants who did not belong to the Church of England.

2 JUNE
John XXIII

25 NOVEMBER 1881—3 JUNE 1963

Defender of the Commonweal

THE PAPACY OF JOHN XXIII was short, but his accomplishments during the nearly five years he sat on Peter's Throne are breathtaking. Although elected as a stopgap pope, John inaugurated the Second Vatican Council, which brought the fresh wind of *aggiornamento* to the Catholic Church. Two months before his death, he released an encyclical, *Pacem in Terris (Peace on Earth)*, which was both an eloquently forceful defense of Christian nonviolence and a timely plea for the Cold War superpowers to pull back from the brink of nuclear disaster before it was too late. It is one of the Church's greatest documents on social justice.

John broke with tradition by addressing *Pacem in Terris* to "all men of good will" rather than only to Roman Catholics. There was good reason for this: the encyclical argues that peace is possible in the world only when nations adopt global rather than narrowly nationalistic perspectives. Political leaders should focus on promoting the commonweal, or "universal common good," and this calls for an end to economic, ethnic, and social inequality. As John wrote, "The fact is that no one can be by nature superior to his fellows, since all men are equally noble in natural dignity. And consequently there are no differences at all between political communities from the point of view of natural dignity." Granted, some individuals are richer than others, just as some nations are wealthier than others. But "that is no valid argument in favor of a system whereby those who are in a position of superiority impose their will arbitrarily on others." On the contrary, the pope wrote, positions of authority bring "a greater share in the common responsibility to help others to reach perfection by their mutual efforts."

One of the greatest threats to global commonweal, John insisted, was the proliferation of nuclear weapons. Their development and maintenance siphon off money that could be used to finance social programs, and their very presence encourages suspicion and enmity between nations. Moreover, their destructive capability is unimaginably horrific. "Hence justice, right reason, and the recognition of man's dignity cry out insistently for a cessation to the arms race." Nuclear weapons should be banned from the face of the earth. Stockpiles of conventional weapons "must be reduced all round and simultaneously by the parties concerned." Nor can the decision be left entirely in the hands of political leaders. Citizens from every nation around the world must "sincerely cooperate in the effort to banish fear" of nuclear holocaust, and this can be done only when hearts and minds are converted to a new vision of peace based not upon the stockpiling of weapons but upon "mutual trust." Only then, John beautifully concluded, will we become "more and more conscious of being living members of the universal family of mankind."

3 June

Satish Kumar

3 June 1935—

Renouncing Realism

WHEN HE WAS IN his mid-twenties, Indian-born Satish Kumar heard that philosopher **Bertrand Russell**, then ninety years old, had been sent to prison for protesting nuclear weapons. Kumar, who came from a Jain background and was a disciple of **Vinoba Bhave**, **Mohandas Gandhi**'s spiritual successor, had long revered all life and practiced nonviolence. But inspired by Russell's example, he felt the need to publicly witness for peace to a world bristling with nuclear weapons.

Along with a friend, Kumar settled on the idea of making a peace walk from Bangalore to the capitals of the four nuclear superpowers: Moscow, Paris, London, and Washington, DC. Following the advice of Bhave, the two youths traveled without passports or money and vowed to keep to a vegetarian diet. Being penniless, they would rely on the hospitality of strangers, with whom they could talk about nonviolence. Refusing meat, they could explain to their hosts that nonviolence meant living at peace with nature as well as with one's fellow humans.

The eight-thousand-mile journey took nearly three years. Kumar and his companion met hundreds of people from different cultures and all walks of life and discovered that "when you dig down, dig deep, and touch the humanity, they are the same everywhere." But they also learned that a genuine meeting of hearts and minds required giving up prejudgments and labels. "If I went as an Indian waving the flag of India, I would meet a Pakistani. If I went as a Hindu, saying that Hinduism is the most supreme religion in the world, I would meet a Christian or a Muslim saying, 'No, no, no! You've got it wrong. We have got the best religion.' If I go as a Socialist I'll meet a Capitalist. If I go as a brown man I'll meet a black man or white man. But if I go as a human being I'll meet only human beings."

Critics during and after Kumar's epic peace walk accused him of being naïve or unrealistic. What good does walking for peace accomplish? His response is that realism is an "outdated and overplayed" concept. "Look at what realists have done for us. They have led us to war and climate change, poverty on an unimaginable scale, and wholesale ecological destruction. Half of humanity goes to bed hungry because of all the realistic leaders in the world."

For the last thirty years, Kumar has been one of the leading voices in the international green movement. Now living in England, he edits *Resurgence,* a journal devoted to ecological sustainability, social justice, and spiritual values. His vision is "what I would call a new trinity, a 'soil, soul, society' philosophy—soil for the environment, soul for the spiritual dimension, and society for the social justice that is essential."

4 June
Jim Wallis

4 June 1948—

Poverty Is the New Slavery

ALMOST SINGLE-HANDEDLY, JIM WALLIS, Christian author, activist, and editor of *Sojourners* magazine, has transformed American evangelicalism. For more than forty years, he's chipped away at the militarism and social conservatism of evangelicals, reminding them that Christian discipleship requires creatively nonviolent resistance to unjust institutions. He worries that traditional evangelicals, obsessed as they are with sexual morality, too frequently ignore core biblical themes. "There are thousands of bible verses on poverty," he notes, "but only about twelve on homosexuality." Poverty is the "new slavery. Poverty and global inequality are the fundamental moral issues of our time." Wallis's firm stand has prompted many, admirers and critics alike, to place him on the left end of the political spectrum. But Wallis rejects such labeling, preferring to call himself a "progressive evangelical."

Raised in a Plymouth Brethren household, Wallis collaborated in 1971 with a few fellow seminarians at Trinity Evangelical Divinity School to found a Christian intentional community called Sojourners. The community also launched a magazine of the same name. Sojourners relocated three years later to inner-city Washington, DC, where it still maintains a program of social outreach. As spokesperson for the community, Wallis early on earned a national reputation for his outspoken criticism of American militarism and his equally passionate advocacy of civil rights and anti-poverty programs.

Wallis's prophetic social commentary is based upon what he sees as the core of the "good news" of Christianity. In his judgment, the life, teachings, death, and resurrection of Jesus highlight a struggle against the powers of destruction and death, demonic as well as human, which seek to stunt human well-being and block a proper relationship with God. Jesus' ministry from first to last was aimed at liberation from these powers, who in turn were so threatened by him that they put him to death. But Jesus' subsequent resurrection demonstrates his ultimate victory over them. The Church is called upon to proclaim this victory, not simply in words but also with deeds. Jesus announced his public ministry by promising relief for the poor, and Christian ministry today should follow his example.

In building his peace and justice agenda firmly on a biblical foundation, Wallis hopes both to make the world a better place for all to live in and to demonstrate that genuine evangelicalism, although decried by many today, is worth taking seriously. As he says, "The answer to bad religion is better religion—prophetic rather than partisan, broad and deep instead of narrow, and based on values as opposed to ideology."

5 June
Angie Zelter

5 June 1951—

Practical Acts of Love

ANGIE ZELTER, WHO CALLS herself a British-born citizen of the world, has been arrested more than one hundred times in several different countries. She's served sixteen prison sentences, totaling nearly two years. Her crimes? Agitating for peace. Zelter is a practitioner of nonviolent direct action against weapons of destruction. As a global citizen, she believes she has a moral duty to persuade governments against "aiding and abetting genocide."

Zelter's resistance began at an early age. In the 1980s she founded the Snowball Campaign, which encouraged British citizens to cut chain fences around U.S. military installations throughout the United Kingdom. In the mid-1990s she helped plan an action against a Hawk jet built by British Aerospace, a U.K. munitions and defense-systems manufacturer. The Hawk had been sold but not yet delivered to Indonesia for use in its struggle against the East Timor independence movement. Using household hammers, three of Zelter's confederates managed to inflict enough damage on the jet to render it inoperative. Their trial, at which they were eventually acquitted, was highly publicized and helped bring the issue of arms control to the public eye.

Zelter founded Trident Ploughshares in 1998 to draw attention to Britain's Trident nuclear weapons submarine system. Each Trident submarine has forty-eight warheads, which are capable of being simultaneously launched at as many targets. Each warhead has an explosive power of one hundred kilotons—eight times that of the bombs dropped on Hiroshima and Nagasaki. Inspired by the prophet Isaiah's vision of a time in which swords will be beaten into ploughshares, Zelter and other members of Trident Ploughshares risk imprisonment by breaking into naval facilities and hammering on docked submarines in symbolic protest. Their hope is that the ensuing publicity surrounding their arrest and trial will focus public attention on the colossal destructiveness of nuclear weapons. Their message, says Zelter, is simple: "Killing is wrong. Mass killing is wrong. Threatening mass destruction is a denial of our own humanity and is suicidal. When something is wrong, we have to stop it."

Under Zelter's direction, Trident Ploughshares also lobbies the UK government for the controlled disarmament of its nuclear arsenal. In 2007, in response to the government's refusal to consider dismantling its nuclear submarine program, Zelter organized a one-year nonviolent blockade of the Trident naval base in Faslane, Scotland.

Zelter was a 2001 recipient of the Right Livelihood Award. In accepting it, she reminded her audience that nonviolent direct action is as much an expression of love as of protest. "Dismantling the machinery of destruction," she said, "is a practical act of love that we can all join in."

6 June
Marian Wright Edelman

6 June 1939—

Standing Up for Children

IN THE UNITED STATES today, 16.5 million children live below the poverty line. Half of them are from families that lack adequate health insurance protection. These kids generally don't attend Head Start programs, and overwhelming percentages of them perform at lower than grade level when they enter public school. Annually, nearly a million of them—that's one every forty-two seconds—is neglected or abused. And all of this in the wealthiest nation in the world.

Marian Wright Edelman, founder and president of the Children's Defense Fund, believes that if we "don't stand up for children," the least empowered members of our society, "we don't stand up for much." Since 1973, her nonprofit organization has served as a research and advocacy center for kids. Through appeals to the public conscience as well as hard-nosed congressional lobbying, the Children's Defense Fund promotes child health care, sponsors youth leadership programs, advocates educational reform, works with communities with high imprisonment rates for youth, and everywhere seeks social programs to better the lives of children in poverty. The organization's motto, sadly co-opted by partisan politics, is "Leave No Child Behind."

Edelman credits her upbringing with her lifelong concern for children. Born into a large South Carolina family, she learned early on the practical and moral value of helping others, a lesson reinforced daily by her Baptist preacher father. "Service," she writes, "was as essential a part of my upbringing as eating and sleeping and going to school." She also witnessed firsthand the developmental harm poverty and lack of educational opportunities inflict upon children.

So no one was surprised that Edelman returned to Mississippi after earning a Yale law degree and began working with the National Association for the Advancement of Colored People (NAACPP) and the Southern Christian Leadership Conference (SCLC). (She was the first black woman admitted to the Mississippi bar, by the way.) After her marriage to one of Robert Kennedy's staffers, she moved to Washington, DC, and shortly thereafter founded the Children's Defense Fund. Her experience as a civil rights attorney, and especially her involvement in **Martin Luther King Jr.**'s Poor People's Campaign for social and economic justice, were important influences in her subsequent advocacy for children.

Although the recipient of dozens of awards and honorary degrees, Edelman sees nothing extraordinary about her life's work. Instead, she believes she's merely paying a debt. "Service is the rent we pay to be living. It is the very purpose of life, not something you do in your spare time."

7 June

Seattle

1785?—7 June 1866

Spokesman for the Earth and Sky

For nearly half a century, Chief Seattle of Puget Sound's Duwamish tribe, had tried to protect his people from the steady inflow of white settlers whose appetite for land seemed insatiable. Although known as a warrior in his youth, Seattle and most of his people had converted to Christianity by 1830. Afterwards, he preferred peaceful solutions to the escalating tensions between Indians and whites. He also saw that armed resistance to the settlers and the American army that backed them up was futile.

In 1855, hoping to avoid armed conflict while ensuring the survival of his people, the aged Seattle signed the Port Elliott Treaty, which ceded lands traditionally held by Indians to the United States government. The treaty was basically an official acknowledgment of what was already de facto: the invasion of Indian territory by white settlers. In exchange for their land, the Duwamish and other tribes were given reservation land that was under the control of federal authorities.

A year earlier, representatives of the U.S. government met with chiefs of the Puget Sound tribes to discuss the terms of what became the Port Elliott Treaty. Listening at that conference to the demands of the whites, a dismayed Seattle rose to speak. His remarks have generated much controversy in the years since. Some historians argue that Seattle's speech was a romantic invention of later commentators. We'll never know with certainty what Seattle actually said. But there's no doubt that the speech as we have it today captures his love of the land and his bewilderment at the abuse of it by white settlers.

The notion of a legal exchange of lands was bizarre to Seattle. "How can you buy or sell the sky, the warmth of the land?" he asked. The very idea was strange because "every part of the earth is sacred." Whereas the Duwamish people looked upon the earth and sky as friends, the white people saw them as things to be mastered and exploited.

In his speech, Seattle invoked the God he worshipped and whom white Christian settlers claimed to worship as well. "He is the God of humanity, and his compassion is equal for the red man and the white. The earth is precious to him, and to harm the earth is to heap contempt on its Creator." The white invasion of Puget Sound, he admitted, had scattered the Indians like storm-swept trees. But he held out the hope of an ultimate reconciliation—one day, "we may be brothers after all"—that would rest upon a shared recognition that "every shining pine needle, every sandy shore, every mist in the dark woods, every humming insect" is sacred.

8 June
John Perkins

16 June 1930—

Helping Justice Roll Down

IF THERE WAS EVER a man who had cause to despise whites, it's John M. Perkins. The son of a Mississippi sharecropper, Perkins' mother died of hunger-related illness when he was less than a year old. Perkins quit school after the third grade. As a child and youth, he bootlegged to supplement his family's meager income. When he was seventeen, his brother Clyde was shot twice and killed by a white deputy marshal. Clyde's crime? Talking too loudly while in a movie theater line. Perkins was packed off to California to keep him out of harm's way.

In California, Perkins became a Christian—a genuine change of life for someone who "had always looked at black Christians as sort of inferior people whose religion had made them gullible and submissive." He came to see the Bible as a chronicle of the progressive liberation of God's children from injustice and oppression, and concluded that it was his duty to carry on the tradition of helping justice roll down to those most in need of it. So when he was thirty, he returned to Mississippi with his wife, Vera Mae, to launch Mendenhall Ministries. Perkins did much more than preach the gospel. He also lived it by throwing himself into community development for poor blacks. Voice of Calvary Ministries, an offshoot of Mendenhall Ministries, sponsored a health center, low-income housing for blacks, a thrift store, and a job training center.

Perkins also became involved in the civil rights movement, working especially for school desegregation, adherence to minimum wage laws, and fair business practices. For Perkins, the struggle for civil rights was more than a campaign for political and economic equality. It was also a test of Christian commitment. "The most terrible thing about the situation in the South was that so many of the folks who were either violently racist or who participated in discrimination called themselves Christian. The question on my mind was whether or not Christianity was a stronger force than racism." Reconciliation was possible, Perkins believed, but only if it followed genuine repentance.

Perkins' activities made him an obvious target for white threats and harassment. The danger in which his ministries placed him finally caught up with him in 1970. Shortly after he participated in a boycott demonstration against white businesses, he was arrested and beaten so badly by police that he nearly died. He required weeks of hospitalization. Afterwards, he and his family returned to California for a few years, where Perkins launched another community development ministry. But they eventually returned to Jackson, Mississippi, where today Perkins heads the John M. Perkins Foundation for Reconciliation and Development. The foundation works in the Jackson area "to develop the lives of youth, leaders and underprivileged in our community and around the world by setting an example of God's love to further his Kingdom."

9 June
Bertha von Suttner

9 June 1843—21 June 1914

Peace Generalissimo

It was the stuff of fairy tales. The beautiful daughter of an impoverished aristocratic family travels from her native Prague to Vienna, glittering capital of the Austro-Hungarian Empire, to tutor the children of a baron. She and the baron's son fall in love, secretly marry, flee the wrath of the young man's father, and live in poverty-stricken exile for several years before all is forgiven. In the meantime, the young wife discovers a talent for writing and ekes out a living for herself and her husband by writing novels. After their return to Vienna, she becomes a best-selling author.

This is a sketch of the first forty-odd years of Bertha von Suttner's life. Except for her romantic elopement, her values during that period conventionally reflected the militaristic aristocratic class into which she was born. She was a loyal daughter of the empire and a privileged member of its upper class. In the 1880s, however, she and her husband Arthur experienced a sea change in their outlook. Persuaded by evolution-inspired arguments that society's advancement depended on a forswearing of war, the two became increasingly involved with European pacifist and disarmament groups.

Wishing to give the movement the aid of her pen, von Suttner published two books in 1889 that established her as one of Europe's leading peace witnesses. The first, *The Machine Age*, was an uncompromising indictment of the European arms race. The other book was a novel titled *Lay Down Your Arms*. In it, von Suttner wrote horrific descriptions of battle scenes remarkably accurate for someone who had never actually witnessed war. The heroine of the novel, a young woman who is clearly von Suttner's fictional avatar, is sickened by the patriotic glorification of war. At one point, the girl and her father listen to a broken-spirited veteran describe his bloodcurdling experiences of battle. Alarmed, the patriotic father exclaims: "The censorship should not allow the publication of things of that sort! It might destroy a man's love for the profession of a soldier!" His daughter sardonically retorts: "And especially the love of war, which would be a pity." The novel was immensely popular, even in the militaristic culture of Austria-Hungary.

In 1891, von Suttner founded the Vienna-based Austrian Peace Society and served as its president for years. A longtime acquaintance of Alfred Nobel, she persuaded him to fund the annual peace prize that bears his name, and she won it herself in 1905 in recognition of her peacemaking efforts. In the final decade of her life, she traveled throughout Europe and the United States to speak at peace conferences. At one of the last she attended before her death, she was warmly greeted by delegates as the "generalissimo" of peace. Many of those who knew and loved her counted it a blessing that von Suttner died just on the eve of the Great War and was consequently spared the horrible devastation of a war that engulfed the entire world in its destruction and death.

10 June
Sumaya Farhat-Naser

11 June 1948—

Activists, Not Victims

BORN IN THE YEAR that Israel became a nation, Sumaya Farhat Naser, a Palestinian Christian, has spent most of her adult life working for a just peace between Palestinians and Israelis. Her efforts have been met at times with suspicion from both sides of the conflict, and her physical activities are now largely restricted by Israeli authorities to the Ramallah district of the West Bank. But she continues to advocate for reconciliation rather than violence.

A trained botanist, Naser has taught at the Palestinian Birzeit University since the early 1980s. In 1991, she cofounded the Palestinian Jerusalem Center for Women, a nongovernmental agency that advocates for a just peace, a protection of human rights, and the advancement of women's interests. One of the center's more exciting initiatives is Jerusalem Link, a collaboration with the Israeli peace organization Bat Shalom. Jerusalem Link brings Palestinian and Israeli women together to design strategies for a just and sustainable reconciliation, which are then taken back to their respective communities. The hope is to encourage fruitful dialogue between Palestinians and Israelis. Jerusalem Link has been periodically suspended by the Israeli authorities, and Naser, because of the difficulty in getting past Israeli security checkpoints, is no longer active in the Jerusalem-based Center for Women. But she continues to work as a peace activist in the West Bank, running workshops for young people on nonviolence, conflict resolution, and leadership.

Naser also continues to be confident that women, Israeli as well as Palestinian, remain the key to ending the decades-long conflict. While acknowledging that peace-building "is not unique to women," she notes that it's "through women's organizations that much of [it] is taking place. This is because the men's organizations are the established ministries and offices—and they're not working across the divide." Her conviction is that women bring a different negotiating style to the table that's more receptive to compromise and agreement. But she admits that it won't be easy. "It's as though the women are ghosts—[the men] don't see us. They don't want to know that we are capable of reaching across the barriers. They don't want to believe that we are working in politics and able to raise our voices. But we are."

In order to be effective, however, Naser thinks it crucial that women see themselves "not as victims, but as activists, as people who can make a difference. So often, people think of women only as victims. We are not victims! We are not weak! Victims need pity. We don't need pity—we need to be independent and functional. We need roles that are challenging and demanding. This is what we want as women."

11 June
Jeanette Rankin

11 June 1880—18 May 1973

Pacifist Congresswoman

WHEN THE U.S. CONGRESS convened after the holidays on 15 January 1968, some five thousand women from all over the nation converged on Capitol Hill to protest the Vietnam War. They were led by a woman in her late eighties, and they called themselves the "Jeannette Rankin Brigade" in her honor.

Rankin was no stranger to Washington, DC. In 1917, she became the first woman in the House of Representatives, sent there by her home state of Montana. In 1941, she was elected to a second term. Before her entry into politics, she worked for the National American Woman Suffrage Association, campaigning in several states for women's voting rights. Her biggest victory was the 1914 referendum that allowed women in Montana to vote a full six years before the Nineteenth Amendment enfranchised women throughout the country.

Rankin's two passions were proposing laws that protected women and children and finding alternatives to war. In her mind, the two went together, since men fight wars but women and children suffer in them. "Peace," she said, "is a woman's job," and by "peace" she meant the total abolition of armed conflict. "There can be no compromise with war; it cannot be reformed or controlled; cannot be disciplined into decency or codified into common sense."

True to her convictions, Rankin was one of only fifty congresspersons who voted against America's entry into World War I, famously observing that "you can no more win a war than you can win an earthquake." Her opposition angered political leaders back in Montana, and she lost her seat in 1919. When she was returned to Congress in 1941, she was the only person in either house to vote against declaring war on Japan. "As a woman, I can't go to war," she stated, "and I refuse to send anyone else." But Rankin was a strong advocate for veterans, whom she thought the victims of warmongering politicians.

In or out of Congress, Rankin devoted herself to working for peace and justice. She helped found the ACLU. She traveled to India seven times to study nonviolent tactics with **Mohandas Gandhi**. In her later years she regularly spoke out against the Vietnam War. A year before she marched to Capitol Hill with the Jeannette Rankin Brigade, she appealed to the nation's women to resist sending their sons and husbands to war. "It is unconscionable that 10,000 boys have died in Vietnam. If 10,000 American women had mind enough they could end the war, if they were committed to the task, even if it meant going to jail."

12 June
Frédéric Passy

20 May 1822—12 June 1912

Apostle of Peace

WHEN MOST PEOPLE THINK of anti-war activists, what comes to mind are countercultural outsiders who work to consolidate public opinion against government-sponsored militarism. But occasionally opponents of warfare focus their energy on converting governments rather than opposing them. Frédéric Passy, who won the first Nobel Peace Prize in 1901 (he shared it with Henri Dunant, founder of the Red Cross), was one of them. Throughout his long life, he labored to create organizations that aimed to convince governments that international peace was in their best interests. His efforts earned him the title of "apostle of peace."

A lifelong Parisian, Passy was an ardent defender of free trade because he saw it as an instrument to persuade nations that armed hostility was detrimental to their economic well-being. Arbitration of international disputes, accepted by nations out of self-interest rather than altruism, became Passy's mantra. As early as the 1853 Crimean War, he urged belligerent nations to seek third-party assistance in ironing out their differences. Later, he founded no fewer than three organizations to promote this vision. The first, the 1867 International League of Permanent Peace, collapsed three years later at the outbreak of the Franco-Prussian War, but was quickly replaced by the French Society of Friends of Peace. The third, founded in 1889, was the French Society for International Arbitration. It was a sister organization to what Passy considered his grandest achievement for peace, the Inter-Parliamentary Union, an association of nations pledged to pursue arbitration beyond conventional diplomatic channels in the event of international disputes.

In addition to his work bringing governments together, Passy also served during the 1880s in the French Chamber of Deputies. His activities there focused on legislation that promoted peace both within France and between France and her European neighbors. He advocated disarmament, opposed his government's colonial policies, and championed French workers' rights.

We sometimes think of a peacemaker like Passy as just another bureaucrat or public policy wonk who's all about treaties and statistics but has little compassion for the actual victims of war. But in Passy's case, nothing could be further from the truth. When he won the Nobel Prize, an article about him appeared in the *New York Times*. The Boer War was then raging in South Africa, and the *Times* reported Passy's reaction to it. "M. Passy said he burst into tears when he saw a picture of a wasted and disfigured Boer child. He declared that science and progress were working in the cause of peace. The abominations of war were formerly known tardily; now the telegraph described them at the very moment they were happening." This isn't the sentiment of a detached bureaucrat, but rather of a passionate advocate—an *apostle*—of peace.

13 June
Dante Alighieri

MID-JUNE 1265—14 SEPTEMBER 1321

World Government, World Peace

The Florentine Dante Alighieri, universally known simply as Dante, is famous for his verse epic the *Divine Comedy*, an imaginative account of traveling through hell, purgatory, and paradise. But besides being a masterful poet, Dante was also a statesman who spent a good deal of his adult life trying to persuade feuding factions to make peace with one another. Elected as one of the rulers of Florence when he was thirty-five, he soon found himself on the losing side of the political infighting that characterized the Florentine politics of his day. Exiled from the city of his birth, Dante spent his remaining years, when he wasn't writing, on a number of peacemaking missions solicited by secular and religious rulers alike.

It was sometime during these years of exile, probably in 1312 or 1313, that Dante wrote a remarkable little book titled *De Monarchia*, usually translated as *On World Government*. The treatise is an eloquent and tightly argued strategy for universal peace. Parts of *De Monarchia* may strike the modern reader as quaintly dated. But its central thesis is as fascinating today as it was seven centuries ago.

Dante argues that lasting peace can never be achieved so long as the human community is split into adversarial nations. What's needed to end international strife as well as conflict between feuding parties within nations is a common set of laws that apply equally to all, and a centralized authority that ensures that the laws are obeyed and justice preserved. This centralized authority is vested in a world-ruler reminiscent of the wise philosopher-king, defended by Plato centuries earlier, whose only desire is that his subjects enjoy genuinely rewarding and enriched lives. In Dante's Christian terms, the world-ruler acts to create a social climate that encourages humans to grow into their Godlikeness by expanding intellectually, morally, and spiritually. The human race as a whole, says Dante, has yet to reach its full potential. The purpose of a single world government is to nurture that potential into full actuality.

Of course, governments, institutions, and philanthropists during Dante's time (and ours) often supported the work of individual artists and intellectuals. Although Dante applauded this sort of sponsorship, he believed that the human task of becoming everything God desires could only be completed when social and economic conditions allow everyone, not just a privileged few, to flourish. And the necessary condition for this, he concluded, was universal peace. "Mankind," he wrote, "is most free and easy to carry on its work when it enjoys the quiet and tranquility of peace." Because our task of becoming fully human is the work that gives us the greatest satisfaction, "it is clear that of all the things that have been ordained for our happiness, the greatest is universal peace." The task of the world government is to ensure universal peace so that a global culture of wisdom and goodness—heaven on earth, if you will—can emerge. Peace, for Dante, isn't simply the absence of conflict. It's the presence of fulfillment.

14 JUNE
David Low Dodge

14 JUNE 1774—23 APRIL 1852

Inhumane, Unwise, and Criminal

THE FIRST PACIFIST ORGANIZATION founded in the United States was the New York Peace Society. Organized in 1815 on the heels of the War of 1812, its leading light was David Low Dodge, a Connecticut native who relocated to New York City in his early thirties. Dodge had almost no formal education. The son of a farmer, he was too busy working in the fields to attend much school. As a young man, he held down a number of jobs in Connecticut before setting up shop as a merchant in New York. But he was a man of intense Christian faith, and the more he read the Bible, the more persuaded he became that war is contrary to Jesus' message.

Even before the New York Peace Society was formed, Dodge was a convinced pacifist and published a couple of pamphlets outlining his reasons for renouncing warfare. The second, which appeared in 1812, was widely read. Matter-of-factly titled *War Inconsistent with the Religion of Jesus Christ,* the book lacked literary grace and occasionally seemed to lose the thread of its argument. But its advocacy of Christian nonviolence was passionate and eloquent in a rough-hewn way.

In his book, Dodge insisted that war was "inhuman, unwise, and criminal," and systematically spelled out his justifications for this claim. War is inhuman (he means "inhumane") because it blunts tenderness of heart; damages God's creation; spreads terror, destruction, and distress; maims or kills youths and men; creates widows and orphans; and everywhere oppresses the poor. War's lack of wisdom consists in its destruction of property, rights, liberties, happiness, and morals. Even worse, in doing all that war obliges us to do—in fact, *rewards* us for doing—we trade the eternal joys of heaven for the temporal triumphs of conquest. Finally, war is criminal because it inflames pride and rancor, dismisses virtues such as forgiveness and patience, renders evil for evil, and most especially violates the Son of God's living example. "If Christians were like Christ," Dodge wrote, "their warfare would not be carnal, but spiritual, corresponding with the armor that he has provided. They would conquer by faith and overcome by the blood of the Lamb, not counting their lives dear to themselves."

In 1828, the New York Peace Society joined other pacifist organizations in New England to form the American Peace Society, which Dodge headed until 1836. Following its opposition to the 1844 Mexican-American War, the Society finally dissolved. But its nearly thirty-year example inspired the subsequent formation of other American peace societies, secular as well as religious.

15 June
Paul Rusesabagina

15 June 1954—

He Stayed

In 1994, the hell that had been threatening to erupt in Rwanda for a generation finally exploded. The two tribal castes that comprised the nation's population, the Tutsis and the Hutus, had a long history of feuding with one another. Tutsis tended to be tall and lighter complexioned than Hutus. They were cattle grazers, favoring open rangeland, while Hutus were farmers and so had interests in enclosing the land. Moreover, the Tutsis had long been the dominant social class in Rwanda, and this predictably generated Hutu resentment.

The spark that ignited the explosion was the assassination of the Hutu president of Rwanda, Juvénal Habyarimana, in April 1994. Almost immediately, angry Hutus used his death as a pretext to begin massacring Tutsis as well as any Hutus viewed as Tutsi-friendly. A ragtag Hutu army known as the Interahamwe militia raced through Tutsi neighborhoods and villages killing any men, women, and children they could find. Their weapon of choice was the machete, the Hutu harvesting tool. There are reports that the Interahamwe often killed their victims slowly, lopping off one limb at a time and forcing Tutsis who wished to end the torture to pay for the privilege of being killed quickly. By the time the butchery ended three months later, over eight hundred thousand Rwandans had been slaughtered in a campaign of genocide that shocked the world.

Hutu Paul Rusesabagina, acting manager of the French-owned Mille Collines, a luxury hotel in Rwanda's capital of Kigali, rushed his Tutsi wife and children to his place of employment as soon as the killing erupted. Planning to keep them there until he could get them out of the country, his hope was that the hotel's status as an internationally owned business would protect it and its guests from Hutu violence. Apparently, hundreds of other Tutsis had the same hope, because it wasn't long before they began flooding into the Mille Collines to seek asylum. Rusesabagina welcomed them all and spent the next one hundred days scrounging to find them adequate food and drink (at one point the refugees had to drink water from the hotel swimming pool) and bribing Interahamwe commanders to keep them from storming the hotel and massacring the refugees. Rusesabagina's life was frequently in danger, despite his being a Hutu. But his efforts paid off; while the killing spree raged throughout the country, he managed to keep his wards safe.

At one point in what amounted to a Hutu siege of the Mille Collines, Rusesabagina had an opportunity to escape with his family. But his conscience wouldn't allow it. "I knew that I would be removing one of the only remaining barriers between the militia and the guests. If I left and people were killed I would never be at peace. My food would never taste good again; I could never enjoy my freedom. It would be as though I had killed those people myself." So he stayed, saving 1,268 Tutsis from an awful death.

16 June
Charles Yale Harrison

16 June 1898—17 March 1954

Chronicler of Stolen Lives

CHARLES YALE HARRISON WAS a nineteen-year-old kid working as a stringer for *The Montreal Star* when he joined the Canadian Expeditionary Force to fight in World War I. A year later, not long before the war ended, he was wounded in France. He returned to Montreal to recuperate, but shortly afterwards relocated to New York City, where he held down a number of jobs during the next ten or so years.

But Harrison couldn't get the war out of his head—the real war, not the sanitized version he read about in the popular and jingoistic press. So he sat down in the late 1920s and began writing an autobiographical novel about the war as he experienced it. Published in 1930, *Generals Die in Bed* became an overnight best seller. Although not as well known today as other anti-war novels to come out of the Great War, it's every bit as powerful.

There are battle scenes in *Generals Die in Bed*. But the novel's genius is its description of the way ordinary men are brutalized by their war experiences. "Our lives are stolen from us," declares the novel's narrator, "taken from us unawares." The stealing of lives doesn't occur just when soldiers are killed or maimed. It also takes place in the way that war stains the innocent goodness of the common soldier. Relentless anxiety, harsh physical conditions, exhaustion, and bad food—not to mention the trauma of killing other human beings, sometimes in hand-to-hand fighting—emotionally and spiritually stupefy the characters in Harrison's novel. They rouse themselves only when ordered to assault an enemy line or when bickering among themselves. Harrison wants his readers to have no illusions: battlefield camaraderie, at least in his own war experience, is largely mythical. Men pushed to the breaking point are much more likely to feud among themselves than to bond. The slightest provocation—a spilled mug of tea, a slightly unequal division of rations, a carelessly chosen word—and the men are at one another's throats.

For Harrison, one of the great tragedies of war is also one of its greatest ironies: in wartime, soldiers are ordered to commit actions that would be condemned as crimes in other contexts. This point is made chillingly at one point in the novel. On leave from the front line, the narrator has a brief fling with a woman he meets in a bar. He says to her, "Did I ever tell you that I committed murder? I came into a place where an enemy of mine was and I stabbed him and ran off." The woman is frightened until the narrator tells her that his "murder" was in fact a wartime killing. Then she calms down. "Her face glows with a smile. 'You silly boy. I thought you had really murdered someone.'"

There's another tragic irony to war that the novel's sadly ironic title is meant to convey: wars are started and armies commanded by powerful men who rarely suffer from the violence they spawn. It's the common foot soldier who pays the cost. This unhappy observation is as true in today's wars as in Harrison's war.

17 June
Viktor Popkov

17 June 1946—2 June 2001

Old Believer Humanitarian

In early February 2000, Russian mercenaries swept through the Novye Aldi suburb of the ruined Chechen capital of Grozny. Battle-hardened by five years of a war that killed forty thousand civilians and displaced half a million more, the soldiers began indiscriminately robbing and shooting residents and burning their homes. Four days later, journalist and advocate of nonviolence Viktor Popkov arrived on the scene with a video camera to document the carnage. His film drew worldwide attention to the massacre and helped build a war crimes case for the European Court of Human Rights.

Popkov was always in the hot spots in the brutal wars between Russia and breakaway Chechnya, pleading for peace, negotiating prisoner exchanges, delivering food and medical supplies to besieged civilians, leading hunger strikes in solidarity with the war's victims, and making sure that the world community knew about the atrocities committed by both sides. He felt a duty, he said, to "strive to help and to defend the people of Chechnya, who are being destroyed by my Russia." He was the war's most outspoken human rights advocate, and his passionate denunciation of violence earned him the anger of both the Russian military and the Chechen rebels.

While at university, Popkov studied physics and seismology, and he worked for a period as a seismologist on the Kamchatka Peninsula. But as a deeply faithful Russian Orthodox Old Believer who believed that Jesus bade his followers to be peacemakers, Popkov left science for humanitarian work. In 1992 he founded Omega, an organization that promoted interdenominational dialogue. At the same time, he affiliated with the Memorial Human Rights Center, which documents past Soviet atrocities as well as monitors current Russian ones, and began writing for *Novaya Gazeta,* a newspaper highly critical of the Russian government.

Popkov, who dressed in a dark monk's habit and had flowing white hair and beard, took as his motto a saying attributed to the thirteenth-century saint Prince Alexander Nevsky: "Not by force, oh God, but in truth." Part of the truth by which Popkov lived was a conviction of the kinship of all humans and the universal application of the nonviolence he practiced. As he said in 1989, "the problems of Abkhazia, Belfast, the Negroes of Harlem, the Japanese Ainu and so on are not merely the problems of one region or another, one ethnic group, one country or another, but to no lesser degree are the shared problems of us all; they will only be solved by the united action of all."

On 18 April 2001, Viktor Popkov was shot by unidentified gunmen while delivering medical supplies in Chechyna. Medical treatment was deliberately delayed by the authorities, causing him to lapse into a coma. Popkov died six weeks later, leaving behind an invalid wife, two children, and thousands of grateful Chechens.

18 June
José Brocca

16 April 1891—June 1950

Standing Fast

Following the horrors of World War I, pacifism enjoyed a period of popularity in Europe. Thousands of people publicly clamored for an end to warfare, and many of them joined the War Resisters' International, formed in 1921. In doing so, they pledged that "war is a crime against humanity. I am therefore determined not to support any kind of war and to strive for the removal of all causes of war."

The first serious challenge to this wave of pacifism was the Spanish Civil War, which erupted in 1936 when a group of fascist generals launched a coup against the Second Spanish Republic. The ensuing bloody war lasted for three years, pitting the conservative "rebels" against the progressive "Republicans." The rebels were heavily financed and armed by Nazi Germany. In light of the fascist threat to liberty playing out in Spain, many European pacifists felt unable in good conscience to hold onto their opposition to war. In their view, the stakes were too high to stand on principle.

Andalusian educator José Brocca, a leader of the Spanish branch of the War Resisters' International, sympathized with the pacifists who felt it their duty to fight for the Republican side. He loathed fascism as much as they did. But he refused to forsake his pacifist convictions and chose to wield the weapons of active nonviolent resistance in the struggle against the rebels. At the beginning of the civil war, he devoted himself, as he said, to works of "information and propaganda" that "spread among the combatants [pacifist] humanitarian ideals and [pacifist] repugnance to oppression and cruelty." Later, he threw his energies into "stimulating, directing, and organizing the peasants so that instead of abandoning their agricultural work, they work to avoid interruption in production and provision of supplies for the towns."

Brocca's greatest form of pacifist resistance to fascism was the establishment of a refuge in the French Pyrenees, just across the Spanish border, for children who had been separated from their parents or orphaned because of the civil war. Hundreds of children passed through the refuge on their way to safety in France or Mexico, or were returned to their Spanish homes when the war ended. Most of them were from Republican families. But Brocca welcomed all children in need of assistance, regardless of the political allegiance of their parents.

After the civil war ended with the triumph of the fascists, Brocca refused to leave the children's refuge until the last of his wards reached safety. He was soon arrested by the Germans, who by this time had occupied France, and was imprisoned in a nearby concentration camp. With the aid of the French Resistance, Brocca eventually managed to escape and make his way to Mexico, where he lived his final eight years in poverty. He remained loyal to the end to his War Resisters' pledge to support no war. At great personal cost, he stood fast by his principles.

19 June
Aung San Suu Kyi

19 June 1945—

Freedom from Fear

BURMA, ALSO KNOWN AS Myanmar, has been ruled by one military junta after another for the past half-century. During that period, dissent has typically been dealt with in ruthlessly violent ways, Muslims and resident Indians have been hounded and driven into exile, civil liberties have been suppressed, and the nation's economy has worsened to the extent that Burma is now one of the poorest countries on the globe. Yet in the midst of this strong-fisted repression, the nonviolent resistance of Aung San Suu Kyi has been a force to be reckoned with by the junta leaders.

For her first forty years, Suu Kyi, the daughter of Burmese independence hero Aung San (assassinated in 1948), was an author and translator who for the most part lived away from her native land. Returning to Burma in 1988 to visit her dying mother, Suu Kyi arrived in the midst of a nationwide nonviolent revolt against the junta and quickly became one of its leading spokespersons. But the pro-democracy movement was soon crushed and hundreds of Burmese were killed. Suu Kyi was too high-profile a figure to murder, so the junta instead tried to silence her with imprisonment. Suu Kyi spent fifteen of the next twenty years in detention of one form or another, but her courage kept nonviolent resistance to the junta alive.

Suu Kyi's nonviolent resistance is founded on her Buddhist-inspired belief that fear is both the greatest weapon of the oppressor and the greatest obstacle to freedom. "It is not power that corrupts," she notes, "but fear. Fear of losing power corrupts those who wield it and fear of the scourge of power corrupts those who are subject to it." One of the more pernicious features of fear is that it's habit-forming. The more we succumb to it, the more entrenched it becomes and the more imprisoned by it we are. Living in fear, either of losing power or becoming the victim of power, impoverishes lives and corrodes society. It becomes such a familiar part of the landscape that it gets confused, as Suu Kyi says, with "common sense or even wisdom, condemning as foolish, reckless, insignificant or futile the small, daily acts of courage which help to preserve man's self-respect and inherent human dignity."

Suu Kyi acknowledges that it's not easy to break free of the iron rule of fear. But she's impressed by how often, "even under the most crushing state machinery, courage rises up again and again." This leads her to conclude and jubilantly proclaim that "fear is not the natural state of civilized man," and neither is the violence it spawns. Humans can achieve freedom from fear and, in so doing, nonviolently liberate themselves from injustice. For the past quarter-century, Suu Kyi's own courageous life has exemplified that conviction. When she was awarded the Nobel Peace Prize in 1991, the award citation got it exactly right: "she has become an important symbol in the struggle against oppression everywhere."

20 JUNE
Jonathan Dymond

1796—1828

"Astonished at the madness of mankind"

TRY TO FORGET EVERYTHING you know about the sorry history of warfare—to become "a being who has never before heard of human slaughter"—and imagine witnessing a vast and bloody battle between opposing armies. What emotions do you think you'd feel?

The nineteenth-century British Quaker Jonathan Dymond asked himself precisely this question, and his answer, recorded in his 1823 *An Enquiry into the Accordancy of War with the Principles of Christianity,* is that the most likely responses would be horror and astonishment. "That several thousand persons should meet together, and then deliberately begin to kill one another, appears to the understanding a proceeding so preposterous, so monstrous, that I think a being such as I have supposed, would inevitably conclude that they were mad. Nor, if it were attempted to explain to him some motives to such conduct, do I believe that he would be able to comprehend how any possible circumstances could make it reasonable. The ferocity and prodigious folly of the act would out-balance the weight of every conceivable motive, and he would turn, unsatisfied, away, astonished at the madness of mankind."

Dymond's *Enquiry,* the first edition of which was published anonymously, is one of the most eloquent statements of Christian pacifism to come out of the Quaker tradition. But it's virtually forgotten today, as are most of the details of Dymond's life. We know that he was a draper, or retailer of cloth, that he wrote in a room adjoining his shop and was frequently interrupted by customers, and that he died of a distressing throat ailment, probably tuberculosis. We also know that a Quaker contemporary described him as a person of rare talent and "exalted piety." But beyond that, we know nothing about the man except, as attested by his book, that he was a vigorous opponent of war.

In the *Enquiry,* Dymond reflects on what he thinks is a sobering paradox: that humans are both the only creatures who regularly wage bloody battle with one another, and the only creatures who are endowed with soul and hence capable of God-like love. The conventional explanation for this strange inconsistency is that sometimes war is necessary to overcome evil. But Dymond is dubious. If the God of peace has mandated nonviolence, he asks, is war ever necessary? As Dymond declares, "supposing the Christian religion to prohibit war, it is preposterous, and irreverent also, to justify ourselves in supporting it, because 'it is necessary.' To talk of a divine law which *must be disobeyed,* implies, indeed, such a confusion of moral principles as well as laxity of them, that neither the philosopher nor the Christian are required to notice it." It's more sensible to take the words of Jesus seriously, as the apostles did, when he bids us not to return evil for evil. If we do that, Dymond says, only one practical and philosophical conclusion is possible: "That war, of every kind, is incompatible with Christianity." There is, in other words, no such thing as a "necessary war."

21 June
Shirin Ebadi

21 June 1947—

Protecting the Limbs of Adam

POLITICAL REVOLUTIONS, EVEN THOSE that end repressive regimes, often wind up devouring their own children. This is precisely what happened in Iran following the 1979 overthrow of the U.S.-backed shah. The post-revolution democracy that many Iranians longed for failed to materialize. Instead, a repressive Muslim theocracy, headed by the Ayatollah Khomeini, seized control.

One of the first casualties of this regime change was Shirin Ebadi. A resident of Teheran, Ebadi was the first woman in Iranian history to become a judge, seated in 1969 when she was only twenty-two years old. She was as brilliant on the bench as she had been as a law student. But after the revolution, Iranian clerics decided that it was unseemly for women to hold public office, and Ebadi was stripped of her judgeship. When she protested, she was offered a job as a government secretary. Ebadi retired in protest and spent the next thirteen years living as a private citizen, raising her two daughters and writing well-received books on children's and refugees' rights.

In 1992, after repeated petitions, Ebadi was finally given a license to practice law. But she soon antagonized authorities by taking on human rights cases that cast shadows on the Iranian government. She represented the families of liberal intellectuals slain by hit squads tied to Iranian intelligence agencies. She also represented victims of child abuse, defended the rights of women, and advocated for members of the persecuted Baha'i faith. (Under Iranian Muslim law, converting from Islam to Baha'ism—or any other religion, for that matter—is a capital offense.) She also began lecturing extensively in Iran and throughout the Middle East on women's rights. She was awarded the Nobel Peace Prize in 2003. An increasingly oppressive Iranian government seized her medal and diploma a few years later and began threatening her family. In 2008, Iranian authorities shut down a human rights agency founded by Ebadi and seized her records. The following year, she went into exile.

Ebadi says that as a child, she "fell in love with a phenomenon I later learned was justice. When I was a child and saw other children fighting I would go aid the underdog, without even knowing what they were fighting about, which would also cause me to get in the middle and get beaten. That is why I later became a student of law. It was the same feeling that encouraged me to become active in defending human rights." In her Nobel acceptance speech, she appealed to the thirteenth-century Persian poet Saadi to express why she believes that human rights are universal and why their protection is the responsibility of everyone.

> The sons of Adam are limbs of one another
> Having been created of one essence.
> When the calamity of time afflicts one limb
> The other limbs cannot remain at rest.

22 June
Paulinus of Nola

355—22 June 431

Soldiering for the Eternal King

There was a time in the early history of the Church when religious leaders were unafraid to follow the teachings of Jesus. Recognizing that war and empire were contrary to Christ's message of peace and reconciliation, they forbade their flocks to serve in the military and urged converts already in the army to leave. One of these leaders was Paulinus, bishop of Nola (near modern-day Naples).

Paulinus, born into an aristocratic Aquitanian family and educated for government service, eventually became governor of Campania. Increasingly dissatisfied with public life, he was converted to Christianity by his wife, Therasia. Shortly afterwards, following the death of their only child, they resolved to withdraw from the world and live monastic lives. They distributed their possessions to the poor and, in 390, moved to Spain. Paulinus was ordained there. Five years later, the couple relocated to Nola, where Paulinus was acclaimed bishop in 409. He and Therasia spent the rest of their lives in the service of the Church, building basilicas and hospitals and ministering to the needy.

In addition to his administrative and pastoral duties, Paulinus was a prodigious writer of both prose and verse. Several of his hymns have survived, as well as fifty letters. One of them (Letter 25) was written to a soldier in the Roman army, Crispianus, exhorting him to forsake campaigning for Caesar and take up soldiering for Christ.

In his message to Crispianus, Paulinus argues that "we ought not to put loyalties or fatherland or distinctions or riches before God." Worldly armies are in the business of subjugating peoples and seizing property. Those who enlist in the army of Christ strive above all else to serve God and establish justice on earth. But those who serve in Caesar's army serve a god of destruction. "He who is a soldier with the sword is the servant of death, and when he sheds his own blood or that of another, this is the reward for his service." The pay and benefits with which Caesar rewards his soldiers are no recompense, earned as they are by "the violence you loathe." Therefore, concludes Paulinus, "change your secular military service into something better. Start being a soldier for the eternal King." If you must be a soldier, be one for Christ. "The soldier who wears armor for Him is never unarmed."

The record is silent about whether or not Crispianus followed Paulinus' advice. If he did, he might well have suffered martyrdom. But Paulinus' reminder of what it means to be a follower of the Prince of Peace speaks eloquently across the centuries to us today.

23 June

William Sloane Coffin

1 June 1924—12 April 2006

Prophet of Wholesale Justice

THE MAN WHOM *The Nation* magazine once called the "only true heir of Martin Luther King, Jr." was born with a silver spoon in his mouth. The child of a wealthy attorney and realtor, Coffin was given a top-notch education at home and in school, including several months studying piano at a Paris conservatory. Returning to the States when war broke out in Europe, he enrolled at Yale School of Music but soon quit to join the U.S. Army. After the war, he returned to Yale and then studied a year at Union Theological Seminary before leaving to join the CIA at the outbreak of the Korean War. His five-year stint in the intelligence agency both disillusioned him—he often said that he had a "lover's quarrel" with the United States—and encouraged him to think deeply about justice.

After leaving the CIA, Coffin was ordained and began a twenty-year career as a college chaplain, first at Williams College and then at Yale. An early opponent of the Vietnam War and the nuclear arms race, he collaborated with other peace activists in the 1960s and early 1970s, and at one point even tried to turn Yale's chapel into a sanctuary for draft resisters. During the same period, he was a staunch advocate of civil rights, helping organize freedom rides through the South. His public witness for peace, disarmament, and civil rights landed him in jail several dozen times. One of his convictions was appealed all the way to the Supreme Court, where it was overturned. After leaving Yale in 1977, he served as senior pastor at New York City's interdenominational Riverside Church. Under his leadership, Riverside became nationally recognized as a progressive Christian church. In his later years, after retiring from Riverside, Coffin devoted himself to the campaign for nuclear disarmament.

Coffin admitted that he was an ambivalent pacifist. He was unquestioningly a nuclear one, but at the same time he recognized that there is "an irremediable stubbornness about evil" that occasionally might demand a militant response. What Coffin wasn't ambivalent about in the least, however, was that the gospel message that he "as a very convinced Christian" embraced had at its core Jesus' call for justice tempered with compassion. "What this country needs," he said shortly before his death, "what I think God wants us to do, is not practice piecemeal charity but engage in wholesale justice. Justice is at the heart of religious faith. When we see Christ empowering the poor, scorning the powerful, healing the world's hurts, we are seeing transparently the power of God at work."

24 June
Raphael Lemkin

24 June 1900—28 August 1959

Naming the Crime of Crimes

EVEN THOUGH WE GENERALLY take them for granted, words are powerful tools. Without them, we'd be helpless when it comes to understanding the world and our place in it. In 1944, the lawyer Raphael Lemkin invented a word that enabled us to name, better comprehend, and do something about a terrible crime against humanity—the "crime of crimes," Lemkin called it. The word was *genocide*, fashioned from the Greek *genos* (tribe, race) and the Latin *cide* (killing). As Lemkin wrote in *Axis Rule in Occupied Europe,* the book in which he coined the term, "Generally speaking, genocide does not necessarily mean the immediate destruction of a nation, except when accomplished by mass killings of all members of a nation. It is intended rather to signify a coordinated plan of different actions aiming at the destruction of essential foundations of the life of national groups, with the aim of annihilating the groups themselves. Genocide is directed against the national group as an entity, and the actions involved are directed against individuals, not in their individual capacity, but as members of the national group."

Lemkin's work wasn't impersonal analysis. Born a Jew in eastern Poland, his older relatives remembered and told him stories about anti-Semitic pogroms they had endured. As a teenager, he was shocked by reports of the Ottoman Empire's systematic destruction of the Armenians. After he became an attorney and international law specialist, Lemkin's memories of these horrors prompted him to prepare a 1933 report for the League of Nations in which he made the case for codifying in international law what he then called the "crime of barbarity." When the Nazis invaded Poland in 1939, Lemkin joined the Polish Army, was wounded in battle, and just managed to escape to the United States via Lithuania and Sweden. Most of his family members weren't so fortunate; nearly fifty of them died in the Nazi genocide.

After settling in the United States, Lemkin made a living by teaching law at Duke, Yale, and Rutgers. But he devoted most of his time and energy to campaigning for international recognition of genocide as a crime. He served as an advisor on genocide to the Nuremburg War Crimes Commission, and unsuccessfully tried to persuade the 1945 Paris Peace Conference to recognize genocide as a crime. Undaunted by his failure, he became a "one-man lobbying machine" (as one admirer put it) to the United Nations, the international body Lemkin correctly saw as having the authority to declare genocide a crime. Although he had difficulty in finding a nation willing to sponsor his proposal, Lemkin finally got his resolution before the General Assembly. His efforts paid off in 1948, when the United Nations approved the Convention on the Prevention and Punishment of Genocide that outlawed the systematic destruction of national, ethnic, religious, or racial groups by murder, deportation, sterilization, or life-threatening oppression. Thanks to the tireless efforts of one man, the world moved one step closer to an internationally codified defense of human life and dignity.

25 June
Lois Marie Gibbs

25 June 1951—

Grassroots Environmentalist

IN 1978, A WOMAN who described herself as "an American housewife buying the American dream" was rocked to discover that her first-grade son, who'd been perfectly healthy until starting school, suddenly developed epilepsy, chronic urinary tract infections, and a dangerously low white blood cell count. When the doctors failed to come up with explanations, she began knocking on doors in her Niagara Falls blue-collar community to see if other children were ill. What she discovered was a nightmare. Since 1974, 56 percent of the neighborhood's pregnancies had ended in miscarriage, stillbirth, or horrific birth defects. Urinary tract disease had increased by 300 percent. Vile odors and oily liquids surfaced in yards. Trees and shrubs blackened and died. Kids came home from the school playground with chemical burns.

Eventually the housewife, Lois Gibbs, discovered that her community of Love Canal was built on a toxic dumpsite containing twenty-one thousand tons of chemical waste. The stockpile included eleven carcinogens, one of them the deadly chemical dioxin. The chemicals had been dumped between 1942 and 1952 in an abandoned, mile-long canal and then buried under twenty feet of dirt. The city managers of Niagara Falls, eager for development property, zoned Love Canal as a residential area. Soon homes and a school were built—and the buried chemicals began seeping.

Gibbs quickly organized and led the Love Canal Homeowners Association, a grassroots organization representing nine hundred families. "Before Love Canal," she said, "my biggest decision was what to make for supper." Now she found herself fighting government and chemical company officials, who refused to take responsibility for the disaster and opposed her every step of the way. But Gibbs persevered—"our children's future and those of their unborn children are at stake"—and after two years of struggle finally persuaded the Environmental Protection Agency to demolish the neighborhood, relocate over eight hundred families, clean up the dumpsite, and create a federal Superfund to locate and clean toxic sites across the nation. "We the community raised our voices, united together, stood together, and demanded that the government do right."

For nearly thirty years, this "American housewife" has led the Center for Health, Environment, and Justice, a grassroots organization that lobbies for environmental responsibility from the government and corporations and educates the public about environmental issues. One of the center's most successful efforts was the 1987 McToxics Campaign, which forced fast food restaurants to quit using dioxin-laced styrofoam containers. Gibbs, nominated for the Nobel Peace Prize in 2003, continues to encourage citizens to recognize that "average people and the average community can change the world. You can do it just based on common sense, determination, persistence, and patience."

26 June
Justin Martyr

103—CA. 165

Murderers No More

IN THE EARLY YEARS of the Christian church, Roman authorities eyed the followers of Jesus with suspicion. The empire was prudently tolerant of the multitude of gods worshipped by the peoples it conquered. All it required was an oath of fealty to the emperor—but an oath so strong that swearing it was tantamount to recognizing him as a deity. Christians refused to do this and thus were seen as seditious. It wasn't their religion that the Romans objected to so much as their refusal to be politically obedient subjects.

One of the many early Christians who tried to persuade officials that the empire had nothing to fear from Christians was the Palestinian-born Greek Justin. Raised in a pagan household and thoroughly schooled in the Greco-Roman philosophical tradition, Justin converted to Christianity as a young man and became one of its leading apologists, or defenders. In his writings, only a handful of which survive, he took on critics of the faith, Roman as well as Jewish, in a sophisticated and sensitive manner.

In a treatise known as the *First Apology*, probably written about a decade before his death, Justin specifically responded to the Roman charge that Christians are seditious and therefore pose a danger to the state. He assured the authorities that Christians had no design upon the empire, no intention of setting up a rival political state, because the kingdom to which they pledged fidelity is of the spirit rather than the flesh. Membership in this kingdom is transformative. It washes away the temptation to violence to which subjects of the empire are susceptible. Consequently, Christians posed no threat to anyone. As Justin memorably wrote, "We who once murdered each other indeed no longer wage war against our enemies." The transformation was so thorough that Christians also renounced the violence of deception, even if doing so put their lives in danger. "So as not to bear false witness before our interrogators," continued Justin, "we cheerfully die confessing Christ."

Roman officials were apparently skeptical of Justin's second claim. It made no sense to them. Why wouldn't someone bear false witness if it meant saving his or her life? But Justin explained that pledging oneself to Christ's nonviolence made perfect sense, despite its immediate legal repercussions. Roman soldiers, he pointed out, take an oath of allegiance for mere corruptible rewards such as money or land. "It would be absurd if we [Christians], who fervently long for incorruption, do not endure all things, so that we will receive what we desire from the One with the power to impart it."

Justin's arguments were of no avail, and he was martyred—hence the name by which he's come to be known—in the reign of the Emperor Marcus Aurelius. Ironically, Marcus, one of the so-called good Roman emperors, was a student of the same philosophical schools Justin had studied before his conversion.

27 June

Geoffrey "Woodbine Willie" Studdert Kennedy

27 June 1883—8 March 1929

Setting Christ Free

MANY COMMITTED PACIFISTS—PERHAPS MOST—HAVE never experienced combat. Geoffrey Studdert Kennedy's pacifism was born in the trenches of World War I. One of the British padres who accompanied troops to the front lines, Studdert Kennedy saw action on the Somme, at Messines Ridge, and in the final allied offensive. He was awarded the Military Cross for bravery and became a national hero. He also became one of the most ardent and influential pacifists of his generation. "There are no words," he wrote, "foul and filthy enough to describe war."

Ordained in 1910 in the Church of England, Studdert Kennedy spent the years before the war as a slum priest ministering to wretchedly impoverished parishes in Leeds and Worcester. Wishing to share the poverty of his flock, he deliberately chose parishes with the smallest income and poorest people and drove his wife to distraction by giving away money and household items.

Afire like most of his countrymen with war fever, Studdert Kennedy enthusiastically enlisted in the British Army in 1916. Many battlefield padres were disdained by British tommies as naïve do-gooders. But they adored Studdert Kennedy as much as his civilian parishioners had, affectionately calling him "Woodbine Willie" after the brand of cigarettes he regularly handed out to them. As the war progressed, he became convinced that the evil of economic injustice he'd witnessed as a civilian priest was matched by the evil of war. The change of heart became total in June 1917 when his batman, Roy Fergusson, "a splendid lad of nineteen," was killed. Studdert Kennedy found him "leaning against a heap of sandbags, his head buried in his hands, and a great hole in his back." He buried the boy with his own hands in a bomb crater.

After the war, Studdert Kennedy took advantage of his status as a national hero to speak and write ceaselessly against war and poverty. In over twenty volumes of prose and verse and hundreds of speeches and sermons, he urged Christians to take Jesus' message of peace and reconciliation seriously. The problem, he said, was that the Church preferred a domesticated, nonthreatening Jesus, safely tucked away "amid the lilies of the altar, with the sweet incense of worship rising round Him, a weekly refuge from a distraught and vulgar world." But, he warned, "You cannot keep Christ in your churches; he will break them into pieces if you try." When Studdert Kennedy died, worn out by his crusade to get Christ out of the churches and onto the streets as much as by asthma and the aftereffects of a trench gassing, thousands of veterans and workers lined the route of his funeral entourage. They covered his casket with lovingly tossed packets of Woodbines.

28 June
Danilo Dolci

28 June 1924—30 December 1997

Fire Beneath Ash

In 1958, a one-time student of architecture led 150 jobless Sicilian men in repairing a neglected road that the government refused to maintain. Enraged by this act of public rebuke, the authorities ordered police to disperse the workers and arrest their leader, who spent the next eight months in prison. But a new tactic in active nonviolence had been launched: the "strike in reverse," in which the unemployed both protested their poverty and demonstrated their willingness to work.

The man who led the strike was Danilo Dolci, whose advocacy for poverty-stricken Sicilian peasants earned him the nickname "The Gandhi of Sicily." Raised in Mussolini's Italy, as a youngster he tore down fascist posters and refused to enlist in the army. He later noted that he was a conscientious objector before he'd ever heard the term. "I felt strongly that it was wrong to kill people and I was determined never to do so."

This commitment to nonviolence led Dolci to abandon his studies in order to work with war orphans. Two years later, in 1950, he moved to his father's native Sicily to share the lives of impoverished peasants and fishermen. Settling in the squalid fishing village of Trappeto, the "poorest place I had ever known," Dolci soon married a widow, Vincenzina Mangano, and adopted her five children. After her death he remarried and fathered two more children.

At the time, Sicily was one of the poorest regions in Europe. Unemployment was rampant, water and electricity scarce, disease and illiteracy abundant, and the Mafia ruled with an iron fist. Northern Italians disdainfully referred to Sicilians as "bandits," "dirt-eaters," and "savages." Dolci immediately began what would become a forty-year campaign of active nonviolence to secure water rights, employment, public housing, and educational opportunities for the poor. He took on both Mafia dons and a corrupt government bureaucracy. In addition to strikes in reverse, Dolci also used hunger strikes, work stoppages, peasant cooperatives, and public demonstrations to draw attention to the desperate economic conditions in Sicily. His hardest battle was a campaign to dam the Iato River so that peasants could irrigate their parched fields. He was also an early pioneer of sustainability, decrying the squander of resources that often accompanied poverty and ignorance.

By the time he died in poverty on 30 December 1997, Danilo Dolci had twice been nominated for the Nobel Peace Prize and was a recipient of the Lenin Peace Prize. Although no communist, Dolci recognized that reality was too complex to fit into a single ideology. "There is some truth in all solutions," he said. "We are all mendicants of truth." To the end, he fought for the Sicilian peasants whom he loved and who had come to love him. "There is God in these people," he said, "like the fire beneath the ashes."

29 June

Samantha Smith

29 June 1972—25 August 1985

Peace Kid

JANE PAULEY OF NBC's *Today* leaned in toward her guest and pointedly asked, "Samantha, do you know what the word 'propaganda' means?"

The guest was eleven-year-old Samantha Smith. The year was 1983. Samantha had just returned from a two-week trip to the Soviet Union at the invitation of General Secretary Yuri Andropov. While there, she'd visited Moscow, Leningrad, and a communist youth camp near the Black Sea. When she returned to the U.S., her message was simple: "none of the [Soviet kids] hated America, and none of them ever wanted war. If *we* could be friends by just getting to know each other better, then what are our countries really arguing about?"

Six months earlier, frightened by the saber rattling from both sides of the Iron Curtain, Samantha had written to Andropov expressing her fears about war. Andropov eventually replied, assuring his young correspondent that he wanted peace and inviting her to visit his country. When she returned, she urged the American people and government to do what she had done: drop the demonizing stereotypes and get to know the Russians personally. "Us kids have made friends, and we're really no different, just smaller versions of grown-ups."

The trip immediately catapulted Samantha into international prominence. The ensuing media frenzy alternated between praising her as the world's youngest goodwill ambassador and dismissing her as the dupe of Soviet propaganda. But the real Samantha defied easy classification. On the one hand, she was a typical kid: a freckled fan of Bugs Bunny cartoons, Cheerios, lavender pajamas, and Michael Jackson who disliked doing homework and who frequently stated in interviews that her fondest hope was for the "destroyment" of nuclear weapons. On the other hand, she was savvy beyond her years. In response to Jane Pauley's question, Samantha replied that she didn't know the meaning of the word *propaganda*. After Pauley explained, Samantha acknowledged that the Soviets probably had taken advantage of her visit. But if they used her, she insisted, "it was propaganda for peace." And that was just fine with her.

Samantha and her father Arthur died in a plane crash two years after her trip to the Soviet Union. At her funeral, a Soviet embassy official said that she "shone like a brilliant beam of sunshine at a time when relations between our two countries were clouded." Mikhail Gorbachev, who presided over the dismantling of the Soviet regime in 1991, acknowledged that her internationally reported peace mission to his country helped ease the way to the democratic reform of *glastnost*.

30 June
Muhammad Yunus

28 June 1940—

Village Banker

THE OLD SAYING "Give a man a fish and you feed him for a day; teach him how to fish and you feed him for a lifetime" has sometimes been used to justify refusing charity to those in need under the pretext that doing so infantilizes them. But even those humanitarians who recognize the sad necessity of charity don't deny that it's more triage than solution. Poverty results from the consolidation of wealth in the hands of a few and a lack of economic opportunity for the many. This fact inspired the Bangladesh economist Muhammad Yunus to do something about helping those people at the bottom of the economic ladder "learn to fish."

The key, he believes, is the extension of microcredit, or very small loans, to the people in developing nations who need them most but who lack the collateral or credit history that most banks require. Under the microcredit system, small loans that finance cottage industries are extended to groups of people, often women, who lack collateral but who serve as one another's co-guarantors. The principle behind this arrangement, tried and tested by experience, is that people are likely to be more diligent in repaying loans if they're held accountable by other members of their local community. The entrepreneurial enterprises financed by these microloans, ranging from the raising of chickens and sheep to the selling of grocery items out of the home, in turn raise the material standard of living of loan recipients and provide them with a stepping-stone for a greater degree of economic security than they have ever known. The goal, as Yunus says, "is creating a level playing field for everybody—rich and poor countries, powerful and small enterprises—giving every human being a fair chance."

Yunus launched his microcredit project in 1976 after begging for financial underwriting from several major banks. By 1982, nearly thirty thousand individuals were in his microcredit network, and in that year he consolidated his operations by opening the Grameen or "Village" Bank. Since then, Grameen has loaned nearly $7 billion to over seven million borrowers in one hundred countries. In 2006, Yunus and Grameen were awarded the Nobel Peace Prize. In its citation, the Nobel Committee noted that "loans to poor people without any financial security had appeared to be an impossible idea. [But] from modest beginnings three decades ago, Yunus has, first and foremost through Grameen Bank, developed micro-credit into an ever more important instrument in the struggle against poverty."

Yunus himself maintains that one of the main reasons the microcredit movement has been so successful is that it bypasses reliance on vast and corruptible state bureaucracies to take care of the poor. Instead, it provides opportunities for people to help one another while helping themselves. That, Yunus believes, is a pretty unbeatable strategy.

1 July

David Brower

1 July 1912—5 November 2000

Friend of the Earth

DAVID BROWER WAS PASSIONATE in his defense of the earth, and that passion frequently got him into trouble. In one of the periodic feuds between conservationists and loggers over the fate of the Northern Spotted Owl, for example, Brower claimed that "loggers losing their jobs because of Spotted Owl legislation is, in my eyes, no different than people being out of work after the furnaces of Dachau shut down." On a different occasion, he insisted that "while the death of young men in war is unfortunate, it is no more serious than the touching of mountains and wilderness areas by humankind." Such bold comparisons rankled many. But what Brower lacked in diplomacy, he more than made up for in his dedication to protecting the environment.

Brower's love of nature was cultivated in his younger years, when he was an avid mountain climber. He made seventy first ascents on the perpendicular rocks at Yosemite, scaled the highest peaks of the Sierra Nevada, and was a member of the first team to make it to the top of Arizona's Painted Rock.

Brower joined the Sierra Club, the organization founded by conservationist John Muir, when he was still in his early twenties. By 1952, after serving on the organization's board and editing its magazine, he became the Sierra Club's executive director and immediately began moving it in the direction of environmental activism. Under his direction, the Club actively opposed the damming of rivers in the Grand Canyon and the construction of power plants in wilderness areas. The Club lobbied for the creation of Redwood National Forest and helped push through the 1964 Wilderness Act, which protected millions of acres of pristine land from logging and mining. Brower's activism attracted thousands of new members to the Club, and their collective voice exerted such political influence that the Internal Revenue Service eventually yanked away the Sierra Club's tax-exempt status.

In 1969, Brower and the Sierra Club went their separate ways. For its part, the Club accused Brower of heavy-handed management. For his part, Brower felt the Club wasn't radical enough in its defense of wilderness. So upon his departure, he founded Friends of the Earth, an international organization that lobbies for environmental protection and sustainable economic justice. In 1986 Brower moved again, this time to Earth Island Institute, an organization he founded to serve as a clearinghouse for innovative social justice and environmental projects. When asked by a reporter to explain his transition from Sierra to Earth Island, Brower responded that each move had been motivated by his desire for a more radical approach to protecting the planet. Given the accelerating rate of environmental degradation, he said, large-scale and revolutionary change was needed. Otherwise, "We're not borrowing from our children, we're stealing from them—and it's not even considered to be a crime."

2 July
Birsel Lemke

4 July 1950—

No!

CYANIDATION IS A MINING technique that extracts gold embedded in rock such as quartz. The rock is ground up and soaked in sodium cyanide, a process that separates the ore from the stone to leave a gold sludge that is then melted into ingots.

It's a simple way to extract gold, but the environmental risks associated with it are colossal. Toxic residue from slag heaps leaches into the earth and contaminates aquifers and streams or rivers. Just how hazardous cyanidation is became eminently clear in 2000, when cyanide from a Romanian gold mine spilled into the Danube River, poisoning drinking water and killing aquatic life for hundreds of miles. It was the worst European environmental disaster since Chernobyl.

In the late 1980s, the multinational corporation Eurogold announced that it intended to develop nearly six hundred gold mines in Turkey, seventy-two of them along the Aegean Coast, all of them extracting gold through cyanidation. The miles-long strip of coastland, stretching from Troy to Pergamon, is one of Turkey's most beautiful natural environments. It's also a major olive-producing region.

Enter Birsel Lemke (whose maiden name, Altin, coincidentally means "gold"), a member of Turkey's Green Party. In response to Eurogold's plans for Turkey, she founded in 1990 the citizens' initiative Hayir ("No!") against gold-mining. Lemke mobilized local farmers, civic leaders, and elected officials within Turkey, and then traveled to Germany to convince the banks underwriting Eurogold to withdraw their funding. Then Hayir sued both Eurogold and the Turkish government, which had signed onto the deal in anticipation of an influx of mining revenue, to close mines already up and running. The Turkish Supreme Court ruled in Hayir's favor and prohibited mining that used the cyanidation process, but Eurogold worked behind the scenes to convince the government to drag its feet in obeying the court order. Lemke and Hayir then took their case to the European Court of Human Rights, which in 2007 upheld the Turkish Supreme Court's decision and censured the Turkish government.

The grassroots resistance Lemke mobilized against Eurogold is a case study in active nonviolence tactics. She organized a meeting in the Aegean Sea of Greek and Turkish ships filled with children to symbolize that cyanidation was an environmental threat that put the children of both countries in danger. She gathered thousands of villagers in a march to Gallipoli, the site of the World War I battle, where they publicly vowed that they too would sacrifice themselves for their country if need be. And in one especially imaginative village, as Lemke describes it, "inhabitants ran unclothed in demonstrations, bearing signs with the slogan, 'Before Eurogold strips us, we'll strip.' The women, who always were at the head of the demonstrations and campaigns, denied themselves to their husbands until the former had expelled the gold mining companies."

In recognition of her nonviolent struggle against a Goliath of industry, Lemke was given a Right Livelihood Award, the alternative Nobel Peace Prize, in 2000.

3 July

Kees Boeke

25 September 1884—3 July 1966

Raising a Peaceful Generation

THE DUTCH QUAKER KEES Boeke spent his first fifty years trying to persuade adults to find nonviolent ways to resolve their conflicts. After his marriage to an heiress to the Cadbury fortune, he and his bride spent two years in the Middle East as Quaker missionaries, returning to her native England when World War I erupted. Once there, Boeke so vigorously protested the war that English authorities sent him back to Holland. Soon afterwards, he helped found the International Fellowship of Reconciliation, and he and his wife used a good deal of her inheritance to build a large conference center to host peace congresses.

Boeke and his wife also lived in voluntary simplicity to avoid having to pay war taxes. They even refrained from buying postage stamps or riding public transportation, lest the money they spent find its way to the military. Eventually they gave away all of the Cadbury money, and for a time they lived in poverty, even losing their home.

A moment of truth came for Boeke nearly a decade after the end of World War I. Looking back on his life, he concluded that neither his work with peace organizations nor his personal lifestyle had done much to prevent violence. They hadn't slowed down the carnage of the war nor prevented the post-war European chaos that Boeke correctly believed would lead to more armed conflict. So he decided to shift gears. If adults were unreceptive to his message of peace, he would try their children. Believing that kids hadn't yet been programmed to assume the moral acceptability of violence, he decided to open a school that would teach nonviolent conflict resolution as a core part of its curriculum.

The school, which admitted its first students in 1926, was called *Der Werkplaats*, the "Workplace." Instead of encouraging a traditional academic environment in which all decisions were made by teachers and administrators and passively accepted by students, the school taught collaboration by creating student-teacher teams to tend the school garden, clean the classrooms, and prepare the daily lunch. Students were encouraged to call teachers by their first names and to look upon them as elder colleagues rather than authority figures. Two principles informed everything the Workshop did: all participants were equal and decisions were made by consensus. The latter was reached by breaking students down into small groups or "circles," where they worked with one another until they reached agreement. Then representatives from each circle met together in a larger one, once again aiming for consensus. The process was often laborious and sometimes frustrating. But it taught young people that disagreements could be resolved in ways that gave everyone a voice and no one an unfair advantage. It was, Boeke hoped, a schooling that would lessen the prospect of future wars.

Nearly a century after its founding, the Workshop continues to school young people in the ways of peace.

4 July
Ron Kovic

4 July 1946—

A Living Reminder of War

THE LAST THING THE organizers of the 1972 Republican National Convention wanted were reminders that the United States had gone down the rabbit hole when it sent troops to Vietnam. So they were anxious to keep anti-war sentiment far away from Miami Beach Convention Center.

But the well-packaged show the Republicans hoped to put on was disrupted by a crowd of khaki-wearing, long-haired veterans who interrupted nomination speeches with shouts of "Stop the bombing!" One of them was in a wheelchair. His name was Ron Kovic, perhaps the best-known war resister of the Vietnam era.

In his autobiography, *Born on the Fourth of July*, Kovic writes that he started out as a patriot who never dreamed of questioning his country's foreign policy. Enlisting in the Marines at age eighteen, he volunteered for two tours of duty in Vietnam, convinced that the war was a selfless crusade against communist aggression. But during his second tour, his confidence in the righteousness of the cause began to crack. At one point, in the midst of a skirmish, he accidentally shot and killed a fellow Marine. When he reported the incident to his company commander, he was told to keep quiet about the incident because it would only make for bad press. Later, he and his platoon were ordered to attack and torch a village suspected of harboring Viet Cong. Kovic was stunned to discover later that the only casualties of the assault were women and children. Then, in 1968, he was hit by a bullet that shattered his spine and paralyzed him from the waist down.

Kovic endured miserable months of recovery and physical therapy in Veteran Administration hospitals. He tried college, but bouts of anger and depression kept him from serious study. Instead, he brooded on the war, and gradually he came to the conclusion that he and all casualties on both sides were victims of an unjust conflict. The war, he believed, was morally wrong.

In 1970 Kovic began appearing in anti-war demonstrations. He protested in front of draft boards, at high schools, at sporting events—anywhere that young, draft-age men were likely to be. He wanted his maimed body to be "a living reminder of war" so shocking that it couldn't be ignored. "I wanted people to understand," he recalled in 2005. "I wanted to share with them as nakedly and openly and intimately as possible what I had gone through, what I had endured. I wanted them to know what it really meant to be in a war—to be shot and wounded, to be fighting for my life on the intensive care ward—not the myth we had grown up believing."

Since the end of the Vietnam war, Kovic has advocated for better medical and psychological services for returning veterans and has publicly protested the two Iraq wars. "I have come to believe there is nothing in the lives of human beings more terrifying than war," he says, "and nothing more important than for those of us who have experienced it to share its awful truth."

5 July
H. H. Dalai Lama

7 July 1935—

The Real Enemy

Although he maintains he is only a "simple Buddhist monk," Tenzin Gyatso, the fourteenth Dalai Lama, has been the Tibetan head of state and spiritual leader since he was fifteen years old.

Born in a remote peasant village on the border of Tibet and China, Tenzin Gyatso was recognized by Tibetan monks as the successor to the thirteenth Dalai Lama when he was only two years old. Believed to be the reincarnation of previous Dalai Lamas and a manifestation of the bodhisattva of compassion—a bodhisattva is an advanced spiritual being who forsakes complete spiritual fulfillment for the sake of helping others achieve enlightenment and liberation—Tenzin Gyatso was brought to the holy city of Lhasa four years later to begin his monastic training. When he was twenty-five he received the equivalent of a doctorate in Buddhist philosophy.

China invaded Tibet in 1949, and the following year the fifteen-year-old Dalai Lama traveled to Beijing as the Tibetan head of state to negotiate a peace treaty with Mao Zedong. But nine years later, Tibetans revolted against their Chinese occupiers, and the Chinese People's Liberation Army brutally suppressed the uprising. The Dalai Lama was forced to flee his country and to seek political asylum in Dharamsala, India, where the Tibetan government-in-exile remains to this day.

The Dalai Lama is internationally known as both a Buddhist scholar and a gentle yet outspoken advocate of nonviolence. He is the recipient of numerous peace prizes, including the 1989 Nobel Peace Prize for his nonviolent struggle for Tibetan independence, as well as dozens of honorary degrees. Remaining firmly rooted in his own Buddhist tradition, he is nonetheless a champion of interfaith dialogue and cooperation. A tireless traveler who has been to over sixty countries, he continues to meet with heads of government and religious leaders from all faiths. Somehow he has also managed to author more than seventy books.

At the heart of the Dalai Lama's message of nonviolence is the very human struggle to manage anger. He refuses to condone or ignore violence and injustice for the sake of a fake peace. But he teaches that when we confront harmful actions or policies, we should do so "without any hatred for those who perpetrate them." Succumbing to hatred ignites anger, and "anger is the real destroyer of our good human qualities; an enemy with a weapon cannot destroy these qualities, but anger can. Anger is our real enemy."

This "simple Buddhist monk" continues to work for the liberation of his people and for the transformation of the "whole of Tibet into a zone of peace" for humans as well as Tibet's natural environment, which has been ravaged by China's use of the nation as a dumping site for hazardous nuclear waste. As a manifestation of the bodhisattva of compassion, the Dalai Lama's concern for well-being extends to all creation.

Elise Boulding

6 JULY

6 JULY 1920—24 JUNE 2010

Pioneer of Peace Studies

BORN IN OSLO, ELISE Boulding's parents immigrated to New Jersey when she was still an infant to escape the Norwegian economic crisis of 1923. As a teenager, she was shocked by the Nazi invasion of neutral Norway. It was then that she realized that there was no "safe place" from war and that human aggression needed to be confronted with nonviolent responses rather than avoided or responded to in kind. Her commitment to world peace eventually led her to the Society of Friends, where she met her future husband, the economist and pacifist **Kenneth Boulding**.

Elise Boulding harbored a dislike of dichotomies in general, whether between the public and private spheres, activism and scholarship, or gendered divisions of labor. So when she married Kenneth in 1941, she saw no problem with becoming a housewife and mother and at the same time throwing herself into other activities outside the home. She became involved with the Women's International League for Peace and Freedom (she was later appointed its international chair) and continued her education, earning a graduate degree in sociology in 1949. Twenty years later, after raising five children, she received a doctorate in sociology from the University of Michigan. Her ability to juggle so many different roles amazed her friends. As one of them remarked, she "stretch[ed] so far the limits of human experience that she could address the United Nations with no problem and then, in the next second, stoop to tie a child's shoe and be aware of the needs of both at the same time."

During the next twenty years, Boulding was instrumental in founding the Consortium on Peace Research, Education, and Development. She also served on the international jury of the United Nations Educational, Scientific, and Cultural Organization's prize for peace, as well as on the congressional committee that led to the creation of the U.S. Institute for Peace. She was nominated for the Nobel Peace Prize in 1990.

Boulding was also a dedicated researcher who authored fourteen books, many of them on peacemaking and women's studies. But perhaps her greatest contribution was the creation at Dartmouth College of the first Peace Studies program in the United States. Her integrative and interdisciplinary approach to peace and conflict resolution studies, her involvement in the women's movement, her advocacy for children, and her concern for the environment shed insight into the building of what she famously called a "culture of peace." Her pioneering contributions to Peace Studies drew attention to women and the institutions of patriarchy, war's effects on families, and the importance of raising children in a climate of "peaceableness." "We need," she wrote, "to have human beings who are oriented [toward peace] from their earliest memories."

7 July

Ben Linder

7 July 1959—28 April 1987

Putting in Light and Hoping for the Best

NEWLY MINTED ENGINEERS USUALLY go straight from college to jobs with corporations and contractors. Ben Linder didn't. He headed instead for Nicaragua to help the country rebuild after years of oppression under the dictator Anastasio Somoza.

Linder, a California-born kid who graduated from the University of Washington, had a quirkiness to him that many people found irresistible. He took up juggling at an early age, and as a college student he sometimes dressed as a clown to entertain children. He mastered the art of balancing on a tall unicycle and frequently surprised both drivers and pedestrians by tooling around Seattle on it. When he left for Nicaragua in 1983, the unicycle went with him, and so did his clown makeup kit.

When Linder arrived in the capital of Managua, it had been four years since the Sandinista revolution overthrew the corrupt Somoza regime. U.S. President Ronald Reagan, an ardent foe of the revolution, was secretly funding and arming the so-called Contras, guerilla insurgents who roamed around the countryside terrorizing Sandinista supporters and wrecking such infrastructure as power stations, hospitals, and schools.

After working on several engineering projects in Managua, Linder left for El Cuá, a village in northeastern Nicaragua, to build hydroelectric dams that would supply electricity to hamlets in the area. Contras were everywhere. As usual, Linder quickly made friends with the children in the area, but he worried about their safety. "I see the kids and I feel like taking them all away to a safe place to hide until the war stops and the hunger stops and El Cuá becomes strong enough to give them the care they deserve," he wrote. "The pied piper of El Cuá. But I can't do that, and even if I could it wouldn't help the neighboring towns. So instead, I try to put in light, and hope for the best."

The best didn't come, at least not for Linder. He was murdered along with two Nicaraguan workers while he inspected a dam construction site. It was obvious that the murderers were Contras and that they specifically targeted Linder, probably with CIA approval. First they tossed grenades to destroy the partially built dam. When Linder fell, wounded by shrapnel, they shot him in the head at close range where he lay.

The death of a young man who went to a foreign country to help its people build a better, just, and nonviolent society might have gone mostly unheralded by the U.S. press had American supporters of the Contras not publicly attacked him. But Florida Congressman Connie Mack went after Linder's mother when she tried to draw attention to what was going on in Nicaragua, presidential press secretary Marlin Fitzwater blamed Linder for his own death, and Vice President George Bush implied that Linder was a traitor who got what he deserved. These public attacks on Linder by people in high places created an unexpected popular backlash against U.S. support for the Contras. In the end, Linder *did* bring light to the people of Nicaragua.

8 July
Peace Pilgrim

18 July 1908—7 July 1981

44,000 Miles for Peace

On the first day of January in 1953, a forty-four-year-old woman started walking for peace. She began her journey in Pasadena, California, and intended to make her way to the East Coast. She carried no food, water, or money, and only one change of clothing and a toothbrush. Her plan was to eat when she was offered a meal and sleep where she was offered shelter. Otherwise, she would fast and take refuge in the open fields or a convenient barn or drain pipe. She had been born Mildred Lisette Norman, but after she began her journey she called herself "Peace Pilgrim."

Peace Pilgrim would traverse the continental United States six full times, averaging around twenty-five miles a day, and was on her seventh circuit when she died. She quit counting the miles in the mid-1960s after she hit the twenty-five thousand mark, but probably added close to another twenty thousand before her death. Everywhere she walked, she spoke to churches, civic groups, student societies, and peace organizations about inner tranquility, nonviolence, reconciliation, and simplicity. After she became better known, she was frequently interviewed by radio and television stations in cities through which she passed, and so her message of peace was heard by thousands more.

Mildred Norman became committed to nonviolence while still a young woman and volunteered with several pacifist organizations, including the American Friends Service Committee. All the while, she strove to live a simple life, believing that excess possessions were not only bad for the soul but also deprived others of goods they needed to survive. In 1952, she walked the entire Appalachian Trail by herself, training her body and mind for the peace witness she intended to undertake the following year.

Why did Mildred Norman become Peace Pilgrim? "I realized in 1952," she said, "that it was the proper time for a pilgrim to step forth. The war in Korea was raging and the McCarthy era was at its height. . . . There was great fear at that time and it was safest to be apathetic. Yes, it was most certainly a time for a pilgrim to step forward, because a pilgrim's job is to rouse people from apathy and make them think."

In order to rouse folks from their fear-inspired apathy—an apathy that, of course, was more repression than indifference—Peace Pilgrim offered a few simple words of counsel. "Hate injures the hater, not the hated," she pointed out. "Prayer is a concentration of positive thoughts. Problems that help us grow are really opportunities in disguise. In all things be thankful. Never be impatient, all good things take time. Be not concerned that you are offended, but that you do not offend." But above all, she advised people to find their calling, that vocation of peace to which they feel especially drawn. For some, it may mean service; for others, simplicity; for still others, witness. Finding it offered a spiritual center of gravity and a deep source of meaning.

Whenever she gave interviews, Peace Pilgrim always refused to divulge her legal name or date of birth. She wasn't important, she insisted. But her message of peace was.

9 July
Shane Claiborne

11 July 1975—

A Simpler Way

THE LAST DECADE HAS seen a reform movement in the American church that resembles the great Franciscan reform of the twelfth century. Called the New Monasticism, the movement focuses on simple, communal living, a lived commitment to serving Christ in the service of others—as a New Monasticism slogan has it, "How can you worship a homeless man on Sunday and ignore another one on Monday?"—and nonviolence in personal lifestyle and social interactions. It has revitalized interest in Christianity among young and old alike, but especially in the young, who also constitute most of the movement's leaders.

One of them is Shane Claiborne. Even before graduating from college, he began rethinking his very conventional evangelical upbringing's near-exclusive emphasis on personal salvation at the expense of social justice advocacy. While still a student, he helped organize a widely publicized campaign against the closure of an abandoned church in which homeless squatters had taken shelter. Claiborne enlisted fellow students to live with the squatters, collect food for them, lobby for their fair treatment, and serve as buffers between them and the authorities. He also worked for nearly a month in Calcutta with Mother Teresa, taking care of the indigent and dying people to whom she and her Missionaries of Charity regularly ministered. He later spent several weeks in Baghdad at the beginning of the Iraq War as a member of a peace delegation.

Claiborne's unique contribution to the New Monasticism was the 1997 establishment of a Philadelphia-based Christian intentional community called The Simple Way. Fellow workers live in community with one another and offer spiritual and material resources to people who need them. Their goal is to create an alternative community that can be a model for the emergence of similar communities—American Christians, laments Claiborne, have generally "not shown the world another way of doing life. Christians pretty much live like everybody else"—as well as a catalyst for overall social change. As Claiborne says, "A gospel that is not political is no gospel at all."

Claiborne and his fellow Simple Wayers hope to halt the retreat of many mainstream Christians into lifestyles indistinguishable from others. Like St. Francis of Assisi and his early followers, they fear that Jesus' message of indiscriminate love and nonviolence has been watered down for the sake of convenience, and that as a consequence the Church has become more of a defender of the status quo than a prophetic voice. "We live in a world of zombies," says Claiborne, "amid a deadness that has infected even the church." His hope is to revitalize the world through a renewal in the Church of the gospel's radical call to justice.

10 July
Toyohiko Kagawa

10 July 1888—23 April 1960

Brotherhood Economics

THE JAPANESE EMPIRE, OR at least its warmongers, was shocked. After the Japanese army's successful and atrocity-filled campaign against China, Toyohiko Kagawa, a middle-aged Christian novelist, author, and social reformer, publicly apologized to the Republic of China. Predictably, he was arrested; upon his release he traveled to the United States in the hopes of preventing the war he feared was coming. His hopes for peace were dashed at Pearl Harbor, but after the war he was a tireless advocate of the proposed article in Japan's new constitution that renounced war forever as a means of resolving international disputes. This time he was successful.

Kagawa's aversion to warfare was based in part on his deep and costly commitment to Christ—when he converted, his entire family disowned him—and his realization that the victims who suffered most during war were the poor. As a young man, he lived in a slum in the city of Kobe for five years, working to relieve the poverty and squalor he found there, opposing prostitution rings, and protecting abused children. Afterwards he published an influential book describing his experiences, and then traveled to Princeton Seminary to study divinity. Back in Japan, he threw himself into peace work, labor union advocacy, environmental conservation, and the struggle for universal suffrage. Arrested several times for these activities, which he considered to be "Good Samaritan" obligations of a Christian, he spent his time in prison writing. A prolific author, Kagawa eventually published over one hundred books.

One of them was a 1936 defense of what he called "brotherhood economics." For Kagawa, none of the predominant political economies of his day—fascism, Soviet-style communism, and capitalism—was either moral or effective. Despite their differences, all of them concentrated wealth and power in the hands of a few and created a permanent poverty-stricken and politically powerless underclass. Moreover, the primary goal in the three predominant models is ever-accelerating growth, a manic pursuit that in turn leads to periodic economic crises.

As an alternative, Kagawa defended an economic model in which he envisioned Christian churches, cooperative movements, and pacifist organizations joining hands to focus on the growth of small, local economies. Instead of massive corporate conglomerates or state-controlled production, Kagawa advocated a network of cooperatives and small, family-owned businesses that focused on collaboration rather than competition. His model closely resembles the distributism endorsed by early twentieth-century English writers such as G. K. Chesterton and Hilaire Belloc as well as the "small is beautiful" model defended by E. F. Schumacher. So far as Kagawa was concerned, it was the political economy most compatible with the Christian ideal of love.

11 July
Abdulkadir Yahya Ali

1957—12 July 2005

"Why Do We Have to Fight?"

THEY CAME FOR HIM in the dead of night. The five intruders rousted him and his wife out of a sound sleep, handcuffed his bodyguards, and then murdered him in front of his wife, spraying him with machine gun fire before shooting him several more times in the face with handguns. Then they left, as quickly as they had come.

Abdulkadir Yahya Ali was murdered because he was a threat to one or more of the factions in the civil war that has been ripping Somalia apart since 1991. Born and bred in the Somali capital of Mogadishu, Yahya, the son of schoolteachers, had been the most visible peace activist in the city during the fifteen years prior to his murder. As founder in 1999 of the Center for Research and Dialogue (CRD), a research and advocacy organization dedicated to nonviolent conflict resolution in the troubled Horn of Africa, Yahya worked tirelessly and cheerfully—all who met him were struck by his perennial optimism—for peace in his war-torn country. The recipient of many death threats who narrowly escaped murder or kidnapping on several previous occasions, Yahya had been advised many times to flee Somalia. But he believed it his duty to remain.

Before his involvement with the Center for Research and Dialogue, Yahya served as a protocol assistant at the U.S. embassy in Mogadishu. During the American military presence in Somalia in the administration of U.S. President Bill Clinton, Yahya actively encouraged the U.S. military to assist in locating and confiscating the tens of thousands of weapons in the hands of the city's feuding warlords, a task that ultimately proved impossible and earned Yahya many enemies. In the final years of his life, Yahya focused his attention on trying to persuade the warlords, many of whom headed clans with long histories of blood feuds, to resolve their differences through peaceful negotiations. As he regularly told them, "I didn't choose to belong to clan X and neither did you, so why do we have to fight?"

Yahya and his family lived in extremely frugal circumstances. Every month he divided his small personal salary up among his extended relatives, reserving the bulk of what donations came in to the CRD to further the organization's mission of reconciliation and peace. After his death, one of his friends described this dedicated man as a "peace warrior." Yahya might have preferred the less militaristic "peace witness."

The CRD continues to advocate for Yahya's vision of a peaceful Somalia. After his murder, the Nabaddoon Yahya Foundation, a Somalian peace institute, was founded in his memory.

12 July
Mitch Snyder

14 August 1943—6 July 1990

Acting Up for the Homeless

THE TURNING POINT FOR Mitch Snyder was meeting **Phil** and **Dan Berrigan** when he was sent to Connecticut's Danbury Prison in 1970 for stealing a car. The Berrigan brothers were behind bars in the same place for burning draft cards. Snyder had been something of a drifter up to that point. Deserted by his father when he was just a boy, he'd grown up in poverty, raised by a single mom and in and out of trouble with the law. But listening to the Berrigans talk about nonviolence and social justice during the long days in prison turned him around. When he was released in 1972, he headed for Washington, DC's Community for Creative Non-Violence (CCNV).

With the Vietnam War tapering off, thousands of returning veterans, many of them addicts or mentally ill, were jobless and on the streets. Snyder's concern for them eventually led to his and the CCNV's full-time advocacy for the homeless. In the years that followed, homelessness became an ever greater problem, and Snyder responded to it with public demonstrations and creative street theater. In 1978, for example, he led a CCNV march in which a coffin representing the homeless was carried through the streets of Washington, DC.

In 1981, the newly elected Reagan administration made severe cutbacks in federal assistance to housing and social service programs, throwing an unprecedented number of people onto the streets. Snyder launched a vigorous campaign for the right of homeless people to decent shelter, food, and medical treatment and badgered the government to repair the Federal City Shelter, an overcrowded and underfunded homeless shelter that had fallen on bad days. The climax of his crusade was a fifty-one-day hunger strike undertaken to compel President Reagan to take the problem of homelessness seriously. Snyder got wide coverage during his fast, eventually winding up on the television program *60 Minutes*, and the resulting public outcry persuaded the federal government to finally renovate the shelter. It helped that Snyder had timed his fast to coincide with the national election in which Reagan ran for a second presidential term.

Everyone who knew Snyder described him as a frequently angry man. His unhappy childhood and youth, combined with his continual frustration over the indifference to homelessness shown by both the government and society at large, sometimes resulted in bouts of dark depression. There was often a belligerent edge to his speech as well as his actions that alienated some of his co-advocates. But most of them recognized that his anger also fueled his activism on behalf of the street people the rest of the country simply wanted to forget.

Shortly before his death, Snyder mentioned to a few friends that he intended to go on retreat at a monastery to battle his personal demons and get reconnected to God. But he never made it. He hanged himself in his room at the CCNV building. After his death, a street in the District of Columbia was renamed in his honor.

13 July

Toma Sik

17 August 1939—13 July 2004

Interpaciganto[1]

CONSCIENTIOUS OBJECTION IS A crime in Israel. Men and women who refuse conscription are handled roughly by tribunals and typically sent to military prisons. They also endure the scorn and even hatred of most Israelis, who see conscientious objection as deplorable cowardice. So it takes a lot of courage for an Israeli to take a public stand against militarism by refusing to serve. Toma Sik had that courage. He not only refused to fight, but counseled similar-minded Israelis for three decades. He headed the Israeli branch of War Resisters International and actively participated in peace demonstrations as well as public protests against the government's treatment of Palestinians.

Believing that competition between nation-states was a leading cause of warfare, Sik was a convinced internationalist who learned and promoted Esperanto as the lingua franca he hoped would draw different peoples and cultures closer together. His commitment to nonviolence extended to the nonhuman animal world as well through his adoption of veganism.

Born into a Jewish-Hungarian family two weeks before World War II erupted, Sik spent his first five years in a Budapest ghetto. After the hunger and fear of the war years, his pro-Zionist family migrated to Israel, where they settled on a kibbutz. But it didn't take long for Sik to reject Zionism for what he took to be its nationalistic chauvinism and militarism. His response baffled and angered his family. It also perplexed him. In his late fifties, Sik wondered why the destruction and brutality he and so many other children experienced during World War II affected them so differently. "How has it happened," he wrote, "that so many Jewish kids, including my brother, and adults, who went through the same horrors, suffering, deaths and what not in the Holocaust, had become immediately after it nationalist, chauvinist, militarist, racist, murderous combatant Zionist; while I, with the same background and experience, became an internationalist, an antimilitarist and pacifist, anti-racist anti-Zionist and vegan." His own assessment was that while the war convinced some of his contemporaries never to bring their own children into such a cruel world and others to raise children and send them into the military to kill or be killed, "my conclusion from my 5 years old child's experience in ghetto Budapest has been, that I didn't wish to inflict such a fate on any 5 years old, younger, or older person."

After years of serving as a public conscience for his fellow Israelis, Sik returned to his native Hungary. He purchased land on which to build a communal "new peasantry" of vegan, egalitarian, and humanist pacifists, but was killed in an accident on the farm a month short of his sixty-fifth birthday.

---

1. *Interpaciganto* is "peacemaker" in Esperanto.

14 July
Woody Guthrie

14 July 1912—3 October 1967

Dust Bowl Troubadour

WOODROW WILSON GUTHRIE'S ITINERANT life was a creative celebration of the "common" men and women who work hard to support their families, and a blistering denunciation of the capitalists and politicians who look down upon and take advantage of them. Few other artists in America's history have so successfully voiced the heartland values of honest work, livable wages, and the dignity of hard labor. His most famous song, "This Land Is Your Land," is both a paean to the beauty of America and a stinging critique of capitalist society.

Guthrie's early years were marred by personal tragedy. When he was a youngster of seven, his eldest sister died in a fire set by their mentally unstable mother. After several more fires, one of which severely injured Guthrie's father, his mother was institutionalized, breaking the family apart. Guthrie never completed high school, preferring to teach himself music "by ear" and to perform on street corners. He married at nineteen and worked odd jobs. But the Dust Bowl forced him, along with thousands of other Okies, to migrate to California in search of work.

Guthrie's travels across the country during the Depression years exposed him to the plight of the working poor. It wasn't long before he became a convinced communist, although never formally affiliating with any communist group. In 1940, he was invited by John Steinbeck, whom he had met in California, to perform at a New York City benefit for migrant workers. The concert not only brought Guthrie national attention. It also introduced him to fellow radical **Pete Seeger**. The two quickly forged a lifelong musical friendship that produced a blend of social commentary and folk music sometimes called "citybilly."

Guthrie's social activism was inextricably linked to his music. As he often said, "Where three communists meet, the fourth one ought to be a guitar player." Music was a way of both spreading a message of social change and giving listeners hope. "In states and countries where it ain't too healthy to speak your mind or even vote like you want to," said Guthrie, "folks have found other ways of getting the word around. One of the mainest ways is by singing."

Guthrie, like so many others, felt obliged to support the war against Hitler. But he concluded that he best served the worldwide struggle against totalitarianism by continuing as a balladeer of freedom and social justice. The ideas embodied in his music, he believed, were every bit as potent as the weapons of armed conflict. As he famously wrote on his guitar, "This machine kills fascists."

After the war, Guthrie continued to write prose, poetry, and songs that spoke to the social injustices of his day. But in 1952, he was diagnosed with Huntington's disease, a neurological disorder that eventually results in madness and loss of muscle control. For the final eleven years of his life, the Dust Bowl troubadour who inspired such later songwriters as Bob Dylan, Bruce Springsteen, and John Mellencamp was silenced by the same illness that maddened and killed his mother.

15 July

Barbara Lee

16 July 1946—

No Blank Check for War

Four days after the 9/11 terrorist attacks in New York City, Washington, DC, and Pennsylvania, Congresswoman Barbara Lee, who represents a blue-collar California district, became the only member of either the House or Senate to vote against a joint resolution granting President George Bush the authority to use "necessary and appropriate force" against the perpetrators of 9/11 and their allies. Members of her own Democratic Party tried to dissuade her from doing so. Afterwards, she was condemned as a traitor by newspaper, radio, and television commentators. For a while she was given round-the-clock protection by District police because of furious threats against her life.

In the aftermath of the terrorist attacks, the entire nation was shocked and outraged. When the White House asked Congress for permission to use military strength in pursuit of the planners of the attacks, there was general agreement throughout the country that this was the right thing to do. But at a Washington National Cathedral memorial service for the victims, Lee was struck by the plea from one of the priests for the U.S. government and people to muster the strength not to return evil for evil. In her judgment, signing on to the authorization *was* returning evil for evil because it gave the president too wide a latitude when it came to waging war. As Lee explained, "It was a blank check to the president to attack anyone involved in the September 11 events—anywhere, in any country, without regard to our nation's long-term foreign policy, economic and national security interests, and without time limit." To bestow such indiscriminate power, Lee believed, would be a failure on Congress's part to properly advise and consent. Her recommendation was to wait for a clearer understanding of who had planned and executed the attacks and to think carefully about the consequences of launching strikes against them.

That recommendation went unheeded, and the United States plunged into a two-fronted, eleven-year war.

Throughout Lee's congressional career, she's voted against a number of military authorizations. In 1999, she refused to support the Clinton administration's request for U.S. airstrikes in Yugoslavia. She consistently defended withdrawal of U.S. troops from Iraq and Afghanistan, and she warned against U.S. involvement in foreign civil wars such as the 2011 conflict in Libya. As an army brat who grew up on a number of military bases, Lee is well aware of the disproportionate number of black and Latino men who traditionally serve and die in America's wars; as a member of the U.S. House of Representatives, she believes it her responsibility to make sure that all avenues of peaceful settlement have been exhausted before she agrees to send blacks and Latinos overseas in future wars. Congresswoman Lee isn't a pacifist. But she's about as close to being one as elected officials are likely to be.

16 July
Bartolomé de las Casas

CA. 1484—18 JULY 1566

Protector of the Indians

THE SPANISH SEIZURE OF the West Indies and regions of Latin America is one of the sorriest chapters in European history. Soldiers of fortune who traveled to the New World slaughtered and enslaved tens of thousands of Indians in a system known as the *encomienda*. Under *encomienda*, the King of Spain granted New World settlers responsibility for natives in the vicinity of their holdings. The grant was ostensibly given to make sure that the natives were instructed in the Christian faith and protected from hostile outsiders. But in practice *encomienda* was a brutal system of slavery that worked natives to death on plantations and in the mines.

Bartolomé de las Casas benefited from the *encomienda* system for years. Born in Seville, he traveled with his father to Hispaniola (present day Haiti and the Dominican Republic) when he was only eighteen and acquired both land and slaves. Ten years later he participated in the conquest of Cuba and enriched himself even further. What's remarkable about this is that Las Casas was a priest, the first one ordained (in 1510) in the New World. But it wasn't until 1514 that he finally realized that the brutalization of natives was contrary in every way imaginable to Christ's message of love. He immediately gave up his *encomienda*, called upon other Spanish landowners to do likewise, and returned to Spain to appeal to the king to outlaw the system. Although the Crown gave him the title "Protector of the Indians" and promised reform, little came of it. Landowner resistance to amending, much less ending, the *encomienda* system was too strong.

In 1523, Las Casas, worn out by his struggle for just treatment of New World natives, entered the Dominican Order and disappeared behind monastery walls for a decade. But the ongoing forced conversion, brutal treatment, and wholesale slaughter of indigenous populations eventually brought him out of retirement. He traveled throughout Central and South America to advocate humane treatment of Indians, helped draft a series of laws aimed at abolishing *encomienda*, and two years later, in 1544, was consecrated the first bishop of Chiapas, Mexico.

In 1552, Las Casas published *A Short Account of the Destruction of the Indies*, a chronicle of the atrocities inflicted on the natives by Spanish conquerors. The book makes for painful reading. Las Casas records seeing Spaniards cutting off the noses of native women for the fun of it, slaughtering infants, burning children alive, and laying wagers as to who could split a man with a single sword blow. The cruel actions of these so-called Christians, Las Casas pointed out, was much greater than any performed by the supposedly "subhuman" natives themselves. In another book published a decade later, Las Casas affirmed that "all people of these our Indies are human" and deserved to be treated with respect, compassion, and justice. His was the first voice against the European imperialism that would run unchecked and cause so much damage over the next four centuries. He truly was the first European "Protector of the Indians."

17 July

Ammon Hennacy

24 July 1893—14 January 1970

One-Man Revolution

Peacemakers come in all shapes and sizes, but Ammon Hennacy broke the mold. An anarchist to the core of his being, he simply defies straightforward classification in anything except his commitment to Christian pacifism. And even that was a while in coming.

Although Hennacy was raised in a religious family, he rejected Christianity from an early age. The tipping point for him was hearing a fire-and-brimstone sermon from the famous evangelist Billy Sunday. He was so repulsed by it that he walked away from faith for years. He became an atheist, a socialist, and an advocate of violent revolution.

Hennacy wound up serving a two-year prison sentence during World War I because he refused conscription on the grounds that the conflict was fought by workers for the benefit of capitalists. While in prison, a Bible was the only book he was allowed. By the time he was released, he had repudiated his earlier allegiance to violence and adopted instead the Christian pacifism he espoused for the rest of his life.

For Hennacy, Christian pacifism went hand in hand with an anarchistic refusal to accept worldly authority, especially when it collided with the teachings of Jesus. To avoid paying taxes to a government that practiced war, capital punishment, and racism, Hennacy deliberately kept his income below the poverty line, earning his living for years as a migrant farmworker. He dressed in secondhand (and sometimes thirdhand) clothes, lived in flophouses, and regularly picketed governmental offices and military installations in defiance of their authority. He refused to register for the draft in World War II, and after the war he protested the buildup of nuclear arsenals. For a decade or so in midlife he converted to Catholicism and worked closely with **Dorothy Day** and the Catholic Workers. But he eventually left the Church, unable to stomach its hierarchical structure. Nonetheless, he opened and ran a Catholic Worker Hospitality House in Salt Lake City for nearly ten years.

Hennacy often called himself a "one-man revolution" because of his countercultural lifestyle and convictions. But the term also sums up his understanding of what it takes to be a peace advocate. Societal reform has to begin, he believed, with an interior change of individual hearts. Ideally, the one-man revolution represented by this change of heart is multiplied tens of thousands of times until there's enough of a critical mass to convert a violence-embracing society. But this demands a degree of wisdom, love, and courage that most people lack. "Love without courage and wisdom is sentimentality, as with the ordinary church member," Hennacy warned. "Courage without love and wisdom is foolhardiness, as with the ordinary soldier. Wisdom without love and courage is cowardice, as with the ordinary intellectual." Still, all it takes to inspire others is the example of a single person—such as "Jesus, Buddha, and Gandhi"—who possesses all three. Then the revolution begins.

18 July
Nelson Mandela

18 July 1918—

Troublemaker for Peace

AT HIS COMING OF AGE ceremony, sixteen-year-old Mandela heard his tribal chief lament that the futures of young South African men had been stolen by the white colonial government's policy of racial segregation. But Mandela didn't really understand apartheid, he later recalled, until he ran away from home in 1941 to escape an arranged marriage and wound up in Johannesburg. For the first time, the relatively sheltered Mandela was confronted by the terrible reality of being black in a racially divided country.

The son of a Xhosa chief, Rolihlahla Mandela—one of his schoolteachers gave him the English name "Nelson"—was sent to live with the leader of the Thembu people when his father died. He was given royal status, allowed to sit on tribal councils, and educated in the best schools available to blacks. From tribal elders, Mandela learned that South Africans once lived and governed themselves peacefully, sharing resources with whites. So when he joined the African National Congress (ANC) in 1944 to participate in its struggle for human rights, he brought to the table a good contemporary education and the memory of the way his ancestors once lived. He hoped to recover that peaceful way of life through the nonviolent strategies taught by **Mohandas Gandhi**.

Mandela reluctantly abandoned his nonviolent stance after the 1960 Sharpeville Massacre of blacks protesting restrictive passbook laws. He became the leader of the ANC's armed wing, the Spear of the Nation, and was responsible for planning several bombings before being arrested in 1962 and sentenced to life imprisonment two years later. He remained behind bars for the next twenty-seven years.

During his imprisonment, the now outlawed ANC continued its violent resistance to apartheid. But Mandela slowly came to the realization that "to be free is not merely to cast off one's chains, but to live in a way that respects and enhances the freedom of others." He concluded that ANC armed militancy neither respected the freedom of others nor was practically effective, and he reembraced his earlier commitment to nonviolence. In 1982 he wrote to the South African Minister of Justice to initiate the slow process of "talks about talks" between the white government and the ANC. The negotiations eventually led to Mandela's release in 1990, the end of apartheid, and the enfranchisement of blacks. Mandela received the 1993 Nobel Peace Prize and was elected president of a democratic South Africa the following year. In his inaugural speech, he praised the sacrifice of all South Africans, black and white, in the cause of justice and peace, and he called on them to continue the struggle. "We must act together for national reconciliation," he said. "Never, never, and never again shall it be that this beautiful land will again experience the oppression of one by another. Let freedom reign."

Mandela's birthname, Rolihlahla, means "troublemaker." What trouble he made during his long life was in opposition to a horribly unjust political system. In the end, this troublemaker became one of the contemporary world's great peacemakers.

19 July
Barbara Deming

23 July 1917—2 August 1984

Respecting Freedom

PERHAPS PART OF THE reason respect for freedom became the center of Barbara Deming's defense of nonviolence is that she spent a good part of her life struggling to protect her own. Born in New York City to a well-to-do, politically conservative Quaker family, she rebelled at any early age against both the conservatism and the religion. When she was seventeen, she announced herself a thoroughgoing secularist as well as a lesbian. For the rest of her life she not only defended her freedom to be who she wanted to be, but also joined others in their struggles for freedom. At one time or another, Deming was involved in the civil rights movement, the anti-Vietnam War movement, the women's movement, the nuclear disarmament movement, and the gay rights movement.

Deming's unique contribution to peacemaking was her insistence that religious belief was not necessary for a commitment to nonviolence. While she applauded the faith-based peace advocacy of such contemporaries as **Dorothy Day**, **Daniel** and **Phillip Berrigan**, and **Martin Luther King Jr.**, she worried that the unintended message they gave was that peace is an exclusively religious concern. Starting in 1959, after a trip to India where she met practitioners of Gandhian strategies of nonviolence resistance, Deming worked to elaborate the theoretical foundation for a secular commitment to nonviolence.

For Deming, the challenge of any practitioner of active nonviolence is "to learn to be aggressive enough." This was a lesson that both King and **Mohandas Gandhi** learned: oppressors aren't likely to give up their power unless they're confronted with a persuasively forceful incentive. Merely appealing to their conscience almost never works; such strategies as economic boycotts, strikes, and international sanctions do.

But if these modes of coercion are acceptable, why isn't violence? Persons of faith can fall back on religious justifications. But Deming's answer to the question is respect for freedom. The goal of any act of resistance is to attain freedom. But violence is an attempt to dominate another person to such an extent that he or she is robbed of free will. So in resorting to violence, the resister undercuts the very reason for resisting. The fundamental respect for freedom upon which Deming rests her argument isn't violated by nonviolently preventing the killing of others. "Some freedoms are basic freedoms, some are not," argued Deming. "To impose upon another man's freedom to kill is not to violate his person in a fundamental way." There's no interference with his free will, no violation of his fundamental personhood. All that nonviolence does is to interfere with a nonbasic freedom of his, the freedom to kill, for the sake of a more basic one, the right of the intended victim to live.

20 July
Mirabehn

22 November 1892—20 July 1982

Gandhi's Daughter

MOHANDAS GANDHI VISITED LONDON in 1931 to attend the Second Round Table Conference, part of a series of talks between Indian and British representatives on constitutional reform in India. Grainy newsreels of his arrival at the conference show a member of his entourage who seemed out of place because of her tall stature and her pale complexion. Although dressed in traditional Indian garb, she was clearly a Westerner.

In fact, she was the daughter of a British admiral, and her birth name was Madeleine Slade. An accomplished pianist who had a passion for Beethoven, Slade first learned about Gandhi when she read **Romain Rolland**'s biography of him. Eager to meet him, she traveled to India in 1925, and after a few days in Gandhi's ashram decided to become his disciple. She shaved her head, adopted Indian dress, and began learning Hindi. Gandhi gave her the new name of Mirabehn, after a sixteenth-century saint noted for her devotion and her musical skills. She became his personal assistant and steady companion. Mirabehn's acquaintances, noting the close relationship between her and Gandhi, called her "Gandhi's daughter."

Mirabehn was often derided by fellow Englishmen, who accused her of "going native." But she proved an invaluable aid to Gandhi in his nonviolent struggle for Indian independence from British rule. She provided him insight into British customs and temperament that a nonnative, even one as familiar with England as Gandhi, might not pick up on. She also wrote hundreds of articles for English-language newspapers, both in India and back in England, which helped familiarize the world with Gandhi's means and aims. But useful as her talents as Gandhi's press agent proved, they also brought her to the attention of the British colonial authorities; she was imprisoned in India several different times for sedition, once for several months.

British contempt wasn't the only burden Mirabehn bore. She was also frequently looked upon with suspicion by native Indians, who questioned her motives and were just as wary as the British of a white woman "going native." But Mirabehn was undaunted, and for years criss-crossed the continent to spread Gandhi's message of nonviolence, truth-power, and self-sufficiency, focusing especially on rural audiences. Her devotion to Gandhi, her embrace of an Indian lifestyle, and her persecution at the hands of the British eventually earned her the trust of most people in her adopted country.

Gandhi's 1948 assassination was a great blow to Mirabehn, but she remained in India for another decade, visiting Gandhian ashrams and teaching his principles of nonviolence. In 1959 she left India and settled in a remote village in Austria, where she lived in seclusion and devoted herself to her music. To the end, she reverently spoke of Gandhi as her spiritual father.

21 July

Albert Lutuli

CA. 1898—21 JULY 1967

Honoring the God-Factor in Humans

IN 1952, THE APARTHEID government of South Africa gave Albert Lutuli a choice: resign his office as Zulu tribal chieftain or leave the African National Congress (ANC), an organization to which he had belonged for eight years. Lutuli had been chieftain since 1936, and there was no immediate event that provoked the government into handing him the ultimatum. What worried authorities was Lutuli's growing reputation, both inside and outside South Africa, as a nonviolent resister to apartheid laws. Lutuli refused to choose either of the ultimatum's options, and so the government removed him from the chieftainship. In response, the ANC elected him president one month later. The struggle was on.

Lutuli was the son of Seventh-Day Adventist missionaries. Well educated as a youth, he went on to teach and administer school, converted to Methodism, and became a lay minister. When the South African government officially enacted apartheid laws in 1948 and began restricting the movement of blacks by requiring them to carry passes, Lutuli became a leader in nonviolent protests. As his stature among South African blacks increased, the government grew more concerned, leading to the 1952 showdown.

For the final fifteen years of Lutuli's life, following his election as ANC president, he would be under official ban—a kind of house arrest that limited his ability to move around the country or meet with more than one or two persons at a time. The first ban immediately followed the ANC election and lasted for four years. When it ended, Lutuli attended an open-air ANC meeting and was arrested, charged with treason, and jailed for nearly a year before charges were dropped. Immediately following the 1960 Sharpeville Massacre, in which nearly seventy men, women, and children were gunned down by police as they protested the pass laws, Lutuli burned his own passbook in protest. The government once again imposed a ban upon his activities.

Although venerated as the ANC's moral leader, the ban's prohibition of Lutuli's overt participation in ANC decision-making eventually led to a decline in the organization's fidelity to his principled nonviolent resistance. **Nelson Mandela**'s formation in 1961 of the ANC's armed wing, the *Umkhonto we Sizwe* ("Spear of the Nation"), shifted the ANC away from nonviolence for the next two decades. In the remaining years of Lutuli's life, this change in ANC strategy was a source of great sorrow to him.

Lutuli was awarded the 1960 Nobel Peace Prize, the first African to be so honored. In his acceptance speech, he noted that his nonviolent resistance to apartheid was inspired by his religious faith. "As a Christian and patriot," he said, he "could not look on while systematic attempts were made, almost in every department of life, to debase the God-factor in man or to set a limit beyond which the human being in his black form might not strive to serve his Creator to the best of his ability. To remain neutral in a situation where the laws of the land virtually criticized God for having created men of color was the sort of thing I could not, as a Christian, tolerate."

22 July
William Wilberforce

24 August 1759—29 July 1833

Anti-Slavery Reformer

ELECTED TO PARLIAMENT WHEN he was only twenty-one, William Wilberforce, wealthy and fond of the good life, later admitted that "the first years in Parliament I did nothing—nothing to any purpose. My own distinction was my darling object." But in 1786 he underwent a religious conversion that changed his direction. For the rest of his life, he displayed a religious fervor that led him, as it did so many nineteenth-century British and American evangelicals, to become a champion of social reform. At one point, he belonged to nearly seventy philanthropic societies, prompting one wit to say that even though Wilberforce never succeeded in becoming prime minister of England, he *was* "prime minister of a cabinet of philanthropists."

Some of Wilberforce's reformist agenda, such as defending what later came to be called "blue laws" that restrict personal behavior and commerce on the Sabbath, strike us today as quaint. He also had a streak of conservatism that led him to frown upon women playing any role in public life. But the very religious zeal that fueled these reactionary causes also fed his dogged thirty-year battle against the buying and selling of human beings. More than any other statesman of his day, Wilberforce was responsible for the end of slavery in the British Empire.

He began researching the British slave trade in the late 1780s. At that time Britain imported upwards of fifty thousand slaves per year to work in its colonies, primarily in the West Indian sugar plantations where they died like flies from exhaustion and disease. He was horrified by what he discovered. "So enormous, so dreadful, so irremediable did the trade's wickedness appear," he later recalled, "that my own mind was completely made up for abolition. Let the consequences be what they would: I from this time determined that I would never rest until I had effected its abolition."

The first legislation to abolish the slave trade was proposed by Wilberforce in 1790. It met with indifference from most Parliament members and hostility from some, and it was easily defeated. As Wilberforce continued pressing the point year after year, his opponents became increasingly fierce, often personally attacking Wilberforce's character. But he persevered, and finally in 1807, working with Quakers and other abolitionists, he succeeded in persuading Parliament to ban the slave trade.

Plagued by ill health his entire life, Wilberforce retired from active politics in 1825. But during the years after the passage of the slave trade ban, he worked, both as a member of Parliament and as a private citizen, to free slaves already captive in the British Empire. This labor bore fruit: slavery ended once and for all throughout the empire in 1833, the same year that Wilberforce died.

23 July

Leopold Engleitner

23 July 1905—

Refusing to Go

He felt unwanted and unloved for as far back as he could remember. Born into an impoverished Austrian family, Leopold Engleitner had a crooked spine that bent his torso to one side and gave him a vaguely dwarfish appearance. His father disliked him, perhaps because of his deformity, and the children in his village mocked and shunned him. By the time he was thirteen, he was forced to take a job to support his family, and young Engleitner found the heavy labor too much for his small frame. He felt utterly alone.

Then, in 1932, he left the Catholic Church to become a Jehovah's Witness. Over the next few years, ardently studying the Bible, he preached throughout Upper Austria. He remained a social pariah, this time because of his abandonment of Catholicism, but his newly found faith gave him the strength to endure both his poor health and his social isolation.

Between 1934 and 1938, Engleitner was arrested four times by Austrian authorities for preaching the "seditious" pacifism and noncooperation with the state characteristic of Jehovah's Witness teachings. After the *Anschluss* of 1938 tied Austria's fortunes to Nazi Germany's, he was arrested for "promotion of a religious sect declared inadmissible by the state." The authorities were ready to drop the charge if Engleitner agreed to military service, but he refused. "I can neither take an oath on military duties nor carry a weapon, since this contradicts my faith, to which I unconditionally adhere. If I were called up to go to the front, I would refuse to go. I am aware that my adherence to this view could cost me my life, but there is nothing I can do about it since life depends on our compliance with God's laws." So the authorities shipped Engleitner off to Buchenwald. He was imprisoned there as well as in two other concentration camps for the next four years. During that time he was starved, worked nearly to death, and physically abused by guards and fellow prisoners alike.

In 1943, Engleitner was released on condition that he agreed to provide what amounted to agricultural slave labor for the rest of his life. Weighing merely sixty-two pounds, he returned to his hometown and was hired out to a local farmer. But within weeks he received notice to report to military authorities for a pre-induction physical examination. Despite his curved spine and poor state of health, he was ordered to the front. Engleitner fled to the mountains, where he hid in caves and abandoned huts until the Nazi defeat in 1945.

SS leader Heinrich Himmler contemptuously referred to Jehovah's Witnesses as "Bible people" too weak and otherworldly to be of any use whatsoever to the Reich. But he was wrong. Conscientious objectors like Engleitner kept decency and the ideal of nonviolent resistance alive in Germany during a time when darkness threatened to extinguish them.

24 July
Stanley Hauerwas

24 July 1940—

Peace Is the Church's Virtue

From the earliest days of Christianity, followers of Jesus have argued about the proper role of the church. Is its sole purpose the glorification of God, or is it also called to convert the world? And if proselytizing is part of its mandate, how should it go about the task? By accommodating itself to the world in order to make its teachings more plausible, or by modeling a radical alternative to the world?

The theologian Stanley Hauerwas, named "America's Best Theologian" by *Time* magazine in 2001, thinks that the business of the church is to obey the commandments of Christ, especially those recorded in the Sermon on the Mount about nonviolence, reconciliation, and forgiveness. Peacemaking, in fact, is the virtue that is "intrinsic to the nature of the church," and it's the business of the Christian community to practice peacemaking in obedience to Christ and to model it to the rest of the world. But it's important for Christian peacemakers to realize that their understanding of peace can't be adjusted to conform to the world's standards, and that the church is not in the business of playing social worker to the world. Christians are "resident aliens," loyal ambassadors of another country, and their primary task is to remain faithful to the story that grounds their identity. It's just that in doing so, they give the rest of the world a glimpse of what God's peaceable kingdom looks like.

The peace taught by Jesus and practiced by the church community isn't the expedient kind so often embraced by the world. Secular peace is typically built on "forgetfulness," an agreement to repress tensions and disagreements for the sake of getting along. This faux peace neither reconciles people to one another nor genuinely resolves the disagreements that are the breeding ground of overt violence. It merely smooths troubled waters temporarily.

The peace that is the church's chief virtue is built not on forgetfulness but forgiveness. Wrongs aren't plastered over with a veneer of forgetfulness, but confronted with honesty, compassion, repentance, and forgiveness. Genuine peace isn't an avoidance of conflict, but an acknowledgment of it whenever and wherever it exists and an earnest effort to heal rather than merely anesthetize wounds. This process of naming and forgiving not only serves as a virtue within the Christian community. It also dictates how the community relates to the world.

Looked at in this way, says Hauerwas, it should come as no surprise that so many Christian peacemakers come across as people who stir up trouble. If the peace that Jesus taught means confronting conflict rather than pretending it doesn't exist, and "if the church is to be a community of peace in a world at war," then the church "cannot help but be a community that confronts the world in an uncompromising manner." Contrary to what many people think, Christian pacifism is not passive. Instead, it's "an active way to resist injustice by confronting the wrongdoer with the offer of reconciliation."

25 July
Walter Rauschenbusch

4 October 1861—25 July 1918

Kingdom before Church

In 1881, a *New York Times* reporter referred to the Hell's Kitchen district in mid-Manhattan as "probably the lowest and filthiest in the city." Rotten tenement buildings loomed over dark and grimy streets. Prostitutes plied their trade at all hours of the day, drunken men and women slumped on doorsteps, and crime was an everyday—and every night—affair. The Gilded Age hadn't touched Hell's Kitchen.

The Reverend Walter Rauschenbusch ministered to a Baptist church in Hell's Kitchen for a full decade, and the experience taught him that the American Protestant emphasis on individual sin, personal salvation, and otherworldliness was overplayed. He never denied the reality of individual sin. But he came to believe that the miserable dramas played out in Hell's Kitchen were as often as not written by unjust social and economic conditions that broke the human spirit and trampled hope. By ignoring these conditions, the Church did more than merely overlook the institutions that created them and profited by them. It collaborated with their evil.

Rauschenbusch's experiences in Hell's Kitchen led him to become the nation's leading exponent of the "Social Gospel," an interpretation of Christianity that focused on the socially transformative message of Jesus. The kingdom of God, he argued, isn't a heavenly reward awaiting humans at the end of time. Instead, it's a state of peace and justice created by men and women of good will in the here and now that mirrors God's intentions. Consequently, Rauschenbusch argued, genuine religion "is not a matter of getting individuals into heaven, but of transforming the life on earth into the harmony of heaven." Forgetfulness of this truth eggs on Christians to "seek to save their own souls and [remain] selfishly indifferent to the evangelization of the world." For Rauschenbusch, "evangelization" meant not only preaching the gospel but using it as a tool of radical social reform—even revolution—against the powers and principalities that ruled society and controlled individual lives.

The powers and principalities standing in the kingdom's way are militarism, individualism, nationalism, and capitalism. The first encourages the violence that Jesus condemned by word and deed; the second justifies a selfish indifference to the needs of others; the third breeds the patriotic zeal that sees other nations as enemies; and the fourth makes greed a virtue. Christian churches, by contrast, ought to teach the Christ-centered alternative virtues of pacifism, community, cosmopolitanism, and socialism, each of which Rauschenbusch believed was practiced by the first Christians. The problem is that Christians have confused the Church with the kingdom and have allowed hierarchy and authority to replace love and a sense of fairness. "We are the church as we worship together; we are the Kingdom as we live justly and lovingly with one another."

26 July
Eberhard Arnold

26 July 1883—22 November 1935

Living the Kingdom Here and Now

In November 1933, the Gestapo raided a small community of Christians who called their rural settlement in central Germany *Der Bruderhof*, the Place of Brothers. Pamphlets, books, and papers were seized, the community's private school was shut down pending the arrival of a Nazi-approved teacher, and Bruderhof members were put on notice that the Third Reich regarded them with deep suspicion.

This small community that Hitler's henchmen found so threatening was founded in 1920 by the Christian visionary Eberhard Arnold. As a youth, Arnold came to believe that the Sermon on the Mount was the "canon within the canon," and that Jesus intended its message of nonviolence, voluntary poverty, and self-giving love to be taken seriously as guidelines for Christian living rather than written off as unattainable ideals. He eventually left the Evangelical State Church of Prussia because he concluded that any alliance of church and state was incompatible with the Sermon, and instead worked for a few years with the Salvation Army ministering to Germany's poor. During this time he continued to study both Scripture and the church fathers, and he wrote voluminously.

In organizing like-minded Christians into the Bruderhof, Arnold's hope was to create a community modeled after the description of the primitive church found in the Acts of the Apostles. Property was held in common, everyone labored for the common good, a policy of noncooperation with secular society was adopted, nonviolence was embraced, and the Sermon on the Mount was taken as the community's normative guide. Arnold was convinced that the Bruderhof's lifestyle wasn't merely a run-up to the kingdom of God, but actually *was* the kingdom. "The character of God's prophetic Kingdom," he wrote, "the future of Christ who shall come again—the future of love and justice—shall and can be lived now and here as a living Church-community!"

Arnold taught that Christians are called to be ambassadors of Christ rather than citizens of nation-states because the interests of Church and State are antithetical. Christ calls on his followers to practice nonviolence and love. The State calls on its followers to bear arms and fight. Consequently, wrote Arnold, "the kingdom of God is not represented by any state of this world, but by the church. This means that we ought to do nothing at all other than what God himself would do for his kingdom." Just as political ambassadors are not subject to the laws of the countries that host their embassies, so Christ's ambassadors are likewise immune from the cultural norms of the nations in which they live. "We are no longer subject to the laws of this world; the grounds of our embassy are inviolable, just as in the residence of an ambassador, only the laws of the country he represents are valid."

It was this conviction that angered the Nazis. After the raid on the Bruderhof, Arnold and his community fled to Switzerland, where he died. His followers then moved to England and Paraguay before settling in the United States, where they dwell to this day.

27 July
George Bernard Shaw

26 July 1856—2 November 1950

The Most Hated Man in England

It was bad enough that George Bernard Shaw was an unembarrassed atheist and that he wrote plays that proper middle-class audiences condemned as too risqué. But he compounded his offensiveness with three additional sins. He defied England's celebration of capitalism and colonialism by being a socialist; he defied the English palate by being a vegetarian; and worst of all, he defied English patriotism by being a pacifist. He was, as the newspapers called him during World War I, the "Most Hated Man in England."

His socialism was of the genteel, Fabian variety, leaning more in the direction of reform than revolution. But it was born of a deep conviction that England's rigid class structure with its inequality of wealth and privilege was fundamentally unjust. He once quipped, with signature Shavian wit, that investors, landlords, and burglars shared at least one thing in common: "all three inflict on the community an injury of precisely the same nature."

Shaw's vegetarianism was a corollary of his distrust of rigid hierarchical distinctions, in this case the conventional assumption that animals, as compared to humans, are owed absolutely no moral consideration. He found the wholesale slaughter of food animals morally objectionable on two grounds: the cruelty to the animals themselves, but also the coarsening effect that their butchery had on workers who killed them and consumers who devoured their flesh without giving a thought to how their mutton or steak wound up on their plates.

But it was Shaw's pacifism that most went against the English grain. Unlike other pacifists of his day, he wasn't motivated by religion. Moreover, his refusal to condone armed conflict extended to both world wars at a time when many pacifists of 1914 endorsed a military response to Hitler. During World War I, Shaw published an anti-war tract, *Common Sense about the War*, that defied the jingoistic boast that the British were noble and the Germans demonic. Shaw pointed out that the British Empire had every bit as shameful a track record as the German one. In a BBC interview at the outbreak of World War II, Shaw the atheist invoked the Sermon on the Mount, knowing that doing so would catch the audience's ear, to push home his pacifism. "The sermon," he said, "is a very moving exhortation, and it gives you one first-rate tip, which is to do good to those who despitefully use you and persecute you. I, who am a much hated man, have been doing that all my life, and I can assure you that there is no better fun; whereas revenge and resentment make life miserable and the avenger hateful. The lesson we have to learn is that our dislike for a certain person, or even for the whole human race, does not give us any right to injure our fellow creatures, however odious they may be."

It's a lesson we're still trying to master.

28 July
Lupus of Troyes

CA. 383—CA. 478

Tamer of God's Scourge

Rheims, Cambray, Besançon, Auxerre, Langres: town after town in Gaul had fallen to Attila the Hun, the self-styled "Scourge of God" whose fearsome warriors cut a swath of death and destruction through fifth-century Europe. A Eurasian nomad who came from east of the Volga, Attila was fierce and ruthless. The very mention of his name was enough to send whole districts into a panic. As one of his contemporaries noted, when he and his army descended on a town, "There were so many murders and bloodlettings that the dead could not be numbered. Aye, for they took captive the churches and monasteries and slew the monks and maidens in great numbers."

And now it was the turn of Troyes, a rich commercial area just one hundred miles southeast of Paris. As word spread throughout the town that Attila was on his way, those with the means to flee did so, and everyone else hunkered down in dreadful anticipation of the storm about to burst upon them. But one among them refused to flee or cower—or to resist with physical weapons. He was Lupus, the town's bishop.

As a young man, Lupus left a marriage (with his wife's consent), renounced his wealth, and entered a monastery. His reputation for holiness spread wide and far, and in 426, much against his will, it got him elected bishop. He quickly gained a reputation as a shepherd who would feed the hungry, give alms to the poor, and protect the defenseless.

A quarter-century after his consecration as bishop, Lupus faced his most formidable challenge: coping with the impending arrival of Attila. After spending a few days in deep prayer and solitude, Lupus dressed himself in his full episcopal regalia and ventured beyond the town gate to meet the newly arrived conqueror. Marching straight up to Attila, who had his entire army behind him ready to descend on Troyes, Lupus introduced himself. Attila did likewise, boastfully calling himself the Scourge of God. Lupus is supposed to have calmly replied, "Let us respect whatever comes to us from God. But if you are the scourge with which heaven chastises us, remember you are to do nothing but what that almighty hand, which governs and moves you, permits." Attila was so impressed by Lupus that he there and then agreed to spare Troyes.

There's a curious and instructive ending to the tale. On the one hand, Attila, struck by the way Lupus' act of nonviolent resistance had dissuaded him, misinterpreted it as some sort of magic and begged Lupus to accompany his army as a sort of living talisman. Roman authorities, on the other hand, interpreted Lupus' stand against Attila as some sort of appeasement and sought to persecute him. Lupus was forced to retreat to the mountains around Troyes and live for two years as a hermit until it was safe for him to return. Nonviolence was apparently as little understood in the fifth century as it is in many parts of the world today.

29 July
Dag Hammarskjöld

29 July 1905 — 18 September 1961

Holiness in Action

Two years after his death in a plane crash while flying to the Congo to broker a ceasefire in that country's civil war, the private diary of Dag Hammarskjöld, second Secretary-General of the United Nations, was published. A combination of prose and poetry, the diary clarified why everyone who met him felt as if they were in the presence of a genuine peacemaker. Shortly after the crash, Hammarskjöld was awarded a posthumous Nobel Peace Prize for his many efforts at international reconciliation during his UN tenure. His diary revealed the hidden spiritual discipline of a man devoted not simply to external peace but also inner equilibrium.

Hammarskjöld was born with a silver spoon in his mouth: his father was once the Swedish prime minister, and many of his ancestors had held prominent positions in the Swedish government. Hammarskjöld, who received an excellent education, eventually earned a doctorate in economics, worked for a few years at Sweden's national bank, followed the family tradition by going into government, and in 1951 became a member of Sweden's delegation to the UN. To his surprise, he was elected Secretary-General three years later.

During his tenure, he negotiated the release of American POWs from the Korean War, tried to do something about the perennial conflict between Israel and her neighbors, resisted Soviet attempts to strong-arm his resignation, intervened in the Suez Canal crisis, and labored for a peace settlement in the Congolese civil war.

A small but significant project undertaken by Hammarskjöld as Secretary-General was the construction of a meditation room in the United Nations, a haven where delegates and others could retreat from their hectic schedules and weighty responsibilities for silence and recollection. The room fittingly expressed Hammarskjöld's conviction that the problems of the modern world call for a marriage of action and contemplation. As he said, "In our era, the road to holiness necessarily passes through the world of action." In order to practice "quiet diplomacy," which Hammarskjöld saw as the only viable alternative to violence, the diplomat needs patience, deep listening, humility, and the conviction that his or her calling is "simple: always to live for others, never to seek one's own advantage." It's one thing to practice these virtues and to desire to do good in the safe seclusion of a monk's cell. But genuine holiness arises when one struggles to remain faithful to them in the midst of a messy and often unpredictable world. Hammarskjöld, who daily lived this challenge, described it the year before he died. "Working at the edge of the development of human society," he said, "is to work on the brink of the unknown. Much of what is done will one day prove to have been of little avail. That is no excuse for the failure to act in accordance with our best understanding, in recognition of its limits but with faith in the ultimate result of the creative evolution in which it is our privilege to cooperate."

30 JULY
Smedley Butler

30 JULY 1881—21 JUNE 1940

War Is a Racket!

SMEDLEY BUTLER WAS A man of contradictions. A descendent of Quaker stock, he quit high school before he was seventeen years old to join the Marines and fight in the Spanish-American War. He served in the Marines Corps for nearly thirty-four years, retiring as a Major General. Although he was a combat veteran in several campaigns—at the time of his death, he was the most decorated Marine in U.S. history; his citations included two Medals of Honor—he was denied battlefield duty during World War I. And after retiring from the military in 1931, he traveled across the nation telling everyone who would listen that the military was in the pocket of corporate interests.

Thirty years before President Dwight Eisenhower gave his famous speech warning the nation against the "military-industrial complex," Butler understood the connection. As he saw it, the whole enterprise of war is a racket. "A racket is best described," he said, "as something that is not what it seems to the majority of the people. Only a small 'inside' group knows what it is about. It is conducted for the benefit of the very few, at the expense of the very many. Out of war a few people make huge fortunes." And war is the biggest racket of them all. "It is possibly the oldest, easily the most profitable, surely the most vicious. It is the only one international in scope. It is the only one in which the profits are reckoned in dollars and the losses in lives."

Butler complained that even though he assumed he'd been serving his nation during his three decades in the military, he'd actually been "a high-class muscle man for Big Business, for Wall Street and the bankers. In short, I was a racketeer, a gangster for capitalism." His combat service in China, Cuba, the Philippines, Nicaragua, and Honduras, he concluded, protected corporate interests that exploited both foreign and domestic labor in the drive to maximize profit. He'd served under the dollar sign, not the American eagle.

In a small book published in 1935, Butler argued that the only way to put an end to the continuous military ventures undertaken in the interests of corporations is to make war unprofitable. In the past, young men with their entire futures ahead of them had been drafted to fight. Butler recommended a different course. "Let the officers and the directors and the high-powered executives of our armament factories and our steel companies and our munitions makers and our ship-builders and our airplane builders and the manufacturers of all other things that provide profit in war time as well as the bankers and the speculators, be conscripted—to get $30 a month, the same wage as the lads in the trenches get." As an additional strategy for cutting down on foreign military adventurism, Butler advocated a constitutional amendment that for the most part restricted military forces to the continental United States and allowed combat for defensive purposes only. His hope was that the crime of war, like any other kind of racketeering, would diminish if opportunity was reduced.

31 July
Ingrid Washinawatok el-Issa

31 July 1957—4 March 1999

Unlocking Indigenous Silence

In February 1999, Ingrid Washinawatok el-Issa, a member of the Menominee Nation, went missing with her two companions. She had traveled with them to Colombia at the request of the U'wa, an indigenous people who live in the cloud forests there. Occidental Petroleum and Shell Oil had negotiated with the Colombian government to drill for oil in U'wa territory, and the natives, numbering only about seven thousand all told, feared that both their land and their traditional way of life would be destroyed. So they asked el-Issa, a well-respected advocate of indigenous sovereignty, to visit and advise them.

But not long after their arrival in Columbia, el-Issa and her companions were kidnapped by guerrilla soldiers of the Revolutionary Armed Forces of Colombia, a rebel army opposed to the Colombian regime. Perhaps out of anger for U.S. support of the regime, the three kidnap victims were tortured and then shot. Their bodies were finally discovered and identified by credit cards found on them.

Known among her own people as Flying Eagle Woman (after her marriage, she took her Palestinian husband's surname), el-Issa was born and raised on a Menominee Reservation in Wisconsin. An early member of the American Indian Movement (AIM), her dedication to upholding the sovereignty of North American Indians soon spread to include concern for the sovereignty of indigenous peoples across the world. She was a leader of the Indigenous Women's Network, a grassroots advocacy group established in 1985; participated in national campaigns for the release of Leonard Peltier, the AIM leader serving a life sentence for the alleged 1975 shooting of two FBI agents; and served as a consultant to the United Nations. One of her dreams was the establishment of a UN "Permanent Forum" for indigenous people that would both protect their cultural integrity and conduct itself in traditional native ways. As she envisioned it, "The Permanent Forum itself could be a model based on Indigenous traditions in the sense that the structure would be complementary to the realities of the 21st century, yet rooted in its foundation of Indigenous thought. If I may use a brief example and if my relatives permit me, the Permanent Forum could be modeled after the Haudenosaunee methods of conflict resolution; Hopi methods of Peacemaking; Kuna methods of negotiation, etc."

El-Issa was well aware of the contemporary world's threat to indigenous culture and constantly stressed the importance of international collaboration between native peoples. For her, the keys to indigenous survival were the preservation of a strong sense of tribal identity and well-established native sovereignty. But indigenous survival wasn't the only end, because el-Issa was convinced that the rest of the world needed the wisdom of native peoples. Natives are "a vast library, a repository of knowledge, intelligence, and an understanding of the earth that is being lost to the world." Lest that wisdom be lost, the "silence of our peoples" must be "unlocked." Ultimate peace, she believed, is possible only when indigenous peoples are allowed to "speak to the world."

1 August
Conrad Grebel

1498—1 August 1526

Father of Modern Christian Pacifism

IN 1524, A POPULAR uprising occurred in areas of what are now Germany, Austria, and Switzerland. Around three hundred thousand peasants, fueled in part by the Protestant Reformation's questioning of traditional authority, revolted against wealthy landowners. The German theologian Thomas Müntzer was a leader in the uprising. His battle cry summed up one of the revolt's ideals: *Omnia sunt communia*, "all things in common."

The revolt captured the attention of Conrad Grebel, the son of a Zurich burgher. In his earlier years, Grebel had studied at universities in Basel, Vienna, and Paris and shown great promise. But disturbing reports of his carousing finally prompted his father to cut off Grebel's funds and bring him home before he took his degree.

Back in Zurich, Grebel underwent a conversion. The former fun-loving student now became a serious reader of the New Testament. His studies convinced him that most of what the Roman church taught lacked a biblical basis. The mass, he believed, was a symbolic memorial rather than a sacrifice; ecclesial hierarchy was a perversion of the egalitarianism defended by Jesus; Christians should remain separate from the world, refusing to fill public office or governmental rank; possessions should be held in common; and baptism should be reserved for adults who explicitly accept the teachings of Christ, not automatically bestowed on infants. This last belief gave Grebel's followers their name: Anabaptists, or "rebaptizers."

Müntzer agreed with all this; however, he and Grebel parted ways over the use of force. Müntzer, citing Old Testament precedents, believed that God sometimes calls for violent opposition to social injustice. But Grebel's reading of the Sermon on the Mount convinced him that Christians are called to nonresistance when confronted by evil. In September 1524, Grebel admonished Müntzer in one of his few surviving letters. "The Gospel and its adherents are not to be protected by the sword," he wrote, "nor are they thus to protect themselves. All killing has ceased with them." True Christians use "neither the worldly sword nor war." Heaven is not to be earned "by killing their bodily enemies; rather they must attain it by killing their spiritual enemies"—and by the latter, Grebel meant passions such as jealousy, anger, greed, and fear that stir men to violence.

Grebel's public ministry was short. He died of the plague in 1526 before he was thirty. But his passionate commitment to nonviolence endured in the Anabaptist tradition. Today's descendants of sixteenth-century Anabaptism—the Amish, the Hutterites, and the Mennonites—continue to preach and practice the Christian pacifism taught by Grebel.

2 August
Niall O'Brien

2 August 1939—27 April 2004

Justice Is the Minimum of Love

THE PHILIPPINE ISLAND OF Negros is a major sugar-producer. Many of the three million souls who live there work on huge sugar cane haciendas owned by wealthy and often absentee planters. The conditions under which they labor and live were, until recently, feudal. Supervised by sometimes brutal overseers, they earned about $1 a day and were often in so much debt to the plantation owners that for all practical purposes they were slaves.

When Irish-born Columban missionary Father Niall O'Brien arrived in Negros in 1964, he was shocked at the poverty endured by the sugar cane workers. Already committed to the nonviolent pursuit of social justice—he once wrote, "The Church's teaching is unambiguous with regard to the pursuit of justice. Christianity is grotesque when it turns its back on justice. It's not Christianity, it's something else"—O'Brien began helping the peasants overcome their oppression. He labored hard to assure them that they were children of a loving God and inherently worthy of respect, truths they found hard to accept after years of internalizing the contempt of the planters they worked for. He worked just as hard at encouraging them to organize into a nonviolent alliance with one another that eventually became known as "People Power." Members of the alliance pledged to stand together against their oppressors. The results were remarkable. When one of the peasants was jailed by a wealthy landowner who wanted to seize his land, dozens of others marched to his farm and planted his crop for him, even though they were threatened the whole time by the landowner's hired thugs.

O'Brien's solidarity with the sugar cane workers, based on his insistence that "justice is the minimum of love," enraged both landowners and governmental leaders. They unsuccessfully tried to stop him many times, but in 1983 they decided enough was enough. He, another Columban priest, and six native members of People Power were arrested on trumped-up murder charges and spent nearly a year in prison before world protest over their incarceration eventually pushed Philippine president Ferdinand Marcos to offer them pardons. O'Neill and his companions refused the offer, even though all of them were facing a death penalty, because accepting it implied guilt. Eventually O'Brien made a deal to protect the six Negrenes arrested with him: he would leave the country if the charges were dropped. They were, and he did.

But O'Brien's imprisonment was a grave strategic mistake for the landowners who wanted to get rid of him. Thousands of visitors flocked to the prison where he was being held, and his Bible readings and discussions with them spread the word of nonviolent resistance to oppression throughout Negros. Moreover, the international publicity generated by his imprisonment focused world attention on the plight of the island's sugar cane workers, and this in turn was a factor in People Power's nonviolent overthrow of Marcos three years later. O'Brien, who had lived in his native Ireland since his exile from the Philippines, returned immediately. In an interview shortly before his departure, he said that he was sad to leave his Irish home. But, he added, he was eager to return to Negros—"my other home."

3 AUGUST

Martin Sheen

3 AUGUST 1940—

Radical Catholic

MARTIN SHEEN HAS BEEN a familiar face to film and television viewers for over forty years. On-screen he's played a variety of intriguing roles that includes villains (*Badlands, The Dead Zone*), military men (*Apocalypse Now, Gettysburg*), and heroes (*The West Wing, Wall Street*). Off-screen, he's a dedicated peacemaker who describes himself as a "radical Catholic," a person who "follows the teaching of the nonviolent Jesus and takes the gospel personally, and then pays the price."

Born of an Irish mother and a Spanish father, Sheen was raised a Catholic but drifted away from his Christian roots while struggling to make a name for himself in his twenties and thirties. In 1979 he suffered a heart attack filming Francis Ford Coppola's *Apocalypse Now*. The experience shook him and awakened a spiritual hunger that eventually led him back to the Catholic Church. For thirty years he's been an almost daily communicant at Mass. He carries a rosary in his pocket wherever he goes and prays frequently. His religion is a deep and integral part of his life.

But for Sheen, Christian commitment necessarily includes modeling Christ's message of nonviolence and social justice. So, since the mid-1980s, he's lived his devotion to Christ by opposing racism, apartheid, nuclear testing, and political repression in Latin America, witnessing for peace and a reduction of weapons worldwide, and advocating for the homeless, the poor, migrant workers, and the environment. He has worked closely with other Christian pacifists such as **Philip** and **Daniel Berrigan**, **John Dear**, and **César Chávez**—he was one of the pallbearers at Chávez's funeral—to make the world a bit more hospitable to those most at risk. "You can't live without seeing the need to do something," he says. "And the underprivileged are always in need. That's why the Church constantly strives to be there for them."

Sheen knows all too well that there's a price to be paid for living as a radical Catholic who devotes a lot of time and energy in hands-on assistance to the needy—what the Church calls "works of mercy"—and who regularly practices nonviolent civil disobedience. Since 1986 he's been arrested more than sixty times while participating in peace and social justice actions. "Once you follow a path of nonviolence and social justice," he says, "it won't take you long before you come into conflict with the culture, with the society. You can't know what is at stake or how much it is going to cost you until you get in the game. That's the only way, and the level of cost is equal to the level of involvement." For Sheen, the level of involvement stretches as high as heaven.

4 August
Raoul Wallenberg

4 August 1912—17 July 1947(?)

To Save Jews

In 1944, residents of Budapest noticed something unusual: building after building in the city began flying the flag of Sweden, identifying them as Swedish diplomatic facilities. Soon, more than thirty buildings were so designated. But it was all a ruse to deceive the Nazi-controlled Hungarian government. The buildings' real purpose was to provide shelter and fake Swedish passports to as many as possible of the quarter-million Jews left in Hungary. This colossal humanitarian effort was largely the brainchild of Raoul Wallenberg.

Wallenberg, a multilingual Swede who studied architecture in the United States, was born into a wealthy and privileged family. In his early thirties he took a job with the Central European Trading Company. Although based in Sweden, the firm was owned by a Hungarian Jew and conducted much of its business in Hungary. As persecution of Hungarian Jews escalated in the months leading up to war, Wallenberg, a Gentile, of necessity became the company's representative in Hungary, traveling there frequently and becoming fluent in the language.

By late 1943, word about the extermination of Europe's Jews was beginning to reach the Allies. In January 1944, President Franklin Roosevelt instituted the War Refugee Board (WRB), whose charge was to come up with a plan to rescue Jews. On the basis of his familiarity with Hungary, Wallenberg was recruited to be the WRB's clandestine agent in Budapest. Shortly afterwards, the Swedish flags and diplomatic outposts began sprouting up around the city.

Working with a crew of people who daily risked their lives to rescue Jews, Wallenberg issued protective passports, successfully demanded that Jews holding them be exempted from wearing yellow stars on their clothing, got Jews out of the country, and bribed German and Hungarian officials or threatened them with war crime persecution in order to rescue Jews from roundups. On more than one occasion he climbed into already loaded cattle cars filled with Jews on their way to Auschwitz, distributed as many fake passports as he had, and demanded that the Jews to whom he gave them be allowed off the trains. The audacity and determination shown by Wallenberg and his collaborators outraged German Nazis and Hungarian fascists, but saved tens of thousands of lives.

Wallenberg disappeared at the war's end. In all likelihood, he was taken prisoner by the Soviet Army and died two years later in captivity. But although the time and manner of his death is unknown, his humanitarian work in Budapest is a living reminder of what persons of good will are capable of doing. As the Israeli attorney who persecuted Adolf Eichmann said with some amazement, Wallenberg "had the choice of remaining in secure, neutral Sweden when Nazism was ruling Europe. Instead, he left this haven and went to what was then one of the most perilous places in Europe—Hungary. And for what? To save Jews."

5 August
Wendell Berry

5 August 1934—

Agrarian Prophet

In the United States, over three hundred small farm owners leave their land each week because they simply can't make enough of an income growing crops or raising animals to support their families. This exile from the land has been going on for a while. Since the 1930s, the number of small American farms has shrunk from five million to two million. The single largest destroyer of these farms has been agri-industry or corporate farming, which buys up immense amounts of acreage to raise monocultural crops sold on the global market.

Poet, novelist, essayist, and small farmer Wendell Berry has been a steady critic since the 1960s of agri-industrial farming. He worries that it not only displaces farmers, destroys local communities and long-standing traditions, and harms the environment because of its heavy reliance on chemical fertilizers, insecticides, and pesticides. It is also yet another aspect of life taken over by the impersonal forces of industrialization and technology that care nothing for cultivating a reflective and grateful relationship with the earth and its living things. When corporations take over, agriculture becomes a factory system in the business of churning out ever increasing quantities of product, regardless of the hidden costs to humans and the environment.

As an alternative to the practices and mindset of agri-industry, Berry advocates an "agrarian" vision that values simplicity in lifestyle, local as opposed to global markets—the "displaced, global economy," he insists, "has no respect for what works in a locality. The global economy is built on the principle that one place can be exploited, even destroyed, for the sake of another place"—and a rural lifestyle that encourages a receptive and respectful relationship with the natural world. For Berry, the consumer- and technology-driven culture that most Americans value leaves no room for solitude, silence, or leisure—no opportunity, as he says in one of his poems, "to ask the world to reveal its quietude." But without the grounding that these experiences provide, a genuinely good life is difficult to attain.

Berry sees a direct link between violence and the urge for more profit, more technology, and more consumer items. If maximization of profit is the chief incentive of both individuals and societies, conflict is inevitable. "Let us have the candor to acknowledge that what we call 'the economy' or 'the free market' is less and less distinguishable from warfare. Though its political means are milder (so far) than those of communism, this newly internationalized capitalism may prove even more destructive of human cultures and communities, of freedom, and of nature. Its tendency is just as much toward total dominance and control." A return to agrarian values of simplicity, self-respect, localism, and cooperation is, for Berry, a rejection of the violence bred by the drive toward globalization. Not everyone need be a farmer. But everyone needs small farm values.

6 August

Hibakusha

6 August 1945

Living Icons

THE STORY HAS BEEN told so many times that there's a certain risk that familiarity may breed indifference. But it's too important not to tell again and again.

At 8:15 A.M. on 6 August 1945, an American B-29 plane named the "Enola Gay" dropped a brand new weapon of war, the atomic bomb, on the large Japanese city of Hiroshima. The explosion was more devastating than had ever been witnessed in the history of humankind. Within seconds, eighty thousand residents were killed. Sixty-nine percent of the city's buildings were utterly destroyed, and another 7 percent were too damaged to be inhabitable. Three days later, another atomic bomb was exploded over the city of Nagasaki, killing another sixty to eighty thousand people.

The physical infrastructures of Hiroshima and Nagasaki have been rebuilt. Today, except for a few memorials, there's no visible sign of the devastation that befell the two cities. But there *is* a living legacy: the people who were directly afflicted by burns, injuries, or radiation poisoning from the two atomic blasts. They are known as *hibakusha*, a word that means "explosion-affected people." Hibakasha include all people who were close to the explosion epicenters when the bombs were dropped or who traveled near the epicenters within two weeks of the explosion. Also included are the children of pregnant women who were subsequently born with birth defects or illnesses because of radiation contamination.

Nearly half a million hibakusha survivors from Hiroshima and Nagasaki are still alive. Their average age now is in the mid-seventies. All of them have serious medical problems such as anemia, blindness, cancer, and atrophic scarring from severe burns. Tragically, their physical wounds are compounded by the fact that they're often looked down upon and shunned by Japanese society as unpleasant reminders of a tragedy that most people want to forget.

Hibakusha are living icons of the horror of nuclear weapons. Their bodies and their suffering provide gruesome testimony to the need to rid the world's arsenals of atomic instruments of mass death. And there are huge numbers of these weapons, despite three decades of disarmament talks and treaties. Although the figures vary depending on who's doing the counting, most experts agree that there are still nearly twenty-four thousand nuclear bombs and missiles in the world. For hibakashua, that's twenty-four thousand too many. As one of them, Toshiko Saeki, says, her suffering often makes her long for death. "But I must live for the sake of the people, all the people who lost their lives then. So I relate my experiences hoping that my talk will discourage people from making war. Our experience must not be forgotten. I went through hell on earth.... Hiroshima should not be repeated again. That is why I keep telling the same old story over and over again. And I'll keep repeating it."

7 August
Helen Caldicott

7 August 1938—

Ending Business as Usual

IN HER 2002 BOOK *The New Nuclear Danger*, anti-nuclear activist Helen Caldicott notes that the U.S. Pentagon recently boasted that it was America's largest company, with a budget in the hundreds of billions, over five million employees, and facilities in 130 of the world's 178 countries. War and war preparation are big business, and one of the most expensive commodities in the business is nuclear weapons. They cost a lot of money to build and even more to maintain. Additionally, the environmental and health costs of using them are nightmarish. The world has already seen this in the atomic bombing of Hiroshima and Nagasaki, the scores of subsequent nuclear tests throughout the world, and the recent use of depleted uranium weapons in Iraq and Afghanistan.

Caldicott has been trying to end the big business of nuclear weapon production ever since she was a young pediatrician in Adelaide, Australia, in the early 1970s. At the time, France was testing nuclear weapons in the South Pacific, and radioactive fallout was detected in Adelaide. As a physician, Caldicott was well aware of how easily radioactive elements can wind up in mothers' milk. Organizing other doctors and concerned citizens, she began a public campaign that eventually led to a ban on nuclear tests in the region. Shortly afterwards, she founded the Women's Action for Nuclear Disarmament, which seeks to persuade governments to siphon off funds earmarked for nuclear research and redirect them toward social programs. She was also involved with Physicians for Social Responsibility for over a decade.

Caldicott argues that even though the end of the Cold War eliminated "official" justifications for nuclear weapons, the profit-driven military-industrial complex—what's sometimes referred to as the "fourth armed service"—keeps their production and maintenance a high national priority. But her anti-nuclear activism doesn't stop with weapons. For the last thirty years she's also been a tireless opponent of the nuclear power industry, which she sees as a lucrative player in the corporate commodification of the atom. Nuclear energy has been touted by its supporters as a green and inexpensive source of energy that can break the world's reliance on fossil fuels. But in fact, says Caldicott, "nuclear energy is one hell of a way to boil water." For her, all nuclear technologies are more dangerous than they're worth, and the wisest course of action is to forgo them rather than face the risk that the use of them poses. "As a doctor as well as a mother and a world citizen," she says, "I wish to practice the ultimate form of preventive medicine by ridding the earth of these technologies that propagate disease, suffering, and death."

Caldicott is passionate in her advocacy of a nuclear-free world, and her critics often object to her strong condemnation of individuals and governments. But Caldicott makes no apologies. When confronting nuclear "business as usual," she says, it's appropriate to get angry.

8 August
Gordon Zahn

7 August 1918—9 December 2007

Dean of American Catholic Pacifists

At the outbreak of World War II, Gordon Zahn, a devout Roman Catholic, decided that he couldn't take up arms and applied to the draft board in his hometown of Milwaukee for conscientious objector status. One of the members of the board, a priest, insisted that pacifism was contrary to Church teaching and rejected Zahn's petition. Zahn appealed and won—he spent the war years at a Civilian Public Service camp fighting forest fires—but this early skirmish signaled the beginning of his lifelong struggle to make pacifism acceptable to a Church that had defended just war doctrine for centuries.

After the war, Zahn enrolled in Minnesota's St. John's College, but was forced to transfer after students and faculty objected to his pacifism. He went on to earn a doctorate in sociology from Catholic University of America and in 1953 landed a teaching job at Loyola University in Chicago. But by 1962, his opposition to war had worn out his welcome there as well. Angry administrators at Loyola tried to block the publication of Zahn's first book, *German Catholics and Hitler's Wars*, an exposé of German Catholic collaboration with the Nazis. Two years later, Zahn published his best-known book, *In Solitary Witness*, a biography of **Franz Jägerstätter**, a young Austrian Catholic farmer beheaded in 1943 for his refusal to serve in the German army.

Zahn relocated to the University of Massachusetts at Boston in the late 1960s, where he taught for several years before becoming president of the Cambridge-based Center on Conscience and War, an organization that counsels and supports conscientious objectors. In 1972 he cofounded Pax Christi USA, the Catholic peace organization. He continued to write until developing Alzheimer's in his eighties, continually encouraging Catholics and others to take Christ's message of nonviolence seriously. A gentle, modest, and soft-spoken man, Zahn's embodiment of the nonviolence he preached was just as persuasive for those who met him as were his writings. Typical of his thought and style is this passage from his book *Vocation of Peace* (1992):

> As a pacifist, I make no claim to having the whole answer to our problems of war and peace; but I'm fairly sure of the indispensable core and center of the answer: a total and unequivocal rejection of war and violence directed against my fellow humans, even (perhaps especially!) the brother who mistakenly sees in me his enemy. Once we get that far, once we exclude options that cannot be reconciled with Christianity, we will be in a better position to explore the broader possibilities for achieving the more positive aspects of the Christian vocation for peace.

9 August
Franz Jägerstätter

20 May 1907—9 August 1943

Refusing to Play the Crooked Game

WHEN WAR FEVER AND patriotic zeal take over a people, anyone who resists the rush to war risks being shunned as a traitor and a coward. It takes nearly unimaginable courage to stand against the tide in such heated situations. The Austrian farmer Franz Jägerstätter had such courage.

Born in Upper Austria to a chambermaid and a farmer, Jägerstätter's childhood and youth were pretty conventional. Although a Catholic like everyone else in his part of Austria, he wasn't particularly pious. But when he married in 1936, things begin to change. His new wife was intensely religious, and the young couple honeymooned in Rome. It was there that Jägerstätter began to take his religion seriously. By 1940 he was a Third Order Franciscan and the sexton in his village church.

From the beginning of their rise to power, Jägerstätter was unafraid to publicly condemn and even mock the Nazis. He voted against the Nazi takeover of Austria in the 1938 plebiscite, so angering local authorities that they refused to count his ballot. Two years later—the same year he joined the Franciscans—he was drafted into the German Army, but he was granted an exemption because he was a farmer and the Third Reich needed food to feed its soldiers. Believing that war in general—particularly the one launched by Hitler—was contrary to Christ's teachings, Jägerstätter was tortured by his military conscription. He sought counsel from a number of priests and his bishop. But each of them advised him to go along by keeping his religious scruples to himself. Finally called up in 1943, Jägerstätter refused to serve. Predictably, he was charged with corrupting the morale of the army and beheaded. He left behind a wife and three children, all of whom were ostracized by their patriotic neighbors.

While in prison awaiting execution, Jägerstätter had time to think, pray, and put his thoughts on paper. In one short reflection, he meditated on the clerical advice he'd received to keep his Christian pacifism to himself and agree to serve in the military. He called this "the crooked game" of living a double life, pretending to believe one thing while secretly holding another. Sometimes, he admitted, the crooked game could be relatively benign and permissible, as when one holds one's tongue in order not to needlessly hurt another's feelings. But the game "should never go so far as to oblige one to perform acts that are actually evil," and hiding one's commitment to nonviolence in order to go along with war-making stepped over that line. It was a "double dealing" that not only betrayed the Prince of Peace and corrupted the game player, but also set a bad example for others who might have similar scruples. "What must people of other faiths think of us and our faith if it means so little to us?" Far better, Jägerstätter concluded, to refuse to play the game than to risk one's soul by safely going along with the crowd. And that's what he did.

10 August

Peter Damian

CA. 1007—1072

Two Gems of Virtue

THE ELEVENTH CENTURY IS a dark period in the history of European Christianity. Priests were corrupt, bishops sold their patronage to the highest bidder, popes and anti-popes angrily excommunicated each other, and monastic communities grew lax, proud, and incredibly wealthy. The end of the century saw the launch of the bloody military campaigns that we know as the Crusades. For all practical purposes, the Church had become just another secular power obsessed with political and economic dominance.

A great movement of reform would sweep through the Church three generations later with the emergence of the Franciscan and Dominican orders. But in the eleventh century, Peter Damian anticipated the revival. A priest, monk, and cardinal (consecrated against his will), Peter made it his life's work to nudge the Church back to righteousness. He wrote books that alternately blasted vice and encouraged virtue—one of his books is descriptively titled *Liber Gomorrhianus* (*Book of Gomorrah*)—visited numerous monasteries to inspect and reform them, and served as counselor to bishops and popes. His message was always the same: the violent and self-serving ways of the world, which the Church ought to condemn, have been scandalously and hypocritically embraced by the Church. This is because clergy have forgotten the two "gems of virtue that our Savior brought from heaven": patience and love. Their recovery can awaken the Church to the fact that its pursuit of the "worthless things" of possessions and power is contrary to its mission. Patience does not greedily grasp after what belongs to others. Love does not go to war over possessions, or anything else for that matter. The temptation to return evil for evil, as proud princes of the Church should know only too well, only breeds the loveless impatience that prompts clergy to forget the teachings of their Lord and "leap up immediately to declare war" at the slightest provocation.

It's far better, said Peter, to be destroyed for the sake of loyalty to the two gems of virtue than to violate them for the sake of worldly advancement. But defeat isn't an inevitable outcome of refusing to use the weapons of the world. In a letter to one Bishop Olderic of Fermo, Peter tells a story of the feud between a proud Gallic abbot and an equally proud nobleman. The source of the feud was disagreement over a piece of land. Eventually the two decided that the only way to settle the dispute was through battle. The nobleman lined his soldiers up. "A forest of swords sprang up all around, shields glistened red, a shouting clamor rose," Peter wrote. But the abbot, repenting his greed, bade his monks congregate on the battle line without armor or swords, "protected only by the breastplate of faith," and asked them to pray. The nobleman was so moved by this humble display of Christian love and patience that he jumped off his horse and threw himself on the ground before the abbot to beg his forgiveness. The two men immediately reconciled.

11 August
Clare of Assisi

16 July 1194—11 August 1253

Holy Poverty

As a child, Clare or Ciara of Assisi—her name means "light"—wouldn't have struck anyone as having the stuff of which saints are made. A daughter of the noble Offreduccio clan, Clare was pampered, coddled, and destined for a marriage that would bring even more prestige and wealth to her family. But all that changed when she heard **St. Francis** preaching in the town square. Francis's recommendation of a life utterly devoted to God and holy poverty touched Clare, and on Palm Sunday, 1212, when she was eighteen years old, she left her family to join him. It wasn't long before other women, likewise attracted to Franciscan spirituality, congregated around her to form a spiritual community.

These Franciscan women dedicated themselves to a life of extreme poverty. They dwelt in an enclosed monastery and supported themselves through manual labor and alms. Throughout her long tenure as the community's abbess, Clare consistently opposed efforts on the parts of popes and prelates to force her and her sisters to accept a less austere Rule. Each time, she managed to convince the authorities that the particular charism of Franciscan spirituality was to live in holy poverty.

Clare's staunch commitment to poverty may seem bizarre to modern sensibilities, but there was nothing life-denying or masochistic about it. On the contrary, Clare saw it as life-affirming on at least two counts. In the first place, voluntary poverty was a renunciation of the social privilege that led to a wildly unequal and unjust distribution of wealth. Holy poverty was no respecter of rank, but it was a radically egalitarian respecter of persons. In voluntarily embracing poverty, Clare and her sisters threw in their lot with those who were born into poverty and misery. Their adoption of a countercultural lifestyle was intended to show solidarity with the poor. It's significant that the monastery in which they dwelt was situated outside the city walls of Assisi, in the surrounding valley where the poor lived.

Voluntary poverty was also life-affirming in that it helped practitioners discriminate between what's really important and what only seems important. Clare realized—she had only to think back to her own pampered childhood—that too often humans are driven by lust for immediate gratification, wealth, power, prestige, and fame. These are not only soul-corrupting objects of desire, but also socially incendiary ones because they're the roots of competition, grudges, anxiety, conflict, and overt violence. To walk away from them is to liberate oneself and to recognize and appreciate the God-given riches with which the world is filled: natural beauty, silence, companionship, and love. Embracing holy poverty isn't so much a relinquishment of desire as a refocusing of it that leads to both inner and outer peace. In reminding the world of this great truth, St. Clare of Assisi was truly a "light."

12 August

Benedict of Nursia

CA. 480—CA. 543

A Ladder of Humility

BENEDICT OF NURSIA, THE founder of Western monasticism, knew that the greatest obstacle any aspiring monk or nun had to overcome was his or her own ego. So when he sat down to write his famous *Rule*, a guidebook of advice for men and women choosing a monastic way of life, he gave some thought on how to break addiction to self.

Benedict realized that egoism is the mother of conflict between individuals and nations. Egoists are the centers of their own world, with everyone else being mere secondary satellites orbiting around them. Arrogance, impatience, a refusal to listen to alternative perspectives or to accept criticism, and a disdainful urge to dominate others are predictable character traits of an egoist. Together, they create a witches' brew that poisons relationships and invites psychological or physical violence.

Benedict was astute enough to realize that egoism is a difficult addiction to break. So he recommended a series of steps—literally, the first "twelve-step program"—as a way out. Each of the steps, which he envisioned as rungs on a ladder, takes the climber progressively away from egoism through the cultivation of progressively ascending levels of humility. Benedict's religious language may strike some modern readers as old-fashioned. But his insights are essential to anyone wishing to be a peacemaker. Humility is a valuable quality in everyone, not only monks and nuns.

The first and most fundamental rung on the ladder of humility is a sense of awed gratitude at the sheer majesty of creation—or, in Benedict's terms, of God. It's difficult for us to take ourselves too seriously if we put our place in the vast cosmos in perspective. Once we're mindful of our relative insignificance in the grand scheme of things, subsequent steps toward humility become easier. We learn to cease insisting on having our own way, to listen to others and patiently accept their instruction, to be honest with ourselves and others about our shortcomings, to endure "wretched and inadequate conditions" when we must, to speak less of ourselves and more of others, to maintain a modest presence, and to avoid gossip and trash talk.

Particularly instructive for contemporary peacemakers is the twelfth and final rung on Benedict's ladder of humility: mindfulness that comportment speaks louder than words. The cultivation of humility isn't merely for personal enrichment; there's also an obligation to model it for others in order to inspire their own liberation from egoism. So Benedict recommends that "the humility of [a humble person's] heart should ever be apparent to all who see them, even in their bodily movements." Regardless of what kind of activity they're engaged in—prayer, work, speaking, standing in solitude—"they should be free of any hint of arrogance or pride in their manner or the way they look about them."

13 August

John Dear

13 August 1959—

Peace Vow

THERE IS A DISTINGUISHED line of U.S. Catholic peacemakers in the twentieth and now the twenty-first century that includes **Peter Maurin** and **Dorothy Day**, **Thomas Merton**, **Philip** and **Daniel Berrigan**, **Richard McSorley**, and **Eileen Egan**. Today, their dedication to peace lives on in the extraordinary Jesuit priest John Dear. In his defense of Christian nonviolence, Dear has been arrested nearly eighty times, once spending eight months behind bars and an additional year under house arrest for a 1993 Plowshares action with Philip Berrigan. He has traveled to Central America, the Philippines, Haiti, and the Middle East on humanitarian missions, advocated pacifism across the world in hundreds of speeches and workshops, and written twenty-five books and scores of articles, popular as well as scholarly, about peace. Dear has been nominated several times for a Nobel Peace Prize. He richly deserves it.

Dear formalized his dedication to peace in 1985, when after two years of spiritual preparation he wrote and embraced a peace vow that bound him to a life of nonviolence and the pursuit of justice modeled on Christ's. It's a vow that, if taken, leads some to civil disobedience—or "divine obedience," as **Roy Bourgeois** says—and imprisonment, and others to quieter lives of compassionate service and interpersonal reconciliation. Peacemaking comes in all shapes and sizes to suit different temperaments and life situations. But however it's lived, the peace vow, as Dear says, "can set us on a new course which will bring immeasurable blessings, perhaps even a lifetime commitment to peace, forgiveness, compassion and suffering love, a true, lifelong fidelity to the nonviolent Jesus." A version of the vow that Dear took, written by himself and Eileen Egan, is reaffirmed by thousands each year:

> Before God the Creator and the Holy Spirit, I vow to carry out in my life the love and example of Jesus:
> - by striving for peace within myself and seeking to be a peacemaker in my daily life;
> - by accepting suffering in the struggle for justice rather than inflicting it;
> - by refusing to retaliate in the face of provocation and violence;
> - by persevering in nonviolence of tongue and heart;
> - by living conscientiously and simply so that I do not deprive others of the means to live or harm creation;
> - by actively resisting evil and working nonviolently to abolish war and the causes of war from my own heart and from the face of the earth.
>
> God, I trust in your sustaining love and believe that just as You gave me the grace and desire to offer this, so You will also bestow abundant grace to fulfill it. Amen.

14 August
Maximilian Kolbe

8 January 1894—14 August 1941

Saint of Auschwitz

It had been an exhausting day for the prisoners of Auschwitz's Block 14A. Up at dawn chopping down huge trees, barely sustained by a midday meal of watery soup, enduring the curses and blows of hostile camp guards, the men of Block 14A were in for a shock when they finally returned to their barracks that night. A prisoner from their work platoon had escaped, and SS Captain Karl Fritzsch, the death camp's deputy commander, was furious.

Fritzsch berated the assembled men of Block 14A for a few minutes and then curtly announced that ten of them would be sent to the "Bunker," an underground starvation cell, in reprisal for the escapee. Striding down the ranks, he randomly pointed at prisoners until he had his ten victims. As the guards were leading the prisoners to the Bunker, one of them, a Pole named Franciszek Gajowniczek, pled for mercy. Immediately, another prisoner, the Polish Franciscan Maximilian Kolbe, stepped up and volunteered to take Gajowniczek's place. Fritzsch, amused by what struck him as an idiotic request, agreed. Kolbe endured starvation, dehydration, and daily beatings in the Bunker for more than two weeks before a camp guard finally finished him off with an injection of carbolic acid.

Ordained in 1918, Kolbe was a rather bookish priest sent by his superiors to establish monasteries in Japan. Recalled to Poland in 1936, he was at a priory near Warsaw when World War II erupted. Starting in December 1939, he spearheaded efforts to shelter refugees from the Nazis, eventually aiding at least two thousand Jews. "We must do everything in our power to help these unfortunate people who have been driven from their homes and deprived of even the most basic necessities," he told his fellow friars. "Our mission is among them in the days that lie ahead." Kolbe eluded Nazi authorities until February 1941, when he was arrested and sent to Auschwitz.

At the camp, Kolbe often shared his meager rations with fellow prisoners and nursed ones who were ill or distraught. Inmates afterwards remarked on his devotion to his fellow prisoners and his equanimity in the face of personal hardship, both of which culminated in his willingness to take the place of a condemned man in July 1941.

Kolbe's faith-based devotion to nonviolence, his conviction that each and every person is worthy of respect and compassion, and his willingness to give up his life for the sake of another person deeply touched the hearts of his fellow Auschwitz prisoners, as well as those who heard of his sacrifice only after the war. He was canonized by Pope John Paul II in 1982.

15 August
Óscar Romero

15 August 1917—24 March 1980

Living On in His People

THE SHEER DARING OF it outraged some and awed others. Archbishop Óscar Romero, the highest ranking churchman in El Salvador, stood in his cathedral to preach a homily denouncing the murder and torture of those who opposed the military junta that controlled his country. At the end of his sermon, Romero called on soldiers to disobey their superiors. "Brothers," he said, "you come from our own people. You are killing your own brother peasants when any human order to kill must be subordinate to the law of God which says, 'Thou shalt not kill.' . . . It is high time you recovered your consciences. . . . In the name of God, in the name of this suffering people whose cries rise to heaven more loudly each day, I implore you, I beg you, I order you in the name of God: stop the repression."

The next day, while serving Mass in a nearby hospital chapel, Romero was murdered by a member of one of the very death squads he'd rebuked. His call for public disobedience had been the last straw; Romero the gadfly, Romero the rebel, had to go.

He hadn't always been such a threat. When he was appointed archbishop in 1977, El Salvador's ruling class rejoiced. In contrast to the "radical" priests in El Salvador who embraced liberation theology, Romero had a reputation for being scholarly, otherworldly, and easily led. But a month after his appointment, his friend **Rutilio Grande**, a Jesuit advocate for the country's poverty-stricken *campesinos,* was murdered by government agents. A grief-stricken Romero vowed to honor Grande's memory by continuing his work. Almost overnight, the meek churchman became the government's most vocal critic. Silence in the face of injustice, he had learned, was culpable. "Peace is not the silence of the graveyard."

For the next three years, Romero devoted himself to speaking out against economic injustice, political repression, and the culture of violence and intimidation created by right-wing paramilitary organizations. He challenged the wealthy landowners for their indifference to the poor, the military for its use of terror and torture, and the Carter administration for supplying the El Salvadoran government with U.S. weapons and advisors. What especially rankled his enemies was Romero's insistence on tracing the injustice back to its sources: the economic and political structures of El Salvador that privileged the wealthy. It was one thing for a churchman to give safe homilies about brotherly love. It was quite another for him to proclaim, as Romero did, that "when the church hears the cry of the oppressed it cannot but denounce the social structures that give rise to and perpetuate the misery from which the cry arises."

Romero knew that his opposition to the government made him a marked man. But he also knew that the gospel of peace and justice would prevail. "If I am killed," he said shortly before his death, "I shall arise in the Salvadoran people."

16 August
E. F. Schumacher

16 August 1911—4 September 1977

Enough Is Plenty

THERE ARE A FEW stock promises that politicians trot out every election cycle. A favorite is the pledge to "grow the economy," which always means to increase individual income, commodity production, and personal consumption. The standard line is that more is better.

But as the German-born economist and philosopher E. F. Schumacher pointed out in the 1970s, more isn't always better. In fact, it so rarely is that we would do better to drop conventional economic models of growth in favor of ones that stress alternative values. Instead of judging economic health in terms of production and consumption growth, we ought to start thinking in terms of well-being and sustainability.

Schumacher began putting together his vision of alternative economies in the early 1950s, when he served as economic advisor to England's National Coal Board. But it was while living in Burma in 1955 that things coalesced for him. Struck by the difference between the Buddhist and the Western capitalist notions of the good life, Schumacher asked himself what an economic model based on Buddhist values might look like. The result was what he called a "small is beautiful" approach to growth.

According to Schumacher, modern capitalist economic models, regardless of whether they lean toward centralization or decentralization, are obsessed with production and consumption. As a consequence, they push technology that progressively streamlines production, regardless of the cost in actual jobs or worker satisfaction and whether or not the commodities that are mass produced and mass marketed are ones that consumers really need. Moreover, the continuous push for production-maximizing technology leaves huge environmental footprints, depleting nonrenewable natural resources and polluting the environment.

The drive to "grow the economy," founded in turn on the "bigger is better" assumption, is best replaced, argued Schumacher, with economic models that focus on local communities, emphasize quality rather than quantity and local needs rather than market manipulation, and utilize green technologies. This "smalling" of the economy, which values the disciplining of desire, simplicity in lifestyle, and modesty in production and consumption, reduces the level of violence in society. As Schumacher wrote, "Simplicity and non-violence are obviously closely related. The optimal pattern of consumption, producing a high degree of human satisfaction by means of a relatively low rate of consumption, allows people to live without great pressure. As physical resources are everywhere limited, people satisfying their needs by means of a modest use of resources are obviously less likely to be at each other's throats than people depending upon a high rate of use. Equally, people who live in highly self-sufficient local communities are less likely to get involved in large-scale violence than people whose existence depends on world-wide systems of trade."

In other words, enough is much better than more than enough.

17 August
Catherine Doherty

15 August 1896—14 December 1985

Poustinik in the World

In the Russian Orthodox tradition in which Catherine Doherty was raised, *poustinia* is a place of solitude and silence where one goes to encounter God. *Poustiniks* often took themselves off to isolated physical locales such as deserts, islands, or caves. But from a spiritual perspective, a *poustinia* is that quiet, still place within the soul—the "cave of the heart," as it's often called—where God can be heard. So a *poustinik* can live in the midst of the busy world while drawing strength from the eternal silence within. This is the spirituality practiced and taught by Doherty.

Doherty, the daughter of aristocratic parents, was born in tsarist Russia, well educated as a youth, married to a second cousin at fifteen, and served with the Red Cross during World War I. After the revolution, she fled Russia, nearly died as a refugee in Finland, wound up in England where she was received into the Roman Catholic Church, and eventually immigrated to Canada, where she took various jobs to support herself, her husband, and their son.

Feeling increasingly called by Jesus' recommendation to "Go, sell everything you have and give to the poor" (Mark 10:21), Doherty founded Friendship House in Toronto at the beginning of the Great Depression, a lay apostolate focused on ministering to the poor. She relocated the house in the mid-1930s to Harlem in New York City. **Thomas Merton**, exploring his own call to ministry, worked with her there for a brief period in 1941.

After her first marriage was annulled in 1942, Doherty married American reporter Eddie Doherty, returned to Canada, and founded the Madonna House settlement, which today has over twenty missions throughout the world. In dozens of books, articles, and retreats, she distilled her approach to *poustinia* spirituality down to a few key principles: practice voluntary poverty, become childlike in faith and trust, pray, and "love, love, love, never counting the cost. Be a light to your neighbor's feet. Go without fear into the depths of men's hearts." She also encouraged what she called the "duty of the moment," a mindfulness of God in even the most mundane or distasteful task. "The duty of the moment," she wrote, "is the duty of God." When we serve others wholeheartedly and single-mindedly, we serve God as well.

Performing one's duty in the moment and lovingly serving one's neighbor ultimately depend on locating and getting in touch with the inner *poustinia*. Doherty believed that the cultivation of inner peace was a necessary condition for doing anything in the world to ease conflict and violence. Renewed by regular retreats into the cave of the heart, peacemakers bring to the world the love and tranquility they discover there.

Doherty is under consideration for canonization by the Roman Catholic Church.

18 August

Mozi

CA. 470 BCE—CA. 391 BCE

As Natural as Fire

The Chinese sage Mozi lived during a time when conflict between regional warlords was so fierce and unceasing that historians call it the Warring States Period. War and preparation for war ate up wealth and lives. Military campaigns were the norm, peace the exception.

A skilled carpenter clever at making such contraptions as mechanical birds, Mozi was often consulted by warlords looking for stronger fortifications of their own cities and better siege instruments to use against the cities of their rivals. But Mozi practiced nonviolent resistance by using his artistic skills to deter rather than encourage battle. He traveled from warlord to warlord, freely sharing with each his latest inventions. His intention was to make sure that each warlord had the same weapon technology so that none would have an advantage and seek to use it by going to war. Mozi came close to death on several occasions at the hands of warlords outraged by his strategy of deterrence.

Mozi studied Confucianism in his youth but eventually broke with it because he found it too formalistic and too exclusive. He believed it substituted ritual for thought, and worried that the Confucian cult of ancestors encouraged individuals to privilege their own family above others. Mozi, on the other hand, taught a doctrine of universal benevolence, claiming that fellow-feeling between humans is as natural as "fire turning upward or water turning downward." All societies that taught partiality and favoritism inevitably sowed the seeds of violence, and the people came to distrust one another. This in turn opened the door to exploitation, crime, competition, and war. But the ideal of universal benevolence, which served as the foundation of Mozi's pacifism, envisioned a quite different model in which "those with sturdy limbs work for others, and those with a knowledge of the way will endeavor to teach others. Those who are old and without wives or children will find means of support and be able to live out their days; the young and orphaned who have no parents will find someone to care for them and look after their needs."

Although Mozi believed that universal benevolence was justifiable on moral grounds alone, he also taught that it had practical advantages over warfare. Armed conflict accomplished little besides taking lives, destroying property and crops, and razing cities. Warlords might claim that their military campaigns were fought for the benefit of their subjects. But, Mozi pointed out, "murdering men is a paltry way to benefit them, and when we calculate the expenditures for such warfare, we find that they have crippled the basis of the nation's livelihood and exhausted the resources of the people." The world, he insisted, is a "commonwealth shared by all," and so the cultivation of peace through acts of benevolence is in everyone's interest.

19 August
Petr Chelčický

c. 1390—c. 1460

Reformation Pacifist

WHEN THE PROTESTANT REFORMATION came to Bohemia, located in what is now the Czech Republic, it brought years of religious warfare. Following the execution of the reformer John Hus in 1415, his followers, initially united by their rejection of Catholicism, broke up into a number of squabbling factions and began fighting one another in what came to be known as the Hussite Wars.

In the midst of this butchery committed in the name of Christ, Petr Chelčický stood out as a man of peace. He was from the village of Chelčice and called himself a peasant, although he was educated and even appears to have known some Latin. He lived for a few years in Prague, but around 1420 he returned to his village and spent the rest of his life there, earning a livelihood by farming and writing books. His two most important ones are *On Spiritual Warfare* (1420) and *The Net of Faith* (1443).

On Spiritual Warfare was Chelčický's response to the wars of religion inflaming Bohemia. In it he argued that the only warfare appropriate to Christians was an interior battle against sin. Especially repugnant was fighting done for the sake of silencing heretics. Invoking Jesus' parable of the wheat and tares (Matt 13:24–30), Chelčický insisted that only God had the right to judge who should live and who die. Any appeal to arms, even for the purpose of self-defense, was absolutely contrary to the spirit of Christ. Christians therefore should refuse military service as well as any governmental appointment that made them accomplices to state violence.

In *The Net of Faith*, Chelčický argued that Christ taught and the apostles lived a radical egalitarianism in which property was communally shared, there were no distinctions of rank or status, and absolute nonviolence was the norm. But this original purity was lost when the Church aligned itself with the State in the fourth century under the Emperor Constantine. This marriage, wrote Chelčický, rent the net of faith. "Christ, by means of his disciples, would have caught all the world in his net of faith, but the greater fishes broke the net and escaped out of it, and all the rest have slipped through the holes made by the greater fishes, so that the net has remained quite empty. The greater fishes who broke the net are the rulers, emperors, popes, kings, who have not renounced power, and instead of true Christianity have put on what is simply a mask of it."

From first to last, Chelčický's thought was based on his pacifist conviction that violence of any kind, whether perpetrated by secular authority or religious sectarianism, was contrary to the teaching of Jesus and forbidden to his followers. His was one of the few authentically Christian voices in an age ripped apart by religious warfare.

20 August

Jonathan Daniels

20 March 1939—20 August 1965

Free to Love the Enemy

In 1965, Lowndes County, Alabama, was one of the most segregated areas in the United States. Although over eighty percent of the population was black, an active Ku Klux Klan ensured that not a single black person was a registered voter. Visitors observed that the county seemed a throwback to pre-Civil War days.

On a sweltering August afternoon in 1965, Jon Daniels, a twenty-six-year-old Episcopal seminarian from New Hampshire, was gunned down in the small town of Hayneville, Lowndes' county seat. Daniels had just been released from jail after being arrested for participating in a public demonstration a week earlier. Hot and thirsty, he and three companions walked toward a store to buy soda. They were stopped at the door by Tom Coleman, a deputy sheriff and notorious racist. Coleman leveled a shotgun at seventeen-year-old Ruby Sales, one of Jon's black companions. Daniels pushed her to one side and took the shotgun blast full in his middle. He died instantly. Although charged with manslaughter, Coleman was later acquitted by an all-white jury.

Daniels had traveled to Alabama six months earlier to participate in the famous Selma to Montgomery march organized by **Martin Luther King Jr**. A bookish young man who planned to teach college after he was ordained, he was shaken by the treatment of Southern blacks he encountered. He decided to stay on to do something about it. The last half-year of his life was devoted to integrating Episcopal churches in Alabama and registering blacks to vote.

Daniels became a devoted advocate of King's strategy of active nonviolence. When he first arrived in the South and witnessed firsthand the brutality of Jim Crow, he admitted to moments of fury "when I'd like to get a high-powered rifle and take to the woods" against white racists. But gradually these urges were replaced with the conviction that the "way of the Cross" was the better option. The breakthrough for him came when he was attacked and gassed in a demonstration. Gazing at his assailants, he found himself "feeling a kind of grim affection" for them, "even though they were white and hateful and my enemy." Daniels suddenly realized that "they were human beings too," and this insight liberated him from anger. "I began to discover a new freedom in the Cross: freedom to love the enemy; and in that freedom, the freedom (without hypocrisy) to will and to try to set him free." Compassion and love, he decided, "will accomplish more for real integration of the races than belligerence."

In sacrificing his life to save Ruby Sales, Daniels practiced the nonviolence he preached. Martin Luther King Jr. described it as "one of the most heroic Christian deeds I have heard in my entire ministry."

21 August
Raymond Hunthausen

21 August 1921—

The Virtue of Nakedness

Roman Catholic Archbishop of Seattle Raymond Hunthausen enraged the Reagan administration in the summer of 1981 when he proclaimed that "Trident is the Auschwitz of Puget Sound." He was referring to the Trident nuclear submarine base then under construction in his diocese.

Many thought that Hunthausen's reference to the Nazi death camp was over the top. But if anything, he understated the case. Each Trident carried multiple nuclear warheads capable of striking 408 separate areas. Together, the warheads had a killing power of over two thousand Hiroshima bombs.

In his 1981 statement, Hunthausen condemned nuclear weapons as "immoral and criminal. They benefit only arms corporations and the insane dreams of those who wish to 'win' a nuclear holocaust." Such weapons, he continued, "protect privilege and exploitation." The very thought of them, much less their production, violates the gospel of love to which Christians are called.

Why, then, do we tolerate them? Because, answered Hunthausen, we live in a state of chronic fear. "To ask one's country to relinquish its security in arms is to encourage risk—a more reasonable risk than constant nuclear escalation, but a risk nevertheless. I am struck by how much more terrified we Americans often are by talk of disarmament than by the march to nuclear war. We whose nuclear arms terrify millions around the globe are terrified by the thought of being without them. The thought of our nation without such power feels naked."

But the vulnerability we so fear, insisted Hunthausen, is an opportunity rather than a threat. Giving up nuclear weapons means getting out from under the constant dread of attack. It means liberating ourselves from the anxiety that safeguarding power necessarily generates. And it also means setting an example for the rest of the world.

This alone would have upset the Reagan administration. But Hunthausen went on to urge the people of Seattle to withhold 50 percent of their income tax—the percentage earmarked for the Pentagon—as a form of nonviolent resistance. Furthermore, he announced that he was holding back half of his own income.

The fallout was swift. Conservative Catholics, munitions manufacturers, military leaders, and right-leaning politicians launched a smear campaign against Hunthausen. The Internal Revenue Service garnished his wages. The Reagan administration brokered a deal with the Vatican to open an investigation into Hunthausen's performance as Seattle's prelate. After a two-year investigation, **John Paul II** significantly sidelined Hunthausen by appointing an auxiliary bishop in Seattle to watchdog him.

Archbishop Hunthausen retired in 1991 but remains active in peace work. His public and costly witness against the madness of nuclear proliferation remains an inspiration to all peacemakers.

22 August

Ouray

CA. 1833—24 AUGUST 1880

Pierced Buffalo

LEADERS OF NATIONS ARE sometimes forced to find ways of dealing with aggressors that, while not desirable, at least ensure the survival of their peoples. Chieftains of American Indian nations, especially those in the western states and territories during the second half of the nineteenth century, learned this bitter lesson time and again. They could wage war against white America and inevitably lose, or they could seek peace and reconciliation, only to be taken advantage of repeatedly. But at least they would survive. It was a terrible choice to have to make.

One of the Indian leaders who found himself in this position was Ouray, Chief of the Uncompahgre Utes of Colorado. Born near Taos in the New Mexico Territory, Ouray was called "Arrow" because on the night he was born, a meteor shower shot stars across the heavens. It was considered a good omen.

Ouray spent most of his youth sheepherding for Mexican ranchers around Taos and protecting their flocks from raiding Sioux and Kiowa. He grew up speaking Spanish and English as well as a couple of Ute dialects. When he was eighteen years old, he relocated to Colorado, where his father was leader of the Umcompahgres. After his father's death around ten years later, Ouray assumed the tribe's leadership.

Partly because of his ability to speak English but mainly because he had a patient and peaceful temperament, Ouray went out of his way to maintain good relations between his people and white settlers. He was a strong negotiator for his tribesmen when it came to hammering out treaties, but he was also a realist who recognized that the Utes were no physical match for the whites and so typically had to settle for what they could get. Even though the treaties he eventually signed advantaged settlers and were nearly always broken in one way or another, he always scrupulously upheld his end of them.

In 1878, gold was discovered in Colorado, and the Utes were faced with an inrush of white prospectors and merchants who began seizing their land. As tension escalated, the U.S. government appointed an Indian agent, one Nathan Meeker, to keep the Utes in line. Meeker's supervision of the Colorado Utes was so tyrannical that several bands of them revolted, killed him and eight other white men, and kidnapped several of their wives and daughters. Chief Ouray, who had earlier tried to calm the waters, now rushed to pacify the rebellious Utes and restrain the U.S. military detachment ordered to defeat them. But it was no use. The Ute war party was tracked down and killed and the entire Ute Nation was ordered onto an even smaller reservation. Ouray's patient and diplomatic efforts for peaceful coexistence between Indians and whites had failed, as he must have known deep down that they would. As he had once sadly noted, "The agreement an Indian makes to a United States treaty is like the agreement a buffalo makes with his hunter when pierced with arrows. All he can do is lie down and give in." Ouray the peacemaker may have finally lain down. But he never gave in.

23 August
Iccho Itoh

23 August 1945—18 April 2007

A Mayor for Peace

IN THE YEAR HE was elected mayor of Nagasaki, one of only two cities ever to endure an atomic bomb attack, Iccho Itoh made a speech that came to be known as the Nagasaki Peace Declaration. In it, he called upon the peoples of the world to rise "above the barriers of age and nationality" and forge "a peaceful future for humankind." Residents of Nagasaki, admiring Itoh's efficiency and integrity, reelected him for two additional terms as mayor. The international community came to know and respect him for his tireless work for global nuclear disarmament and his eloquent championing of the **hibakusha**, or survivors, of Nagasaki's atomic blast.

Convinced that "nuclear weapons are instruments of indiscriminate genocide" and that "the human race cannot co-exist" with them, Itoh served as vice president of the international organization Mayors for Peace during the last twelve years of his life. Founded in 1982, Mayors for Peace encourages cities across the world to declare in favor of total nuclear weapons abolition. Today, thanks in large part to Itoh's efforts, over four thousand cities in 144 countries have done so.

One of Itoh's most important victories as a proponent of peace occurred in the early summer of 2005, when the Nuclear Non-Proliferation Treaty was up for review by its signatories. Enacted in 1970 and currently endorsed by 189 nations, the treaty aims at the non-proliferation of nuclear weapons, the disarmament of existing nuclear stockpiles, and the peaceful use of nuclear technology. One of the major issues on the table in the 2005 review was the desire of the United States to develop nuclear weapons effective in destroying such deeply buried targets as Taliban and al-Qaeda strongholds in the mountain caves of Afghanistan. Traveling to New York City and speaking at both the United Nations and to a peace march forty thousand people strong, Itoh pled for renewed commitment to the Non-Proliferation Treaty. Addressing the American people, he said, "We understand your anger and anxiety over the memories of the horror of the 9/11 terrorist attacks. Yet, is your security enhanced by your government's policies of maintaining 10,000 nuclear weapons?"

In April 2007, while campaigning for reelection to a fourth term as mayor, Itoh was shot outside Nagasaki's train station. He died a few hours later. His assassin was a gangster whose motive was vengeance for a perceived slight on the part of the city's bureaucracy. The supreme irony of Mayor for Peace Itoh's life was that he died violently in the city he so loved.

24 August
Howard Zinn

24 August 1922—27 January 2010

The Highest Form of Patriotism

In 1976, the publishers of the *Boston Globe* fired a columnist because of the uproar one of his pieces had generated. The columnist was Howard Zinn, Boston University professor, anti-war activist, and human rights advocate. His essay was titled "Whom Will We Honor Memorial Day?" In it, Zinn challenged the holiday's glorification of militarism. "Memorial Day will be celebrated," he wrote, "by the usual betrayal of the dead, by the hypocritical patriotism of the politicians and contractors preparing for more wars, more graves to receive more flowers on future Memorial Days." But the "memory of the dead deserves a different dedication. To peace, to defiance of governments." To that end, Zinn recommended that "no politician who voted funds for war, no business contractor for the military, no general who ordered young men into battle, no FBI man who spied on anti-war activities, should be invited to public ceremonies on this sacred day."

It was strong stuff. But Zinn made a career out of defying the American government. He considered it a moral obligation to speak truth to power when political leaders misled the public or embraced unjust policies. Dissent, he was fond of saying, is "the highest form of patriotism."

Service in World War II as a bombardier who flew on missions that carpet bombed cities in Europe gave Zinn his first exposure to the possibility that his government could endorse immoral actions. The experience soured him on war for the rest of his life and started him on his long career of dissent. After the war he studied history and political science and taught at Georgia's Spelman College, an historic all-black women's institution. He threw himself into the civil rights movement. In 1963, Zinn was fired after helping his students organize anti-segregation demonstrations, despite the fact that he was tenured. He relocated to Boston University, where his outspoken criticism of national policy was a perpetual source of irritation to the institution's administration and trustees.

Zinn was particularly active in opposing the Vietnam War. In 1967 he published one of the first book-length denunciations of U.S. involvement in Southeast Asia, and the following year he traveled to Hanoi with **Daniel Berrigan** to negotiate the release of American POWs. He regularly participated in anti-war demonstrations, marches, and sit-ins. When **Daniel Ellsberg** was prosecuted for leaking the Pentagon Papers in 1971, Zinn was called in by Ellsberg's defense team as an expert consultant.

Zinn's most far-reaching legacy is undoubtedly his 1980 *A People's History of the United States,* which tells the story of America through the eyes of "common people"—workers, immigrants, women, Indians, blacks—rather than from the usual perspective of the wealthy and empowered. Zinn said that his intention in writing the book was to inspire a "quiet revolution" in which ordinary patriots would nonviolently take back their government from the powerbrokers who start wars and tolerate social injustice. Dissent, after all, is patriotic.

25 August
Ginetta Sagan

1 June 1925—25 August 2000

The Little Mouse Who Roared

IN EARLY 1945, A nineteen-year-old girl named Ginetta despairingly crouched in a filthy prison cell. A member of the Italian Resistance, she'd been arrested a month earlier by Mussolini's Black Brigade. Her parents, both physicians in Milan, were also arrested; her Catholic father was shot outright and her Jewish mother sent to Auschwitz. The girl, barely five feet tall and affectionately called *"Topolino"* or "Little Mouse" by her friends, had been repeatedly tortured and raped during her imprisonment. "My greatest fear, greater even than the fear of death, which seemed almost a certainty," she remembered years afterwards, "was that I would betray my comrades to the Black Brigade."

Suddenly a guard opened her cell door and tossed her a loaf of bread. When she tore it in two she discovered a matchbox containing a scrap of paper with a scrawled message: "*Coraggio!* Courage! We are working for you!" The note gave her the strength to endure her ordeal a little longer. Shortly afterward, two resistance fighters disguised as Nazis rescued Ginetta and got her to England, where she worked with traumatized concentration camp survivors and resistance fighters.

After studying psychology at the Sorbonne, the Little Mouse moved to the United States in 1951 where she met and married an American medical student named Leonard Sagan. For the next few years she raised a family and counseled juvenile offenders. But she was increasingly drawn to human rights work, and in 1967 she helped found Amnesty International USA, started building its membership, and edited its first national newsletter, which she called *Matchbox*. The name was significant. She wanted Amnesty International to be the unexpected message of hope for prisoners of conscience throughout the world.

Over the next few years, Sagan was present wherever human rights were abused, advocating for prisoners and publicly chastising their oppressors, regardless of whether they came from the political left or right. In the late 1960s and early 1970s, she investigated and publicized the crimes of the Greek military junta. In the 1970s she exposed CIA complicity in the Chilean coup that toppled President Salvador Allende and brought General Augusto Pinochet to power. In the 1980s she worked to rescue prisoners in Vietnam's "reeducation" gulags and channeled funds into Poland for Solidarity, the workers movement. On at least one occasion she smuggled cash into the country herself. And in the last decade of her life, she worked tirelessly for human rights in Algeria, Ethiopia, and Tibet. All prisoners of conscience were her concern, but she especially advocated for women and children. When asked once why she labored so tirelessly for human rights, she replied: "Silence in the face of injustice is complicity with the oppressor."

In 1996, Ginetta Sagan's *coraggio* as a peacemaker was recognized when Bill Clinton presented her with the Presidential Medal of Freedom and Italy awarded her the *Grand Ufficiale del Merito della Repubblica*.

26 August
Jinzaburo Takagi

18 July 1938—8 October 2000

Anti-Nuclear Energy Activist

PRIOR TO THE 2011 earthquake that crippled the Fukushima-Daiichi nuclear plant, the worst nuclear energy accident in Japan's history occurred in 1999 when an explosion and fire shook the nuclear reprocessing plant at Tokai. (A reprocessing facility separates uranium and plutonium from waste in spent nuclear fuel.) Two employees were killed, and the plant was closed down for a few months pending an official investigation by Japanese authorities.

When the government released its report on the Tokai accident, Dr. Jinzaburo Takagi made headlines by publicly accusing it of whitewashing the dangers involved in the production of nuclear energy and the disposal of spent fuel. Takagi's name was well known in Japan. For a quarter of a century he had been watchdogging the nuclear energy industry as well as government regulatory offices. An advocate for green energy sources, Takagi argued that plutonium-based nuclear energy was dangerous on any number of levels: accidents such as the one at Tokai were always a threat, and plutonium is a known cancer-causing element as well as an essential component in nuclear weapons. If there was a nation on the face of the globe that should be wary of nuclear energy, it was Japan, Takagi believed.

Takagi hadn't always been an opponent of nuclear energy. As a young man, he believed that plutonium's promise of abundant energy would make it the "gold of the nuclear age." But by the mid-seventies the rush to build nuclear energy plants, coupled with the Japanese government's blithe disregard of warnings about the environmental and human risks of producing plutonium, persuaded Takagi that he had an obligation to leave pure research to become a "citizen scientist." In 1975 he resigned a professorship of nuclear chemistry at Tokyo Metropolitan University and joined the Citizens' Nuclear Information Center (CNIC), a nongovernmental organization designed to educate the public about the hazards of nuclear energy. Takagi subsequently became the CNIC's executive director, a position he held until cancer forced him to step down in 1998. But even in his final illness he continued to advocate for sustainable energy sources. "Since the start of my social activities," he said shortly before his death, "a sense of responsibility as a nuclear chemist for the future generation has always occupied my mind in regard to the vast amount of plutonium stockpile which our generation had accumulated and is still going to produce."

In 1997, Takagi's advocacy for a nuclear-free world was recognized with a Right Livelihood Award, the alternative Nobel Prize. The award citation praised him for his efforts "to overcome the threat to humanity posed by the manufacture, transport, use and disposal of plutonium."

27 August
Mother Teresa

26 August 1910—5 September 1997

The Fruit of Service

SHE WAS A TINY woman, and old age and hard work bent her back so that she looked even smaller. But Mother Teresa of Calcutta's moral stature was colossal. A Roman Catholic nun for nearly seventy years and head of the Missionaries of Charity for forty-five years, she set up over six hundred missions in 123 countries to serve the dying, the homeless, and the indigent. Although often burdened with a desolate sense of God's absence—spiritual dryness, as it's often called—Mother Teresa persevered in her ministry of treating others as the images of the suffering Jesus she believed them to be. God, she was convinced, "identified himself with the hungry, the sick, the naked, the homeless."

Teresa, who was born in Albania and christened Agnes Gonxha Bojaxhiu, joined the Sisters of Loreto when she was eighteen years old. After learning English, she was sent to India to teach school, which she did for nearly two decades. But she eventually felt she was called to a life of total dedication to the poor and ill of India, and she received permission to leave her teaching position, move to a Calcutta slum, and begin her new ministry. Before long, like-minded women joined her, and the Missionaries of Charity order was born.

The new order combined action and contemplation. So far as Teresa was concerned, the two necessarily complemented one another, the Martha of action being sustained by the Mary of contemplation. As she once put it, "The fruit of silence is prayer; the fruit of prayer is faith; the fruit of faith is love; the fruit of love is service; the fruit of service is peace." Never willing to shirk even the most unpleasant of chores when it came to taking care of the sick and dying, Teresa always found time after a grueling day's work to sit quietly in prayer, sometimes for hours.

Asked once why she never seemed to judge others despite the violence she saw in the world, Teresa responded that judging was such all-consuming work that it would leave her no time to love. Compassionate love, not judgment—much less bombs and guns—was the key to overcoming the world's violence. Once we recognize that we are kin to all other humans, bound to them by virtue of sharing the same divine Parent, love replaces judgment. "If we have no peace," she said, "it is because we have forgotten that we belong to each other—that man, that woman, that child is my brother or my sister. If everyone could see the image of God in his neighbor, do you think we would still need tanks and generals?"

International awards and honors, including the 1979 Nobel Peace Prize, were poured upon Mother Teresa in the final twenty-five years of her life. She was thankful for the purses attached to the awards—every cent of the money went to support the work of the Missionaries of Charity—but was otherwise unimpressed. Her job, she believed, was just to do "something beautiful for God." That was simply what she was called to do, and it deserved no special recognition.

28 August
Smaragdus of Saint-Mihiel

CA. 760—CA. 840

Spiritual Warfare

THE EMPEROR CHARLEMAGNE'S FRANKISH kingdom, which united much of western and central Europe, brought a period of stability and peace to a war-torn region and even ushered in a short-lived revival of learning known as the Carolingian Renaissance. But the empire began to break apart after Charlemagne died in 814, and warfare and pillage returned.

One of the learned monks who lived during this period was Smaragdus, abbot of the Benedictine monastery of Saint-Mihiel, located near modern-day Verdun. In reaction to the violence that began to fracture Charlemagne's empire following his death, Smaragdus wrote a commentary on the Rule of St. Benedict that drew a clear distinction between worldly warfare and spiritual warfare. "The world," he noted, "has its soldiers and Christ has his. Now the world's soldiers take up weak and slippery weapons, whereas Christ's soldiers take up strong and bright ones. The former fight against their enemies, and the result is they bring themselves and those they kill to eternal punishment; the latter fight against the vices, so that after death they may be able to gain eternal life."

Both the worldly soldier and the Christian soldier follow orders. The former submits himself to his military superiors and the discipline of army life, while the latter submits to religious superiors and the gospel's teachings. Popular opinion has it that the worldly soldier is stronger in courage and resolve than the Christian one. But Smaragdus disagreed. "What can be stronger," he asks, "than that when struck on one cheek he should offer the other, should surrender his cloak to one who is taking away his tunic, that for one who is forcing him to go one mile he should go two?" Moreover, the worldly soldier obeys, but often in a grumbling sort of way. The Christian soldier, on the other hand, rejoices to obey and is "content with great poverty and hardship," because his service is performed out of love rather than coercion or fear. Finally, whereas the worldly soldier's rewards are material and fleeting, the Christian soldier's reward, inner peace, is spiritual and enduring. "Peace is mind's serenity, spirit's tranquility, heart's simplicity, love's bond, charity's fellowship."

It may be regretted that Smaragdus chose to use military language to contrast the way of Christian love with the way of worldly violence. The notion of spiritual warfare has become especially unpalatable to many post-9/11 Western ears because of its unpleasant association with the way Islamicists have appropriated the term *jihad*. But even St. Paul used military metaphors to describe the human struggle to tame tendencies and drives that break the peace. Smaragdus, equally concerned with promoting inner and outer harmony, followed his lead.

29 August
Arndt Pekurinen

29 August 1905—5 November 1941

He Refused to Butcher

Few pacifists have suffered more for their convictions than the Finnish conscientious objector Arndt Pekurinen. Executed in the first years of World War II and forgotten for nearly fifty years, Pekurinen's principled refusal to bear arms is a story of heroic resolve from first to last.

Pekurinen was barely twenty when he first ran afoul of military authority. Called up for mandatory service in the Finnish army, he refused conscription. At the time, Finnish law granted religious conscientious objectors military deferment. Although religious himself—Pekurinen's pacifism was inspired especially by the Sermon on the Mount and the writings of **Leo Tolstoy**—he refused to go this route. Believing that all pacifists, religious or otherwise, should have the right to refuse to bear arms, he chose to base his opposition to war on purely ethical grounds: war is evil and direct or indirect participation in it immoral. "As people are not eaten," he said, "butchering them is of no use."

Pekurinen successfully resisted conscription for three years before he was finally arrested and forcibly inducted into the army in 1929. An advocate of nonviolent resistance, he refused to strip for the required military physical examination and to wear the uniform, and eventually went on a hunger strike to protest his treatment. Sent first to a mental hospital for observation, then to a military disciplinary unit where he was barracked with criminals and savaged by right-wing soldiers who disapproved of his anti-militarism, Pekurinen was finally sentenced to a series of prison sentences that totaled three years.

During his time in prison, Pekurinen's story was picked up by the press and generated an outcry of support throughout Europe. Eventually the publicity created such an uproar that the Finnish parliament rewrote the conscription laws in 1931 to grant conscientious objector status to those who objected to war on moral rather than only religious grounds. That same year, Pekurinen was released from jail.

For the next eight years, he enjoyed a normal life. He married, had two children, and supported his family by driving taxis. He remained active in peace work and also became involved in the temperance movement. Then the first of two wars between Finland and the Soviet Union—the so-called Winter War—erupted against the backdrop of World War II, and Pekurinen was drafted.

Bizarrely, the 1931 law on conscientious objection was applicable only during peacetime. During wartime, conscientious objection was legally unrecognized. Once again Pekurinen resisted the call-up, and once again he was imprisoned. Finally, the army ordered him to the front line, even though he'd never had a single day of combat training. Once there, he again refused to serve, and was summarily executed.

Nearly a half-century after his death, the city of Helsinki named a park after Pekurinen in honor of his principled stance against war.

30 August

Gene Sharp

21 January 1928—

Pragmatic Nonviolence

Many practitioners of active nonviolence are motivated by religious beliefs or ethical ideals. Perhaps as a consequence of this, there tend to be more philosophical and theological analyses of pacifism than concrete guidelines for nonviolent resistance to injustice and oppression. But Gene Sharp, whom many consider to be the world's leading expert on nonviolent revolutions, ignores motives and focuses squarely on the pragmatics of nonviolence. His analysis provides both an explanation of why nonviolence is an effective tool and how to go about wielding it in different circumstances.

Sharp believes that any powerful institution, be it a totalitarian regime, a democratically elected government, or even a corporation, rules only with the consent of those whom it governs. There's nothing magical about power. It arises from the relationship between those who rule and those who are ruled. What needs to be remembered is that the real leverage is controlled by those who are ruled. If they withhold their consent, then any regime must inevitably topple. Dictators will find themselves overwhelmed by massive protest, democratic officeholders will find themselves voted out, and corporations will lose revenue through consumer boycott.

Obviously, withdrawal of consent isn't easy in most situations. Dictators have armed thugs they can call upon, clever officeholders can manipulate public opinion, and the artificial need for commodities created by corporations can make it hard for consumers to say no. But effective organization as well as incentives strong enough to outweigh risks can maximize the possibility of withdrawing consent, and "once there has been a major reduction of or an end to the subjects' fear, and once there is a willingness to suffer sanctions as the price of change, large-scale disobedience and noncooperation become possible."

But what are the specific nonviolent tactics involved in "large-scale disobedience and noncooperation"? Sharp recommends a kind of "political jiu-jitsu" that deflects an opponent's assault, throws him off balance, and redirects his own strength against him. Obviously, the appropriate jiu-jitsu move depends on the nature of the aggressor. Sharp suggests a number of them, ranging from speeches, letters, petitions, marches, leaflets, skywriting, and social media, to walkouts, ostracism, economic boycotts, strikes, civil disobedience, and seizure and occupation of property. In discussing these tactics, he stresses, as **Mohandas Gandhi** did before him, that participants must be prepared to suffer psychologically, economically, and physically. But the suffering itself becomes yet another weapon of nonviolent resistance, pricking as it can the consciences of oppressors and outside observers.

Sharp believes that nonviolent resistance has historically been "partly spontaneous, partly intuitive" and nearly always with "no advance preparations or training." His life's work has been to provide the focus on technique that will make the active nonviolence of the future a science.

31 August
Jaime Sin

31 August 1928—21 June 2005

The Philippines' Moral Compass

In 1989, a number of "velvet revolutions" swept through Poland, East Germany, Bulgaria, and Czechoslovakia that used nonviolent tactics to overthrow their Soviet-style communist governments. They were inspired by the nonviolent People Power Revolution that brought down the corrupt Marcos regime in the Philippines three years earlier. One of the leaders of that revolution was Cardinal Jaime Sin, Roman Catholic Archbishop of Manila.

Ferdinand Marcos was elected president of the Philippines in 1965, and he was reelected four years later. His second term was marred by allegations of governmental corruption and the enactment of policies that favored the rich and exploited the poor. Barred by the Philippine constitution from seeking a third term, Marcos declared martial law in 1972, shut down the country's congress, suppressed civil rights, and arrested his political opponents. Backed by the United States, Marcos, became the virtual dictator of the Philippines for the next fourteen years. Along with his extravagant wife, Imelda, and their political and military cronies, he bankrupted the nation.

The People Power Revolution was sparked by a 1985 phony presidential election engineered by Marcos. When Marcos was predictably declared the winner, opposition leaders called for a nationwide protest strike. In response, Marcos called out the military. Cardinal Sin, citing Jesus' example of nonviolence, led Filipinos into the streets to kneel and pray the rosary in front of advancing tanks. Marcos' soldiers backed down; many of them joined the protesters. Eventually Marcos and his wife fled the country for U.S. asylum in Hawaii, and in early 1986 Corazon Aquino became the first legitimate president of the Philippines in nearly fifteen years.

In the years that followed the People Power Revolution, Cardinal Sin continued to be a spokesperson for the poor, making sure that their voices were heard by the nation's leaders. He returned to the public arena in 2001 to lead opposition to Philippine president Joseph Estrada, who was charged with graft and corruption. Speaking on the radio, Sin prayed, "May God show him the heroic value of relinquishing his post for the sake of our people." Shortly afterwards, Estrada resigned.

Throughout his career, Sin's political activities were motivated by what he called "a moral dimension." Disclaiming partisan allegiance, his only loyalty was to Christ and Christ's message of nonviolence and love. But he always insisted that the Church had an obligation to intervene in the public arena to champion society's least privileged and to speak truth to power. The Church, he said, "cannot proclaim eternal salvation to our flock when we are blind to the physical realities which deny them that very salvation here on earth."

By the time he retired in 2003, Cardinal Sin was one of the most beloved public figures in the Philippines. When he died a few months later, the *Chicago Sun-Times* praised him as "the Philippines' moral compass."

1 September
Siegfried Sassoon

8 September 1886—1 September 1967

Finished with War

On the eve of World War I, young Siegfried Sassoon seemed the perfect British gentleman, respectable in every aspect. He came from a good family, excelled on the cricket field, followed the hounds with enthusiasm and skill, and put in a couple of years reading history at Cambridge, though he left without taking a degree. When war clouds loomed over Europe, he enlisted in the British army in a burst of patriotism, was commissioned, and was sent to France in 1915.

And then the bottom began to fall out of Sassoon's respectability. His younger brother was killed in action, a tragedy that knocked the wind out of him. His own experiences of trench warfare soon convinced him that there was nothing at all noble or grand about combat. Sassoon had dabbled in verse before his enlistment, but his time at the front helped him find his poetic voice. The poetry he began to write described in sometimes excruciating detail the terror and muck of war. His brutally honest portrayals of young recruits who despairingly shot themselves or who, exhausted, fell asleep while on guard duty, as well as his thunderous denunciations of civilian warmongers who encouraged young men to enlist, reflected his growing disenchantment. At the same time, however, he was cited on numerous occasions for extraordinary bravery, earning the Military Cross and being recommended for the Victoria Cross, England's highest military decoration for valor.

By 1917, Sassoon had had enough. In July of that year, he wrote a short statement titled "Finished with the War: A Soldier's Declaration," which he sent to his military superiors. In short order it was read in the House of Commons and published in the *London Times*. In his letter, Sassoon declared that he was willfully defying military authority by refusing to fight any longer in a war he considered unjust. After writing it, he clinched his defiance by tossing his war medals into a river.

"Finished with the War" caused an immediate scandal, written as it was by a member of the upper class as well as a decorated war hero. Authorities were eager to avoid the public embarrassment of a court martial, so they expediently announced that Sassoon was suffering from shell shock and hustled him off to a secluded military hospital for battle-fatigued soldiers. While there, Sassoon met and befriended the young poet Wilfrid Owen, who was subsequently killed in battle.

Sassoon eventually returned to the front, not because he changed his views about the war but because he felt an obligation to look after the men under his command and to share the dangers and hardships they faced each day. He was accidentally wounded by friendly fire almost a year to the day after the appearance of "Finished with the War." Years later, he wrote a thinly fictionalized account of his war experiences titled *Memoirs of an Infantry Officer*. It remains one of the best British anti-war books of the twentieth century.

2 SEPTEMBER
Dick Sheppard

2 SEPTEMBER 1880—31 OCTOBER 1937

Peace Pledger

In October 1934, the Reverend Hugh Richard Lawrie Sheppard, known to everyone as Dick, received a phone call from the local post office informing him that several huge bags of mail were on their way to his London home. When they arrived, Sheppard found they were stuffed with thousands of postcards from people across the United Kingdom.

The avalanche of postcards—135,000 in all—was in response to a letter published earlier that month in the *Manchester Guardian* (the *London Times* refused to print it) in which Sheppard decried "the almost universally acknowledged lunacy of the manner in which nations are pursuing peace" and declared that it was essential "to discover whether or not it be true, as we are told, that the majority of thoughtful men in this country are convinced that war of any kind or for any cause, is not only a denial of Christianity, but a crime against humanity which is not to be permitted by civilized people." Sheppard ended the letter by inviting anyone interested in joining him in a public demonstration renouncing war to drop him a postcard.

The public witness for peace Sheppard called for took place the following July, and it birthed what became known as the Public Pledge Union. People who signed up pledged to refuse participation in armed conflict and promised to work for an end to the armaments race. Thousands took the pledge, many of them young men of draft age, and thousands more read and admired Sheppard's anti-war book, *We Say "NO!": The Plain Man's Guide to Pacifism*.

Sheppard had been a Christian pacifist since his service as a battlefield chaplain during World War I. Ill health plagued him throughout his life, periodically forcing him into periods of inactive convalescence. But in his more or less healthy intervals he was one of Britain's leading advocates for the poor—while rector of St. Martin-in-the-Fields in London's Trafalgar Square, for example, he transformed the church's cellar into a homeless shelter—and a tireless defender of nonviolence. Both his compassion for the poor and his pacifism were fueled by his Christian faith—as he said in 1929, "I do not think a Christian can take part in any work of killing, or do anything he cannot believe that Christ would have done"—but he was happy to work with people from any or no religious tradition. In 1932, for example, he issued a public invitation to all persons, regardless of their spiritual beliefs, to stand as physical buffers between the opposing forces in the Japanese-Chinese War.

Dick Sheppard died in 1937, beaten down by overwork and chronic asthma. It is, perhaps, a blessing that he didn't live to see the outbreak of World War II. But his efforts on behalf of peace created a movement that still endures; the Public Pledge Union remains vibrantly active in England to this day.

3 September

e. e. cummings

14 October 1894—3 September 1962

A Conscientious Object

The American poet e. e. cummings, although notorious for his unusual syntax and punctuation, was actually pretty conventional in the themes he wrote about. But on one subject he was quite unconventional: he was a steadfast opponent of warfare, militarism, and jingoistic patriotism, and he mocked all three in his writing. It's not entirely clear whether he objected to them because he was a principled advocate of nonviolence or a temperamental rebel against any form of authority. Most likely both were factors.

In the spring of 1917, during World War I, cummings joined an ambulance corps that served French troops on the front line. His enlistment wasn't a sign of support for the war, but rather an attempt to avoid the U.S. draft. While a member of the corps, cummings wrote a number of indiscreet letters strongly condemning the war and what he took to be the bloodthirsty and stupid willingness of French officers to throw wave after wave of troops into hopeless assaults against enemy fortifications. The French censors read his letters, and within a short time after his arrival in Europe he was arrested on rather vague charges of espionage and disloyalty. Shipped off to a prison in Normandy, cummings spent nearly five months in a detention camp before he was finally released through the intervention of U.S. President Woodrow Wilson. His memoir *The Enormous Room*, whose title is a reference to the prison barracks in which he and other prisoners were housed, describes his ordeal. Ironically, cummings was drafted almost immediately after his return to the United States, but the war ended before he could be shipped overseas as a combat troop.

e. e. cummings' best-known anti-war poem—and, in fact, one of the best-known of all English anti-war poems—is "i sing of Olaf glad and big." It's a heartbreaking and chilling account of a conscientious objector—a "conscientious object," as he's disdainfully called by military superiors—named Olaf, "whose warmest heart recoiled at war." After being drafted into the army, Olaf refuses to cooperate and is systematically abused, with the implicit approval of officers, by noncoms and privates in an effort to break him. He's knocked about, submerged in icy water, scrubbed with filthy bristle brushes until his skin is raw, kicked, cursed, and even sodomized with bayonets. But Olaf refuses to budge from his refusal to cooperate with the military—"I will not kiss your fucking flag!"—and eventually, the president of the United states "threw the yellowsonofabitch into a dungeon, where he died." Olaf, concluded cummings, was as brave as any soldier in battle. But struggles such as his too often go unsung.

4 SEPTEMBER
Albert Schweitzer

14 JANUARY 1875—4 SEPTEMBER 1965

To Reverence All Life

ALBERT SCHWEITZER WAS A renaissance man of the twentieth century. An expert on the music of J. S. Bach, an accomplished organist, an ordained theologian and biblical scholar, and a medical missionary to equatorial Africa, Schweitzer combined throughout his long life a deep erudition with an abiding humanitarianism. He expressed both in his famous "ethic for the reverence of life," for which he was awarded the 1952 Nobel Peace Prize.

Schweitzer's starting point is his realization that all his actions are motivated by a deep-seated and unquenchable will to live, a "yearning for more life, a mysterious exaltation" of life itself. He concluded that a similar will to live is present in all organic beings. Consistency demanded that he value and respect all other wills to live in the same way that he valued his own, and this conclusion resulted in what Schweitzer maintained was the "fundamental principle" of morality: "It is good to maintain and cherish life; it is evil to destroy and to check life." Thoughtless injury to life is always condemnable.

Schweitzer's argument for the reverence of life, which he saw as "the ethic of Jesus brought to philosophical expression," has been criticized by many for what they see as its philosophical incoherence. The standard objection is that Schweitzer's fundamental principle is too vague. Should we reverence a cancer cell to the same degree that we do a blue heron? Or a blue heron equally with a human?

But this criticism misses Schweitzer's point. Reverencing all life means opening oneself to the awe that contemplation of the mystery of life brings, fully appreciating the living world not merely for its beauty and grandeur, but also for its dark and dangerous aspects. Fundamentally, Schweitzer's point is that the proper attitude towards life is one of immense gratitude. Even when it's necessary to take life—in chemotherapeutic destruction of cancer cells, for example—the awesomeness of all life-forms shouldn't be trivialized. As Schweitzer says, "Whenever I injure life of any kind I must be quite clear as to whether this is necessary or not. I ought never to pass the limits of the unavoidable, even in apparently insignificant cases." It may, for example, be necessary to "mow down a thousand blossoms" in order to cut hay for cattle to eat. But it's not necessary to absent-mindedly "switch off the head of a single flower growing on the edge of the road." To do so is to indulge in a "wanton pastime."

Cultivation of the awed gratitude that Schweitzer says is the proper response to life encourages an overall sensibility that he believed grounds the practice of nonviolence in both everyday and extraordinary contexts. He realized that "by itself, the affirmation of life can only produce a partial and imperfect civilization." But in a world that increasingly holds life cheap, encouraging reverence for life is a very good start.

5 September

Jonathan Kozol

5 September 1936—

Educational Advocate

In 1964, Jonathan Kozol took a job teaching fourth grade in Roxbury, Massachusetts. His move surprised family and friends. Kozol, after all, was a Harvard-educated Rhodes Scholar, and the troubled Roxbury public school system primarily served black kids from low-income families. But Kozol, inspired by the expanding civil rights movement in the South, wanted to put his elite education to good use.

What he discovered in Roxbury shook him to his core. The physical infrastructure of the school was literally crumbling. Textbooks were outdated and falling apart, school supplies for his class were in such short supply that Kozol purchased them with his own money, illiteracy was high, teacher morale was low, and the curriculum was unimaginatively restrictive. Before the year was out, Kozol was fired, ostensibly for violating the set curriculum by reading Langston Hughes's poems to his students. Angry, not so much at what happened to him as what the kids at Roxbury were enduring, he spent the next few months writing an exposé titled *Death at an Early Age*. His book, now a classic, appeared in 1967 and won a National Book Award the following year.

Death at an Early Age launched Kozol into the educational advocacy that's become his lifework. In several subsequent books, including *Amazing Grace* (1995), which he refers to as a "theology of children," Kozol continues his documentation of what he calls "educational apartheid" in the United States. He argues that there is "savage inequality" in educational opportunities for black and white students. Although racial segregation has been illegal for several decades, Kozol's examination of schools in cities such as Chicago, New York, Boston, Detroit, and Washington, DC, has convinced him that it nonetheless exists de facto. Public schools that serve mainly white student bodies are better funded than primarily black schools. The quality of education funded for these schools is as poverty-stricken as the neighborhoods that the students who attend them generally live in. In effect, the system's failure of these students robs them of their childhood and youth. "For the children of the poorest people," Kozol protests, "we're stripping the curriculum, removing the arts and music, and drilling the children into useful labor." We're treating them, in other words, as commodities rather than humans. But "children aren't commodities to be herded into line and trained for jobs that white people who live in segregated neighborhoods have available."

Gandhi once said that the seriousness with which a society takes justice can be gauged by how it treats its least empowered citizens. Most people agree that children fall into that category. Jonathan Kozol's tireless critique of the public educational system's habit of treating some children as more equal than others reminds us that we've got a long way to go when it comes to taking justice seriously.

6 September
Jane Addams

6 September 1860—21 May 1935

Founder of Hull House

THERE ARE FEW AMERICANS in the Progressive Era, that period of social reform that flourished in the late nineteenth and early twentieth centuries, more impressive than Jane Addams. The daughter of a wealthy Illinois businessman who was a friend of Abraham Lincoln, Addams was uncertain about what she wanted to do with her life until her late twenties. But in 1888 she visited a "settlement house" in London and was inspired to open one in the United States.

Settlement houses were experiments in what was then called the "social Christianity" movement. Adherents of social Christianity weren't concerned with converting others to their faith so much as practicing Jesus' self-giving love to reform unjust social and economic conditions. The settlement houses were basically hostels in which Christians lived side by side with the poor and the homeless. They were inspired by scriptural descriptions of early Christian communities in which possessions were shared equally by all.

In 1889, Addams and her close friend Ellen Gates Starr founded the first settlement house in the United States. Located in Chicago, it was called Hull House after its builder, and it was intended to be a woman's shelter as well as a community center for the surrounding immigrant neighborhood. But as time passed, Hull House grew into a thirteen-building complex that housed a public kitchen, a night school, a recreation hall, and a library, with an average of two thousand visitors each week. It became the model for dozens of other settlement house communities across the nation.

Addams wasn't content just to offer service to those in need. In keeping with what she called the three ethical principles for settlement houses—"to teach by example, to practice cooperation, and to practice social democracy, that is, egalitarian, or democratic, social relations across class lines"—she also worked toward reforming the social and economic institutions that caused poverty in the first place. To that end, she regularly collected statistical information about drug addiction, child mortality, and diseases among the less privileged, and she bombarded Chicago authorities with her findings. She fought the corrupt political bosses who exploited some of the most poverty-stricken wards in Chicago. And when World War I erupted, she not only condemned it for its waste of human life and squandering of physical resources that could have been used to feed the poor, but also defended foreign-born citizens against war-inspired discrimination. In recognition of her efforts, she won the 1931 Nobel Peace Prize, the first American woman to do so.

One of Addams's greatest accomplishments was to offer a living alternative to the rugged individualism so valued in the American tradition. For her, communities, such as the one built at Hull House, are the keys to human flourishing. As she once said, "The good we secure for ourselves is precarious and uncertain until it is secured for all of us and incorporated into our common life."

7 September

Asoka

CA. 304—232 BCE

Dharma King

THE WAR WAS OVER. After a particularly fierce battle, King Asoka had finally subdued the last kingdom standing between him and the conquest of nearly all of the Indian subcontinent. But as he strode across the battlefield and surveyed the thousands of bloodied and mutilated corpses, something broke within him. Instead of feeling a sense of triumphant exultation, he felt only shame at the destruction he'd wrought, and compassion for its victims. According to legend, he cried out: "What have I done? If this is a victory, what's a defeat then? Is this a victory or a defeat? Is this justice or injustice? Is it gallantry or a rout?"

Asoka, who up to that point had been a ruthless and feared ruler, walked away from the battlefield a changed man. He adopted Buddhism, proclaimed it the official religion of his empire, and for the rest of his life tried his best to rule in accordance with the *dharma,* or central precepts of the Buddha. *Ahimsa* or nonviolence became the empire's fundamental policy, and Asoka extended its application to animals as well as humans. He was little interested in the religious ceremonies and rituals associated with Buddhism. What fueled his new style of governance was the Buddha's ethical vision of compassion for all living things.

To announce that his kingdom was now under the rule of *dharma,* Asoka ordered that large stone tablets be erected throughout the land detailing his intentions. Known as the "Stone Edicts," they are remarkable documents. Declaring that his primary goal as a ruler was the happiness and welfare of his people, Asoka renounced warfare and embraced instead a policy of reconciliation and alliance with neighboring kingdoms. He ended royal hunts, drastically curtailed the number of animals slaughtered for the royal table, banned sports involving animal fighting, and issued laws protecting the lives and well-being of animals that weren't eaten. He worked hard to make sure that laws were just and uniformly applied and that slaves and servants were treated well. He tolerated all religious sects within his borders, asking only that they extend the same toleration to one another. Asoka was confident that the *dharma* could be found in them all. Universities and libraries were built across the land.

In order to better serve his "children," as he referred to his subjects, Asoka also improved the quality of medical care throughout his kingdom. As he proclaimed in one of the Stone Edicts, "I made provision for two types of medical treatment: medical treatment for humans and medical treatment for animals. Wherever medical herbs suitable for humans or animals are not available, I have had them imported and grown. Wherever medical roots or fruits are not available I have had them imported and grown. Along roads I have had wells dug and trees planted for the benefit of humans and animals."

"For the benefit of humans and animals": this was the guiding principle of Asoka, the *Dharma* King.

8 September
Mother Ann Lee

29 February 1736—8 September 1784

Of One Heart and Soul

In 1780, Mother Ann Lee, leader of the charismatic Christian group known as the Shakers, was thrown into a New York jail for refusing to pledge allegiance to America in its revolutionary war against Britain. The imprisonment, which lasted several months until New York governor George Clinton finally ordered her release, completely broke her already frail health. But it didn't damage her spirit. Over the next three years, Mother Ann and Shaker elders embarked on a missionary tour of New England. They were met with opposition everywhere they went, frequently mobbed, and sometimes physically abused. At one point, Mother Ann was actually tied by her heels to a wagon and dragged several miles over an icy road.

What was it about this diminutive woman that stirred up such rage? Partly it was her gender. In the eighteenth century, it was unusual to the point of scandal for a woman to be a religious leader. Not only had Ann ably shepherded her followers from England to the American colonies in 1774, but she was also recognized by them as the embodiment of the feminine aspect of Christ. As a consequence, she was their unchallenged spiritual and ethical mentor. All this stuck in the craw of her non-Shaker contemporaries.

But mainly it was the beliefs lived and preached by the Shakers that infuriated their critics. Founded in 1747, the Shakers (so called because they often trembled and ecstatically danced during worship services) were Christians who practiced celibacy, radical egalitarianism, and lived in close community with one another. They adopted simple lifestyles that they believed liberated them from distracting passions such as greed and envy; a well-known line from one of their hymns is "'Tis the gift to be simple, 'tis the gift to be free." They took seriously Jesus' command to refrain from returning evil for evil and adopted a radical pacifism that forbade them from serving in the military or supporting it indirectly through labor or taxes. And they tried to practice in thought, word, and deed the two great commandments: love of God and humanity. As one 1823 Shaker document put it, "the greatest practical evidence of genuine love and disinterested benevolence that can be manifested on earth, is found where all are of one heart and one soul; where the rich and the poor can meet together, and eat and drink at one table, and mutually share in each other's comforts and afflictions."

Mother Ann led the Shakers for nearly thirty years and founded several communities throughout New England in the last decade of her life. Eventually, there were nineteen different communities with upwards of six thousand members. One of them, located at Sabbathday Lake, Maine, still remains. Shakers at the Sabbathday community continue to practice the simple living, communitarianism, and nonviolence that Mother Ann taught and suffered for.

9 September

Ruth Fry

4 September 1878—26 April 1962

Victory without Violence

ALTHOUGH SHE WAS ONE of the most active Quaker peace advocates between the two world wars, Ruth Fry is nearly unknown today, even to Quakers. Born into a London middle-class family, she learned from an early age the value of dialogue and compromise as ways of settling disputes. Her father, a Quaker attorney and judge, often collaborated in conflict resolution negotiations at The Hague.

Fry cut her teeth as a peace activist during the Second Boer War (1899–1902). When World War I erupted a decade later, she served during its duration and for six years afterwards as the head of the Friends War Victims Relief Committee, a Quaker organization devoted to aiding war refugees. During this time she worked closely with the American Friends Service Committee to make sure that food and medical supplies got through to people, especially children, displaced by the war.

In 1921, when famine broke out in the fledgling Soviet Union—before it was over, it claimed the lives of five to ten million peasants—Fry chaired the British-based Russian Famine Relief Fund, working closely with other international relief agencies to gather and ship grain to Russia. She visited the Soviet Union on three different occasions during the famine and later wrote a book describing in poignant detail what she saw there. The book was just one of Fry's many works; she was a prolific author.

In the 1920s and 1930s, she was an active participant in anti-war organizations such as **Dick Sheppard**'s Peace Pledge Union, the War Resisters League, and the Fellowship of Reconciliation.

Fry's characteristic approach to peacemaking, influenced by both her father's work at The Hague and her Quaker background, is nicely expressed in the title of one of her books, *Victory without Violence*. Fry was convinced that "moral enthusiasm," by which she meant a principled embrace of pacifism, was a more effective route to peace than coercion. She not only condemned the blatant coercion of warfare, but also the "peacekeeping" coercion exercised by international police forces.

But Fry was also a realist, and she acknowledged that sometimes Christian pacifists like herself had to make compromises, either because of the urgency of crisis situations or because they found themselves in the minority. She insisted, however, that any compromise should point, howsoever minimally, in the direction of the ultimate goal of absolute nonviolence, and that any compromise that represented a step in the opposite direction had to be rejected. As she wrote, "the ideal Quaker method" of peacemaking is waiting for an enlightenment that convinces with absolute certainty. But short of that, any advance towards peace is "a stepping stone, although only methods consistent with Quaker ideals"—nonviolent resistance, for example—may be used. Sometimes, she admitted, it's difficult to know where to draw the line. But "doing anything tinged with evil that good may come," she warned, "is entirely contrary" to peace work.

10 September
Jean Vanier

10 September 1928—

Celebrating People as They Are

Most of us who are "normal" have a hard time dealing with people with intellectual developmental disabilities. We feel awkward or embarrassed in their presence and relieved when we can get away from them. So we tend to pack them safely out of the way in institutions and hospitals.

Jean Vanier, the Canadian founder of the international organization L'Arche, thinks this is a grave mistake. When we segregate the intellectually disabled, we not only fail to love them—what we do to people with handicaps, warns Vanier, is "a measure of how hard and broken society is"—but we also deprive ourselves of opportunities for spiritual growth.

Vanier gave up a promising naval career to open the first L'Arche house, which also happened to be his personal home, in 1964. The L'Arche philosophy is to create a community in which the developmentally disabled live with one another and their care providers, and everyone learns to affirm each other's unique gifts. For Vanier, this nonjudgmental affirmation is a celebration of people as they are as well as what they have to teach the rest of us. It is, as he says, "to give thanks for the gift God has given us in having brought us together from a place of loneliness into a sense of belonging. I know that you have accepted me and I you. I know your gifts, and I also know your darkness. Yet I accept you as you are, not expecting more and not weeping because you are not exactly what I wanted you to be. So to celebrate is to give thanks for all you are and all we are together."

Although it sounds strange to celebrate and give thanks for what society sees as brokenness, Vanier insists that there's good reason to do so. All of us are poor in one way or another. All of us are spiritually disabled to a certain extent. Until we get in touch with and acknowledge our own brokenness, we are unable to reach up to God or out to others. "The presence of God," Vanier believes, "is in our own littleness and poverty." Consequently, cultivating relationships with those whose obvious brokenness reminds us of our own is a blessing rather than a burden. "The poor are not people whom we have to change from our pedestal and make them like us but people from whom we can drink."

Apparently, Vanier's message resonates with many people. Today, there are 137 L'Arche communities in over forty countries. Each of them continues the L'Arche tradition modestly started by Vanier in 1964: to "foster the acceptance of each person as a unique and valuable individual, whatever his or her abilities or disabilities." For Vanier, this is just another way of saying that all persons are made in God's likeness, and consequently both deserve our love and have great gifts to offer us.

11 September
Vinoba Bhave

11 September 1895—15 November 1982

Peace Army Visionary

Considered the spiritual successor of **Mohandas Gandhi**, Vinoba Bhave continued his teacher's nonviolent reform agenda in India. He's perhaps best known for his 1951 inauguration of *Bhoodan* or the Land Gift Movement. Believing that the single greatest cause of Indian poverty was land monopoly, Bhave began a nationwide campaign to persuade wealthy landowners in India to donate a portion of their acreage to landless members of the lower castes. Bhave traveled the length and breadth of India, mostly on foot, to lobby for the land reform. In the end, the ownership of more than five million acres was transferred.

Bhave was also a scholar of religion who wrote insightful commentaries on the Christian Bible, the Qur'an, and the classics of Hinduism, especially the Bhagavad Gita, a text he once described as his "life's breath." Bhave's sympathetic study of the major world religions' holy books made him a staunch defender of interfaith dialogue and tolerance.

But his greatest contribution was his call for a *Shanti Sena,* or Peace Army. Bhave was convinced that peace is more an absence of fear than an absence of war and that genuine peacemaking called for an eradication of the psychological and social causes of fear. Following a suggestion made by Gandhi, Bhave proposed the formation of a Peace Army soldiered by men and women—especially the latter, because Bhave believed them less prone to violence than men—dedicated to creating a world "in which no part fears or is exploited by another part."

How would the Peace Army go about accomplishing this? "It will be the *Shanti Sena's* task," wrote Bhave, "to remove the root causes of unrest: the gulf between the haves and the have-nots, the pride of ownership, the insistence of 'mine' and 'thine,' on high and low, on caste distinction, on religious differences and disputes. These are all causes of unrest, some economic, some social, some religious. The *Shanti Sena* will, therefore, be a full-time service army, working to remove these causes of dissensions and to find peaceful solutions to national problems. The result will be a cleansing of the national mind and growth of mutual goodwill. When that takes place, the government will not have to spend much on the army; the moral strength of the nation will be increased and it will be able to make its influence felt in the international field."

Soldiers in the Peace Army, Bhave continued, should take a pledge to trust one another, consider no person their enemy, and practice love, even at the risk of their own well-being and life. They should be totally devoted to serving needs "impartially, distinterestedly, without asking for any reward." The whole vocation of a peace soldier was to confront hatred with love.

Shanti Sena was more than just an inspired idea. Bhave actually organized it in 1957 and it endured for close to forty years. At its height, it boasted more than six thousand dedicated recruits.

12 SEPTEMBER
Solange Fernex

15 APRIL 1934—11 SEPTEMBER 2006

Mother of the French Anti-Nuclear Movement

ON 6 AUGUST 1983, the anniversary of the atomic blast that destroyed Hiroshima, thirteen anti-nuclear activists began a forty-day fast to draw public attention to the stockpiling of nuclear weapons by the United States and the Soviet Union. The activists lived in Paris, Toronto, Bonn, and San Francisco. Their fast attracted worldwide media attention, and thousands of people showed solidarity by fasting along with them for a few days. Their action raised consciousness about the deadly threat of nuclear weapons to a new level.

One of the fasting activists was Solange Fernex, who has been called the "mother of the French anti-nuclear movement." Nearly fifty when she participated in the fast, Solange had already established herself as an advocate of human rights, environmental protection, and nuclear disarmament. In the 1960s she worked in Africa with Terre des Hommes, a nonprofit organization concerned with protecting children's rights. Returning to Europe, she became involved in the fledging anti-nuclear movement and quickly established herself as a leader.

One of her early concerns was the environmental impact of nuclear weapons testing. After the 1986 accident at the Chernobyl nuclear power plant in Ukraine, she grew increasingly alarmed about the effects of nuclear power on both the environment and human health. Along with other anti-nuclear activists, she collected and published scientific data about the short- and long-term effects of the radiation leak from Chernobyl's reactor No. 4. She also championed the Russian scientist Yuri I. Bandazhevsky, who was censured and then sentenced to eight years in a Soviet prison for his public declaration that stillbirths, birth defects, and fetal malformations had escalated in the Chernobyl region following the accident. As Fernex saw it, neither the world's two political superpowers nor the corporations financially invested in nuclear power wanted scientists casting doubt on the safety of nuclear energy. So Bandazhevsky had to be made a chilling example. In a public statement she released after his sentencing, Fernex blasted his persecution. "The times when Galileo Galilei was persecuted by the Holy Inquisition for his scientific findings should be past," she said. "The truth of the health consequences of Chernobyl cannot be concealed, as this was possible, centuries ago, for the movements of the earth around the sun. Science must cease to be silenced by the economic interests of the promoters of nuclear energy."

In recognition of her long and dedicated advocacy of a nuclear-free world, Fernex was awarded the Nuclear-Free Future Lifetime Achievement Award in 2000. She died six years later, still at work. As her biographer put it, when it came to the struggle for social justice and a nuclear-free environment, she was *insoumise:* "unsubdued."

13 September

Aristophanes

CA. 448 BCE—388 BCE

Make Love, Not War

WAR IS NO LAUGHING matter. But comedy can be a great conveyor of truths, even ones about something as horrible as warfare. The Greek playwright Aristophanes proved as much in his anti-war play *Lysistrata*.

Actually, *Lysistrata* is one of three anti-war plays written by Aristophanes that together make up what's often called his "peace and war series." All three of them were provoked by the war between the city-state of Athens and the Spartan-led Peloponnesian League. Despite periodic negotiations, the war dragged on for nearly a quarter of a century. We don't know if Aristophanes actually served as a soldier in the war. But as an Athenian, he must have been affected by it—and, judging from his peace and war series, sick of it, too.

The plot of *Lysistrata* is simple, bawdy, funny, and insightful. The title character concocts a scheme to end the seemingly never-ending war: she and the other Athenian wives, in coordination with Spartan ones, will withhold sexual favors from their husbands until an armistice is signed. Nor will they simply refrain from sex. They'll also torture their husbands by dressing provocatively in "saffron-colored gowns" to inflame passion that will then go unconsummated. If their lust-filled husbands force them, they will simply lie under them, "cold as ice and never stirring a limb." All of the women take a solemn (but hilarious) oath, chanting in unison, "I will not lift my legs in air" and "Nor will I crouch with bottom upraised."

The reactions of their men are predictable. The old men of Athens and Sparta, long past their sexual prime, howl with indignation that women would dare to interfere with the masculine work of making war by refusing to make love. The younger men, warriors all, are equally defiant at first, but as the play progresses their spirits wilt as their unsatisfied ardor rises, metaphorically and literally. Their moan, "What a dreadful, dreadful torture it is!" is soon replaced with a nearly frenzied agreement to the women's demands for peace. As one of the Athenian soldiers says, speaking in ribald double entendre, "Oh, I'm ready now to remove my armor and cultivate my land!" Athenian and Spartan couples happily fall into one another's arms once the peace is made, and Lysistrata joyfully cries out, "Dance, dance, to celebrate our bliss, and let us be heedful to avoid like mistakes for the future." The wisdom of women has conquered the hotheadedness of men.

Sigmund Freud once argued that humans are ruled by two opposing tendencies, which he called eros, or creation, and thanatos, or destruction. In individuals as well as cultures, these two psychic drives dance in dynamic tension with one another. Sometimes eros is in the ascendency, sometimes thanatos. To his credit, Aristophanes recognized the tension centuries ago, and in *Lysistrata* he offered a funny but thought-provoking suggestion about how to control the one by wielding the other.

14 September
Cyprian of Carthage

Died 14 September 258

What Iron Is For

PEACEMAKING TAKES COURAGE, AND for most of us, courage doesn't come quickly or easily. Like all virtues, it's something we have to work at. Along the way, there may be moments in which our spirits falter. But the quality of our characters is ultimately judged by the strength of our perseverance.

Cyprian, bishop of Carthage, is a good example of this. Born into a wealthy patrician family in the North African city of Carthage, he practiced law before converting to Christianity about a decade before his death. In quick order he became a priest and then bishop of the city. During a persecution of Christians, sparked because of their refusal to recognize the divinity of Caesar, Cyprian fled, claiming that a divine revelation had given him permission to forsake his flock until the danger passed. Cyprian wasn't the only priest who evaded persecution. So many others did, in fact, that the Church debated for years about what to do with them. But Cyprian seems to have felt particularly shamed by his cowardice, and spent the rest of his life atoning for it by preaching Christ's message of peace with justice and thereby courageously defying the secular authorities.

One of the more dangerous themes of this preaching was his condemnation of warfare. "The world," he said, "is wet with mutual bloodshed. Homicide is a crime when individuals commit it, but it is called a virtue when it is carried on publicly" by armies. But all homicide is both unnatural and wicked. "God wished iron to be for the cultivation of the earth, and for that reason acts of homicide ought not to be committed." Christians ought not to misuse iron; it is a sin for them to spot their hands with blood after receiving the Eucharist. Likewise, torture, a common interrogatory technique under Roman law, was also an abomination that inflicts "more punishment for the one body of man than it has limbs!"

Christians renounce such violence, noted Cyprian, because "it is not lawful for us to hate." Violent response to injustice is forbidden "although our people are numerous and plentiful." Instead, "enemies are to be loved," and "when an injury has been received, patience is to be kept and vengeance left to God." Moreover, enemies are to be treated with the same love that Christians give one another. When a plague erupted in Carthage, Cyprian urged his flock to attend to the medical needs of Christian and pagan alike.

In the final two years of Cyprian's life, the Emperor Valerian launched a new persecution of Christians. This time the bishop refused to flee. He remained in Carthage to prepare his flock for the coming storm. When it arrived, he was imprisoned and eventually sentenced to death. Before the sword descended on him on 14 September 258, his last words were "Thanks be to God!" Both his death and the way in which he lived in his final years demonstrated that there was iron in the soul of this third-century peacemaker.

15 September
Jean Renoir

15 September 1894—12 February 1979

Cinematic Public Enemy #1

When filmmaker Jean Renoir's *Grand Illusion* was released in 1937, Joseph Goebbels, Nazi propaganda chief and self-proclaimed movie expert, angrily condemned it as "Cinematic Public Enemy #1." That Goebbels disliked the film was unsurprising. In addition to being a cinematic masterpiece, *Grand Illusion* is one of the most powerful anti-war movies ever made.

Renoir, son of the impressionist painter Pierre-Auguste Renoir, knew something about war. When World War I erupted, he was already a French cavalryman. He saw combat but eventually suffered a leg wound that laid him up for a long time. It was during his recuperation, while watching dozens of silent films to wile away the time, that he became interested in cinema. Immediately after the war he began making his own films, often selling paintings he'd inherited from his father to finance them.

During the 1930s, Renoir became one of France's most popular directors, despite the fact that most of his films reflected his unpopular left-wing politics. But it was *Grand Illusion*, released on the cusp of World War II, that brought him international fame.

The film centers on the escape of French World War I soldiers from a German prisoner of war camp. One of the French prisoners, de Boeldieu, and the German commandant, von Rauffenstein, represent the old, aristocratic order that sees soldiering as an honorable and noble profession. But warfare in the twentieth century, with its mass slaughter, horrible weapons, and wanton destruction of civilian lives and properties, has put the lie once and for all to such a romantic view. In this new way of making war, de Boeldieu and von Rauffenstein are dinosaurs, holdovers from a dead past. Renoir symbolizes this by giving the German horrible battle wounds and by actually killing off the Frenchman towards the end of the film. Before he dies, de Boeldieu prophetically declares that the era of "noble" warfare is over.

Opposed to the romanticized notion of warfare represented by the two officers is the perspective of the film's other main characters, a couple of low-born French soldiers who despise the aristocratic valorization of war and want only to flee both the prisoner of war camp and the horror of the battlefield. They manage to escape and make their way to neutral Switzerland. They are not cut from the same "heroic" cloth as de Boeldieu and von Rauffenstein. They want life, not medals and military glory. But they are precisely the sort of men, Renoir implies, who are forced to fight in the wars aristocrats start. It's the suffering, hatred of battle, and lost future endured by the common fighting man, not the martial strutting of a professional warrior class, that reveals the true nature of armed conflict. To suppose otherwise is to be sucked in by the "grand illusion."

16 September
Ursula Franklin

16 September 1921—

Cartographer of Peace

As a metallurgist, Ursula Franklin has been fascinated her entire adult life by structure, "the arrangement and interplay," as she says, "of parts within a whole." But her fascination isn't only about the structure of metals. It includes the ideological structures that humans create to justify social systems and public policies. As a Quaker and pacifist, and as someone who suffered under the Nazi regime, she has especially focused on structures that encourage obedience or acquiescence to unjust social and economic institutions—what she calls "cultures of compliance." These cultures prescribe supervision in all aspects of life. Labor is supervised by managers, knowledge by scholars, democracy by representatives, nations by statesmen, economies by brokers.

But for Franklin, the grids or maps drawn by supervisory structures and generally accepted as conventional wisdom are oppressive. Genuine freedom can flourish only when new maps are drawn. As she notes, "The social maps of gain and success are unhelpful for charting co-operation, compassion, and friendship." So Franklin calls upon her Quaker heritage and her commitment to nonviolence to help her chart new ways of thinking about the world in which we live. One fundamental question guides her peace cartography: "How can one live and work as a pacifist in the here and now and help to structure a society in which oppression, violence, and wars would diminish and co-operation, equality, and justice would rise?"

Like all maps, Franklin's contains lines of latitude and longitude that orient the map reader. A conversion of heart is the new map's latitude, and specific times and contexts its longitude. Peacemaking requires a sincere interior will on the part of individuals to build a society based on cooperation and compassion rather than competition and enmity. Translation of that will into concrete works and social structures demands adaptability to time and place instead of a "dogma of unvarying rules of conduct." Applying these new grid points, Franklin has devoted herself to presenting ways of thinking about women's rights, the environment, technology, and warfare that fall outside the culture of compliance's map of the world.

One of the new ways in which Franklin believes the map of war-making needs to be reimagined, for example, is in the recognition that not all warfare is carried out with soldiers and bombs. Globalization is a new kind of war fought by corporations and governments against the "commons." The goal is privatization of the public sphere—"publishing, culture, health care, prisons, education"—and absorption of it into "the empire of marketeers" who will "transform the ill health or misery of our neighbors into investment opportunities." Thinking of globalization as an "occupation," Franklin says, "is something that helps me to decide what I can do with my limited time and energy."

The new points on her world map offer, she hopes, "a path into a constructive and creative future."

17 September

Ron Sider

17 September 1939—

Evangelical Activism

For years, American evangelicals were relatively indifferent to peace- and justice-related social issues. Instead, their focus was on the cultivation of a personal relationship with God. Believing that the concerns of this world were distractions and hence risks to their salvation, they tended to have little time for such problems as armed conflict, economic inequality, political suppression, and environmental degradation.

Evangelicals became more socially conscious in the 1970s and 1980s with the rise of Jerry Falwell's Moral Majority and the "religious right," but the movement's political conservatism focused on issues such as abortion and sexuality to the virtual exclusion of all others.

At about the same time, though, a fresh wind began to blow through the evangelical world with the publication of Ron Sider's *Rich Christians in an Age of Hunger*. In it, Sider argued that concern for the one billion chronically hungry people in the world is a legitimately Bible-based one that disciples of Christ are called to take seriously. It isn't enough to chalk up poverty, squalor, and disease to individual sinfulness. As Christ recognized, there is institutional as well as personal sin, and building the beloved community requires recognizing and combating both. This is a particularly urgent religious duty when Christians benefit from institutional structures that oppress others. "If the church wants to be faithful to the Bible," concluded Sider, "then it has no choice" but to attend to those most in need, extending them charity but also working to eradicate the institutional causes of their suffering. The message of *Rich Christians in an Age of Hunger*, originally published in 1977 but revised several times since, has infuriated some evangelicals, but it has become a sort of manifesto for a great many others. In 2000 the leading evangelical magazine *Christianity Today*, founded by Billy Graham, called it one of the "books of the century."

Even before writing *Rich Christians*, Sider was instrumental in bringing socially conscious evangelicals together in Evangelicals for Social Action, a national organization founded in 1973 whose mission is "to serve as a catalyst and connector of a community of Christian leaders, educating and equipping them to do holistic ministry, work for social transformation, and challenge others to do the same." He also inspired the founding of Christian Peacemakers Team, an organization that sends witnesses to troubled areas of the world in the hope that their presence will inhibit violence. In addition to being a leader in Evangelicals for Social Action, Sider has continued to write books and articles that prod evangelicals in the direction of environmental stewardship, nonviolence, and a consistent respect for life. Under his wise direction, the evangelical movement has come a long way toward seeing authentic, Bible-based Christianity as a vehicle for both spiritual regeneration and social transformation.

18 September
Chris Hedges

18 September 1956—

The War Habit

Psychologically, war is paradoxical. On the one hand, it churns up terror, fury, hatred, and panic, emotions that are so unpleasant that any reasonable person tries to avoid situations that cause them. But on the other hand, there's a strangely seductive quality to war that many people, both those in the thick of fighting and those who sit on the sidelines and observe, find appealing. War correspondent Chris Hedges knows full well both of these responses. As he notes in his 2002 anti-war study *War Is a Force that Gives Us Meaning*, "The rush of battle is a potent and often lethal addiction, for war is a drug, one I ingested for many years."

What is it about war that humans find alluring—so alluring, in fact, that we buy into what Hedges calls the "myth of war," the claim that combat ennobles us, brings out our best qualities, and tempers the steel of our characters? Hedges, who has covered wars in Central America, the Middle East, and the Balkans, argues that its primary appeal is its capacity to infuse a false sense of meaning into our lives. War divides the world up into good guys and bad guys, eliminating moral ambiguity by drawing clear and distinct divisions between "us" and "them." In doing so, it provides us with a definite sense of self, both as members of a nation at war and as individuals. Our patriotic identities and our personal identities in turn orient us in an often bewildering world. War likewise provides our otherwise normal lives with a sense of purpose and excitement that we otherwise might not experience as individuals. I may feel as if I'm a total failure as an individual—bad marriage, insignificant job, boring life—but when my country goes to war, even if I don't directly participate in it, I suddenly become a part of something bigger, something that transcends my humdrum existence and makes my life worthwhile. This is a heady feeling, notes Hedges, that's hard to resist.

But of course the myth of war, like all addictions, can feel good while being horribly destructive in actuality. War doesn't merely destroy lives and property, argues Hedges, although that would be bad enough. It also destroys the spirit. "It cripples and perverts whole societies," he writes. The experience of combat brutalizes soldiers and noncombatant observers to such an extent that genuinely noble human qualities fall victim. As Hedges puts it, "War ascendant wipes out Eros. It wipes out all delicacy and tenderness. And this is why those in war swing from rank sentimentality to perversion, with little in between." In war, "we deform ourselves" by subverting everything that's good in life—"passion, loyalty, and love"—to an enterprise that's destructive of them all. War doesn't truly enhance our meaning, although it may well give us a rush; instead, it destroys it. Like the chemical addict, we have a hard time controlling our craving for the high, even when it becomes apparent that its pursuit is killing us. For Hedges, a necessary step for breaking the addiction is nurturing humility, compassion, and repentance.

19 September

Paulo Freire

19 September 1921—2 May 1997

Critical Pedagogue

The Martiniquo revolutionary Franz Fanon became well known in the 1960s for his argument that liberating native peoples from colonial rulers requires violence. Decolonization has to be purchased in blood, first because violence is the only language oppressors understand, but second because violence is the only tonic strong enough to purge the oppressed of the low self-esteem bred in them by years of colonial rule.

The Brazilian pedagogue Paulo Freire was just as concerned about liberating the bodies and minds of people burdened for generations by economic and political injustice. But unlike Fanon, Freire was a Christian and consequently saw appeals to violence as another form of enslavement. He agreed that the oppressed had to take charge of their lives and participate in their own liberation if they were ever to shuck off their internalized subservience. But for Freire, the key to this liberation was through the rejuvenation of the mind rather than violence.

Freire was trained as a lawyer but never actually practiced his craft. Instead, while still in his twenties, he began working with the illiterate poor in Brazil. For the next two decades he explored new teaching techniques to raise literacy rates and empower peasants. Forced into exile in 1964 by a right-wing military coup whose leaders saw Freire's work with the poor as communist subversion, he lived abroad for fifteen years and wrote several books on what he came to call "critical pedagogy." When he returned to Brazil in 1979, he resumed his educational work.

Freire's basic idea was that education is always a political and never a neutral enterprise. Conventional education—what he called the "banking" model—encourages mindless conformity to the status quo by stuffing students' heads with predigested, canned, and above all safe ways of viewing the world. But a "pedagogy for the oppressed," recognizing that the conventional model in fact seeks to program students into silently accepting unjust institutions and discriminatory policies, refuses to deposit chunks of information into passive student-vaults. Instead, it demands that students actively participate in the learning process. They must be encouraged to question, to go beyond accepted norms, and to scrutinize their own roles in society. In the process, they come to take charge of their own intellectual liberation and form their own identities, even if it means that they reject conventional social structures and beliefs. Beginning to see through society's myths—that ethnicity is a gauge of worth, that violence is an acceptable response to violence, or that poverty is an inescapable fact about the world—is the mark of an educated, and liberated, person. And such persons are empowered to change the world in which they live.

20 September
Henry Salt

20 September 1851—19 April 1939

Bridging the Gulf between Animals and Humans

ONE OF OUR MOST common assumptions—so common that it seems part of the natural landscape—is that animals fall outside the moral community. We treat them in ways that we would never dream of treating human beings. We perform medical and commercial experiments on them, put them down when they're ill or even when they've simply become inconvenient, and cage or tether them without a second thought. Most commonly, we slaughter and eat animals—billions of them—each year. Humans have rights that demand our moral consideration. Animals don't.

Henry Salt, a man sadly almost forgotten today, dared to disagree with this received wisdom. Beginning in the 1880s and continuing to the end of his long life, Salt argued that "the great [moral] gulf" conventionally fixed between animals and humans is "an antiquated notion" in need of serious reconsideration. Far from deserving no moral consideration, animals possess rights just as surely as humans do. "There is nothing quixotic or visionary in this assertion," insisted Salt. "It is perfectly compatible with a readiness to look the sternest laws of existence fully and honestly in the face."

Salt's argument is that all living beings, if left undisturbed, "live a natural life—a life which permits of their individual development." An undisturbed "natural life," in other words, allows them to flourish, and their well-being is stunted to the extent that their natural development is thwarted. Because we value well-being, it follows that any living being can be said to have a natural right to develop as nature intends it to develop. This applies to humans as well as animals.

But organisms live in relationship to one another, and that means there are appropriate limitations "imposed by the permanent needs and interests of the community." My right to develop naturally is restricted by your equal right to flourish. Consequently, both humans and animals have a "restricted freedom" to live natural lives, and humans, as moral agents, ought to respect that freedom as much as circumstances allow. If we occasionally must eat animals or inflict pain on them, "let us do what is inevitable without hypocrisy, or evasion, or cant." Let us, in other words, acknowledge that they have rights that we are sometimes forced to violate, that doing so is always a moral tragedy, and that such violations must be kept to a bare minimum.

Salt's attempt to bridge the great moral gulf between animals and humans was consistent with his broader moral outlook. A pacifist, socialist, and ethical vegetarian, Salt believed that the abuse of animals is cut from the same cloth as mistreatment of such socially marginalized humans as prisoners and the poor. The generally unspoken assumption in all three cases is that some living beings are more deserving of rights than others. Salt correctly saw that this arbitrary moral division is an act of violence.

21 September
Henri Nouwen

24 January 1932—21 September 1996

Defeating the Powers of Death

The Dutch priest and popular author Henri Nouwen was a trained clinical psychologist, and his many books on the spiritual life draw on his understanding of the mechanisms of repression, guilt, and fear. Nouwen realized that our psychic wounds, just as much as our individual and corporate sins, alienate us from God. Our inability to truly believe that we are loved by the deity—that we are in any way lovable to *anyone*—fragments our motives and inhibits our ability to enter into healthy, enriching relationships.

Nouwen was no armchair theorist. Although he spent several years in the academy, teaching at both Yale and Harvard, he also served in Central America as a missionary, and as chaplain and caregiver at a L'Arche community for the mentally and physically disabled. In addition, Nouwen himself suffered from several bouts of serious depression throughout his life. He knew from firsthand experience how entangled psychological distress and spiritual yearning can become.

He also knew that before would-be peacemakers can begin to change patterns of social and economic violence, they must deal with the demons that haunt their inner psychological landscapes. One of the most powerful of the interior "powers of death" is the urge to judge others, to divide the world into good guys and bad guys, and to morally privilege the group to which one belongs. Our judgmental divisions typically spring from our own insecurity and fears. If I can classify others I find threatening, I deceive myself into thinking that I've acquired power over them and that I can keep them safely imprisoned in the cubbyhole into which I've thrust them.

But these sorts of judgments, says Nouwen, are violent. They are "a form of moral killing" that always precede and justify acts of actual killing in the world. "Long before we start a war," Nouwen observes, "we have already killed our enemies mentally by making them into abstractions with which no real intimate human relationship is possible." We freeze-frame those with whom we disagree, reducing them to caricatures that we then feel no compunction about treating violently. They become the "enemy," and we may in good conscience kill, wound, torture, oppress, or discriminate against them. But the more we do so, the more sovereignty we grant to both the power of death within us and the power of death we unleash upon the world.

For Nouwen, "peacemaking requires clear resistance to death in all its manifestations," psychological as well as physical. Peacemakers never kill by judging. Instead, their "hearts are so anchored in God that they do not need to evaluate, criticize, or weigh the importance of others." Secure in their knowledge that God loves them, peacemakers don't need to pump themselves up with mental violence and can approach the world with the love and equanimity necessary to heal the wounds of others. This, says Nouwen, is the secret of peacemaking.

22 SEPTEMBER

James Lawson

22 SEPTEMBER 1928—

Nonviolent Tactician

DURING THE FIRST HALF of 1960, the nation watched, mesmerized, as black students defied Jim Crow by sitting down at segregated lunch counters in Nashville department stores and asking to be served by white waitresses. At first the sit-ins were without incident. But soon angry whites began to retaliate with jeers and physical blows. Blacks were pulled from lunch counter stools, thrown on the floor, kicked, and then hauled off by the police for disturbing the peace. But others took their place, and the demonstrations, nonviolent to the core, continued until downtown merchants agreed to desegregate their luncheonettes. It was one of the first victories of the civil rights movement. It was also a striking example of the power of nonviolence.

The man most responsible for the success of the Nashville sit-ins was a Vanderbilt divinity student named James Lawson. A cradle Methodist, Lawson early on came to the conclusion that violence was contrary to the teachings of Jesus. Drafted during the Korean War, he spent over a year in federal prison for refusing to serve. After his release, he finished his undergraduate studies and then traveled to India, where he taught for two years and learned firsthand the principles and tactics of Gandhian nonviolence. Returning to the United States in 1956, he enrolled in the Oberlin School of Theology. But a meeting with **Martin Luther King Jr.** convinced him that he needed to be on the front lines of the civil rights movement. So he moved to Nashville, studied at Vanderbilt University, opened an office of the Fellowship for Reconciliation, and began teaching his fellow students the methods of nonviolent resistance he'd learned in India.

Lawson knew that effective nonviolence requires training and discipline. Because most of us have been raised in a culture of violence, we've been programmed to respond to aggression in kind. It takes mindfulness, commitment, and courage to successfully resist the urge to protect ourselves against violence by going on the offensive. In late-night training sessions, Lawson schooled protesters in how to respond nonviolently to what awaited them at the lunch counters.

He knew that Gandhi's nonviolence had to be translated into an idiom that would resonate with Southern blacks, and that idiom derived from the Christian story. So Lawson argued that nonviolence was "deeply rooted in the spirituality of Jesus and the prophetic stories of the Hebrew Bible." Sit-ins at lunch counters, he told the students who came to him for training, were earth-shaking actions, representing "a moment in history when God saw fit to call America back from the depths of moral depravity and onto his path of righteousness."

Vanderbilt officials expelled Lawson for his participation in the Nashville protests. (The university offered an official apology in 2006.) But he continued training civil rights activists in nonviolence throughout the 1960s. No single person on the American scene was more instrumental in ensuring that the civil rights movement achieved its end through peaceful means.

23 September

Eric Bogle

23 September 1944—

Anti-War Balladeer

THE SLAUGHTER AND DESTRUCTION that took place during World War I—the "war to end all wars," as many contemporaries described it—truly defies description. Battle lines became frozen almost immediately with no significant movement on either side. Assaults against enemy entrenchments were usually feckless and costly, leading to great loss of life and achieving little if any strategic or even tactical advantage. As the war stalemated, generals on all sides recklessly sacrificed their troops, hoping for breakthroughs.

One of the most sickening squanderings of life in the entire war began at the end of April 1915. British and French forces sought to secure the Gallipoli Peninsula in order to control the Ottoman capital of Constantinople. For nearly nine months, Allies and Turks hammered at one another. Finally, the Allies withdrew and the Turks celebrated their retreat as a victory. But there really was no winner in the battle for Gallipoli; 220,000 British and French, or 59 percent of the Allied force, were casualties. A full quarter million, or 60 percent of the Turkish army, fell.

The British force at Gallipoli included soldiers from the different nations of the empire. Among them was a large contingent of troops from ANZAC, the Australian and New Zealand Army Corps. Most of the Australians at Gallipoli were green recruits. Over eight thousand of them died.

Singer-songwriter Eric Bogle, who was born in Scotland but moved to Australia while still a teenager, has made a well-deserved name for himself as an anti-war balladeer. In several of his popular songs—"No Man's Land" and "Green Fields of France," for example—he poignantly explores the tragedy of war. But the anti-war song that has especially captured the hearts of his audiences is "And the Band Played Waltzing Matilda," a ballad about the Gallipoli tragedy. It derives its inspiration from the fact that ANZAC soldiers boarding troop ships on their way to war were frequently serenaded by bands playing "Waltzing Matilda," the unofficial anthem of Australia.

In his song, Bogle hauntingly juxtaposes the high spirited patriotism with which recruits go off to war and the nightmarish reality that confronts them once they arrive. The song's narrator tells of sailing off triumphantly "amidst all the cheers, the flag-waving and tears," only to be "showered with bullets," rained on with shell, "and in five minutes flat blown all to hell." Jingoistic war-fever quickly gives way to hopeless assaults and exhausted efforts simply to remain alive in a "mad world of blood, death, and fire." The narrator sees the corpses of his mates piling up around him higher and higher until he himself becomes a casualty of a Turkish shell, which we learn in the final stanza blows off both his legs. "Never knew there was worse things than dyin'," he sadly tells us. "No more waltzing Matilda for me."

24 September
Hildegard of Bingen

1098—17 September 1179

Sybil of the Rhine

HILDEGARD, FUTURE THEOLOGIAN, SCIENTIST, philosopher, mystic, composer, and diplomat, was "tithed" by her noble parents to a Benedictine convent when she was only eight years old. She suffered from poor health as a child. But Abbess Jutta von Spanheim took Hildegard under her wing and educated her in music, Latin, Scripture, and the medical arts. When Jutta died in 1136, Hildegard succeeded her as abbess. Chafing under the male supervision of a nearby abbot, Hildegard led a campaign, fiercely resisted by him, to relocate the convent. She finally succeeded in 1150. The hardwon autonomy of the new convent at Bingen on the Rhine enabled Hildegard to go on four preaching missions during the course of her life and to counsel kings and popes, actions unheard of from a twelfth-century nun.

Even as a child, Hildegard was predisposed to visions or "illuminations," and they continued for most of her life. At the age of forty-three, she experienced a particularly powerful one, "a fiery light [that] flashed from the open vault of heaven" to give her "insight into the meaning of Scripture." Encouraged by Bernard of Clairvaux, Hildegard began documenting this and other visions in several books, the best known of which is the *Liber Scivias,* or *Knowing the Way.* She also wrote on medicine, cosmology, botany, pharmacology, and Scripture, invented a language that used a contrived alphabet that served as a kind of shorthand, and composed music, some of which is considered a medieval precursor to opera. Despite these accomplishments, Hildegard routinely referred in her correspondence to her lack of education or exegetical skills. This humility was probably genuine. She once beautifully described herself as nothing more than "a feather on the breath of God." But it may also have been a self-effacing strategy designed to make her voice more acceptable to men in an age in which women were expected to remain silent.

Hildegard's learning and mysticism strengthened both her appreciation of God's creation as well as her commitment to social justice. Her writings reveal a deep love of the earth and the plants that grow in it, and in one of her visions she prophetically warns against the sins of indifference and injustice to the earth, for God's creation demands veneration. "The earth must not be injured," she wrote. "The earth must not be destroyed." She also corresponded with popes, bishops, emperors, and kings on theological as well as political matters, not hesitating to rebuke them when necessary for their mistreatment of their subjects. Like another great medieval woman, Catherine of Siena, Hildegard believed it the God-designated duty of rulers to treat their subjects in accordance with the teachings of Christ. The advice she gave to commoners she also gave to them. "Be not lax in celebrating. Be not lazy in the festive service of God. Be ablaze with enthusiasm. Let us be an alive, burning offering before the altar of God."

In 2012, Hildegard was canonized and declared a Doctor of the Church by Benedict XVI.

25 SEPTEMBER
Erich Maria Remarque

22 JUNE 1898—25 SEPTEMBER 1970

Butterfly

IN MAY 1933, SCARCELY four months after taking control of Germany, the Nazis began burning books they considered threats to their racist regime. One author whose works were fed to the flames was the novelist Erich Maria Remarque. His novel *All Quiet on the Western Front,* certainly the best-known anti-war book to come out of World War I and quite possibly the most famous one ever written, was a direct challenge to the militaristic culture encouraged by Hitler and his cronies.

By the time the Nazis burned his books, Remarque was already safely out of the country, living for a time in Switzerland before immigrating to the United States. But a decade later Hitler's henchmen were still so offended by Remarque's novel that they struck back at him by arresting his sister, a mother of two. Accusing her of subverting the war effort because she had said that the war was lost, they beheaded her. As one of her judges sneered, "Your brother has unfortunately escaped us. You, however, will not."

What was it about *All Quiet on the Western Front* that so infuriated the Nazis? It wasn't so much Remarque's depiction of the horror of battle, the filth and tedium of the trenches, or the lack of hot food and adequate medical treatment for troops. His descriptions were accurate; drafted into the German army during the war and serving for two years until shrapnel wounds took him out of the fighting, he knew firsthand what he was talking about. Nor were they especially brutal. Similarly disturbing portrayals could be found in dozens of other anti-war novels.

What was dangerous about Remarque's novel was his claim that war didn't just kill bodies, but also destroyed souls. In *All Quiet on the Western Front*, he describes with merciless precision how the war has shattered the characters' dreams, hopes, and sheer ability to imagine any other life except that of the trenches. Typical of this decay of spirit is the fate of protagonist Paul Baumer, a nineteen-year-old who, fired up by the patriotic harangues of his schoolmaster, enlists in the army with several of his classmates. An idealistic young man who before the war dreamt of becoming a writer, the death and destruction of battle eventually sap Paul of both artistic ambitions and sense of self. He, like his companions in the trenches, no longer feels at home anywhere. He, like they, will be killed off before the novel's end. Their souls wither long before their bodies die.

But perhaps not entirely. Remarque allows for a spark of hope at novel's end. In the scene in which Baumer is killed by a sniper, the bullet hits him as he reaches out of the trench for a butterfly. Remarque's suggestion is that the tiny creature's beauty awakens something in him that the warmongers had tried to extinguish. This affirmation of the human spirit, sober and muted as it is, most likely infuriated the Nazis just as much as Remarque's explicit challenge to their deification of the state and war.

26 September
Paul VI

26 September 1897—6 August 1978

The New Name for Peace

POPE PAUL VI HAS been overshadowed by his immediate predecessor, the lovable John XXIII, and his immediate successor but one, the magisterial John Paul II. In contrast to them, Paul VI is often perceived as aloof, conventional, and even reactionary. If people remember anything about him at all, it's likely to be his controversial condemnation of artificial birth control in the 1968 encyclical *Humanae Vitae*.

This is unfortunate, because Paul was actually one of the great humanitarians in the history of the Roman Catholic papacy. He embraced and carried out the reformist agenda of the Second Vatican Council inaugurated by John XXIII. He advocated and strongly encouraged both ecumenical and interfaith dialogue. He urged world peace and condemned the Vietnam War and imperialism. And most impressively, he wrote an encyclical, published one year before *Humanae Vitae*, that stressed the connection between economic justice and peace and called upon the wealthy nations of the world to take greater responsibility for the well-being of poorer ones.

The encyclical, *Populorum Progressio* ("On the Development of Peoples"), begins by embracing the basic social teachings of the Church first spelled out in Leo XIII's 1891 *Rerum Novarum* and reaffirmed by every pope since: the rich have a duty to the poor; uncontrolled capitalism is destructive; and the common good trumps individual aggrandizement.

But Paul went on to defend specific recommendations for eliminating the egregious disparity in international wealth distribution. He argued that the wealthy should accept higher taxation so that foreign aid to impoverished nations can be increased, that the interest on international loans financially crippling developing nations should be eased if not outright eliminated, and that poorer nations should be allowed to sell their exports at legally protected higher prices. He insisted that the global economy should be managed to ensure developmental equality, and that individual entrepreneurs, pursuing as they do the bottom line, couldn't and shouldn't be entrusted with the task. Instead, governments need to step up with more generous aid packages and with legislation that protects the economic interests of disadvantaged nations.

If wealthy countries aren't willing to help poorer ones out of a sense of fairness, Paul suggested, they ought to do so out of self-interest because "extreme disparity between nations in economic, social and educational levels provokes jealousy and discord, often putting peace in jeopardy." Peace isn't "simply the absence of warfare." It's an end to the poverty and unfair advantages that cause misery and discontent in the first place. This realization of the inseparable connection between ending poverty and securing peace is what fuels the "new humanism" Paul advocated in *Populorum Progressio*. Economic development, he said, needs to be understood for what it is: "the new name for peace."

27 September
Nujood Ali

1998—

Resisting Child Marriage

The Universal Declaration of Human Rights recognizes the right of "free and full" consent to marriage, which in turn implies that partners in any marriage contract must at least have reached an age where they're capable of giving or withholding consent. But in many African and Asian countries, child brides are common. Some of these nations have laws that stipulate a minimum age for entering into marriage, but tribal traditions often trump them. Other nations such as Yemen have no laws at all.

In Yemen, girls may be married at any age, although the law *does* forbid intercourse with child brides until they've reached pubescence—which Yemeni officials claim arrives at nine years of age. Every year, impoverished Yemeni parents sell their young daughters to much older men.

When she was eight years old, Nujood Ali was promised by her Yemeni father, an unemployed street sweeper with sixteen children, to a motorcycle deliveryman in his mid-thirties. The couple was married two years later. The bridegroom promised to abstain from sex with his bride until she was older, but he lied. He forced Nujood almost immediately after the wedding and every night thereafter for two months. When she protested, her in-laws beat her. Her own father refused to take her back, saying that doing so would bring dishonor on the family. So one day little Nujood caught a bus to a local courthouse and demanded a divorce. It was a remarkably brave thing for any kid to do. But for a Yemeni child bride, it was a defiance of centuries of tradition.

The judge before whom she appeared was startled and saddened by Nujood's story. Not quite knowing what to do, since the law was clearly on the side of her husband, he took her home with him for a few days, where she played with his children. In the meantime, Yemeni human rights lawyer Shada Nasser took up Nujood's case. Arguing that the ten-year-old had been criminally raped, Nasser asked the court to grant a decree of divorce. Nujood's husband refused to let the child go unless he was paid several hundred dollars in compensation. The divorce became official in April 1998.

Nujood's initiative in seeking a divorce created a storm of international publicity that brought the ugliness of child marriage to light. Predictably, her actions angered traditional Yemenis and even prompted angry death threats against her and her family, to whom she returned after the divorce. But as Shada Nasser pointed out, Nujood's stand also encouraged other child brides to seek legal release from their sexual enslavement. She said it's as if the ten-year-old "opened the window" for other girls to come forth and demand that one of their most basic human rights be honored.

Nujood currently attends a private school in Yemen, paid for by royalties from a book about her case written by a French journalist. Inspired by Shada Nasser, she hopes to become a human rights lawyer.

28 September
Lillian Smith

12 December 1897—28 September 1966

Resurrecting the Dream

LILLIAN SMITH WAS A lightning rod. When her novel *Strange Fruit,* a tale of illicit interracial love, was published in 1944, the U.S. Post Office refused to mail it and Massachusetts banned its sale. Five years later, when she published *Killers of the Dream,* a collection of essays that explored the effects of segregation on Southern culture, she was reviled as a race traitor. Hate mail and death threats poured in, and in 1955 two angry white arsonists torched her house.

What provoked people was Smith's bold claim that the South's troubled history of racism, violence, and oppression was a destroyer of the "dream" of freedom and dignity. Southern culture, she argued, explicitly condemned blacks to lives of frightened servitude. Everyone recognized this, whether they were bothered by it or not. But the climate of hate also poisoned Southern whites, especially women—who were nearly as powerless as blacks—and children. "Segregation is evil; there is no pattern of life which can dehumanize men as can the way of segregation." Its legacy of hatred and oppression, she concluded, warped Southern values to the point where a complete overhaul was necessary to get things back on track. She saw the civil rights movement, which began in 1955 with the Montgomery bus boycott, as the beginning of that change, and she was an early and enthusiastic supporter. In her final book, 1964's *Our Faces, Our Words,* Smith especially praised the active nonviolence practiced by **Martin Luther King Jr.** and his coworkers.

Smith lived in the South her whole life except for a two-year stint teaching music at a Methodist mission house in China. Born in Florida, she relocated with her family to Georgia after her father fell on hard times. He opened a summer camp there for girls as a source of income for the family. Following his death in 1930, Smith took charge of the camp, and it soon became her avenue for resurrecting the dream. Through the classes and instruction she offered, she hoped "to wake up the little sleeping beauties that our Anglo-American culture has anesthetized, or rather put in a deep freeze."

In collaboration with her life partner, Paula Snelling, Smith also launched a literary magazine that appeared for nearly a decade in the 1930s and 1940s. In it, the two women published articles that quickly earned the magazine a reputation for being out of step with the segregated South. The magazine folded when Smith devoted herself to full-time writing following the publication of *Strange Fruit.*

Smith was one of the few white Southerners of her generation courageous enough to stand against racism and segregation. She once described herself as a "tortured Southern liberal." There's no doubt that she suffered for her efforts to bring racial justice to the South, and to that degree she was "tortured." But she at least had the inner peace that comes from doing what she knew was right.

29 September
Lech Walesa

29 September 1943—

Solidarity

For nearly fifty years, Poland was under the heel of the Soviet boot. Although officially granted autonomy in 1952, Poland remained a Soviet satellite until 1990 when the USSR broke apart. Thousands of Soviet troops were stationed within its borders, the Communist Party was the only recognized political entity, and only officially approved trade unions were permitted.

Soviet dominance began to creak and sway in 1980 at the Lenin Shipyard in the Baltic coast city of Gdansk. Lech Walesa, a former employee who had been fired for labor agitation, organized a strike there that swiftly spread throughout the country. Gdansk workers demanded the right to form an independent trade union and the right to strike. Anticipating a massive shutdown of industry that they feared would anger their Soviet masters, Polish authorities capitulated. The so-called Gdansk Agreement was signed at the end of August, and the free trade union Solidarity was born. It was a coalition of different groups with different ideologies, but everyone shared a moral and practical commitment to the strategy of active nonviolence. Walesa was elected president of the union, and for the first time in a generation freedom blossomed in Poland.

Fourteen months later, the bottom fell out. Walesa had been traveling abroad, meeting world leaders and garnering support for the Solidarity movement and bad press for the Soviets. The Polish government, under the leadership of General Wojciech Jaruzelski, received orders from the Kremlin: get the workers back in line. Martial law was declared, Solidarity was outlawed, and Walesa was arrested. The small window of freedom slammed shut.

Or so the authorities thought. But protest work slowdowns and stoppages across the country sent an already unstable economy into a spiral. Before long the panicked government defied Moscow by beginning a series of concessions—the release of Walesa, his return to the Gdansk shipyard as an employee, amnesty for Solidarity activists—that eventually culminated in negotiations that reinstated Solidarity and for the first time in Soviet-dominated Poland allowed non-Communists to run for public office. By 1989, Solidarity had won a majority in the Polish parliament, Jaruzelski had resigned, and a non-Communist prime minister was elected. A year later, Walesa was overwhelmingly elected president of Poland.

Walesa was awarded the Nobel Peace Prize in 1983. His wife accepted it for him, because he feared that if he left Poland to attend the Stockholm ceremony, he wouldn't be allowed to return. In presenting the prize, the Nobel committee praised Walesa and his fellow Solidarity members for their reliance on "spiritual and intellectual power" rather than force of arms. "The courage which Lech Walesa showed in stepping forward openly and unarmed," continued the committee, "was overwhelmingly rewarded by the millions of Polish workers and farmers who joined him in his struggle." And they joined him because Walesa showed them the strength and promise of nonviolence.

30 September
Elie Wiesel

30 September 1928—

Our Gift to Each Other

In 1960, a slim book with a small printing—only three thousand copies—appeared in the United States. It was titled *Night* and written by an unknown author named Elie Wiesel. It took three years for the publisher to sell all the copies of *Night*. But soon afterwards, thanks to good reviews and word of mouth, the book caught on. Since then, it's been printed in the millions.

Night became such a success because it's one of the most gripping accounts ever written of what can happen when ordinary human decency is corrupted by hatred and fear. The book is a partly fictional, partly autobiographical account of Wiesel's experiences in the Nazi concentration camps of Auschwitz and Buchenwald. When the Nazis took over his Transylvanian hometown of Sighet in 1944, he and his family were initially confined to a Jewish ghetto, but then sent to Auschwitz. His mother and one of his sisters were gassed immediately upon arrival; Wiesel and his father were kept alive as slave laborers. Wiesel just barely survived the ordeal. His father died of overwork, illness, and abuse just a few months before the camp was liberated by Allied troops.

At war's end, the young Wiesel settled for a while in France and worked as a journalist. He had vowed not to write about his Auschwitz experiences for at least a decade because he wasn't sure he could trust himself to give an objective account of what happened to him and his father. But the French novelist Francois Mauriac convinced him that he had a duty to tell his story to the world. The result was *Night*.

Wiesel, who eventually moved to the United States, is acknowledged as the best of the Holocaust authors. In nearly sixty books—novels, plays, essays, and the retelling of Hasidic stories—he has unforgettably warned the world of the horrors that can erupt when humans lose their compassion for one another. Wiesel knows that his message is a hard one to hear. But as he said when he accepted the 1986 Nobel Peace Prize, after his experiences at Auschwitz, "I swore never to be silent whenever and wherever human beings endure suffering and humiliation. We must always take sides."

An activist for peace as well as an author, Wiesel used the Nobel Prize money to establish the Elie Wiesel Foundation for Humanity, whose mission, "rooted in the memory of the Holocaust, is to combat indifference, intolerance and injustice through international dialogue and youth-focused programs that promote acceptance, understanding and equality." He speaks to audiences around the world, especially to young people, about nonviolent resistance to evil, reminding them that one person—a **Raoul Wallenberg** or an **Albert Schweitzer**—can make a huge difference. There may be times, he acknowledges, when nonviolence is ineffective, "but there must never be a time when we fail to protest." Our responsibility to prevent war and the social and economic injustices that provoke it can never be ignored or piously palmed off on God. "A destruction only man can provoke, only man can prevent. Mankind must remember that peace is not God's gift to his creatures, it is our gift to each other."

1 October
Vida Scudder

15 December 1861—9 October 1954

True Pacifist

It speaks well for the authorities at Wellesley College that they refused to fire English professor Vida Scudder in 1912, despite cries by alumni for them to do so, when she publicly supported the great textile workers strike in Lawrence, Massachusetts. Organized by the International Workers of the World (I.W.W.), the strike was blasted by both press and governmental leaders. But Scudder, who visited Lawrence to see the strike for herself, enthusiastically endorsed it: "I speak for thousands besides myself when I say that I would rather never again wear a thread of woolen than know my garments had been woven at the cost of such misery as I have seen in this town."

Scudder's defense of the Lawrence strikers was a reflection of her deep commitment to both socialism and Christianity. A devout Episcopalian, Scudder embraced the Social Gospel movement, which emphasized Christian responsibility for redressing violence and injustice, at an early age. She founded and lived in one of the first settlement houses in the United States, facilities that provided food and shelter for homeless men, women, and children. She was active in several ecumenical groups focused on alleviating misery in the world. And she was a prolific author, publishing volume after volume of theology and social commentary.

Scudder was convinced that reformist tinkering with capitalism, much less philanthropy that did nothing to change the very unjust system which created the need for philanthropy in the first place, was insufficient. She allowed that charity, which she scornfully described as "the long-accredited solution of all our troubles," might occasionally "hold greed in check." But more commonly, she warned, it "involves the more subtle and profound temptation to the use of power." Only a thoroughgoing revolution, a complete overthrowing of the social and economic power structures that perpetuate class distinctions and wealth concentration, would do.

For a period in her life, Scudder's anger at social inequality drove her towards Marxism, even though its materialism was utterly incompatible with her Christian faith and even though it advocated violent revolution. But by the end of World War I, deep immersion in the Franciscan spiritual tradition made her a convinced pacifist—one, however, who still believed that a revolutionary change was necessary. "The only true pacifist," she wrote, "is he who sees that no campaign against war can be effective which views war in isolation. He is forced by the exigency of the times into a constructive social radicalism; his vision travels past the battlefield, past the political relationships of nations. These are to him part of a universal struggle, result of a system that drives peoples, classes, and individuals alike, into a defensive and potentially hostile attitude towards one another. Faith in brotherhood, however ardent, will not prevent war till it prevents also what lies behind war. So long as conflicting interests are the ruling principle of the economic order, it is hopeless to expect the political order to escape the curse of war."

2 October
Mohandas Gandhi

2 October 1869—30 January 1948

Great Soul

MOHANDAS GANDHI, WHO EVEN during his lifetime was called the Mahatma or "Great Soul," is beyond doubt the best recognized icon of peace in the contemporary world. Everyone seems to know that his nonviolent defiance of the British Empire won freedom for India. This was, of course, a stunning accomplishment. But even greater was his demonstration that nonviolence is a practical social and political tactic.

The two great principles of Gandhi's nonviolence are *ahimsa* and *satyagraha*. *Ahimsa*, which Gandhi derived from Jainism and Buddhism, is the cultivation of peaceful love for all living beings. The person who practices *ahimsa* honors the life force in all beings and desires to protect, preserve, and enhance their existence. The love that flows from a person of *ahimsa* is profligate, drawing no distinction between friend and foe. Traditional ways of dividing the world into opposite and frequently adversarial factions is rejected in favor of seeing reality as a unity.

Satyagraha, often translated as "truth-force," is love-in-action grounded in *ahimsa*. The great truth or fact about the unity and lovability of all living beings is the spiritual impetus for the exertion of nonviolent and non-vengeful power on their behalf. As Gandhi once noted, "Strength does not come from physical capacity. It comes from an indomitable will." In the struggle to liberate humans from oppression and injustice, the indomitable will grounded in *satyagraha* suggests two fundamental tactics: civil disobedience and noncooperation with evil. Resistance to unjust laws, on the one hand, and noncooperative acts such as boycotts or strikes, on the other, are the nonviolent weapons of *satyagraha*. It's true that practitioners of these tactics may suffer for their convictions. But the suffering, argued Gandhi, if accepted by victims in the spirit of *ahimsa* as the price for change, can exert a powerful influence on both public opinion and oppressors. Seeing the voluntary suffering of people who resist injustice can prick the conscience and awaken moral sensitivity in those who hold the reins of social and political power.

Gandhi practiced *ahimsa* and *satyagraha* in both his private and public life. He became a vegetarian and embraced voluntary poverty in order to ensure that his personal desires harmed no other living being. His efforts on behalf of "colored" citizens of South Africa, his famous 1930 salt march in India, the years of imprisonment he endured for civil disobedience, the fasts he undertook in order to discourage Indians from violent rampages against their British colonial rulers or one another, his refusal to hate or abuse the British either before or after independence, and his efforts toward the end of his life to reconcile Indian Muslims and Hindus, all speak to his public practice of truth-force.

Gandhi recognized all too well that nonviolence is not always successful. He was an idealist but also a shrewd man of the world when it came to political struggle. Even when nonviolence fails, however, *ahimsa* and *satyagraha* enable their practitioners "not to bow their heads" before evil. And this in itself is a great victory.

3 October
Robert Barclay

23 December 1648—3 October 1690

Conscience May Not Be Coerced

GEORGE FOX FOUNDED THE Society of Friends in 1647, and for an entire generation the Quakers were fiercely persecuted in Britain. Accused of disturbing the peace, blasphemy, and refusal to swear an oath of allegiance to the Crown, they were fined, imprisoned, and sometimes beaten. Even after the period of official persecution ended, Quakers were looked at suspiciously for no other reason than that they held religious beliefs that differed from those of the general population.

The Scotsman Robert Barclay joined the Society when he was nineteen, shortly after returning from a period of study in Paris. Graced with a deep intellect and skilled pen, he quickly became a leading apologist for the movement, writing books and pamphlets that explained and defended Quaker principles such as the Inner Light. He was imprisoned several times for his pains but eventually found favor with the future James II, under whose reign the Toleration Act of 1689, which allowed religious freedom of conscience to Quakers and other dissenters, was passed. With James' approval, Barclay served during the final decade of his life as the nominal or nonresidential governor of the American colony of East Jersey.

Ground for the passage of the Toleration Act was cleared by the 1676 publication of Barclay's masterpiece, *An Apology for the True Christian Divinity*. Written in lucid and irenically toned prose, the *Apology* defended Quakerism in fifteen "Propositions" that covered topics such as revelation, Scripture, grace, original sin, worship, and baptism. But it was the fourteenth Proposition, "Concerning the Power of the Civil Magistrate in Matters Purely Religious and Pertaining to the Conscience," that directly addressed the topic of religious persecution. In it, Barclay argued that only God has "dominion of the conscience." Therefore, "all killing, banishing, fining, imprisoning, and other such things which are inflicted upon men for the exercise of their conscience or difference in worship or opinion proceedeth from the spirit of Cain, the murderer, and is contrary to the truth."

Barclay's passionate defense of freedom of conscience not only helped temper public animosity toward Quakers. It also began a conversation about the right of all people to believe what they wish in religious matters that influenced the separation of church and state debate in the early American republic. It would be too much to say that Barclay's defense of freedom of conscience ended religious intolerance in the English-speaking world. But after him, efforts to coerce religious belief through physical threat or legal intimidation were no longer respectable.

4 October
Francis of Assisi

CA. 1181—3 OCTOBER 1226

Wolf-Tamer

As a young man, Francis Bernardone longed for military glory. Although not a member of the nobility, he was the son of an ambitious cloth merchant who gladly outfitted him in a splendid suit of armor and sent him on his way to battle. But his military career was short. Francis was captured during his first melee and held prisoner for a year in miserable conditions. Shortly after his release, he had a vision that turned him away from martial dreams and toward God. In just a few years he founded a new religious order that stressed poverty, simplicity, and nonviolence.

Two aspects in particular of Francis' spirituality testify to his commitment to nonviolence. In the first place, he labored hard to purge himself of violent desires that encourage egoism and competitiveness, and on more than one occasion he offered himself as a peacemaking arbitrator in disputes. In the second place, he saw all of creation as worthy of respect, friendship, and protection. Nothing was foreign to him except hatred and malevolence.

Francis' effort to liberate himself from interior seeds of violence took many forms. In addition to turning his back on military ambition, he willingly relinquished any claims on his father's wealth, lived in voluntary impoverishment, endured the scorn of family, friends, and acquaintances, and famously forced himself to overcome his aversion to lepers to such an extent that he personally dressed their wounds. All of these episodes were efforts to tame the wolf within so that the child of a peaceful God could emerge.

But there were wolves on the outside as well. In one charming story, Francis makes peace between the townspeople of Gubbio and a ravenous wolf who was terrorizing them. He secured a compromise: the townspeople agreed to feed the wolf in exchange for the wolf's promise to leave their flocks alone. In 1219, Francis traveled to Egypt to arbitrate a ceasefire between Muslims and Christian crusaders. At still another time, Francis invited a band of cutthroat thieves to sit and break bread with him and his fellow friars. Francis the peacemaker was always ready to reconcile adversaries.

The love that he displayed in seeking peace among humans extended to nature as well. In his famous "Canticle of the Sun," he embraced the moon, stars, sun, wind, rain, fire, earth, and even death itself as his brothers and sisters. A story has it that once, while sitting next to an open fire, Francis' threadbare habit caught fire. When his alarmed brothers quickly rolled him on the ground to extinguish the flames, he rebuked them for their violence toward "Brother Fire." Stories of Francis' love of animals are legendary. He often preached to the birds of the air and protected rabbits and other small animals from predators. As Bonaventure once wrote of Francis, "At the beginning and end of every sermon he announced peace; in every greeting, he wished for peace; in every contemplation, he sighed for ecstatic peace." All of creation spoke to Francis of the God of love, and love, never violent, always strives for reconciliation and transformation.

5 October
Philip Berrigan

5 October 1923—6 December 2002

FBI's Most Wanted Pacifist

CHRISTIAN PACIFIST AND ANTI-WAR activist Philip Berrigan was once asked why people in such states as Iowa, far removed from East Coast centers of power, should be concerned about militarism. His response was decisive. "There is no place in this country where the Pentagon does not have its presence. The military industrial complex is everywhere. You just have to look."

Berrigan spent most of his life looking. Shocked by his two years of combat experience as an artillery officer in World War II, he entered seminary upon his discharge. Following ordination, he worked closely with several poor black congregations in the Deep South and became involved in the civil rights movement. His superiors relocated him to a parish in Baltimore in 1966, partly because of his active participation in marches, sit-ins, and boycotts.

As the war in Vietnam heated up, it became apparent to Berrigan that poor blacks were being sent there in disproportionate numbers. Berrigan's battle experiences as well as his Christian faith convinced him that war was wrong, especially when it singled out society's most disempowered members. So on 27 October 1967, Berrigan and three others witnessed publicly against both the Vietnam War and racism in America. They poured blood on draft files in the Baltimore Customs House, prayed, and handed out New Testaments while awaiting the police. Berrigan was sentenced to six years. Six months later, he joined his brother **Daniel Berrigan** and seven other anti-war activists in burning draft files in Catonsville, Maryland. Before his arrest for this witness, he was placed on the FBI's Ten Most Wanted fugitive list. The Catonsville protest got him three and a half additional years.

For the rest of his life, Berrigan was in and out of prison or jail—he ultimately spent over eleven years behind bars—for protesting the Vietnam War and trespassing on federal property to pour blood on the nose cones of nuclear missiles. Leaving the priesthood after nearly two decades—the church, he wrote, "is a major bureaucracy, and major bureaucracies are disobedient to the gospel"—he married former nun Elizabeth McAlister, with whom he had three children, all of whom are also peace activists. Berrigan and McAlister founded Jonah House, an intentional community in Baltimore dedicated to anti-war witness. Berrigan worked as a painter and construction laborer, and he and McAlister refused tax payments that were earmarked for the Department of Defense budget.

Although he left the priesthood, Berrigan remained a committed Christian. It was his faith, in fact, that fueled his commitment to nonviolence and justice. In a final statement, dictated shortly before his death, he reaffirmed his commitment to the kingdom of God by announcing one last time his belief that the use of nuclear weapons is "a curse against God, the human family, and the earth itself."

6 October
Fannie Lou Hamer

6 October 1917—14 March 1977

A First-Class Citizen

IT WAS AN ELECTRIFYING moment. A heavy-set black woman stood up in front of the Credentials Committee at the 1964 Democratic National Convention and for nearly ten minutes eloquently explained why the all-white delegation from Mississippi, her home state, didn't represent all Mississippians. Along the way she told of the struggle that she and other blacks in the Lower South fought to be recognized as "first-class citizens." President Lyndon Johnson was furious with "that illiterate woman," fearing that she would alienate the Southern Democratic vote, and called a last-minute press conference during her speech in the hopes that it would deflect media attention away from her. But the tactic didn't work. Her message came across loud and clear: "Is this America, the land of the free and the home of the brave, where we [blacks] are threatened daily because we want to live as decent human beings?"

The woman was Fannie Lou Hamer, the daughter of a Mississippi sharecropper who began working in the fields when she was six, dropped out of school when she was twelve, and with her husband, Perry, sharecropped on a plantation until she was in her mid-forties. Then, in 1962, her life changed. Stating that she was "sick and tired of being sick and tired," she volunteered in the campaign launched by SNCC (Student Nonviolent Coordinating Committee) and SCLC (Southern Christian Leadership Conference) to register Southern blacks to vote. She threw herself into the work with such dedication that she was soon traveling across the South challenging county voting boards and advocating for blacks.

Years later, Fannie Lou half-jokingly said that she'd have been frightened about getting involved in the civil rights movement if she'd "had any sense." The plantation owner for whom she worked immediately fired her, she received numerous threats on her life, and at one point she was kidnapped and so severely bludgeoned by three white men, one of whom was a state trooper, that she nearly lost sight in one eye and suffered permanent kidney damage. But she persevered, and by 1964, when she spoke at the Democratic National Convention, she'd become one of the nation's most electrifying champions of civil rights.

Fanny Lou died too young, succumbing to breast cancer when she was only fifty-nine. But in her final decade she accomplished more than many people manage in a long life. She created a food co-op in Mississippi to help poor blacks get more protein in their diets; founded the Freedom Farm Co-op, which offered low-interest loans to black farmers so they could buy land and escape sharecropping; and worked for school desegregation, affordable day care, and low-income housing. At her funeral, U.S. Ambassador to the United Nations Andrew Young correctly noted that "she shook the foundations of the nation."

7 October
Desmond Tutu

7 October 1931—

Restorative Justice

In his 1984 Nobel Lecture, Desmond Tutu told the story of a Zambian and a black South African swapping boasts. The Zambian brags about his nation's Minister of the Navy. The South African protests, "But Zambia has no coastline. How can you have a Naval Minister?" The Zambian replies, "So what? You have a Minister of Justice, don't you?"

The story captures the heart of what Tutu, retired archbishop of Cape Town, is all about. His entire adult life has been spent opposing fake justice, which privileges some at the expense of many others, and promoting genuine justice, which is egalitarian on the one hand and focuses on reconciliation rather than retribution on the other.

The fake justice Tutu struggled to reform was, of course, the apartheid laws of South Africa. He endured them as a young man—they were enacted when he was seventeen—and he spoke against them as a young priest and university instructor. But it was the 1976 Soweto Uprising, in which some five hundred protesting blacks were murdered by police, that galvanized Tutu. As bishop of Lesotho, then Secretary-General of the South African Council of Churches, and finally archbishop of Cape Town, Tutu became an increasingly harsh critic of apartheid and a vocal advocate of international divestment from South African holdings. At the same time, he denounced violent resistance to apartheid perpetrated by the African National Congress (ANC). Tutu consistently said that the enemy was apartheid, not South African whites. They too were victims of apartheid, which had robbed them of their humanity.

Tutu's struggle for genuine justice began in 1994 when apartheid was dismantled, the first election in which blacks could vote was held, and **Nelson Mandela** became South Africa's first democratically elected president. Now that political power had shifted from whites to blacks, the temptation to seek revenge against white South Africans who had persecuted blacks under apartheid was nearly overwhelming. But Tutu lobbied for a model of justice based on restoration rather than retribution. He argued that the nation's healing and embrace of its identity as a "rainbow" culture of many different ethnic groups depended on an honest dialogue between victims and perpetrators of apartheid, which could open the door to the healing of old wounds and the possibility of reconciliation. Convinced by Tutu's argument, President Mandela authorized the creation of a national Truth and Reconciliation Commission (TRC) and appointed Tutu its chair. Over the next few years, the TRC heard testimony from thousands of people.

Tutu believes that reconciliation "can happen only between persons who assert their own personhood and who acknowledge and respect that of others." The beauty of the TRC is that it works with victims and aggressors to achieve these goals. In bringing their stories to the light of day, victims feel empowered as human beings. In listening to the victims' stories and in turn publicly acknowledging their own culpability, aggressors take responsibility for their actions and begin the journey back to their own humanity. Under a system of genuine justice, the truth indeed does set people free.

8 October
Penny Lernoux

6 January 1940—9 October 1980

The Third World's Galilean Vision

In 1980, President Jimmy Carter shipped arms to the repressive military junta in El Salvador, and Archbishop **Óscar Romero** was assassinated one day after publicly rebuking him. In Nicaragua, the Sandinista revolutionaries were learning how to run a democracy and build a new society. And Penny Lernoux published *Cry of the People*, an exposé of how U.S. political and corporate interests controlled Latin America. In chapter after chapter, she documented the torture, human rights violations, corporate exploitation, political repression, and military domination endured by Latin Americans.

Had *Cry of the People* merely recorded the abuses, it would have been a useful document. But Lernoux's most significant contribution in the book was drawing attention to the way in which the dreadful poverty and repression were giving rise to a new way of thinking about God and the struggle for justice. As she discovered, "For Latin American Christians who view the world through the eyes of the poor, who see the slums beyond the glass skyscrapers, the next logical step is to reexamine their faith in the light of reality, and this leads them to reread the Bible. Gradually the biblical story is perceived to be more than a history lesson; it also describes the contemporary scene." The Old Testament prophets who denounced the rich and powerful, and Jesus of Nazareth, who privileged the poor and the outcast, became the historical and spiritual lenses through which liberation theologians began to read the political and corporate abuse of Latin America. They transformed the gospel from a tool that vested interests used to placate the disadvantaged into a powerful call for peace with justice achieved through nonviolent means.

Somewhat to her surprise, Lernoux, who originally set out only to chronicle the transformation, was changed by it herself. As a lukewarm cradle Catholic who found the North American church unimaginatively conservative, she had pretty much given up on religion. But her discovery of liberation theology reawakened her. She wrote that it "changed my life, giving me new faith and a commitment as a writer to tell the truth of the poor to the best of my ability." It showed her that nonviolent resistance to social and political oppression, although frequently condemned by ecclesiastical authority, was in fact an obligation for followers of Christ.

But Lernoux was no visionary idealist. She recognized that the institutional Church would resist—violently, if necessary—challenges to its entrenched power. In a book left unfinished because of her early death, she saw a great struggle coming that would originate in the Third World but eventually spread throughout the globe between the Constantinian "church of Caesar, powerful and rich" but spiritually impoverished, and the "living, poor, [but] spiritually rich" church of Christ. Lernoux died confident that the Third World's "Galilean vision" would eventually triumph, "even if [I] never see that world but have only carried [my] grain to the building site."

9 October
Jody Williams

9 October 1950—

Banning the "Perfect Soldier"

THERE ARE SOMEWHERE BETWEEN 100 and 110 million unexploded landmines in seventy countries, relics of past wars or terrible guardians of national borders. Moreover, a further two to three hundred million landmines are stockpiled by the nations of the world. Placed under or on the ground, landmines explode when stepped on. Some are hair-triggered to detonate simply from nearby vibrations.

Vermont-born Jody Williams is one of the most influential voices in the worldwide movement to ban the construction and use of landmines. She is the founding coordinator of the International Campaign to Ban Landmines (ICBL), an organization that has more than one thousand centers in seventy countries. The purpose of the ICBL is to draw attention to the horrible effects of landmines on both military personnel and civilians, especially children. Thanks largely to its lobbying and educational efforts, 121 countries signed a 1997 agreement known as the Ottawa Treaty that pledged them to cease using landmines. The three superpowers—the United States, Russia, and China—declined to ratify the treaty.

Williams and the ICBL were joint recipients of the Nobel Peace Prize the year the Ottawa Treaty was signed. In her acceptance speech, she chillingly explained why landmines are such a threat. "Landmines distinguish themselves because once they have been sown, once the soldier walks away from the weapon, the landmine cannot tell the difference between a soldier or a civilian—a woman, a child, a grandmother going out to collect firewood to make the family meal. The crux of the problem is that while the use of the weapon might be militarily justifiable during the day of the battle, or even the two weeks of the battle, or maybe even the two months of the battle, once peace is declared the landmine does not recognize that peace. The landmine is eternally prepared to take victims. In common parlance, it is the perfect soldier, the 'eternal sentry.' The war ends, the landmine goes on killing."

In recent years, Williams and the ICBL have turned their attention to another "perfect soldier": cluster bombs, explosive canisters that explode in midair. Many of the individual bomblets or "submunitions" within the canisters fail to explode on impact, in effect becoming landmines that maim and kill civilians unfortunate enough to stumble across them. In 2008, 108 countries signed on to the Convention on Cluster Munitions, agreeing to reduce and eventually eliminate their stockpiles. Thus far, ten nations have destroyed their cluster bomb arsenals, and ten more, including Germany and Great Britain, are in the process.

10 October
Ken Saro-Wiwa

10 October 1941—10 November 1995

An Environmental David

IN THE NIGER DELTA region of Nigeria lies Ogoniland, traditional home of the Ogoni people. Forty years ago, engineers discovered a huge reservoir of oil under its soil, and a multinational conglomerate headed by Shell quickly signed contracts with the Nigerian government to begin extraction. Since then, over $30 billion in oil has been mined, and huge royalties have flowed into the hands of Nigeria's rulers. But next to none of the profits have trickled down to the half-million Ogoni whose land and water have been progressively polluted by Shell's drilling.

By 1990, the Ogoni people had decided that enough was enough. The Movement for the Survival of the Ogoni People (MOSOP), a grassroots organization that advocated environmental reform, was founded. The Nigerian educator, businessman, and author of the anti-war novel *Sozaboy* (*Soldier Boy*) Ken Saro-Wiwa soon became its president and leading spokesman. In dozens of articles, speeches, and rallies, Saro-Wiwa led a nonviolent campaign against the twin goliaths: the oil industry and the corrupt Nigerian government. He went after the Shell Corporation for its disregard of the devastating environmental effects caused by its drilling, and he took on Nigerian rulers for their kickback-inspired refusal to rein Shell in through environmental laws and regulations. He soon became one of the world's most respected environmental advocates. But he also made powerful enemies who, he knew, would do anything to silence him. As he told a reporter a couple of years before his death, "They'll kill me, you know. They'll kill me."

He was right. In 1994, Saro-Wiwa and fourteen other environmental activists were arrested on trumped-up murder charges. After a yearlong imprisonment during which he was regularly tortured, Saro-Wiwa was tried by a military tribunal and sentenced to death. His judges ignored the confession of two chief prosecution witnesses who claimed they'd been bribed by Shell to give false testimony. Ten days after the guilty verdict, to the horror of the world, Saro-Wiwa was hanged. At his trial, when given a final opportunity to speak, Saro-Wiwa reminded his accusers that he wasn't the only one on trial. Shell also stood in the dock, and world opinion was its judge. "The [Shell] Company has, indeed, ducked this particular trial," he said, "but its day will surely come, for there is no doubt in my mind that the ecological war that the company has waged in the Delta will be called to question sooner than later and the crimes of that war be duly punished. The crime of the Company's dirty wars against the Ogoni people will also be punished."

Nearly two decades after Saro-Wiwa's murder, Shell Oil and the Nigerian government are still earning huge profits at Ogoniland's expense.

11 October
Thich Nhat Hanh

11 October 1926—

Engaged Buddhist

Vietnamese Buddhist monk Thich Nhat Hanh, affectionately known to students and friends as Thay ("teacher"), has been an influential champion of nonviolence for over half a century. A scholar, contemplative, and activist, Nhat Hanh's life and teachings exemplify what he calls "engaged Buddhism," the conviction that the detachment and universal compassion taught by the Buddha can and should engage with unjust social and economic institutions. His approach has sometimes been called "mindfulness in action" and rests upon the fundamental insight of "interbeing," the unbreakable connectedness of all things. Because I "inter-be," says Nhat Hanh, rather than exist as an isolated individual, everything I do or fail to do affects everything else in the world. Consequently, I have a great responsibility to engage with the world responsibly so as not to inflict on it unnecessary damage.

Nhat Hanh's engaged Buddhism was first formulated and tested in the chaos of civil war. Ordained a Zen monk in 1949 and later sent to Princeton for advanced studies, by 1963 he was back in Vietnam actively protesting the increasingly fierce war between the north and the south. He founded the School for Youth of Social Services (SYSS), a peacekeeping organization that sent relief workers into bombed-out rural villages to offer medical aid and to rebuild infrastructure. The SYSS maintained strict neutrality in the civil war, provoking both South Vietnamese and American authorities to label Nhat Hanh a communist.

Nhat Hanh attended the Paris Peace Talks, the negotiations that eventually led to the end of the Vietnam War, as a member of the Buddhist Peace Delegation. When the Peace Accords were signed in 1973, he was denied reentry to Vietnam and afterwards lived in exile at Plum Village, a monastic community in France. Nhat Hanh was finally allowed to visit Vietnam in 2005, although his reception there was less than enthusiastic.

In the years since the Vietnam War, Nhat Hanh has traveled the world teaching the active mindfulness of engaged Buddhism. The spiritual discipline has fourteen precepts that students are asked to meditate on and practice. They include warnings against egoism, intolerance, dishonesty, narrow-mindedness, greed, and violence in thought, deed, or livelihood. Above all, practitioners of engaged Buddhism are encouraged to be so aware of their interconnectedness with the world that they experience the suffering of others as their own. As the Fourth Precept recommends, "Do not avoid suffering or close your eyes before suffering. Do not lose awareness of the existence of suffering in the life of the world. Find ways to be with those who are suffering, including personal contact, visits, images and sounds. By such means, awaken yourself and others to the reality of suffering in the world." Co-suffering with others is not an end in itself, but a means of awakening the compassion necessary for the redress of injustice.

12 October
Edith Stein

12 October 1891—9 August 1942

Going for Her People

WHEN HITLER BECAME CHANCELLOR of Germany in January 1933, he wasted no time in putting into practice the repressive measures against Jews he'd advocated for years. In February, he pushed through legislation that drastically curtailed civil liberties for all Germans, especially Jews. A month later, he ordered the construction of Dachau. A month after that, the Nazi government sponsored a nationwide boycott of Jewish stores.

Remarkably, there was little protest. Most people were either too indifferent or cowed to speak out. But that spring a Jewish convert to Catholicism named Edith Stein wrote a letter to Pius XI begging him to condemn Nazi anti-Semitism. "For weeks," she wrote, "not only Jews but also thousands of faithful Catholics in Germany, and, I believe, all over the world, have been waiting and hoping for the Church of Christ to raise its voice to put a stop to this abuse of Christ's name. Isn't the effort to destroy Jewish blood an abuse of the holiest humanity of our Savior?" Those who kept silent, she warned, would share responsibility.

There was no reply from the pope. Shortly afterwards Stein, a trained philosopher who ten years earlier abandoned a university career to teach in a Dominican girls school, entered the Discalced Carmelite Order. She sensed that Christ's cross "was now being laid upon the Jewish people," and as a Jewish-Catholic she wanted to carry it with them by living a life of austerity, sacrifice, and prayer. "I myself was willing to do this," she wrote, "if only [the Savior] would show me how." In 1938, she was transferred from her convent in Germany to one in Holland. On her arrival, she wrote a prayer in which she offered herself "to the Heart of Jesus as a sacrifice of atonement" for the persecuted Jews and for the war she saw coming.

Although the Nazis rounded up most of Holland's Jews soon after they occupied the country in mid-1940, they spared Jewish-Christians in hope that the Church would refrain from publicly rebuking the regime. But in July 1942, the Dutch Bishops' Conference publicly blasted Nazi racism. In retaliation, all Jewish converts, including Stein and her sister Rosa, a laywoman who lived with Edith, were rounded up for deportation to Auschwitz. When the Gestapo hammered on their convent door, Stein said to her terrified sister, "Come, Rosa. We're going for our people."

Edith was gassed in Auschwitz immediately on her arrival in early August, sharing, as she had prayed for, the fate of millions of other Jews. John Paul II canonized her in 1989.

13 OCTOBER

Mordecai Vanunu

14 OCTOBER 1952—

"Traitor" for Peace

IN 1988, MORDECAI VANUNU, a thirty-four-year-old nuclear facility technician, was convicted of treason and espionage against the State of Israel. He spent the next eighteen years in prison, eleven of them in solitary confinement. Since his release from prison in 2004, he has been obliged to live under a number of restrictions: he's forbidden to leave Israel or even to come within five hundred meters of its borders; he may not have contact with non-Israeli citizens, either in person or by phone; he is not allowed to use the Internet; and he must steer clear of foreign embassies in Israel. Vanunu has been arrested several times for alleged violations of these rules.

Vanunu's "treasonous" offense was committed in 1986, when he went public with information about Israel's secret nuclear weapons program. For the previous ten years, he'd worked as a technician at the Negev Nuclear Research Center, primarily involved in the refinement of plutonium. Increasingly disturbed by Israel's steadily growing stockpile of nuclear weapons—at the time of his arrest, Vanunu estimated that there were between 150 and 200 warheads in the nuclear arsenal—he traveled to England and leaked photographs and data to *The Sunday Times*. He did so, he said, "to expose the danger of nuclear weapons which threatens this whole region. I acted on behalf of all citizens and all of humanity."

Israel responded quickly with a public denial and a fierce denunciation of Vanunu that blasted him as mentally unstable. Less publicly, a Mossad agent code-named "Cindy" was sent to London to seduce and lure Vanunu to Rome, where he was drugged, kidnapped, and whisked away to Israel to stand trial. During his subsequent imprisonment, he was subjected to what he later called "cruel and barbaric treatment" such as sleep deprivation and isolation.

Vanunu is a not a native Israeli. Born in Marrakesh, Morocco, the son of a Sephardic rabbi, his family immigrated to Israel in 1963. After completing his mandatory three years of military service, he began work at the Negev Nuclear Research Center and also enrolled at Ben Gurion University of the Negev, where he became involved in the peace movement. He received his university degree in 1985. Troubled by his participation in Israel's manufacture of nuclear weapons, Vanunu left Israel, traveling to Burma and Thailand and eventually settling for awhile in Australia. While there, he converted to Christianity and made the decision to tell the world about Israel's nuclear program.

Vanunu, who has been nominated for the Nobel Peace Prize several times, rejects the label of "traitor." He was glad, he says, "to reveal [Israel's] nuclear secrets to all the world. The real traitors are Israel's government who was behind this nuclear weapons policy for 40 years, and continues. They are betraying the Israeli citizens, and betraying the Arab community, and betraying all of humanity and the world, the human beings of all the world. They are the real traitors."

14 October
William Penn

14 October 1644—30 July 1718

Arms or Toga?

WILLIAM PENN IS PROBABLY the most famous of all Quakers. His name is even more familiar to the general public than that of **George Fox**, the founder of the Society of Friends. Penn is best known, of course, as the proprietor of Pennsylvania, the founder of Philadelphia, and the author of a charter of liberties for the colony that guaranteed fair trial by jury, religious freedom, freedom from unjust imprisonment, and free elections.

But Penn was also the author of a remarkable essay, published when he was nearly fifty years old, that advocated the formation of a European Union whose purpose would be to ensure peace among member nations. The treatise, rather cumbersomely titled *An Essay Towards the Present and Future Peace of Europe, by the Establishment of an European Diet, Parliament, or Estates*, was a practical application of Quaker pacifism. The essay's central message was nicely expressed by the Latin tag Penn quoted on the title page: *Cedant Arma Togae*, or "Let arms yield to the toga." So far as Penn was concerned, the only hope for European peace was a laying aside of the weapons of war and a taking up of the tools of diplomacy and international cooperation (the "toga").

Penn's starting point in the *Essay* is a denial that war is ever a "procurer" of genuine peace. This is because the fundamental aim of war is to destroy lives and property. Justice, on the other hand, is a "preserver" of peace because it ensures that no person's ambition or desire trumps another person's safety or health. Just as good governments uphold internal justice for the sake of their citizenry's well-being, so a confederacy of governments can uphold international justice for the sake of European well-being.

There are three fundamental urges, says Penn, that break the peace: the desire of a sovereign to keep what he already has, to recover what has been taken from him, or to seize that which belongs to another sovereign. A league of nations in which each sovereign is the equal of all others and all agree to abide by certain rules of arbitration can substitute diplomacy for war-making when the peace is at risk of being violated. Unbridled urges to add or recover territory can be checked. Assaults aimed at seizure can be preempted. The peace of international justice instead of the warfare of nation against nation can finally be achieved.

Penn noted that his plan for the establishment of a European Diet would give rise to actual advantages that far outweigh any of those that might be gained by warfare. First and foremost, a league of peace would reduce the shedding of blood. But it would also save European nations the huge expense of maintaining vast armies, not to mention the colossal cost of war itself; it would preserve infrastructure otherwise damaged in war; it would benefit trade by making travel safer; and it would encourage "friendship" between nations. A confederacy of peace is not only morally right, concluded Penn. It's also smart from a practical point of view.

15 October

Mahavira

CA. 599 BCE—527 BCE

"Great Hero" of Nonviolence

Sometime between the ninth and sixth centuries BCE, a reform movement in Vedic Hinduism arose that took as its fundamental spiritual insight the importance of nonviolence to all living things. This doctrine of nonviolence, or *ahimsa*, is scrupulously followed today by practicing Jains, and it has influenced millions of Hindus, Buddhists, Christians, and secularists who accept it as an ideal, even if they don't always practice it.

According to Jain tradition, certain sages periodically appear to teach the way of holy living. Because these sages have achieved enlightenment themselves, they're qualified to serve as guides for others. The twenty-fourth and final sage or *Tirthankara* (one who helps others across the river of mystery) is the Indian Vardhamana, better known by his title of Mahavira or "great hero." Born a prince, Vardhamana relinquished wealth and position and spent twelve years as a wandering ascetic before achieving enlightenment. He then devoted the rest of his life to teaching others the insights he achieved.

Under Mahavira's spiritual leadership, the Jain way of nonviolence was codified into five fundamental principles. Lay Jains observe them as best they can; Jain monks and nuns embrace them as mandatory vows. The first and most important of these three principles is the great vow of nonviolence or *ahimsa*: "I renounce all killing of living beings, whether subtle or gross, whether movable or immovable. Nor shall I myself kill living beings nor cause others to do it, nor consent to it." The great vow in turn lists five specific obligations: to walk carefully, lest creatures be trodden underfoot; to cleanse one's mind of hurtful thoughts and grievances; to guard one's speech against angry and cruel words; to sit carefully lest creatures be harmed; and to inspect food and drink lest living beings be devoured. The remaining four fundamental principles encourage Jains to walk in the ways of truthfulness, honesty, chastity, and nonattachment. All of them are aimed at cultivating nonviolence, assuming as they do that lying and stealing damage the well-being of victims, while licentiousness and attachment destroy inner tranquility.

Nonviolence is central to Mahavira's teaching because he was convinced that all living beings are karmic reincarnations of human beings slowly working their way to an end to rebirth. To harm or kill a creature, however insignificant it may seem, is to violate a soul. Moreover, he recognized the dangerous connection between passionate attachment to the things of the world and violent thoughts and behavior. Defending *ahimsa* as the first great principle was his way of encouraging self-discipline when it comes to the desires that stir up animosity between humans and other living things.

Mahavira achieved *moksha*, or liberation from the cycle of rebirth, shortly before his death. Jains celebrate the event at the annual festival of Diwali, which falls between mid-October and mid-November.

16 October
Günter Grass

16 OCTOBER 1927—

Remembering the Past for the Sake of the Future

AT ONE POINT IN *The Tin Drum* (1959), his most famous novel, Günter Grass has the main character, Oskar, disrupt a rigidly orchestrated Nazi rally by beating a sensuous rhythm on his drums. The implication is that the power of art is capable of defeating social and political evil. As a novelist, sculptor, and graphic artist, Grass has devoted his life to helping others envision a new world in which poverty and warfare no longer oppress the human spirit.

But in order to build a noble future, one must come to terms with the sometimes blighted past. In Grass's case, the past is Nazi Germany and World War II. In nearly all of his novels—but particularly in the Danzig Trilogy, which includes *The Tin Drum*, *Cat and Mouse* (1961), and *Dog Years* (1963)—Grass remembers and writes about the era of Nazi rule. His intention is to keep ever present in his readers' minds what happens when the public, through indifference, fear, or complacency, hands absolute power to corrupt governments.

Grass was born in the town that serves as the setting of his Danzig Trilogy a scant six years before the Nazis came to power. Less than a month after his seventeenth birthday, he was drafted into the Waffen-SS and served in a Panzer division until he was wounded in April 1945. After the war, he worked a variety of jobs while trying to establish himself as an artist. The publication of *The Tin Drum* brought him international fame.

Not content with simply using his pen to promote peace, Grass got involved in German politics in the 1960s, supporting the Social Democratic party and advocating for a moderate position that condemned extremism from either the right or the left. In the early 1980s he joined hands with the peace and environmental movements. In the late 1980s, he unpopularly opposed the reunification of Germany out of fear that it would encourage a resurgence of nationalism and militarism.

One of the most profound experiences of Grass's life was the six-month period (in 1987–88) during which he lived in Calcutta. While there, he was horrified by the squalor and poverty that surrounded him. "All framed and pedestaled works of art should be forced to compete with such scenes from reality," he later wrote.

Grass has long held that the developed countries of the world are largely responsible for the impoverishment and oppression in the developing ones. In his acceptance speech for the 1999 Nobel Prize in Literature, he warned that "the affluent North and West can try to screen themselves off in security-mad fortresses, but the flocks of refugees will catch up with them: no gate can withstand the crush of the hungry." Nor, if Grass is correct, of art.

17 October
Richard McSorley

2 October 1914—17 October 2002

Exposing the Taproot of Violence

FBI DIRECTOR J. EDGAR Hoover called him a "disgrace." Some of his Jesuit colleagues at Georgetown University publicly denounced him. The Church hierarchy was embarrassed by him. But Jesuit priest Richard McSorley, one of the most persistent late twentieth-century champions of the gospel of peace and justice, remained undaunted. He labored for over fifty years to "expose," as he said, the "taproot of violence" in American culture. Along the way, he witnessed for an end to racism (at one point so angering the Klan that members conspired to murder him), the Vietnam War, the nuclear arms race, and economic injustice.

McSorley was born into a large Catholic family from Philadelphia. While still a seminarian, he was sent to teach school in the Philippines. Captured by the Japanese just a few days after the attack on Pearl Harbor, he remained a prisoner of war until February 1945. While a captive, McSorley was tortured, starved, and nearly executed on three different occasions.

After ordination he served a parish in southern Maryland. The experience, he wrote, changed his life by awakening him to the reality of racism in both American society and the Church. He later worked closely with **Martin Luther King Jr.**, whom he once described as "a great Christ figure. King showed us how to live the gospel."

In 1961, McSorley began teaching at Georgetown University, and he remained there until his death. Joining **Daniel** and **Philip Berrigan** in opposing the Vietnam War, he encouraged conscientious objection, participated in dozens of peace witnesses, began teaching courses on Christianity and nonviolence, and helped found Pax Christi USA, the national Catholic peace organization. McSorley was also the tireless author of hundreds of articles and several books. His *The New Testament Basis for Peacemaking* (1979) is a classic in the Christian peace movement.

In his final three decades, McSorley turned his attention to the nuclear arms race. "It is a sin to build a nuclear weapon," he argued, because doing so signals a soul-destroying intent to use it. Nuclear bombs and missiles, like all weapons of mass destruction, are indiscriminate in their killing. So even if a nation insists that its nuclear arsenal is purely defensive, the mere "possession of weapons which cannot be morally used is wrong."

McSorley's criticisms of nuclear weapons didn't mean that he approved of conventional warfare. He saw no scriptural basis for the just war doctrine accepted by some secular and religious authorities, arguing that the same rationale used to justify it could also be invoked in the defense of other kinds of behavior prohibited by Scripture, such as adultery. "To be a Christian means to have respect for life in all its forms," he wrote. "That means that Christians must become active witnesses for peace and firmly oppose all forms of war."

18 October
René Ngongo

October 1961—

Advocate for the Rainforest

THE DEMOCRATIC REPUBLIC OF Congo (DRC) is home to the second largest rainforest in the world. Only the Amazonian one is bigger. The forest covers 57 percent of a country the size of Western Europe. Tens of thousands of animal and plant species can be found there, including elephants, great apes, and chimpanzees. Two-thirds of the DRC's sixty million people rely on the forest for food, medicine, and shelter. Its huge canopy's capacity for absorbing CO_2 plays an important role in regulating global climate.

Yet in spite of its importance, the forest is in grave peril. Ignoring environmental protection laws, the DRC government regularly signs "contracts of shame" with multinational corporations that grant logging and mining rights to a piece of the forest roughly the size of England. The ensuing deforestation has created environmental and social disaster, devastating the land, polluting ground water, and dispossessing already poverty-stricken Congolese who, although living in a country rich in natural resources, derive little benefit from them.

In 1994, a University of Kisangani–trained biologist named René Ngongo decided enough was enough. He founded a nongovernmental organization known as OCEAN (*Organisation Concertée des Ecologistes et Amis de la Nature*). OCEAN lobbies for stricter enforcement of the DRC's environmental protection laws, trains farmers in alternatives to slash-and-burn agriculture, and watchdogs government-awarded contracts to foreign corporations. One of its primary programs is the promotion of agroforestry, an agricultural technique similar to permaculture that grows food in the rainforests without destroying them. OCEAN volunteers have also planted tens of thousands of seedlings in denuded rainforest land.

Ngongo is motivated by a deep and abiding love for the "precious heritage" of the rainforests. "Those forests should not be considered merely as raw material to be exported and should neither only be seen as a carbon reservoir," he says. "Before anything else, it is a living environment, a grocery store, a pharmacy, a spiritual landmark for millions of forest communities and aboriginal peoples, those who are our forest's main guardians. Destroying the forest means destroying lifestyles that are worth as much as others." He's become a thorn in the side of both government agencies and international corporations, and his life is regularly threatened. But he continues advocating for the rainforests.

In 2009, Ngongo was presented with a Right Livelihood Award "for his courage in confronting the forces that are destroying the Congo's rainforests and building political support for their conservation and sustainable use."

19 October

John Woolman

19 October 1720—7 October 1772

Quaker Man of Peace

ONE OF THE EARLIEST foes of slavery in the American colonies was the clerk, tailor, and Quaker minister John Woolman. Convinced that slavery is "a practice inconsistent with the Christian religion," he spent the better part of his adult life traveling throughout the colonies preaching against it. As a Quaker, he believed that each human possesses an Inner Light that, if heeded, reveals that all persons—and all animals as well—deserve moral consideration. Each of God's creatures, he believed, exemplifies the majesty and goodness of God. To harm any of them is an assault upon their Creator.

Born into a farming family in New Jersey, Woolman thought for a while about reading law but eventually became a clerk and tailor. Early on in his career he made the decision to refuse any work that involved writing bills of sale for slaves or wills that bequeathed slaves. Doing so, he believed, implicated him in a practice he considered evil. He also tried to live as best he could without using any products made by slave labor. He dressed in plain white woolen clothes, because cotton was picked by slaves and dye was made by them. He avoided sugar and rice since they too were planted, tended, and harvested by slave labor. During his travels, whenever he accepted hospitality from slave owners, he always insisted on paying the slaves who tended to him during his visit. And everywhere he went, he urged an end to the enslavement of humans, sometimes appealing to his listeners' sense of basic decency, other times warning them of God's wrath. "Many slaves on this continent are oppressed," he wrote, "and their cries have reached the ears of the Most High. Such are the purity and certainty of his judgments, that he cannot be partial in our favor."

Woolman was convinced that one of the root causes of slavery was human greed. He practiced and recommended to others a lifestyle of voluntary simplicity. "Wealth," he wrote, "is attended with power, by which bargains and proceedings, contrary to universal righteousness, are supported; and hence oppression, carried on with worldly policy and order, clothes itself with the name of justice and becomes like a seed of discord in the soul." Warfare was another of the worldly policies generated by the desire for wealth, and Woolman remained a staunch pacifist all his life, even refusing to pay taxes during the French and Indian War. Hostility toward Native Americans was another greed-inspired policy Woolman opposed. To the astonishment of his peers, who for the most part insisted on seeing Indians as ignorant savages, Woolman frequently visited Native American villages. He never failed, he said, to learn something of spiritual value from these trips.

Toward the end of his life, Woolman traveled to England on a preaching mission. While there, he characteristically insisted on walking to his various destinations on the grounds that horses that pulled coaches were misused by their handlers.

20 October
Wayne Morse

20 October 1900—22 July 1974

The Senator Who Said No

IN LATE SUMMER OF 1964, relations between the United States and North Vietnam were tense. President for less than a year, Lyndon Johnson had already made it clear that he had no intention of letting Vietnam become communist.

On 2 August, the tension erupted in a naval battle between the U.S. destroyer *Maddox,* cruising in the Gulf of Tonkin off the Vietnamese coast, and three North Vietnamese torpedo boats. The Vietnamese vessels fired first, claiming that the *Maddox* had wandered into Vietnam's territorial waters. Two days later, word of a second battle reached Washington, DC. The report was later discovered to be false, but by then President Johnson had asked for and received from Congress authorization to deploy regular combat troops in Vietnam. For all practical purposes, the Gulf of Tonkin Resolution, as it came to be called, was the start of a war that would last a decade and claim over fifty thousand American lives and over a million Vietnamese ones.

During the congressional debate on Johnson's request, Wayne Morse, senior senator from Oregon, questioned the reliability of the second report. On the floor of the Senate, he also warned that granting Johnson the power he requested in the absence of an official declaration of war was a violation of Article One of the Constitution. In effect, he argued, Congress gave Johnson a blank check to wage war, and no one person should have that much power. "Under our constitution," he said, "the president is the administrator of the *people's* foreign policy." Morse's arguments failed to persuade his colleagues. When the vote on the resolution came up, Morse and Alaska's Ernest Gruening were the only two senators to vote against it.

Until his death, Morse spoke out against the Vietnam War on both the Senate floor and in the public arena. He often took part in anti-war demonstrations and condemned the American presence in Vietnam in media interviews. Never one to let party loyalty override what he thought was the right thing to do, he usually defended his opposition to the Johnson administration's war policy by appealing to conscience. "People say, 'we've got to back our president.' Since when do we have to back our president? Or *should* we, when the president is proposing an unconstitutional act?" He also condemned the secrecy surrounding the United States' entry into war with Vietnam as well as the subsequent conduct of the war. "My charge against the government is we're not giving the American people the facts."

Morse's courageous opposition to the Vietnam War provoked Johnson to order the FBI to dig up information on him that could be used for political blackmail. But it was wasted energy, because his anti-war position cost Morse his Senate seat in 1968. He accepted electoral defeat but continued speaking out against the war with what the *New York Times* later called "a fierce integrity."

21 October
Ernest Fremont Tittle

21 October 1885—3 August 1949

War Defeats Freedom and Justice

Ohio-born Methodist minister Ernest Fremont Tittle was one of his generation's greatest champions of progressive Christianity. In a steady stream of sermons, articles, and books, he defended civil rights, ecumenism, and Christian pacifism. At various times during his career, he also spoke out against racism, anti-intellectual Christian fundamentalism, and anti-Catholicism. He was a proud member of both the American Civil Liberties Union and the National Association for the Advancement of Colored People. He also publicly declared himself a socialist at a time when it was dangerous for Americans, especially clergy, to do so.

Tittle came by his liberal pacifism on the battlefields of World War I. In 1917 he left his wife and three children to serve as a chaplain and first-aid station worker on the French front. He went believing that "war was the only means of preserving a humane and civilized culture." He returned knowing that the war had solved nothing. "Men were killed, millions of them. Women were left desolate. Wealth was destroyed. Hunger stalked and pestilence raged. But justice was not achieved." War, he concluded, not only was a "defiance of the righteousness of God," but also a certain defeater of "the ends of freedom and justice."

Maintaining his pacifism even in the face of Nazi aggression twenty years later, Tittle insisted that peace rather than warfare ought to be the national policy of the United States. To those who charged that such a suggestion was an unrealistic response to Hitler's belligerence, Tittle made two replies. First, he said, it's naïve to assume that any society that engages in "a long-drawn-out orgy of indiscriminate killing and wholesale destruction" can suddenly return to normalcy simply because it signs a peace treaty. The psychic and moral scars of violence endure. Second, it's foolish to assume that war eradicates evil. It only contributes to it by treating human beings "as if they were things."

To his critics who claimed that peace as a national policy meant either cowardly appeasement or irresponsible isolationism, Tittle replied that peace meant working to reconcile hostile nations rather than kowtowing to thuggish leaders, and that far from being isolationist, a national policy of active nonviolence would legislate "relief of human suffering in war-stricken regions through gifts of food, clothing, and medical supplies." The building of good will and trust is a much surer ground of national security than conquest. Peace as a national policy would not be an act of insanity, as critics maintained. Rather, said Tittle, "it would be an act of high statesmanship" that demonstrates faith in "the power of justice and good will, not merely in human cunning and brute force."

22 October
Eileen Egan

1912—7 October 2000

Peaceful Table

Since its founding in 1943, Catholic Relief Services' mission has been "to cherish, preserve and uphold the sacredness and dignity of all human life, foster charity and justice, and embody Catholic social and moral teaching." Eileen Egan, who was with the organization from the very beginning, embodied that Christ-inspired dedication. During her long involvement with Catholic Relief Services, she was instrumental in getting aid to distressed people in Europe, the Middle East, and the Far East. She was a confidante of **Dorothy Day** and a regular contributor to the *Catholic Worker* newspaper, marched with **Martin Luther King Jr.** during the civil rights movement and with **César Chávez**'s striking farm laborers in the early days of the United Farm Workers movement, and was largely responsible for the United Nations' recognition of conscientious objection to conscription as a universal human right. Her energy was as inexhaustible as her dedication.

Egan's commitment to gospel nonviolence—she preferred the term to "pacifism" because of the latter's phonic similarity to "passivity"—was firmly grounded in her Christian faith. For her, the centerpiece of liturgical worship, the Eucharist, was a re-creation of Christ's call to fellowship and reconciliation. "The Lord's Supper," she wrote, "is the very heart of a theology of nonviolence. As the memorial of the act of sacrificial, redemptive love on the cross, it is the central act which convenes the community of those who have been baptized." Whoever approaches the altar table, she said, draws close to the "heart of peace, the great peace between God and man."

Experiencing communion with God through the Eucharist and thereby building "the great peace" between God and oneself is a transformative moment that in turn helps transform an aggressive and unjust society into the "beloved community." Anyone who feeds on Christ's body and blood, noted Egan, is incorporated into the body of Christ and bound to fellow communicants by their shared union with the mystical Christ. The bond puts "all enmity to death," replacing it with "the way of non-retaliation, of no revenge-taking, of forgiveness, and of a love that would enfold the enemy and persecutor." When a communicant experiences the Eucharist in its full reality, it is unlikely that he or she can ever justify the killing of anyone, much less fellow communicants.

For Egan, the words and teachings of Jesus recorded in the gospels, inspiring as they are, may not by themselves be enough to strengthen a disciple in the hard slog of daily peacemaking. But the eucharistic food served at the altar's peace table provides the spiritual nourishment "to meet the demands of living according to Jesus's way."

23 October
Anita Roddick

23 October 1942—10 September 2007

Entrepreneurship with a Social Conscience

Born in a British bomb shelter during World War II to parents who had fled Mussolini's Italy, Anita Roddick, founder of The Body Shop, became socially conscious at an early age. As a girl she read a book on the Nazi holocaust and was filled with "a sense of outrage and a sense of empathy for the human condition." As the CEO of one of the most successful businesses in the world, that same empathy made her a leader in the Responsibility in Business movement, a progressive alternative to the bottom-line mentality defended by the International Chamber of Commerce. Her goal, she said, was "to put idealism back on the [business] agenda."

Roddick founded The Body Shop, a cosmetic company, in 1976. Inspired by the "decency" of seventeenth- and eighteenth-century Quaker merchants, she insisted from the very start on corporate ethical standards that protected people, animals, and the environment. She refused to sell cosmetics that had been tested on laboratory animals, and she dealt only with vendors who practiced fair trade in developing countries. The Body Shop regularly supported organizations such as Amnesty International and Greenpeace and eloquently advocated a nonviolent and earth-friendly lifestyle in its catalogs and publications. It quickly became known as a commercial venture with a social conscience, and Roddick, because of her outspoken concern for environmental sustainability, was dubbed by journalists the "Queen of Green."

To the astonishment of the conventional business world, The Body Shop thrived. By the time Roddick sold it in 2006, the firm had over two thousand branches in fifty-five countries with nearly eighty million customers. It was the second most trusted brand in England and the twenty-eighth top brand in the world. Roddick's efforts proved that a business could succeed not *in spite of* but *because of* its commitment to nonviolence.

In the last two decades of her life, Roddick threw herself into charity work and philanthropy. She said many times that she wished to give away the fortune she'd made, valued at $100 million, and in her will she did precisely that. In 1990 she founded Children on the Edge, an organization to aid disadvantaged, ill, and orphaned children in Eastern Europe. The venture was inspired by several trips to Romanian orphanages Roddick made in the wake of the Soviet Union's breakup. And she spent hundreds of hours speaking to audiences around the world about the differences that individuals of good will can make. "If you think you're too small to have an impact," she told them, "try going to bed with a mosquito."

24 October
Denise Levertov

24 October 1923—20 December 1997

Our Lungs Are Pocked with War

The British-born American poet Denise Levertov wrote some of the most beautiful and haunting anti-war verse that's ever been penned in the English language. Unlike many poets, she had firsthand experience of what she was writing about. She lived through the London Blitz while serving as a nurse in several hospitals and first aid stations.

Levertov came from a family passionate about social justice on the one hand and intensely religious on the other. She remembered her mother and siblings joining in Hyde Park demonstrations against fascism and offering aid to refugees from Germany and Italy. Her father, a scholarly Hassidic Jew who become an Anglican priest, infused her with a deep streak of mysticism. Levertov didn't actually consider herself a professing Christian until 1984. But from the very beginning, her poetry reflects the religious influence of her father as well as her mother's thirst for justice. In her poetry, themes of sacrifice, suffering, silence, holiness, and rapture regularly interplay with darker ones of violence, oppression, and cruelty. In many ways, Levertov's poeticizing was a lifelong reflection on the search for personal and social salvation.

In 1948, Levertov married an American and moved to the United States, where she eventually became a citizen. The characteristic themes in her poetry came together in the 1960s and early 1970s in a stream of anti-war verse. The immediate impetus for the verse was the Vietnam War, a conflict that Levertov believed to be an unjust war of imperialism. During these years she joined the War Resisters League, allied with other writers and poets in publicly refusing to pay taxes, and spoke frequently at rallies and demonstrations against the American presence in Vietnam. After the war officially ended in 1975, she continued her poetic and activist resistance to violence and injustice around the world.

Although much of Levertov's anti-war poetry was inspired by the horrific destruction of the Vietnam War, her denunciations of armed conflict are universal. She believed that war, regardless of where or when it erupted, was like an insidious disease that saps the moral and spiritual health of everyone involved. In a poem titled "Life at War," she tells us that the grit of wars past and present so saturates the air of our culture that we can't help breathing it in. We are, she wrote, "filmed over with the gray filth" of armed conflict. Her life's work as a poet was to offer a tonic to the culture of war that so pollutes our imagination that we can't envision alternatives to armed conflict.

25 October

Micah

8th Century BCE

What the Lord Truly Wants

PROPITIATION OF THE GODS is as ancient as religion. Sometimes an offering is made because worshippers believe it's the only way to protect themselves from the gods' capricious mood swing. But more often, gifts are laid on altars as atonement or reparation. They represent a sort of celestial payment to make up for sins of omission and commission. They are blood money.

The ancient Hebrew prophets, or *nevi'im*, those inspired men of whom God said, "I will put My words in [their] mouth, and [they] shall speak unto the people all that I shall command [them]" (Deut 18:18), served as the conscience of the ancient kingdoms of Judah and Israel. As mouthpieces of God, their mission was to speak truth to power, even when doing so put them in danger from the political and priestly authorities they challenged. The Hebrew prophets frequently accused the aristocrats and wealthy of living off the backs of the poor, of worshipping idols of gold, gratification, and power, and of ignoring the Mosaic commandments. They knew well that the burnt offerings the rich dedicated to Yahweh were more often self-protective bribes than genuine expressions of repentance for misdeeds, and they said time and again that the smoke of such offerings was an affront to God's nostrils.

One of the most memorable of these prophets was Micah. Born in the southern kingdom of Judah, Micah appears to have lived in the countryside all of his life, even though he frequently traveled to Jerusalem to preach. The northern kingdom of Israel had already ceased to exist, having been swallowed for its sins by the ferocious Assyrian Empire. Micah warned Judah that its turn was next if it continued to mock God by cannibalizing the poor—"Listen, you heads of Jacob and rulers of the house of Israel! You who tear the skin off my people, and the flesh off their bones; who eat the flesh off my people, break their bones in pieces, and chop them up like meat in a kettle, like flesh in a caldron" (3:1–3)—and then trying to pay off a wrathful God with cheap gifts. God requires neither young, plump calves, nor thousands of fatted rams, nor even the sacrifice of the firstborn, thundered Micah. A gift much more precious than any of these, and yet one within the reach of everyone, is what God really desires. As Micah famously said:

> He has showed you, O man, what is good.
> And what does the Lord require of you?
> To act justly and to love mercy
> and to walk humbly with your God. (6:8)

Social and economic fairness, lovingkindness to all, and an honest self-appraisal that rejects the egoism that breeds violence: these are the qualities, according to Micah, most pleasing to God.

26 October
Paul Farmer

26 October 1959—

Health as a Human Right

Haiti is easily the poorest country in the Americas. Hunger is widespread, public facilities and sanitation primitive (especially after the devastating 2010 earthquake), and illness and disease rampant. HIV infection and multi-drug resistant tuberculosis are especially common, but so are less deadly illnesses that could easily be prevented by vaccinations or inexpensive medicines. The trouble is that the average Haitian has no way of getting them.

In 1987, Dr. Paul Farmer, a physician and medical anthropologist who is also a Harvard professor, cofounded Partners in Health (PIH), a nonprofit health organization "relentlessly committed," as its mission statement says, "to improving the health of the poor and marginalized." PIH "works closely with impoverished communities to deliver high-quality health care, address the root causes of illness, train providers, advance research and advocate for global policy change." PIH's first clinic was established in Haiti.

The Haiti center concentrated in its early years on simply providing free health care to local patients. But its focus soon expanded beyond the clinic to the community. Farmer and his associates recognized that illness and disease arise in a social context. For a developing nation like Haiti, that context typically includes poverty, malnutrition, unclean drinking water, a lack of essential sanitation, and inadequate shelter. So in addition to treating existing illnesses, Farmer also began practicing preventative medicine by working to improve patients' living conditions.

Health care, Farmer believes, is a fundamental right that can't be separated from other basic human rights. Consequently, his goal goes beyond immediate patient care. The aim, he says, is "nothing less than the refashioning of our world into one in which no one starves, drinks impure water, lives in fear of the powerful and violent, or lives ill and unattended." As a Haitian volunteer once told Farmer after a patient died of an infection that could have been easily treated had antibiotics been available, "This is a stupid death." Farmer wants a world in which there are no more stupid deaths. For him, "every premature, preventable death is a rebuke."

In 1993, Farmer was given a MacArthur Fellowship (the so-called genius grant), and he used the funds awarded him to found the Institute for Health and Social Justice. Its purpose is to analyze more closely the relationship between poverty and health, to recommend public policy, and to work more closely with local communities in the struggle against poverty and illness. PIH clinics are now located in Malawi, Rwanda, Siberia, Peru, and the Dominican Republic. In each of them, volunteers offer immediate care to patients and search for creative ways to break the cycle of poverty and illness.

27 October
Klas Pontus Arnoldson

27 October 1844—20 February 1916

Founder of the World's Oldest Peace Society

WHEN SIXTEEN-YEAR-OLD KLAS PONTUS Arnoldson's father died, he was forced to quit school to support his relatively impoverished Swedish family. For the next twenty years, he drudged for a railroad, managing to move up from a clerk's position to that of railway inspector.

But his heart was never in the work. In his off time, he read avidly in philosophy, history, politics, and theology; he was a self-taught man in every sense of the word. Inspired by his reading, he started to contribute occasional essays on politics and theology to local newspapers. Repulsed by the Danish-Austrian-Prussian War of 1864, and confident that education, freedom of conscience, and arbitration could eliminate armed conflict, Arnoldson became a pacifist. His journalistic criticism of all things military soon reflected his newly found allegiance. "The relation between the pressures of militarism and the deterioration of social conditions becomes more and more apparent," he wrote. "Vast resources are absorbed by militarism, without benefit to anyone. If these were set free, we could double the harvests of the nourishing earth, harness the power of roaring rivers for mills and factories, and open up undreamt of opportunities to challenge the finest talents possessed by man."

In 1883, Arnoldson was one of the founders of the Swedish Peace and Arbitration Society. Its aims then (and now) were peace, disarmament, and democratization. For a while, Arnoldson served as the society's secretary as well as the editor of its newspaper, tasks he undertook on top of serving for five years in the Swedish Parliament. But his experience as both editor and politician soon convinced him—and others—that he had little talent for administration. The final thirty years of his life were devoted to the tasks he did best: writing and speaking in defense of peaceful arbitration of international disputes.

In addition to hundreds of journalistic articles, Arnoldson also wrote several peace-themed novels and a number of philosophical and theological works. Two of his books, *Pax Mundi* (1890) and *Hope of the Centuries* (1901), a history of pacifism, were especially popular. In recognition of his labors on behalf of international peace, he received the 1908 Nobel Peace Prize. His faith in the promise of pacifism never wavered, even after the outbreak of World War I. Despite the jingoistic patriotism with which many citizens of warring nations welcomed the conflict, Arnoldson remained convinced that the commandment "common to the whole of mankind" is "Thou shalt not kill! You are all of one blood. Love one another. People can. Nations can. All this is eminently possible because love is as natural as national hatred is the most unnatural of all human feelings."

28 October
Desiderius Erasmus

28 October 1466—12 July 1536

In Praise of Peace

The Protestant Reformation launched by Martin Luther in 1517 ignited a firestorm of sectarian warfare that blazed across Europe for the next two centuries. Protestants fought Catholics and different Protestant sects fought each other. All disputants ardently believed that God was on their side, and this conviction too often fueled horrendous atrocities.

The Christian humanist Desiderius Erasmus was one of the few voices of reason in this troubled era. While many of his peers (including Martin Luther) defended religious persecution, Erasmus pled for tolerance and an end to the "great madness" of sectarian violence. It makes no difference, he argued, whether one appeals to arms for political gain or for religious reasons. Warfare of any kind is "a monstrous pursuit" suitable only "for beasts, not men." It's "so infectious that it spreads moral corruption far and near, so unjust that it's most effectively waged by the most cruel of thieves, so impious that it's utterly detestable to Christ."

Erasmus, the illegitimate son of a Rotterdam priest, came by his pacifism from two sources. As a youth he was educated by the Brethren of the Common Life, a Catholic religious community that emphasized voluntary simplicity, the cultivation of a rich interior life, and the foreswearing of violence. After studying at the University of Paris, where he immersed himself in classical literature, Erasmus traveled to England and fell under the influence of the humanist John Colet, who believed that the use of violence to correct social injustice and religious corruption only led to more evil. The Brethren convinced him that living a genuinely Christian life meant embracing the lovingkindness preached and practiced by Jesus. Colet persuaded him that violence, besides being immoral, was also impractical.

During his last twenty years, Erasmus was one of the most widely read authors in Europe, and he took advantage of his popularity to condemn warfare and advocate Christian nonviolence. In his 1502 *Handbook of the Militant Christian* (the title's "militant" is synonymous with "dedicated," not "martial"), he argued that peace is "the highest good." In his 1511 *The Praise of Folly*, perhaps his best-known work, he argued that violence, especially when it's committed in the name of religion, hypocritically contradicts Christ's teachings. Five years later, in his *Education of a Christian Prince*, Erasmus urged secular rulers to so focus on the art of peacemaking that the science of war becomes obsolete and forgotten. At around the same time, Niccolò Machiavelli wrote *The Prince*, a guide for secular rulers that cynically advised them to practice deception and violence in pursuit of their aims. Unfortunately, Machiavelli's has proven to be the more influential of the two manuals.

29 October

Clarence Jordan

29 July 1912—29 October 1969

Building the Community of Love

The Acts of the Apostles record that the earliest followers of Christ lived in community, shared property, looked out for the needy, and regularly worshipped together (2:42–47). Although this description of Christian living has been admired throughout the centuries, it's been imitated only occasionally. One of those rare Christians who took it as a blueprint for living was Clarence Jordan (pronounced Jurdan), founder of an interracial Christian community in Georgia.

Born in rural Georgia of relatively well-to-do parents, Jordan was disturbed from an early age by the racism and economic injustice of the Deep South. Determined to help black sharecroppers improve their quality of life, he studied agriculture in college. But he became convinced that the source of racism was as spiritual as it was material, and he went on to earn a doctorate at a Baptist seminary.

In 1942, Jordan, his wife, and a couple of friends purchased land near Americus, Georgia, and launched Koinonia Farm. *Koinonia* is Greek for "communion" or "fellowship," and the name attested to the farm's goal of emulating the first Christians' lifestyle. Jordan worried that Christian faith had come to be little more than an abstract way of thinking when, in fact, Christ intended it as a way of acting. He hoped to recapture this original sense at Koinonia.

The day-to-day living at Koinonia was pretty much what one would expect at a farm: up early, lots of physical labor throughout the day, following the seasonal cycle of planting, tending, and harvesting crops. But the farm's spiritual center of gravity was something special: absolute equality of farm members, black and white; active nonviolence; regular worship and study times; and common ownership of all property. The energizing force was the daily practice of Christ's love. As Jordan said, "Even though people about us choose the path of hate and violence and warfare and greed and prejudice, we who are Christ's body must throw off these poisons and let love permeate and cleanse every tissue and cell. Nor are we to allow ourselves to become easily discouraged when love is not always obviously successful or pleasant. Love never quits, even when an enemy has hit you on the right cheek and you have turned the other, and he's also hit that."

Jordan and the other members of Koinonia Farm paid a high price for their countercultural practice of Christian love. The citizens of Americus, enraged by the farm's interracial egalitarianism, refused to sell Jordan supplies or to buy his crops. Buildings at the farm were periodically sprayed by shotgun pellets and even bombed. Death threats were common. But Jordan and his coworkers persevered, and Koinonia Farm thrives today as a community that takes Christ's message of loving nonviolence seriously.

30 October
Marcellus the Centurion

Died 298

Serving Christ, Not Caesar

St. Hippolytus, one of the first bishops of Rome, is said to be the author of a second-century text, the *Apostolic Tradition*, that catalogs the earliest beliefs of the Church. Much of the text is missing. But in the surviving fragment of the book's sixteenth chapter, there's a clear statement of what the Church expected from soldiers who converted to the faith. "A soldier under authority shall not kill a man. If he is ordered to, he shall not carry out the order, nor shall he take the oath. If he is unwilling, let him be rejected. Catechumens or believers who want to become soldiers should be rejected because they have despised God."

Roman soldiers who became Christians during their time in service must have experienced great inner turmoil because of the clash between their military oath and the pacifism of their faith—not to mention the unhappy fact that refusal to perform their military duties meant death. No doubt many of them remained silent, keeping their faith a secret and living with the contradiction as best they could. But some of them chose to be witnesses—martyrs—by publicly proclaiming their religious objections to violence.

Marcellus the Centurion, whose feast day is 30 October, is one of them. He may have been a northern African by birth. At any rate, the surviving record of his military trial tells us that he was stationed in what is now Tangiers, Morocco, when he ran afoul of the authorities. Apparently he was attending a banquet in celebration of the Emperor Maximian's birthday when he suddenly stood up, threw his sword and emblem of rank on the floor, and proclaimed: "I am a Christian and I serve Jesus Christ!"

Marcellus may have chosen the moment deliberately, knowing that the banquet would give him a large audience, or his public confession may have been unpremeditated. Either way, it landed him in big trouble. He was immediately arrested. At his trial, he reaffirmed his Christian faith, adding, "It is not proper for a Christian man to engage in earthly military service." The judge, astounded that a centurion in the Roman army could violate military discipline so blatantly, asked, "What madness possessed you to cast aside your oath and say such things?" Marcellus replied: "No madness possesses him who fears God." He was beheaded shortly afterwards.

Legend has it that the scribe charged with recording the trial proceedings, a man named Cassian, was so outraged at the injustice of Marcellus' sentence that he protested and was also executed.

31 October

Dick Gregory

12 October 1932—

"I don't eat colored people"

THE WEAPONS OF NONVIOLENT resistance generally aim to deflect an aggressor's blows if they're physical or deflate them if they're ideological. One of the most effective deflationary tactics is humor. It's not the same thing as ridicule or mockery, which often spawn only resentment and dissatisfaction. But humor can help the aggressor see the absurdity of his anger or prejudice without humiliating or defaming him. It invites him to take himself a little less seriously so that he can be a little more open to other points of view.

Few social activists have been better at wielding the weapon of humor than comedian Dick Gregory. He discovered his comedic voice in the mid-1950s while serving in the army. In the early 1960s, a three-year stint at Chicago's Playboy Club, television appearances, and comedy records made his name familiar to hundreds of households. Gregory took advantage of his fame to put his comedic skills at the service of the civil rights movement. He became adept at using humor to show the ridiculous and hurtful nature of racial discrimination without antagonizing white audiences. One of his classic routines included a gag that nicely illustrates his talent for making racial discrimination seem laughably ridiculous. "Last time I was down South," Gregory would say, "I walked into this restaurant and this white waitress came up to me and said, 'We don't serve colored people here.' I said, 'That's all right. I don't eat colored people. Bring me a whole fried chicken.'"

Gregory soon became a regular speaker at civil rights rallies and anti-Vietnam War protests. Despite his advocacy of nonviolence, he was often arrested. It wasn't unusual for him to go to jail, post bail, and then entertain audiences with an account of the day's events in night clubs later that night.

In 1968, at the height of the Vietnam War, Gregory ran for president as a write-in candidate of the Freedom and Peace Party. He traveled across the nation speaking against the war and racial discrimination, everywhere combining humor and serious social commentary. At one point one of his campaign gags put him on the wrong side of federal law. In Chicago, his supporters printed hundreds of mock dollar bills with his picture substituted for George Washington's. The problem was that the bills looked so much like real currency that for a time the feds thought of prosecuting Gregory for counterfeiting. The investigation was eventually dropped. Gregory characteristically joked that the bills couldn't have really passed for actual money because everyone knew that a black man's image would never make it onto American money.

Throughout his career as a peacemaker, Gregory has taken on many causes, often using another nonviolent tactic, fasting, in his support of them. He has been a consistent opponent of U.S. military intervention in Vietnam, Panama, and Iraq. He has protested economic inequality, especially the disparity between whites and blacks, as well as sexism. And he is a longtime anti-drug activist.

1 November
Collateral Damage Victims

ALL SAINTS' DAY

Centuries of Slain Civilians

HISTORIANS ESTIMATE THAT IN the last three and a half millennia, the world has been entirely at peace for about 268 years. Warfare, in others words, has been a nearly continuous occurrence, erupting in one place or another for 92 percent of recorded history. It's impossible to estimate the total number of people who have perished in war, but scholars estimate somewhere between 150 million and 1 billion.

There's little doubt, regardless of what the total casualty figure is, that war in the twentieth century was the fiercest the world has ever seen. An estimated 105 to 110 million people perished in its dozens of "little" wars and two worldwide ones, a full six times more than died from war in the preceding century. Even more chillingly, two-thirds of those killed were noncombatant civilians—children, women, the elderly, and the disabled.

The killing of civilians in war is an ominously growing trend. In the nineteenth century, civilians accounted for approximately 10 percent of war deaths. That figure rose to 50 percent in World War II. In the wars fought in the last decade of the twentieth century, 75 percent of those killed were civilians. Noncombatant mortality in war has become so commonplace that the United States Department of Defense coined the deceptively neutral term *collateral damage* to refer to it. As defined by the DoD, collateral damage is the "unintentional or incidental injury or damage to persons or objects that would not be lawful military targets in the circumstances ruling at the time." But such "damage" does not violate the rules of war "so long as it is not excessive in light of the overall military advantage anticipated from the attack."

One of the reasons more civilians than soldiers die in today's wars is that weapons such as "bunker-busters" and satellite launched air-to-ground missiles have such enormous, sometimes near-nuclear, explosive power. Western military powers brag about the "smart" technology that allows them to hone in on specific targets. But the killing force of the weapons used, their mediocre success rate in actually hitting what they aim for, and the accelerating practice of shielding soldiers behind noncombatants, suggests that civilians will continue to be victims when armies fight.

In dozens of countries throughout the world, Christians remember their dead on All Saints' Day. In many cultures, it's customary to visit the graves of loved ones, light candles, and eat a commemorative meal. The day has been observed in the West since the beginning of the seventh century. This All Saints' Day, remember the millions of noncombatants caught in history's crossfire.

2 November
Samuel Ruiz García

3 November 1924 – 24 January 2011

"Tatic" to the Mayans

SAMUEL GARCÍA, ROMAN CATHOLIC bishop of Chiapas, Mexico, was a physically small man with great moral stature. Shepherd for forty years of what was thought of as a backwater diocese, his nonviolent struggle for justice for his impoverished Mayan flock meant that he defied authorities in both the Mexican government and in Vatican City. Grateful Mayans affectionately called him *tatic* or "father."

Consecrated bishop in 1960, García was highly influenced by the Second Vatican Council's emphasis on social justice. His diocese was one of the poorest in all Mexico, in large part because of discrimination against the indigenous Mayans who made up the bulk of its population. Their misery was so great that once, when García was asked by a journalist what the face of Christ looked like in his parish, he responded, "It is not really Christ risen. It is still the Passion. He is on the cross, suffering." But he quickly added that resurrection follows the passion. "When we see people with hope, we know there is still the possibility for change. We can see the pain of Christ in the community, but also the hope."

García's service to the Mayans of Chiapas was tireless. He learned four different Mayan dialects so that he could speak with them in their own tongue during his many trips by mule across his diocese. An enthusiastic proponent of liberation theology, he encouraged his people to interpret the gospel in light of their own experiences of poverty and injustice. He also commissioned scores of lay catechists to travel throughout the diocese ministering to Mayans in remote, priestless areas.

Just as importantly, García listened to his Mayan flock and encouraged them to embrace their own culture and traditions. He believed—and helped them believe—that they had much to teach the rest of the world. "After 500 years of oppression," he declared, "Indian people are still alive—and not just alive but proposing ideas for the whole culture such as keeping commitments; justice, not only for their own change but the change of governments as well; reconciliation to be worked out within the community. These are some of the values they want to offer."

García's advocacy of liberation theology got him in hot water with the Church. He was even asked to resign in 1993; he declined. His efforts at mediation and his outspoken defense of indigenous rights during the Chiapas uprising also angered the Mexican government, which accused him of fomenting violence. García was no advocate of violence—quite the contrary—but he well understood that peace is inextricably linked with justice. "There can be no peace if there is no justice," he said. "Justice means bringing down from their throne those who are privileged and elevating those who are humble to the same heights." In saying this, García was simply appealing to the Magnificat, the Virgin Mary's song of liberation found in Luke's Gospel.

3 November
Martin de Porres

9 December 1579—3 November 1639

Compassion Trumps Obedience

As a lay Dominican brother, Martin de Porres took obedience to his superiors and the Rule of his Order seriously. But he placed even more weight on what he owed Christ. Martin had been blessed with a great gift for healing and an enormous capacity for compassion. Besides tending to infirm Dominicans in the Lima, Peru, monastery where he lived, he frequented the city streets in search of the ill, old, and forgotten. Frequently he would take them back to the monastery and nurse them in his own cell. Once, after he had put an ulcerous beggar in his bed, one of his exasperated brothers rebuked him for breaking the house rules against visitors. Martin is said to have replied, "Compassion takes precedence over obedience."

It's remarkable that a person to whom so little compassion was shown had so much to give. The son of a Spaniard and a freed black slave, he was an outcast from both white and black communities as a youngster. As a mulatto and the bastard son of a noble father, Martin was viewed with suspicion by Lima's blacks, free or slave. But he was also an inconvenient embarrassment to his politically ambitious father. So Martin was apprenticed out to a physician-barber as soon as he was old enough, and it was then that he learned the surgical and medical techniques he would practice in the years to come. When he was fifteen, he entered the Dominican monastery as a lay brother, remaining there for the rest of his life.

Probably because of his own mixed blood, Martin was especially concerned for the well-being of Indians, African slaves, and mulattoes. He often visited them, sharing his food, treating their sicknesses, and generally offering them hope. Like St. Francis of Assisi, whom he resembles in so many ways, Martin's compassion also extended to animals. His fellow Dominicans soon ceased being surprised at the sick mongrels, cats, fowls, and donkeys he brought back to the monastery to nurse. It was as if Martin recognized that compassion properly has no bounds or limitations. If a creature was in distress, it made no difference whether it was human or animal. This holistic regard for all beings, and especially for those generally forgotten and neglected by the rest of society, was the hallmark of Martin's ministry. Nor did he stop simply with compassion. On at least one occasion, he offered to have himself sold as a slave in order to raise funds for the monastery. His prior refused the offer but was deeply moved by Martin's willingness to sacrifice himself for others.

John XXIII canonized Martin in 1962, just as the civil rights movement was gaining ground in the United States. It was a fitting coincidence.

4 November
James Groppi

16 November 1930—4 November 1985

Fair Housing Advocate

Visitors to the city of Milwaukee riding the municipal bus system were sometimes startled in the early 1980s to hear regular passengers greet one of the drivers as "Father Jim." The man behind the wheel was James Groppi, a former Roman Catholic priest and civil rights advocate whose efforts helped end segregation in housing and public schools in Milwaukee.

Groppi's interest in civil rights began during his seminary days when he worked with black youths in Milwaukee's inner city. He was disturbed and then angered by the obvious difference between their living conditions and those of the city's white kids. Appreciating how well he related to African Americans, his superiors assigned him to a mostly black parish shortly after his ordination. By 1963, Groppi was heavily involved in the struggle for civil rights. In 1965 he traveled to Alabama to participate in the Selma to Montgomery march and to help register Southern black voters. Closer to home, he became advisor to the local NAACP chapter and organized and led protests against segregated schools and social clubs.

Groppi's most notable campaign was his advocacy of fair housing opportunities for Milwaukee's blacks. In the 1960s, most of the city's African American population, routinely discriminated against by realtors and landlords, was denied access to property in white neighborhoods and were overcharged for shoddy rented apartments in black ones. Groppi regularly led nonviolent marches across the 16th Street Viaduct, which separated white from black Milwaukee, to protest the segregation. The federal Fair Housing Act of 1968 finally outlawed housing discrimination. In honor of his efforts, the viaduct bridge over which Groppi and other housing advocates marched was later renamed the James E. Groppi Unity Bridge.

Like many other racially segregated cities during the 1960s, Milwaukee had its share of race riots, which often devolved into looting and arson sprees. While approving of demonstrations and sit-ins, Groppi condemned violence to persons or property. He organized a group of black men that came to be known as the Milwaukee Commandos to keep a lid on the violence. The commandos accompanied Groppi and others during peaceful marches to protect them from angry onlookers, but they also worked to channel the African American community's resentment in nonviolent and fruitful directions.

Although Groppi's superiors in the Church initially encouraged his ministry to Milwaukee's African American community, they became concerned after his civil rights work began to make national headlines. His civil disobedience, which led to a number of arrests, embarrassed his superiors and angered many influential Catholic laypersons. Relations between Groppi and the archdiocese of Milwaukee became so strained that in 1976 he left the priesthood, married, and fathered three children. From 1979 to his death Groppi worked as a bus driver for the city he'd done so much to liberate from the evil of segregation.

5 NOVEMBER
Vandana Shiva

5 NOVEMBER 1952—

Alter-Globalizationist

THE GLOBALIZATION MOVEMENT HAS been criticized for enriching developed countries at the expense of developing ones by imposing industrial and corporate values and policies that tend to damage local communities and ecosystems. The alter-globalizationist movement embraces the notion of economic cooperation between nations, but argues that this is best done using "alternative" strategies that protect local communities and customs, the environment, and the rights of native and indigenous peoples. One of the leaders in this movement is the Indian ecologist and activist Vandana Shiva.

A major focus of Shiva's attention is food and food production. In recent years, agribusiness has steadily discouraged developing nations from growing food for domestic consumption and moved them instead in the direction of monocultural cash crops for exportation. Hybridized seeds for which food corporations hold patents, chemical fertilizers, pesticides, and insecticides, and water- and soil-depleting irrigation techniques have become normative. All of them lead to larger harvests in the short run but damage the environment and oppress local farmers in the long run. Consequently, the "cheap" food that such practices produce isn't cheap at all. Shiva writes that "globalized, industrialized food is not cheap: it is too costly for the earth, for the farmers, for our health. The earth can no longer carry the burden of groundwater mining, pesticide pollution, disappearance of species and destabilization of the climate. Farmers can no longer carry the burden of debt, which is inevitable in industrial farming with its high costs of production. It is incapable of producing safe, culturally appropriate, tasty, quality food. And it is incapable of producing enough food for all because it is wasteful of land, water and energy. Industrial agriculture uses ten times more energy than it produces. It is thus ten times less efficient."

In 1982, Shiva founded the Research Foundation for Science, Technology and Ecology, a think tank and advocacy group that seeks to preserve biodiversity of native seeds by monitoring the "biopiracy" practices of agribusiness. The foundation also examines challenges to democracy posed by the globalized economy, especially when it comes to the production and availability of food. Democracy, says Shiva, isn't the freedom to do whatever one wishes. This is the unbridled and unprincipled outlook of capitalism run amok. Instead, authentic democracy ensures "freedom from hunger, freedom from unemployment, freedom from fear, and freedom from hatred" on which "good human societies are based." Finally, Shiva's foundation has helped the world understand the central importance of women in developing countries, who are often the primary food producers in their communities. For her alter-globalization emphasis on ecology and women, Vandana Shiva received a richly deserved Right Livelihood Award in 1993.

6 November

Lucretia Mott

3 January 1793 — 11 November 1880

No Advocate of Passivity

LUCRETIA MOTT WAS ONE of those nineteenth-century women who seemed to infuriate men on several different counts. In the first place, she was outspoken, unafraid to voice her opinions either at the public lectern or in print. (In her time, such behavior was styled "promiscuous" by outraged men.) In the second place, she was a supporter of abolitionism, a movement that most Americans, even those who opposed slavery, disliked. Finally—and this was perhaps the cause of greatest fury—Mott was a defender of women's rights, especially their right to property and to vote. She was indeed, as she once proudly declared, "no advocate of passivity" who would "tamely" submit to "injustice inflicted either on me or on the slave." Instead, she was a skilled practitioner of nonviolent resistance.

Born into a New England Quaker family, Mott became involved in abolitionist activities in the early 1830s. Although frequently refused permission to speak publicly because she was a woman, she made special efforts to address audiences on the evils of slavery. Licensed as a Quaker minister in 1831, Mott found receptive audiences among her fellow Quakers.

It was as a member of the 1840 World's Anti-Slavery Convention in London—where she was not only denied permission to speak or vote, but was forced to sit in a segregated "women's" gallery—that Mott met and struck up an alliance with Elizabeth Cady Stanton. The two began planning a conference that would defend women's rights in the same way that abolitionist groups defended freedom for slaves. The conference finally met in 1848 and was known as the Seneca Falls Convention after the New York town in which it was held. Lasting two days, the convention ratified a "Declaration of Sentiments" that urged women's suffrage and the rights to hold and bequeath property, to receive a university education, to exercise leadership in churches, and to divorce without prejudice or loss of children. At first Mott balked against suffrage, not because she believed women incapable of making rational electoral decisions but because she repudiated the American political process for its refusal to condemn and put an end to slavery. But she eventually capitulated and signed the Declaration of Sentiments, a document that a local newspaper referred to as "the most shocking and unnatural event ever recorded in the history of womanity."

Throughout her long life, one of Mott's abiding convictions was that the oppression of women and blacks revealed a serious flaw in the American understanding of what it meant to be a Christian. "It is time," she once said, "that Christians were judged more by their likeness to Christ than their notions of Christ. Were this sentiment generally admitted we should not see such tenacious adherence to what men deem the opinions and doctrines of Christ while at the same time in everyday practice is exhibited anything but a likeness to Christ."

7 NOVEMBER
Eleanor Roosevelt

11 OCTOBER 1884—7 NOVEMBER 1962

Defender of Human Rights

IN SEPTEMBER 1948, ELEANOR Roosevelt stood before the General Assembly of the United Nations to announce the ratification of the Universal Declaration of Human Rights. The document, she said, "may well become the international Magna Carta for all men everywhere."

Roosevelt had long been a champion of human rights, both in the United States and abroad. After the death of her husband, President Franklin Roosevelt, in 1945, she was appointed a delegate to the United Nations by Harry S. Truman. Beginning the following year, she chaired the commission eventually tasked with writing the Universal Declaration.

Roosevelt was no figurehead chair. She was actively engaged in writing the Declaration from the very start, putting in long hours with such fellow commissioners as Jacques Maritain, René Cassin, and especially John Peters Humphrey, the Canadian delegate who sketched a first draft of the document. She later told a friend that she was a hard taskmaster who pushed her fellow commissioners so energetically that she and they sometimes spent weeks "arguing over the weight of each word, as well as the legal meaning of every phrase." One of the many heated debate points during the commission's work was whether a philosophical discussion of the origin of rights should be included in the final document. Ultimately, the decision was made to use language reminiscent of the U.S. Declaration of Independence, which claimed that universal and "inalienable" rights are based upon "the inherent dignity" of all humans.

One point that Roosevelt especially wanted to press home to people and nations around the world was that "universal" rights shouldn't be thought of as abstract or mysterious. They're grounded in very specific and local situations, "in small places, close to home—so close and so small that they cannot be seen on any maps of the world. Yet they are the world of the individual person; the neighborhood he lives in; the school or college he attends; the factory, farm, or office where he works. Such are the places where every man, woman, and child seeks equal justice, equal opportunity, equal dignity without discrimination. Unless these rights have meaning there, they have little meaning anywhere. Without concerted citizen action to uphold them close to home, we shall look in vain for progress in the larger world."

The U.N. General Assembly discussed the Universal Declaration of Human Rights for two months before ratifying it in December 1948. The vote was unanimous, although eight nations, including the USSR, South Africa, and Saudi Arabia, abstained. Eleanor Roosevelt continued as a delegate to the U.N. for another five years before retiring in 1953. She always considered her work on the Declaration to be her life's greatest achievement.

8 November

Dorothy Day

8 November 1897—29 November 1980

Works of Mercy and Justice

LEFTIST JOURNALIST, NOVELIST, SUFFRAGIST, and bohemian: Dorothy Day wore several hats in her first thirty years, ever trying to find creative ways to marry her political passions and artistic talents. But she never quite succeeded in filling what she later called "the long loneliness," the sense that something essential was missing from her life. Her conversion to Roman Catholicism at the age of thirty, which coincided with the birth of her only child, didn't relieve her of the long loneliness, but it did help her understand it. She realized that it originated from a deep longing for God and God's kingdom.

In 1933, inspired by the vagabond philosopher **Peter Maurin**, Day launched the Catholic Worker Movement and devoted the rest of her life to it. It was the perfect vehicle for her leftist political views, her artistic genius, and her deep religious faith. Catholic Workers then and now live with the poor, the marginalized, and the hopeless. They minister to their needs by exercising the works of corporal and spiritual mercy commanded by Jesus: feeding the hungry, sheltering the homeless, nursing the sick, clothing the naked, visiting the imprisoned, instructing the ignorant, bearing wrongs patiently, comforting the afflicted, and so on. The work is performed out of love, but it isn't easy. Day, who knew firsthand how difficult it could be, often quoted Dostoevsky's warning that "love is a harsh and dreadful thing."

But Day and her Catholic Workers didn't stop at works of mercy. They also focused on the unjust political and social institutions that made the works necessary in the first place. Traditionally, the Church spent a lot of energy trying to remedy evils instead of nipping them at their source. But where, asked Day, "were the saints to try to change the social order, not just to minister to the slaves, but to do away with slavery?" So in addition to ministering to the poor, Day went after the sources of their poverty. She criticized a judicial system that hammered at the poor but frequently exonerated the wealthy, a government that favored big business at the expense of workers, and a military that devoured millions of dollars that otherwise could go to social services. Although she remained a loyal daughter of the Church, she also took it to task for too frequently aligning itself with political powers and corporate principalities. And Day consistently advocated nonviolence. She was one of the few religious leaders in the United States to staunchly oppose participation in World War II—a pacifist stand that cost the Catholic Worker Movement many supporters—and she continued her opposition to war during the Korean and Vietnam conflicts. She also witnessed against the Cold War's nuclear buildup.

Day's hope was to "build the new in the shell of the old," to subvert the foundations of a society indifferent to the works of mercy and justice by raising up a vibrant alternative to it—by helping to build, in short, the kingdom of God. Catholic Workers continue that vision to this day.

9 November
Thomas Berry

9 November 1914—1 June 2009

Earth's Storyteller

Eleven-year-old Thomas Berry was standing in a meadow in his native North Carolina when he experienced an epiphany that shaped the rest of his life. He suddenly understood that the Mystery that created and guides the physical world was discernible within the physical realm itself. The wind blowing in trees, the emergence of supernovas, birds in flight: everything in the material world carried the imprint of the dynamism, the Spirit, underlying it. The evolution of the universe, if read correctly, discloses the Creator's consciousness. This insight was the nucleus of the "New Story" that Berry would spend the rest of his life telling.

One of thirteen children, Berry entered the Roman Catholic Passionist order when he was twenty and was ordained eight years later. Recognizing his intellect, his superiors sent him to the Catholic University of America for advanced study, and he eventually earned a doctorate for a thesis on the philosophy of Giambattista Vico. Vico's division of human history into various periods proved a major influence on Berry's own exploration of the evolution of human consciousness and what he feared was a deepening historical alienation of humans from the earth.

Shortly after World War II, Berry traveled to China to learn the language and study the culture. He also mastered Sanskrit and immersed himself in Indian philosophy and religion. His affinity for Asian thought and his deep love of the earth naturally drew him to a study of Native American and other indigenous religions as well. All were grist for his growing understanding of the insight he had as a boy about the deep interconnectedness of humanity, the physical cosmos, and God.

Preferring to call himself a "geologian" because of his conviction that the Divine is discoverable through an examination of physical nature, Berry worried that the current technological assault upon the planet—what he called a "barbarism of reflection"—was the symptom of an underlying loss of cultural and historical earth wisdom. Instead of thinking of the universe in holistic terms, humans increasingly reduce it to mindless matter distinct from and decidedly inferior to human consciousness. Berry believed this pervasive cultural attitude both encourages our abuse of nature and our distorted understanding of what it means to be human. Only through a recovered awareness of our deep and intertwined genetic and spiritual connection to the earth can we remember who we are and prepare the way for a sustainable future. This shift in humanity's self-perception and relationship to the earth is, said Berry, the next stage in the evolution of consciousness—"the New Story of the universe." He was confident that the shift would occur, despite the current depth of human forgetfulness, because the "same dynamism" that "awakened life in the primordial cell, and then brought into being the unnumbered variety of living beings, and finally brought us into being and guided us safely through the turbulent centuries" will also "awaken" us in good time. Then we will be at peace with the earth.

10 November

Seneca

4 BCE—65 CE

War Is Madness

THE ROMAN PHILOSOPHER LUCIUS Annaeus Seneca had an impossible job. As tutor and advisor to Nero, his task was to teach the young emperor to exercise his absolute power with justice, wisdom, and compassion. He failed, of course, but not for want of trying.

Born in present-day Spain to wealthy and cultured parents, Seneca and his family moved to the city of Rome when he was still a boy. Like most lads of his class and rank, he studied rhetoric, then considered a necessary schooling for a career in both law and politics. But he also immersed himself in philosophy, particularly the writings of the Stoic school, whose members emphasized self-discipline, freedom from disruptive passions, and the exercise of virtue.

The Emperors Caligula and Claudius both found Seneca objectionable. The first nearly executed him, and the second exiled him from Rome for nearly a decade, a period in which Seneca devoted himself to study. But Claudius' successor, Nero, recalled him to the imperial city in 49 and made him an advisor. At the start of Nero's reign, Seneca's influence worked some good. Under his tutelage, Nero really did seem to want to be the sort of philosopher-king admired by Stoics. But as the years progressed and Nero's self-indulgence and megalomania grew, Seneca's moderating advice became unwelcome. By 62, he had ceased to have any influence at all with Nero. Three years later, Nero rid himself once and for all of Seneca by requiring him to commit suicide.

In the years between his banishment from court and his death, Seneca, sobered by his unhappy relationship with Nero, wrote a series of moral essays that have come to be called the *Letters to Lucilius*. In them, he reflected on a number of themes, but one in particular stands out. In the ninety-fifth epistle, Seneca blasts the conventional double standard that condemns individual acts of brutality but valorizes collective ones. "We are mad, not only individually, but nationally," he wrote. Manslaughter and isolated murders are punished. "But what of war and the much vaunted crime of slaughtering whole peoples?" Individual crimes are often less cruel and always less widespread than the cruelties "practiced in accordance with acts of senate and popular assembly"—and, Seneca could have added, imperial decree—but the one is discouraged by punishment and the other encouraged by rewards.

As a Stoic, Seneca believed that the good life is lived in accordance with nature. But warfare is unnatural for both humans and animals. It runs against our grain because humans are "the gentlest class of being," and "even dumb beasts and wild beasts keep the peace with one another." When we go to war, "reveling in the blood of others," we do so only because we are confused about what's truly in our best interests. Even worse, we corrupt the younger generation into betraying its finest nature by "entrusting the waging of war to our sons." And this, concludes Seneca, is worse than tragic. It's madness.

11 November
Martin of Tours

316—8 November 397

Early Conscientious Objector

THE EMPEROR JULIAN WAS furious. Known as "the Apostate" for his renunciation of the Christian religion, which his predecessor Constantine had legalized a quarter-century earlier in 313, Julian and his mighty Roman army were squaring off against invading Gauls in front of the city of Worms—and suddenly one of his young officers refused to go into battle.

The officer was Martin, the twenty-year-old son of a Roman cavalry leader who named his son after Mars, the god of war. Born in Hungary, Martin became a catechumen in the Christian faith while still a boy. His angry father strong-armed him into enlisting in the cavalry when he was only fifteen, hoping that military life would cure his son of his unmanly attraction to the Christian faith. But the plan didn't work. Martin used most of his pay to feed and clothe the poor. He refused to let the servant allotted him wait on him. One freezing day at the gates of Amiens, he tore his heavy military cloak in two and gave half of it to a shivering beggar. That night, he dreamt that Christ wore the half-cloak.

Although increasingly uncomfortable with military service, he stuck it out for two more years. Finally, in 336, he'd had enough. "I am the soldier of Christ," he told Julian the day before the anticipated battle at Worms. "It is not lawful for me to fight." When Julian accused him of cowardice, Martin volunteered to face the enemy unarmed. The seething Julian agreed, evidently hoping that the Gauls would save him the trouble of executing the young officer. But the Gauls unexpectedly surrendered that night and the battle never occurred. Martin spent some time in jail while Julian cooled off. Eventually, probably as a favor to his father, Julian released Martin from both jail and the military.

Martin, who went on to become a monastic, was elected bishop of Tours in 371. As bishop, he was known as a man of great holiness. He regularly cared for the poor, refused to persecute heretics, and lived an austere life in the Abbey of Marmoutier, one of the monasteries he founded. But none of his accomplishments matched the courage and devotion he'd exhibited when he stood up to Julian by refusing to fight.

Although Martin renounced the sword, history has insisted on remembering him as a warrior saint. One of his relics, his half-cloak *(cappa Sancti Martini)*, was regularly used as a battle banner by Frankish kings. In the Franco-Prussian War of 1870–71, France heralded him as the spiritual protector of her soldiers. The U.S. Army Quartermaster Corps has adopted him as a patron saint. And his feast day, 11 November (the day he was buried), coincides in the United States with Veterans Day. It's unlikely Martin would have wanted these sorts of memorials.

12 November

Baha'u'llah

12 November 1817—29 May 1892

Manifestation of God's Peace

THE FOUNDERS OF ALL faith traditions claim peace as a fundamental ingredient of a holy life, and the founder of the Bahai faith is no exception. The son of a high-ranking government official, Husayn Ali, whom his followers would call Baha'u'llah, "the glory of God," was born in Tehran and displayed remarkable precocity and wisdom as a child. Once after watching a puppet show that featured warring kings, young Husayn observed the puppet master exiting the tent, box under arm, and was told that everything he'd just witnessed was inside it, the intriguing kings and the powerful princes. Ever since that day, the adult Baha'u'llah recalled, "all the trappings of the world have seemed akin to that same spectacle. All this conflict, contention, and vainglory have ever been and will ever be, like the play and pastimes of children."

After his father's death, Baha'u'llah rejected the governmental position offered him and instead worked for several charitable organizations. In 1844 he became a follower of the "Bab," a charismatic religious leader who proclaimed he was the "promised one" sent by God and who broke with Islam. Predictably, the Bab was executed for his heresy, and many of his followers, including Baha'u'llah, were jailed. While in a Tehran dungeon, he experienced a mystical vision that convinced him he was the "manifestation of God," a messenger of divine revelation.

The revelation that came to Baha'u'llah was that unity was the great principle of reality: the unity of God, religion, and humanity. Although many religions have different notions of what God is, they all refer to one and the same Creator, who is essentially unknowable except through messengers like Baha'u'llah. Similarly, despite their specific differences in beliefs and forms of worship, all religions point to the same deity, share similar basic values, and are destined to shed their differences and converge. Finally, Baha'u'llah taught that God privileges no group or race of people. Valued equally by a transcendent God, humans should transcend their individual prejudices and group loyalties to see one another as God sees them. When we finally are able to view one another through God's eyes, world peace will be achievable. In an astounding series of letters he sent in 1867 to world leaders, Baha'u'llah outlined his vision of unity and appealed to them to abandon war and the pursuit of wealth that leads to war.

Sadly, Baha'u'llah's teachings on the unity of God, religion, and humanity brought him persecution, exile, and imprisonment. But throughout all his ordeals, he remained loyal to his central conviction that "these fruitless strifes, these ruinous wars, shall pass away, and the 'Most Great Peace' shall come. Let not a man glory in this, that he loves his country; let him rather glory in this, that he loves his kind."

13 November
Karen Silkwood

19 February 1946—13 November 1974

Whistleblower

Karen Silkwood, a lab tech at the Kerr-McGee Cimmaron River plutonium processing plant, had been collecting reports of safety violations in the plant for several months. Putting all her documentation in a manila envelope, she hopped in her car one night in mid-November 1974 to drive from her home in Crescent, Oklahoma, to Oklahoma City. There she was to meet a reporter from the *New York Times* who was interested in publishing her story.

She never arrived. She was found the next morning, dead behind the wheel of her car. The official report concluded that she ran off the road and plunged down an embankment. The back of her white Honda was banged up, leading some to suspect she had been pushed off the road by another vehicle. The manila envelope was never found.

Silkwood took a job at the Cimmaron facility in 1972 following the breakup of her marriage. The plant manufactured fuel rods used in nuclear fission reactors; the rods contained particles of radioactive plutonium, a heavy-duty carcinogen. Silkwood later said that neither she nor any of her follow employees were fully briefed on the dangers of working with plutonium, despite the fact that there were at least seventeen documented exposures to plutonium involving nearly eighty employees during her two years at the facility. Plutonium dust was even found in the employee cafeteria.

Silkwood's specific job was quality testing the fuel rods to make sure there were no cracks in them that might cause them to shatter when used in nuclear power plants. She discovered that instead of discarding defective rods, Kerr-McGee was grinding down the blemishes in them and selling the rods as if they were in prime condition. After meeting secretly with officials from her labor union as well as the Atomic Energy Commission (AEC), Silkwood agreed to collect proof of the cover-up by taking before and after microphotographs of the rods.

A few weeks after agreeing to collect data, Silkwood triggered radiation alarms on two separate occasions at the Cimmaron facility. Tests indicated that she had traces of plutonium on the surface of her body as well as in her lungs and organs. Silkwood feared that her plans to whistleblow had been discovered and that plutonium had been smuggled into her home in order to contaminate her and frighten her off her crusade to improve safety conditions at the plant. A week later, she was killed in the car accident.

After her death, the story of Silkwood's concerns about the nuclear facility went public, launching widespread concern about safety standards in the nuclear industry and prompting the AEC to tighten up national regulatory standards. The AEC confirmed her charge that Kerr-McGee was falsifying quality reports on its fuel rods and concluded that the radiation contamination she suffered was most likely the result of deliberate poisoning by parties unknown. Three years later, a jury awarded Silkwood's estate nearly $100 million in damages.

14 November

Pedro Arrupe

14 November 1907—5 February 1991

Defender of Liberation Theology

HE WAS THREE YEARS into medical school in Madrid when a miraculous healing he witnessed at Lourdes sparked Pedro Arrupe's call to the Society of Jesus. He entered the order at the age of nineteen and was ordained seventeen years later after studying in Holland and Belgium.

Following doctoral studies in the United States, Arrupe was sent as a missionary to Japan. He was serving in a Hiroshima suburb on the day the atomic bomb fell and later described the horror as "a permanent experience outside of history, engraved on my memory." Calling on the skills he had acquired years earlier as a medical student, he quickly converted a damaged chapel into a makeshift hospital for the bomb blast's victims. Arrupe remained in Japan after the war years and was named Jesuit provincial there in 1958. Seven years later, fellow Jesuits elected him Father General of the entire order.

During his leadership of the Jesuits, Arrupe was particularly supportive of his brethren who worked with the poor in Central and South America. These Jesuits combined spiritual ministry with social activism, convinced as they were that the poor were oppressed by wealthy landowners who acted with the tacit approval of the Church. The Roman hierarchy condemned this political involvement as well as the liberation theology, or gospel-based privileging of the poor, that justified it. The worry was that the Jesuits who embraced this approach were pawns of communist aggression. Arrupe disagreed, and he vigorously defended his priests, even after the Congregation for the Doctrine of the Faith officially condemned liberation theology. He also refused to withdraw Jesuits serving in El Salvador, despite persistent death threats against them, insisting that the people of that war-torn and oppressed nation needed them. Six Jesuits who remained, including noted theologian Ignacio Ellacuría, were murdered in 1989.

Described by one of his friends as "a second Ignatius" who "refounded" the Jesuit Order "in the light of Vatican II," Arrupe focused the Jesuits during his term as Father General on both renewed spirituality—as a result of his years in Japan, Arrupe himself practiced Zen meditation daily—and social justice advocacy. Along with other proponents of liberation theology, he identified the suffering endured by the victims of war and poverty with Christ's Passion and taught that alleviating the one through justice was honoring the other in faith.

Arrupe's leadership of the Jesuits and his quiet but persistent defense of their involvement in liberation theology came to an end in 1981 when a massive stroke left him paralyzed and mute. In resigning as Father General, he offered this prayer: "More than ever I find myself in the hands of God. This is what I wanted all my life from my youth. But now there is a difference; the initiative is entirely with God. It is indeed a profound experience to know and feel myself so totally in God's hands." He died ten years later.

15 NOVEMBER
Paul Moore

15 NOVEMBER 1919—1 MAY 2003

Social Gospel Bishop

NOTHING IN HIS BACKGROUND suggested the passion with which blue-blooded Paul Moore would advocate for the poor and oppressed. Paul Moore was born into one of America's richest families, attended the finest boarding schools money could buy, graduated from Yale, and became a highly decorated Marine hero in World War II. Following his discharge from the military, he attended seminary and was ordained an Episcopal priest in 1949.

It was his first assignment, to an inner-city parish in Jersey City, that transformed Moore from a loyal establishment figure into an ardent proponent of the Social Gospel. While there, he encountered for the first time the misery of poverty and the injustice of racism. His experiences in Jersey City primed him for an active role in the civil rights movement, and he traveled south to join **Martin Luther King Jr.** on several marches, including Selma. After being named Suffragan Bishop of Washington, DC, in 1964, he gained national notoriety for his vocal opposition to the Vietnam War. Some of the antiwar protests he organized were controversial. In 1970, he staged a short play by Norman Mailer that used language so indecent that Tennessee Williams, certainly no prude, stalked out in disapproval.

In 1972, Moore was appointed bishop of the diocese of New York. He used his position as one of the most powerful leaders in the Episcopal Church to continue advocating for social justice. Under his guidance, the Cathedral Church of St. John in New York City became a center where the homeless could find safe and clean shelters and inner-city youth could learn job skills. The cathedral became known as an oasis of music, art, and culture, but also as an activist headquarters from which rallies against racism and the nuclear arms race were launched. Critics argued that a bishop had no business involving the church in political matters. But Moore replied that the gospel of Jesus obliged Christians to speak against and redress injustice whenever they encountered it.

Moore, a closeted bisexual, advocated for gay rights and was the first Episcopal bishop to ordain an openly gay woman. In 1986, he clashed with Roman Catholic Cardinal John J. O'Connor, who publicly stated that homosexuals had no right to legal protection against hate crimes directed at them. Moore countered that it was morally wrong not to grant all citizens equal legal rights.

After his 1989 retirement, Moore wrote his memoirs and continued witnessing for peace and justice as much as his declining health permitted. One of his final public statements was a stinging criticism of President George W. Bush's claim of divine approval of the 2003 invasion of Iraq. "It appears that we have two types of religion here," Moore said. "One is a solitary Texas politician who says, 'I talk to God and I am right'; the other involves millions of people of all faiths who disagree."

16 November
Adolfo Sansolini

15 November 1966—

Animal Activist

A NATIVE OF ROME, Sansolini has been an animal rights advocate since he was a teenager. Horrified at the violence involved in the factory farming and slaughter of food animals, he has waged many campaigns for more humane treatment of them. But his most dramatic campaign was in 1999, when he fasted to protest the use of egg battery cages.

In an egg battery system, hens are confined in tiny wire mesh cages not much larger than a sheet of ordinary-sized paper. The cages are stacked on top of one another, and the birds are fed hormones to keep them laying eggs at a continuous and unnatural rate. Because of the filth and confinement, the hens suffer from osteoporosis, infections, and blindness, and display uncharacteristically aggressive behavior toward one another.

In 1999, a European Commission met to determine whether nor not to outlaw egg batteries. Sansolini feared that Italian egg producers would pressure the Italian government to instruct its representatives on the commission to vote against a ban. So he went on a hunger strike to exert some counterpressure. Recalling his decision years later, Sansolini said, "I knew I was risking a lot. But living is about using life. If you believe in something you should invest in it to make it happen. What I could invest at that moment wasn't anything else but putting my life on the table."

Soon alarmingly weak from his highly publicized hunger strike, Sansolini was called to the Italian prime minister's office, collapsing twice in route. A glass of water was placed on a table next to him. If he ended the strike, he was told, Italian commissioners would be instructed to vote for the cage ban. But Sansolini refused. "If you do something before I leave," he replied, "I'll be happy to drink it. But I won't drink it now." Worried about the public outcry if Sansolini's strike continued, the appropriate phone call was made, Sansolini ended his hunger strike, the Italian vote swayed the commission's final decision, and three hundred million birds across Europe were rescued from battery cages.

Sansolini believes that the concern for animal rights is closely linked to concern for human ones. As he sees it, Christians and members of the LBGTQ community in particular—the first because of the teachings of Jesus and the second because of their own experiences of persecution—should be especially attuned to the sufferings of animals. As he says, "I oppose all violence, be it violence against animal victims in the laboratory or violence towards people outside the laboratory. The differences between races, sexuality, or religion have long been used to justify prejudice and exploitation. The argument that we have the right to experiment on animals because they are a different species is just the same."

In 2004, Sansolini was called to London as the first non-British CEO of the British Union for the Abolition of Vivisection and Chairman of the European Coalition to End Animal Experiments. He is currently an independent consultant focusing on the impact of trade rules on animal welfare.

17 November

Origen

CA. 185—CA. 254

All Sheep, No Goats

RECOGNITION OF EVIL IN the world, both the kind perpetrated by individuals and the kind institutionalized by unjust social and economic structures, can inspire persons of good will to work for its eradication. But there's a great temptation that must be avoided in responding to evil: the trap of thinking that those who commit evil are irredeemable and deserve unqualified condemnation.

There are many problems with this way of thinking, but the most obvious is that it divides the world into good sheep and bad goats, with the former typically being "us" and the latter "them." Such a division distorts human nature by shoving it into one-dimensional categories—after all, no person is exclusively good or exclusively evil—and it unnecessarily fosters suspicion, hostility, and violence between humans. Dividing humans into sheep and goats is the stuff from which crusades are spawned.

The early church father Origen rejected this sheep/goat division of humanity. He learned firsthand how dangerous it is while still a youth in Alexandria after his father and hundreds of other "evil" Christians were murdered in a state-approved pogrom. Later, as a priest and theologian, he personally experienced its effects when he himself was persecuted for heresy by fellow Christians and imprisoned and tortured by pagan Roman authorities.

In light of this, Origen denied that people can ever properly be judged utterly evil, totally condemned, and viciously punished, and he did so in a theologically radical way: he defended universalism, the belief that no one, neither humans nor demons, will ultimately be consigned to hellish darkness. Everyone capable of sin will finally be saved; salvation is universal. The obvious ethical implication is that if God forgives everyone, humans have no reason whatsoever for condemning one another in a once-and-for-all way.

Origen argued for universalism in his book *On First Principles*. His argument is that no one made in God's likeness is capable of utter corruption and that all humans and fallen angels, no matter how much evil they may commit, will eventually remember who they are and embrace the God from which they come. True, it may take some longer than others. As Origen says, some will "outstrip others, and tend by a swifter course towards perfection, while others again follow close at hand, and some again a long way behind." But given enough time—for God is infinitely patient—everyone, even Satan, will be redeemed.

Ironically, Origen was persecuted for his refusal to divide the human race into sheep and goats. One of the reasons so few of his works survive, in fact, is that most were burned as heretical. But his central message survived: if no one is beyond God's redemption, no one should be absolutely judged and unequivocally condemned by his or her fellows.

18 November
Howard Thurman

18 November 1899—10 April 1981

Opening the Door of the Heart

In the fall of 1935, Howard Thurman, dean of Howard University's chapel, met **Mohandas Gandhi**. Thurman, the grandson of a slave, implored Gandhi to visit the United States and tackle the race issue. Gandhi gently declined the invitation, pointing out that his first obligation must be to India. He told Thurman that it was up to African Americans to find a nonviolent solution to the problem of racism.

Thurman was anxious to meet Gandhi because, as a Quaker, he was also an advocate of the nonviolence Gandhi had used so effectively in India. Educated at Haverford College, Thurman had imbibed the Quaker tradition of active nonviolence that speaks truth to power. Gandhi's words encouraged him to use that tradition in the struggle against racial discrimination.

Already enjoying a national reputation as a gifted speaker and religious leader, Thurman left Howard in 1944 to co-minister San Francisco's newly founded Fellowship of All Peoples Church, the nation's first interracial and intercultural congregation. He found it an exciting experiment in Christian living and worship. The church, he wrote, "was timeless and time-bound, the idiom of all creeds and totally contained in none, the authentic accent of every gospel but limited to none." It was, he concluded, a "breathless moment in time" in which people forsook differences and focused on what they held in common. His heart remained at Fellowship Church even after he returned east to become Boston University's chaplain, where he would meet and influence **Martin Luther King Jr**.

Like all Christian pacifists, Thurman wanted to see an end to physical violence. But he believed that an even greater threat was psychological violence. To hate, scorn, or despise another person, he believed, is to deny that person's being. It is to see him or her as nothing more than a noxious obstacle worthy only of being swept out of the way. Physical violence seeks to kill the "enemy's" body. But the psychological violence that motivates it has already reduced the "enemy" to the status of disposable vermin.

Nonviolence, on the other hand, is based on a "mood" of "reconciliation." It is an "affirmation" of the humanity of even the person of violence, and this essential affirmation always contains within it the possibility of dialogue. But as Thurman learned from Gandhi, nonviolence is more than a mood. It's also a "technique" that rejects physical force or coercion and substitutes an appeal to conscience. Its purpose is "to open the door of the heart" so that "what another is feeling and experiencing can find its way" into the aggressor's mind and soul. Someone who is thus "faced with nonviolence is forced to deal with himself; every way of escape is ultimately cut off," prompting self-examination, conversion, and community.

At the end of the day, Thurman said, the work of reconciliation is "to find a way to honor what is deepest in one person and to have that person honor what is deepest in the other." Martin Luther King Jr.'s leadership of the civil rights movement would be founded on that basic principle.

19 November
Gillo Pontecorvo

19 NOVEMBER 1919—12 OCTOBER 2006

De-Romanticizing War

ITALIAN-BORN GILLO PONTECORVO PLANNED to follow in the footsteps of his two elder brothers by becoming a scientist. But after flunking out of the University of Pisa, he instead traveled to Paris, hobnobbed with left-leaning intellectuals and artists, and began assisting a number of filmmakers. During World War II, he returned to Italy and eventually became one of the leaders of the Milan underground resistance. After the war, he turned his energy to writing and directing a number of films that reflected his leftist sympathies. The two best known were *The Wide Blue Road*, which focused on poverty, and *Kapo*, a study of anti-Semitism.

Pontecorvo's cinematic masterpiece is his 1966 *The Battle of Algiers*. Shot on location in the Casbah and using local residents rather than professional actors, the film focuses on the Algerian War of Independence, a brutal eight-year conflict in which native Algerians fought against French colonial settlers (the so-called *pied-noirs*) as well as the French army. Like most civil wars, this one was savage. Atrocities were committed by all sides. The Algerian independence movement didn't hesitate to kidnap, torture, and kill *pied-noirs*. The French army utilized covert assassination in some instances and blanket executions in others to destroy the insurgents. The *pied-noirs* threatened, bullied, and murdered Algerians in an effort to intimidate them from joining the liberation forces. From first to last, the Algerian War was one outrage after another. No one was safe. Women and children as well as Catholic and Muslim religious leaders were all considered fair targets. The rules of warfare, arguably never of much use in any armed conflict, were utterly disregarded in Algeria.

Although Pontecorvo clearly sympathized with the native Algerians—his leftist politics made him a sworn enemy of all colonialism—it's to his credit that he didn't shrink from an honest and sometimes shocking portrayal of the brutality practiced by all sides in the war. Adopting a semi-documentary style shot in black-and-white, Pontecorvo filmed scenes depicting the torture of prisoners, the assassination of leaders, the guillotining of prisoners, children shooting soldiers at point-blank range, women exploding bombs in crowded cafés, and the cynical way in which ordinary people were blackmailed or terrorized into becoming informants. At no time does Pontecorvo succumb to the temptation to glorify either the Algerian guerrillas or the French soldiers. The entire film destroys any romantic notions of war that viewers might bring with them into the theater, making the movie one of the strongest anti-war statements ever shot.

Ironically—and sadly—*The Battle of Algiers* became a favorite not only of war resisters but also of guerrilla advocates of violence in the 1960s and 1970s. Organizations such as the Black Panthers, the Baader-Meinhof Gang, and the IRA were reportedly inspired by Pontecorvo's cinematic depiction of guerrilla tactics and determination.

20 November

Leo Tolstoy

9 September 1828—20 November 1910

Obeying the Law of Love

To the general reading public, Leo Tolstoy is the great Russian novelist who wrote such masterpieces as *War and Peace* (1869) and *Anna Karenina* (1877). But in the final twenty-five years of his life, he was also the leader of a pacifist movement that attracted thousands of "Tolstoyans" throughout Russia and around the world.

Born the son of a nobleman, the first forty years of Tolstoy's life pretty much reflected the values of his social class. He was an indifferent student, served in the military and saw action in the Caucasus, drank too heavily, incurred huge gambling debts, settled down on the family estate of Yasnaya Polyana, married, and fathered children. But beginning in the 1870s, Tolstoy began to undergo a philosophical and religious conversion. Although he broke with the Russian Orthodox Church, he became a deeply devoted follower of Christ and especially of the moral principles espoused by Christ: love of neighbor and enemy, simplicity in lifestyle, and nonviolence. They provided him with a sense of meaning and purposefulness for which he'd been searching all his life.

Following his conversion, Tolstoy's writing changed. Although he continued to publish some fiction, most memorably the religiously themed novel *Resurrection* (1899), he increasingly turned his attention to works of philosophy and religion such as *A Confession* (1882) and *The Kingdom of God Is Within You* (1894). Additionally, he became a public champion of social reform, actively campaigning against militarism, private property, capital punishment, and aristocratic privilege. He signed away all of his own property, including royalties from his writings, and tried to cultivate the simple, peasant-like lifestyle that he recommended to others.

Tolstoy's religious sensibilities, and particularly his pacifism, were ultimately founded on what he called the "law of love" taught by Jesus and encapsulated in the Sermon on the Mount. According to the law, wrote Tolstoy, "man should always do unto others as he would that they should do unto him; he should always cooperate in the development of love and union among created beings." Yet despite being given this "one definite, indubitable law," humans override it for the sake of personal advancement, social conformity, or sometimes a misguided idealism that assumes for itself the right to break the law of love for expediency's sake. They break the law of love and follow instead the law of violence.

But Tolstoy believed that none of this can be justified. The real question, he said, is not what will advance my personal interests or even what will be good or bad for society. The question that must be asked of each person is this: "do you wish now, immediately and entirely, to obey the law [of love] of Him who sent you into life and who clearly showed you his will; or do you prefer to resist?" For Tolstoy, the answer was a no-brainer.

21 November
Menno Simons

1496—31 January 1561

A Child of Peace

HIS EXTANT WRITINGS BEGIN with a quotation from Paul's first letter to the Corinthians (3:11): "No other foundation can anyone lay than that which is laid, which is Jesus Christ." Menno Simon's rootedness in the person of Jesus Christ led him to understand pacifism as the calling of every Christian. Such a calling is not a helpless resignation in the face of violence, but rather the strenuous practice in the world of works of mercy and justice. "True evangelical faith cannot lie dormant," wrote Simons. "It clothes the naked, it feeds the hungry, it comforts the sorrowful, it shelters the destitute, it serves those that harm it."

Born in Friesland in present-day Holland, Simons was ordained a Roman Catholic priest in 1524. He later confessed that even though he was trained in Latin and Greek and had studied some of the church fathers, he performed his parish duties without ever really reading the Bible carefully. He resisted doing so, he said, because he feared the gospels might confuse and mislead him. Besides, he was too busy—"playing cards, drinking, and in diversions as, alas, is the fashion and usage of such useless people"—to take his priestly duties seriously.

It was the theological questions raised by the Reformers that led Simons to begin studying Scripture. When he did, he found himself sympathizing with a new sect that taught that only adults were capable of making the decision to follow Christ. Because members of this sect believed that adults who had been baptized as infants needed to be baptized again, they were known as Anabaptists (from the Greek *ana,* "again"). Simons' brother Peter became a member and was among a group of Anabaptists killed in 1535 by Roman Catholics. His brother's murder brought about a spiritual crisis in Simons' life, leading to his rejecting the Catholic Church, renouncing his priestly orders, and joining the Anabaptists. A year later, he reluctantly allowed himself to be designated an elder, and from then until his death he traveled throughout present-day Holland and northern Germany, preaching to anyone who would listen to his message of peace and reconciliation. His followers began to be called "Mennonites." Today, the denomination is one of Christianity's traditional peace churches. Mennonites are leaders in Christian social activism as well as peace-building.

Simons, like all Anabaptists, believed that Christians are called to live apart from the world in voluntary simplicity, forsaking recourse to violence and coercion in the promotion of their own interests or even in self-defense. Today, when it comes to nonviolence, more than one and a half million Mennonites identify with the words of their founder: "We who were formerly no people at all, and knew no peace, are now called to be a church of peace. True Christians do not know vengeance. They are the children of peace. Their hearts overflow with peace. Their mouths speak peace, and they walk in the way of peace."

22 November

Aldous Huxley

26 July 1894—22 November 1963

One Generous Gesture

The British author Aldous Huxley is probably best known for his dystopian novel *Brave New World*, which portrays a culture held together by false peace. Its social harmony is based on soulless uniformity, and the personal tranquility of its citizens comes from their daily ingestion of drugs.

Brave New World reflects Huxley's lifelong commitment to genuine peace. From his youth to his dying day, he was troubled that humans too often settle for false peace—political order and inner contentment, regardless of how these are achieved—instead of the real thing. Throughout his life, but particularly in the 1930s when he was involved in England's Peace Pledge Union, Huxley wrote essays and pamphlets that analyzed the nature of genuine peace and advocated for what he usually called "constructive pacifism."

One of the myths that Huxley especially wanted to prick is the belief that war is an inevitable part of the natural order of things. On the contrary, he argued, "war is a purely human phenomenon. Animals kill for food [and] fight duels in the heat of sexual excitement," but only humans indulge in "the mass murder" of their own species. Looked at from an evolutionary perspective, the notion that war is a natural law is especially absurd, since "active warfare tends to eliminate the young and strong." It doesn't select the fittest. Instead, it indiscriminately kills them.

So if war is a human artifact that's avoidable because not written into the fabric of nature, how do we go about eliminating it? In the long run, Huxley believed, "constructive pacifism is based on a consideration of the facts of personal relationship" between people. It's foolish to presume that a government can consistently work for peace if the individuals who comprise it "are tyrants in their families." Peace "must be first of all a personal ethic." Otherwise, any political peace that might be brokered rests on an unreliable foundation that can collapse at any moment.

But Huxley wasn't naïve. He recognized that personal, interior conversion to pacifism is a slow and halting process and that sometimes political circumstances demand a swifter response. So in the short run, while waiting for individuals to arrive at a personal commitment to peace, responsible governments in moments of crisis must be willing to sheath their swords and make sacrifices for the sake of avoiding war. The more powerful the nation, the greater the sacrifice owed. There's no guarantee that this willingness on the part of any government to act humbly will keep the peace, but there's at least the chance that it might break the escalation of violence-prone tension. Huxley's hope was that "one generous gesture on the part of a great nation might be enough to set the whole world free." There's risk involved, of course. But "which is better," Huxley asks, "to take a risk for a good cause, or to march to certain perdition for a bad one?"

23 November
Maude Royden

23 November 1876—30 July 1956

Pacifist, Suffragist, Religious Reformer

It was a spiritual crisis that brought a young Maude Royden together with the man who would become one of the two loves of her life and launch her career as a lecturer, author, and preacher. A friend to whom Royden had confessed her desire to become a Roman Catholic suggested that she seek counsel from Hudson Shaw, an Anglican priest who lectured at Oxford. The two impressed one another. Shaw persuaded Royden to remain within the Church of England, and Royden gladly accepted his invitation to move into his rectory as parish secretary and companion to his wife, the second (platonic) love of her life. Shaw was also pivotal in arranging for Royden to lecture on literature for Oxford's extension university.

Royden was an early supporter of voting rights for women. She began speaking nationwide for the suffragist movement in 1908, and she edited the suffragist weekly paper, *The Common Cause,* between 1912 and 1914. She considered the struggle for women's rights to be "the most profound and moral movement since the foundation of the Christian church." Her advocacy extended beyond obtaining the right to vote to an endorsement of birth control and the sexual rights of women within marriage. She also brought her struggle for women's rights to the very church that Shaw had persuaded her not to leave, protesting that although women performed most parish work and were numerically predominant in congregations, they were nonetheless barred from the priesthood and church councils.

Royden was shocked when World War I erupted. Believing that the Christian ideal of nonviolence should never be trumped by national interest, she toured the country speaking for the Fellowship of Reconciliation. In 1915 she published *The Great Adventure: The Way to Peace,* a call for Christian heroism as opposed to militaristic heroism. Taking her cue from the Sermon on the Mount, Royden argued that England could have offered nonviolent resistance to the evil of war instead of entering into battle. "We could have called for the peace lovers in the world to fling themselves, if need be, in front of the troop trains. If millions of men will go out to offer their lives up in war, surely there are those who would die for peace! And if not men, we could have called out women!" In fact, Royden believed that women and the women's movement were natural alternatives to a masculine culture of "might makes right."

Although Royden felt obliged in 1939 to endorse the war effort against Hitler, she never renounced her conviction that violence in nearly all circumstances is both impractical and non-Christian. Between the two wars, she became a noted author and preacher, beginning a career in religious radio broadcasting in 1936 that continued for fifteen years. Although she might have secured ordination in other Protestant denominations, she remained loyal to the Church of England. In 1944 Royden married Hudson Shaw after the death of his wife, who had been Royden's dear friend.

24 November

Arundhati Roy

24 November 1961—

Not Looking Away

INDIAN-BORN AUTHOR ARUNDHATI ROY started out writing for television, but her 1996 Booker Prize–winning *The God of Small Things* established her as a serious novelist. Since then, she has devoted most of her writing to political and social analysis, especially in advocacy of environmental protection and human rights. She credits her courage for taking on justice issues to her mother's colorful and unconventional lifestyle.

One of Roy's first campaigns after winning the Booker award was trying to halt the Narmada dam project. The partially built dam—which, if completed, will be one of the largest in India—could eventually displace half a million people and disrupt ecosystems all along the Narmada River. Roy donated a substantial amount of her Booker Prize money to the campaign to stop the dam's construction, earning the admiration of environmentalists and human rights activists alike. But other causes with which she's associated herself have proven more controversial.

In 1998, for example, Roy staunchly condemned India's development and testing of nuclear weapons. Many admirers of her opposition to the Narmada dam project, as well as others who had celebrated her authorial fame as a cause of national pride, condemned her as a traitor. What especially stunned her was the criticism of her fellow artists. "I was shocked at how even musicians and painters were celebrating the nuclear test," she later said, "and I could smell fascism on the breeze."

Ten years later, her sympathetic description of "Maoist" guerillas—actually, little more than a coalition of tribal communities—in the jungles of India's Chhattisgarh State once again shocked her fellow countrymen. Roy is a passionate advocate of nonviolence. But after spending three weeks with the guerillas, she publicly endorsed their grievance that the Indian government was conniving with corporations to forcibly mine tribal land. The guerilla "army," she said, was "more Gandhian than any Gandhian. Even their sabotage techniques are Gandhian." She argued that the government's portrayal of the guerillas as dangerously violent was a smokescreen to draw attention away from the mining controversy.

Roy hasn't published a novel since *The God of Small Things*, although she began a new one in 2007. Each time she hopes to return in earnest to her fiction, some new crisis clamors for her attention. So for the last fifteen years she's devoted her energy to exposing the relationship between governments and corporations, on the one hand, and economic, environmental, and political oppression, on the other. She misses writing fiction. But when confronted with the world's injustices, she says, "it's not an easy thing to do—to just look away." Her willingness to put her craft at the nonviolent service of justice is a reminder to the rest of us not to look away.

25 NOVEMBER
Paul Jones

25 NOVEMBER 1880—4 SEPTEMBER 1941

More than a Scrap of Paper

CHRISTIAN PACIFISM WAS AN unpopular position in England and France at the start of World War I. But it was condemned by many in the United States as well, including religious leaders from nearly all Christian denominations who gladly used their pulpits to declare that war against Germany was a moral duty. Episcopal bishop Paul Jones was one of the few clergymen who refused to endorse the war. "War," he proclaimed, "is entirely incompatible with the Christian profession." Just because Germany had "ignored her solemn obligations" was no justification for Christians to treat "the sermon on the mount as a scrap of paper."

Jones was born in Pennsylvania and studied at Yale and the Episcopal Divinity School in Cambridge, Massachusetts. After ordination, he served a mission church in Logan, Utah, and in 1914 was consecrated bishop of the large and thinly populated Missionary District of Utah.

Jones's condemnation of the European war ruffled feathers, but his outspoken witness to the gospel of peace after the United States entered the conflict directly contravened the Episcopal Church's House of Bishops, one of the denomination's two governing bodies. America, the bishops publicly stated, had the right to "expect of every one of her citizens some true form of national service," which could be neither commuted nor delegated. Shirking military duty was a sin. But Jones was undeterred in his opposition to war. "I believe most sincerely that German brutality and aggression must be stopped," he declared, "and I am willing, if need be, to give my life and what I possess to bring that about." But what he wasn't willing to do was "aid or encourage the way of war."

By 1917, Jones had so alienated some of the largest and most powerful parishes in Utah that they demanded that he cease speaking publicly against the war, charging that he was mixing religion and politics. Jones replied that "as a Christian bishop, charged with the responsibility of leadership, I would be deserving only of contempt did I remain silent in the present crisis." He believed it his duty to publicly condemn the war, "no matter what opinion may stand in the way." But the House of Bishops disagreed, and in April 1918 forced Jones to resign his bishopric. He became a casualty of the war he opposed.

Three years before his ouster, Jones cofounded the interfaith Fellowship of Reconciliation, and he faithfully served on its board in the years following World War I. In 1939, seeing another war on the horizon, he helped found the Episcopal Pacifist Fellowship, later renamed the Episcopal Peace Fellowship. In the months leading up to his death, Jones aided in resettling Jews displaced by the Nazis, and he worked hard to ease the growing tension between Japan and the United States. He died two months before the United States entered into its second worldwide conflict.

26 November
Adolfo Esquivel

26 November 1931—

God Does Not Kill

SCULPTOR, ARTIST, AND PROFESSOR of architecture Adolfo Esquivel taught for twenty-five years in Buenos Aires before resigning his university post in 1974 to take on the leadership of *El Servicio de Paz y Justicia* (SERPAJ), an ecumenical organization dedicated to protecting human rights in Latin America. An outgrowth of the work of Christian pacifists **Jean Goss** and **Hildegard Goss-Meier** nearly a decade earlier, SERPAJ's advocacy on behalf of rural farmers and urban workers is grounded in the Christian principle of nonviolence.

Raised a Roman Catholic by his Guaraní Indian grandmother after the death of his mother, Esquivel early on absorbed the two cultures, one indigenous and the other Christian, that later informed both his art and his political activism. The two came together dramatically in the 1970s while he was working with indigenous people in Ecuador. In a vivid dream, he saw the crucified Christ dressed in native clothing, a vision he later described in the appropriately titled book *Christ in a Poncho*.

As leader of SERPAJ, Esquivel was especially outspoken in 1976 during Argentina's "Dirty War," which brought the country under the control of a military junta. Championing the families of the *desaparecidos*, those who were "disappeared" because of their opposition to the regime, Esquivel created a Permanent Assembly for Human Rights to monitor government actions. He traveled to the United States and Europe to expose the Argentinian junta's excesses and to seek support for his Permanent Assembly. But in 1977, as he tried to renew his passport, Esquivel was himself disappeared, imprisoned for a whole year, and tortured for days on end. His Christian faith sustained him. "In the torture center," he recalls, "there were times when the morning light shone on the walls and I could see names of loved ones, essays, insults, the names of favorite soccer teams. But what impressed me most was a big message written in blood: 'God does not kill.'" Pressure from Amnesty International finally led to Esquivel's release in 1978.

The Argentinian military dictators, not to mention oppressive leaders everywhere in Latin America, were shocked when the still relatively obscure Esquivel won the 1980 Nobel Peace Prize. In his acceptance speech, he boldly accepted the award "in the name of the poorest and smallest of my brothers and sisters." The international recognition that the Nobel brought Esquivel turned the spotlight of the world's scrutiny on the repressive nature of the Argentine government. The ensuing international condemnation of the regime aided in the restoration of civilian rule in 1983.

Since democracy returned to Argentina, Esquivel and SERPAJ have devoted their energy to reducing the gulf between rich and poor nations exacerbated by globalization. "Governments of the world must come to their senses and construct a new economic order," he says. "They must rediscover the virtue of sharing."

27 November
Thich Quang Do

27 November 1928—

Living for Others

VIETNAM HAS A HIGHER percentage of atheists than any other nation in the world. This is largely because religious organizations, Christian as well as Buddhist, have been persecuted by the communist government since 1975. But one of the leaders of the Unified Buddhist Church of Vietnam (UBCV) has refused to remain silent about the regime's repression of religious freedom and other human rights. He is the Venerable Thich Quang Do.

Quang Do's struggle with Vietnamese communists is a long-standing one. When he was a Buddhist novice of barely seventeen, his spiritual master was brutally tortured and slain by them. Fleeing to the South after the 1954 communist takeover of Hanoi, Quang Do's high profile as a Buddhist leader made him a marked man when the communists gained control of the entire country in 1975. In 1977, after a two-year period of governmental crackdown on religion, Quang Do and several other UCBV leaders were arrested and tortured. That same year, the revolutionary government issued a decree, Resolution 297, that confiscated religious property and denounced the "spread of superstition."

Five years later, surprised by the tenacity of religion despite Resolution 297, the revolutionary government decided to control the UCBV by co-opting it into a more easily controlled state-run church. Anticipating his opposition, the authorities arrested Quang Do and sent him into exile in the hopes of keeping him quiet and out of the public eye. Clandestinely returning to Saigon in 1992, he issued a pamphlet recording the regime's crimes against religious people since it seized power in 1975. Arrested again, he was sentenced to five years in prison, but released three years later when an amnesty for "common criminals" was declared. He has been under house arrest ever since in a Ho Chi Minh City monastery.

Although the communist regime has accused him of being a politically motivated puppet of the CIA, Quang Ho's opposition to human rights abuses is based squarely on his Buddhist convictions. "In Vietnam," he says, "Buddhists do not live for their own life. They only think of the life of the people in general. And as long as the Vietnamese people suffer, we suffer with them." The "important thing for a human being," he observes, "is freedom. If you have no freedom, life becomes meaningless. All the Vietnamese people are living under a yoke." As one of the nation's spiritual leaders, Quang Do believes it his duty to help "bring about real freedom."

But the key to his Buddhist resistance to the regime is nonviolence. "In my mind," Quang Do says, "I have no hate. No hate. I try to love everyone"—even the communists who killed his spiritual master. This gentle monk who has endured oppression for most of his life knows that love is more powerful than the violence of the totalitarian regime he opposes. Love will eventually "peel away the regime's hatred," exposing its deeper Buddha nature. Then, Quang Do says, "love will be released."

28 November
Arthur Carman

2 August 1902—28 November 1982

Rugby, Not War

For over thirty years, a bookshop in Lambton Quay, Wellington, was a meeting place for dozens of New Zealand's leftists and pacifists. They congregated there to discuss local politics, strategize election campaigns, and speculate about the future of socialism. The man at the center of the gatherings was Arthur Carman, the shop's owner. Along with **Ormond Burton** and **Archibald Baxter**, he is New Zealand's best-known conscientious objector.

One of Carman's lifelong passions was sports, especially rugby and cricket, both of which he played as a young man before bad eyesight forced him off the field. As early as 1923 he began reporting on games for local newspapers, and by the 1930s he was recognized as one of the nation's top sports journalists. It was during that decade that he began publishing the annual *Rugby Almanack of New Zealand*, a compendium of rugby statistics that became the bible for fans for years to come. Carman soon began publishing an annual cricket almanac as well.

His other passion was socialism. For Carman that meant a commitment to pacifism as well, because like many socialists of his generation, he was convinced that wars were essentially struggles between capitalist nations vying for control of world markets. His pacifism was also fed by a strong Christian faith—he was a Methodist for the first half of his life but became a Quaker during the war years—and the conviction that participation in violence was forbidden to Christians. In 1936, he became a founding member of New Zealand's Christian Pacifist Society and an active member of the pacifist No More War Movement.

When Germany invaded Poland on 1 September 1939, England declared war. As a member of the British Commonwealth, New Zealand began drafting young men to serve in the military. Almost immediately, Carman denounced both the war and the call-up, and by October of the following year had cofounded the Conscientious Objectors Advisory Board to assist young men who objected to war for reasons of conscience. The New Zealand government tolerated his anti-war activity for a while, but in March 1942 he was arrested while speaking on a Wellington Street and charged with conducting an unlawful meeting. For good measure, he was also charged with subversion because of an anti-war pamphlet published by the Christian Pacifist Society. He was found guilty and sentenced to a year in jail, which the presiding judge offered to suspend if Carman would cease his public opposition to the war. Carman refused, and spent the next twelve months behind bars. After his release, the army called him up, almost certainly in retaliation for his pacifist stand, and the draft board refused to grant him a deferment as a conscientious objector. But his age and poor eyesight eventually got him a medical exemption.

Carman never lost either of his two passions. To the end of his life he was a fan and chronicler of New Zealand rugby as well as a committed and courageously outspoken pacifist.

29 November
Elias Chacour

29 November 1939—

Peace Needs Actors

Although Elias Chacour allows that he is a Palestinian-Arab-Christian citizen of Israel, he quickly points out that none of these labels, which can so easily polarize, ultimately defines him. He prefers to think of himself as merely a peasant from a Galilean village. Although ordained a priest in the Melkite tradition of the Catholic Church, he's even uneasy about embracing the label "Christian," preferring to say that he "was born a baby in the image and likeness of God, not more, and not less either."

After ordination and study at Jerusalem's Hebrew University—Chacour was the first Arab to earn a higher degree there—he was sent as a parish priest to the Galilean village of Ibillin. Once there, he was dismayed to discover that there were few educational opportunities for Arab youths, and he determined to change the situation. For six years he tried to obtain a building permit from the government to build a school. Blocked by red tape, he began construction without official permission. When work was halted by Israeli police, Chacour continued by night. Government officials again stopped the work. In desperation, Chacour appealed to the U.S. Secretary of State, who later made a personal appeal to the Israeli government. Chacour got the building permit he needed and finished his school. Within just a few years, its enrollment was nearly five thousand students coming from both Muslim and Christian families.

Chacour, an advocate of Christian nonviolence, has been saddened to see Israel burdened by eight wars and two intifadas during his lifetime. As director of the Mar Elias Educational Institutions in Ibillin and as archbishop of Akko, Haifa, Nazareth, and all Galilee, he travels throughout the Middle East and elsewhere, speaking about reconciliation between Jews—"who wanted and won physical independence"—and Arabs, who are "still struggling for independence, for liberation." He encourages active peacemaking wherever he speaks and urges his audiences to get involved at both local and national levels. There are plenty of scholars who write about peace, he says, and their work enhances our understanding of the nature of nonviolence. But peace work also "needs actors, people who are willing to get their hands dirty, to get up and do something."

Chacour's efforts on behalf of nonviolent conflict resolution in the Middle East have earned him several international awards and honorary doctorates. He continues to advocate for peaceful coexistence between Jews and Arabs, avowing that "you see God on your neighbor's face. The face of the other is the face of God." Understood in this way, no person can properly be thought of as an alien or an "other." All are related to one another through God.

30 November

Etty Hillesum

15 January 1914—30 November 1943

Radical Gratitude

Hitler's army rolled over Holland in May 1940, and within a few days the tiny nation was conquered. Nearly immediately, its Jewish population began to feel the bite of Nazi occupation. At first severe curfews were imposed on Jews. Then they were forbidden to use public transportation or to appear in public without the infamous yellow star sewn on their clothing. Inevitably, they were rounded up and sent to local camps for eventual transport to Auschwitz. The primary transit camp was a place called Westerbork, located in northeastern Holland. Tens of thousands, including Anne Frank and her family, passed through Westerbork on their way to their deaths.

One of them was a young university student named Etty Hillesum. In a handful of diaries and letters, Hillesum recorded a remarkable conversion during the final three years of her life. Born into a secular Jewish family, she discovered during the years of Nazi occupation a religious faith that not only sustained her spiritually but also allowed her to see the German soldiers who controlled her destiny as fellow humans rather than alien enemies. Although bewildered by their animosity, she felt no hatred for them.

Hillesum earned a law degree from the University of Amsterdam in the mid-1930s but was relatively indifferent to the law. Her real interest was literature, and she hoped to become an author herself. So she began studying Russian literature—her mother was Russian and had tutored her in the language—but was forced to put everything on hold once the Nazis invaded Holland. Instead of despairing, however, she became progressively aware that there was something deep within her—and in others, too, she believed—which she called "God." Six months after the invasion, she suddenly and to her surprise found herself on her knees, praying for the first time in her life.

This conversion allowed Hillesum to begin seeing the world as a gift. She had always had a keen sense of beauty, and wrote lovingly of sunlight against tree branches, flowers in bloom, the song of birds. But before her conversion, she had wanted to analyze the beauty. She wanted "to subject nature, everything, to myself." Afterwards, "the quite simple fact is that now I just let it happen to me," gratefully accepting it.

Opening herself to the beauty of creation, even after she was sent to Westerbork, awakened in Hillesum a profound sense of gratitude and love that prevented her from demonizing the Germans or from despairing over the hopeless plight of her and her fellow Jews. Hillesum's gratitude wasn't denial. She was perfectly aware that she would be transported to Auschwitz and would in all likelihood die there. But she refused to allow her own fate to poison her appreciation for life or her conviction that despite all of the horrors humans perpetrate against one another, life is a gift that calls for radical gratitude. No matter how things turned out, she wrote, "It all comes down to the same thing: life is beautiful. And I believe in God. And I want to be there right in the thick of what people call 'horror,' and still be able to say: life is beautiful."

1 December
Peter Rideman

1506–1 December 1556

No Need for Many Words

THE GREAT ANABAPTIST MOVEMENT of the sixteenth century birthed several Christian denominations that have since become known as "peace churches" because of their practice of nonviolence. One of them, the Hutterites, named after founder Jacob Hutter, posed a special threat to established church and state authorities. Modeling themselves on the communism of the early church, Hutterites lived in rural communities, held property in common, and embraced absolute pacifism. The only fealty they were willing to swear was to Christ—not to kings, princes, popes, or bishops.

Along with **Jacob Hutter** (who died in 1536), Peter Rideman—called "Tall Peter" because of his height—was the most important figure in the early days of the Hutterites. Born in Silesia and trained as a shoemaker, he became affiliated with the Anabaptist movement while still in his early twenties, eventually becoming a Hutterite three years before Hutter's death.

Rideman was a gifted and prolific writer of devotional tracts, hymns, sermons, letters, and books. Apparently, he was also a talented speaker, because he spent most of the final twenty-five years of his life as a Hutterite missionary throughout present-day Germany, the Czech Republic, Slovakia, and Austria. Shortly after his death, he was described by those who heard him preach as "rich in all divine secrets, and the gift of the spiritual language issued forth from him like a spring which gushes over. All souls who heard him gained peace." Much of his preaching was done during an intense period of persecution. Not surprisingly, Rideman was imprisoned many times, eventually spending a total of nine years behind bars.

In one of his books, *Confession of Faith*, written in 1540–41 during one of his periods of imprisonment, Rideman eloquently defends the absolute pacifism of the Hutterites. In the new kingdom inaugurated by Christ, he writes, "all worldly warfare hath an end. Therefore, a Christian neither wages war nor wields the worldly sword to practice vengeance." This is because the disciples of Christ are called "to show forth the nature of him who, though he could, indeed, have done so, repaid not evil with evil." Nor can Christians appeal to the instances of war or violence chronicled in the Old Testament as justifications for practicing violence themselves. David and the other Old Testament "saints" may have gone to war, but Christ himself forbids his followers to follow in their footsteps. To defend this conclusion, Rideman cites Matthew 5:38–39, in which Jesus tells his followers that the old eye-for-an-eye and tooth-for-a-tooth law has been replaced by the law of love. "There is therefore no need for many words, for it is clear that Christians can neither go to war nor practice vengeance."

2 December

Gamaliel

1ST CENTURY

The Virtue of Forbearance

Forbearance or patience isn't a virtue that many of us are eager to exercise, especially when we run across an individual or group with convictions that challenge our own. Humankind's history is sprinkled with ugly periods in which people were socially ostracized, legally persecuted, and even tortured and slain because they held beliefs that ran contrary to conventional ones. Sadly, similar chapters are still being written today. This makes it important to remember the example of Gamaliel.

We don't know much about this first-century Pharisee. He was called "the Elder" and was a member of the Sanhedrin, Jerusalem's judicial assembly charged with, among other tasks, keeping an eye out for heretics. He was a Pharisee at a time when the Sanhedrin was dominated by Sadducees, but was nonetheless revered for his piety and learning. After his death, it was said that "the honor of the Torah ceased and piety became extinct."

What we *do* know about Gamaliel is that he is an exemplar of forbearance in a world that too often allows impatience and intolerance to explode into violence. After Jesus' death and resurrection, his apostles went around Jerusalem jubilantly proclaiming the good news of his resurrection and performing many miracles in his name. The Sanhedrin, as anxious to silence them as it had been to get rid of their master, threw them into prison. But the doors of their cells mysteriously unlocked, and they walked out of the jail to resume their public preaching. The members of the Sanhedrin, bewildered and enraged, clamored for the apostles' execution. But the Acts of the Apostles tells us (5:35–39) that at this point Gamaliel stood up in the Sanhedrin and addressed its members. "Men of Israel," he said, "consider carefully what you intend to do to these man. Some time ago Theudas appeared, claimed to be somebody, and about four hundred men rallied to him. He was killed, all his followers were dispersed, and it all came to nothing. After him, Judas the Galilean appeared in the days of the census and led a band of people in revolt. He too was killed, and all his followers were scattered. Therefore, in the present case I advise you: Leave these men alone! Let them go! For if their purpose or activity is of human origin, it will fail. But if it is from God, you will not be able to stop these men; you will only find yourselves fighting against God." The Sanhedrin found Gamaliel's reasoning persuasive, and the apostles were released.

The Acts of the Apostles also tells us (22:3) that Gamaliel was the teacher of Saul of Tarsus, renamed Paul after his conversion. But Gamaliel's peaceful forbearance when it came to the followers of Jesus was so starkly different from Saul's intolerant persecution of them that it's hard to take the claim seriously. At best, if it's true, we can conclude that Saul was an inattentive student. Unfortunately, so were thousands of others down the centuries who have read and ignored Gamaliel's sage advice.

3 December
Aelred of Rievaulx

CA. 1110—1167

Deep Friendship

THE WORD FRIEND TENDS to be trivialized these days. Perhaps because of the influence of social media, we often claim as friends people who may be no more than passing acquaintances. Even worse, we may cultivate "friendships" with others solely for what we think we can get out of them. We become predators, and our "friends" are prey. Or, finally, we mistake what's merely an expedient alliance against a perceived common enemy for friendship.

These and similar perversions of friendship inevitably result in an erosion rather than a strengthening of bonds between people. They too often cultivate conflict and enmity, or at best indifference, between individuals as well as cultures. They are examples of shallow friendship masquerading as deep ones, and they breed violence rather than nurture peace.

Nine centuries ago, the Cistercian Aelred of Rievaulx was abbot of Rievaulx monastery, and for twenty years he was charged with making sure that some three hundred monks and lay brothers lived together harmoniously, genuinely seeing one another as friends. In a little book that he worked on for years, *On Spiritual Friendship*, he recorded his insights.

For Aelred, friendship is never only between two individuals. Because genuine friendship is an act of love, God, who *is* love, is always present as well. What this implies is that the love between friends participates in the same kind of love that God has for us. At one point, in fact, Aelred says that if it makes sense to say that God is love, it's also perfectly sound to say that God is friendship.

Because genuine friendship reflects something of God's love, a friend is someone whom we trust utterly. As Aelred says, a friend is "another self to whom you can speak on equal terms, to whom you can confess your failings, to whom you can make known your progress without blushing, one to whom you can entrust all the secrets of your heart." This trust endows friendship with four additional qualities: loyalty, discretion, patience, and right intention. Friends support one another, come what may; they understand that sometimes friends may be called upon to share grief and suffering; they honestly give and gratefully accept criticism from one another when criticism is due; and they cherish the friendship in and of itself, not because of any secondary and incidental benefits it might bring.

Aelred never intended his discussion of deep friendship to apply only to one-on-one relationships. For him, the love, trust, loyalty, patience, discretion, and right intention two friends feel for one another is a microcosm of rightly ordered communal and social arrangements. The good society is one in which all people are looked upon as friends, other selves rather than strangers, equals rather than subordinates, trustworthy rather than suspicious.

4 December
Benjamin Britten

22 November 1913—4 December 1976

Pacifist Composer

In May 1962, twenty years after Coventry Cathedral was destroyed by German bombers, composer Benjamin Britten debuted his *War Requiem* in the new, rebuilt one. A large-scale orchestral piece in six parts, the *Requiem's* subject, as Britten noted, was "War, and the pity of War." With breathtaking music and somber texts taken from the Latin Mass for the Dead and verse by Wilfred Owen, a poet killed in the final days of World War I, Britten's *Requiem* conveyed the tragic senselessness of warfare. After the performance, Britten said of his musical prayer for peace: "I hope it'll make people think a bit."

The *War Requiem* was not only one of Britten's finest musical compositions. It was also a statement of his lifelong pacifism. Even as a youth, Britten was profoundly committed to nonviolence. He refused to take part in his school's popular officer training program, and he wrote an essay (to which his teacher gave a failing mark) passionately condemning hunting. As a child prodigy—Britten started writing music at the age of five—he studied under the eminent composer Frank Bridge, also a pacifist. Entering the Royal College of Music on a scholarship when he was sixteen, Britten associated with other pacifists, and in 1937 composed a *Pacifist March* for the Peace Pledge Union, an anti-war organization founded in 1934 by **Dick Sheppard**.

By the late 1930s, Britten was recognized as one of the most promising composers in England. But his dismay at the coming war with Germany prompted him to sail for the United States in 1939. Along with tenor Peter Pears, his companion of nearly forty years, Britten stayed in America until 1942, until homesickness drove him back to England. Upon arriving, he immediately applied for conscientious objector status, writing in his application that "the whole of my life has been devoted to acts of creation (being by profession a composer) and I cannot take part in acts of destruction." Although initially rejected, his application was accepted on appeal, thereby rescuing him from the prison term his refusal to serve would have inevitably earned.

Britten spent the next two decades writing symphonies, concerti, choral works, and operas before finally tackling the large anti-war piece he'd had in mind for some time. His *War Requiem*, although first performed in a cathedral and invoking the Mass for the Dead, was a sober, nonromantic indictment of the killing and destruction that occurs in war. For Britten, there was no resurrection after death and no redemptive purpose behind the slaughter of battle. War is death without rebirth, and all lives lost in it criminally squandered. It is the message proclaimed by pacifists throughout the centuries. But few have done so with as much haunting and unforgettable beauty as Britten.

5 December
Clement of Alexandria

CA. 150—CA. 215

Soldiers of Peace

Most of Clement of Alexandria's life is hidden in the obscurity of time. What we do know about him is that he was born in Athens to heathen parents and from an early age thirsted for knowledge of God. He traveled a great deal in his youth in southern Italy and Palestine, seeking out teachers of wisdom. The Egyptian city of Alexandria became his new home when he met Pantaenus, head of the city's Christian catechetical school. Under his influence, Clement was baptized in his thirtieth year. Within a decade he was ordained and teaching alongside Pantaenus. But the wave of Christian persecution launched by the Emperor Septimius Severus closed the catechetical school in 203, and Clement fled to Cappadocia, where he died some ten years later.

Clement was a deeply learned man, well versed in the various schools of Greek philosophy. Unlike some of the early church fathers, he believed that the best of heathen thought was compatible with the gospel. In much of his writing, Clement sought to show that there's no irreconcilable difference between Athens and Jerusalem.

When it came to war and violence, however, Clement was firmly convinced that the gospel of Christ parted company with both Greek philosophy and Roman culture. The Roman Empire was built on the strength of the sword, and the trumpets of war calling men to battle sounded all too frequently. But the Christian, Clement insisted, heeds a different call. "If a loud trumpet summons soldiers to war, shall not Christ with a strain of peace issued to the ends of the earth gather up his soldiers of peace? By his own blood and by his word he has assembled an army which sheds no blood in order to give them the Kingdom of Heaven. The trumpet of Christ is his Gospel. He has sounded it and we have heard it. Let us then put on the armor of peace."

Clement was all too aware that Christians who answered Christ's trumpet call by refusing to serve in the emperor's armies faced swift and certain punishment. But he reminded them that their baptismal vows trained them "in peace, not in war," enlisted them in God's army rather than Caesar's, and bound them to a heavenly set of statutes that superseded earthly ones. "If you enroll as one of God's people, heaven is your country and God your lawgiver. And what are His laws? You shall not kill; you shall love your neighbor as yourself. To him that strikes you on the one cheek, turn to him the other also." Obedience to these divine laws, even if it means disobeying human ones, is the real duty of a soldier of peace.

6 December
Ryan White

6 December 1971—8 April 1990

AIDS Activist

As he took his seat to testify before the ten-member President's Commission on AIDS, all eyes were riveted on the small sixteen-year-old boy with brown spiked hair. "My name is Ryan White," he said. "I am sixteen years old. I have hemophilia, and I have AIDS."

As a hemophiliac, Ryan had received numerous transfusions throughout his childhood. Somewhere along the way, he picked up the HIV virus. He was diagnosed with full-blown AIDS in December 1984 after being hospitalized for acute pneumonia. Doctors told him and his family that he had less than six months. "I spent Christmas and the next thirty days in the hospital," he told the President's Commission on AIDS. "I came face to face with death at 13 years old."

Little was known about the transmission of AIDS in the mid-1980s. When Ryan surprised his doctors by recovering enough to resume school in his hometown of Kokomo, Indiana, he became the victim of fear and ignorance. Initially forbidden by school authorities to return on the grounds that he was a risk to students and teachers, the decision was eventually overturned by the Indiana Department of Education. But even then school officials insisted that Ryan eat with disposable utensils, use a separate bathroom, and refrain from taking gym classes. Teachers and students avoided physical contact with him, and he soon became the victim of vicious bullying. After a bullet was fired through a window of his home, Ryan and his family relocated to Cicero, Indiana. He lived his last three years there in relative peace.

President Ronald Reagan had largely ignored the AIDS epidemic during most of his two terms. But he finally agreed to the creation of a presidential commission on AIDS in 1987, and Ryan White, whose struggle against discrimination had become national news, was one of the first people to testify before it. He became a national spokesperson for AIDS education, appearing many times on television to urge the importance of learning the facts about the disease so that patients suffering from it weren't treated like pariahs. Ryan knew that it was a hard job chiseling away at intolerance born of panic. As he told the presidential commission, he learned that "listening to medical facts was not enough. People wanted one hundred percent guarantees." But he persevered, even after his health began to break for the final time, and by the time he died, one month short of his high school graduation, he'd helped move the country toward a more compassionate treatment of AIDS patients. As the commission's chair James Watson said, "Semen, blood, and ignorance surround this epidemic." Before Ryan White's crusade, "we were in this last category."

7 December
Ivo Markovic

1952—

Soul Bridges

BY THE TIME THE three-year Bosnian War ended in 1995, more than two million people were displaced, one hundred thousand soldiers and civilians dead, and thousands of women raped. The fighting had been fierce because it was fueled by white-hot ethnic and religious hatred. Catholic Croats fought with Orthodox Serbs and Muslim Bosniaks. It was a horrible time of mass murder, torture, ethnic cleansing, and destruction of property.

Franciscan priest Ivo Markovic, a Croat who had been a priest and professor since 1976, worked hard to prevent atrocities during the war and to build bridges afterwards. In both enterprises he was fearless, empowered by his religious conviction that the price of war is always too great to be paid. He personally knew the cost well: his father and several relatives perished during the fighting.

Expelled in 1992 from his Sarajevo seminary by advancing Serbs, Markovic relocated to Zagreb, which remained his base of operation throughout the war. He made frequent trips to the front lines to offer aid to prisoners and lead refugees to safety. He also served as a guide for international journalists wishing to travel to the war zones. Markovic believed that one of the best ways to minimize atrocities was to ensure the steady presence of journalistic witnesses. He also spoke across Europe and North America to expose audiences to the horrors of the Bosnian War and to plead with them for aid for the war's victims. And he risked his life more than once to cross battle lines in order to broker ceasefires between opposing armies.

After hostilities ceased, Markovic knew that many people from each of the three ethnic and religious groups still felt bitter animosity for one another. So in 1996 he organized an interfaith choir named Pontanima, from the Latin words for bridge and soul, to begin bringing them together. Pontanima includes performers from all of the religious groups in the Balkans, and its repertoire includes songs from the Christian, Muslim, and Jewish traditions. By inviting the different religious groups to share their songs, Pontanima aims to "enter into the heart of what is different in order to receive these differences in the heart of one's own being, to feed the soul with the highest spirituality of different people."

Pontanima is part of a larger ministry called Face-to-Face, which hosts workshops, retreats, and interfaith religious services, all aimed at healing the wounds inflicted by the Bosnian War. Markovic says that during the war, he "simply stopped acknowledging the boundaries that divide people and create phobias." Since then, he has "felt called to cross those boundaries and to invite others to do so." The music and shared worship offered by Face-to-Face are two of the bridges by which he hopes to link the souls of a divided people together again.

8 December
Elihu Burritt

8 December 1810—6 March 1879

Communicating Peace

Born in New Britain, the same small Connecticut town in which he would die, Elihu Burritt was trained in blacksmithing—the trade of his father—and occasionally resorted to it as an adult when money was tight. But his heart was in books, ideas, and the vision of a world free from violence and injustice. He was largely a self-taught man. Although he had very little formal schooling, he read voraciously and early on displayed an astounding talent for picking up languages. As an adult he was fluent in most European languages as well as Hebrew, Chaldaic, and Syriac. Among his contemporaries, he was known as the "learned blacksmith."

Burritt became convinced at an early age of the power of words and public discourse. He believed that much of the hostility between individuals and between nations was fueled by a breakdown in dialogue, and that injustice was prevalent because otherwise decent people simply didn't know how badly its victims suffered. Information and conversation, he concluded, were the keys to overcoming violence and inhumanity.

Beginning in his mid-thirties, Burritt became a vocal catalyst of the conversation he hoped would ameliorate the world's ills. In 1846 he launched a newspaper, the *Christian Citizen*, that explored political and religious issues. After a visit to Ireland at the height of the potato famine, he wrote a pamphlet, *Four Months in Skibbereen*, in which he described the famine's horrific impact on the people of Ireland and pled for Americans to welcome immigrant Irish with open arms. The following year, in 1848, Burritt organized the first international Friends of Peace Congress. Representatives from a number of countries met together in Europe to talk with one another about strategies for world peace and adopted resolutions calling for arms limitations and banning foreign loans for war purposes. Five more peace congresses would follow.

Burritt was also an eloquent champion of the abolition of American slavery, advocating peaceable emancipation by way of federal compensation to slave owners. Other abolitionists objected to his plan, arguing that any government-backed purchase of slavery, even if the purpose was to free slaves, was a tacit acknowledgment that the slave owner had a right to his human property. But for Burritt, the objection was moot in light of the suffering endured by slaves.

In later life, Burritt campaigned for an international penny postage standard, believing that cheap postal rates would encourage communication between people in different countries and build characters devoted to peace and justice in everyone involved. "Forming characters!" he wrote. "And in that momentous fact lies the peril and responsibility of our existence."

9 December
Dalton Trumbo

9 December 1905—10 September 1976

Halleluja Dirge

WHEN THE UNITED STATES entered World War I in 1917, the entertainer George M. Cohan wrote a patriotic song, "Over There," that became an instant popular hit. Its jingoistic lyrics, which included "Johnny get your gun, get your gun, get your gun... Pack your little kit, show your grit, do your bit," aimed at encouraging young men to enlist in a war that was the most brutal the world had seen up to that time.

In 1939, as war clouds gathered once more over Europe, screenwriter and novelist Dalton Trumbo published a novel whose title, *Johnny Got His Gun,* intentionally evokes Cohan's song. But Trumbo pushed beyond the song's sloganeering glorification of war to offer in its place one of the most chilling descriptions ever written of war's havoc.

The novel's protagonist is Joe Bonham, a Canadian soldier in World War I whose face and all four limbs have been torn off by an artillery explosion. Bonham survives and resides in an institution for maimed veterans. His mind is clear, but it's locked inside a maimed torso. Unable for much of the novel to communicate with the outside world, Bonham is forced to imaginatively relive over and over the horrors of war that ripped apart his life. Finally able to work out a means of communication by lifting and lowering his head to spell out words, Bonham tells his caregivers that he wants to be allowed to die. But short of that, he asks to be put in a glass case and carted all over the country as a warning to all those who think war a noble and glorious thing. He wishes especially to be displayed to the pious folks who believe that God sanctions warfare. "Take me into your churches," he signs, "your great towering cathedrals that have to be rebuilt every fifty years because they are destroyed by war. Carry me in my glass box down the aisles where kings and priests and brides and children at their confirmation have gone so many times . . . Chorus out the hallelujas I can't sing. Bring them out loud and strong for me your hallelujas all of them for me because I know the truth and you don't you fools. You fools you fools you fools . . ." But neither of Joe's wishes, to die or to be used as an anti-war warning, is granted. He remains imprisoned in his body and is thought of as a war hero.

Trumbo would go on after the war to be blacklisted and jailed for defying Joe McCarthy's House Un-American Activities Committee. Resettling in Mexico after his release, he was forced to write many of his Hollywood screenplays under a pseudonym. He was a master of his craft, eventually winning two Academy Awards for movie scripts. But his masterpiece remains *Johnny Got His Gun,* one of the most shocking anti-war novels ever published.

10 December
Thomas Merton

31 January 1915—10 December 1968

Proclaming the Kingdom

Thomas Merton broke any number of molds. After a hell-raising youth, he renounced the pleasures of the flesh for the ascetic life of a cloistered Trappist monk. Although absolutely secluded from the world behind the walls of Gethsemane Monastery in Kentucky's knob country, he wrote book after book that touched the lives of tens of thousands of people throughout the world. A contemplative by temperament and training, he also championed such social causes as nuclear disarmament in the 1960s. A man thoroughly grounded in the Western Christian tradition, he was fascinated by Buddhism.

Merton broke the mold in one other way as well: he challenged the traditional Christian endorsement of the just war doctrine by arguing that no act of violence, however justifiable it may seem at the time, is compatible with the life and teachings of Jesus. Violence, he argued, is always sectarian. It's always a struggle of *us* against *them*. Its basis is division. But Christian nonviolence "is not built on a presupposed division, but on the basic unity of man. It is not out for the conversion of the wicked to the ideas of the good, but for the healing and reconciliation" of humans with one another and with God.

For Merton, Christian nonviolence is ultimately founded on Jesus' message that the kingdom of Heaven is for everyone, not just for an exclusive few (part of what he means by the "basic unity of man"), as well as Jesus' recommendation in the Sermon on the Mount and elsewhere of the virtue of meekness. The inclusiveness of the kingdom creates a radical equality between humans that leaves no room for adversarial divisiveness. The virtue of meekness is recognition that the ways in which worldly evil should be resisted should be determined by God, not humans.

Too frequently, Christian meekness is interpreted as either a passive submission to unjust social oppression or a psychological cowardice that inhibits standing up for oneself and others. But Merton points out that this is a misunderstanding. Christian meekness is neither submission nor cowardice, but instead a courage practiced by "the oppressed who have no human weapons to rely on and who nevertheless are true to the commandments of Yahweh." Nonviolent meekness isn't passive acceptance of the world's evil, but rather a profound awareness that it ought not to be fought with conventional human weapons that kill and maim but with spiritual ones that heal and transform. This is what it means to "remain true to the commandments" of God: to resist evil in such a way that the mode of resistance is a proclamation of the kingdom of God, a "formal profession of faith in the Gospel message that the Kingdom has been established." Thus Christian meekness and Christian hope are, as Merton says, inseparable.

11 December
Martyrs of El Mozote

11 December 1981

Mama, They're Killing Me!

CIVIL WAR RIPPED EL Salvador apart for nearly fifteen years. Atrocities were committed by both sides in the conflict, the military-led government and the coalition of leftist militias known as the Farabundo Marti National Liberation Front (FMLN). The worst atrocity of all wiped out the village of El Mozote in December 1981. It was perpetrated by the Atlacatl Battalion, an El Salvadoran counterinsurgency unit on a search-and-destroy mission against FMLN guerrillas. The battalion's officers had been trained by the U.S. army at the infamous School of the Americas.

The Atlacatl Battalion rolled into El Mozote, a settlement high in the El Salvadoran mountains, on 10 December. They forced the village's nearly one thousand inhabitants into the square, interrogated them about local guerrillas, and then ordered them into their homes. When the troops left at day's end, everyone in El Mozote breathed a sigh of relief. The danger, they believed, was past.

But they were wrong. At dawn the next day, the Atlacatl Battalion returned. This time they separated the village's men from its women and children. Marched into the surrounding forest, the men were tortured and executed. Then the troops returned for the women and young girls, some of them no more than ten years old, and systematically raped and murdered them all. Finally, the children, screaming in terror for their mothers, were machine-gunned. The corpses were piled up and burned, and the village's now empty houses and church were torched.

Only one person survived the El Mozote massacre, thirty-eight-year-old Rufina Amaya. It's because of her testimony that we know the details of what happened. She managed to escape at the last minute, as she was standing in line to be shot, and hid in a tree just on the edge of the village. Afraid to flee lest the soldiers spot her, Amaya saw or heard most of what happened that day, including the murder of her husband, son, and three young daughters. As her nine-year-old son Cristino was taken away, she heard him scream, "Mama, they're killing me! They've killed my sister! They're going to kill me!"

The fire-scorched bones of the El Mozote victims lay in the village's ruins for weeks afterward. The El Salvadoran government denied that the massacre had taken place, and the Reagan administration, while conceding that something had happened, downplayed the number of victims. But FMLN members smuggled American reporters from the *New York Times* and the *Washington Post* to the scene of the massacre. The story hit the wire services in late January 1982, and the world was reminded yet again of the nightmare of armed violence. The martyrs of El Mozote, innocent victims all, testify to the brutality and waste of war.

12 December
Hafsat Abiola

1974—

KINDness

An entire generation of war and corruption followed the 1960 end of British colonial rule in Nigeria. Traditional tribal tensions erupted into civil war. Military leaders replaced one another, sometimes with breathless swiftness, in a series of *coups d'état*. When free elections were finally held in 1993, the president-elect, Chief Moshood Abiola, was overthrown by yet another military coup. Tossed into prison, he died there in 1998. His wife, Alhaja Kudirat Abiola, died in a political demonstration two years earlier.

Their daughter, Hafsat Abiola, had been sent to the United States, partly for her education but also to get her out of harm's way. She had just graduated from Harvard when her mother was killed.

One year later, Abiola launched the Kudirat Initiative for Democracy (KIND). Named after her mother, KIND was founded to oppose the military rule of Nigeria. When democracy was finally restored to the nation in 1999, KIND focused its efforts on finding ways to encourage democratic sensibilities in a country that had been under the dominion of one military strongman after another for forty years.

Under Abiola's leadership, KIND concentrated its resources on Nigerian women. The reasoning behind this decision was simple but insightful: traditionally disempowered as they were, Nigerian women were much less likely to be tainted by, as KIND's website says, the "dysfunctional political leadership culture that undermined Nigeria" for so many years. Additionally, since they and their children were the ones who suffered most from the years of oppression, they had the most legitimate stake in social and political reform. "Consequently, they would be the most open to learning new ways of leading and, by participating in the public domain, will be able to influence a change in the culture to one that can deliver development dividends to Nigerians."

Abiola believes that increased democratization will help heal Nigeria's national wounds and historical clan tensions and bring peace to the region. This is because democracy invites participation from everyone, utilizing talents and skills that can benefit the commonweal but that are either unnoticed and untapped or actively suppressed in totalitarian or corrupt regimes. "Peace comes," she says, "from being able to contribute the best that we have, and all that we are, toward creating a world that supports anyone. But it is *also* securing the space for others to contribute the best that *they* have and all that *they* are." Her campaign of KINDness aims to secure that space.

13 December
Archibald Baxter

13 December 1881—10 August 1970

War Is the Devil's Philosophy

New Zealand farmer Archibald Cox was thirty-two when World War I erupted. As a lifelong Christian pacifist who believed that "all war is wrong, futile, and destructive alike to victor and vanquished," he immediately declared himself a conscientious objector. But when military conscription was introduced in the war's second year, Cox was arrested, held in a military prison in Wellington for a few months, and then shipped to France and put on the front line.

Once there, Cox began a program of passive resistance. He refused to wear a military uniform or carry a weapon. His commanding officer, determined to break his spirit, punished him savagely. Cox was routinely beaten, starved, and verbally abused by fellow soldiers egged on by officers. When this didn't work, "Field Punishment #1," commonly called the "crucifixion," was repeatedly inflicted. A soldier sentenced to this ordeal was tied to a stake, hands bound behind back and rope circling ankles, knees, and chest, for up to four hours. Cox endured the crucifixion again and again, in all kinds of weather, during his time at the front. But still he refused to play the part of a soldier.

Finally, Cox's commander ordered him to one of the most heavily shelled sectors of the front. While in the trenches there, Cox was again beaten and denied rations on a regular basis. The physical and mental abuse he endured eventually landed him in a military hospital in April 1918, where his refusal to serve was discredited with a diagnosis of "mental weakness and confusional insanity." Transferred to a mental hospital in England, Cox was finally shipped back home to New Zealand when the armistice was signed. He'd persevered in his pacifism to the very end; he'd beaten the military machine.

In 1939, as another world war was about to explode, Cox published a memoir of his ordeal titled *We Will Not Cease*. In it, he asserted that war was "the devil's philosophy" because it claims to protect life by destroying it. "The military machine is turned against that communal life which is the seed-bed of future generations. The only apparent justification that war ever had was that by destroying some lives it might clumsily preserve others. But we make war chiefly on civilians and respect for human life seems to have become a thing of the past."

Most of the first run of Cox's book, which was published by a London firm, was destroyed in the Blitz (the bombing of the United Kingdom by Germany). But it's been reprinted several times since, and stands as a great testament to the spirit of nonviolent resistance to war.

14 December
Andrei Sakharov

21 May 1921—14 December 1989

Bridging Divisions

For the first twenty years of his adult life, Andrei Sakharov was a rising star in the Soviet Union. A brilliant young nuclear physicist, he worked on the research teams that developed atomic and hydrogen bombs for the Soviet arsenal. By the time he was forty, he'd been elected to the prestigious Soviet Academy of Sciences, given three Hero of Socialist Labor awards, and received the Lenin Prize, the Stalin Prize, and the Order of Lenin.

But in the mid-1960s, Sakharov grew disturbed by the moral implications of his work. He became convinced that "the division of mankind"—especially the tension between the Soviet East and the capitalist West—"threatens it with destruction." So he began to urge Soviet authorities to halt the proliferation of nuclear weapons, to ban atmospheric testing, and to negotiate with the United States to halt the arms race.

In 1967, Sakharov sent a document to the Soviet authorities outlining his reasons for believing that nuclear weapons are morally unjustifiable. When it was ignored, he began circulating underground copies of the document throughout the Soviet Union. Eventually one of them made its way to the West and was published in 1968 by the *New York Times*.

Sakharov's essay, "Reflections on Progress, Peaceful Coexistence, and Intellectual Freedom," pled for a "convergence, a rapproachement of the socialist and capitalist systems" that would reduce the danger of "thermonuclear extinction, ecological catastrophe, famine, alienation, and dogmatic distortion of our conception of reality." But such a convergence is impossible, argued Sakharov, without open dialogue and the unafraid expression of ideas. Intellectual freedom is a necessary condition both for ending the arms race and the flourishing of society. It is "the only guarantee against an infection of people by mass myths" that encourage the growth of "bloody dictatorship."

Immediately after the publication of Sakharov's daring essay, Soviet authorities removed him from all military-related research and began systematically hounding him. He was placed under constant surveillance by the secret police and denied the right to travel outside the country. When he was awarded the Nobel Peace Prize in 1975, his wife Yelena Bonner traveled to Oslo to accept it for him. He also found it increasingly difficult to get official permission to publish even scientific essays. The final straw for the government was his public protest of the Soviet invasion of Afghanistan in 1979. Despite his failing health, enraged authorities banished Sakharov to the city of Gorky, where he was kept under close KGB supervision and lived in near isolation. His exile was finally ended in 1986 by Mikhail Gorbachev. Until his death three years later, Sakharov traveled extensively in both the Soviet Union and abroad, speaking everywhere he went about the need for nuclear disarmament, the inviolability of human rights, and the necessity of intellectual freedom. Up to the very end, he labored to bridge divisions.

15 December
Ludovic Lazarus Zamenhof

15 December 1859—14 April 1917

Filologiisto por paco[2]

As a Jew born in the Russian Empire city of Bialystok (in present-day northeastern Poland), L. L. Zamenhof grew up hearing four different languages—Yiddish, Polish, German, and Russian—spoken by four different ethnic groups. Tensions between the groups ran high, and outbreaks of violence occurred regularly. While still a youngster, Zamenhof became convinced that a primary cause of the hostility was the lack of a common language. Language barriers encouraged insularity and xenophobia. Break them down, and crosscultural communication and peace became real possibilities. The way to do that was through the use of a universal language. Zamenhof decided to invent one.

While still in primary and secondary school, Zamenhof learned as many languages as he could, mastering or achieving competence in Russian, Yiddish, Polish, French, Latin, Greek, Hebrew, English, Italian, Spanish, German, and Lithuanian. By the time he was nineteen, he'd worked out the basics of his universal language. It took another decade of labor to refine the details. In the meantime, Zamenhof trained as an ophthalmologist, opened a medical practice, and got married. But in 1887, he finally published a primer titled *Lingvo internacia* under the pseudonym "Doctor Esperanto." "Esperanto" means "someone who hopes," and it became the official name of Zamenhof's new language, reflecting its inventor's hope that it would encourage reconciliation between the peoples of the world.

Even though Esperanto is influenced by a number of languages, Zamenhof made sure that it privileges no single one of them and thus remains culturally neutral. Moreover, he labored to make Esperanto's grammar and vocabulary relatively easy to learn and accessible to everyone. His ultimate goal was what he called *homaranismo*: a universal linguistic bond that encourages crosscultural communication and friendship without threatening cultural identities.

Zamenhof never claimed that Esperanto was *the* solution to conflict and violence. In a 1906 address to the Second World Congress of Esperanto, he said, "We are not so naive as some think of us; we do not believe that a neutral base will turn men into angels. But we believe that communication and knowledge based upon a natural tool will prevent at least the great quantity of brutality and crimes which happen not because of ill will, but simply because of lack of knowledge." Four years later, he was nominated for the Nobel Peace Prize.

Today, Esperanto is the most widely spoken constructed language, with two million fluent speakers and another ten million who have some level of competency. Over twenty-five thousand Esperanto books are in print, and there are scores of regional and international Esperanto newspapers, magazines, and societies. Recent popes include Esperanto in their multilingual *Ubi et orbi* annual addresses. Zamenhof's dream of crossing linguistic borders to form bonds of friendship lives on.

2. Philologist for Peace, in Esperanto.

16 December

Kabir

CA. 1440—1518

The Same Clay

MOHANDAS GANDHI CLAIMED THAT much of what he knew about nonviolence, or *ahimsa*, he learned from the fifth-century poet and wisdom teacher Kabir. In both his life and his teachings, Kabir tried to show that the squabbles and divisions that separate humans into conflicting factions are based on illusion. There are no essential divisions, because all humans are connected with God and one another. Reality and truth are one.

Legends about Kabir's life are plentiful, making it difficult to separate fact from fiction. One of the most common stories told about him has it that he was born in Benares, India, to a Hindu mother who abandoned him at birth, but that he was discovered and raised by a Muslim family. We're also told that he persuaded—some say tricked—a Hindu Brahmin to accept him as a disciple, despite the fact that he was a Muslim. Both of these tales symbolize Kabir's refusal to take sides in the sectarian strife between Indian Hindus and Muslims. In his life, as in his poetry, he celebrated them both.

In his poems—called *banis*, or "utterances," because Kabir never learned how to write—he taught that the goal of humans is to awaken to our intimate connectedness to God; God is a "moon" or "sun" inside the soul that illuminates us even if we're only dimly aware of its presence. The crucial task is to make contact with God, not through sectarian forms of worship or theologies, but through *bhakti*, or personal devotion. Once this is done, the presence of God in all of creation is recognized, and the devotee overflows with such love that *ahimsa* becomes his or her default position. In the absence of this love, said Kabir, religion is heresy and such spiritual disciplines as yoga, fasting, and almsgiving are empty.

Ahimsa born of awareness of the essential unity of creation is the key to ending sectarian intolerance and violence. Muslims, Hindus, and Buddhists, all of whom Kabir encountered in Benares as well as in his travels, were "pots shaped from the same clay." In his own spiritual devotions, he happily incorporated elements from all three traditions without preference or prejudice. His rejection of sectarian-bound forms of piety earned him the enmity of some. At one point in his life, he was especially persecuted by devout Hindus, and only the intervention of the Muslim emperor saved his life. But his message of unity and love spread during his own lifetime and afterwards. His *bhakti* path influenced both the Sikhs and the Kabir Panth, a religious family of ten million members who come from the Hindu, Muslim, Buddhist, and Sikh backgrounds. Both revere Kabir as a spiritual mentor.

17 December
Craig Kielburger

17 December 1982—

Children Helping Children

Part of the mission statement of Free the Children, the advocacy and development group founded by Craig Kielburger in 1995, is a declaration of "shameless idealism." Idealism is a virtue that's often in short supply among adults. So who better than unjaded youngsters to launch an organization that seeks to improve the quality of life for children across the world? That's exactly what Free the Children is all about: idealistic children helping children in need.

Kielburger, a native of Canada, was twelve years old when he read about the murder of **Iqbal Masih**, the Pakistani boy who launched a crusade in his country against child labor. Inspired by Masih's example, Kielburger began collecting information about child exploitation around the world and enlisted some kids at his school to help him publicize the problem. Soon the group graduated from passing information to collecting relief funds, and Free the Children was born. The organization gained widespread recognition when Kielburger traveled to South Asia to investigate child labor firsthand. While there, he publicly challenged Canadian Prime Minister Jean Chrétien, who was also visiting the region as a member of a trade delegation, to speak out against child labor. Four years later, Kielburger published *Free the Children,* an account of how he came to found his organization.

In its early years, Free the Children focused primarily on exposing and eliminating child labor. While still involved in that campaign, the organization has broadened its scope to stimulate education and development in the developing world. It has built nearly seven hundred schools, and its Adopt a Village program helps rural communities in such countries as Haiti, Kenya, and Ecuador to build local economies, clean water facilities, schools, and health care.

Kielburger has been a frequent critic of the global imbalance of wealth that privileges the developed world at the expense of poorer nations. Of the one billion inhabitants of the planet who live in abject poverty on less than $1 per day, approximately 70 percent are women and children. These people could be fed, and the children educated, for only a few billion dollars per year—a pittance when one stops to consider that each year the world spends $160 billion on beer, $400 billion on cigarettes, and $40 billion playing golf.

Some people contend that children ought not to become activists because they're too young to cope with the world's darker side. Kielburger disagrees. "If you expose young people to the issues of poverty, war, violence and child labor, it's not as if you're taking away their childhood. Young people see it in the world. We know there are social injustices. Free the Children is trying to help young people not just close their eyes and feel powerless, but to realize that they do have a positive role to play through very simple, very concrete, actions." Shameless idealism.

18 December
Junsei Terasawa

1950—

Holy Peace Fool

IN THE CHRISTIAN TRADITION, there is a class of saints known as "holy fools," people so intoxicated with God and so intent upon doing God's work that they appear outlandish and even crazy to the rest of the world. Junsei Terasawa qualifies as a Buddhist holy fool. His entire adult life has been a worldwide pilgrimage on behalf of peace. He travels without money, banging on a prayer drum and chanting Buddhist sutras, building peace pagodas, leading long and sometimes dangerous peace marches, and everywhere urging both individuals and governments to reconcile. By the standards of the world, his lifestyle and message are crazy.

Born in Japan, Terasawa attached himself while still a young man to a Buddhist master who at one time had studied nonviolence in **Mohandas Gandhi**'s Indian ashram. Terasawa lived for six years in the cities of Hiroshima and Nagasaki, sites of the atomic blasts, and then six more years in India, practicing meditation, studying Gandhian nonviolence, and ministering to the untouchables. He was in Bombay when India tested its first atomic weapon in 1975. After he participated in public opposition to the test, Terasawa was kicked out of the country.

Since then, he has roamed around the world with his message of peace. He has built peace pagodas, public memorials of the need for disarmament and reconciliation, in England and France. In 1983, in response to NATO's decision to deploy intermediate nuclear weapons in Europe, he organized an international peace march that began from points within the East and West and culminated at the Berlin Wall. All the participants from the Eastern bloc eventually dropped out, leaving Terasawa to march alone through Poland and East Germany.

In 1998, Terasawa organized another peace march. This one originated from Leo Tolstoy's estate in Russia and ended at Lumbini, the Buddha's birthplace in present-day Nepal. The Eurasian pilgrimage, which took months to complete, was intended as a peace witness to open the hearts of the adversaries in the Chechen conflict.

Terasawa was on the road again in 2002, this time on a three-month trek from Pakistan to India in order to calm dangerously tense relations between the two nations. Both India and Pakistan had amassed hundreds of thousands of soldiers at their borders in preparation for an armed showdown that, if it had occurred, could well have turned nuclear. Within a week of the completion of Terasawa's peace pilgrimage, both nations stood down.

In recent years, Terasawa has witnessed for peace in the Middle East, the United States, Canada, and again in India and Nepal. Everywhere he goes, this holy fool's message of peace inspires a change of heart from some but provokes laughter and even derision from many more. So why does he persevere? His answer is simple. "What will be the future of mankind if we fail to address this issue? No more empty principles! No more empty declarations on paper! Military and violence will never give the answer. What we need today is a proof of the victory of nonviolence and truth."

19 December
James Peck

19 December 1914—12 July 1993

Non-Utopian Peacemaker

James Peck, Harvard dropout, World War II conscientious objector, and early civil rights activist, was refused treatment by a Birmingham, Alabama, hospital in 1961. At the time, Peck was a participant in the famous Freedom Ride, a public protest in which blacks and whites rode together on interstate buses into the South to challenge segregation laws. When the bus carrying Peck pulled into Birmingham, Alabama, he was savagely beaten by furious Klansmen. Rushed by fellow Freedom Riders to the hospital, administrators refused to admit him when they discovered who he was and why he'd been attacked, despite the fact that he was bleeding badly from a head wound that eventually required over fifty stitches.

Peck was accustomed to paying a high price for his principles. During World War II his commitment to nonviolence earned him two years in a Connecticut prison. While incarcerated, he volunteered to serve as a human guinea pig in a series of medical experiments aimed at finding a cure for jaundice. Although his participation in the experiments permanently damaged his liver, Peck never regretted it. He believed he was morally obliged, even while in prison, to serve humanity as best he could—including that portion of humanity that persecuted him for his pacifism.

In 1946, Peck was one of a handful of whites who joined the Congress of Racial Equality (CORE), a civil rights organization founded four years earlier. A few months later, he took part in the CORE-sponsored Journey of Reconciliation, a precursor of the 1961 Freedom Ride, and was arrested by Southern authorities for violating segregation laws. He was the only person, white or black, to participate in both of the bus protests. Peck served as an active member of CORE for nearly twenty years until he and other whites were purged in the mid-1960s when the organization's leadership embraced the ideal of black nationalism.

During the Vietnam years, Peck became a prominent voice in the anti-war movement, working closely with the War Resisters League. After the war, he allied himself with Amnesty International to draw attention to violations of civil liberties across the globe. His activism came to a close in 1983 when a stroke paralyzed one side of his body.

Peck's lifelong commitment to nonviolent direct action against war, racism, and injustice was based on what he saw as rugged realism. He was idealistic to the extent that he envisioned a future society in which violence and oppression were reduced. But he also knew that the distance between his ideals and the actual state of affairs in the world precluded a naïve optimism. "My life has been nonviolent direct action to try to make this a better world," he once said. "It is my philosophy that the struggle has to be a non-ending one, because I am not one of those idealists who envision a utopia."

20 December
Sidney Lewis Gulick

10 April 1860—20 December 1945

Blue-Eyed Ambassadors of Peace

THE HATRED AND MISTRUST of others that breeds violence is learned, not innate. It's often difficult for adults to break free of prejudices that are habits of a lifetime. But children are a different matter. They're teachable because their natural openness to others hasn't yet been closed down by religious, ethnic, and political divisions. They're innocent, and as such are each generation's greatest resource for peace.

The Congregationalist missionary Sidney Lewis Gulick knew as much. Gulick lived in Japan for twenty-five years, preaching, writing, and teaching. His time in Japan gave him immense respect and affection for its culture. He went there to convert Japanese to Christianity. Along the way, he fell in love with them.

On his return to the United States in 1913, Gulick was utterly shocked by the anti-Japanese sentiment he encountered. California, especially, was a hotbed of discrimination against Asians. Gulick immediately began campaigning against anti-immigration legislation being proposed there as well as in other states. Just as he earlier had served as a missionary to Japan, he now saw himself as a missionary of peace and reconciliation to his own countrymen.

In 1924, President Calvin Coolidge signed legislation that became known as the Immigration Act. The new law set restrictive caps on the numbers of new immigrants allowed in the United States and expressly prohibited the immigration of Middle Easterners and Asians. Gulick was horrified by the enthusiasm with which the public greeted the new law. Recognizing that there was little he could do to influence adult attitudes, he launched a campaign to reach children.

Under the auspices of the Committee on World Friendship Among Children, an organization he cofounded, Gulick hit upon the idea of encouraging dialogue and understanding between Japan and the United States by encouraging the children of each nation to exchange dolls. The exchange was scheduled to coincide with the annual Japanese doll festival in March 1927. Schoolchildren and their parents from around the country gathered nearly thirteen thousand blue-eyed dolls as ambassadors of good will to Japan. Each doll had a name, passport, and handwritten letter from the doll's sender. Japanese children in return sent nearly sixty dolls to the United States, each with its own trunk of clothes and tea ceremony dishes.

Kids in both nations were enthusiastic about the project, and the dolls in many cases sparked pen-pal correspondence between Japanese and American girls and boys that lasted for years. The dolls were cherished by their recipients, and many of them were sent on national tours so that large numbers of people could see and admire them. When war between Japan and the United States erupted fourteen years later, some Japanese hid the blue-eyed dolls to protect them from destruction. The surviving dolls are treasured today as symbols of international peace.

21 December
Emma Tenayuca

21 December 1916—23 July 1999

La Pasionaria de Texas

In the 1930s, half of the pecans sold in the United States were grown in Texas. The city of San Antonio was the nation's pecan-shelling capital with over four hundred factories employing thousands of workers, mainly women. Working conditions were harsh. Tuberculosis and other respiratory diseases were common because of the fine pecan dust the shelling process released into the air, the factories were dark and squalid, and wages were abysmal, generally between $2 and $3 a week.

Emma Tenayuca, a San Antonio native, had been active in organizing Mexican workers in Texas from the time she was just a teenager. In only a few years she became known as a major player in the struggle to improve working conditions for Tex-Mexicans and to persuade U.S. trade unions to accept them as full-fledged members.

In January 1938, the San Antonio–based Southern Pecan Shelling Company announced a 50 percent wage cut for its shellers. Under Tenayuca's leadership, a protest strike that included 130 plants and twelve thousand laborers was launched. Tenayuca worked hard to make sure that strikers remained nonviolent. But San Antonio authorities made no such commitment, and picketers were regularly spray-hosed, teargassed, clubbed, and hauled off to jail. The violence against strikers intensified when police chief Owen Kilday frightened the public by accusing the strike of being part of a "Red plot."

But Tenayuca's strategic nonviolence paid off. After two months, the Southern Pecan Shelling Company agreed to increase rather than cut wages, and the strike ended. The next year, largely because of the Fair Labor Standards Act passed by Congress that mandated a minimum wage of $.25 an hour, the company began replacing workers with cost-effective automated cracking machines. Tenayuca angered city officials and factory owners by publicly protesting the layoffs. In retaliation, they blacklisted her from employment, harassed her with death threats, and finally ran her of town. She relocated to San Francisco where she taught school—education, she believed, was another way of empowering workers—and returned to San Antonio only thirty years later.

Recalling her participation in the great Pecan Shellers' Strike years later, Tenayuca remarked, "I was arrested a number of times. I never thought in terms of fear. I thought in terms of justice." Her courageous advocacy for social justice earned her the title of "La Pasionaria de Texas" ("The Passionflower of Texas"). At her funeral Mass, one speaker said, "she was our passion, because she was our heart—speaking out at a time when neither Mexicans nor women were expected to speak at all."

22 December
Francis Sheehy-Skeffington

23 December 1878—26 April 1916

Fighting Pacifist

IN THE EARLY HOURS of 26 April 1916, a handsome bearded man named Francis Sheehy-Skeffington was marched into the courtyard of Dublin's Portobello Barracks, stood before a seven-man firing squad, and shot to death. His body was stuffed in a gunnysack and buried on the barracks grounds. Details of his murder only gradually came to light.

Sheehy-Skeffington, called Skeffy by his friends, was a journalist noted in Dublin for his outspoken support of pacifism and women's rights. (When he married, he added his wife's surname to his, something unheard of at the time.) James Joyce, whom Sheehy-Skeffington knew when both were students at University College Dublin, lampooned his idealism in *Portrait of the Artist as a Young Man*. But Sheehy-Skeffington's commitment to peace and justice was anything but naïve. He knew that it often meant placing reputation and well-being in danger, and he was willing to risk both. His wife called him a "fighting pacifist." He himself said, "I advocate no mere servile lazy acquiescence to injustice. I want to see the age-long fight against injustice clothe itself in new forms, suited to a new age. I want to see the manhood of Ireland no longer hypnotized by the glamour of the 'glory of arms,' no longer blind to the horrors of organized murder."

Sheehy-Skeffington's new style of fighting for peace and justice drew him into three dangerous situations in his final years. In 1913, he tried to reconcile both factions in the great Dublin lockout, a strike that involved over twenty thousand workers and three hundred employers. It was the largest and most violent work stoppage in Ireland's history. At the outbreak of World War I, he was charged with sedition while campaigning against recruitment. Sentenced to six months of hard labor, he went on a hunger strike and was eventually released.

His final battle came a year later. In the spring of 1916, Irish republicans staged an insurrection against British rule that became known as the Easter Rising. Although Sheehy-Skeffington sympathized with the aim of the republicans, he deplored their use of violence and refused to condone it. On Easter Monday, the insurrection's first day, he went to Dublin's city center to see what could be done to prevent the looting of shops. While there, he was arrested by a British military unit and taken as a hostage on a raiding party against a suspected republican stronghold. In the brief gun battle, the soldiers killed three people, including a young boy. It's doubtful that any of them were rebels. Sheehy-Skeffington, who witnessed the murders, was executed a few hours later to preemptively silence his testimony.

The British officer who ordered the execution later pled shell-shock before a military court of inquiry and was exonerated. Parliament offered Sheehy-Skeffington's widow financial compensation, but she scornfully refused it and to the end of her days honored the sacrifice of her fighting pacifist husband.

23 December
Abraham Joshua Heschel

11 January 1907—23 December 1972

Praying with the Legs

ONE OF THE BEST-KNOWN photographs to come out of the 1965 civil rights march from Selma to Montgomery shows five men striding forward, arm in arm, leading the procession. Four of them are African Americans: Ralph Bunche, **Martin Luther King Jr.**, Ralph Abernathy, and **Fred Shuttlesworth**. The fifth, a man with a mane of white hair and a thick goatee, is Rabbi Abraham Joshua Heschel, the Jewish philosopher and theologian. Heschel later wrote that the march was "both protest and prayer. Legs are not lips, and walking is not kneeling. And yet our legs uttered songs. Even without words, our march was worship. I felt my legs were praying." He awakened his generation to its prophetic obligation to pray with one's lips *and* one's legs.

Heschel, who came from a long line of Polish Hasidic rabbis, studied at both an Orthodox yeshiva in Warsaw and the University of Berlin. Fleeing the Nazis in 1940, he relocated to the United States where he taught first in Cincinnati and then in New York City and wrote books on prayer, mysticism, and philosophy that influenced Jews and Christians alike.

Perhaps his most famous book is on the prophets of the Hebrew Bible. In it, he argued that the prophets weren't foretellers of the future so much as religious activists who exhorted the Israelites to peace and social justice. Read in this light, Heschel argued, they still speak to us today. "The prophets remind us of the moral state of a people. Few are guilty, but all are responsible."

His own sense of prophetic responsibility led Heschel to champion civil rights for black Americans—racism, he believed, is "the maximum of hatred for a minimum of reason"—and to speak out for the right of Russian Jews to leave the Soviet Union for Israel. Additionally, Heschel believed it was his duty to protest war and witness for peace. In the same year that he marched with King in Selma, he cofounded Clergy and Laymen Concerned about Vietnam. The war in Southeast Asia that was quickly consuming the resources of the United States and devastating the people of Vietnam was a source of great heartache for Heschel. His daughter, Susannah, recalled that she often found her father pacing in the middle of the night, unable to sleep because of his anxiety about the war. So far as Heschel was concerned, "to speak about God, and remain silent on Vietnam, is blasphemous." His work with the Clergy and Laymen Concerned about Vietnam was one of the many ways he tried to make sure that his actions in the world were compatible with both his convictions and his preaching. To the very end of his life, Heschel prayed with both his lips and his legs.

24 December
Benjamin Rush

24 December 1745—19 April 1813

National Peace Office

ONE OF THE MOST remarkable Founding Fathers of the United States—and one most Americans have never heard of—was the physician and humanitarian Benjamin Rush. An early practitioner of psychiatry, founder of Pennsylvania's Dickinson College, professor of chemistry at the University of Pennsylvania, physician to the Continental Army during the War of Independence, and defender of the rights of Native Americans and slaves, Rush was also deeply suspicious of the necessity or virtue of a standing army. So in response to the 1789 creation of a federal War Department (the precursor of today's Department of Defense), Rush penned a plea for the establishment of a Peace Office.

Rush proposed that the Peace Office be headed by a professional educator skilled in teaching the "youth of our country" that "the Supreme Being alone possesses a power to take away human life, and that we rebel against his laws, whenever we undertake to execute death in any way whatever upon any of his creatures." Just as the Peace Office would positively instruct American citizens in the ways of peace, so it would also monitor and check legally institutionalized violence, such as the death penalty, or excessive displays of militarism, such as patriotic parades.

To "inspire a veneration for human life and a horror at the shedding of blood," Rush suggested, "an inscription would be carved above the door of every courthouse throughout the land: 'THE SON OF MAN CAME INTO THE WORLD, NOT TO DESTROY MEN'S LIVES, BUT TO SAVE THEM.'" Moreover, a large sign would be posted on the door of the War Department that suggested a number of alternative names for the bureau. Some of Rush's suggestions included "An office for butchering the human species," "A Widow and Orphan making office," "An office for creating public debt," "An office for creating famine," and "An office for creating poverty, and the destruction of liberty, and national happiness." To press the point home, Rush also advocated a mandatory display for the lobby of the War Department: "let there be painted representations of all the common military instruments of death, also human skulls, broken bones, unburied and putrefying dead bodies, hospitals crowded with sick and wounded soldiers, villages on fire, mothers in besieged towns eating the flesh of their children, ships sinking in the ocean, rivers dyed with blood, and extensive plains without a tree or fence, or any object, but the ruins of deserted farm houses." And above this display, another large sign, "painted in red characters to represent human blood": NATIONAL GLORY.

Nearly two centuries after Rush's death, there is still no cabinet Department of Peace. The U.S. Institute of Peace, a nonpartisan, federally sponsored institution, was founded in 1984, but its funding is at the mercy of Congress. In early 2011, the House of Representatives voted to eliminate its budget, even though the money allocated to the USIP is one-hundredth of one percent of the Pentagon's budget.

25 December
Jesus the Christ

1ST CENTURY

Prince of Peace

Today in the town of David a Savior has been born.... Glory to God in the highest, and on earth peace to men on whom his favor rests." (Luke 2:11, 14)

"Blessed are the merciful, for they will be shown mercy." (Matt 5:7)

"Blessed are the peacemakers, for they will be called sons of God." (Matt 5:9)

"You have heard that it was said to the people long ago, 'Do not murder,' and anyone who murders will be subject to judgment. But I tell you that anyone who is angry with his brother will be subject to judgment. Therefore, if you are offering your gift at the altar and there remember that your brother has something against you, leave your gift there in front of the altar. First go and be reconciled to your brother; then come and offer your gift." (Matt 5:21–24)

"You have heard that it was said, 'Eye for eye, and tooth for tooth.' But I tell you, Do not resist an evil person. If someone strikes you on the right cheek, turn to him the other also. And if someone wants to sue you and take your tunic, let him have your cloak as well. If someone forces you to go one mile, go with him two miles. Give to the one who asks you, and do not turn away from the one who wants to borrow from you." (Matt 5:38–42)

"You have heard that it was said, 'Love your neighbor and hate your enemy.' But I tell you: Love your enemies and pray for those who persecute you, that you may be sons of your Father in heaven. He causes his sun to rise on the evil and the good, and sends rain on the righteous and the unrighteous. If you love those who love you, what reward will you get? Are not even the tax collectors doing that? And if you greet only your brothers, what are you doing more than others? Do not even pagans do that? Be perfect, therefore, as your heavenly Father is perfect." (Matt 5:43–48)

"Then the King will say to those on his right, 'Come, you who are blessed by my Father; take your inheritance, the kingdom prepared for you since the creation of the world. For I was hungry and you gave me something to eat, I was thirsty and you gave me something to drink, I was a stranger and you invited me in, I needed clothes and you clothed me, I was sick and you looked after me, I was in prison and you came to visit me.'

"Then the righteous will answer him, 'Lord, when did we see you hungry and feed you, or thirsty and give you something to drink? When did we see you a stranger and invite you in, or needing clothes and clothe you? When did we see you sick or in prison and go to visit you?'

"The King will reply, 'I tell you the truth, whatever you did for one of the least of these brothers of mine, you did for me.'" (Matt 25:34–40)

26 December
Walter Wink

21 May 1935—10 May 2012

Busting the Myth of Redemptive Violence

According to the Methodist biblical scholar Walter Wink, the belief that violence can fix bad situations and be used for noble purposes "is the real myth of the modern world. It, and not Judaism or Christianity or Islam, is the dominant religion in our society today." This belief that violence is redemptive finds expression in the mundane—Popeye beating the villainous Bluto to a pulp—and in matters of real consequence, such as going to war for "humanitarian" reasons. But regardless of whether it plays out in children's cartoons or international relations, the myth persuades us that only violence can bring order, peace, and justice out of chaos, disharmony, and oppression. As Wink says, "It enshrines the ritual practice of violence at the very heart of public life, and even those who seek to oppose its oppressive violence do so violently."

Given the prevalence of the myth, cultures have typically recognized only two ways of responding to chaos, fight or flight, with the latter nearly always being condemned as craven and cowardly and the former nearly always applauded as noble and courageous. But according to Wink, Jesus offered a "third way," and in so doing busted the myth of redemptive violence wide open. The third way is the strategy of active nonviolence. The famous passage from the Sermon on the Mount typically translated as "resist not evil" (Matt 5:39) is better translated, says Wink, as "don't resist evil with evil." Instead, find a nonviolent alternative that goes beyond both fight and flight, one that hopefully pricks the conscience of the aggressor and, if nothing else, subverts the aggressor's alleged authority and deflects potential violence.

Take one of Jesus' most famous recommendations in the Sermon on the Mount: if someone strikes you on the right cheek, offer him the left (Matt 5:39). Wink argues that Jesus' intent, far from counseling meekness, was to shame the aggressor by forcing him to strike the second time with a full-bodied punch rather than with a backhanded slap.

Any blow to the left cheek would likely come from the right hand. The only non-awkward way to strike a right cheek with the right hand is to backhand it, which was a disdainful blow reserved for slaves and menials too lowly to merit the honest punch reserved for social equals. But if the left cheek is offered after the first slap, the only non-awkward way to strike it is with a full-bodied punch or open-palmed slap, and this immediately puts the aggressor in the uncomfortable spot of acknowledging with the type of blow he uses that his victim is his equal. In offering the left cheek, the victim forces the aggressor to acknowledge his humanity. It's a beautiful piece of subversion. It's a nonviolent third way that avoids fight or flight. And it shows up the notion of redemptive violence for the myth it is. Nonviolent resistance to evil can chip away at the authority of evil until it collapses under its own weight.

27 December

Lactantius

CA. 240—CA. 320

Religion Cannot Be Imposed by Force

ADMIRED DURING HIS LIFETIME as the "Christian Cicero," the eloquent Lucius Caecilius Firmianus Lactantius came to Christianity late, probably in middle age. Until then, he had been a respected teacher of rhetoric and a member of the Emperor Diocletian's court. But he either lost or quit his position in 303 when Diocletian issued an edict commanding all Christians to offer traditional sacrifices to the gods, including divinized emperors. The new wave of persecution that ensued when thousands of Christians refused was the final one that would sweep through the empire, but in many ways it was also the worst. It ended only in 313 when Emperor Constantine declared religious toleration throughout the land. Constantine rescued Lactantius from penury and appointed him tutor to his son.

During the years of persecution, Lactantius turned his considerable stylistic and philosophical skills to the writing of *The Divine Institutes,* an apologetic work that argued that Roman had nothing to fear from Christians and that religious belief cannot be forcibly coerced. Along the way he made some telling and, under the circumstances, quite courageous criticisms of Roman culture.

The Roman glorification of war, said Lactantius, is irrational. "The more men they beat up, rob or kill, the more distinguished and famous they think they are." A man who kills "countless thousands" is hailed as a hero. But a man who "throttles a single individual is considered a vile criminal." Perhaps the Romans so feared and persecuted Christians because they believed that followers of Christ likewise revel in mass killing. But nothing is further from the truth. Christians may not kill, not even when they're allowed or even commanded by the law of the land. They know that all humans are made in God's likeness. Each person, therefore, is a "sacred animal."

So there's no need, continues Lactantius, for the persecution. Moreover, it's futile, "for religion cannot be imposed by force; the matter must be carried on by words rather than by blows, that the will may be affected." A far more effective way to convert is through the "weapons of intellect." Bloodshed does nothing but pollute and profane religion. But kindness, patience, and a willingness to die for one's faith offer a compelling witness.

Although Lactantius wrote seventeen centuries ago, his words still speak today. Our society continues to glorify martial ardor and still fails to see the inconsistency in praising wholesale slaughter, on the one hand, while condemning individual acts of violence, on the other. Moreover, Lactantius' warning against violence perpetrated in the name of religion, although leveled by him against pagan Rome, should also be taken to heart by modern-day believers in all faith traditions. Antiquity had no monopoly on religious persecution and sectarian conflict.

28 December

Child Soldiers

Slaughter of the Holy Innocents

Rachel Weeping

December 28 is recognized by Roman Catholics, Anglicans, and Lutherans as the Feast of the Holy Innocents. The day commemorates the New Testament story (Matt 2:16–18) of Herod the Great's order to execute all male children two years and younger in Bethlehem after he heard that a "King of the Jews" had been born there. The innocent children were mercilessly torn from their mothers' arms and put to the sword, prompting the gospelist to write that the tragedy was a fulfillment of one of the prophecies of Jeremiah (31:15): "A voice is heard in Ramah . . . , Rachel weeping for her children and refusing to be comforted, for they are no more."

Matthew's story reminds us that innocent children have long been brutalized by war. When conflicts erupt, they're frequently caught in the crossfire. Even if they manage to avoid death from bombs and bullets, they often fall victim to the disease and hunger brought about by war's destruction.

Children have been brutalized by war in another way as well: they've been forcibly recruited by warring factions as "child soldiers" in parts of Africa, the Middle East, Latin America, and Europe. The typical child soldier is between the ages of fourteen and eighteen, can be either a boy or a girl, and is often terrified into "joining up" or is kidnapped and beaten into submission. One boy from the Congo, forced into the army when he was only thirteen, testified: "When they came to my village, they asked my older brother whether he was ready to join the militia. He was just 17 and he said no; they shot him in the head. Then they asked me if I was ready to sign, so what could I do? I didn't want to die." Another child, also from the Congo, reported that his abductors threatened "that they would come back and kill my parents if I didn't do as they said." A boy from Colombia, recruited into a paramilitary group when he was only seven, testified: "They give you a gun and you have to kill the best friend you have. They do it to see if they can trust you. If you don't kill him, your friend will be ordered to kill you. I had to do it because otherwise I would have been killed."

Once recruited, the child soldier is usually trained as an active combatant, but can also be used as a human shield, messenger, porter, servant, or sex slave. According to Human Rights Watch, there are two to three hundred thousand child soldiers throughout the world, and tens of thousands have been killed or wounded in the first decade of the twenty-first century. This despite the fact that the Geneva Convention, the UN Convention on the Rights of the Child, and the International Criminal Court have condemned the practice.

Rachel still weeps.

29 December
John Howard Yoder

29 December 1927—30 December 1997

Recovering the Nonviolent Jesus

WORLD WAR II NEARLY killed Christian pacifism in the United States. Reinhold Niebuhr, America's leading theologian and long a proponent of nonviolence, spoke for many when he said that Nazism was so evil that war against it was not only justified but obligatory. The eventual defeat of Hitler vindicated the use of military force in the minds of many Christians.

The recent renewal of Christian pacifism in the United States is due primarily to the writings of John Howard Yoder. A Mennonite who studied under Karl Barth, worked with Mennonite relief teams in Europe and northern Africa, and taught for years at the University of Notre Dame, Yoder consistently defended nonviolence as the lifestyle practiced and recommended to his followers by Jesus. Authentic Christianity is so inescapably nonviolent that the very term "Christian pacifism" is a redundancy.

In his 1972 masterpiece, *The Politics of Jesus*, and in subsequent works, Yoder argued that the thoroughgoing pacifism of the first Christians was lost in the fourth-century shift to a "Constantinian" merger of the political interests of the Roman state with those of the Church. But the Church, Yoder maintained, is called to be *in* the world, yet not *of* it. Its identity is a community that embodies values antithetical to the political ones of worldly institutions. The Church is built upon forgiveness, love, and a willingness to sacrifice in obedience to God. Its purpose isn't to act as a social relief organization, although it certainly practices charity, or a political commentator, although it is called upon to witness to the truth about God's justice. Instead, the Church is a community centered on radical obedience to God, and God calls us to love everyone, including our enemies. As Yoder wrote, "Christians love their enemies not because they think the enemies are wonderful people, nor because they believe that love is sure to conquer these enemies. The Christian loves his or her enemies because God does, and God commands his followers to do so. The Christian has no choice. If the Lord's strategy for dealing with his enemies was to love them and give himself for them, it must be ours as well."

The Christian mandate to love everyone as God loves them sometimes puts the lover in danger. Resisting the Nazis nonviolently, for example, is a risky business (but so is resisting them violently, Yoder pointed out). Still, Christians are called to take up their crosses and follow Jesus. Many Christians consider these crosses to be personal tribulations such as illness or financial misfortune. But Yoder, citing the example of Jesus, argued that the cross we're obliged to carry is the disdain the world has for anyone who responds to hatred with love and to violence with nonviolence. The cross Christians are called to bear is Christ's.

30 December
Maurice McCrackin

1 December 1905—30 December 1997

A Very Contrary Angel

When the Korean War broke out in 1950, Maurice McCrackin, a Cincinnati-based Presbyterian pastor and pacifist, believed he was conscience-bound to oppose it with more than mere words. Realizing that a huge percentage of the federal budget was earmarked for the war effort, he decided to withhold 80 percent of his taxes. "To give financial support to war while at the same time preaching against it," he explained, "is, to me, no longer a tenable position."

It wasn't long before the IRS caught up with McCrackin. Its officers summoned him to meetings. He ignored them. The IRS garnished his wages. But McCrackin, a bachelor, lived such a frugal lifestyle that he didn't miss them. Finally, the government prosecuted him. The judge hearing the case was so bewildered by tax resistance to war, an action he'd never heard of, that he ordered McCrackin to undergo psychiatric testing. When McCrackin was declared perfectly sane, the judge sentenced him to five months in a federal penitentiary.

This was just one of more than twenty times that McCrackin went to jail for following his conscience. Throughout his long life, he resisted violence in all its forms—war, the arms race, poverty, capital punishment, inequality, racism—all in the name of the Prince of Peace. A continuous gadfly to the establishment—he was, as one of his friends put it, a "very contrary angel"—McCrackin continued his witness for peace and justice right up to the end. In 1983, he was arrested for trespassing on the grounds of a U.S. Department of Energy nuclear power plant. Two years later, when he was eighty-five, he was arrested after scaling the fence around the White House to dump red dye into the fountain as a protest against the Persian Gulf War. Even in his final years, when confined to a wheelchair and nearly blind, he spoke at peace rallies, encouraging his audiences to persevere in peace work and prodding authorities to reform public policy.

Born and raised in rural Ohio and ordained in his early twenties, McCrackin spent five years as a missionary in Iran and then moved on to parishes in the American Midwest before finally settling in Cincinnati in 1945. Within a few months he had integrated his church, St. Barnabas, and launched his lifelong peace witness. He lived unpretentiously in one of Cincinnati's most impoverished areas, the West End, casting his lot with the men, women, and children forgotten by society. In 1962, his social activism prompted the Cincinnati Presbytery to defrock him and remove him from St. Barnabas. He founded the Community Church of Cincinnati, pastoring it until his retirement in 1989. In 1987, the Cincinnati Presbytery publically apologized and reinstated him. It was a long overdue vindication of his years of loyalty to the gospel of peace.

31 December
John Timothy Leary

1958—31 August 1982

Unsung Peace Hero

Although they're rarely recognized as such in our culture, peacemakers are genuine heroes. We tend to think of heroism almost exclusively in terms of battlefield valor. In the popular imagination, the hero is a larger-than-life Rambo figure who, pitted against incredible military odds, muscles his way through to victory.

But of course most heroes are quite ordinary folks who see injustice and violence in the world and take responsibility for doing something about it. They could easily turn a blind eye to the world's pain. But they don't. Instead, they dedicate themselves to alleviating suffering, even if only in a small way that may be confined mostly to their tiny corner of the world. These heroes do great but unglamorous things that, consequently, for the most part go unsung.

One of them was a young man named John Timothy Leary, who died of sudden cardiac arrest while jogging in Boston. He was only twenty-four years old, but he crammed more peacework into his short life than most of us do in threescore and ten.

Born into a Catholic family in Connecticut, John became interested in social issues as early as the seventh grade. By the time he arrived at Harvard as a freshman, he was ready to change the world. Inspired by such peacemakers as **Dorothy Day**, **Thomas Merton**, and **Martin Luther King Jr.**, he threw himself into a prison tutoring project, regularly invited homeless people to share his meals and his succession of low-rent apartments in poor Boston neighborhoods, participated in anti-war and anti-nuclear witnesses, and became a staunch advocate of respect-for-life issues. He worked for a miniscule salary at Boston's Center on Conscience and War, practiced voluntary poverty, and dressed in secondhand clothes. Although tempted at one point to drop out of Harvard and devote himself full time to working with the poor and homeless—he once described his daily routine as a continuous race "from seven in the morning until one the following morning spending all my time calling people or going to meetings or working at the jail"—he persevered and graduated *magna cum laude* a year before his death. After graduation he lived in a Boston Catholic Worker house, since renamed in his honor.

A deep religious faith fueled John's peace activism. He attended Sunday Mass at a Melkite Catholic church and daily Mass at a Latin rite one. An avid jogger, he told a friend shortly before his death that he always prayed the Jesus Prayer during his runs. He was most likely praying it when his heart stopped.

Of all the peacemakers profiled in this book, John may well be the least known and least praised. But it's precisely anonymous, good-hearted people like him who keep alive the hope that peace may prevail. After his death, one of his acquaintances said of him that "he dared to take on tasks he knew were beyond his, and probably anyone else's, capacity to complete." That kind of commitment to a better world, even in the face of what seem impossible odds, enriches and blesses us all.

For Further Reading

1 January — Telemachus
Theodoretus, *A History of the Church in Five Books, 322–427*. Ann Arbor: University of Michigan Press, 2009.

2 January — Willi Graf
Annette E. Dumbach and Jud Newborn, *Shattering the German Night: The Story of the White Rose*. New York: Little Brown, 1986.

3 January — Takashi Nagai
Takashi Nagai, *The Bells of Nagasaki*, trans. William Johnston. Tokyo: Kodansha, 1994.

4 January — Albert Camus
Albert Camus, *Neither Victims Nor Executioners: An Ethic Superior to Murder*, trans. Dwight MacDonald. Eugene, OR: Wipf & Stock, 2005.

5 January — Lanza del Vasto
Lanza del Vasto, *Warriors of Peace: Writings on the Techniques of Nonviolence*. New York: Knopf, 1974.

6 January — Jacques Ellul
Jacques Ellul, *Anarchy and Christianity*, trans. Geoffrey W. Bromiley. Grand Rapids: Eerdmans, 1991.

7 January — Sadako Sasaki
Eleanor Coerr, *Sadako and the Thousand Paper Cranes*. New York: Puffin, 2004.

8 January — Emily Greene Balch
Mercedes M. Randall, *Improper Bostonian: Emily Greene Balch, Nobel Peace Laureate, 1946*. New York: Twayne, 1964.

9 January — Rigoberta Menchú Tum
Rigoberta Menchú and Elisabeth Burgos-Debray, *I, Rigoberta Menchú: An Indian Woman in Guatemala*, trans. Ann Wright. London: Verso, 2010.

10 January — Henry Scott Holland
Edward Lyttelton, *The Mind and Character of Henry Scott Holland*. New York: Morehouse, 1926.

11 January — Aldo Leopold
Julianne Lutz Newton, *Aldo Leopold's Odyssey: Rediscovering the Author of* A Sand County Almanac. Washington, DC: Island, 2006.

12 January — Benny Giay
John Braithwaite, Valerie Braithwaite, Michael Cookson, and Leah Dunn, *Anomie and Violence: Non-Truth and Reconciliation in Indonesian Peacebuilding*. Canberra: ANU E Press, 2010.

13 January — Tom Hurndall
Josie Sandercock, et al. (eds.), *Peace under Fire: Israel, Palestine, and the International Solidarity Movement*. London: Verso, 2004.

14 January — Martin Niemöller
James Bentley, *Martin Niemöller*. New York: Free Press, 1984.

15 January — Nathan Soderblöm
Bengt Sundkler, *Nathan Soderblöm: His Life and Work*. London: Lutterworth, 1968.

16 January — Ormond Burton
Ernest A. Crane, *I Can Do No Other: A Biography of the Reverend Ormond Burton*. Auckland: Hodder & Stoughton, 1987.

17 January — William Stafford
Kim Stafford (ed.), *Every War Has Two Losers: William Stafford on Peace and War*. Minneapolis: Milkweed, 2003.

18 January — Kenneth Boulding
Robert Wright, *Three Scientists and Their Gods: Looking for Meaning in an Age of Information*. New York: HarperCollins, 1989.

For Further Reading

19 January—Helen Mack Chang

Myrna Mack Foundation. Online: http://www.myrnamack.org.gt/index.php.

20 January—Khan Abdul Ghaffar Khan

Eknath Eswaran, *Nonviolent Soldier of Islam: Badshah Khan, A Man to Match His Mountains.* Tomales, CA: Nilgiri, 1999.

21 January—Hildegard Goss-Mayr

Richard Deats, *Marked for Life: The Story of Hildegard Goss-Mayr.* Hyde Park, NY: New City, 2009.

22 January—U Thant

U Thant, *View from the UN.* Garden City, NY: Doubleday, 1978.

23 January—María Julia Hernández

Guerra de El Salvador / María Julia Hernández. Video. Online: http://www.youtube.com/watch?v=ZjcQVPJTRCY.

24 January—Absalom Jones

Harold T. Lewis, *Yet with a Steady Beat: The African American Struggle for Recognition in the Episcopal Church.* Harrisburg, PA: Trinity, 1996.

25 January—Rufus Jones

Kerry Walters (ed.), *Rufus Jones: Essential Writings.* Maryknoll, NY: Orbis, 2001.

26 January—Thomas Gumbleton

Thomas Gumbleton, "Sermons." From "The Teaching and Ministry of Bishop Thomas Gumbleton: A Living Archive." Online: http://bishopgumbleton.org/sermons.html.

27 January—Roy Bourgeois

James Hodge and Linda Cooper, *Disturbing the Peace: The Story of Father Roy Bourgeois and the Movement to Close the School of the Americas.* Maryknoll, NY: Orbis, 2004.

28 January—Isaac of Nineveh

Sebastian P. Brock, *The Wisdom of Isaac of Ninevah.* Piscataway, NJ: Gorgias, 2006.

29 January—Romain Rolland

Romain Rolland, *Above the Battle,* trans. C. K. Ogden. Chicago: Open Court, 1916.

30 January—Vallalar

Vallalar, *Thiruvarutpa: Holy Book of Grace.* Tamil Nadu, India: Annamalai University, undated.

31 January—Donald Soper

Donald Soper, *Calling for Action: An Autobiographical Enquiry.* London: Robson, 1984.

1 February—Yevgeny Zamyatin

Yevgeny Zamyatin, *We,* trans. Clarence Brown. New York: Penguin, 1993.

2 February—Maximilian Vanka

"The Murals of Maxo Vanka." Online: http://vankamurals.org/.

3 February—Carlos Filipe Ximenes Belo

Arnold S. Kohen, *From the Place of the Dead: The Epic Struggles of Bishop Belo of East Timor.* New York: St. Martin's, 2001.

4 February—Rosa Parks

Douglas G. Brinkley, *Rosa Parks: A Life.* New York: Penguin, 2005.

5 February—John Nevin Sayre

Charles F. Howlett, "John Nevin Sayre and the International Fellowship of Reconciliation." *Peace and Change* 15 (1990) 123–49.

6 February—Asha Hagi Elmi

Asha Hagi Elmi, "Power of the People Over Power of the Gun." *New Statesman* 19 (2008). Online: http://www.newstatesman.com/society/2008/09/peace-somalia-women-/power-asha.

7 February—Dom Hélder Câmara

Francis McDonagh (ed.), *Dom Hélder Câmara: Essential Writings.* Maryknoll, NY: Orbis, 2009.

For Further Reading

8 February—Martin Buber

Asher Biemann (ed.), *The Martin Buber Reader.* New York: Palgrave Macmillian, 2002.

9 February—Alice Walker

Evelyn C. White, *Alice Walker: A Life.* New York: Norton, 2005.

10 February—Frances Moore Lappé

Frances Moore Lappé, *Hope's Edge: The Next Diet for a Small Planet.* New York: Tarcher, 2003.

11 February—Muriel Lester

Richard Deats (ed.), *Ambassador of Reconciliation: A Muriel Lester Reader.* Philadelphia: New Society, 1991.

12 February—Dorothy Stang

Roseanne Murphy, *Martyr of the Amazon: The Life of Sister Dorothy Stang.* Maryknoll, NY: Orbis, 2007.

13 February—Emil Fuchs

Emil Fuchs, *Christ in Catastrophe.* Pendle Hill Pamphlet 49. Wallingford, PA: Pendle Hill, 2003.

14 February—Valentine

Ruth Styles, "How to Have an Eco-Friendly Valentine's Day." *Ecologist*, 10 February 2011. Online: http://www.theecologist.org/green_green_living/how_to/764844/how_to_have_an_ecofriendly_valentines_day.html.

15 February—Ben Salmon

Torin R. T. Finney, *Unsung Hero of the Great War: The Life and Witness of Ben Salmon.* Mahwah, NJ: Paulist, 1989.

16 February—Simone Weil

Sian Miles (ed.), *Simone Weil: An Anthology.* New York: Grove, 2000.

17 February—Jonah Jones

Jonah Jones, *The Gallipoli Diary.* Bridgend, Wales: Seren, 1989.

18 February—Julia Butterfly Hill

Julia Butterfly Hill, *The Legacy of Luna.* San Francisco: HarperSanFrancisco, 2000.

19 February—Krishnammal and Sankaralingam Jagannathan

1998 Right Livelihood Award Interview with Krishnammal Jagannathan. Online: http://shantinik.blogspot.com/2008/09/opus-prize-questionnaire.html.

20 February—A. J. Muste

Nat Hentoff (ed.), *The Essays of A. J. Muste.* Indianapolis: Bobbs-Merrill, 1967.

21 February—John van Hengel

Feeding America. Online: http://feedingamerica.org.

22 February—Menachem Froman

Yossi K. Halevi, *At the Entrance to the Garden of Eden: A Jew's Hope for Christians and Muslims in the Holy Land.* New York: Harper, 2002.

23 February—Wulfstan of Worchester

William of Malmesbury, *Saints' Lives,* trans. M. Winterbottom and R. M. Thompson. New York: Oxford University Press, 2002.

24 February—Monika Hauser

Medica Mondiale. Online: http://www.medicamondiale.org/index.php?id=7&L=1.

25 February—Jacob Hutter

John A. Hostetler, *Hutterite Society.* Baltimore: Johns Hopkins University Press, 1997.

26 February—Naim Ateek

Naim Ateek, *A Palestinian Christian Cry for Reconciliation.* Maryknoll, NY: Orbis, 2008.

27 February—Gautama Siddhartha

Kenneth Kraft (ed.), *Inner Peace, World Peace: Essays on Buddhism and Nonviolence.* Albany: State University of New York Press, 1992.

For Further Reading

28 February—Linus Pauling

Clifford Mead and Thomas Hager (eds.), *Linus Pauling: Scientist and Peacemaker*. Corvallis: Oregon State University Press, 2008.

1 March—Loung Ung

Loung Ung, *First They Killed My Father: A Daughter of Cambodia Remembers*. New York: HarperCollins, 2001.

2 March—Judi Bari

Judi Bari, *Timber Wars*. Monroe, ME: Common Courage, 1994.

3 March—Miriam Makeba

Miriam Makeba and Nomsa Mwamuka, *Makeba: The Miriam Makeba Story*. Johannesburg: Real African, 2004.

4 March—Ludwig Quidde

Ludwig Quidde, 1927 Nobel Peace Prize Acceptance Speech. Online: http://www.nobelprize.org/nobel_prizes/peace/laureates/1927/quidde.html#.

5 March—Hussein Issa

Hope Flowers School. Online: http://www.hopeflowersschool.org/intro.html.

6 March—Sulak Sivaraksa

Sulak Sivaraksa, *Seeds of Peace: A Buddhist Vision for Renewing Society*. Berkeley: Parallax, 1992.

7 March—Stanley Kubrick

Stanley Kubrick (director), *Dr. Strangelove or: How I Learned to Stop Worrying and Love the Bomb*. Columbia Pictures, 1964.

8 March—Maria Skobtsova

Jim Forest (ed.), *Mother Maria Skobtsova: Essential Writings*. Maryknoll, NY: Orbis, 2003.

9 March—Tom Fox

Tricia Gates Brown, *118 Days: Christian Peacemaker Teams Held Hostage in Iraq*. Telford, PA: Cascadia, 2009.

10 March—Asghar Ali Engineer

Asghar Ali Engineer, *The Prophet of Non-Violence: Spirit of Peace, Compassion, and Universality in Islam*. New Delhi: Vitasta, 2011.

11 March—Rutilio Grande

Anna L. Petersen, *Martyrdom and the Politics of Religion: Progressive Catholicism in El Salvador's Civil War*. Albany: State University of New York Press, 1996.

12 March—Preah Maha Ghosananda

Preah Maha Ghosananda, *Step by Step: Meditations on Wisdom and Compassion*. Berkeley: Parallax, 1991.

13 March—Ham Sok-Hon

Kim Sung-Su, *Ham Sok-Hon, Voice of the People and Pioneer of Religious Pluralism in Twentieth-Century Korea: Biography of a Korean Quaker*. Seoul: Samin, 2001.

14 March—Walter Brueggemann

Walter Brueggemann, *Peace*. Understanding Biblical Themes. St. Louis: Chalice, 2001.

15 March—SuAnne Big Crow

Ian Frazier, *On the Rez*. New York: Picador, 2001.

16 March—Rachel Corrie

Rachel Corrie, *Let Me Stand Alone: The Journals of Rachel Corrie*. New York: Norton, 2009.

17 March—Bayard Rustin

John D'Emilio, *Lost Prophet: The Life and Times of Bayard Rustin*. Chicago: University of Chicago Press, 2004.

18 March—Fred Shuttlesworth

Andrew M. Manis, *A Fire You Can't Put Out: The Civil Rights Life of Birmingham's Reverend Fred Shuttlesworth*. Tuscaloosa: University of Alabama Press, 2001.

19 March—Vera Brittain

Vera Brittain, *Testament of Youth*. New York: Penguin, 1994.

20 March—John Middleton Murry

Sharron G. Cassavant, *John Middleton Murry*. Tuscaloosa: University of Alabama Press, 1982.

21 March—Pocahontas

Camilla Townsend, *Pocahontas and the Powhatan Dilemma*. New York: Hill & Wang, 2004.

22 March—John McConnell

John McConnell and John C. Munday Jr., *Earth Day: Vision for Peace, Justice, and Earth Care: My Life and Thought at Age 96*. Eugene, OR: Wipf & Stock, 2011.

23 March—David Suzuki

David Suzuki, *The Sacred Balance: Rediscovering Our Place in Nature*. Vancouver: Greystone, 2002.

24 March—Kalle Lasn

Kalle Lasn, *Culture Jam*. New York: HarperCollins, 2000.

25 March—Norman Borlaug

Leon Hesser, *The Man Who Fed the World: Nobel Peace Prize Winner Norman Borlaug and His Battle to End World Hunger*. Dallas: Durban House, 2009.

26 March—Kate Richards O'Hare

Sally M. Miller, *Prairie to Prison: The Life of Socialist Activist Kate Richards O'Hare*. Columbia: University of Missouri Press, 1993.

27 March—Wally and Juanita Nelson

Billy Joe Mills, "Radical Stories #1: Wally Nelson." *Urbanagora*, 8 December 2006. Online: http://www.urbanagora.com/2006/12/radical-stories-1-wally-nelson.html.

28 March—Pelagius

Pelagius, "On Riches." In Andrew Bradstock and Christopher Rowland (eds.), *Radical Christian Writings: A Reader*, 15–33. Oxford: Blackwell, 2002.

29 March—R. S. Thomas

Byron Rogers, *The Man Who Went into the West: The Life of R. S. Thomas*. London: Aurum, 2006.

30 March—Dith Pran

Sydney H. Schanberg, *The Death and Life of Dith Pran*. New York: Viking, 1985.

31 March—César Chávez

Frederick John Dalton, *The Moral Vision of César Chávez*. Maryknoll, NY: Orbis, 2003.

1 April—Wangari Maathai

Wangari Maathai, *Unbowed: A Memoir*. New York: Vintage, 2007.

2 April—John Paul II

John Paul II, *No Peace without Justice, No Justice without Forgiveness*. Dublin: Veritas, 2005.

3 April—Jane Goodall

Jane Goodall, *Reason for Hope: A Spiritual Journey*. New York: Warner, 2000.

4 April—Martin Luther King Jr.

James M. Washington (ed.), *A Testament of Hope: The Essential Writings and Speeches of Martin Luther King, Jr.* New York: HarperCollins, 1991.

5 April—Pythagoras

Kenneth Sylvan Guthrie, *The Pythagorean Sourcebook and Library: An Anthology of Ancient Writings which Relate to Pythagoras and Pythagorean Philosophy*. Grand Rapids: Phanes, 1988.

6 April—Daniel Ellsberg

Daniel Ellsberg, *Secrets: A Memoir of Vietnam and the Pentagon Papers*. New York: Penguin, 2003.

7 April—André Trocmé

Philip Hallie, *Lest Innocent Blood Be Shed*. New York: Harper & Row, 1979.

For Further Reading

8 April—Ivan Supek
Bojan Marotti, "Ivan Supek, 1915–2007." *Prolegomena* 7 (2008) 89–100.

9 April—Dietrich Bonhoeffer
Larry L. Rasmussen, *Dietrich Bonhoeffer: Reality and Resistance*. Nashville: Abingdon, 1972.

10 April—Jessie Wallace Hughan
Kathleen Kennedy, *Disloyal Mothers and Scurrilous Citizens: Women and Subversion during World War I*. Bloomington: Indiana University Press, 1999.

11 April—Kurt Vonnegut
Kurt Vonnegut, *Armageddon in Retrospect*. New York: Berkley, 2009.

12 April—Frederick Franck
Frederick Franck, *The Zen of Seeing*. New York: Vintage, 1973.

13 April—Amy Goodman
Amy Goodman, *Breaking the Sound Barrier*. Chicago: Haymarket, 2009.

14 April—Arun Gandhi
Arun Gandhi, *Legacy of Love: My Education in the Path of Nonviolence*. El Sobrante, CA: North Bay, 2003.

15 April—Robert Purvis
Margaret Hope Bacon, *But One Race: The Life of Robert Purvis*. Albany: State University of New York Press, 2007.

16 April—Iqbal Masih
Andrew Crofts, *The Little Hero: One Boy's Fight for Freedom*. London: Vision, 2006.

17 April—Albert Einstein
Otto Nathan and Heinz Norden (eds.), *Einstein on Peace*. New York: Random House, 1988.

18 April—Margaret Hassan
Jason Burke, "Margaret Hassan: Obituary." *The Guardian*, 17 November 2004. Online: http://www.guardian.co.uk/society/2004/nov/17/internationalaidanddevelopment.guardianobituaries.

19 April—Meng Tzu
James Legge (trans.), *The Works of Mencius*. Mineola, NY: Dover, 2011.

20 April—Lady Godiva
Daniel Donoghue, *Lady Godiva: A Literary History of the Legend*. Malden, MA: Blackwell, 2003.

21 April—Helen Prejean
Helen Prejean, *Dead Man Walking: An Eyewitness Account of the Death Penalty in the United States*. New York: Vintage, 1993.

22 April—Käthe Kollwitz
Hans Kollwitz (ed.), *The Diaries and Letters of Käthe Kollwitz*, trans. Richard Winston. Evanston: Northwestern University Press, 1989.

23 April—Adin Ballou
Adin Ballou, *Christian Non-Resistance*. Providence, RI: Blackstone, 2003.

24 April—Margaret Fell
Elsa F. Glines (ed.), *Undaunted Zeal: The Letters of Margaret Fell*. Richmond, IN: Friends United, 2003.

25 April—Ernesto Balducci
"The Words of Balducci." Online: http://freaknet.org/martin/books/wordsof.html.

26 April—Amy Biehl
Frances Reid (director), *Long Night's Journey into Day: South Africa's Search for Truth and Reconciliation*. Iris Films, 2000. (This documentary devotes one of its four parts to Amy Biehl.)

27 April—Dorothee Soelle
Dorothee Soelle, *The Silent Cry: Mysticism and Resistance*, trans. Barbara and Martin Rumscheidt. Minneapolis: Fortress, 2001.

28 April—Oskar Schindler
David Crowe, *Oskar Schindler: The Untold Account of His Life, Wartime Activities, and the True Story Behind the List*. New York: Basic Books, 2007.

29 April—Gordon Kiyoshi Hirabayashi

"45 Years Later, An Apology from the U.S. Government." *A & S Perspectives*, University of Washington Newsletter (Winter 2000). Online: http://www.artsci.washington.edu/newsletter/Winter00/Hirabayashi.htm.

30 April—Immanuel Kant

Immanuel Kant, *Toward Perpetual Peace and Other Writings on Politics, Peace, and History*, trans. David L. Colclasure. New Haven: Yale University Press, 2006.

1 May—Albert Bigelow

Lawrence S. Wittner, *Resisting the Bomb: A History of the World Nuclear Disarmament Movement, 1954–1970*. Stanford: Stanford University Press, 1997.

2 May—Benjamin Spock

Thomas Maier, *Dr. Spock: An American Life*. New York: Basic Books, 2003.

3 May—Anthony Benezet

Maurice Jackson, *Let This Voice Be Heard: Anthony Benezet, Father of Atlantic Abolitionism*. Philadelphia: University of Pennsylvania Press, 2009.

4 May—Carl von Ossietzky

Carl von Ossietzky, *The Stolen Republic: Selected Writings*. London: Lawrence & Wishart, 1971.

5 May—Pete Seeger

Alec Wilkinson, *The Protest Singer: An Intimate Portrait of Pete Seeger*. New York: Vintage, 2010.

6 May—Ariel Dorfman

Ariel Dorfman, *Death and the Maiden*. New York: Penguin, 1991.

7 May—Carl Upchurch

Carl Upchurch, *Convicted in the Womb: One Man's Journey from Prison to Peacemaker*. New York: Bantam, 1997.

8 May—Pat Barker

Pat Barker, *Regeneration*. New York: Plume, 1993.

9 May—Sophia Scholl

Annette Dumbach and Jud Newborn, *Sophie Scholl and the White Rose*. Oxford: Oneworld, 2007.

10 May—Beyers Naudé

Colleen Ryan, *Beyers Naudé: Pilgrimage of Faith*. Trenton, NJ: Africa World Press, 1990.

11 May—Mychal Judge

Michael Ford, *Father Mychal Judge: An Authentic American Hero*. Mahwah, NJ: Paulist, 2002.

12 May—Brother Roger

Marcello Fidanzio (ed.), *Brother Roger of Taizé: Essential Writings*. Maryknoll, NY: Orbis, 2006.

13 May—Fridtjof Nansen

Michael R. Marrus, *The Unwanted: European Refugees from the First World War through the Cold War*. Philadelphia: Temple University Press, 2001.

14 May—Peter Maurin

Peter Maurin, *Easy Essays*. Eugene, OR: Wipf & Stock, 2010.

15 May—Frances Crowe

"You Have the Right to Be a Conscientious Objector." 2004 Audio Interview with Frances Crowe. Online: http://www.grassrootspeace.org/frances_crowe.html.

16 May—Nhat Chi Mai

Thich Nhat Hanh and Daniel Berrigan, *The Raft Is Not the Shore: Conversations toward a Buddhist-Christian Awareness*. Maryknoll, NY: Orbis, 2001.

17 May—Daniel Berrigan

Daniel Berrigan, *The Trial of the Catonsville Nine*. New York: Fordham University Press, 2004.

For Further Reading

18 May—Bertrand Russell

Bertrand Russell, *Why Men Fight*. London: Allen & Unwin, 1916.

19 May—Laozi

Stephen Mitchell (trans.), *Tao Te Ching: A New English Version*. New York: HarperPerennial, 2006.

20 May—Wei Jingsheng

Wei Jingsheng, *The Courage to Stand Alone: Letters from Prison and Other Writings*, trans. Kristina M. Torgeson. New York: Penguin, 1998.

21 May—Elizabeth Fry

Anna Isba, *The Excellent Mrs. Fry: Unlikely Heroine*. New York: Continuum, 2010.

22 May—Betty Williams

Susan Muaddi Darraj, *Mairead Corrigan and Betty Williams: Partners in Peace in Northern Ireland*. Philadelphia: Chelsea House, 2006.

23 May—Max Walters

"Max Walters: Obituary." *The Independent*, 13 December 2005. Online: http://www.independent.co.uk/news/obituaries/max-walters-519286.html.

24 May—Harry Emerson Fosdick

Robert Moats Miller, *Harry Emerson Fosdick: Preacher, Pastor, Prophet*. New York: Oxford University Press, 1985.

25 May—David Dellinger

David Dellinger, *Revolutionary Nonviolence: Essays*. Indianapolis: Bobbs-Merrill, 1970.

26 May—Utah Phillips

Utah Phillips, *I've Got to Know*. Audio CD. Daemon Records, 2003.

27 May—Julia Ward Howe

Valarie H. Ziegler, *Diva Julia: The Public Romance and Private Agony of Julia Ward Howe*. New York: Continuum, 2006.

28 May—Rachel Carson

Linda J. Lear, *Rachel Carson: Witness for Nature*. New York: Henry Holt, 1997.

29 May—Leó Szilárd

William Lanouette and Bela Silard, *Genius in the Shadows: A Biography of Leó Szilárd, the Man Behind the Bomb*. Chicago: University of Chicago Press, 1994.

30 May—Ruth Manorama

Ruth Manorama, 2006 Right Livelihood Award Acceptance Speech. Online: http://www.rightlivelihood.org/manorama_speech.html.

31 May—Jean-Pierre Willem

Medecins aux Pieds Nur. Online: http://www.mapn.org.

1 June—Mary Dyer

Ruth Talbot Plimpton, *Mary Dyer: Biography of a Rebel Quaker*. Boston: Branden, 1994.

2 June—John XXIII

John XXIII, *Pacem in Terris*. New York: America Press, 1963.

3 June—Satish Kumar

Satish Kumar, *No Destination: An Autobiography*. Devon, UK: Green Books, 2004.

4 June—Jim Wallis

Jim Wallis, *God's Politics: Why the Right Gets It Wrong and the Left Doesn't Get It*. San Francisco: HarperSanFrancisco, 2006.

5 June—Angie Zelter

Angie Zelter, *Trident on Trial: The Case for Peoples' Disarmanent*. Edinburgh: Luath, 2001.

6 June—Marian Wright Edelman

Marian Wright Edelman, *The Measure of Our Success*. New York: William Morrow, 1993.

For Further Reading

7 June—Seattle

Warren Jefferson, *The World of Chief Seattle: How Can One Sell the Air?* Summertown, TN: Native Voices, 2001.

8 June—John Perkins

John Perkins, *Let Justice Roll Down*. Ventura, CA: Regal, 1976.

9 June—Bertha von Suttner

Bertha von Suttner, *Lay Down Your Arms: The Autobiography of Martha von Tilling*. Charleston, SC: Nabu, 2011.

10 June—Sumaya Farhat-Naser

Sumaya Hanna Farhat-Naser, *Daughter of the Olive Trees*. Basel: Lenos, 2003.

11 June—Jeannette Rankin

Norma Smith, *Jeannette Rankin: America's Conscience*. Missoula, MT: Montana Historical Society, 2002.

12 June—Frédéric Passy

Sandi E. Cooper, *Patriotic Pacifism: Waging War on War in Europe, 1815–1914*. New York: Oxford University Press, 1991.

13 June—Dante Alighieri

Dante Alighieri, *On World Government*, trans. Herbert W. Schneider. Indianapolis: Bobbs-Merrill, 1957.

14 June—David Low Dodge

David Low Dodge, *War Inconsistent with the Religion of Jesus Christ*. Charleston, SC: Nabu, 2010.

15 June—Paul Rusesabagina

Paul Rusesabagina, *An Ordinary Man: An Autobiography*. New York: Viking, 2006.

16 June—Charles Yale Harrison

Charles Yale Harrison, *Generals Die in Bed*. Buffalo, NY: Annick, 2007.

17 June—Viktor Popkov

Stanislav Bozhko, "He Died for His Ideals." *St. Petersburg Times*, 22 June 2001.

18 June—José Brocca

Devi Prasad, *War Is a Crime against Humanity: The Story of War Resisters' International*. London: War Resisters' International, 2005.

19 June—Aung San Suu Kyi

Justin Wintle, *Perfect Hostage: A Life of Aung San Suu Kyi, Burma's Prisoner of Conscience*. New York: Skyhorse, 2008.

20 June—Jonathan Dymond

Jonathan Dymond, *An Enquiry into the Accordancy of War with the Principles of Christianity*. Charleston, SC: Nabu, 2010.

21 June—Shirin Ebadi

Shirin Ebadi, *Iran Awakening: A Memoir of Revolution and Hope*. New York: Random House, 2006.

22 June—Paulinus of Nola

Dennis E. Trout, *Paulinus of Nola: Life, Letters, and Poems*. Berkeley: University of California Press, 1999.

23 June—William Sloane Coffin

William Sloane Coffin, *Credo*. Louisville: Westminster John Knox, 2005.

24 June—Raphael Lemkin

John Cooper, *Raphael Lemkin and the Struggle for the Genocide Convention*. New York: Palgrave Macmillan, 2008.

25 June—Lois Marie Gibbs

Lois Marie Gibbs, *Love Canal: The Story Continues*. Gabriola Island, BC: New Society, 1998.

26 June—Justin Martyr

C. John Cadoux, *The Early Christian Attitude to War*. New York: Seabury, 1982.

27 June—Geoffrey "Woodbine Willie" Studdert Kennedy

Kerry Walters (ed.), *After War, Is Faith Possible? The Life and Message of Geoffrey "Woodbine Willie" Studdert Kennedy*. Eugene, OR: Cascade Books, 2008.

For Further Reading

28 June—Danilo Dolci

James McNeigh, *Fire Under the Ashes: The Life of Danilo Dolci*. London: Hodder & Stoughton, 1965.

29 June—Samantha Smith

Samantha Smith, *Journey to the Soviet Union*. Santa Fe, NM: Ocean Tree, 2005.

30 June—Muhammad Yunus

Muhammad Yunus, *Banker to the Poor: Micro-Lending and the Battle against World Poverty*. New York: Public Affairs, 2003.

1 July—David Brower

David Brower, *Let the Mountains Talk, Let the Rivers Run: A Call to Save the Earth*. San Francisco, CA: Sierra Club, 2007.

2 July—Birsel Lemke

Birsel Lemke, 2000 Right Livelihood Award Acceptance Speech. Online: http://www.rightlivelihood.org/lemke_speech.html.

3 July—Kees Boeke

Wyatt T. R. Rawson, *The Werkplaats Adventure*. London: Vincent Stuart, 1956.

4 July—Ron Kovic

Ron Kovic, *Born on the Fourth of July*. New York: Akashic, 2005.

5 July—H. H. Dalai Lama

H. H. Dalai Lama, *Beyond Religion: Ethics for a Whole World*. New York: Houghton Mifflin Harcourt, 2011.

6 July—Elise Boulding

Elise Boulding, *Cultures of Peace: The Hidden Side of History*. Syracuse: Syracuse University Press, 2000.

7 July—Ben Linder

Joan Krukewitt, *The Death of Ben Linder: The Story of a North American in Sandinista Nicaragua*. New York: Seven Stories, 2001.

8 July—Peace Pilgrim

Peace Pilgrim, *Peace Pilgrim: Her Life and Work in Her Own Words*. Sante Fe, NM: Ocean Tree, 1994.

9 July—Shane Claiborne

Shane Claiborne, *The Irresistible Revolution: Living as an Ordinary Radical*. Grand Rapids: Zondervan, 2006.

10 July—Toyohiko Kagawa

Robert D. Schildgen, *Toyohiko Kagawa: An Apostle of Love and Social Justice*. Berkeley: Centenary, 1988.

11 July—Abdulkadir Yahya Ali

Center for Research and Dialogue (Somalia). Online: http://www.crdsomalia.org/.

12 July—Mitch Snyder

Victoria Rader, *Signal through the Flames: Mitch Snyder and America's Homeless*. Chicago: Sheed & Ward, 1986.

13 July—Toma Sik

Toma Sik, "Puzzles of a Lifetime." Online: http://www.wri-irg.org/news/2004/toma-en.htm.

14 July—Woody Guthrie

Joe Klein, *Woody Guthrie: A Life*. New York: Delta, 1999.

15 July—Barbara Lee

Barbara Lee, *Renegade for Peace and Justice: A Memoir of Political and Personal Courage*. Lanham, MD: Rowman & Littlefield, 2011.

16 July—Bartolomé de las Casas

Helen Rand Parish (ed.), *Bartolomé de las Casas: The Only Way*. Mahwah, NJ: Paulist, 1992.

17 July—Ammon Hennacy

Ammon Hennacy, *The One-Man Revolution in America*. Salt Lake City: A. Hennacy, 1970.

18 July—Nelson Mandela

Nelson Mandela, *Long Walk to Freedom*. Boston: Little, Brown, 1995.

19 July—Barbara Deming

Jane Meyerding, *We Are All Part of One Another: A Barbara Deming Reader*. Gabriola Island, BC: New Society, 1984.

20 July—Mirabehn

Mirabehn, *The Spirit's Pilgrimage*. Salt Lake City: Great River, 2010.

21 July—Albert Lutuli

Albert Lutuli, *Let My People Go: An Autobiography*. New York: HarperCollins, 1987.

22 July—William Wilberforce

Eric Metaxas, *Amazing Grace: William Wilberforce and the Heroic Campaign to End Slavery*. New York: HarperOne, 2007.

23 July—Leopold Engleitner

Bernhard Rammerstorfer, *Unbroken Will: The Extraordinary Courage of an Ordinary Man*. Beverly Hills, CA: Grammaton, 2006.

24 July—Stanley Hauerwas

John Berkman and Michael Cartwright (eds.), *The Hauerwas Reader*. Durham: Duke University Press, 2001.

25 July—Walter Rauschenbusch

Benjamin E. Mays (ed.), *A Gospel for the Social Awakening: Selections from the Writings of Walter Rauschenbusch*. Eugene, OR: Wipf & Stock, 2008.

26 July—Eberhard Arnold

Johann Christoph Arnold (ed.), *Eberhard Arnold: Selected Writings*. Maryknoll, NY: Orbis, 2000.

27 July—George Bernard Shaw

Michael Holroyd, *Bernard Shaw*. New York: Norton, 2005.

28 July—Lupus of Troyes

Alban Butler, *The Lives of the Fathers, Martyrs, and Other Principal Saints*. Vol. 7. Dublin: James Duffy, 1866.

29 July—Dag Hammarskjöld

Brian Urquhart, *Hammarskjöld*. New York: Norton, 1994.

30 July—Smedley Butler

Smedley Butler, *War Is a Racket*. Los Angeles: Feral House, 2003.

31 July—Ingrid Washinawatok el-Issa

Ingrid Washinawatoki el-Issa, "The roots of war and violence go deep . . ." In Michael Collopy (ed.), *Architects of Peace*, 102–3. Novato, CA: New World Library, 2000.

1 August—Conrad Grebel

John Landis Ruth, *Conrad Grebel: Son of Zurich*. Eugene OR: Wipf & Stock, 2000.

2 August—Niall O'Brien

Niall O'Brien, *Revolution from the Heart*. New York: Oxford University Press, 1987.

3 August—Martin Sheen

"Martin Sheen Interview with David Kupfer." *The Progressive*, July 2003. Online: http://progressive.org/mag_intvsheen.

4 August—Raoul Wallenberg

John Bierman, *Righteous Gentile: The Story of Raoul Wallenberg, Missing Hero of the Holocaust*. New York: Penguin, 1996.

5 August—Wendell Berry

Norman Wirzba (ed.), *The Art of the Commonplace: The Agrarian Essays of Wendell Berry*. Berkeley: Counterpoint, 2002.

6 August—Hibakusha

Gaynor Sekimori (trans.), *Hibakusha: Survivors of Hiroshima and Nagasaki*. Tokyo: Kosei, 1989.

For Further Reading

7 August—Helen Caldicott

Helen Caldicott, *A Desperate Passion: An Autobiography*. New York: Norton, 1997.

8 August—Gordon Zahn

Gordon Zahn, *Vocation of Peace*. Baltimore: Fortkamp, 1992.

9 August—Franz Jägerstätter

Gordon Zahn, *In Solitary Witness: The Life and Death of Franz Jägerstätter*. Collegeville, MN: Liturgical, 1964.

10 August—Peter Damian

Peter Damian, "Letter to Bishop Olderic." In Michael G. Long (ed.), *Christian Peace and Nonviolence: A Documentary History*, 61–62. Maryknoll, NY: Orbis, 2011.

11 August—Clare of Assisi

Ilia Delio, *Clare of Assisi: A Heart Full of Love*. Cincinnati, OH: St. Anthony Messenger, 2007.

12 August—Benedict of Nursia

Joan Chittister, *The Rule of Benedict: A Spirituality for the Twenty-First Century*. New York: Crossroad, 2010.

13 August—John Dear

John Dear, *A Persistent Peace: One Man's Struggle for a Nonviolent World*. Chicago: Loyola, 2008.

14 August—Maximilian Kolbe

Patricia Treece, *A Man for Others: Maximilian Kolbe, Saint of Auschwitz, in the Words of Those Who Knew Him*. New York: Harper & Row, 1982.

15 August—Óscar Romero

Scott Wright, *Óscar Romero and the Communion of the Saints*. Maryknoll, NY: Orbis, 2010.

16 August—E. F. Schumacher

E. F. Schumacher, *Small Is Beautiful: Economics as if People Mattered*. New York: Harper Perennial, 2010.

17 August—Catherine Doherty

Catherine Doherty, *Poustinia: Encountering God in Silence, Solitude and Prayer*. Combermere, ON: Madonna House, 1975.

18 August—Mozi

Ian Johnston (trans.), *The Mozi: A Complete Translation*. New York: Columbia University Press, 2010.

19 August—Petr Chelčický

Murray L. Wagner, *Petr Chelčický, A Radical Separatist in Hussite Bohemia*. Scottdale, PA: Herald, 1983.

20 August—Jonathan Daniels

William J. Schneider, *American Martyr: The Jon Daniels Story*. Harrisburg, PA: Morehouse, 1992.

21 August—Raymond Hunthausen

Raymond Hunthausen, "Trident Is the Auschwitz of Pugent Sound." Speech given 12 June 1981. Online: http://sniggle.net/Experiment/index.php?entry=16Mar09.

22 August—Ouray.

P. David Smith, *Ouray: Chief of the Utes*. Ouray, CO: Wayfinder, 1986.

23 August—Iccho Itoh

Mayors for Peace. Online: http://www.mayorsforpeace.org/.

24 August—Howard Zinn

Howard Zinn, *The Zinn Reader: Writings on Disobedience and Democracy*. New York: Seven Stories, 1997.

25 August—Ginetta Sagan

Nat Hentoff, "The Passion of Ginetta Sagan." *Village Voice*, 5 December 2000. Online: http://www.villagevoice.com/2000-12-05/news/the-passion-of-ginetta-sagan/2/.

26 August—Jinzaburo Takagi

Citizens' Nuclear Information Center (CNIC). Online: http://cnic.jp/english/cnic/index.html.

For Further Reading

27 August—Mother Teresa

Kathryn Spink, *Mother Teresa*. New York: HarperOne, 1998.

28 August—Smaragdus of Saint-Mihiel

Smaragdus of Saint-Mihiel, *Commentary on the Rule of Saint Benedict*, trans. David Barry. Kalamazoo, MI: Cistercian, 2007.

29 August—Arndt Pekurinen

Katri Silvonen, "Conscientious Objection in Finland." *Peace Review* 16 (2004) 207–9.

30 August—Gene Sharp

Gene Sharp, *The Politics of Nonviolent Action*. 3 vols. Boston: Porter Sargent, 1973.

31 August—Jaime Sin

Felix B. Bautista, *Cardinal Sin and the Miracle of Asia: A Biography*. Manila: Vera-Reyes, 1987.

1 September—Siegfried Sassoon

Max Egremont, *Siegfried Sassoon: A Life*. New York: Farrar, Straus & Giroux, 2005.

2 September—Dick Sheppard

Carolyn Scott, *Dick Sheppard*. London: Hodder & Stoughton, 1977.

3 September—e. e. cummings

e. e. cummings, *The Enormous Room*. New York: Penguin, 1999.

4 September—Albert Schweitzer

Marvin Meyer and Kurt Bergel (eds.), *Reverence for Life: The Ethics of Albert Schweitzer for the Twenty-First Century*. Syracuse: Syracuse University Press, 2002.

5 September—Jonathan Kozol

Jonathan Kozol, *Amazing Grace: The Lives of Children and the Conscience of a Nation*. New York: Harper, 1995.

6 September—Jane Addams

Jean Bethke Elshtain (ed.), *The Jane Addams Reader*. New York: Basic Books, 2001.

7 September—Asoka

Dhruv Raina, *King Asoka, A Love Story: A Glimpse into the Golden Past of India*. New York: Oxford University Press, 2010.

8 September—Mother Ann Lee

Nardi Reeder Campion, *Mother Ann Lee: Morning Star of the Shakers*. Hanover, NH: University Press of New England, 1990.

9 September—Ruth Fry

Theodore Paullin, *Introduction to Non-Violence*. Middlesex, UK: Echo Library, 2008.

10 September—Jean Vanier

Carolyn Whitney Brown (ed.), *Jean Vanier: Essential Writings*. Maryknoll, NY: Orbis, 2008.

11 September—Vinoba Bhave

Vinoba Bhave, *Moved by Love: Memoirs*. Devon, UK: Green Books, 1994.

12 September—Solange Fernex

Elisabeth Schulthess, *Solange, l'insoumise: écologie, féminisme, non-violence*. Paris: Yves Michel, 2006.

13 September—Aristophanes

David Stuttard (ed.), *Looking at Lysistrata: Eight Essays and a Provocative New Version of Aristophanes' Provocative Comedy*. London: Duckworth, 2010.

14 September—Cyprian of Carthage

C. John Cadoux, *The Early Christian Attitude to War*. New York: Seabury, 1982.

15 September—Jean Renoir

Jean Renoir, *My Life and My Films*. New York: Atheneum, 1974.

For Further Reading

16 September—Ursula Franklin

Ursula Franklin, *Pacifism as a Map: The Ursula Franklin Reader*. Toronto: Between the Lines, 2006.

17 September—Ron Sider

Ron Sider, *Rich Christians in an Age of Hunger*. Nashville: Thomas Nelson, 2005.

18 September—Chris Hedges

Chris Hedges, *War Is a Force that Gives Us Meaning*. New York: Public Affairs, 2002.

19 September—Paulo Freire

Anna Maria Araujo Freire and Donaldo P. Macedo (eds.), *The Paulo Freire Reader*. New York: Continuum, 2000.

20 September—Henry Salt

Henry Salt, *Animals' Rights, Considered in Relation to Social Progress*. Clarks Summit, PA: Society for Animal Rights, 1980.

21 September—Henri Nouwen

Henri Nouwen, *The Road to Peace*, ed. John Dear. Maryknoll, NY: Orbis, 1998.

22 September—James Lawson

Taylor Branch, *Parting the Waters: America in the King Years, 1954-1963*. New York: Simon & Schuster, 1989.

23 September—Eric Bogle

Eric Bogle, *At This Stage*. Audio CD, 2 discs. 2005.

24 September—Hildegard of Bingen

Carmen Acevedo Butcher (ed.), *Hildegard of Bingen: A Spiritual Reader*. Brewster, MA: Paraclete, 2007.

25 September—Erich Maria Remarque

Erich Maria Remarque, *All Quiet on the Western Front*, trans. Brian Murdoch. New York: Ballantine, 1987.

26 September—Paul VI

Karl A. Schultz (ed.), *Pope Paul VI: Christian Values and Virtues*. New York: Crossroad, 2007.

27 September—Nujood Ali

Nujood Ali and Delphine Minoui, *I Am Nujood, Age 10 and Divorced*. New York: Three Rivers, 2010.

28 September—Lillian Smith

Lillian Smith, *The Winner Names the Age*. New York: Norton, 1982.

29 September—Lech Walesa

Lech Walesa, *The Struggle and the Triumph: An Autobiography*. New York: Arcade, 1994.

30 September—Elie Wiesel

Elie Wiesel, *All Rivers Run to the Sea: Memoirs*. New York: Knopf, 1995.

1 October—Vida Scudder

Vida Scudder, *The Church and the Hour: Reflections of a Socialist Churchwoman*. New York: Dutton, 1917.

2 October—Mohandas Gandhi

Thomas Merton (ed.), *Gandhi on Non-Violence: Selected Texts from Mohandas K. Gandhi's Non-Violence in Peace and War*. New York: New Directions, 2007.

3 October—Robert Barclay

D. Elton Trueblood, *Robert Barclay*. New York: Harper & Row, 1968.

4 October—Francis of Assisi

Paul Moses, *The Sultan and the Saint: The Crusades, Islam, and Francis of Assisi's Mission of Peace*. New York: Doubleday, 2009.

5 October—Philip Berrigan

Philip Berrigan, *Fighting the Lamb's War: Skirmishes with the American Empire*. Bloomington, IN: iUniverse, 2011.

For Further Reading

6 October—Fannie Lou Hamer

Kay Mills, *This Little Light of Mine: The Life of Fannie Lou Hamer.* Lexington: University Press of Kentucky, 2009.

7 October—Desmond Tutu

Desmond Tutu, *No Future without Forgiveness.* New York: Image, 2000.

8 October—Penny Lernoux

Penny Lernoux, *People of God: The Struggle for World Catholicism.* New York: Penguin, 1990.

9 October—Jody Williams

Shawn Roberts and Jody Williams, *After the Guns Fall Silent: The Enduring Legacy of Landmines.* Washington, DC: Vietnam Veterans of America Foundation, 1995.

10 October—Ken Saro-Wiwa

Onookome Okome, *Before I Am Hanged: Ken Saro-Wiwa, Literature, Politics, and Dissent.* Trenton, NJ: Africa World Press, 1999.

11 October—Thich Nhat Hanh

Thich Nhat Hanh, *Interbeing: Fourteen Guidelines for Engaged Buddhism.* Berkeley: Parallax, 1987.

12 October—Edith Stein

John Sullivan (ed.), *Edith Stein: Essential Writings.* Maryknoll, NY: Orbis, 2002.

13 October—Mordechai Vanunu

Yoel Cohen, *The Whistleblower of Dimona: Israel, Vanunu, and the Bomb.* Teaneck, NJ: Holmes & Meir, 2003.

14 October—William Penn

William Penn, "An Essay Towards the Present and Future Peace of Europe by the Establishment of an European Diet, Parliament, or Estates." In *The Political Writings of William Penn*, ed. Andrew R. Murphy. Indianapolis: Liberty Fund, 2002.

15 October—Mahavira

Ranchor Prime, *Mahavira: Prince of Peace.* San Rafael, CA: Mandala, 2006.

16 October—Günter Grass

Julian Preece. *The Life and Work of Günter Grass: Literature, History, Politics.* New York: Palgrave Macmillan, 2004.

17 October—Richard McSorley

Richard McSorley, *My Path to Peace and Justice: An Autobiography.* Washington, DC: Rose Hill, 1996.

18 October—René Ngongo

René Ngongo, 2009 Right Livelihood Award Acceptance Speech. Online: http://www.rightlivelihood.org/ngongo_speech.html.

19 October—John Woolman

John Woolman, *The Journal and Major Essays of John Woolman*, ed. Phillips P. Moulton. Richmond, IN: Friends United, 1989.

20 October—Wayne Morse

Mason Drukman, *Wayne Morse: A Political Biography.* Portland: Oregon Historical Society, 2004.

21 October—Ernest Fremont Tittle

Ernest Fremont Tittle, "If America Is Drawn into the War, Can You, as a Christian, Participate in It, or Support It?" In *Christian Peace and Nonviolence: A Documentary History*, ed. Michael G. Long. Maryknoll, NY: Orbis, 2011.

22 October—Eileen Egan

Eileen Egan, *Peace Be with You: Justified Warfare or the Way of Nonviolence.* Maryknoll, NY: Orbis, 1999.

23 October—Anita Roddick

Anita Roddick, *Business as Unusual: My Entrepreneurial Journey, Profits with Principles.* London: Anita Roddick, 2005.

For Further Reading

24 October—Denise Levertov

Denise Levertov, *Selected Poems*, ed. Paul A. Lacey. New York: New Directions, 2003.

25 October—Micah

James C. Howell, *What Does the Lord Require? Doing Justice, Loving Kindness, and Walking Humbly*. Louisville: Westminster John Knox, 2012.

26 October—Paul Farmer

Tracy Kidder, *Mountains beyond Mountains: The Quest of Dr. Paul Farmer, a Man Who Would Cure the World*. New York: Random House, 2009.

27 October—Klas Pontus Arnoldson

Klas Pontus Arnoldson, *Pax Mundi: A Concise Account of the Progress of the Movement for Peace by Means of Arbitration, Neutralization, International Law and Disarmament*. London: Cousens, 2011.

28 October—Desiderius Erasmus

Desiderius Erasmus, *The Complaint of Peace*. New York: Cosimo, 2004.

29 October—Clarence Jordan

Faith Fuller (director, executive producer), *Briars in the Cotton Patch: The Story of Koinonia Farm*. Cotton Patch Productions, 2005.

30 October—Marcellus the Centurion

Tom Hostetler, "The Passion of Saint Marcellus." *In Communion* (Fall 2007). Online: http://www.incommunion.org/2007/10/27/saint-marcellus-military-martyr/.

31 October—Dick Gregory

Dick Gregory and Robert Lipsyte, *Nigger: An Autobiography*. New York: Dutton, 1964.

1 November—Collateral Damage

Robert S. McNamara and James G. Blight, *Wilson's Ghost: Reducing the Risk of Conflict, Killing, and Catastrophe in the Twenty-First Century*. Cambridge: Public Affairs, 2001.

2 November—Samuel Ruiz García

Gary MacEoin, *The People's Church: Bishop Samuel Ruiz of Mexico and Why He Matters*. New York: Crossroad, 1996.

3 November—Martin de Porres

Brian J. Pierce, *Martin de Porres: A Saint of the Americas*. Hyde Park, NY: New City, 2008.

4 November—James Groppi

Jackie DiSalvo, "Father James Groppi (1930–1985): The Militant Humility of a Civil Rights Activist." In Philip Cannastraro and Gerald Myers (eds.), *The Lost World of Italian-American Radicalism*, 229–44. Westport, CT: Praeger, 2003.

5 November—Vandana Shiva

Vandana Shiva, *Earth Democracy: Justice, Sustainability, and Peace*. Cambridge: South End, 2005.

6 November—Lucretia Mott

Carol Faulkner, *Lucretia Mott's Heresy: Abolition and Women's Rights in Nineteenth-Century America*. Philadelphia: University of Pennsylvania Press, 2011.

7 November—Eleanor Roosevelt

Mary Ann Glendon, *A World Made New: Eleanor Roosevelt and the Universal Declaration of Human Rights*. New York: Random House, 2002.

8 November—Dorothy Day

Robert Ellsberg (ed.), *Dorothy Day: Selected Writings*. Maryknoll, NY: Orbis, 2005.

9 November—Thomas Berry

Thomas Berry, *The Dream of the Earth*. San Francisco, CA: Sierra Club, 2006.

10 November—Seneca

Seneca, *Letters from a Stoic*, trans. Robin Campbell. New York: Penguin, 1969.

11 November—Martin of Tours

Sulpicius Severus, *Life of St. Martin*. In *Early Christian Lives*, ed. Carolinne White. New York: Penguin, 1998.

For Further Reading

12 NOVEMBER—BAHA'U'LLAH

Shoghi Effendi (trans.), *Gleanings from the Writings of Baha'u'llah*. Wilmette, IL: Baha'i, 2005.

13 NOVEMBER—KAREN SILKWOOD

Richard Rashke, *The Killing of Karen Silkwood: The Story behind the Kerr-McGee Plutonium Case*. Ithaca: Cornell University Press, 2000.

14 NOVEMBER—PEDRO ARRUPE

Kevin F. Burke (ed.), *Pedro Arrupe: Essential Writings*. Maryknoll, NY: Orbis, 2004.

15 NOVEMBER—PAUL MOORE

Paul Moore, *Presences: A Bishop's Life in the City*. New York: Farrar, Straus & Giroux, 1997.

16 NOVEMBER—ADOLFO SANSOLINI

British Union for the Abolition of Vivisection. Online: http://www.buav.org/.

17 NOVEMBER—ORIGEN

Origen, *On First Principles*, trans. G. W. Butterworth. Gloucester, MA: Peter Smith, 1973.

18 NOVEMBER—HOWARD THURMAN

Luther E. Smith Jr. (ed.), *Howard Thurman: Essential Writings*. Maryknoll, NY: Orbis, 2006.

19 NOVEMBER—GILLO PONTECORVO

Piernico Solinas (ed.), *Gillo Pontecorvo's The Battle of Algiers*. New York: Scribner, 1973.

20 NOVEMBER—LEO TOLSTOY

Leo Tolstoy, *The Law of Love and the Law of Violence*. Mineola, NY: Dover, 2010.

21 NOVEMBER—MENNO SIMONS

Helmut Isaak, *Menno Simons and the New Jerusalem*. Kitchener, ON: Pandora, 2006.

22 NOVEMBER—ALDOUS HUXLEY

Aldous Huxley, *What Are You Going to Do about It? The Case for Constructive Peace*. London: Chatto & Windus, 1936.

23 NOVEMBER—MAUDE ROYDEN

Sheila Fletcher, *Maude Royden: A Life*. New York: Blackwell, 1989.

24 NOVEMBER—ARUNDHATI ROY

Arundhati Roy, *The Cost of Living*. New York: Modern Library, 1999.

25 NOVEMBER—PAUL JONES

John Howard Melish, *Bishop Paul Jones, Witness for Peace*. Cincinnati, OH: Forward Movement, 1992.

26 NOVEMBER—ADOLFO ESQUIVEL

Adolfo Esquivel, *Christ in a Pancho: Testimonials of the Nonviolent Struggles in Latin America*. Maryknoll, NY: Orbis, 1984.

27 NOVEMBER—THICH QUANG DO

Scott A. Hunt, *The Future of Peace: On the Front Lines with the World's Great Peacemakers*. San Francisco: HarperSanFrancisco, 2002.

28 NOVEMBER—ARTHUR CARMAN

Arthur H. Carman, *A Full Life: Three Score Years and Ten, One Man's Life*. Chapel Hill, Queensland: R. Carman, 1994.

29 NOVEMBER—ELIAS CHACOUR

Elias Chacour, *Blood Brothers*. Grand Rapids: Chosen, 2003.

30 NOVEMBER—ETTY HILLESUM

Klaas A. D. Smelik (ed.), *Etty: The Letters and Diaries of Etty Hillesum, 1941-1943*. Grand Rapids: Eerdmans, 2002.

1 DECEMBER—PETER RIDEMAN

Peter Rideman, *Confession of Faith*. Rifton, NY: Plough, 1970.

For Further Reading

2 December—Gamaliel
Gerald Heard, *The Gospel According to Gamaliel*. Eugene, OR: Wipf & Stock, 2009.

3 December—Aelred of Rievaulx
Aelred of Rievaulx, *Spiritual Friendship*, trans. Dennis Billy. Notre Dame: Ave Maria, 2008.

4 December—Benjamin Britten
Humphrey Carpenter, *Benjamin Britten: A Biography*. London: Faber & Faber, 2003.

5 December—Clement of Alexandria
C. John Cadoux, *The Early Christian Attitude to War*. New York: Seabury, 1982.

6 December—Ryan White
Ryan White and Ann Marie Cunningham, *My Own Story*. New York: Signet, 1992.

7 December—Ivo Markovic
Keziah Conrad, "Ivo Markovic." *Beyond Intractability*. Online: http://www.beyondintractability.org/node/2818.

8 December—Elihu Burritt
Peter Tolis, *Elihu Burritt: Crusader for Brotherhood*. Hamden, CT: Archon, 1968.

9 December—Dalton Trumbo
Peter Hanson, *Dalton Trumbo: Hollywood Rebel*. Jefferson, NC: McFarland, 2007.

10 December—Thomas Merton
Thomas Merton, *The Nonviolent Alternative*, ed. Gordon Zahn. New York: Farrar, Straus & Giroux, 1981.

11 December—Martyrs of El Mozote
Mark Danner, *The Massacre at El Mozote*. London: Granta, 2005.

12 December—Hafsat Abiola
Kudirat Initiative for Democracy (KIND). Online: http://kind.org/newsite/index.php.

13 December—Archibald Baxter
Archibald Baxter, *We Will Not Cease*. Baker City, OR: Eddie Tern, 2000.

14 December—Andrei Sakharov
Andrei Sakharov, *Memoirs*. New York: Knopf, 1990.

15 December—Ludovic Lazarus Zamenhof
Arika Okrent, *In the Land of Invented Languages: Esperanto Rock Stars, Klingon Poets, Loglan Lovers, and the Mad Dreamers Who Tried to Build a Perfect Language*. New York: Spiegel & Grau, 2009.

16 December—Kabir
Linda Hess and Shukdev Singh (trans.), *The Bijak of Kabir*. New York: Oxford University Press, 2002.

17 December—Craig Kielburger
Craig Kielburger, *Free the Children: A Young Man Fights against Child Labor and Proves that Children Can Change the World*. New York: HarperCollins, 1999.

18 December—Junsei Terasawa
Metta Spencer, "That Peace Monk: Junsei Terasawa." *Peace Magazine*, July-September 2001, 16.

19 December—James Peck
James Tracy, *Direct Action: Radical Pacifism from the Union Eight to the Chicago Seven*. Chicago: University of Chicago Press, 1996.

20 December—Sidney Lewis Gulick
Committee on World Friendship Among Children, *Dolls of Friendship: The Story of a Goodwill Project between the Children of America and Japan*. New York: Friendship, 1929.

21 December—Emma Tenayuca
Selden Menefee and Orin C. Cassmore, *The Pecan Shellers of San Antonio: The Problem of Underpaid and Underemployed Mexican Labor*. Washington, DC: Government Printing Office, 1940.

22 December—Francis Sheehy-Skeffington

Leah Levinson, *With Wooden Sword: A Portrait of Francis Sheehy-Skeffington, Militant Pacifist*. Gallway, Ireland: MW Books, 1983.

23 December—Abraham Joshua Heschel

Edward K. Kaplan, *Spiritual Radical: Abraham Joshua Heschel in America, 1940–1972*. New Haven: Yale University Press, 2009.

24 December—Benjamin Rush

Benjamin Rush, "Plan of a Peace-Office." In *The Selected Works of Benjamin Rush*. New York: Philosophical Library, 1947.

25 December—Jesus the Christ

The Gospels of Matthew, Mark, Luke, and John.

26 December—Walter Wink

Walter Wink, *Jesus and Nonviolence: A Third Way*. Minneapolis: Fortress, 2003.

27 December—Lactantius

Lactantius, *The Divine Institutes*. In vol. 7 of *The Ante-Nicene Fathers*, ed. Alexander Roberts and James Donaldson. Buffalo: Christian Leadership, 1885.

28 December—Child Soldiers

P. W. Singer, *Children at War*. Berkeley: University of California Press, 2006.

29 December—John Howard Yoder

John Howard Yoder, *The Politics of Jesus*. Battle Creek, MI: Eerdmans, 1994.

30 December—Maurice McCrackin

Judith Blackburn and Robert Coughlin, *Building the Beloved Community: Maurice McCrackin's Life for Peace and Civil Rights*. Bloomington, IN: Trafford, 2006.

31 December—John Timothy Leary

Gordon C. Zahn, "John Leary: A Different Sort of Hero." In *Vocation of Peace*, 152–71. Baltimore: Fortkamp, 1992.

Alphabetical Index

(Month/Day)

Abiola, Hafsat	12/12	Burton, Ormond	01/16
Addams, Jane	09/06	Butler, Smedley	07/30
Aelred of Rievaulx	12/03	Caldicott, Helen	08/07
Ali, Nujood	09/27	Càmara, Dom Hélder	02/07
Aristophanes	09/13	Camus, Albert	01/04
Arnold, Eberhard	07/26	Carman, Arthur	11/28
Arnoldson, Klaus Pontus	10/27	Carson, Rachel	05/28
Arrupe, Pedro	11/14	Chacour, Elias	11/29
Ashoka	09/07	Chang, Helen Mack	01/19
Ateek, Naim	02/26	Chávez, César	03/31
Baha'u'llah	11/12	Chelčický, Petr	08/19
Balch, Emily Greene	01/08	Child Soldiers	12/28
Balducci, Ernesto	04/25	Claiborne, Shane	07/09
Ballou, Adin	04/23	Clare of Assisi	08/11
Barclay, Robert	10/03	Clement of Alexandria	12/05
Bari, Judi	03/02	Coffin, William Sloan	06/23
Barker, Pat	05/08	Collateral Damage Victims	11/01
Baxter, Archibald	12/13	Corrie, Rachel	03/16
Belo, Carlos Filipe Ximenes	02/03	Crowe, Frances	05/15
Benedict of Nursia	08/12	cummings, e.e.	09/03
Benezet, Anthony	05/03	Cyprian of Carthage	09/14
Berrigan, Daniel	05/17	Dalai Lama	07/05
Berrigan, Philip	10/05	Daniels, Jonathan	08/20
Berry, Thomas	11/09	Dante Alighieri	06/13
Berry, Wendell	08/05	Day, Dorothy	11/08
Bhave, Vinoba	09/11	de Porres, Martin	11/03
Biehl, Amy	04/26	Dear, John	08/13
Big Crow, SuAnne	03/15	del Vasto, Lanza	01/05
Bigelow, Albert	05/01	Dellinger, David	05/25
Boeke, Kees	07/03	Deming, Barbara	07/19
Bogle, Eric	09/23	Dith Pran	03/30
Bonhoeffer, Dietrich	04/09	Dodge, David Low	06/14
Borlaug, Norman	03/25	Doherty, Catherine	08/17
Boulding, Elise	07/06	Dolci, Danilo	06/28
Boulding, Kenneth	01/18	Dorfman, Ariel	05/06
Bourgeois, Roy	01/27	Dyer, Mary	06/01
Brittain, Vera	03/19	Dymond, Jonathan	06/20
Britten, Benjamin	12/04	Ebadi, Shirin	06/21
Brocca, José	06/18	Edelman, Marion Wright	06/06
Brother Roger	05/12	Egan, Eileen	10/22
Brower, David	07/01	Einstein, Albert	04/17
Brueggemann, Walter	03/14	El-Issa, Ingrid Washinawatok	07/31
Buber, Martin	02/08	Ellsberg, Daniel	04/06
Burritt, Elihu	12/08	Ellul, Jacques	01/06

Alphabetical Index

Elmi, Asha Haji	02/06	Hibakusha	08/06
Engineer, Asghar Ali	03/10	Hildegard of Bingen	09/24
Engleitner, Leopold	07/23	Hill, Julia Butterfly	02/18
Erasmus, Desiderius	10/28	Hillesum, Etty	11/30
Esquivel, Adolfo	11/26	Hirabayaski, Gordon Kiyoshi	04/29
Farmer, Paul	10/26	Holland, Henry Scott	01/10
Fell, Margaret	04/24	Howe, Julia Ward	05/27
Fernex, Solange	09/12	Hughan, Jessie Wallace	04/10
Fosdick, Harry Emerson	05/24	Hunthausen, Raymond	08/21
Fox, Tom	03/09	Hurndall, Thomas	01/13
Francis of Assisi	10/04	Hutter, Jacob	02/25
Franck, Frederick	04/12	Huxley, Aldous	11/22
Franklin, Ursula	09/16	Isaac of Nineveh	01/28
Freire, Paulo	09/19	Issa, Hussein	03/05
Froman, Menachem	02/22	Ito, Iccho	08/23
Fry, Elizabeth	05/21	Jagannathan, K. & S.	02/19
Fry, Ruth	09/09	Jägerstätter, Franz	08/09
Fuchs, Emil	02/13	Jesus the Christ	12/25
Gamaliel	12/02	John XXIII	06/02
Gandhi, Arun	04/14	John Paul II	04/02
Gandhi, Mohandas	10/02	Jones, Absalom	01/24
García, Samuel Ruiz	11/02	Jones, Jonah	02/17
Gautama Siddhartha	02/27	Jones, Paul	11/25
Ghosananda, Preah Maha	03/12	Jones, Rufus	01/25
Giay, Benny	01/12	Jordan, Clarence	10/29
Gibbs, Marie Lois	06/25	Judge, Mychal	05/11
Godiva, Lady	04/20	Justin Martyr	06/26
Goodall, Jane	04/03	Kabir	12/16
Goodman, Amy	04/13	Kagawa, Toyohiko	07/10
Goss-Mayr, Hildegard	01/21	Kant, Immanuel	04/30
Graf, Willi	01/02	Khan, Khan Abdul Ghaffar	01/20
Grande, Rutilio	03/11	Kielburger, Craig	12/17
Grass, Günter	10/16	King, Jr., Martin Luther	04/04
Grebel, Conrad	08/01	Kolbe, Maximilien	08/14
Gregory, Dick	10/31	Kollwitz, Käthe	04/22
Groppi, James	11/04	Kovic, Ron	07/04
Gulick, Sidney Lewis	12/20	Kozol, Jonathan	09/05
Gumbleton, Thomas	01/26	Kubrick, Stanley	03/07
Guthrie, Woody	07/14	Kumar, Satish	06/03
Ham Sok-Han	03/13	Lactantius	12/27
Hamer, Fannie Lou	10/06	Laozi	05/19
Hammarskjöld, Dag	07/29	Lappé, Frances Moore	02/10
Harrison, Charles Yale	06/16	Las Casas, Bartolomé de	07/16
Hassan, Margaret	04/18	Lasn, Kalle	03/24
Hauerwas, Stanley	07/24	Lawson, James	09/22
Hauser, Monika	02/24	Leary, John Timothy	12/31
Heschel, Joshua Abraham	12/23	Lee, Barbara	07/15
Hedges, Chris	09/18	Lee, Mother Ann	09/08
Hennacy, Ammon	07/17	Lemke, Birsel	07/02
Hernández, María Julia	01/23	Lemkin, Raphael	06/24

Alphabetical Index

Leopold, Aldo	01/11	Pauling, Linus	02/28
Lernoux, Penny	10/08	Paulinus of Sola	06/22
Lester, Muriel	02/11	Peace Pilgrim	07/08
Levertov, Denise	10/24	Peck, James	12/19
Linder, Ben	07/07	Pekurinen, Arndt	08/29
Lupus of Troyes	07/28	Pelagius	03/28
Lutuli, Albert	07/21	Penn, William	10/14
Maathai, Wangari	04/01	Perkins, John	06/08
Mahavira	10/15	Peter Damian	08/10
Makeba, Miriam	03/03	Phillips, Utah	05/26
Mandela, Nelson	07/18	Pocahontas	03/21
Manorama, Ruth	05/30	Pontecorvo, Gillo	11/19
Marcellus the Centurion	10/30	Popkov, Viktor	06/17
Markovic, Ivo	12/07	Prejean, Helen	04/21
Martin of Tours	11/11	Purvis, Robert	04/15
Martyrs of El Mozote	12/11	Pythagoras	04/05
Masih, Iqbah	04/16	Quang Do, Thich	11/27
Maurin, Peter	05/14	Quidde, Ludwig	03/04
McConnell, John	03/22	Rankin, Jeannette	06/11
McCracken, Maurice	12/30	Rauschenbusch, Walter	07/25
McSorley, Richard	10/17	Remarque, Eric Maria	09/25
Menchú Tum, Rigoberta	01/09	Renoir, Jean	09/15
Meng Tzu	04/19	Rideman, Peter	12/01
Merton, Thomas	12/10	Roddick, Anita	10/23
Micah	10/25	Rolland, Romain	01/29
Mirabehn	07/20	Romero, Óscar	08/15
Moore, Paul	11/15	Roosevelt, Eleanor	11/07
Morse, Wayne	10/20	Roy, Arundhati	11/24
Mother Teresa	08/27	Royden, Maude	11/23
Mott, Lucretia	11/06	Rusesabagina, Paul	06/15
Mozi	08/18	Rush, Benjamin	12/24
Murry, John Middleton	03/20	Russell, Bertrand	05/18
Muste, A.J.	02/20	Rustin, Bayard	03/17
Nagai, Takashi	01/03	Sagan, Ginetta	08/25
Nansen, Fridtjof	05/13	Sakharov, Andrei	12/14
Naser, Sumaya-Rarhat	06/10	Salmon, Ben	02/15
Naudé, Beyers	05/10	Salt, Henry	09/20
Nelson, Wally and Juanita	03/27	Sansolini, Adolfo	11/16
Ngongo, René	10/18	Saro-Wiwa, Ken	10/10
Nhat Chi Mai	05/16	Sasaki, Sadako	01/07
Nhat Hanh, Thich	10/11	Sassoon, Siegfried	09/01
Niemöller, Martin	01/14	Sayre, John Nevin	02/05
Nouwen, Henri	09/21	Schindler, Oscar	04/28
O'Brien, Niall	08/02	Scholl, Sophia	05/09
O'Hare, Kate Richards	03/26	Schumacher, E. F.	08/16
Origen	11/17	Schweitzer, Albert	09/04
Ouray	08/22	Scudder, Vida	10/01
Parks, Rosa	02/04	Seattle	06/07
Passy, Frédéric	06/12	Seeger, Pete	05/05
Paul IV	09/26	Seneca	11/10

Alphabetical Index

Sharp, Gene	08/30	Trocmé, André	04/07
Shaw, George Bernard	07/27	Trumbo, Dalton	12/09
Sheehy-Skettington, Francis	12/22	Tutu, Desmond	10/07
Sheen, Martin	08/03	Ung, Loung	03/01
Sheppard, Dick	09/02	Upchurch, Carl	05/07
Shiva, Vandana	11/05	Valentine	02/14
Shuttlesworth, Fred	03/18	Vallalar	01/30
Sider, Ron	09/17	van Hengel, John	02/21
Sik, Toma	07/13	Vanier, Jean	09/10
Silkwood, Karen	11/13	Vanka, Maximilian	02/02
Simons, Menno	11/21	Vanunu, Mordechai	10/13
Sin, Jaime	08/31	von Ossietzky, Carl	05/04
Sivaraksa, Sulak	03/06	von Suttner, Bertha	06/09
Skobtsova, Maria	03/08	Vonnegut, Kurt	04/11
Smaragdus of St. Mihiel	08/28	Walesa, Lech	09/29
Smith, Lillian	09/28	Walker, Alice	02/09
Smith, Samantha	06/29	Wallenberg, Raoul	08/04
Snyder, Mitch	07/12	Wallis, Jim	06/04
Soderblöm, Nathan	01/15	Walters, Max	05/23
Soelle, Dorothy	04/27	Wei Jingsheng	05/20
Soper, Donald	01/31	Weil, Simone	02/16
Spock, Benjamin	05/02	White, Ryan	12/06
Stafford, William	01/17	Wiesel, Elie	09/30
Stang, Dorothy	02/12	Wilberforce, William	07/22
Stein, Edith	10/12	Willem, Jean-Pierre	05/31
Studdert Kennedy, G. A.	06/27	Williams, Betty	05/22
Supek, Ivan	04/08	Williams, Jody	10/09
Suu Kyi, Aung San	06/19	Wink, Walter	12/26
Suzuki, David	03/23	Woolman, John	10/19
Szilárd, Leó	05/29	Wulfstan of Worchester	02/23
Takagi, Jinzaburo	08/26	Yahya Ali, Abdulkadir	07/11
Telemachus	01/01	Yoder, John Howard	12/29
Tenayuca, Emma	12/21	Yunus, Muhammad	06/30
Terasawa, Junsei	12/18	Zahn, Gordon	08/08
Thant, U	01/22	Zamenhof, Ludovic Lazarus	12/15
Thomas, R. S.	03/29	Zamyatin, Yevgeny	02/01
Thurman, Howard	11/18	Zelter, Angie	06/05
Tittle, Ernest Fremont	10/21	Zinn, Howard	08/24
Tolstoy, Leo	11/20		

www.ingramcontent.com/pod-product-compliance
Lightning Source LLC
Chambersburg PA
CBHW060453300426
44113CB00016B/2576